*Workers of the World and Oppressed Peoples, Unite!*

VOLUME TWO

The Communist International
in Lenin's Time

# WORKERS OF THE WORLD AND OPPRESSED PEOPLES, UNITE!

PROCEEDINGS AND DOCUMENTS OF
THE SECOND CONGRESS, 1920

VOLUME TWO

*Edited by John Riddell*

PATHFINDER
New York London Montreal Sydney

ISBN 978-0-87348-941-6
Two-volume set: ISBN 978-0-87348-942-3
Library of Congress Catalog Card Number 91-66263
Manufactured in the United States of America

First edition, 1991
Twelfth printing, 2025

COVER PHOTO: Delegates leave opening session of Second Congress, Petrograd, July 19, 1920. (Internationaal Instituut voor Sociale Geschiedenis)

COVER DESIGN: Toni Gorton

**PATHFINDER**
pathfinderpress.com
Email: pathfinder@pathfinderpress.com

# Contents

## VOLUME 1



## PROCEEDINGS

## VOLUME 2

## APPENDIXES

# MAJOR REPORTS

# MAJOR RESOLUTIONS

**Europe in 1920**

*Frontiers of Poland are those of October 1920*

N
W
E
S
SWEDEN
FINLAND
SOVIET
RUSSIA
Petrograd
ESTONIA
Baltic Sea
Moscow
LATVIA
LITHUANIA
BELO-
RUSSIA
GERMANY
Bialystock
Warsaw
POLAND
Kiev
UKRAINE
GALICIA
CZECHOSLOVAKIA
AUSTRIA
HUNGARY
ROMANIA
Black Sea
YUGOSLAVIA
BULGARIA
Constantinople
TURKEY
ALBANIA
GREECE

**Asia in 1920** *Detail below.*

SOVIET RUSSIA
MONGOLIA
CHINA
KOREA
(Occupied by Japan)
JAPAN
Pacific Ocean
PHILLIPINES
SIAM
INDOCHINA
(French colony)
DUTCH EAST INDIES

SESSION 11

AUGUST 3, 1920 (MORNING)

# Trade unions and factory committees

*(Part 1)*

ZINOVIEV: I declare the session open. Permit me to read the following telegram bringing greetings from the Working Group of Revolutionary Social Democrats of Austria, along with the Third International's reply.

"July 31, 1920

"The Congress of the Communist International:

"The Social Democratic Working Group of Revolutionary Workers Councils of Austria, a majority at the last congress of [workers'] councils, is fighting as the extreme left wing of the [Social Democratic] party for the dictatorship of the councils and for affiliation to the Communist International. Closely linked with you in spirit, we hope to be represented at the next congress. We enthusiastically greet the fighting proletariat of Soviet Russia and long for the moment when our united struggle will achieve the final victory of the world revolution. We wish your conference complete success.

"Revolutionary greetings! On behalf of the Working Group of Revolutionary Social Democrats of Austria,

*"Franz Rothe*
*Josef Benisch*
*Ernst Fabri"*

(*Zinoviev reads the reply.*)

"Dear Comrades:

"The congress of the Communist International is pleased to acknowledge your greetings. At this conference, the parties of all countries affiliated to the Communist International have voted to make the idea of soviets a reality in every country through unconditional discipline and solidarity in action. In Austria the Communist Party is conducting this struggle. If you are truly in earnest in your longing for the final victory of the world revolution, then your solemn and most sacred duty in Austria is to wage a struggle to the death against the section of Austrian Social Democracy represented by the reformist and social-traitor leaders Renner, Bauer, Fritz Adler, Hueber, Tomschik, and Domes, to name only the best known. You must break unconditionally with the reformist Social Democracy, unite with the Communist Party of Austria, and fight in the workers' councils for communist demands. Not lip service but ruthless revolutionary action will bring a speedy victory of the world revolution."

(*A vote is taken on the reply proposed by the Bureau. It is adopted.*)

ZINOVIEV: We will now go to the next point on the agenda, which is the trade union question. The reporter, Comrade Radek, has the floor.

## REPORT ON THE TRADE UNIONS AND FACTORY COMMITTEES

RADEK: Comrades, the Communist International's relationship to the trade unions is the most serious and important question facing our movement. The unions are the proletariat's largest mass organizations. They play the decisive role in economic struggles, which are the most important factor in capitalism's disintegration. After the revolution triumphs the unions will be in the forefront of the mass organizations called on to work for the economic construction of socialism. The importance of unions in the ever-intensifying economic struggles and in the construction of socialism decrees that we can approach this question only through the closest scrutiny of conditions within the unions, if we aim to be guided not by our wishes but by an objective evaluation of possibilities for further development.

When the war began many of us thought that the trade union movement was finished. Many thought the unions—which had relied primarily on their treasuries in the fight against capital—would collapse when the war ended in view of the enormous tasks they would face. And when the German revolution erupted, no less a figure than Rosa Luxemburg believed that the unions were done for.[1] Very characteristically, even in the debates at the KPD founding congress, this question played no role.

If we review union development in the most important countries for the periods before the war, during the war, and during the revolution, we obtain the following approximate figures: In Germany before the war broke out, the trade unions were 2.25 million strong. During the war the curve fell considerably and the number was lower. After the war, in December 1918, the unions numbered fewer than 2 million; since then they have grown to 8 million. In Britain they have grown from 4.5 million at the beginning of the war to 6.5 million. In France the number of organized workers has increased from 400,000 to 2 million today; in Italy from 450,000 to 2 million. Even in America the trade unions have grown from approximately 2 million at the beginning of the war to 4 million.

One leader of the KAPD, Schröder, said in his pamphlet on the factory committees that these figures do not express a healthy growth process but an "unhealthy puffing up."[2] If it were only a matter of issuing a bad bill of health to historical events we dislike, we could be content to regard the trade unions as a tumor on the cadaver of capitalism. But since something else is at stake, the following facts must be recognized.

Although the working masses witnessed the union leaders' betrayal during the war and are for the most part full of bitterness toward the union bureaucracy, at the same time the war taught them to act in an organized fashion—as a battalion, as an army corps. Now, faced with immense economic battles, forced to endure the onslaught of enormous price increases, the many difficulties of the housing question, and economic chaos, they are looking for ways to expand and strengthen their power in struggle. They have no choice but to join the unions and turn them into big, mass formations. And that is the road the masses are taking. It is typical that in no country do we see any particular growth of the so-called revolutionary unions. The Industrial Workers of the World in America is very weak organizationally, which cannot be explained by government persecution alone. The syndicalists in Germany, it is true, have grown in size but only to a very limited extent. The working masses go directly into the big unions.

That of course does not answer the question of what the trade unions are and what their functions are. In assessing our attitude toward them, we must begin with an analysis of the possibilities and paths of communist struggle. We must answer whether there is any road to the emancipation of the working class other than the one the unions are following by intensifying the methods of struggle they have used until now. Reduced to a political formula, the question could be posed this way: What are the tasks of revolutionary unions?

Often revolutionary unions are counterposed to trade unions in general. Let us ask ourselves: What does the decline of capital consist of? What are the working class's methods of struggle and what can the unions accomplish if they want to conduct this struggle?

First, we know that the trade union bureaucracy, in keeping with its counterrevolutionary outlook, tries to escape from the situation by abolishing economic struggle in general. After the [November 1918] triumph of the revolution the German unions began to strengthen the Labor Boards. These organizations aim to achieve lasting reconciliation with the capitalists, in which of course the working class is at a disadvantage. In Britain the Whitley committees developed into the Joint Industrial Councils, which correspond perfectly to the concept of "labor boards":[3] the attempt to create lasting agreement between workers and capitalists through an organization that can settle disputed questions.

This tactic of the union leaders aims at dismantling the class struggle, and it goes without saying that we can have nothing in common with it but must wage the sharpest possible struggle against such efforts. This struggle does not need to be waged under the banner of a new trade union policy, however, for in this case the novelty is on the other side—that of the union leaders.

As for a new trade union policy and the possibility that there may be some special, revolutionary union tactic, we have this to say: The process of capitalist decay consists of a disorganization of the continuity of the economic process. By trying to eliminate from the economic process the half of the European continent that supplies world markets with most of the raw material for industry and by trying to enslave these countries, Anglo-Saxon capital interrupts the division of labor in the entire world economy. The only conceivable outcome of this effort is the collapse of the capitalist system in America and Britain as well. Huge unemployment and the disruption of production leave no doubt that these countries are headed for a great economic crisis. In American literature there are now studies (such as Spargo's book) that present Russia as an "American affair" and try to show that America is on the verge of a crisis.[4]

This interruption of the economic process on a world scale is accompanied by a virtually insane rise in prices. We witnessed the colossal increase of all prices on the world market, aggravated by the differences in currency exchange rates between the defeated and "victorious" countries. Now we are beginning to see a drop in prices. The rise in prices created a kind of phony prosperity while bleeding the Central Powers dry. Now, the drop in prices means another crisis in production.

Given the general condition of the working class, any thought of reformist tactics, of gradually raising its real wages, its standard of living, is a completely opportunist illusion. The hope of gradually improving the condition of the working class is a reactionary utopia. This statement is confirmed by a review of Kuczynski's statistical data, which lead him to the conclusion that in Germany a family of four requires sixteen thousand marks a year for a bare subsistence standard of living, lower than before the war, and also that only about 10 percent of the population earns that much.[5]

If we then take the figures for America, that is, compare the most highly developed defeated capitalist nation on the one hand with the conqueror in the war on the other, this finding is completely confirmed. "The High Cost of Labor," an article in the Washington magazine the *Nation* of June 19, 1920, gives the following figures: According to statistical surveys for 1919, the minimum subsistence for a family of husband, wife, and three children was $2,500 per year, a level defined not as the American standard of living but as one "below which the family would be in danger of physical and moral degeneration." Other statistics cited in the article arrive at the figure $2,180. Next, calculating wages for 103 occupations, the magazine concludes that a wage corresponding to such an annual budget, $6.50 to $8.50 [per day], is earned by only 10 percent of all metalworkers. Consequently—at least according to the *Nation*'s calculations—90 percent live under conditions that put them, in the opinion of American statisticians, in danger of physical and moral degeneration. This bourgeois magazine goes on to say that even today a quarter of the working class suffers from undernourishment and lack of clothing. That was the situation in America before the crisis began.

It is clear that in this situation the trade unions' tactics and the tasks of communist struggle cannot be to make repairs on the capitalist structure but must be to work consciously for the overthrow of capital.

Along what road can we wage this struggle? On our "left" wing we frequently encounter the idea that since it is impossible to improve the condition of the working class by an increase in wages, there is no point fighting for that. Economic struggles are futile; it is necessary to wait until so much resentment has accumulated that the working class dispatches capitalism with a single blow. Then again we find propaganda for sabotage (of work or industry) as the road leading to a rapid collapse of capital.

One notion is as incorrect as the other. Even if the working class cannot save itself by seeking an increase in wages, there are still sound reasons why it should not remain indifferent to that struggle. For example, if the Berlin metalworkers cannot raise their wages in step with price increases, they will undoubtedly be worse off in March than they were in January. So, while raising wages may not solve the question, still it is a way to maintain the workers' ability to struggle.

Furthermore, for mechanical reasons alone it is inconceivable that capital will collapse immediately, just as a building from which the pillars have been removed does not collapse at once. Capitalism could encounter the gravest difficulties in the world and still survive for years if its decline did not unleash forces opposed to it. The working class will become convinced of the hopelessness of capitalism's situation only if, driven by necessity, it goes into struggle and becomes convinced in the course of this struggle that it cannot save itself within the framework of capitalism. *The main significance of struggles to raise wages is that they mobilize large masses of workers for revolutionary struggle.*

At the same time, the slogan of sabotage, at least sabotage of equipment, is directly counterrevolutionary. By this route our inheritance will be pretty small, since civil war is bound in any case to result in destruction of values and of means of production. Therefore, it is the working class's responsibility to destroy this equipment only when absolutely necessary.

Sabotage is not a slogan of struggle. It is certainly not our duty to tell workers to exert themselves for the capitalists, but passive resistance is not a method that can lead to a collapse of capital. The working class's methods of struggle are active methods: broadening the front of the struggle by mobilizing millions of fighting workers, intensifying and prolonging that struggle, and forging unity among the struggling masses.

The question is this: Struggles, though fruitless, will lead ultimately to a general attack by the working masses on capitalism. In this struggle there is no new method. If we rid those great mass formations, the trade unions, of the bureaucracy's counterrevolutionary tendencies, if we depose the bureaucracy, these mass proletarian organizations will become the organs best able to lead the proletariat's struggle on a broad front.

We come now to the question of the practical possibilities of transforming reactionary trade unions into institutions of the revolution. In the theses we are submitting to the congress, we give Communists the following slogan as a guideline: Join the trade unions and struggle in the big unions to win control of them. But in establishing this guideline, we should not close our eyes to the difficulties that became clear to us particularly in the course of our commission's lengthy deliberations. The difficulties lie in the fact that, in drafting the theses, perhaps we had the Russian and German experiences too much in mind. The German trade unions with their eight million organized workers encompass the great mass of the German workers—more than half of the German proletariat—and thus they are no longer merely organs of the labor aristocracy. More than 600,000 agricultural workers are in unions, and the mere fact that the great masses belong to unions opens the best of prospects.

But if we recall that in America there are only four million organized workers, and if we recall that they are dispersed in craft unions, we face the fact that at present in America organized workers constitute the labor aristocracy. Secondly, they are hermetically sealed off from the great masses of workers. And thirdly, even this labor aristocracy is scattered among a great many small organizations of the old type. In America and Britain there are union organizations in which the bureaucracy is appointed for life. Thus, while adhering to the theses in general, we must authorize the American Communists, in cases where such general tendencies continue to prevail, to consider the possibility or even the necessity of forming new unions.[6] A fine arena for this lies open before us, namely, the trades in which the labor aristocracy voluntarily relinquishes its leading role as organizer, that is, the many trades of unskilled, untrained workers.

We cite only a single case in our theses, namely, one where unskilled workers are oppressed by the union bureaucracy and the only way out is to organize new unions. In that regard, we must tell the American Communists, "It is your duty to take the initiative in organizing unskilled workers." The IWW is one organization there that is tackling this job. It is certainly the most persecuted organization, one whose breast is pierced by every spear of American capitalism. Therefore we should not be put off by the IWW's revolutionary romanticism. Instead, we tell our comrades to throw their full weight into supporting these organizations in their efforts to organize the masses. A united policy is possible only if we bring our efforts to organize the broad masses of unskilled workers into harmony with those of the IWW.

But unlike the IWW, we affirm that Communists' efforts to organize the broad masses of unskilled workers must not lead them to become isolated from the American Federation of Labor (AFL), from the Anglo-American labor organizations. Through the new organizations we must not only storm capitalism, we must also join the federation of labor.

In response to this the American comrades say they have been trying to transform the AFL for decades. But this argument is hardly convincing. Insofar as the AFL is concerned, workers always went into the unions with the good intention of taking up arms immediately. But not all the forces that did so were revolutionary. And do not forget that all these efforts were made in the epoch of peaceful development, when workers in Britain and America were unable to conceive of revolution at all.

Now the AFL itself is undergoing a transformation. I have authoritative witnesses for this in the *Times* of London, which wrote in its anniversary edition last year:

"During the war and presumably as a result of it the trade unions grew enormously. Strikes became far more numerous than in normal times, and discontent with Mr. Gompers was loudly voiced—if not formally and publicly, then at least privately. . . . The existence of a strong Socialist group in the federation has been evident for some time, finding expression in the repeated efforts to unseat Gompers as chairman. Furthermore, experienced observers believe that this group is far stronger than the actions of the convention, its resolutions, or its elections for chairman and executive board would indicate. In addition, in a number of cases capable and experienced chairmen of craft unions were defeated in elections and replaced by men of the extreme, Socialist type. . . ." That was written on July 4 of last year.

I have a report on the last AFL convention, held in January of this year. This report, which appeared in Sydney

Webb's publication the *New Statesman,* discusses the fact that, by a vote of 29,000 to 8,000, the convention adopted a proposal not just to nationalize the American railroads but to do so under the supervision of a joint commission of labor and management representatives. This project, in itself reformist, has revolutionary significance, representing a breach in the American union movement. The *New Statesman* has this to say about the outcome of the convention discussions: "Mr. Gompers was reelected as chairman. Mr. Gompers for the first time in his career expressed the desire to lay down the scepter. *He senses that his throne is shaky and that his time is past.* The radicals departed in jubilation. They had won their first big, decisive victory at a convention of the AFL and, as one delegate put it, had showed 'how to throw a monkey wrench into the works.'"

I do not want to be identified in any way with this optimistic appraisal. It is quite possible that things will develop differently. In any case, these events show that the AFL is no longer a monolithic bloc. There are rifts in it, and it is the American Communists' duty to widen them.

When American Communists ask me what means can be used to transform the bureaucracy in the AFL or to get rid of it, I reply that if the Communists begin by going into the AFL with the slogan of destroying it, they will destroy their own work. However, if as a result of their struggle it turns out to be necessary to destroy the federation, they should do so. But no tactical consideration requires us to take a hard stand against joining the federation. The task is to work *within it* as the factor unifying those acting on it from the outside with the body of British and American workers organized in the labor federation. The aristocratic arrogance of these organized workers will be broken by all the suffering brought down on them, even in America, by a capitalism that is collapsing. Thus, we make it a general rule to fight to win over the trade unions.

The other question we face is that of the spontaneously formed organizations. Originating in quite different ways, they are emerging out of the struggle during the war and today. As new phenomena, they require our closest attention. These are organizations such as the Shop Stewards and factory committees in Britain or the factory committees in Germany. Initially their composition is chaotic, but such a chaos engenders new life, and only the most thickskulled German trade unionist would fail to see new life in this movement.

We saw how the Shop Stewards arose when the British union bureaucracy renounced the strike weapon during the war. The workers themselves formed the committees that led the strike. After the war these shop committees became the center of the most active forces in the British working class, as those forces set out to organize strikes. Once again with no help from the union bureaucracy, they took on the task of working consciously to neutralize the bureaucracy and push it back. Because of this the Shop Stewards are an organization called on to renew British trade union life. As the struggle unfolds and this movement becomes consciously revolutionary, the Shop Stewards come to see themselves as the leaders of revolutionary political activity as well. They become the center of direct action by the masses in Britain.

Turning to Germany, we see that the rise of the factory committees can in large measure be ascribed to disillusionment with the trade unions. As new, unorganized masses pour into the unions, we see that the core of thinking workers senses that the unions are inadequate because they are dominated by a counterrevolutionary bureaucracy, because they are craft organizations, and because they splinter and fragment the masses. In many cases this recognition causes workers to turn away completely from these trade unions. We see how the factory committee movement tries, under the yoke of capitalism, under Noske's rule, to lay the foundation of the future socialist economic order.

Now we face the principled question of judging and evaluating the opportunities for work in the trade unions in the capitalist countries. There is no need to dwell on our duty to support every factory organization that emerges among the proletariat with the goal of breaking the omnipotence of the union bureaucracy—not only in Britain but also in Germany, France, and every other country. When we consider the question of the factory committees' relationship to the trade unions in Germany, when we see not only the Legiens but also the right Independents (the Dissmanns and others) trying to integrate these organizations into the union apparatus on grounds of economizing revolutionary strength—saying that struggles must be led in a more unified way—we know these crafty people too well not to see through their intentions. If it were to happen that the Legiens and Dissmanns became leaders of the proletariat's revolutionary struggle, we would tell the factory committees to join their ranks. But that is not the case. The Legiens lead the German counterrevolution. Look at the right Independents' practice, examine Dissmann's policies in the metalworkers' union, and you will not see the slightest difference between his policies and those of the Legiens. Under these circumstances, the effort to fit the factory committees into the union apparatus is an attempt to destroy these revolutionary organizations, which in time of struggle can act as organs of the revolution.

As for the effort to turn these factory committees into a systematic organization able to facilitate the transition to socialism (an effort that belongs properly to a transitional epoch)—that was an illusion, as I believe will be recognized even by comrades who worked for that goal. Under the sword of capitalism and the state of siege, it is impossible to construct an organization that can be the apparatus of the future socialist economic order. The point is that the movement is growing, growing for a variety of reasons. It encompasses the most active parts of the proletariat, it combats the leaden weight of the union bureaucracy, and, as it grows, it increasingly organizes the struggle and exercises control over production. If the capitalist economic system continues to decline, not only conscious workers but every single worker in the factory will face the question: Where can coal, raw materials, and so on be obtained?

For all these reasons a struggle arises and percolates through the factories, and the masses become its vehicle. The trade unions alone cannot be that vehicle, for they do not encompass the entire mass of workers in the factory; they are still craft organizations. Here a revolutionary organization is required that acts as a revolutionary force and that on a question like this takes as its primary task setting the *masses* in motion and leading them in struggle. Just as we said that it is the task of Communists to march at the head of the trade unions—not to be satisfied with communist propaganda but to attempt to become the movement's leading part—so too, where the factory committees and Shop Stewards are concerned, the initiative clearly falls to the Communists.

When we are asked whether new organizations should be created alongside the trade unions and what their relationship to each other should be, our answer is that these new organizations will be our bases against the union bureaucracy as long as the bureaucracy dominates the unions. However, when the Communists become the leaders of the movement, then it will be time to let the two streams merge and turn the factory committees into organs of the trade unions.

But today, any attempt to deliver the councils into the hands of the trade unions is counterrevolutionary.

There is one more question on which we must take a position, namely that of industrial unionism and the industrial unions. When we hear propaganda for industrial unionism from various quarters, it makes us think we are dealing with a new fetish. It is claimed that the craft unions can no longer serve the revolution, that the industrial unions are exalted and perfect. That is a completely metaphysical position. It has already been shown in practice that there can be such a thing as reactionary industrial unionism. If the workers organize themselves into industrial unions in order to make a pact with the capitalists, there is nothing revolutionary about that. On the other hand, it is possible for union organizations that are even more backward than the craft unions to unite in revolutionary struggle if they are filled with a revolutionary spirit.

The ideology of these industrial unions can in fact be traced to a very simple fact: it is better if workers are organized by industry, not by craft. The tendency toward industrial unions is progressive. We want to support them, but we must not make a shibboleth of them. If we do, instead of preventing fragmentation we will create in addition to twenty craft unions a twenty-first, industrial union encapsulating yet another one-hundredth of the masses. The road to industrial unions leads through our struggle in the trade unions. If we were to split the unions in order to found an industrial union, the result would be the opposite of what we desire. We see this in the case of America, where after the rise of industrial workers' unions—which were supposed to unite all the workers—the unions remained as fragmented as ever.

The question of industrial unionism is related to that of syndicalism, and the fact that some of our comrades talk about it constantly indicates to me that they incline toward the syndicalist movement, which opposes the proletarian state and the dictatorship of the proletariat. It is very difficult to struggle against this current in the Anglo-Saxon countries, where the workers have never had a really revolutionary party nor seen a revolutionary struggle. We should not make such a struggle more difficult for them by adopting syndicalist ideology.

The Communist International's position on the syndicalist currents is established by the congress resolution admitting syndicalist organizations to the International.[7] By adopting this resolution the Communist International showed that the old spirit of the Social Democracy is completely alien to it. Because we see syndicalism as a transitional ailment of the revolutionary workers' movement, we try to approach the syndicalists, to form a bloc with them, and when possible to struggle shoulder to shoulder with them. But at the same time we must point out to them all the unclarity of the road as they see it. With respect to the union movement we must recall that the great masses of workers are not in the syndicalist camp. We must take that into account, and direct our organizational efforts toward reaching the masses.

I am coming to my conclusion. The task of communism with respect to the trade unions is both very difficult and very rewarding. Here in the unions we see the convergence of millions of workers destined by history to become the main contingent of the social revolution. They bring with them all of their prejudices, clumsiness, and changing moods. Nevertheless, these masses will wage the decisive struggles, and for that reason it is the Communists' duty not just to see the Legiens in the leadership. The Communists' task is to keep their eyes on the masses and work in the trade unions as long as necessary. The comrades say, "Yes, if we had time for that, a few years in which to work, we could win over those organizations." No one can say how long it will be before the victorious social revolution sets its foot on capitalism's throat; and if the masses must be won over to the idea of communism, that will take no less time than winning over the trade unions. There is only one road: shrink from no difficulty, go into these organizations, and conduct the struggle.

To my German comrades I say: To this day you have not started even a weekly trade union newspaper that could lead the struggle systematically. Where are the united fractions of Communists and Independents in the unions? Where has anyone tried to break up the organization of the union bureaucracy from below? We are only at the beginning of our systematic struggle and have no right to complain about the modest results. As for the situation in the Anglo-Saxon countries, we must say that less despair and more communist optimism would certainly do you good.

Let me sum up. The USPD press expressed the position on the trade union bureaucracy that we are taking now. This brings us to the last question on the union movement, which of course is that of communism. Here we are separated by an abyss from the theory and practice of the USPD—not so much in form as in deed. It is not solely a matter of whether or not we join the trade unions but rather what we will do in those unions. What the USPD accomplished in the trade unions was no more than the replacement of Schlicke by Dissmann.[8] The point is not merely to go into the trade unions but rather to take up the struggle against the old trade union bureaucracy and its spirit, even at the risk of a split—which we do not fear, if it arises from the struggle.

Satisfied by their victory at the metalworkers' congress, the USPDers immediately reattached the leaden weight of proportional representation by leaving the old bureaucracy on the executive board. Their membership in the General German Trade Union Federation binds them in practice to the Labor Boards. They look over their shoulder at every step. None of this, of course, is winning over the trade unions but signifies only that the USPD is replacing the Legiens and will continue their policy.

We are in favor of entering parliaments, and so are the Independents. But we do this in order to conduct revolutionary agitation and propaganda there, to provoke clashes. If necessary we will even participate in the commissions, since that is the best place to gather information. The Independents, however, behave differently. Let me give an example. During the war Comrade Haase was in the commission for foreign affairs, but he took care not to reveal the commission's secrets in parliament, even when they were directed against the German people. Keeping the government's secrets was very important to him. I think that when our comrades take part in those commissions, they will act differently.

It is the same with the trade unions. We join the unions in order to overthrow the bureaucracy there and, if necessary, to split the unions. We go into the unions in order to turn them into weapons of struggle. The result of the USPD's first year of work in the trade unions, however, is that they want to put the factory committees, revolutionary organizations of the proletariat, under the thumb of the union bureaucracy. It is a matter of the difference in spirit, in the will to act and struggle, the will to turn the trade unions into an instrument of the revolution.

The Communist Party advances its policies by utilizing elements left over from bourgeois society. We will try to convert the unions into organizations of struggle. If the bureaucracy's resistance proves stronger than we think, we will not be afraid to smash them, because we know that the most important thing is not the form but rather the workers' capacity to organize and their will to organize the revolutionary struggle. We will join the trade unions and try with all our might to win them over, without tying our hands. We will not let the trade union bureaucracy bind us hand and foot, and if it tries to restrict our possibilities for revolutionary struggle, we will lead the masses in driving it out of the unions. We go into the unions not to preserve them but rather to promote working-class solidarity—the only basis on which the big industrial unions of the social revolution can be formed.

It is most essential to combine two things: to be with the masses and go with them, yet not to lag behind them. That is the direction of communist policy in the trade unions. We see the councils as spontaneous organizing by the proletariat, and as long as the unions fail to serve the revolution, as long as the union bureaucracy stands as a bulwark against the revolution, we will keep the councils separate and help them, so that along with them we can lead the masses in struggle.

That is what I wanted to say.

Now a few formal things. The commission elected by the congress had to overcome big problems. These originated in the fact that the resolutions were written too narrowly. Our theses gave too little consideration to British-American conditions, and I admit that for a long time it was difficult for me to figure out what these comrades wanted. We finally realized that there are no principled differences between our position and theirs. All agreed it is our duty to work in the trade unions. Only one American comrade proposed in his theses that Communists should remain outside of the AFL.[9]

Then the question arose of determining in which cases they should work outside the unions. One case had already been incorporated into our theses, namely, when the union bureaucracy suppresses our agitation. We established a second case when we learned that 80 percent of workers in America are unorganized and that the AFL consciously rejects organizing large masses by demanding very high initiation fees. In such a situation it is clear that Communists have the obligation to organize those masses.

The final problem, which we could not settle in the commission, is that the American comrades insist that numerous union statutes prevented their working in the unions, that the bureaucracy there is irremovable, that no conventions have been called in years, and so on. We acknowledge that such cases are theoretically possible, but I told the comrades frankly that I suspect they have a tendency to take the easy way out and run away from the unions. So I take no responsibility for this amendment. The American comrades should be specific here about this case. If the situation is as they report, then we cannot refuse to let them form separate unions in such cases.

The other question concerned the factory committees. The resolution describes the final phase of the factory committees, when their task is to struggle for control of production. The passage gives the impression that this is a prospect for the future. We therefore agreed that the resolution should also take into account the factory committees' earlier phases of development.

The final point concerns the question of international trade union organization. On this there are two points of view. The Russian commission on unions submitted a version that takes as its starting point the statement by the unions of Britain, Italy, Russia, and Bulgaria, which have called a congress.[10] The Russian resolution points out that the unions must become part of the Communist International. The American comrades object to the call by the Italian, Russian, and British unions. They made quite a few criticisms of it. These comrades will present these problems here themselves, and we will let the congress settle it.

I will not read the motions individually, simply because the commission must first edit them in any case. Therefore, I will merely repeat that they include the cases in which special organizations should be formed, that is, cases in which revolutionary union organizing is suppressed. They also mention the need to support the Shop Stewards and factory committees as organizations of proletarian struggle. Further, they say these organizations must remain separate as long as the counterrevolutionary bureaucracy dominates the unions. Finally, they deal with the still-undecided question of the trade union International.

*(The next speaker is Baba Akhunde Samilov, representing the Khorezm delegation. He presents the following greetings.)*

## GREETINGS FROM THE TOILERS OF KHOREZM

BABA AKHUNDE SAMILOV: Dear comrades, we, the authorized representatives of Khorezm, bring you warm greetings on behalf of Khorezm's toiling poor.[11] This Second Congress of the Communist International symbolizes the unity of the toilers of the whole world. We therefore congratulate you for having the opportunity to come together in this great assembly, and we consider it our great good fortune that we can be present here on this happy occasion.

Comrades, when the European capitalists ruled, we the toilers of Khorezm were oppressed under the political and economic yoke of their tsars and parliaments, for they made small nations like ours languish in chains and granted freedom only to the rich.

Today, with the help of soviet power in Russia, we the oppressed have raised ourselves up, freed ourselves from the oppressors' heavy hand, and declared our country an independent soviet republic.

We sincerely believe that assistance from the East, which thanks to soviet power in Russia has recently awakened, will help to bring about in the near future the liberation of the toilers of the whole world from the rapists and capitalists. We believe that the peoples of the East will not lay down their weapons until the toilers of the whole world have united into a single family.

Long live the unity of the toilers of the whole world!

Long live the European proletariat and the vanguard of the world revolution, the Communist Party!

Long live the Communist International!

Long live the world soviet republic!

Long live Comrade Lenin, leader of the world revolution, and Comrade Broido, consolidator of the revolution in Khorezm!

Long live the Communist Party of Khorezm and the soviet republic of Khorezm!

## MINORITY REPORTS ON THE TRADE UNIONS AND FACTORY COMMITTEES

FRAINA: After the discussion in the trade union commission we found ourselves much more in agreement than we expected.[12] The differences that still persist are largely differences of emphasis and practice, not of principle.

The differences first developed out of the declaration convening a conference to organize an International of revolutionary labor unions. Some of the fundamental features of this declaration were totally unacceptable. For example, the condemnation of revolutionists' leaving the trade unions was put in such a form as to exclude construction of a new labor organization.[13] This would cripple the American movement, since in our country, where 80 percent of the workers are unorganized and the trade unions are dominated by the labor aristocracy, the construction of a new revolutionary labor organization is an imperative revolutionary task. Furthermore, the admission of separate industrial unions to the conference is made conditional upon the consent of the central labor organization of each country.[14] Moreover, no provision is made for a representative on the organizing committee of that labor International from both the IWW and the Shop Stewards of England—two movements of vital importance in the development of the revolutionary struggle.[15]

Our objections to Comrade Radek's theses (only some of which were met by his accepting several of our amendments) pertained, above all, to his conception of unionism. Radek approached the problem almost exclusively from the standpoint of winning the masses in the unions to communism. That, of course, is fundamental. But it is also fundamental to consider the unions in relation to our task—as organs of revolutionary struggle and as factors in the economic reconstruction of society after the conquest of political power. Radek also made the conditions under which new labor unions may be organized too narrow and artificial. And, finally, it appeared in Radek's theses as if our task was to capture the trade union bureaucracy. The theses reveal no understanding of and no provision for extraunion organizations (such as the shop committees, shop stewards, and so forth) as means of aggressive struggle against the bureaucracy and for the mobilization of the masses for action.

In the United States revolutionary conceptions have been spread through revolutionary unionism. These conceptions were the necessity of extraparliamentary action to conquer political power, destruction of the bourgeois state machinery, and organization of the proletarian state not on geographical but on industrial divisions. These conceptions made it easy for us to understand the fundamental tactics of the Russian revolution. But at the same time we were compelled to carry on a severe theoretical struggle against the IWW conception that the overthrow of capitalism requires only the industrial unions, without soviets and proletarian dictatorship. The American Communist movement has done very important work in reconciling the old revolutionary conceptions of industrial unionism with the new conceptions of Bolshevism. And a necessary part of our work is to recognize the revolutionary functions of the labor unions.

The IWW in the United States has been a real revolutionary force, but not primarily because of its agitation for industrial unionism nor because it tried to boycott and destroy the American Federation of Labor—in neither of these things has it been very successful. The IWW has been a tremendous revolutionary force in the American movement primarily because it expressed the awakening to consciousness and action of the great masses of unorganized, unskilled workers excluded from the American Federation of Labor. All movements to break the AFL by leaving the old unions have been a failure. During the war when the old unions made a partnership with the government, the IWW members were compelled to join the old unions, and by agitating from within, these IWWs developed very powerful revolutionary movements in the old unions.

American experience, accordingly, emphasizes the necessity of working within the old unions (in a revolutionary way). But this experience equally emphasizes the necessity of constructing new unions (in accord with objective conditions) in order to unite revolutionary work within the old unions with work from without.

There is no controversy on the need to work in the old unions. On that we are all agreed. For the American Communist movement to reject working in the old unions and adopt the slogan "Destroy the American Federation of Labor" would destroy the Communist movement and not the reactionary labor unions.

The controversy centers on the methods and purposes of working in the old unions. We maintain that the emphasis must be not on capturing the bureaucracy but on liberating the masses from the domination of this bureaucracy and mobilizing the masses independently of it.

In the old unions the bureaucracy is practically immovable, imposed upon the masses and a barrier to action. In the United States in addition to constitutional provisions, long-term offices, and parliamentary tricks, the trade union bureaucracy uses gunmen to suppress the rebel opposition in the unions. I mention this not as an argument against working in the reactionary unions but as an argument against the idea of capturing the bureaucracy. We must fight this bureaucracy in the unions, but it will be impossible to capture or destroy this bureaucracy until the revolution itself or after.

Really revolutionary work in the trade unions has two important aspects:

1. The organization of Communist groups (necessary in all workers' organizations).

2. The formation of extraunion organizations—shop committees, shop stewards, and so forth. These are organizations of workers in the unions expressing the requirements of the immediate economic struggle of the workers, and their struggle is against the bureaucracy and the limitations on trade union forms of organization.

The formation of extraunion organizations does not mean that the workers leave the old unions; on the contrary, the workers stay in the unions but organize their opposition in a different way. Moreover, these extraunion organizations act inside and outside the trade unions, and if in a crisis they cannot get the unions to act, they act independently of the unions and of the bureaucracy. They are the most adequate means of driving the unions to more revolutionary action and of mobilizing the masses for the aggressive struggle against capitalism. In England and the United States these extraunion organizations have been produced by life itself, by the experience of the workers' struggle. It is through the creation of such extraunion organizations that the Communists can best become the leaders of the immediate economic struggle of the working class.

What we insist upon is not leaving the old unions, but organizing an aggressive, decisive struggle in the unions and against the bureaucracy.

It is also necessary to carry on this struggle outside of the old unions. This is accomplished by the organization of new, independent unions. It is absolutely necessary that the organization of such unions (and secessions from the old unions) should be based upon objective conditions and express the struggle itself. But it is equally necessary not to be afraid of new unions. It is just as harmful to act in general against splits and new unions (where these concern the masses) as it is to insist upon splits and new unions as a doctrinaire proposition, thereby isolating ourselves from the masses. A split, after all, is a decisive, aggressive act, and may accomplish more revolutionary agitation than years of peaceful routine work in the unions. Moreover, by uniting the independent industrial unions with the extraunion organizations in the old unions, we perfect a force that will batter from inside and outside and that, inspired and dominated by the Communists, will constitute a powerful factor in mobilizing the masses for action. We are in a revolutionary epoch, and our fundamental task is to liberate the masses for action. We cannot depend upon the peaceful prolonged process of capturing the bureaucracy.

Parallel with this problem of extraunion organizations is the problem of industrial unionism as against the craft form of unionism. This problem has three aspects:

1. Industrial unionism is the organizational expression of the unorganized, unskilled workers, which in the United States comprise the majority of the industrial proletariat. The construction of new unions generally implies the adoption of industrial unionism. Industrial unionism is the basis for the development of revolutionary unionism.

2. Agitation for industrial unionism is a necessary part of our work in the old unions. These unions, mostly organized on the antiquated basis of crafts, are, under the pressure of concentrated industry, unable to really unite the workers in unions and carry on an aggressive struggle. Workers in the old unions revolt against the limitations of the craft forms as well as the purposes of the trade unions, and we must urge upon them the industrial union form

of organization—an indispensable phase of our struggle to transform and revolutionize the old unions.

3. After the conquest of political power the unions will become organs for the administration of industry under the proletarian state. Because their organizational form does not correspond to integrated industry, craft unions cannot function in the management of industry. Industrial unions are necessary, as is proved by the Russian experience. The larger the industrial unions and the greater the understanding of industrial unionism, the easier will be the task of economic reconstruction after the revolutionary conquest of power.

This is the conception of unionism developed and formulated by the American movement, and we are convinced that it is an indispensable phase of communist tactics.

TANNER: I speak in the name of the Shop Stewards' committees. I wish to emphasize that after the speech of Comrade Radek it has become clear to me that there can be no question of differences in principle. The main thing is to ascertain the relations between the Communists, the Shop Stewards, and the revolutionary organizations now coming into existence. It has been pointed out that there must be relations between the Communists and all revolutionary organizations. During the war, after the Shop Stewards came into existence, some people suggested that with the end of the war their role too would be finished. But this is not in accordance with the truth. They are called upon to play their revolutionary role now as well. As regards the purpose of all such organizations, one of their most difficult duties is to fight bureaucracy in the trade unions. But in spite of the difficulty, they must strive for great results in this respect.

Now what is the attitude of the Shop Stewards' supporters toward the question raised here? Although the trade unions are not organized democratically, we are far from saying that no one should belong to them under any circumstances. We hold the view that one must leave them, but we understand that the situation varies in each case. We put the main stress on the revolutionary class struggle, a struggle that must also be carried on against the bureaucracy of the old trade unions.

It has been pointed out that the conference of the Shop Stewards together with that of the factory committees should emphasize once more their attitude and tactics toward the soviet movement. Their purpose is to overcome capitalism and root out the wage system. Considering the fact that the revolution can be realized only by the mass actions of the workers, the Shop Stewards' attitude toward already existing organizations cannot be inimical. But it can be said that the movement of the Shop Stewards and factory committees aims at reorganizing the trade unions on a revolutionary basis, changing their structure. This revolutionary purpose can be realized only if vigorous propaganda is carried on within the old trade unions and if there is more active participation in the work inside these organizations.

The Shop Stewards are in no way opposed to all work whatsoever within the trade unions. But they are against the Red trade union International and refuse to take part in it. The attitude expressed in the proclamation under consideration is unacceptable for the Shop Stewards because it contains the assertion that one must not leave the old trade unions.[16] Given this condition the Shop Stewards cannot accept the proposal. The fact that such a passage has been included proves that the conditions in the various countries have not been taken into consideration. This proclamation should be submitted to criticism by the congress and be handed over to the commission. The comrades who have worked in the commission have proved that they do not share the standpoint of this proclamation.

SESSION 12

AUGUST 3, 1920 (EVENING)

# Trade unions and factory committees

*(Part 2)*

*(The session opens at 10:00 p.m.)*

WALCHER: Comrades, this morning the reporter referred to the important fact that at the beginning of the revolution many of us believed that in the future the trade unions had no further role to play. But he is mistaken if he believes Comrade Rosa Luxemburg as well was among those who supported this idea. Let me state here that at the party's founding congress she expressly opposed those who envisaged solving the whole question with the slogan: "Get out of the trade unions."[1]

On the question at hand, I would like to say that I am skeptical of Comrade Radek's report and of the remarks made by subsequent speakers indicating that the commission achieved unity in principle on the disputed questions. It was evident from several comments made in the commission that the comrades in Europe and America are inclined to struggle against the old, ossified trade union bureaucracy by founding new unions and withdrawing from the old ones. Several comments made there breathed the KAPD spirit and sounded very familiar to me.

The situation in Britain and America is certainly very complicated, but if the British comrades want to remain in the trade unions while working in the Shop Stewards' movement as well, I do not understand why they spoke out so harshly and emphatically against the theses right from the beginning.

We have already stated the principle that it is the duty of Communists to form Communist cells in all organizations and carry out propaganda there. Thus the British comrades, whatever their activity in the unions, have not only the right but the duty to work for our ideas in the Shop Stewards' committees. If they nonetheless oppose the theses on principle, then I think that proves that the British and American comrades are as emotional about the trade union question as they are about the question of parliamentarism. In my opinion, we must take care not to look at this question in an emotional way, especially in a time of revolution.

As Marxists we must not forget that the unions did not become what they are today by accident. Rather, we see the results of a reformist era that lasted for decades, during which the unions grew together with capitalist society to an ever greater degree. The objectively revolutionary situation we face today gives us the opportunity to revolutionize the old trade unions. If some comrades doubt this is possible, they are overlooking the fact that the objective situation has changed fundamentally, transforming what may have seemed utopian before the war into our duty today. These comrades feel that it is taking too long, that the road is too hard. But by now every comrade should know that without the millions in the unions we cannot carry out our task. That is why we absolutely must do this difficult work there. The slogan to quit the unions is an attempt to circumvent troublesome obstacles; unfortunately, however, it fails to remove them from our path.

I do not understand how those who say the masses are ready and we can conquer the whole world can deny that it is possible to win the minds of the masses in the unions. I say it is possible and we can and must do it. The argument continues, "Well, we do not need the broad masses; revolutions are always the work of small minorities." I think that when comrades say this they are thinking of a palace revolution like the one in Portugal or elsewhere.[2] The kind of revolution that we must carry out can be the work only of the great masses.

It will be said, "Yes, the masses are ready, but the leaders are to blame." This notion leads to the assumption that it is enough to eliminate the leaders, and then everything will be fine. The German Independents' entire trade union policy is oriented to filling individual leadership posts with their followers. They neglect revolutionary activity among the masses themselves. The Wolffheims and Rühles, on the other hand, say that even if the bureaucracy is eliminated, that will not change the essence of the matter.[3] The British comrades reason the same way in their theses. This is a strange contradiction. On the one hand it is the leaders' fault; on the other, it does not matter whether there are leaders or not. In Germany the Wolffheims and Rühles put this to the test. It is our duty to issue a strong warning against following their example.

We have fought hard over precisely this question, and the split in the KPD was caused primarily by its position on the trade union question. We have not just one example but hundreds to prove that the day the Communists leave the ranks of the unions the bureaucracy will hold a joyous celebration. I personally had to fight for a long time for my membership in the metalworkers' union. We will not do the union bureaucracy that favor. Our comrades know that this would be like uncoupling the locomotive from the train and driving it around by itself, leaving the train to its fate.

In both the theses and the reporters' remarks it was very correctly pointed out that we must not only conduct communist propaganda in the unions but look after all of the proletariat's interests and vigorously take up all questions. Precisely in the unions—my own experience has shown me this—the more selflessly and energetically Communists advocate all their co-workers' concerns and needs, the more rapidly they win the confidence of the masses.

Now, I also wish that what Comrade Radek said about sabotage and passive resistance had been included in the theses. After the experiences we have had with sabotage as a weapon in union struggles, that seems highly advisable to me. Of course there are situations in which we must use sabotage, but in general it is unsuitable and we should warn against using it.

Finally I would like to say a word about the position of the factory committees. The theses we have before us say quite correctly that the division of tasks between the factory committees and the trade unions is the result of historical development. But Comrade Radek said that any attempt to turn the factory committees over to the trade unions would be counterrevolutionary. In principle this statement seems to me to be correct, but in a situation like the one that exists in Germany at the present time it could well cause misunderstandings.

A debate has been under way in Germany for several months over whether the factory committees should exist as independent organizations or be incorporated into the unions. It is a struggle between the union bureaucracy and the central leadership of the factory committees. We supported the effort of the left Independents to unite the factory committees as independent organizations, but to this day the effort has not been successful for reasons I will not go into here. I will say only that it is true that in this struggle—and earlier as well—half of the USPD took one side and half the other. They canceled each other out, and in practice the trade unions, supported by the right wing of the USPD, were able to impose their views.

The struggle can now be regarded as finished. And we must say that Legien emerged from it as the provisional victor, because the federation of the old German trade unions adopted his platform unanimously, and it has already been announced that a national congress of factory committees will be held soon. Our comrades are inclined to participate in it and continue the struggle against Legien on that terrain. The Legiens are trying to turn the factory committees into organs of "civil peace" and collaboration,[4] but we are certain that they will not succeed. We will try to prevent them from doing this by firmly uniting our comrades everywhere and also by uniting our comrades in the factory committees into fractions. And if they become champions of all the proletariat's needs arising from the decay of the capitalist order, we are certain to succeed in turning the factory committees and trade unions into organizations that direct their full force against capitalist society in a fully conscious way and consciously advocate communism.

BOMBACCI: I would like to explain in a few words why I cannot accept Comrade Radek's theses. What was proposed here does not correspond either to the evolution of the trade unions over time or to the present stage of historical development in general. I fear—and I think that this applies to all of western Europe—that a danger can be seen in Radek's theses of substituting the trade unions for the party. I stress that I understand his thinking well enough to see that these theses do not imply simply substituting the unions for the party. But that is the tendency.

I absolutely deny that trade unions have any revolutionary function whatever. I am referring to the examples of America and western Europe. Precisely in Russia, where there certainly is a trade union movement, it did not carry out a truly revolutionary function. The unions were a sort of intermediary between the workers and the bourgeoisie. I repeat, it would be a mistake to attribute a revolutionary function to the unions, and it would be an even greater mistake to permit the unions to replace the parties. The unions represent a platform for propaganda. In parliament propaganda is limited in that it is addressed only to a certain number of people, whereas in the unions it is addressed to the entire working class.

During the war a movement developed in Italy to form a workers' party based on the unions. In Germany, too, during the events around the Kapp conspiracy, the unions said that if they took power, they would exercise it in the name of these same unions. I see a dangerous symptom in all these manifestations. Trade unions must not be allowed to exercise political functions; they develop a reformist activity and are not qualified for revolutionary tasks. I would like to draw the attention of the British and American comrades to this danger, and I point to the Italian experience, during which efforts were made to unite the most varied movements, efforts that naturally failed.

What is the task of Communist parties in the trade unions? The example of Italy shows us that certain unions were syndicalist and others reformist. Above all the opportunist heads of the unions must be replaced by Communists so that there is a Communist leadership in the unions as well. But the trade unions as such are unable to play any political role.

LOZOVSKY: Comrades, the question of the trade unions and what they mean for the revolution we are now experiencing is extremely important not only for this congress but also in the struggle now occurring in every country.

In my opinion, many comrades who have spoken on the union movement make a great error by looking at it from an incorrect point of view. Comrade Bombacci, for example, who just spoke on the union movement, asserted that it is absolutely impossible to win the trade unions—in Italy, for example—to the Communist movement. Other comrades, mainly the American and British, after studying the union movement in their countries, also reach very pessimistic conclusions. They say that the union movement cannot be used for the social revolution.

Do these conclusions correspond to the truth?

When we use the words "trade union" and "trade union movement," do we mean the organizational structures—the unions, the councils, and so on? If we have only the leaders in mind, then it is clear that they are not the material for the social revolution. But when we speak of the union movement and the unions, we want to talk about the masses in these organizations. The pessimistic comrades say it is absolutely impossible to win over the unions and, moreover, the unions in France and Italy are reformist and will always remain so. If this is so, they must necessarily conclude that the social revolution is completely impossible in those countries, since modern trade unions are not small but are mass bodies encompassing millions of workers. And if it is true that we cannot win over these organizations, we must despair of the world revolution.

At the same time, however, Comrade Bombacci tells us that the revolution in Italy is making progress and will be realized in a matter of weeks. Let me then ask him: With whom will you make your revolution? And who will make it? What will the trade unions do in the revolution? What role will they play? The comrade must answer these questions. Certainly we would be wrong to assert that these bodies are beyond all hope.

We will not point to the Russian unions, scarcely three years old, as an example. In fact, we were born only in 1917. We are still quite young.

Turning our attention to the old capitalist countries, especially America or Germany, where the unions have already existed for a long time, or to Britain, where they have existed for a century already, we see that in recent years, in the last few months, millions of workers have joined the trade unions and are changing them. We are not talking about the leaders here. We must drive them out. The important thing is to win over the masses.

Any tactic aiming to encourage the most advanced elements to leave the unions is a reactionary tactic, an admission that we are so weak that we cannot win over the masses. Comrades, the more difficult the task, the harder one must work to carry it out. It is necessary to go into the unions and conquer them. If we have a wonderfully organized union such as the metalworkers in Germany, should we form a new one alongside it? If we have a solidly organized union in Britain, must we start a new one?

From all of this it is plain that some comrades, who seemed in their speeches to be very revolutionary, are in reality proposing a reactionary tactic that must be rejected.

A Communist, who understands the situation and hopes and believes that the masses of workers will march hand in hand with the Communists, says, "Join the unions and win them to our cause!" That is a primary condition for seizing power and overthrowing the bourgeois state.

This is where the question of the factory committees comes up, and it takes different forms in different countries. I asked a German comrade, "How many workers have you organized in these factory committees in Germany?" He answered, "There were seventeen million."

Mention was also made of the Shop Stewards' committees in Britain. Unlike the factory committees in Russia and the factory committees in Germany, these are groups of like-minded workers who have united to form bodies called Shop Stewards' committees. These are not factory committees but Communist or revolutionary fractions in the factories, which is not quite the same thing. When people talk to us about the Shop Stewards' committees, we reply that it is a very particular question since their situation has nothing in common with that of the factory committees in Germany and the factory committees in Russia.

We must reach agreement on this question. If you mean to say that a Communist or vanguard fraction must be formed in the unions, go ahead and do it. But if you want to organize factory committees outside of the unions, committees that encompass all workers,[5] we reply that you are wrong to form them outside of the unions. Some people say that the unions are reactionary and that it is therefore necessary to form a counterorganization outside of the unions. No, this organization must be formed *inside* the unions themselves. If you establish factory committees as organizations standing outside the unions, the masses of workers in the unions will be *against* you. But if you organize factory committees in the shops and factories, if they function as auxiliary bodies, doing the same work as the unions, and if their work also transforms and arouses the unions, then in the end your perseverance, your labor, and your propaganda will revolutionize the unions.

Such a result is possible not through speeches but only through actions. And this action must be carried out by the soviets and factory committees. Only from this point of view can the work of the factory committees be understood; only thus can the need to organize them be grasped.

We reshaped the factory committees before the October revolution. We will reorganize the trade unions before the social revolution—not through propaganda of words but rather through deeds—because the unions must become the organ of this revolution. If we do not win the unions *before* the decisive battle, if we cannot make use of the unions' discipline for the social revolution in every country, we will be defeated. These unions must be won before the social revolution in order to constitute the basis for the dictatorship of the proletariat. That is the lesson that can be drawn from the Russian revolution.

Finally, a few words on the international movement.

We discussed with several American comrades the prospects for an international trade union organization. They said the organization that has been created is not revolutionary enough.

Here in Moscow we laid the basis for a new organization.

We had discussions with the British comrades for six days and six nights. What were our differences? I will tell you. The same comrades who today accuse us of not being revolutionary enough did not want to sign the point on the dictatorship of the proletariat. They said that the state must be overthrown. "Which state?" we asked them. We said, "The bourgeois state must be overthrown," explaining that we want a revolution, but we do not want ambiguities.[6]

Those are the differences of opinion that prevented the Shop Stewards' committees and the IWW from supporting the statement we signed. I hope this statement will be included in the congress proceedings. Two questions in it are of great importance.

This statement, signed by the delegates of seven countries, makes three important points:

1. We are now creating an organization opposed to the Amsterdam International.

2. This organization is based on the concept of the dictatorship of the proletariat and the violent overthrow of bourgeois society.

3. The main elements of the vanguard must not withdraw from the workers' trade unions but must win them.

Those who feel too weak to fight to win the unions do not share this position. We, however, believe that the workers' movement is making great strides forward in all countries, driving the workers toward social revolution. It is up to the Communists to do everything possible to win the unions (that today still have such an opportunist orientation) and utilize union discipline for the greatest possible good of the social revolution.

I have not said everything that I wanted to say, but it is almost everything that I could say in the short time allotted me.

ZINOVIEV: The Presiding Committee proposes ending debate and proceeding to the vote. There are sixteen more speakers on the list. We have heard a report and two coreports, which presented the positions adequately. The commission held six meetings, each five hours long, and in addition the question is sufficiently explained in the literature.

REED: I have nothing to say against closing the list, but I am against ending debate. The discussion is being closed on purpose, to avoid discussing this point with the English and American delegations. During the commission sessions Comrade Radek refrained from discussing the trade union question, pretending there were differences over principles, and today he declared there are no differences. All of this proves that a discussion is necessary, even if it lasts all night, because this subject has not really been discussed here at all.

RADEK: Reed's speech is certainly not distinguished by excessive fear of distorting the truth. The whole description of what happened in the commission is an objective falsehood. The situation in the commission was this: For two sessions no amount of massaging could coax a single idea out of Comrade Reed. Finally Comrade Reed and his comrades put forward theses. The principled position they developed was that the trade union organizations must be demolished. He defended the principled position of smashing the unions. I then stated that there was a difference in principle between his theses and ours. Consequently, there seemed to be no purpose in a point-by-point discussion. Comrades Murphy and Fraina were also present in the commission. You could detect a factual content in their remarks that could not be gotten from Reed's speeches.

Yesterday we devoted a session to this question. The American and British delegates were of the opinion that we had reached an agreement and that there was no disagreement on principle. Reed's position was dropped. Reed himself put forward not a single motion. Even though no alternative position was before us, the British and American comrades had two coreporters today. After this, if Reed has the temerity to say discussion is being cut off for fear of the great genius John Reed, that is shameless. He may have the time to continue discussion until tomorrow morning, but other people do not.

MACALPINE: I ask that we close the speakers' list but not end the discussion. Radek's speech, which lasted two hours, was given to us in a twenty-minute translation. It strikes me as rather strange that time is being valued so highly here, because on the whole it is hard in Russia to notice any such economizing of time. I urgently ask that six or seven hours more be given for the discussion and that the English-speaking comrades be given the chance to express their opinion.

GALLACHER: I think Radek should play fair here. He gave a bad translation in the commission too. They did not want to allow us time for the discussion of the theses. And we English-speaking comrades have the impression that the theses are simply going to be railroaded through. We therefore ask that the debate be continued and that Comrade Reed be given a chance to explain his standpoint.

ZINOVIEV: The commission met six times; today we had discussion all day long in plenary session; and now we are told, "You want to shut us up, you do not want to play fair," and so forth. There should be discussion, but not until we drop. We have had seven speakers: three from the British-American group, three supporters of Radek's theses, and the seventh was Bombacci, who took a position rather close to that of the English delegates. The discussion was apportioned quite fairly. The English-speaking comrades had half of the speakers or even more. So I think that our English friends are in the wrong to make such heated speeches. After we have had so much discussion here, they now declare that we are being disloyal toward them. It is outrageous on their part to take such a position after so many concessions have been made to them. I suggest we resolve to end the discussion.

Tanner: I insist on our request that we receive the floor and that the list of speakers not be closed. In the commission we were promised that the question would be discussed in detail, because it is admitted to be one of the most important. The theses, the amendments, the motions have not been translated. And the members of the commission have hardly had the chance to become familiar with them. I believe that if two and a half days were spent on the question of the admission of the French Socialists and the Independent Socialist party then this question, which is of greater importance, must be discussed at greater length.

RADEK: Never before have I heard of a group disavowing its own reporters. The British-American group appointed two reporters. After they spoke Tanner came forward and said their arguments had not been adequately presented.

Does Reed think it takes two days to present his ideas? That does not require long discussions. Reed is not a separate political party or tendency. The tendency he represents was defended by the British-American reporters. The fact that they did not appoint Reed as a coreporter showed that they do not see him as a representative of a separate tendency. They had the opportunity to explain their position here. It was Fraina and Tanner who spoke for the group.

If anyone claims it is not true that Reed demanded leaving the trade unions, I have here the theses that he submitted. They say, "The trade union apparatus must be destroyed as surely as we must destroy the bourgeois state." I do not understand what will remain of the trade unions after the trade union apparatus has been destroyed.

Moreover, it should be borne in mind that in today's session we will not adopt any final resolutions. I will not give a summary. The issue goes back to the commission because prolonging the discussion will not settle the matter.

ZINOVIEV: No one has asked for the floor. The vote will now be taken. All in favor of the Bureau's recommendation to cut off discussion and vote on the theses, raise your hands. I ask all in favor of closing the debate to hold up their red cards.

In favor, 50; against, 25. The discussion is closed. (*Reed asks to make a statement.*) We now come to the vote on the theses. If various groups want to make statements on the vote, I will grant them two minutes.

REED: On behalf of the American delegation I declare that we decline to take part in the vote on these theses.[7]

TANNER: On behalf of the British delegation I declare that, since the Bureau considers the subject of so little importance, we decline to participate in the commission and in the voting.

SERRATI: I will vote for Comrade Radek's theses. I had not proposed any amendment, but I think the theses will need to be amended subsequently. We will see at the next congress what amendments we will have to submit. The American delegation can view the question in exactly the same way. I do not completely agree with Comrade Radek, since I question the possibility of changing the orientation of the [American] Federation of Labor. It is a narrow organization that has not changed for twenty-five years and remains reactionary. Nothing can be done to change it. I will vote for the theses because they correspond to the direction of our party; we never stopped supporting them. But I will reserve judgment on the question of the Red International of Labor Unions. In my opinion, this organization should not be dependent on the Third International but should be an autonomous and fraternal organization.

RADEK: I believe there is a misunderstanding here. Comrade Serrati did not know that the vote was final; he thought that the motions would be referred back to the commission as has been done with all other questions and as I announced.

WIJNKOOP: When Radek spoke, I understood that he meant to say that we would vote on these motions and not on his theses. I am sorry that now, after Radek introduced the matter that way, further amplification is impossible and the discussion is being cut off like this. As I understood the matter, Radek himself proposed not voting on his theses at this time. If what he said was that a vote would be taken on the theses only as a basis, then the procedure followed here would have been no different from the one followed for the other theses. But I thought he wanted to proceed differently here. I believe that several other members, when they voted to end the discussion, also understood that a commission would meet here at six o'clock, at which time the discussion that is being denied now would be continued. However, since the vote is to be taken without discussion, I do not believe that we will be able to cast our vote under such conditions.

PESTAÑA: I protest against the irregular manner in which the debates are being conducted. Nothing is being translated into French for us. However, the trade union question is of fundamental importance. It is even the most important question debated at the congress. Given this irregularity, I will abstain on the vote.

ZINOVIEV: We will vote on the theses as a basis. The question will be referred to the commission and will be dealt with further there. I would also like to point out that one should be sparing with threats to leave the congress—first because no one is afraid of threats and second because it will not be tolerated at a Communist congress.

MARING: Comrades, I believe that a solution can be found to this matter. There was the same problem with the colonial question, and the matter was referred back to the commission. If complete unity had not been achieved there, the commission would have had to come before the congress again. Thus, if the trade union commission does not now reach complete agreement—and so far I see no possibility that it will—then the question will come back from the commission to the congress. If that is how it will be, then I can state my agreement with the proposed arrangement.

ZINOVIEV: We will come to a vote. All in favor of making Comrade Radek's theses the basis, in favor of referring the amendments to the commission for further discussion, and—if agreement cannot be reached—bringing them back here, raise your hands. (*Vote*) The motion carries with 64 votes in favor and 13 abstentions.[8]

The Bureau wishes to make the following proposal. We must have an accurate text of all of our resolutions. We have four main groups, and we ask each of them to name one comrade to a committee that will be responsible for taking in hand all the texts, checking them, and preparing the final texts in the four languages.

The plenary session on the agrarian question will be tomorrow at eleven o'clock. The session on the organization question will be tomorrow afternoon.

(*The session adjourns.*)

## THESES ON THE TRADE UNION MOVEMENT, FACTORY COMMITTEES, AND THE COMMUNIST INTERNATIONAL

### I

1. The trade unions created by the working class during capitalism's period of peaceful development were workers' organizations for the struggle to raise the price of labor power on the labor market and improve its conditions

of employment.[9] Revolutionary Marxists strove to draw the unions, along with the political party of the proletariat, the Social Democracy, into a common struggle for socialism. International Social Democracy turned out to be, with few exceptions, not a tool of revolutionary proletarian struggle to overthrow capitalism but an organization that serves the bourgeoisie by holding back the proletariat from revolution. For the same reasons, the trade unions in wartime became in most cases part of the bourgeoisie's war apparatus, helping it squeeze as much sweat as possible out of the working class so that war could be waged as vigorously as possible in the interests of capitalist profit.

The unions were made up chiefly of the skilled, most highly paid workers. Limited by their narrow trade union outlook and fettered by a bureaucratic apparatus, these workers were divorced from the masses and led astray by their opportunist leaders. These unions betrayed not only the cause of social revolution but even the struggle to improve living conditions for their worker members. They abandoned trade union struggle against the employers, replacing it with a program of making peaceful deals with the capitalists at any price. This type of policy was pursued not only by the liberal unions in Britain and America, not only by the ostensibly socialist Free Trade Unions in Germany and Austria, but also by the syndicalist unions in France.

2. The economic consequences of the war—complete disorganization of the world economy, insane inflation, increased use of female and child labor, deterioration of housing conditions—all drive the broad masses of the proletariat onto the road of struggle against capitalism. This struggle, by the scope and character it acquires in greater measure every day, is revolutionary, objectively destroying the foundations of the capitalist order. Wage

increases won today through economic struggle by one or another category of workers are outstripped tomorrow by inflation. This inflation can only intensify because the capitalist class of the victorious countries, while destroying central and eastern Europe with its exploitative policy, is not only incapable of reorganizing the world economy but disorganizes it without letup.

In order to succeed in the economic struggle, very broad masses of workers who formerly remained outside the unions are pouring into their ranks. Trade unions have registered enormous growth in all capitalist countries. They are now no longer organizations only of the advanced part of the proletariat but of its main masses.

Streaming into the unions, the masses seek to turn them into their weapon of struggle. Sharpening class antagonisms[10] compel the unions to lead the strikes that are sweeping the entire capitalist world in a great wave, continually interrupting the process of capitalist production and exchange. In pace with quickening inflation and their own growing exhaustion, the working masses are escalating their demands, thereby destroying the basis of all capitalist cost calculations, which are an elementary precondition of any orderly economy.

During the war the unions became instruments for influencing the working masses in the interests of the bourgeoisie.[11] Now they are becoming instruments for the destruction of capitalism.

3. This change in the unions' character is impeded in every possible way by the old trade union bureaucracy and the old organizational forms. In many cases the old bureaucracy tries to preserve the unions as organizations of the labor aristocracy, retaining the regulations barring the poorly paid working masses from joining unions.[12] Even now, the old bureaucracy still tries to replace the workers'

strike battle—which daily acquires more of the character of a revolutionary struggle between the proletariat and the bourgeoisie—by a policy of making deals with the capitalists and signing long-term contracts—contracts made meaningless simply by the constant, insane leaps in prices.

The bureaucracy tries to impose on the workers the policies of Labor Boards, of the Joint Industry Council and, aided by the capitalist state, tries to place legal obstacles in the way of conducting a strike.[13] At moments of greatest tension in the struggle, the bureaucracy sows dissension in the masses of struggling workers, preventing the different categories of workers from uniting their struggles into one general class struggle. It is aided in this by the trade unions' old craft form of organization, which divides workers in one branch of industry into separate groups by occupation, even though the process of capitalist exploitation unites them. It relies on the power of ideology passed on by the old labor aristocracy, even though that aristocracy is constantly weakened as individual groups of the proletariat lose their privileges due to the general collapse of capitalism,[14] the leveling of conditions of the working class, and the generalization of their hardship and insecurity.

In this way the union bureaucracy splits up the powerful stream of the labor movement into weak rivulets, trades the movement's overall, revolutionary goals for reformist partial demands, and in general hinders forging the proletariat's struggle into a revolutionary struggle for the destruction of capitalism.

4. Given the influx of huge masses of workers into the unions, given the objectively revolutionary character of the economic struggle that these masses are waging in spite of the bureaucracy, Communists in every country must join the unions in order to turn them into instruments of conscious struggle for the overthrow of capital-

ism and for communism. They must take the initiative in forming trade unions where none exist.[15]

Shunning the union movement by choice poses an enormous danger for the Communist movement. So too do attempts to create separate unions artificially, unless this is made necessary by unusually outrageous actions on the part of the union bureaucracy (the disbanding of individual revolutionary union locals by the opportunist central leaderships)[16] or by narrow-minded, aristocratic policies barring the great masses of less-skilled workers from membership in the organizations. Such actions threaten to separate the most advanced, most class-conscious workers from the masses who are on the road to communism, leaving them at the mercy of opportunist leaders, who play into the hands of the bourgeoisie.

The inadequacies of the masses of workers, their ideological irresolution, their openness to the pretexts offered by the opportunist leaders can be overcome only in the process of sharpening struggle; only as the broad layers of the proletariat come to understand through their own experience—their victories and defeats—that decent living conditions can no longer be achieved under the capitalist economic system; only if the advanced Communist workers learn not just to be prophets of communist ideas in the economic struggle but also to become the most resolute leaders of that struggle and of the trade unions. This is the only possible way to remove the opportunist leaders from the unions. It is the only way Communists can gain the leadership of the union movement and turn it into an instrument of the revolutionary struggle for communism. Only in this way will they be able to overcome the unions' fragmentation and replace it with industrial unions. Only thus can they eliminate the bureaucracy, which is divorced from the masses, and replace it with an apparatus of factory representatives, leaving only the most essential functions to the head offices.

5. Since Communists put the aim and nature of trade union organizations ahead of their form, they must not shrink from a split in the unions if avoiding a split would mean abandoning revolutionary work in the unions, abandoning the effort to make them into a tool of revolutionary struggle,[17] and abandoning organization of the most exploited part of the proletariat. But even if such a split should prove necessary, it should be carried out only when the Communists succeed—through unrelenting struggle against the opportunist leaders and their policies and through vigorous participation in the economic struggle—in convincing the broad masses of workers that the split is being undertaken not for the sake of distant, revolutionary goals that they still do not understand but rather in the concrete, immediate interest of advancing the working class's economic struggle. In the event that a split becomes necessary, Communists must examine with constant attention whether it will lead to their becoming isolated from the masses of workers.

6. When there has already been a split between the opportunist and revolutionary union leadership, when—as in America—unions with revolutionary (although non-Communist) tendencies exist alongside opportunist unions, Communists are obligated to support revolutionary unions, helping them to shed their syndicalist prejudices and to take the side of communism, the only reliable compass in the chaos of the economic struggle. Wherever organizations such as the Shop Stewards or factory committees emerge in the factories, inside or outside the union framework—bodies that adopt the aim of struggling against the counterrevolutionary tendencies of the trade union bureaucracy and support direct, spontaneous

actions by the proletariat—Communists must of course support them with all their energy.[18] But supporting revolutionary trade unions must not mean that Communists resign from the opportunist trade unions, which are in a state of ferment and are beginning to support class struggle. On the contrary, by seeking to accelerate this development in mass unions on the road to revolutionary struggle, Communists will be able to play the role of uniting union workers ideologically and organizationally for the common struggle to destroy capitalism.

7. In the epoch of capitalism's decline, the proletariat's economic struggle turns into political struggle much more rapidly than was possible in the age of its peaceful development. Every major economic clash can confront the workers directly with the question of revolution. Therefore, it is the duty of Communists to point out to the workers in every phase of the economic struggle that it can be successful only if the working class defeats the capitalist class in an open contest and begins the work of socialist construction through the dictatorship of the proletariat. Proceeding from this, Communists must strive to bring about the most complete unity possible between the unions and the Communist Party, subordinating the unions to the party's leadership as the vanguard of the workers' revolution. To this end, Communists must form Communist fractions in trade unions and factory committees[19] everywhere and with their help take control of the trade union movement and lead it.

## II

8. The proletariat's economic struggle for higher wages and an overall improvement in living conditions of the

masses of workers is more and more coming up against a dead end. The economic ruin spreading to country after country on an ever larger scale shows even backward workers that it is not enough to fight for better wages and a shorter working day: the capitalist class is daily less able to restore economic life and guarantee workers even the living conditions they had before the war. The growing realization of this by masses of workers gives rise to efforts on their part to create organizations that can take up the struggle to save the economy by means of workers' control of production through factory committees. The desire to form factory committees, which is spreading to more and more workers of different countries,[20] has many sources: struggle against the counterrevolutionary bureaucracy; discouragement after union defeats; the striving to create an organization encompassing all workers. Ultimately, however, it leads to the struggle for control of industry—the factory committees' special historic task. It is therefore a mistake to want to organize factory committees only among workers who already support the dictatorship of the proletariat. On the contrary, it is the Communist Party's task to organize *all* workers on the basis of the economic crisis, prepare them for the struggle for the dictatorship of the proletariat, and do this by broadening and deepening the struggle for workers' control of production, which they all understand.

9. The Communist Party will accomplish this task if, through the factory committees' struggle, it deepens the masses' understanding of the fact that systematic restoration of the economy on the foundation of capitalist society—which would mean a new subjugation of the workers by the government in the capitalists' interests—is now impossible. Organizing the economy in the interests of the masses of workers will be possible only when

the government is in the hands of the working class and when the firm hand of the workers' dictatorship begins to abolish capitalism and carry out socialist reconstruction.

10. The factory committees' immediate general goal in the struggle against capitalism is workers' control of production. Workers in every enterprise and every branch of industry, whatever their job, suffer from sabotage of production by the capitalists, who often find it more profitable to discontinue production in order to starve the workers into agreeing to the most oppressive working conditions or to avoid making new capital investment in a time of generalized inflation. Defense against the capitalists' sabotage of production ties the workers together, whatever their political views. Factory committees elected by all the workers of a particular enterprise are therefore the proletariat's broadest mass organizations.

Disorganization of the capitalist economy, however, results not only from the conscious will of the capitalists but to a much greater extent from capitalism's irrepressible decay. Thus, in their struggle against the consequences of that decline, the factory committees will have to go beyond the bounds of controlling individual factories. Factory committees in each factory will soon face the question of workers' control over entire branches of industry and over industry as a whole.

The workers' attempts to regulate supplying the factories with raw materials or to audit the factory owners' financial operations will provoke vigorous measures against the working class by the bourgeoisie and the capitalist governments. The struggle for workers' control over production thus leads to the struggle of the working class to take power.[21]

11. Agitation for factory committees must be conducted in such a way as to fix in the minds of the broadest pos-

sible popular masses, even if they do not belong to the factory proletariat directly, the conviction that blame for the crisis rests on the bourgeoisie whereas the proletariat, by raising the slogan of workers' control of industry, is fighting to organize production and to eliminate speculation, disorganization, and high prices. The Communist parties' task is to struggle for control of production around the burning questions of the day, such as the shortage of heating fuel and the decline of the transportation system. They must link the isolated parts of the proletariat with one another and win to their side broad layers of the petty bourgeoisie, which is becoming more proletarianized every day and suffers immensely from the economic decay.

12. Factory committees cannot replace the trade unions. Only in the process of struggle can the councils go beyond the framework of individual factories and workshops, unite by branch of production, and create an overall apparatus to direct the struggle as a whole. The unions are already centralized organs of struggle, although they do not encompass such large masses of workers as can the factory committees, which are a loose organization accessible to all the workers in an enterprise.

The division of tasks between the factory committees and the unions results from the historical evolution of the social revolution. The unions organize the masses of workers to struggle on the basis of demands for higher wages and a shorter working day in the entire country. The factory committees are organized to exercise workers' control over production, for the struggle against economic crisis. They include all the workers in an enterprise, but only gradually can their struggle become national in scope. Communists should support efforts to turn the factory committees into trade union factory groups only to the extent that the unions overcome the counterrevolutionary tendencies of their bureaucracy and become conscious instruments of the revolution.[22]

13. The task of Communists is to inspire the unions and the factory committees with an identical spirit of resolute struggle and with knowledge and understanding of the best methods for its pursuit—in short, with the spirit of communism. In carrying out this task, Communists must, in fact, subordinate the factory committees and unions to the Communist Party's leadership, thus creating a proletarian mass organization, the basis for a powerful, centralized party of the proletariat embracing all organizations of proletarian struggle and leading them all along the same road: toward the victory of the working class through the dictatorship of the proletariat, toward communism.

14. By turning the trade unions and factory committees into powerful weapons of the revolution, Communists prepare these mass organizations for the great task that will devolve upon them after the proletarian dictatorship is established, that of being a principal element in reorganizing economic life on a socialist basis. The unions, consolidated into industrial unions and based on the factory committees as their factory organizations, will then acquaint the working masses with their production tasks and train the most experienced workers as managers of the factories. They will supervise the technical specialists and, together with representatives of the workers' government, design and execute the plans of socialist economic policy.[23]

## III

Even in time of peace, the unions were already striving to unite internationally because the capitalists resorted during strikes to recruiting workers from other countries as strikebreakers. But before the war the trade union International was of secondary importance. It tried to encourage unions to support each other financially, to organize social statistics, but not to organize the common struggle. This was because the unions, led by opportunists, sought to avoid all revolutionary struggle on an international scale.

The opportunist union leaders—who during the war, each in their own country, were lackeys of the bourgeoisie—are now endeavoring to reestablish the trade union International, trying to make it a weapon for international, direct struggle by world capital against the proletariat. Under the leadership of Legien, Jouhaux, and Gompers, they are forming a "labor office" of the League of Nations, that organization of international capitalist banditry. In every country they try to strangle strikes with laws and try to oblige workers to submit to courts of arbitration made up of representatives of the capitalist state. Everywhere they try to win concessions for the skilled workers through agreements with the capitalists, hoping that this will shatter the growing unity of the working class. Thus, the Amsterdam trade union International is a replacement for the bankrupt Second International of Brussels.

Communist workers, in contrast, who belong to the unions in every country, must strive to create a front for international trade union struggle. The question is no longer one of financial support in the event of a strike. Rather, when danger threatens the working class of one country, the unions of other countries, as organizations of the broad masses, should help to defend them and prevent the bourgeoisies of their own countries from aiding another country's bourgeoisie that is locked in struggle against the working class.

Every day, the proletariat's economic struggle becomes more and more a revolutionary one. Therefore, the trade unions must consciously exert all their strength to support every revolutionary struggle, in their own country as well as in others. Toward this end they must strive for the greatest possible centralization in struggle, not only in each country but also on an international scale. They must do this by joining the Communist International, fusing with it to form an army whose separate parts support one another and conduct the struggle as one.

SESSION 13

AUGUST 4, 1920 (MORNING)

# The agrarian question

(*The session opens at 12:30 p.m.*)

ZINOVIEV: The session is open. Comrade Balabanoff has the floor to deliver a message.

BALABANOFF: Comrades, unfortunately we are in the most unhappy position of having to share news that is as distressing for you as it is for us. The day before yesterday, one of our best and most active comrades, Comrade Augusta Åsen, who came from Norway and has been active in the movement for twenty years, was visiting the airport to view our Red air force. An accident occurred that claimed her life. We do not need to tell you how dreadfully and how deeply we feel this great loss. We ask you to stand in honor of the memory of the deceased. (*All present stand.*) Thank you. We ask all comrades to take home with them the assurance that the Russian proletariat will not forget our deceased comrade. Though her death was the result only of an unfortunate accident, she came here and died in struggle for the proletariat and out of love for the Communist International.

ZINOVIEV: The Bureau proposes that we express in the name of the congress our deepest condolences to our sister party in Norway.

We will now move to the next point on the agenda. The topic is the agrarian question. The reporter, Comrade Ernst Meyer, has the floor.

## REPORT ON THE AGRARIAN QUESTION

MEYER: Comrades, since the proper reporter for this question, Comrade Marchlewski, is prevented from speaking in connection with the encouraging advances of the Red Army,[1] I will deliver a report in his place briefly summarizing Comrade Lenin's theses and the work of the commission.

The social revolution in eastern and central Europe has placed the agrarian question on the agenda. It requires a solution not merely in theory but in practice. Very little preliminary work has been done on this question until now. The Second International did practically nothing here. It was usually satisfied with drawing beautiful pictures of agrarian production in the future after the advent of socialism. But as to how the rural population can be won to the proletarian revolution and what struggles must be waged to attain this splendid goal, the Second International said very little and made no practical preparations.[2]

The best forces in the Second International were content to polemicize against the opportunist wing, who, based on a distorted reading of the statistical data, claimed that socialization of rural property was out of the question and, furthermore, that the social revolution could not establish a base in the countryside. Using German statistics, the revisionists tried to prove that Marxist theories do not apply to the countryside and, on the basis of these theories, they gave up the social struggle and the social revolution. Those who contradicted these reformists, such as Kautsky, did so basically to prove only that Marxist theory still applies to this field.[3] Further practical conclusions were not drawn, however.

The Communist International's position on this question is different. We believe that the countryside must be truly revolutionized, because there is no doubt that without the active participation of broad layers of the rural population, it is not possible to achieve and consolidate the dictatorship of the proletariat. For us, the Communist International, what is most important is achieving the revolution, and only from this perspective is it possible to examine and resolve all aspects of the agrarian question. The Communist International's tasks with respect to the agrarian question can be summarized by asking: How do we carry the class struggle, the revolutionary struggle, into the countryside?

Revolutionizing the rural population, whose needs can be satisfied only through the revolution, is on history's agenda. Even the limited experiences here in Russia and the experiences with agrarian reform in central Europe bear out the thesis that guides all the proceedings at this congress: bourgeois democracy cannot solve this problem, and a satisfactory solution can be achieved only through the revolution and the dictatorship of the proletariat. The parties that supposedly represent the interests of the rural population, such as the Socialist Revolutionaries in Russia and the bourgeois peasant parties in Europe, betrayed their own programs when they got into power and could have put them into practice.

Bourgeois democracy is unable to solve this question. Not only is this shown by the conduct of the Socialist Revolutionaries in the countries bordering on Russia. In addition, all attempts at an agrarian reform in the other countries amount to dividing up and distributing part of the large landholdings in order to create a new proletarian or semiproletarian layer that can be a source of cheap labor for exploitation by the remaining large landowners. The measures prescribed by Germany's Settlement Laws either were never implemented or provided labor for exploitation by the large landowners.[4] The single exception, where an agrarian reform law that appeared to be more serious was put into effect, was in Bohemia [Czechoslovakia]. But even it was adopted only to aggravate national conflicts between the Czechs on the one hand and the Jewish and German population on the other. The Czech peasants were partially satisfied by expropriating the Jews and Germans.

The Communist International must go beyond what bourgeois democracy has done; in particular it must strive to overcome the differences between city and country. It must forge unity between urban and rural proletarian populations for the common struggle, for the proletarian revolution. That will happen if we see to it that rural workers are given all the advantages available to urban workers, and if we raise the consciousness of the urban proletariat regarding the importance of rural labor.

The question of how the proletarian revolution can be taken to the countryside and village can be answered only by making a precise analysis of the different layers of the rural population. The theses you have before you attempt to separate the rural population into different layers: first, the agricultural proletariat, or wageworkers; second, the semiproletarians and the peasants with small plots; third, the small peasants; fourth, the middle peasants; fifth, the large peasants; and sixth, the large landowners. Naturally the theses provide only a general framework. Since the composition of the rural population varies widely from one country to another, conditions in each country must be carefully studied in order to determine how to begin revolutionizing the rural population in each case. Only a general outline for assessing where things stand in the rural population can be given here at the congress for consideration by the Communist parties.

The groups that are important for the proletarian revolution are first and foremost the farm workers, forest workers, and also workers active in industrial enterprises connected with agriculture, such as dairies, distilleries, and so on. The large market farms, which employ a great many wageworkers, should be included here. The social conditions of this layer of the rural population are very difficult and very harsh, but this is so well known that we do not need to discuss it further. The miserable economic situation, low wages, and bad living conditions combine with political and social oppression by the large landowners to ensure that these proletarian forces will rally to the revolution automatically. This layer is one of the most active forces in the proletarian revolution, and today, despite its inexperience, its ability to organize is very great. I need recall only that the farm workers' union in Germany is one of the largest free trade unions today, numbering 500,000 members. In a country as small as Italy the farm workers' union includes more than 800,000 members. This shows how important this layer is to the social revolution and also how relatively easy it will be to integrate it into our ranks. Not only should these masses be organized into unions, but even more important, they must be drawn into our political bodies, the Communist parties. And every effort should be made in all other areas of work (education and so on) to win them over.

I would like to add something here about work among women in the countryside. Farm girls and the wives of small peasants have been forced by the war and present social conditions to do a good part of the farm labor on their own. Prospects for recruitment among them are very promising and should certainly not be neglected.

In this framework the questions already resolved by the congress (work in the trade unions and in parliament) acquire added importance. Those opposing work in the unions argue that even outside the unions there are ample opportunities to organize the proletariat and carry on agitation. This may hold true for the industrial proletariat. Reaching the rural proletariat, however, can most easily be done by Communists collaborating in the farm workers' unions and participating in election campaigns. Both of these are excellent avenues for reaching broad layers of the rural population with revolutionary agitation. Systematic agitation will be very successful.

Consider the experiences in Russia and Germany. In March, in beating back the Kapp putsch, Germany's rural proletariat conducted itself very courageously. Estate owners were driven out or locked up, while farm production was maintained. The farm workers unhesitatingly delivered surplus food to the cities. In addition, farm workers came together and provided fighting cadres to the proletariat in the cities. Not only in struggles preceding the seizure of power, but also thereafter, the rural proletariat will be one of the main pillars of soviet power. Our task is to give this movement of the rural proletariat, which at first is largely spontaneous, an organizational form. The best way to bring together these tempestuous, spontaneous forces is to build estate councils.

The second layer of the rural population, the semiproletarians and peasants with small plots, will be won to the proletarian revolution in a similar manner, though not as easily as the farm workers. These toilers are also dependent on the large landowners, suffering the same hardships as farm workers. Indeed, their situation is perhaps even more difficult, because they have the additional worry over their individual speck of land. In most countries it would be advantageous to incorporate these semiproletarian forces into the organizations of the farm workers in the narrower sense of the word.

Somewhat more difficult is the question of the small peasants and tenant farmers who can just barely earn their living by working their land, but employ no outside labor. Included here are also the small tenant farmers and market farmers who grow vegetables and fruit. They are not revolutionary-minded, but a portion of them should still be counted among our ranks in the struggle. The task is to teach them about the need for social revolution and about their own interests. In reality these small peasants suffer greatly under present conditions. They are also dependent on the large landowner and on capital—though indirectly for the most part—and they also perform unpaid labor in that they must come up with mortgage interest, pay high prices for agricultural machinery, and so forth. The standard of living of this layer is often strictly proletarian. The burden of taxes, the purchase fees and other such obligations, and the general inflation that this layer suffers are questions that we must help them understand through systematic agitation. Forming a union among this layer is not excluded either. An association for farm workers and small peasants was formed in Germany last year. It became apparent that it was inappropriate to organize a special association outside the trade unions, and it was dissolved. Nevertheless, the small peasants in southern Germany asked us to maintain it and to continue to publish our magazine for them,[5] explaining that they were very interested in our ideas. And so in Germany we ended up creating an organization for the peasants, which though somewhat looser, is important.

In Germany we also encourage the small peasants to form small peasant councils, not only to pursue economic interests but also to take up the political and social struggle. I must add that so far this work has had no success. We had estate councils in a great many villages. Although small peasants have not yet participated, we are not slackening off this agitation. Occasionally we have succeeded in convincing the small peasants that they would not benefit very much from dividing the land and that they would gain by uniting in small peasants' councils and cooperatives to work in common the large landholdings, which should be expropriated.

Admittedly, it must be emphasized that in many countries, especially in the small western democracies, the small peasants are very reactionary, and in general it is therefore to be assumed that during the struggle for the dictatorship of the proletariat, this layer will vacillate between private property and communism. These small property owners are demoralized by individual-capitalist views. To overcome their vacillation and win their support, we must help them realize that they are suffering under the present system, telling them what advantages they will gain with the dictatorship of the proletariat and the consolidation of the proletarian state power.

We must assure them that they can keep their small plots. It would serve no purpose to expropriate them, because during the period of the struggle it is neither politically nor technically possible to work the plots collectively against the will of their owners. Not only must we promise that they can keep their property, but we must also do everything we can to eliminate the usurers that oppress these small peasants. Liberation from the burden of taxation, rent, mortgages, and purchase fees are gains for the small peasant that the proletariat must grant without hesitation. Furthermore, they must be freed from dependence on large landowners for the right to use field and forest. They also must be promised that help will be provided in the form of buildings, machinery, tools, and seed taken from the large landholdings. Finally, they must be told that the cooperatives, which today in virtually every country are in the hands of the rich peasants, must be transformed into organizations that serve the interests of the small peasants exclusively. In countries where there are restrictions on free trade and where peasants are required by law to deliver foodstuffs, they must also be told that this obligation must remain in force, but the organizational apparatus necessary to carry it out will be taken away from the bureaucracy and placed in the hands of the small peasants themselves.

The small peasants must be made aware of the benefits they will derive from socialization of the large enterprises and reduction of the cost of agricultural machinery. Therefore, methodical educational work should be conducted among the small peasants. They must be made conscious of their particular place in society. If agitation is carried out in this manner, some peasants can be expected to side with the proletariat or at least not oppose the proletarian dictatorship. As a whole, farm workers, semiproletarians, and smallholders are an excellent arena for Communist Party work, and after the conquest of power by the proletariat, all three layers will see that supporting proletarian state power is the best way to satisfy their particular interests.

More complicated than the question of the small peasants is that of the middle peasants. They use some outside labor power and have enough land to be able to produce a surplus of food. This layer is by no means small. The theses point out that in Germany this middle layer, with holdings between five and ten hectares [twelve and twenty-four acres], numbers more than half a million people.[6] Clearly it is impossible to drive this layer from its land, since that would mean reducing food production. So we must treat this layer differently; we must try to neutralize them. Kautsky pointed out that the peasantry must be approached in such a way that they do not actively support the bourgeoisie. For these middle peasants, too, the immediate abolition of private property is out of the question. It will even be possible to give the middle peasants somewhat more land, as long as it is land they already rent. The middle peasants will also benefit from having their rent eliminated. Obviously all these advantages can be accorded to the middle peasants only on the condition that they recognize soviet power, supply food, and offer no resistance.

Here again the experience in Russia shows that such a course can cause the middle peasants to adopt a loyal attitude toward soviet power. This stance toward the middle peasants, that of preserving their private property, is essential. The attitude of this layer of peasants can be summed up as a Russian peasant did in a bad joke: We are for soviet power, but against communism. The example of Russia shows that these peasants adjust and reconcile themselves to proletarian state power when they are treated wisely. A large number of the middle peasants are in the Red Army doing their duty in the struggle against the external enemy.

The large peasants, on the other hand, who as a rule employ outside labor, are among the most numerous and determined opponents of soviet power. It is to be expected that, not only now but also later, after the establishment of soviet power, they will engage in every kind of sabotage and also offer military resistance. This danger must be kept clearly in mind, and every preparation must be made to thwart and defeat this resistance wherever it appears. The large peasants must be disarmed.

But even for these large peasants, expropriation is excluded as an immediate task of the revolution. The parcels of land they offer for rent must be taken away if the small and middle peasants need them. If they offer stubborn resistance, they will be immediately and totally expropriated. If their land is not needed, however, the large peasants may keep it. It is important that the political and military resistance of this layer be eliminated. And there again the experience in Russia shows that it is possible to elicit such halfway loyal conduct from this layer. As soon as the victory of the proletarian revolution is achieved or certain to be achieved, even the large peasants will accept the new relations.

The large landowners, some of whom made large land purchases during the war, must be immediately expropriated, without exception and without compensation. Expropriation with compensation, as proposed by Kautsky and other Independents, is out of the question. What should be done with the expropriated land? The most natural and useful thing is to hand it over in its entirety to the farm workers who previously worked it. Soviet enterprises must be organized that function as organs of the proletarian state and on its instructions. These enterprises will operate the estates, provide for their own needs, and supply the surplus to the soviet government. Perhaps it will be possible to establish collective enterprises that work the land cooperatively. These two solutions are best, not only for farm workers and semiproletarians but also for the urban population, who will thereby gain partial independence from the peasantry with regard to food supplies.

A precondition for this solution is that the rural proletariat must have accumulated a certain amount of technical experience. Since this prerequisite is not always present, we must be prepared to make exceptions in some cases. Such exceptions were made in Russia, where the large landholdings were sometimes divided up. This is not a violation of the principles of communism, as Kautsky wanted to prove, because the main task of the proletarian state is to consolidate itself and the proletarian revolution and lay the basis for communism. All other questions are secondary to this central point. Even a reduction in agricultural production, which today can be so painful, is not too important to be subordinated to this question.

When may large landholdings be divided up? A division can be considered only when the land has been rented to small peasants, that is, when the large landholdings are not being farmed as a unit. In that case dividing it up does not mean renunciation of large-scale production at all. Such division is also possible when a large landholding is broken up and wedged between small-peasant settlements. In these cases the hunger for land is so great that sometimes it must be satisfied in order to preserve the revolution. In southern Germany it is conceivable that the few existing large estates will be divided up. Finally, where the rural proletariat is too backward, dividing the land among experienced peasants can be considered. In any case, the main thing is that the estate owners may not keep their estates; they must be driven out. If the large holdings cannot be farmed without the estate owners, the peasantry must be persuaded to work this land. After the proletarian state has been established, it will become possible to obtain the cooperation of bourgeois specialists, under the supervision of the soviet state.

The precondition to winning the rural proletariat is a determined struggle by the urban proletariat for social revolution, without fear of sacrifices, and here the Communist parties must take the lead and be the vanguard.

In order to win over the layers that are still vacillating or are open to communist ideas, they must be accorded economic benefits immediately after the victory of the proletarian revolution. The semiproletarians and the small and middle peasants must feel that they have a stake in the new order. These benefits must be granted at the expense of the exploiters.

To advance this movement Communists must link up with economic struggles in the countryside, above all the strike movement. In almost every country great strike movements have begun. They must be used by the Communist parties to convince the rural proletariat that a real improvement in its conditions will be achieved not by higher wages but only by the victory of the proletarian revolution. To link up with these economic struggles, the Communist parties must go into the rural areas and create their own organizations. The rural proletariat has to be convinced that it must organize itself into estate councils for the liberation struggle.

Rural industrial workers, most of whom come originally from the urban population, will have a special role to play in strengthening this movement in the countryside. The Communist parties must appeal to them for help in taking the movement into the rural areas and strengthening it. Special agitation is also necessary among the small peasants, and it must be carried out with all available means. The theses make additional suggestions about revolutionizing the countryside through agitation, meetings, the collaboration of trade unions, and by raising the agrarian question in parliament.

These, in brief, are the tasks presented to the congress in the theses. The commission spent many sessions going over the theses thoroughly and made a large number of changes, most of which were stylistic alterations in the original German text. The theses should set only the general framework for the activity of the Communist parties in the countryside. It would be useful if Communists of all countries would write their own agrarian programs with specific proposals. I would like to point out, for example, that in Germany the Communist Party already has such an agrarian program.[7]

As for substantive changes: in thesis 2, on page 33, after "wage labor in capitalist farming" insert "and related industrial enterprises." Further, after "the organization of this class," insert "including craftsmen on the estates, forest workers, and so on."

On page 34, we added, "In some countries the first and second groups are not sharply differentiated. Therefore, under special circumstances it is permissible to organize them together."

On page 38, thesis 4, several passages were struck in which the interests of the middle peasants were compared to those of the wageworkers, that is, from the phrase, "because the world outlook and sentiments of the property owners are prevalent among this stratum" to the words "the victorious proletariat."

On page 39, we inserted, "In most capitalist states it is out of the question for the proletarian state to abolish private property immediately."

The most important changes are in thesis 6. The original version put much too much emphasis on the exceptions to the rule that the land should not be divided. The commission struck the sentence that said it would be a mistake not to divide the land and replaced it with: "the principle that the large-scale enterprise must be maintained."[8]

The changes are so numerous that I do not want to read out this whole new version. They correspond almost verbatim to a proposal by Comrade Marchlewski. In the German edition everything was deleted from where the paragraph begins on page 43, "It would nevertheless be a big mistake," to the point on page 45, "the inventory of the large-scale enterprises." It has been replaced with a new version. From there on the old text remains with few changes.

Then on page 46 a polemic against the Second International, the German and British Independents [Independent Labour Party], and the French Longuetists was struck because the same idea was expressed in other places.

Those are the main changes.

In conclusion I would like to point out again how important it is that the Communist parties carry the social revolution into the countryside. Victory cannot be ensured, especially in central and western Europe, unless the rural proletariat is incorporated into the urban proletarian vanguard. Especially favorable conditions existed in Russia because the peasantry also had a stake in proletarian power, through the questions of peace and land, which are to some degree absent in central and western Europe. This makes it all the more important that Communist parties base themselves, in the countryside, on *those* sections of the rural proletariat that under present conditions suffer as much as urban workers and sometimes even more. And the commission hopes that the application by the different Communist parties in each country of the proposals that were made here will also bear fruit.

GRAZIADEI: I am speaking only for myself. First I must state that in general I accept the theses proposed to us by Comrade Lenin, especially after the very significant changes made by the commission, particularly to thesis 6.

Although the subjects are very different, there are striking similarities between Comrade Lenin's theses on the national and colonial questions and Comrade Meyer's on the agrarian question. It is the same method applied to different questions, which consists of dividing the opponents and making concessions according to the needs of the moment and the character of those to whom they are made.

This method can be called economizing efforts in order to facilitate and accelerate the seizure of power and to create conditions favorable to holding power once it is conquered.

I will limit myself to noting that there is a danger in this method, which could be called that of left opportunism.

But because these theses and their application are entrusted to such comrades as Lenin and other Russian comrades, we can be very sure that this danger will remain only theoretical. Certainly I can tell you that there are other countries and other situations where I will not express so much confidence.

In order to facilitate the taking of political power by the proletariat, Comrade Lenin's theses analyze the peasant masses quite correctly and divide them into several parts. He tells us, "We can draw some of them over to our side, and neutralize others. But one portion will always be our enemy, and it is against it that we must fight untiringly."

The second part of Lenin's thesis concerns the question of what to do once power has been conquered. Given the proposed corrections, this thesis can be accepted. Nevertheless, I must make some practical observations.

In the thesis on the small and middle proprietors, Lenin shows himself to be very original. He tries to avoid two counterposed errors that Socialists have made up to now.

Many Socialists believed they could get rid of the important question of the small proprietors by saying that they are, in fact, destined to disappear in bourgeois society, and we therefore do not have to be concerned about them. That conception was completely wrong, above all because the law of concentration of capital does not unfold everywhere as described by Marx. In any case, the way people tried to apply the law of concentration to small proprietors was utterly absurd. Furthermore, you understand very well that if we say the small peasants are destined to disappear, we will fall into one of two dangers: either we will pay no attention to them at all, or we will drive them into the arms of our adversaries. If we tell the small proprietors that they are going to disappear and that we want to make them disappear artificially, obviously such a policy will turn millions of people against us.

The opposite mistake, the one committed by the Socialists, was to think that since the small peasants are not bound to disappear, they must be organized, and we cannot make the revolution until that is done. That is the same as saying that we must postpone the revolution indefinitely. That is unacceptable.

Comrade Lenin proposes a position that falls between these two diametrically opposite mistakes, and I find it fairly precise and acceptable. He says we should show the small peasants that they have everything to gain from following us. That is good. But I must express several reservations about the passage on the forms of organization and the struggle in the period before the conquest of political power.

The next to last thesis, thesis 8, talks of strikes by agricultural wageworkers, which the small proprietors may join in some cases. Far be it from me to deny the revolutionary importance of rural strikes. In Italy there have been significant ones, and these vast movements have had far-reaching consequences.[9] All the same, I will raise two objections. I do not understand why we say that in some cases small proprietors might participate in strikes. I do not believe they will. It is also an error to claim that striking is the only major weapon in all countries. In some countries organizations of agricultural wageworkers are so strong that they are preparing for revolution and even now, in bourgeois society, are able to begin the process of instituting proletarian dictatorship.

In Italy some workers' organizations organize public works directly. Similarly, there are cooperatives that buy or rent land and cultivate it collectively. These are extremely important forces both in the struggle and in reconstruction, and we should not ignore them.

That is why I would like to propose that the following be added in thesis 8 [at the end of paragraph 1]:

"Under certain conditions and in certain countries, the most exploited rural masses, if their organizations are quite advanced, may also organize themselves in cooperatives to carry out public works, to cultivate collectively part or all of lands purchased or rented, and so on. Communists should take an interest in these organizations and try to lead them, among other reasons in order to prevent their making shady political compromises."

I want to discuss the question of the small proprietors as well. In many countries small proprietors are already organized in cooperatives that buy, sell, and process goods. Very often they are organized by our opponents.

Organizing small proprietors is not the Socialists' primary task. But if small proprietors begin to organize, we should join their organizations, because we should take part in all organizations where there are toilers. Therefore, I propose that we make the following addition at the end of thesis 8:

"As for the small peasants, Communists join their organizations (cooperatives for buying and selling) in order to increase our influence over these forces, neutralize opponent tendencies there, and try to limit their fixation on private property."

Let me mention another point. I accept the conception, as amended by the commission, regarding what the proletarian government should do as soon as it is in a position to take up the agrarian question. But in thesis 6, at the end of the second paragraph, I would like to make a small addition regarding reconstruction.

It is very correct that we oppose compensating former large landholders. I believe it is correct to remind Socialists and Communists that this is an antisocialist and, moreover, an anticommunist act. And I find it strange that the proposal to give monetary compensation was supported by the comrades from Italy, Austria, and Germany. That would place an enormous burden on the rural masses. But since we must ease the transition as much as possible, we should try, after the first period of struggle, to use the talents of some of the proprietors. We should take note of this situation. I therefore propose this addition to the end of the second paragraph of thesis 6:

"Although the idea of monetary compensation must be absolutely ruled out, the possibility of granting a personal pension to former large landowners is admissible, if their age does not permit them to work and adapt rapidly to the new conditions of existence."

Of course it will all depend on their political conduct, since it would be ridiculous to grant anything to counterrevolutionaries. But if there are some who accept the new situation, we should ease their conditions somewhat.

Finally, I believe that in thesis 3, line 2, we should not say "in all capitalist countries," but rather "in almost all capitalist countries," because it is not accurate that in all capitalist countries the rural masses make up the big majority of the population.[10] In Britain, particularly, the rural masses are the minority.

SHABLIN: Comrades, although there is considerable industry in Bulgaria's cities, the predominant form of property in the villages is small landholdings. The workers are concentrated in the cities, and it is from them that the Communist Party draws most of its forces. But the Communist Party is beginning to extend its influence into the countryside, because the proletarianization of the small peasants is advancing very quickly, and as a result of the war the position of small peasants who succeeded in holding on to their plot of land has become very difficult.

The predominant form of land ownership in Bulgaria is the small holding. In Bulgaria there are 495,000 landowners, and the average area of each holding is 90 decares.[11] But these holdings are distributed as follows: 225,000 holdings up to 50 decares; 175,000 up to 100 decares, 95,000 up to 1,000 decares, 936 more than 1,000 decares.

The first category, which is also the largest, consists of semiproletarians, whose land is not even sufficient for their own needs. They are forced to work a good part of the year either for the rich peasants or in the mines, factories, and cities. Most of our rural cadres come from this group.

The second category is the small landholders, whose land is barely enough to satisfy the needs of their families. They do not exploit the labor of others; they cultivate their land themselves. The Communist Party works among this layer and has remarkable results to show for it. As a result of a significant decline in agricultural productivity, which resulted from the destruction of livestock during the war, the economic situation of this category has actually become very insecure.

These two categories, semiproletarians and small peasants, make up about four-fifths of the entire peasant population of Bulgaria. All they can expect from the bourgeoisie and the bourgeois state is intensified taxation to cover war expenditures, which will deepen their impoverishment. The Communist Party is carrying out active agitation and intensive propaganda among them. Our party does not hide from the semiproletarians and small peasants our maximum program, namely the socialization of the land.[12] In our country the profitability of small agricultural holdings is so slim and the poverty of semiproletarians and small landowners so great that the idea of increasing agricultural productivity through common ownership of the land is gaining ground every day.

At the same time, we tell them that the proletariat, once in power, will expropriate the large landowners, not the small peasants and semiproletarians, and will even allow the middle peasants free use of their land. The semiproletarians and small landowners will come to the idea of collective ownership and cultivation of the land of their own accord, once the proletarian state shows them by its actions the advantages of the new socialist order, and once the use of improved agricultural machinery, electrification of the farm, and the development of agricultural knowledge make collective ownership and cultivation of the soil economically feasible.

That is the basic direction of our agitation, which takes into account the real situation of the semiproletarians and small landowners. We also strive to break the working masses of the peasant population away from the influence of the urban and rural bourgeoisie and the bourgeois and petty-bourgeois parties and win them over to the cause of the proletarian revolution. I must emphasize in particular that we have already been very successful in this respect. The Communist Party has begun to publish a Communist newspaper for the peasants;[13] it has approximately a thousand Communist organizations and groups in the countryside, embracing twenty-five thousand farm workers, semiproletarians, and small landowners, and it is preparing them for the revolution. The slogan of workers' and peasants' councils is greeted enthusiastically by these masses, who have lost confidence in the bourgeoisie, the bourgeois state, and the bourgeois parliament. We are working to have the majority of these masses on our side at the moment of the revolution, and with their help we will thwart the bourgeoisie's efforts to use the peasantry to strangle the revolutionary proletariat in the cities—a proletariat, I must add, that has already been completely won to communist ideas.

The middle peasants—that is, those who sell their agricultural products on the market—amassed no small amount of bank notes during the war, and many of them became rich. They represent the reactionary classes in the countryside, but in our country they are a numerically weak and insignificant layer.

Even fewer in number are the large landowners, who together with the middle peasants constitute the peasant reaction on which the power of the Bulgarian bourgeoisie rests today. In our country—just as in the other capitalist countries—the peasant bourgeoisie (middle and large landowners) exerts a rather large influence and plays a greater political role because of its predominance in the market for agricultural products, whose prices have undergone an incredible increase. These peasant bourgeois are in the camp of reaction and counterrevolution. Today they are allied with the urban bourgeoisie, through the banks and corporations, both in speculation and exploitation of the masses and in bloodthirsty policies to suppress the proletarian revolution with the most gruesome methods available to the bourgeois dictatorship.

But I must repeat: in our country the peasant bourgeoisie is only a very thin layer of the rural population, and if we succeed in winning over the majority of the semiproletarians and small peasants, we will be able to break the resistance of the peasant bourgeoisie when the revolution occurs. For these reasons we are making the greatest efforts in the countryside to organize the farm workers, who are united in a union. But what we want most of all is to draw over to our side and win for communism the semiproletarians and small peasants in the countryside, who constitute the big, overwhelming majority of the rural population.

We also clearly recognize the need to neutralize the middle peasants in the revolution. We are not frightening them with the idea of expropriating their land, for with the technical means now at our disposal we cannot immediately organize collective agricultural production in place of private agricultural production. Our goal is to expropriate the large landowners. Should we succeed in neutralizing the middle peasants, we will have split in two the forces of the reactionary bloc and will more readily defeat them.

As for forming peasants' councils, in our view this is closely tied to the creation of workers' councils in the cities. Workers' and peasants' councils can exist as revolutionary organs for the conquest and exercise of proletarian power only if they are defended arms in hand by the workers and peasants. When the revolutionary struggles reach their high point, when the working class and the urban poor resolve, as their struggle broadens, to go all the way to the creation of soviets and armed insurrection, only then will it be possible and permissible to proceed to establishing peasant councils, consisting of the poor, the proletarians, and the semiproletarians in the countryside.

Therefore the Bulgarian delegation adopts and supports the theses submitted to the congress by the Executive Committee with the commission's amendments presented by the commission reporter, Comrade Meyer.

SERRATI: I asked for the floor so that Comrade Wijnkoop could not come and reproach me for making a statement at the time of the vote.

In my opinion, this question does not interest the congress. This is a congress of comrades from industrial countries who do not know how important the question is.

As for me, I will just make a statement. I think that the next congress should discuss this question more thoroughly, when we have acquired more experience.

I will abstain on the vote. Personally I am against the theses, which do not seem to me to correspond sufficiently to the needs of the revolution in the western countries. Our party in Italy has not yet come to a final decision on this very serious question, and I do not think I have the right to substitute my personal will for that of the comrades who sent me to the congress as their delegate.

In general it seems to me that the needs of the postrevolutionary period, during which the proletarian state is forced to adapt to certain circumstances, are being confused with those of the prerevolutionary period, during which Communists must follow a precise and sharply defined line against all bourgeois and petty-bourgeois parties.

The theses on the agrarian question, just like those on the national and colonial questions, do not take into account that the concessions made to certain social layers to influence them in our favor, or at least to neutralize them at the time of the revolutionary melee, can be very dangerous for the proletarian layers and start them on a road of increasingly opportunist concessions.

In general the small peasants of western Europe are very grasping and know very well what political position to take to defend their interests. It is not enough to make declarations of sympathy for them—they want something practical. They are for high tariffs and administrative autonomy and against industrializing the land. That is what they were promised by the parties that organized them. Can we in turn promise them the same? Would they believe us? Furthermore it is necessary to recall that in the most advanced countries, the peasants—small and middle proprietors—already have their parties. That is the case in Switzerland and France.

The small and middle proprietors and the tenant farmers in these countries are fighting against the agricultural wageworkers, who want to dispossess them right now. In Italy this struggle has been going on for twenty years and occasionally has bloody consequences. Can we go and say that we were wrong?

The small landholding is an economic form that exists for a reason in certain areas, especially in the mountains. The Communists should not harm the small peasants. They should accept certain inevitable solutions during and after the revolution. They should understand and make others understand that after the fall of the bourgeois regime, compromises should be possible with even the middle peasants. But especially *before the revolution* the Communists have a particular duty not to make concessions to the agricultural petty bourgeoisie so as not to harm the interests of the proletarian masses.

It is for these reasons and because I am not adequately acquainted with the opinion of our party's leadership on this subject that I will abstain on the vote.

GRIGORY SOKOLNIKOV [COMMUNIST PARTY OF RUSSIA]: Comrade Graziadei tells us that he considers Marxist theory, in its application to the agrarian question, as childishness.

GRAZIADEI: I did not say that. I said that the theory of the concentration of capital has not proved correct everywhere in the manner contemplated in *Capital*. I said that it is childishness on the part of certain comrades to conclude, based on the law of the concentration of capital, that all the petty proprietors must disappear in the bourgeois world.

SOKOLNIKOV: Which word is used is not of great importance. Comrade Graziadei says that Marxist theories are wrong on the concentration of capital in agriculture.

Comrade Graziadei is, if I am not mistaken, an outstanding professor of political economy, but in the present case, which concerns Marxist theory, I really think that it is he who is wrong, and that he is following the example of professors of political economy who have so often declared that in general Marxist theory is of no value when applied to a specific question.

If it were really true that Marxist theory proved not to apply to the question of agriculture, then we would have to draw the necessary conclusion: we would have to admit that the entire socialist and communist conception must fall, since Marxist theories do not hold up on the question of agriculture.

If it is impossible to organize socialist production in agriculture from the foundations left by capitalist development, that obviously means the collapse of the socialist system in industry. Furthermore I believe that when Comrade Graziadei spoke against applying Marxist theories to agriculture, he failed to note that the centers of agricultural production have shifted. Central Europe has ceased to be the grain basket of Europe. Large-scale agricultural production now is located on the other side of the ocean. It is North America and in recent years South America that feed European industry and make possible the provisioning of the European working masses. This forces us to talk about the change that has taken place in Europe and America during the war and in the last few years.

I would also like to comment on Comrade Serrati's remark that the war did not proletarianize but, on the contrary, enriched the peasants. He gives the example of the Italian peasants whose wool socks are full of gold. I think he is mistaken there. It is true that a portion of the peasants—those who were able to sell their grain, the products of their small holdings—enriched themselves, but in a completely conventional manner. I will return to this point, but I want to point out that, quite the contrary, a large portion of the peasants were ruined by the war. The war snatched away hundreds of thousands of the peasant masses, and that means a terrible blow, a death blow, for all small proprietors.

They are condemned to the depths of poverty. A great many peasants are emigrating or going to work in the factories. The war has certainly dealt the small proprietors and peasants a terrible blow, driving them to ruin.

If you now look at the mass of those who were able to sell their agricultural products, you can be sure that they put a lot of money into their wool socks. But I doubt it is gold. It is bank notes—paper. And this is a form of expropriating the peasant holdings through the imperialist war. In reality they became propertyless and their holdings were expropriated. In return for their real goods they received paper that is of little value and that increasingly depreciates. You mentioned the example of Switzerland, which did not even participate in the war and, moreover, is a small country. It is indisputable that in France, Germany, and Russia the war was a form of expropriation of the small peasant.

When Comrade Serrati tells us that he does not believe that the change in our policy toward the small peasants has real merit, I must point out that there is a change in our policy nonetheless. There is no change in the policy of the Communist Party, but there is a change in the conditions of the small peasants. You cannot compare the conditions of a small peasant in Europe in 1851, at the time of Napoléon's coup d'état, with the present situation of a small peasant in Europe.[14] A great change took place during the development of capitalism. The small peasant was proletarianized in very specific ways and became greatly dependent on capitalism.

The great banks, the export companies, and the capitalist organizations have in various ways brought the small peasants, the petty proprietors, to a situation that is not far from that of a proletarian. And because of this change in the small peasant's conditions of life, he has become the slave and enemy of capitalism. That is why the Communist Party turns to these petty proprietors, these small peasants, with great prospects of success.

The situation of the small peasant was changed by the development of capitalism in recent years. The war transformed him even more deeply. Hence the proletarianization of the peasant that we now see. The war was the cause of the expropriation of the small peasant. That is why the Communist Party today can count on the small peasant and the semiproletarian entering its ranks and fighting together with the workers in the cities against capitalism and for the social revolution.

LEFEBVRE: I am taking the floor to comment on certain of Serrati's statements. His intransigent argumentation was founded on opportunist considerations, proposing that communist policy be based solely on the alliance with farm workers against small peasants. His key reason was that small peasants will not accept the Communists' word the day after we take power when we come and say to them, "You will preserve your privileges—and even get new ones."

It seems to me to be (please excuse my using the term) shameless demagogy to not say and not support something except to the degree that you hope it will pay off immediately and will be useful for current propaganda. We are here not only to prepare today's propaganda, aimed at taking power, but equally to establish under what conditions we can organize a communist society in our countries.

What is more, Serrati spoke in the name of western Europe. It seems to me that you said that the situation in western Europe is such that the policy advocated in the theses could not satisfy propaganda needs.

I do not share this view. I believe on the contrary that—I can speak only of France, because that is the country I know fairly well—this policy fits the situation in France pretty well. First, it seems to me virtually impossible to undertake anything at all if we have the mass of French petty proprietors against us. Furthermore, I think—without going as far as Comrade Sokolnikov and without sharing his optimism—that things could soon be that way in France. I would say that even if the war has not proletarianized small proprietors in France, it could be that it has had a big effect.

Obviously, the French small peasant appears to have been enriched by the war. But in a society in decomposition, wealth, once born, withers again just as quickly, and we can already foresee for what reason and by what process small-peasant property is going to find itself injured by what we could call the postwar period.

In France, for electoral reasons, the big bourgeoisie appeared to support the interests of the small peasantry. But now, since discussion of a law about a month and a half ago, we have seen the big bourgeoisie drop the interests of the small peasantry on the wheat question in such a way that the situation of the small peasantry is soon going to be quite serious in our country.[15]

Sokolnikov is right to say that the wealth of the peasants is paper wealth. We should add that, up to now, the small proprietors have really benefited from the war in the sense that they have paid off their mortgages with paper. Now, the repayment of the mortgages in France is an accomplished fact, and the paper is in the peasants' strongboxes. And now that the French peasant has to keep this paper at home, he is greatly concerned to know how much it is worth.

So, in our country—and I think that this is international—the peasant feels contempt for those who borrow. This leads the peasant to hold the capitalist state in contempt because in France it has no policy beyond a continuous stream of borrowing.

For this reason, communist propaganda is finding a very attentive reception in France. Where there was no sympathy before, today this propaganda is received with respect. Pamphlets are bought, groups are formed. A policy that would lead to turning this class into an implacable enemy would be an absolute disaster.

Furthermore, it would be impossible to organize agrarian production after taking power without the total collaboration of the small peasants.

I do not protest against the point of view of Comrade Graziadei, who would like to put a paragraph into the theses benefiting the large landowners. Obviously, the collaboration of those among them who rally to the soviet regime will be welcomed and they can be given government posts. But there is no point in putting into the theses a paragraph on them that would imply some sort of right.

## SUMMARY

MEYER: Comrades, I will be brief. I am glad that the Italian comrades participated in the discussion and told us something about the agrarian question in Italy. Unfortunately, for factional reasons, they did not send their representatives to the commission.[16] I hope they will make further information available to the agrarian commission. I recommend that Comrade Graziadei's proposals be referred to the commission for consideration. I agree with Comrade Lefebvre that there is no need to mention compensation of former large landowners. The other addition, on cooperatives, will be made by the agrarian commission in one form or another, since the commission also discussed this question.

As for the role of the small peasants, I agree with what Comrade Sokolnikov laid out. It is true that during the war, in the belligerent as well as the neutral countries, a portion of the small peasantry not only covered their own needs out of their production, but also transformed the surpluses into capital. That happened and continues to a certain degree even today. In the meantime, however, the prices for all consumer goods, especially clothing and agricultural implements, have risen so sharply, and the tax burden for all low-income layers has become so much heavier, that gains won previously by the small peasants have been canceled out. If that is not yet evident in all countries, in the coming period it will and must increasingly become the case. I share Comrade Sokolnikov's view that the small peasant must be made aware of the drop that can be expected in his own standard of living.

There is no break with the program of socialism in these theses. Comrade Serrati opposes them because he believes the Communist International has given up the idea that the large enterprises should be nationalized. That is not at all true. The point was only that in fact it is impossible to socialize small landholdings right now. That is because the rural proletariat in general is not sufficiently prepared and also lacks the technical means for collective farming. Therefore we make concessions that preserve for now the private property of the small and middle peasants and a portion of the large peasants. We project making all the preparations to overcome this transitional stage, to influence the small and middle peasantry in favor of the cooperative enterprise, and to show them the advantages of collective farming.

That is one course that was proposed. Second, the technical preparation to expand rural large-scale enterprises must take place through consolidating proletarian power, even though this entails concessions to different layers of the rural population. Proletarian state power must be consolidated to the point that it completely dominates heavy industry, so that it can produce more machines for agriculture. As soon as these technical preconditions are at hand, it will be possible to fuse together these small and middle farms. There is thus no break with our earlier program; rather we are being shown in detail how we arrive at socialization of agriculture. That is the meaning of the theses.

With that I think I have answered the questions raised in the discussion. I propose that you adopt the theses in principle and refer Comrade Graziadei's motions to the commission. No further substantive changes will be made.

ZINOVIEV: Now we come to the vote on the theses.

(*The theses are adopted unanimously with 1 abstention. The session adjourns at four o'clock.*)

## THESES ON THE AGRARIAN QUESTION

1. Only the urban and industrial proletariat, led by the Communist Party, can free the toiling masses of the countryside from the yoke of capital and landlordism and protect them from ruin and imperialist wars, which are always and forever inevitable so long as the capitalist system endures.[17] The toiling masses in the countryside can find their salvation only in alliance with the Communist proletariat, in wholeheartedly supporting its revolutionary struggle to throw off the yoke of the Junkers (large landowners) and the bourgeoisie. Conversely, the industrial workers cannot carry out their world-historic mission of freeing humanity from the yoke of capital and war if they confine themselves to their crafts and their narrow, trade union interests and complacently limit themselves to trying to better their conditions, which are sometimes tolerable in a petty-bourgeois sense.

But in many advanced countries that is precisely the situation with the "labor aristocracy," which constitutes the base of the so-called Socialist parties of the Second International. In reality these parties represent socialism's worst enemy—its betrayers, petty-bourgeois jingoists, and agents of the bourgeoisie within the workers' movement. The proletariat acts as a truly revolutionary and truly socialist class only by taking a stand and acting as the vanguard of all toilers and exploited, as the leader in the fight to overthrow the exploiters. But this cannot be accomplished without carrying the class struggle into the countryside, without rallying the rural toiling masses, without the Communist Party of the urban proletariat, without the urban proletariat educating that of the countryside.

2. The toiling and exploited masses of the countryside, whom the urban proletariat must lead in struggle or at least draw over to its side, are represented in the capitalist countries by the following groups:

First, the agricultural proletariat—the wageworkers (seasonal, migrant, and day laborers) who make their living by wage labor in agricultural and related industrial enterprises. The basic task of the Communist Party in all countries is to organize this class—including forest workers, estate workers, and so on—independently and separately from the other groups of the rural population, in political, military, trade union, cooperative, and educational organizations. The Communist Party also must increase propaganda and agitation among this group and win it over to the side of soviet power and the dictatorship of the proletariat.

Second, the semiproletarians or smallholders, who make their living partly from wage labor in agricultural, industrial, and capitalist enterprises and partly by toiling on their own or a rented scrap of land that yields only a portion of their family's needs. This group of rural toilers is very numerous in all capitalist countries. Its existence and particular conditions are hushed up by the representatives of the bourgeoisie and Socialists belonging to the Second International. They do this in part consciously, to mislead the workers, and in part blindly, because they give in to the conventional philistine viewpoint that confuses this group with the mass of the peasantry in general.

This method of bourgeois deception of the workers can be seen most clearly in Germany and France, but it also takes place in America and other countries. This group can become a solid supporter of the Communist Party if the party's work is properly organized, because the conditions of these semiproletarians are very hard, and the benefits that soviet power and the dictatorship of the proletariat bring them are significant and immediately effective.

In some countries the first and second groups are not sharply differentiated. Therefore, under special circumstances it is permissible to organize them together.[18]

Third, the small peasants—farmers who own or rent small parcels of land that barely cover their families' needs and who hire no outside labor. They gain implicitly and immediately from the victory of the proletariat in the following ways: (a) they are freed from paying rent or a portion of their crops to the landowners (for example the *métayers* [sharecroppers] in France and Italy, and so forth); (b) they are freed from the burden of mortgages and purchase fees; (c) they are freed from the yoke of dependency on the large landowners in its various forms (use of forest and pasture, for example); (d) the proletarian state immediately helps small peasants' farms by, for example, enabling them to use agricultural equipment and a portion of the lands of the large capitalist enterprises expropriated by the proletariat, and the proletarian state immediately transforms the consumer and agricultural cooperatives, which under capitalism have mainly served the rich and powerful peasants, into organizations that primarily help the poor, that is, the proletarians, semiproletarians, small peasants, and so forth.

At the same time, the Communist Party must be conscious that during the transition period from capitalism to communism—that is, during the period of the dictatorship of the proletariat—at least part of this layer will inevitably waver toward full freedom of trade and free use of private property. This layer, which acts, even if only on a small scale, as a seller of food, has been corrupted by speculation and the habits of proprietorship. However, if there is a firm proletarian policy, a decisive settling of accounts by the victorious proletariat with the landowners and large peasants, the waverings of this layer cannot be significant and cannot in any way change the fact that for the most part the small peasant will be on the side of the proletarian overthrow.

3. The three above-mentioned groups taken together constitute the majority of the rural population in all countries. That is why the ultimate success of the proletarian overthrow is ensured not only in the cities, but also in the countryside.

The contrary opinion is widespread, but it persists only because of, first, systematic deception by bourgeois science and statistics, which does all it can to conceal the deep gulf between these rural layers and the exploiters, landowners, and capitalists as well as between the semiproletarians and the small peasants, on the one hand, and the large peasants on the other.

Second, it survives because the heroes of the Second International and the "labor aristocracy," corrupted by imperialist prerogatives, are unwilling and unable to carry out truly proletarian, revolutionary propaganda and agitational and organizational work among the rural toiling population. The opportunists' whole attention was and is directed at concocting an agreement, in theory and in fact, with the bourgeoisie, including with the large and middle peasantry, and not at the revolutionary overthrow by the proletariat of the bourgeois government and the bourgeoisie.

Third, this false opinion persists as a result of an obstinate prejudice, linked to all bourgeois-democratic and parliamentary prejudices. This view resists the following truth, fully proven by Marxist theory and entirely confirmed by the experience of the proletarian revolution in Russia. The fragmented, oppressed, and intimidated rural population of the above-mentioned groups, condemned to a semibarbaric standard of living in even the most advanced countries, stand to gain economically, socially, and culturally from the victory of socialism. But except for the rural workers, who today already support the revolution, this population can give decisive support to the revolutionary proletariat only after the proletariat has conquered power, the large landowners and capitalists have been decisively dealt with, and these layers see in practice that they have an organized leader and defender who is powerful and firm enough to help them and guide them on the correct course.

4. The middle peasantry refers in the economic sense to the small farmers: owners or renters of small pieces of land that under capitalism usually not only ensure the upkeep of the family and farm but also yield a small surplus which, at least in good years, can be transformed into capital. These farmers are often in a position to hire outside labor. An example of the middle peasantry in an advanced capitalist country is the layer in Germany which, according to the 1907 census in Germany, has farms of from five to ten hectares of land, of which about one-third employ agricultural wage labor.[19] In France, where there is specialized cultivation (vineyards, for example) requiring a particularly great expenditure of labor, this group probably uses outside, hired wageworkers on an even greater scale.

The revolutionary proletariat cannot take on the task of winning this layer over, at least not in the immediate future and in the opening stage of the dictatorship of the proletariat. On the contrary, the proletariat must restrict itself to the task of neutralizing this layer, of preventing it from actively assisting the bourgeoisie in the latter's struggle against the proletariat. The vacillations of this layer are unavoidable, and at the beginning of the new epoch its prevailing tendency in the developed capitalist countries will be to favor the bourgeoisie, because the outlook and frame of mind of property owners are predominant here.[20] The victorious proletariat will improve this layer's lot by abolishing rent and mortgage debts, providing machinery, introducing electricity in agricultural production, and so on.

In most capitalist states it is out of the question for the proletarian state to abolish private property immediately. But the proletarian state power certainly will abolish all obligations this layer is subject to because of private property rights.[21] In any case, the proletarian state guarantees the small and middle peasants not only that they will retain their piece of land but also that it will be enlarged to encompass the land they previously rented (by abolishing rents).

Combining measures of this sort with the relentless struggle against the bourgeoisie guarantees the success of the policy of neutralization. The transition to collective farming can be implemented by the proletarian state only gradually and with great care, without any force, and through example, by providing machinery and introducing technical improvements and electrification.[22]

5. The *large peasantry* comprises the capitalist agricultural enterprises, which as a rule employ several wageworkers

and are connected with the peasantry only through their level of culture, way of life, and through personal, physical work on their farm.

This is the most numerous of the bourgeois layers, and it is a direct and decided enemy of the revolutionary proletariat. Freeing the toiling and exploited majority of the rural population from the spiritual and political influence of these exploiters and struggling against this layer must be the main goal of the Communist Party's work in the countryside.

After the proletariat's victory in the cities, it is inevitable that this layer will carry out every possible form of resistance, sabotage, and direct, counterrevolutionary armed struggle. Therefore, the revolutionary proletariat must immediately begin the intellectual and organizational preparation of the necessary forces to disarm this group and, in addition to overthrowing the capitalists of industry, to deal it a decisive, ruthless, devastating blow at the first expression of resistance. For this purpose the rural proletariat must be armed and organized into soviets (estate councils), in which there can be no place for exploiters, while the proletarians and semiproletarians must be ensured predominant influence.

Nevertheless, expropriating the large peasants should not be the immediate task of the victorious proletariat, because the material, especially technical, but also social conditions for socializing such farms are still lacking. In certain cases, probably exceptions, the parts of their lands that they rent out or that are especially needed by the small peasantry in the area will be expropriated. These small peasants must also be ensured the free use, under certain conditions, of a portion of the large peasants' agricultural machinery. In general the proletarian state power can allow the large peasants to keep the land

and will expropriate it only if they resist the power of the toilers and exploited. The experience of Russia's proletarian revolution, in which the struggle against the large peasants was especially complicated and protracted by a number of special conditions, accordingly showed that this layer, when taught a resounding lesson for the slightest resistance, is capable of loyally fulfilling the tasks set by the proletarian state and even begins to feel respect for this power that protects all who work and ruthlessly prosecutes the idle rich.

The particular conditions in Russia impeding the proletariat, after its victory over the bourgeoisie, in its fight against the large peasants were by and large the following: After the uprising of November 7, 1917 [October 25, old style], the Russian revolution went through the stage of the general democratic—that is, basically, bourgeois-democratic—struggle of the entire peasantry against the estate owners. The urban proletariat was culturally and numerically weak. The distances, given the extremely poor means of communication, caused great difficulties.

The revolutionary proletariat of Europe and America must energetically prepare for total victory over the large peasants' resistance, eliminate any attempt at even the slightest resistance, and achieve victory significantly more quickly, decisively, and successfully. Such a complete victory of the masses of rural workers, semiproletarians, and small peasants is essential. Without it the proletarian state cannot be considered secure or sturdy.

6. The revolutionary proletariat must immediately, without exception and without any compensation, expropriate all the lands of the large landowners, estate owners, and those people who, performing no physical labor themselves, directly or through rents systematically exploit the labor power of wageworkers and the neighbor-

ing small (and often middle) peasantry. Here are found most of the descendants of the feudal lords—the nobles in Russia, Germany, and Hungary, the restored former feudal large landholders in France, the landlords in Britain, the former slaveholders in America, and, in addition, financial magnates grown rich—hybrids of these two varieties of exploiters and loafers. Propaganda for or implementation of any compensation to the large landowners for expropriated landed property must not be allowed in any form in the ranks of the Communist Party. In the present situation in Europe and America, that would be tantamount to betraying socialism and imposing a new burden on the toilers and exploited masses. These masses have already been burdened more than enough by the war, in which the number of millionaires and their wealth proliferated.[23]

For the most advanced capitalist countries, the Communist International recognizes it as correct to preserve for the most part the large agricultural enterprises and to run them along the lines of the Soviet enterprises in Russia.

It would also be appropriate to support the formation of collective enterprises (agricultural cooperatives and communes).

In Russia the economic backwardness of the country made it necessary to divide these lands among the peasants for their use. Only in comparatively few exceptional cases was it possible to utilize these lands to establish a so-called Soviet enterprise, run by the proletarian state on its own account. The former wageworkers thereby become both workers for the state and members of the soviets that administer the state.

Preserving the large landed enterprises best protects the interests of the revolutionary layer of the rural population, the propertyless farm workers and the semiproletarian plot owners, who earn their livelihood mainly from wage labor in the large enterprises. Furthermore, nationalizing the large enterprises makes the urban population at least partially independent of the peasantry for provisions.

On the other hand, where vestiges of the medieval order such as the corvée system lead to special forms of exploitation, where servitude or sharecropping or the like exist, it may be necessary to turn over to the peasants part of the land of the great estates.

In countries and regions where the large agricultural enterprise plays a relatively small role, but there are, on the other hand, a great many small peasant owners striving for land, distributing the large landowners' land will prove to be the surest method of winning the peasantry for the revolution, while preserving the large enterprises has no particular significance for supplying the cities.

The proletariat's first and most important task is to secure a lasting victory, come what may. For the sake of the revolution, the proletariat must not hesitate even at a temporary decrease in production. Only by keeping the middle peasants neutral and winning the support of the majority of the small peasantry, if not all of it, can the proletarian state achieve lasting stability.

In any case, whenever large landholdings are distributed, the interests of the rural proletariat must be safeguarded first and foremost.

The assets of the large enterprises absolutely must be transformed, without compensation, into state property with the vital stipulation that, after the needs of the large state enterprises have been met, these assets can be used without charge by the small peasants, subject to conditions worked out by the proletarian state.

In the period right after the proletarian uprising, it is absolutely necessary that the large landowners be immediately expropriated without compensation, and that in general they be expelled and interned as leaders of the counterrevolution and ruthless tyrants of the entire rural population. In addition, as proletarian power is consolidated not only in the city but also in the countryside, the effort must be made systematically to involve in the establishment of large socialist agricultural enterprises men from the bourgeoisie with useful experience, knowledge, and organizational ability, under the special surveillance of reliable Communist workers and under the supervision of estate councils.

7. Socialism will defeat capitalism definitively and be secure forever only after the proletarian state has broken all resistance by the exploiters, securing total dominance and complete obedience, and reconstructed industry on the basis of scientific, large-scale enterprises and the most modern achievements of technology (electrification of the entire economy). This is the only way the city can offer the more backward and dispersed rural population the technical and social assistance that will create the material basis for significantly increasing productivity in agriculture and of rural labor in general. This is also the way that the smaller landowners will be induced by force of example and self-interest to change over to large, cooperative, mechanized enterprises.[24]

Especially in the countryside, effectively carrying out the successful struggle for socialism requires the following: The Communist parties must instill in the industrial proletariat a recognition of the need for sacrifices in order to overthrow the bourgeoisie and to consolidate proletarian power. For the dictatorship of the proletariat signifies both the proletariat's ability to organize and guide all toiling and exploited masses and the vanguard's capacity to make the greatest efforts and heroic sacrifices for the sake of this goal. Success imperatively requires that the conditions of the toiling and most exploited rural masses be immediately and significantly improved by the proletariat's victory at the cost of the exploiters, because without this, the industrial proletariat cannot be certain of the support of the countryside and cannot count on provisions for the cities.

8. The tremendous difficulty of organizing and training in revolutionary struggle the masses of the rural population, who because of capitalism are intellectually undeveloped, scattered, oppressed, and often held in a condition of medieval dependency, demands that the Communist Party give special attention to the strike movement in the countryside and energetically support and broaden the mass strikes of the rural proletarians and semiproletarians. The experience of the Russian revolutions of 1905 and 1917, now confirmed and developed by the experiences in Germany, Poland, Italy, Britain,[25] and other developed countries, proves that only the advancing strike movement of the masses (under certain circumstances with the participation of the small peasants) is capable of awakening the slumbering village, arousing class consciousness and an understanding of the necessity for the rural exploited classes to organize along class lines, and making clear, in word and deed, the importance of their unifying with the urban workers. Therefore, demanding the trade union organization of the farm workers and collaboration by the Communists in farm and forest workers' unions is especially necessary. The Communist parties should also support the formation among the exploited rural population of production cooperatives that work closely with the revolutionary workers' movement. Furthermore, there should be agitation aimed particularly at small peasants.[26]

The congress of the Communist International brands as traitors and turncoats those Socialists—found not only in the Second International but also in the parties, very important for Europe, that have left that International—who manage not only to watch the strike movement in the countryside with indifference, but who (like the trade union bureaucracy, the Scheidemanns, and Kautsky), oppose the strikes, seeing them only in terms of the danger of a decrease in food production.[27] No program whatsoever and no declaration, however solemn, has the slightest value unless the Communists and workers' leaders prove in practice that they put the development of the proletarian revolution and its victory before everything, and that they therefore are ready to make the greatest sacrifices, since there is no other way and no other means of overcoming hunger and ruin once and for all and preventing new imperialist wars.[28]

9. The Communist parties must do all in their power to proceed as soon as possible to form soviets in the countryside, primarily estate councils of representatives of the wageworkers and semiproletarians. The formation of small peasant councils should also be promoted.[29] Only when linked to the mass strike movement and when acting together with the most oppressed classes will the soviets be able to perform their functions and become consolidated, bringing the small peasants under their influence and later drawing them into their ranks through the fusion of the small peasants' soviets with those of the farm workers.[30] So long as the strike movement is not yet strong, however, and the agricultural proletariat is still poorly organized because of both heavy pressure by landowners and large peasants and insufficient support from industrial workers and their organizations, forming soviets in the countryside will require painstaking preparation. This preparation

must take place by creating Communist Party cells, even if they are very small at first, through active propaganda that presents the demands of communism in popular form and uses examples to illustrate the various methods of exploitation and subjugation, and furthermore by using systematic agitational tours of industrial workers to the countryside, and so on.

SESSION 14

AUGUST 4, 1920 (EVENING)

# Statutes

ZINOVIEV: On behalf of the Bureau I move that the following comrades do the final editing of all theses: Meyer (German); Rosmer (French); Reed (English); and Sokolnikov (Russian).[1] (*Vote*) We proceed now to the question of the statutes. Comrade Kabakchiev has the floor to give the report.

## REPORT ON THE STATUTES

KHRISTO KABAKCHIEV [COMMUNIST PARTY OF BULGARIA]: Comrades, first of all, I will review the main considerations that speak in favor of the Statutes of the Communist International as proposed by the Executive Committee, and then I will spend some time on the most important objections raised in the commission.

The defeat of the Second International occurred when the bourgeoisie succeeded in destroying the proletariat's international solidarity. One of the Communist International's first tasks, therefore, is the restoration of proletarian solidarity. Only revolutionary struggle for the overthrow of capitalism will make it possible to create the necessary preconditions for solidarity and unity of the proletariat in different countries. Clearly, the mere existence of a counterrevolutionary international alliance makes it necessary that there be unity in revolutionary struggle of the proletariat of all countries. This alliance is organized and led today by the Entente, by the Supreme Council of the governments of the big capitalist countries, and by their creation and agent, the League of Nations. Unification and centralization of proletarian forces is the main condition necessary for the success of the proletariat's revolution against the counterrevolutionary united front of the bourgeoisie. The Communist International is the only organ capable of making unity among the proletarian forces of the world a reality.

There is another reason for the defeat of the Second International. The Second International admitted all parties on the strength of their spoken or written statements but never took the trouble to learn the real policies pursued by parties that joined. It tolerated in its midst parties whose policies and practice were in obvious conflict with the policies of the revolutionary proletariat. Moreover, it admitted petty-bourgeois parties that had nothing in common with socialism. The experience with the Second International teaches us that if the Communist International is to carry out its tasks and achieve its goal, it must become a strictly disciplined and tightly centralized organization. It must oversee, lead, and bring into harmony the practical activity and revolutionary action of the proletariat of all countries.

The triumph of the revolutionary proletariat in Russia showed us clearly that strong centralization is needed in each Communist party and consequently also in the Communist International itself. The Communist Party of Russia can serve us as a model and an inspiration not only because its policies are farsighted and its actions strictly Marxist but also because of its iron discipline and strict centralism. The Russian Communist Party's principle of centralism and its discipline, which was displayed in all the Russian proletariat's revolutionary activity, was further strengthened after the conquest of power; it was extended to the organization of the Soviet republic, which helped to consolidate the revolutionary victory and make it unshakable. Without a centralized and disciplined organization, the Russian proletariat would never have triumphed. Without a centralized and disciplined organization, the international proletariat will never break capitalist rule. It is impossible to imagine how the proletariat could overthrow bourgeois rule and triumph over the capitalist state—a class tool that wields centralized and powerful means of coercion—without centralization.

We all agree that the victory of the proletarian revolution is impossible without the dictatorship of the proletariat. But anyone who says "dictatorship" must presuppose that the class that exercises this dictatorship and the party that leads that class have a centralized and strictly disciplined organization. Without such iron discipline and such a centralized organization, the Communist International cannot look forward to the advent of the proletarian dictatorship. The task of the Communist International is to unite the proletarian parties and other revolutionary proletarian organizations of all countries and fuse them into a bloc of struggle.

The economic crisis, a consequence of the imperialist war, created a revolutionary situation in most capitalist countries, ensuring in turn the rapid growth of the Communist International. The International has the duty to attract the mass organizations of the proletariat. The most effective—and perhaps only—way to shield the Communist International from the danger that rapid growth will threaten the purity of its revolutionary policies is to organize it on the basis of firm centralism. Merely adopting the theses proposed at this congress will not assure that the parties that have joined the Communist International will also remain true to its principles and policies. On the contrary, only organizational centralism and voluntary and sincere subordination to the Statutes of the Communist International provide a foundation for the parties that have already affiliated to communism and those that will do so in the future.

The proposed statutes establish the organizational foundation of the Communist International. But the Communist International, especially in the future, must develop in step with the expansion of the international revolutionary proletarian movement.

One of the most important principled objections to the draft statutes concerns the passage after the introduction that says, "The Communist International takes as its goal to struggle with all possible means, including with arms in hand, for the overthrow of the international bourgeoisie and the creation of an international soviet republic as a transitional step toward complete destruction of the state." The comrades that raised objections concerning this question reasoned as follows: First, the Communist International must not openly state and concede that it will employ force of arms in order to attain its goals. Second, the statutes must not talk exclusively about armed struggle; this could lead to the conclusion that other weapons of struggle do not come in question and that the Communist International knows no methods of struggle other than rifles and machine guns.

The first argument requires no detailed refutation. Seventy years have passed since the founders of revolutionary socialism, Marx and Engels, ended the renowned Communist Manifesto with this declaration: "The communists disdain to conceal their views and aims. They openly declare that their ends can be attained only by the forcible overthrow of all existing social conditions."[2]

Today we have before us the example of the Russian proletarian revolution, a revolution that triumphed through force of arms. The great, victorious Red Army is dealing mortal blows to the imperialism of the Allies and clearing the way for the world proletarian revolution. We claim we are going through a revolutionary epoch in which the bourgeoisie is openly organizing White Guards against us and civil war is flaring up in country after country. Is it possible today, after all this, to propose that we remain silent, to have the Communist International remain silent on the need to utilize the mightiest and most effective means of struggle, the one weapon above all others upon which the actual, ultimate success of the proletarian revolution depends?

No, comrades! In its statutes, the Communist International must refer quite explicitly to the need to engage in armed struggle. Hypocrisy concerning the use of such means will not spare us persecution by the ruling bourgeoisie. We must state plainly that the bourgeoisie understands what is at stake and thus knows our true revolutionary aims and methods of struggle perfectly well. It organizes White Guards to press other institutions into its service. The Communist International must declare openly, before the whole world, that the marching orders for the revolution can be only: Struggle to the death; struggle, arms in hand, against capitalism and for communism.

In the same manner we can answer the comrades on the commission who thought it would be dangerous to express the need to form illegal organizations alongside legal ones. (See article 12 of the statutes.) When the bourgeoisie of a given country found it convenient and in its interests to proscribe the Communist Party, it did so; when it thinks this a good idea in the future, it will do so, as it has already in several countries.

But is this really cause for the Communist Party to conceal its objectives and refrain from disseminating the idea that armed struggle is necessary? Not at all. Under such circumstances, to remain silent on the need to form illegal organizations is needless caution and causes confusion. What is more, comrades, we say that such diplomatic caution is dangerous, for today the illegal organization is just as important as the legal one. And it is not just important but indispensable and imposed on us by necessity. And as you know, the congress has already adopted theses that settle this question and require the formation of illegal organizations. Comrades who have already voted for these theses would find themselves in a contradiction, as would the congress that adopted them, in rejecting the corresponding article of the statutes. We will parry the bourgeoisie's blows not by discarding the article in the statutes on illegal organizations but by learning, by becoming accustomed to forming illegal organizations, which will frustrate the bourgeoisie's investigations and vigilance. And for that we need revolutionary experience and revolutionary skill.

The question of the composition of the Executive Committee generated a lively discussion in the commission.

I will repeat the most important objections made there. Several comrades believe that because the Communist Party of their country is currently weak, it is impossible to release a member to be a permanent representative to the Executive Committee. Others say that since the Communist parties of each country cannot maintain regular correspondence with their delegates to the Executive Committee, those delegates will have little information about the situation in their country and the state of the revolutionary movement.

To me these considerations do not seem very sound compared to the role that the Communist International and its Executive Committee plays and must play. We live in a revolutionary epoch in which the Communist International has important and immediate tasks to perform every day, in which questions of worldwide significance constantly arise that absolutely must be answered. The Communist International must be a powerful, centralized organization of struggle. It must therefore be led from a center that is representative and in which the largest Communist parties have permanent representatives.

The tasks of the Communist International are so important that every Communist party must select from its ranks a comrade of merit, equal to the magnitude of the assignment, so that this party can be represented on the Executive Committee and thereby maintain close contact with the Communist International. The Executive Committee will not be able to base its decisions on the real international situation unless it includes representatives of the large Communist parties of different countries. On the contrary, there is a danger that in certain cases Communist parties not represented on the Executive Committee will not recognize its decisions as binding, on the excuse that the Executive Committee does not know the true situation in their countries and makes decisions without first consulting them.

Several comrades demanded that the Executive Committee be composed of representatives from every party that belongs to the Communist International, every representative having decision-making vote. Otherwise, these comrades fear, the small countries and small parties will be left with no representation on the Executive Committee. I represent a small country, but the Communist Party there is tightly organized and unites the workers and peasants. I am certain that in appointing members to the Executive Committee the congress will take into account not a country's geographic size but rather the real strength of the Communist Party. If every party that belongs to the Communist International is given the right to have representatives with decision-making vote on the Executive Committee, it will become a cumbersome apparatus, in danger of being dominated by a majority of small and weak parties and never having a clearly defined composition. The congress must make a final decision on the size of the Executive Committee, selecting not which individuals but which parties should belong to it. The statutes give all parties the right to representation on the Executive Committee with consultative vote. That is sufficient.

The question was posed in the commission whether the Executive Committee should be given the power to expel from the Communist International individuals, groups, or even parties that "contravene decisions of the world congress" (article 9 of the statutes). But it is this power that gives the necessary effective force to all the other powers granted by the statutes to the Executive Committee. How can its decisions have the necessary authority and binding force if the committee does not have the power of expulsion? Not to give the Executive Committee this power would be to return to the old practices of the Second International.

Finally, the statutes give the Executive Committee the power to involve representatives of organizations and parties sympathetic to communism by giving them consultative vote.

The question was also raised whether the Executive Committee has the power to admit two parties from the same country with decisive vote. The commission did not resolve this question; it is left open in the statutes. I think that only one Communist party in each country should belong to the Communist International. This is absolutely necessary to preserve the unity of the Communist movement in each country. If the Communist International begins to follow the example of the Second International, admitting into its ranks two or more competing parties from the same country, whose differences are sometimes fabricated by less conscious elements and sometimes inspired and sustained by the bourgeoisie itself, that will hamper the development of the Communist movement.

The Executive Committee's experiences with the auxiliary bureaus in Amsterdam and Berlin show that all organs and bureaus it creates must be directly subordinate to it and act only within the guidelines it establishes. That is the only way we can create a centralized and disciplined international Communist organization.

SIEGFRIED BAMATTER [SOCIALIST YOUTH ORGANIZATION, SWITZERLAND]: The commission on statutes instructed the editing commission to incorporate the editorial changes and motions into the statutes. This was no easy task for us, because our only basis was the three drafts that had been translated from the Russian, and not one of the translations was correct. For that reason we cannot present the statutes in their final form. Instead, I will read you only the editing commission's motions and those of its changes in wording that bear on principle. The statutes must go back to the commission again.

In the second paragraph on page 1, a sentence is missing from the German translation and must be inserted into the quotation. This sentence does appear in the French statutes.

Several small stylistic changes were made, which I will not enumerate. A change was made on page 2 that provoked a major debate in the commission. The line in question, which began, "The Communist International takes as its goal," was changed to begin, "The Communist International takes as its goal to struggle with all possible means, including with arms in hand." Another change was made on page 3 in the last sentence of the first paragraph, which now reads, "The Communist International pledges to support every soviet republic, wherever one is created." Articles 1, 2, and 3 were adopted unanimously without change.

In article 4, second sentence, the following change was inserted. Instead of, "The world congress usually meets," it now says, "The world congress meets regularly once a year." The third sentence in article 4 was deleted, as was the last sentence. Articles 5, 6, and 7 were adopted with no substantial changes.

A few stylistic changes were made in article 8. For example, the first sentence began, "The main burden and responsibility . . ." It now begins, "The party . . . bears the main burden of the Executive Committee's work." Then, further on, in the next-to-last sentence of article 8, it now reads, "the ten to thirteen most important Communist parties," instead of, "the ten largest parties."

At the end of article 9 the following motion was added: "Executive Committee representatives discharge their political duties in the closest possible communication with the party leaderships of their respective countries." The last sentence of article 10 now says, "that, although not members of the Communist International, are in close sympathy with it." Article 11 was adopted unchanged.

Article 12, which reads, "The general situation in all of Europe and America compels Communists around the world to form illegal Communist organizations parallel to the legal ones," now continues, "The Executive Committee must see that this is done everywhere." In the first sentence of article 13, instead of beginning, "As a rule all important political communications," it now begins, "As a rule, political relations between individual parties belonging to the Communist International are conducted through the Executive Committee of the Communist International."

The first sentence of article 14 states, "Under the Communist International's leadership," instead of "Under the supervision . . ." The second sentence now says, "These unions appoint," instead of "The Communist unions appoint . . ." Article 15 is changed to read, "The Communist Youth International is a member of the Communist International with full rights, subordinate to its Executive Committee." The last sentence of article 15 was deleted. Articles 16 and 17 were adopted with no change. That completes the changes. The final version of the statutes will be presented later.

ALEXANDER BILAN [COMMUNIST LABOR PARTY, UNITED STATES]: The statutes of our organization is one of the most important questions we have to decide. The reporter pointed out that the discipline of the Communist Party of Russia helped it play such an important role. We must therefore study the statutes carefully. If we adopt them, we must treat them seriously, be prepared to carry them out to the fullest extent, and not regard them as simply a piece of paper.

In several of the articles, the way the statutes were edited differed from one language to another, and therefore it was not possible for the members of the commission to reach agreement on several questions.

An editorial change must be made on the question of armed struggle. In my opinion, the wording of this article confuses the concept of ends with that of means. The concepts must not be confused. We want to pose armed struggle not as the goal of the revolutionary movement but rather as a means forced upon us. We must also clarify the circumstances under which such armed struggle becomes a necessity. Otherwise, if we call for it in general, we could experience what sometimes has happened in the past, when anarchists brandish hand grenades and that is seen as the Communist International's conception of armed struggle.

If we establish armed struggle as a general rule without taking into account the situation in each country, that is, whether conditions are sufficiently mature and whether such an armed struggle is really necessary and practically possible, then in some countries, where such struggle is not yet possible, the call to armed struggle could have the effect of a provocation. I point to the example of the KAPD, in which the concept of armed struggle is not understood in a mature and serious way and produces only harmful effects.

I proposed several amendments to articles of the draft statutes to the commission, but it did not adopt them. I would like to bring them before the plenary session now. I move that the following sentences be added: "The Communist International's objective is to overthrow the international bourgeoisie in order to liberate humanity from the fetters of slavery and exploitation. It is determined to make use of armed struggle against the international bourgeoisie as the best possible way to achieve this objective."

Article 12 of the statutes reads, "The general situation in all of Europe and America compels Communists around the world to form illegal Communist organizations." There are countries where opportunities still exist to agitate and work legally for communist ideas. If we retain this article in its present form, we will enable governments to claim that the parties in their respective countries belong to the Communist International, which calls upon them to build illegal organizations. This could serve governments as a pretext to persecute very harshly comrades who might otherwise be able to struggle legally. Therefore, I propose to make a slight change in this section, striking from the passage the words implying that it is obligatory for parties belonging to the Communist International to form illegal organizations. With my change the article reads, "The general situation in all Europe and America compels the Communists of the whole world to form Communist organizations."

WIJNKOOP: I did not vote on this point in the commission, and in my opinion it cannot be voted on. Instead, the question must first be referred to the parties in each country for study. Statutes are very important, in my view, and comrades in every country must know exactly what they have all agreed to in this matter. That can happen only if the parties in every country hold discussions on it. The discussion we had tonight and the discussion in the commission are not enough. That is why I did not vote and will abstain in the plenary session, too.

I say that statutes are very important because I believe they must be implemented and made reality. In this case the statutes must reflect what the different parties in various countries, after a thorough discussion, declare to be their will.

The key question for me is article 8, which reads, "The party of the country where, by decision of the world congress, the Executive Committee is located bears the main burden of the Executive Committee's work." In my opinion, although this gives the impression that an international Executive Committee is being formed, the reality is quite different; we are setting up an expanded Russian Executive Committee. Now please understand me. I have no objection to a Russian Executive Committee if that is necessary, and perhaps now it is necessary. If we really cannot have an international Executive Committee, we must have a Russian one, because the Russian party is the most revolutionary and the most powerful. I have nothing against that, but then it should be stated. We should not act as if we were getting an international Executive Committee. It should be stated that at this time we cannot have anything other than a Russian Executive Committee and that this congress places power in the hands of the Russian Executive Committee. I would be for that without hesitation.

But all we will have is an expanded Russian Executive Committee; here, at this time, we can have no other Executive Committee. Why do I believe this? Because I am not as optimistic as some comrades about the blockade. For Russia it is a reality and may not be eased for some time—although some believe that it has already eased. If that were true, then of course my argument would no longer be appropriate. For the moment, however, it is not true.

I will give only one example. When delegates are here, that is, if delegates from the largest parties are sent here, they cannot monitor the world situation because they receive no reports on world politics. They do not hear enough about the organization in each country. They get reports only on what happens here. If it is possible for ten of the best men in the international movement to be sent here, they will lose contact with their own countries and will be informed only about Russia. And whether their character and intelligence are great or small, they will necessarily be guided by Russian information and therefore by the Russian Executive Committee. That cannot be otherwise, and nothing else is conceivable, because they will lose touch with their own country.

When this Executive Committee makes decisions, it might be said in those countries, "So-and-so, one of our leaders, is there, and he was present there. Yet such and such a decision was made, and it is a bad one, because he is not taking into account the situation in the countries of Europe and America." The workers in these countries would become even more separated from their leaders—who came here after all in order to maintain contact between Moscow and the rest of the world. They would become convinced that their leaders had lost their sure perception of the world situation. So I do not believe that we can proceed this way.

I proposed that the Executive Committee be located outside of Russia, and I think this question should be discussed here. I suggested Italy or Norway as a site for the Executive Committee because I think that the workers' movement in those countries is strong enough now to make it possible to hold meetings of an international Executive Committee there. Comrade Levi proposed Germany as the Executive Committee's location. Indeed I would agree to Germany as readily as to Norway or Italy—for one thing because the workers' movement of those countries is sufficiently strong, and for another because people there are well informed about the world situation. The Russian delegation can certainly come to Norway or to Italy. Comrade Levi thinks they could come to Germany too.

I propose that this question be discussed. If the congress believes that changing the seat of the Executive Committee is impossible, then there cannot be a truly international Executive Committee at this time, and we will have to be satisfied with a Russian one. This question is very important, because we are giving this Executive Committee a great deal of authority, authority so broad that the Executive Committee can even expel entire parties, groups, and individuals. But surely it can do this only if it knows the situation in the various countries extremely well. That is why I feel that the statutes cannot simply be adopted in their present form.

ZINOVIEV: It has been moved that the speakers' list be closed. Is there any objection? (*The motion carries.*)

LEVI: The questions under discussion here are so important that it is a shame they are being taken up when the delegates are in such a state of exhaustion that they cannot follow them properly.

First, I propose deleting from article 8 the words "not less than." The sentence that concerns me would read, "The party of that country sends five representatives . . ." Adding the words "not less than" could result in a misunderstanding. Although I certainly do not think this was intended by those who proposed it, it could be inferred that the country where the Executive Committee resides may assign as many representatives to the committee as it likes. Five representatives is what it should be, no more and no less.

Furthermore, in my opinion, part of what Comrade Wijnkoop said is right. After a time, the representatives assigned here from abroad will lose living contact with the parties in their countries. I would not put it the way Comrade Wijnkoop did, that after a while a delegate sent here would be dependent solely on Russian information. Rather, I would say that from the moment he sets foot on Russian soil he has exactly the same sources of information as the Russian comrades.

As for Comrade Radek's objection that it would be no different in any other country, that is correct in principle but looks quite different in practice. Nowhere else for example, does it take ten days for letters or newspapers to arrive—even from Germany. And there is no doubt, in my opinion, that this will cause big problems, because when the Executive Committee must make decisions, the inadequacy of sources of information could, undoubtedly, influence the outcome.

How very true that is was shown by an example I raised in the commission yesterday. The Russian comrades gave credentials to the Dutch comrades. When we in Germany saw that decision, we said right away it was an error. And when the comrades in the Netherlands saw their credentials, they immediately said the same thing.[3]

I do not conclude from this that the Executive Committee should not remain here—other considerations speak too strongly in favor. No, I favor its staying here. But I believe that we must find a way to make important, unpostponable decisions. Representatives who come here to make decisions must be able to do that. And that is why my other motion reads, "The Executive Committee must meet in plenary session every three months." That, in my opinion, is what needs to be said to make sure that particularly important decisions are made by party representatives who are very well informed about these questions and have close contact with their party.

I also move that article 12 of the statutes be amended by striking the words up to "the Executive Committee" and replacing them with "The Executive Committee must see that . . ."

In my opinion, there is no need to give a special place in the statutes to the illegal organizations provided for here. What we have to say about illegal organizations is found anyway in another one of our resolutions, so it is quite enough to state in general that the Executive Committee has to see to it that the congress resolutions are carried out. That says everything, and I believe that for many parties affiliated to the Communist International, omitting mention of these illegal organizations can entail only advantages.

GALLACHER:[4] With regard to the statutes read out here, which demand establishment of a united Communist party, I must say that the British communists who are marching under the banner of the British Communist Party are in fact holding on to the Communist International with one hand and the Second International with the other. They have not decisively adopted the platform of the Communist International. The British Socialist Party too is considered a communist party and at the same time is affiliated to the Labour Party. The Labour Party is a conglomeration of quite diverse parties standing on conflicting platforms. I see this as a contradiction and as a reason to ask whether the British Socialist Party can be regarded as a truly communist party. Comrade Radek asked me whether I am not myself in the Labour Party as a trade union official. My reply is that I am not an official but a member of the union. There is a difference between someone who is forced to join a labor organization and someone who joins a noncommunist organization voluntarily.

In order to get real power into our hands, we must first of all make sure that we rouse the masses to fight vigorously against the capitalists and industrialists. That is the first and most important step. Then we must see to the creation of an organization with the material strength needed to undertake armed struggle. The British Socialist Party, which is regarded here as a communist party, is in fact not at all in favor of armed or physical struggle. It is pacifist, although Comrade Quelch may deny it, for he himself said that he opposes the use of any force in this struggle.

The trade union movement in Britain can never be won over to communism. On the contrary, this whole organization must be regarded as capitalism's most powerful bulwark for defense against social revolution. Several delegates representing the union movement, who were received here with open arms, upon their return to Britain appeared at large meetings and recounted how they were received here with such honor.[5] When it is really necessary to fight for the workers' cause, they participate in arbitration boards, thereby harming the revolutionary struggle.

REED: I disagree with those who do not want to include the point on armed insurrection in the theses. I base my position especially on experience in America. The workers will not understand why something like this is passed over in silence. And if they knew it, they would take it to mean that the party is afraid of the consequences. Experience shows that no matter how legally you express yourself, whenever the government wants to pass state-of-emergency laws against Communists or revolutionaries, it finds a way to turn the most legal thing into something completely illegal. That is why I am against saying nothing.

In addition I propose that article 14, which talks of a Red trade union International, not be incorporated into the statutes, or at least that it not be voted on until the whole trade union question has been considered in the commission and discussed here. Yesterday it was said here clearly that all questions concerning the unions would first be dealt with in commission and then presented to the congress.

I also wish to point out that it was said that in general the trade union International should have a looser relationship to the Communist International. But according to article 14 it would appear that the union International is going to become a section of the Communist International. According to the new statutes, even the youth International will have much greater autonomy than the union International. For this reason, I would like to ask that no vote be taken on this point at present.

FRAINA: First of all, I would like to emphasize what Reed has said concerning the trade union International. This is a vital question. Precisely as we broke the Second, Socialist International, we must now break the Amsterdam trade union International—an indispensable condition for our struggle against world imperialism. I am absolutely in favor of the proposed plan for the Communist International to organize the labor unions of the world. But we feel that this question should be considered separately and not as part of the statutes, since it deserves serious consideration, and we would like to put forward certain proposals.

Concerning the statutes, I totally disagree with Comrades Wijnkoop and Levi in their suggestion that the Executive Committee of the International should be elsewhere than in Russia. Before the congress many comrades feared that because of the blockade, lack of adequate information on the world movement, the requirements of "practical politics," and so forth, it might be necessary to have the Executive Committee in some other country. But now everyone must conclude that all these fears were imaginary. The Russian comrades know precisely what is going on, and no one in this congress has shown a finer international spirit than the comrades of the Russian party.

Moreover, the argument was advanced that the Executive Committee should be in the country that is currently the center of the world revolution. This argument is sound. We are past the stage of mere agitation; now is the stage of actual action. The world revolution is a fact, and the strategy and tactics of the Communist International must conform to this fact. Upon the country that is for the moment the center of the world revolution (in this case Russia) play all the world forces of imperialism and revolution, compelling the Communist movement in that country to adhere absolutely to an internationalist standpoint, failing which it will meet disaster.

Everything that happens in the world intimately concerns the Russian comrades, not as a matter of theory and tendency of coming events, but as a matter of life and death. What happens in England today immediately concerns Russia much more intimately than the United States; what happens in the United States concerns Russia much more intimately than England. And so with every country. World politics converge upon Soviet Russia. In intimate matters of the policy of our own imperialist governments, the Russian comrades are frequently more informed than we ourselves. Objective conditions, if nothing else, impose an international standpoint upon the Russian comrades, and with them in control of the Executive Committee we have a guarantee that problems will be met in the spirit of the International. It is absurd to suggest that the Executive Committee should be transferred to Berlin. They have had a West European Secretariat in Berlin, and it has been parochial, narrow, to some degree nationalistic, and not international.

It is surprising that any delegate to this congress would oppose inserting in the statutes the clause concerning illegal work. Not only is the combination of illegal and legal work absolutely necessary, but it should be openly proclaimed and made mandatory. Where a party is legal, a tendency develops against illegal work, and where a party is illegal there develops a tendency against utilizing legal opportunities. We must insist upon the combination of the two. Let there be no illusions: your party may be legal today, but tomorrow it can become illegal. We suffered greatly because of this in America, where we recognized that we would ultimately become illegal, but in practice had not done enough to prepare for this. As a result we were caught unawares when the great repression came. Moreover, even where a party is perfectly legal, there are indispensable forms of work—such as agitation among soldiers and sailors—that require illegal organization.

I am firmly convinced that centralization is our fundamental problem. The great difference between the Second and the Third International is precisely this matter of centralization. It may be objected that centralization is a purely organizational problem and not fundamental, but that argument is sheer Menshevism. Centralization is a revolutionary necessity. The Communist International is a highly centralized organization precisely because it is revolutionary, while the Second International was decentralized and autonomous because it was a loose federation of reformist and nonrevolutionary organizations. World imperialism is centralizing. This is only partial, since rivalry of interests prevails, but centralization of imperialism is a fact insofar as the opposition to world revolution is concerned.

The proletariat and Communist parties of the world have a complete identity of interests and can achieve a centralization impossible to imperialism, a fact that gives us an enormous advantage. The world revolution is a problem that requires flexibility, adaptation to each peculiar development of the world situation, and unified strategy and tactics. Unless the International is firm, centralized, and moving as one in a particular direction determined by events, we shall never conquer. There must be concentration of forces and unity of command so that the International and its affiliated organizations will move unitedly, focusing on each specific phase of the world revolution. The International must have the right to issue orders to each national organization. It must have the authority to say, in accord with events, whether a certain thing should or should not be done. Only in this way will we conquer.

## SUMMARY

ZINOVIEV: Comrades, three objections have been raised on points of principle. First, by the American comrades, who propose deleting article 14 and not taking up the trade union question at all. These comrades said we promised to wait until the trade union commission had completed its work. Comrades, I believe that is not correct. Article 14 says:

"Trade unions that uphold communism and that are united internationally under the Communist International's leadership constitute a trade union section of the Communist International. These unions appoint representatives to the world congresses of the Communist International through the Communist parties of their respective countries. The trade union section of the Communist International appoints a representative with decisive vote to the Executive Committee of the Communist International. The Executive Committee has the right to designate a representative with decisive vote to the trade union section of the Communist International."

We really need not wait until the trade union commission has concluded its labors before stating this, for it should be clear to every Communist. We want the Communist International not only to organize political parties but also to encompass every mass organization of the proletariat that takes a communist position. That is the first principle of the Communist International. Or do Comrade Fraina and Comrade Reed want to dispute that?

As has been mentioned several times, we build on the same foundation as the First International; we seek to continue its traditions. Well, one of the First International's most important traditions was that it sought to organize not only political parties but all proletarian mass organizations that took a communist position. That is what is stated here; no more, but no less either. If we were to call that into question, we could not build the Communist International. We must encompass not only political parties but revolutionary proletarian trade unions as well. And it is quite clear that if unions come to us, we must organize them in some way as a section of the Communist International, as part of the Communist International. Can anyone challenge that? Not at all.

All questions such as whether to remain in the American unions, whether or not the British unions should be split at once—all the questions that have been raised here have nothing to do with this. These questions are issues that must be discussed again in the commission. Only one thing is stated here: In the Communist International we want not only political organizations but all proletarian organizations and above all the trade unions. That is the ABC of the Communist International.

Our first principle is that the trade unions must send delegations to the world congress and constitute themselves as a section of the Communist International. Each must be represented on the other's Executive Committee. That is incontestable. And every serious Communist must accept it. Otherwise our practice will be like that of the Second International.

But we want to renew the practice of the First International under new historical conditions and to carry on the traditions of Marx, namely that the Communist party leads not only in politics, but in every aspect of the workers' movement, and that we must organize every branch of the workers' movement in the world within the Communist International.

Let us turn to the second question, to article 8, regarding the Executive Committee. Comrade Wijnkoop suggested here that the Executive Committee be moved, perhaps to Norway. Any number of proposals could be made, and various exotic republics could be located. But I must point out that here in article 8, as in the statutes in general, there is not a word about Russia. That is a different question, which we must discuss and decide separately. The statutes say, "The location of the Executive Committee of the Communist International shall be determined by each world congress of the Communist International." If it should happen that the proletarian revolution is victorious in France or Britain, we will of course agree to the Executive Committee being moved to one of those countries. Russia is not mentioned here at all. That is a separate question. Therefore, it is not anticipated here. The principle advanced here is that the congress must decide where the Executive Committee shall be located.

Now we come to the composition of the Executive Committee. The statutes read, "The Executive Committee shall consist of five comrades from the country where the Executive Committee resides and of one comrade from each of the ten largest parties." I agree with Comrade Levi's motion to delete "not less than five comrades" and say "five comrades." Wijnkoop says that the Executive Committee will be an expanded Russian committee. But I say that perhaps it will be an expanded Dutch committee. The point is simply that the Executive Committee shall have fifteen members: five from one country and ten from other parties of the different countries belonging to the Communist International. That will be an international committee. So how can anyone claim that this will be merely an expanded Russian committee? It will be an international committee if all ten of these parties send delegates, and they should do that.

It was said here that it is impossible for all parties to send one comrade each. I take issue with that. Apparently it is considered a luxury to have a qualified comrade here, because he is needed in Germany or somewhere else. This will not do. We regard the Executive Committee as the foremost instrument of the workers' movement. Every important party should thus find a prominent comrade to participate in it. It is the most important organization of the international movement and also has great significance for every Communist movement. We are asking for only one comrade from each country, and if the parties rotate their delegates regularly, I think it will always be possible to find the number required by the statutes. We should and must make this sacrifice for the Communist International.

I also deny that it is correct to say that a comrade who stays here will lose contact with his organization. You do not lose contact in two or three months, especially if you are a veteran militant. We lived in exile for many years and did not lose contact. Today the movement is much broader. As we envisage it, each delegate to the Executive Committee should become the first secretary of the committee for his country. The German comrade should be secretary for Germany, and so forth. Obviously, it would be best if comrades were not changed too often. But it is possible that even if the comrade in question changed places with someone else, he would remain secretary. He can have a technical assistant, but the leadership should be entrusted to the party representative in question. Only if this is the case will we have a real Executive Committee.

In some cases the Executive Committee is more important even than the congress. We have discussed a number of questions here, but we cannot foresee everything. In two weeks the most important questions might be posed anew under entirely different circumstances. Just now we stressed that we are acting in an epoch of revolutionary struggles. The Executive Committee must give help and answers to immediate questions, and therefore its composition too must be such that it has the formal and moral authority to speak in the name of the Communist International. That is why we must insist that it consist of fifteen members and that the ten most important parties actually send comrades to serve on the Executive Committee. If that does not happen, half of the meaning of our work will be lost.

The very meaning of our congress is that we want to construct a tightly knit organization, an international general staff of the fighting proletariat. If we are unable after the congress to form an Executive Committee, we will have destroyed at least half of our work. During the first year we were only a propaganda society. The Executive Committee could not function as a centralized body. It was a Russian institution—we state this frankly. That is exactly what we want to change now. We have said so openly. Now we want to have a centralized international organization, always able to give direction. We have vested great authority in the Executive Committee, including even the power to expel entire parties. Therefore the parties must see to it that they have a representative here. Otherwise our work has been in vain and we will not be able to tell the world proletariat, "Now we have a centralized International."

That is why I am against the motion by Comrade Levi that there be a plenary session of the Executive Committee once every three months. Yesterday in the commission I wavered a bit. I thought we should make concessions to our German friends. But if you think over Comrade Levi's proposal—that the party send representatives only in special cases or only once every three months—it is clear that every party will do that. Once every three months there will be a full session, but between sessions we will not have a functioning Executive Committee.

Thus we must tell our friends, "Although it will be difficult for you to keep a comrade here at all times, you must make this sacrifice, because it is in the interest of your own party." Communists will not pose this question as do the Independents, for example, who play a double game, saying the electoral struggle is one thing and the Communist International quite another. The point is to see that they are one and the same. We are a united international party with branches in different countries. The work of the International is just as important for Germany as it is for Russia. Thus we must insist categorically that the wording remain as it is, so that we have an Executive Committee of five members from one country and ten from others, all of whom are secretaries for their countries and who all work together.

We now come to the last disputed point, in article 12, on the illegal organizations. Article 12 states: "The general situation in all of Europe and America compels Communists around the world to form illegal Communist organizations parallel to the legal ones. The Executive Committee must see that this is done everywhere." We in the commission also considered perhaps phrasing this a bit more cautiously. My opinion, after having listened to everything, is that we should leave it as it is. There may be some negative considerations, but the positive ones outweigh them.

In countries like Britain and America, the so-called classic countries of bourgeois freedoms, it had not occurred to anyone to form illegal organizations. Perhaps it was accepted in theory, but it was never carried out in practice. Only now, when five thousand Communists are in jail in America, is it beginning to be understood there that we cannot do without illegal organizations. Experience in Germany also confirms this. There the party is legal at some times and illegal at others. And there is a lesson in this for the proletariat of the world: we must have an illegal organization no matter what the circumstances. It is important for every country. That is the lesson of the Communist International's fifteen months of existence. It is important to say this and put it into action. We must make it as binding as possible on all of us so that we know it and carry it out.

Practical considerations have been advanced, such as, "We shall see, perhaps we can get by with a legal organization." That is not the case. Comrade Levi said of Germany that he believes the bourgeoisie there has become so accustomed to Communists' legal work that it will not venture to take any action against it. Consequently, the German comrades say, whether or not we mention illegal organizations in the statutes, the bourgeoisie cannot deny us our legal status. In Italy the party is so strong that the bourgeoisie cannot take away its legal status. Then there is the experience of Bulgaria, where we have an old party that is legal and has forty or more deputies that have been subjected to much persecution.

We are in favor of expressing this point clearly and openly. The experiences in the Balkans, in Germany, Austria, and Italy should be decisive for us. Perhaps this clause will cause one or another party some difficulty, but the positive side is much more important for us.

And experience tells us we must make it mandatory in the statutes, because, to the bourgeoisie, whether we hang them illegally or legally is not a decisive question. What is important to them is whether we really hang them, whether we fight for communism. To them our form of organization is not the most important thing. That is something we have already learned, arms in hand. In any case, comrades, the prosecutor will quote these theses—it will amount to the same thing. We can only lose by failing to state clearly what every man and woman worker should and must know. That is why we insist that the wording remain as it is.

We must tell proletarians around the world, "Now that you have entered the epoch of decisive struggles, you should understand that you must develop an illegal organization systematically and everywhere. For when the decisive hour strikes, the bourgeoisie will trample on your legality and you will be left with nothing and have no organizations." That is why we must express this clearly.

I believe the congress can confidently approve what was decided by a large majority of the commission, which unanimously adopted the statutes in general, with one abstention. I propose that the congress adopt the statutes unanimously. It is important that we adopt the constitution of our international party unanimously if at all possible and show the whole world that we are no longer merely an amorphous propaganda society.

We have matured and become a united international party that has statutes, that knows what it wants and what its international obligations are, whose members have bound themselves together by a mutual pledge and in comradely discipline in order from this hour forward, truly united, to fight for communism.

First I will call for a vote on the different motions, beginning with those pertaining to article 8.[6] (*The text is adopted unanimously in the original version.*)

Now the vote will be taken on the statutes as a whole, which read as follows:

## STATUTES

The International Working Men's Association, also called the First International, was founded in London in 1864.[7] The General Rules of the International Working Men's Association state:

"That the emancipation of the working classes must be conquered by the working classes themselves; that the struggle for the emancipation of the working classes means not a struggle for class privileges and monopolies, but for equal rights and duties, and the abolition of all class rule;

"That the economical subjugation of the man of labour to the monopolizer of the means of labour, that is the sources of life, lies at the bottom of servitude in all its forms, of all social misery, mental degradation, and political dependence;

"That the economical emancipation of the working classes is therefore the great end to which every political movement ought to be subordinate as a means;

"That all efforts aiming at that great end have hitherto failed from the want of solidarity between the manifold divisions of labour in each country, and from the absence of a fraternal bond of union between the working classes of different countries;

"That the emancipation of labour is neither a local nor a national, but a social problem, embracing all countries in which modern society exists, and depending for its solution on the concurrence, practical and theoretical, of the most advanced countries;

"That the present revival of the working classes in the most industrious countries of Europe, while it raises a new hope, gives solemn warning against a relapse into the old errors and calls for the immediate combination of the still disconnected movements."[8]

The Second International, which was founded in 1889 in Paris, pledged to continue the work of the First International. But in 1914, as the world slaughter began, it suffered a complete collapse. Undermined by opportunism and broken by the betrayal of its leaders, who went over to the side of the bourgeoisie, the Second International collapsed.

The Communist International, founded in March 1919 in Moscow, capital of the Russian Soviet Federated Socialist Republic, solemnly proclaims to the whole world that it undertakes to carry forward and complete the great work begun by the First International, the International Working Men's Association.

The Communist International was formed at the end of the 1914–18 imperialist war, in which the imperialist bourgeoisie of different countries sacrificed twenty million human beings.

"Remember the imperialist war!" That is the first appeal that the Communist International addresses to every toiler, no matter where he lives, no matter what language he speaks. Remember that because the capitalist order exists, a handful of imperialists was able for four long years to force the workers of different countries to cut each other's throats. Remember that the bourgeoisie's war wrought the most dreadful famine and the most terrible misery throughout Europe and the entire world. Remember that unless capitalism is overthrown, a repetition of such predatory wars is not only possible but inevitable.

The Communist International takes as its goal to struggle with all possible means, including with arms in hand, for the overthrow of the international bourgeoisie and the creation of an international soviet republic as a transitional step toward complete destruction of the state. The Communist International believes that the dictatorship of the proletariat is the only means offering the possibility of freeing humanity from the horrors of capitalism. And the Communist International regards soviet power as the historically determined form of the dictatorship of the proletariat.

The imperialist war created a particularly close bond between the fate of proletarians in one country and that of proletarians in all countries. The imperialist war has reaffirmed what was said in the General Rules of the First International: The emancipation of the workers is neither a local nor a national but an international problem.

The Communist International breaks once and for all with the traditions of the Second International, which in reality recognized the existence only of people with white skin. The Communist International sets as its task the liberation of the toilers of the whole world. People of white, yellow, and black skin color—the toilers of the whole earth—are fraternally united in the ranks of the Communist International.

The Communist International supports completely and wholeheartedly the conquests of the great proletarian revolution in Russia, the first victorious socialist revolution in world history, and calls upon proletarians of the whole world to take the same path. The Communist International pledges to support every soviet republic with all its strength, wherever one is created.

The Communist International knows that in order to achieve victory more rapidly, the international workers' association that fights to destroy capitalism and create communism must have a strictly centralized organization. The Communist International must be, truly and in fact, a united Communist party of the whole world. The parties that work in each country are only its individual sections. The organizational apparatus of the Communist International must guarantee the workers of every country that at any given moment they will receive maximum assistance from the organized proletarians of other countries.

To this end, the Communist International adopts as its statutes the following points:

1. The new international workers' association was founded to organize the common activity of the proletarians of different countries who strive for one single goal: overthrowing capitalism and establishing the dictatorship of the proletariat and an international soviet republic to completely abolish classes and realize socialism, the first stage of the communist society.

2. The new international workers' association is called the Communist International.

3. All parties belonging to the Communist International bear the name Communist Party of such and such a country (Section of the Communist International).

4. The highest authority of the Communist International is the world congress of all parties and organizations belonging to it. The world congress meets regularly once a year. Only the world congress is empowered to change the program of the Communist International. The world congress shall discuss and decide the most important questions of program and policy affecting the work of the Communist International. The number of decisive votes allotted to each party or organization is determined by a special congress decision.

5. The world congress elects the Executive Committee of the Communist International, the governing body of the Communist International between world congresses. The Executive Committee is responsible only to the world congress.

6. The seat of the Executive Committee of the Communist International shall be determined by each world congress of the Communist International.

7. An extraordinary world congress of the Communist International can be convened either by decision of the Executive Committee or by demand of one-half of the parties belonging to the Communist International at the time of the last world congress.

8. The party of the country where, by decision of the world congress, the Executive Committee is located bears the main burden of the Executive Committee's work. The party of that country appoints five representatives with decisive vote to the Executive Committee. In addition, the ten to thirteen most important Communist parties—a list that will be approved by the regular world congress—shall each send one representative with decisive vote to the Executive Committee.[9] Other organizations and parties accepted into the Communist International have the right to appoint one representative apiece with consultative vote to the Executive Committee.

9. The Executive Committee directs all the activities of the Communist International from one congress to the next, publishes the central organ of the Communist International (the magazine *Communist International*) in at least four languages, issues in the name of the Communist International such appeals as are required, and issues directives binding on all organizations and parties belonging to the Communist International. The Executive Committee of the Communist International has the authority to demand of its member parties the expulsion of groups or individuals that breach international discipline, as well as the authority to expel from the Communist International any party that contravenes the resolutions of the world congress. Such parties have the right to appeal to the world congress. As necessary, the Executive Committee organizes in different countries technical and other auxiliary bureaus, which are strictly subordinate to the Executive Committee. Executive Committee representatives discharge their political duties in the closest possible communication with the party leaderships of their respective countries.

10. The Executive Committee of the Communist International has the authority to co-opt representatives with consultative vote from organizations and parties that, although not members of the Communist International, are in close sympathy with it.

11. Publications of all parties and organizations that belong to the Communist International or are among its sympathizers are required to print all official resolutions of the Communist International and its Executive Committee.

12. The general situation in all of Europe and America compels Communists around the world to form illegal Communist organizations parallel to the legal ones. The

Executive Committee must see that this is done everywhere.

13. As a rule, political relations between individual parties belonging to the Communist International are conducted through the Executive Committee. In urgent cases such contact may be direct, but the Executive Committee of the Communist International shall be informed simultaneously.

14. Trade unions that uphold communism and that are united internationally under the Communist International's leadership constitute a trade union section of the Communist International.[10] These unions appoint representatives to the world congresses of the Communist International through the Communist parties of their respective countries. The trade union section of the Communist International appoints a representative with decisive vote to the Executive Committee of the Communist International. The Executive Committee has the right to designate a representative with decisive vote to the trade union section of the Communist International.[11]

15. The Communist Youth International is a member of the Communist International with full rights, subordinate to its Executive Committee. The Executive Committee of the Communist Youth International shall appoint a representative with decisive vote to the Executive Committee of the Communist International. The Executive Committee of the Communist International has the authority to designate a representative with decisive vote to the Executive Committee of the Communist Youth International.

16. The Executive Committee of the Communist International shall approve the international secretary of the Communist Women's Movement and shall organize the women's section of the Communist International.

17. Any member of the Communist International who moves from one country to another shall receive

fraternal assistance from members of the Communist International there.

(*The statutes are adopted unanimously.*)

ZINOVIEV: Comrades, we now have statutes for the Communist International. We have finally organized ourselves as an international party. I congratulate the congress on this occasion. I believe that this is one of the international proletariat's most important conquests. At last we have organized ourselves formally. Long live the Communist International!

(*End of session.*)

SESSION 15

AUGUST 5, 1920

# Forming workers' councils; Part 3 of trade unions and factory committees

SERRATI: The session is open. Comrade Radek has the floor on behalf of the Credentials Commission.

## REPORT OF THE CREDENTIALS COMMISSION

RADEK: The Credentials Commission had to decide the question of the Americans' credentials. Both American parties, the Communist Party and the Communist Labor Party, are represented here. A delegate from America, Comrade Flynn, has now arrived with the news that the two parties have united into one. But one portion of the Communists declared it would not go along with this unification, placing itself outside the United Communist Party. Therefore, the Communist Party representatives want to keep their old credentials. Comrade Flynn, however, moved that the credentials of two comrades, Fraina and Stoklitsky, be revoked.

In the commission we decided to continue to recognize these comrades as delegates for the following reasons: In America we face a situation that is changing rapidly. In this specific case the only fact before us is that the United Communist Party has been formed. We are unable to judge here to what extent there were compelling reasons for a minority of the Communist Party to remain outside the united party. To take away their credentials would be to declare from the outset that we are in solidarity with the United Communist Party as the only Communist party. That may prove necessary when we receive more detailed reports, but we cannot disqualify a Communist organization on the strength of information that is insufficient. For that reason, we voted to recognize the credentials of both parties.

And since Comrade Fraina by no means denies that—as he understands the situation—the majority of organized Communists are in the ranks of the United Communist Party, we divided the credentials so that the United Communist Party representatives received 6 votes and the Communist Party representatives 4. Comrade Fraina, by the way, declared that although he and Comrade Stoklitsky do not in any way support the split, they cannot join the United Communist Party without discussions. On behalf of the Credentials Commission, I ask the congress to approve this decision without delay.

The Ukrainian comrades insist that I make one other announcement, which is that the Credentials Commission did not recognize the credentials of the Ukrainian Communist Party [Ukapists]. As comrades may know, there is a large Communist Party [Bolsheviks] of the Ukraine, and in addition to it a group has formed that numbers between one hundred and five hundred members. Clearly, what is involved is a very small group that has nothing to do with actual Communist work.

FLYNN [EDWARD LINDGREN, UNITED COMMUNIST PARTY, UNITED STATES]:[1] I protest against recognizing the credentials of the Communist Party of America or adopting Comrade Radek's motion. After several attempts, a United Communist Party was finally formed from thirty thousand members of the Communist Party and twenty thousand members of the Communist Labor Party.[2] It took up illegal work, and a kind of separation developed in the party itself because only one part of it wanted to do illegal work. Consequently, a part of the Communist Party split away from the united party.

Now, one could understand the Communist Party's credentials being recognized here if the American comrades had initiated the party unification. But that was not so. A delegate from the Communist International was sent to America to bring about this fusion. Since the fusion has already taken place, we cannot understand why the Communist International sanctions the split by recognizing the part that split away.

FRAINA: It is very unfortunate that this controversy should come before the plenary session of the congress, all the more since the Credentials Commission has settled the matter already. When I arrived in Moscow, Comrade Stoklitsky and I discussed the situation with delegates of the Communist Labor Party. We proposed to them (before Comrade Flynn's arrival) that we, as representatives from both parties of the American Communist movement, come to an agreement, first, to recognize the necessity of complete and final unification, second, to appear and work in the congress as one group, third, to call upon the Executive Committee of the International to act for complete unity among Communists in America, and fourth, to pledge to fulfill the decisions of the Executive Committee.

Flynn speaks as a factionalist, not in the interests of the American Communist movement as a whole. Recognition of the Communist Party will not create more discord. On the contrary, it will facilitate complete unity, and what is more, promote clear and uncompromising understanding of revolutionary principles and tactics, since the Communist Party is more consistent than the other organization. None but a factionalist of the worst sort would make a proposal to exclude the Communist Party from this congress.[3]

Comrade Stoklitsky and I have an unassailable right to sit in this congress as the representatives of our party. The question of how large or small the Communist Party may be is unimportant in this connection; no one but a Menshevik would speak in that way. It may be that the majority of the Communist Party has united with the Communist Labor Party, but I do not know, and Flynn's factional spirit makes me doubt his statement.

We can be excluded from the congress only if the Communist Party itself withdraws us as delegates, only if the Executive Committee decides to exclude the Communist Party of America from the International. But otherwise its representatives have the right to demand that they remain here as delegates.

The Communist Party, historically and actually, represents the most consistent Communist elements in the American movement, whereas the former Communist Labor Party represented the less consistent and developed elements. In this sense the Communist Party is of vital importance to the American movement. It must be given the opportunity to impose upon the coming unity its consistent understanding of the revolution.

(*A motion is made to end the debate.*)

REED: I oppose the motion of closure. I wish to give a few reasons why Radek's proposition should not be adopted.

(*The motion to close debate carries. The Credentials Commission report is then adopted by a vote of* 19 *to* 9.)

## REPORT ON FORMING WORKERS' COUNCILS

ZINOVIEV: Comrades, I hope that the conditions under which workers' and soldiers' councils should be formed are known to all of you—they are on pages 73 to 77 in the German edition. I venture to voice the hope that for once we may be able to adopt these theses without discussion, because from all the discussions we have had with various delegates we have determined that there is unanimity on this question. The point of these theses is that we must tell all our comrades that soviets can and should be created only when the historical conditions for them are present. Such formations should not be created artificially; that would compromise the idea of soviets.

We all know that the entire working class of Europe—and perhaps of the whole world as well—has been won to the idea of soviets. The working class has grasped that in the next historical period political life will unfold in the form of soviets. It is to the Communist International's good fortune that this idea has stirred the masses. Now that the working masses have made this idea their own, it possesses great power. Today, however, we see powerless groups in various countries forming soviets, doing so where the historical preconditions do not exist at all. This was the case in France and in other countries too. In the name of the entire congress, we want now to emphasize to the workers of the world that propaganda must always be made for soviets (the time is always right for that) but that unfortunately the historical conditions for the forming of soviets are not always and everywhere present.

In my theses I refer briefly to the history of these new ideas.

As all of you well know, the idea of workers' councils was born in 1905; in other words, it is only fifteen years old. In 1905, during the first Russian revolution, the first, temporary formation was created, the Petrograd soviet, and its history shows us that special historical conditions are required for soviets. The soviets of 1905 were destroyed immediately. They died after tsarism triumphed over the revolution. Once the revolutionary flood began to ebb, it became clear that the soviets could not be maintained.

The brilliant idea that the soviets are merely class organizations and cannot be organizations of the state, defended today by Mensheviks and right Independents, was expressed back then too. "The soviets should act as the proletariat's class organization but not as a state organization." That is what Kautsky and many of his supporters promoted during the German revolution.[4] The history of the past fifteen years has shown that the soviets acquire significance only if they become not ordinary, everyday class organizations like the trade unions, but *state* organizations, *a form of the proletarian dictatorship*. That was shown by the first Russian revolution, by the first stage of our new revolution (the historic first eight months, those of the Kerensky government).[5] And it is also shown by the history of the German and Austrian revolutions—especially the German revolution.

When the working class in Germany achieved a victory in November 1918, workers' and soldiers' councils arose of their own accord. But the Social Democracy betrayed the workers' cause, and the bourgeoisie together with the counterrevolutionary Social Democracy defeated the workers. The soviets then began at once to die out. During the Kapp days the soviets summoned their last spark of life. That is only a brief episode in history, but the fate of the soviets is reflected in it in miniature. When the workers were advancing toward victory, the soviets tended to revive, but when the jackboot of reaction triumphed, immediately they began to die away again. This episode shows that the soviets become important only when they are carried by a really large mass movement that is moving toward turning them into a state power.

At the beginning of 1917, when we were still in exile, when the revolutionary movement in Russia was already very intense and our comrades had already begun to form councils of workers' deputies, we told our comrades, from abroad, that the idea would not last. We should make propaganda for the idea of soviets, we said, but the call to form them should be issued only when we are convinced that the preconditions exist and that the masses themselves are for them and want to fight for that cause.

That is why we are against the efforts being made by our comrades in France. Although only a small group, they publish a paper in which they present themselves as a soviet, on behalf of a few hundred members, and call that a "soviet" movement.[6]

I read several leaflets that our Swiss comrades issued during the election campaign in Switzerland. When everyone is going to the polls, our party raises the slogan "We demand soviets." Here we see soviets are being demanded of the bourgeoisie, of the government. But soviets are not something you demand. They are created when the working class is ready to make the revolution. Is it perhaps communist to raise such a demand? First the working class must be organized, aroused, and prepared; then, when the moment arrives, it is not necessary to raise the demand.

Today the moment has arrived when the question of revolution, the struggle for power, is becoming acute and the working class in many countries has already been won to the idea of soviets. Therefore I believe that the Communist International's task is no longer to popularize this idea, as it was for the First and Second Internationals. That is already taken care of; the idea is popular enough. Something much bigger is at stake: *it is a matter of impressing upon the working class of the whole world what conditions are necessary for the formation of soviets.* That is the second step we must take.

The purpose of the theses is to lay the basis for this. We must tell the working class clearly the conditions under which we can and must form such soviets. Because forming soviets artificially serves only those who oppose this idea. We will be ridiculed, as has happened already in some countries. That would compromise this great idea. We should not play with this word. We should show the working class a clear road forward, explaining under what conditions soviets may be formed.

In these theses we have tried to analyze the experiences of several parties. There is a peculiar situation in Austria, approximately like the one that existed here during the first stage of the Kerensky period. A rather powerful workers' council exists there, in which the social patriots and the Center hold the majority. The Communists are in the minority but are growing every day. The soviets there have a certain amount of power, rivaling the legitimate government of Messrs. Renner and company; they are a sort of parallel government. We had an analogous situation here, in different historical circumstances, during the first eight months of the revolution. Such a movement is a weighty matter, and our comrades must participate in it. They must try to bring their influence to bear in the soviets and fight for power in them.

A different situation where soviets exist can be found in Germany. A number of books, good and bad, have been written on the soviet system there. Our German comrades always talk about it as "the system." Well, they have a system, but no soviets. We would prefer it if they had a worse system and better soviets. All schemes for fitting the soviet system into the bourgeois Social Democratic counterrevolutionary republic are artificial. Thus, objectively speaking, the soviets sometimes even play a counterrevolutionary role, because the working class is not told what are the only conditions under which soviets can be established.

We tried to incorporate into the theses the experience in Germany and of course above all the experience in Russia, where the soviet idea was born. With the aid of these examples—the Russian revolution of 1917 and the two revolutions in 1918 in Germany and in Austria—we want to show the working class the circumstances under which we can form soviets.

I am convinced that the Second Congress of the Communist International is the precursor of an international congress of soviet republics. Those of us who are not yet too old will live to see the moment when we will have such an international congress of soviet republics. But to hasten that moment, we must see the way clearly, keep the idea pure, and present to the working class concretely the road we really should follow in order to achieve an international soviet republic.

(*The vote is taken on the theses. The theses are adopted unanimously.*)[7]

## THESES ON THE CONDITIONS UNDER WHICH WORKERS' COUNCILS MAY BE FORMED

1. Councils of workers' deputies (soviets) originated in Russia in 1905 at the height of the Russian workers' revo-

lutionary movement.[8] In 1905 the Petersburg [Leningrad] soviet was already taking the first, instinctive steps on the road toward the conquest of power. The Petersburg soviet was powerful then only to the extent that it had the prospect of conquering power. As soon as the tsarist counterrevolution gained strength and the workers' movement began to ebb, the soviet, after a brief stagnation, ceased to exist altogether.

2. In 1916, at the beginning of a broad, new, revolutionary upsurge in Russia, the idea arose that workers' soviets could be organized immediately. The Bolshevik Party warned the workers against this, pointing out that this would be appropriate only when the revolution had already begun and the immediate struggle for power was on the agenda.

3. When the 1917 revolution began, the soviets of workers' deputies in Russia immediately turned into soviets of workers' and soldiers' deputies; brought the broad, popular masses under their influence; and instantly commanded enormous authority, because the real power was on their side and in their hands. But when the liberal bourgeoisie recovered from its surprise at the first blows of the revolution, and when the social traitors—the Socialist Revolutionaries and Mensheviks—helped the Russian bourgeoisie get the power into its hands, the importance of the soviets began to diminish. Only after the events of July 1917 and the failure of Kornilov's counterrevolutionary campaign, when the broad popular masses came into motion and the collapse of the counterrevolutionary government of bourgeois and compromisers became acute, did the workers' soviets begin to revive. Soon thereafter they acquired decisive importance throughout the country.

4. The history of the German and Austrian revolutions shows the same thing. When broad masses of workers

rose up, when the revolutionary wave climbed especially high and washed away the citadels of the Hohenzollern and Hapsburg monarchies, workers' and soldiers' councils were formed spontaneously in Germany and Austria. Initially, the councils had real strength and were on their way to gaining genuine power. But when a combination of historical circumstances caused power to pass to the bourgeoisie and counterrevolutionary Social Democrats, the councils soon began to fade, and they dwindled to nothing. At the time of the abortive counterrevolutionary Kapp-Lüttwitz putsch, for a few days the councils in Germany began to revive. As soon as the struggle ended in another victory for the bourgeoisie and the social traitors, however, the councils that had begun to raise their heads withered away.

5. These facts show that specific preconditions are necessary to create soviets. It is possible to organize workers' soviets and transform them into soviets of workers' and soldiers' deputies only when the following three conditions are present:

a) A revolutionary mass upsurge of broad layers of men and women workers, soldiers, and the toiling population generally.

b) The political and economic crisis is so acute that power begins to slip from the hands of the old government.

c) A firm will to begin a decisive, systematic, and well-planned struggle for power has matured among significant layers of workers and, above all, in the ranks of the Communist Party.

6. When these preconditions do not exist, Communists can and must propagate the idea of soviets systematically and persistently, popularize this idea among the masses, and show the broadest possible layers of the population that soviets are the only practical form of the state dur-

ing the transition to complete communism. But it is not possible to organize soviets directly without the conditions specified above.

7. Objectively, the attempt by the social traitors in Germany to clip the soviets' wings, debase them, and incorporate them into the overall bourgeois-democratic constitutional system is a betrayal of the workers' cause and misleads the workers. For real soviets are possible only as a form of state organization that supersedes bourgeois democracy, shatters it, and replaces it with a *workers' dictatorship*.

8. The propaganda by right-wing leaders of the Independents (Hilferding and Kautsky, among others) aimed at demonstrating that the "soviet system" is compatible with a bourgeois national assembly either shows a complete lack of understanding of the laws of development of the proletarian revolution or is a conscious effort to mislead the working class. *Soviets* mean the *dictatorship of the proletariat. National assembly* means the *dictatorship of the bourgeoisie.* It is not possible to unite and reconcile workers' dictatorship with dictatorship by the bourgeoisie.

9. The propaganda by some representatives of the left USPD in Germany—who give the workers a contrived, paper plan for a "council system" that has no connection with the real course of civil war—is pedantry. It distracts the workers from the tasks of the day in the real struggle for power.

10. The attempts by some communist groups in France, Italy, America, and Britain to create soviets that do not encompass the broad masses and are therefore unable to launch a direct struggle for power only harm the real work of preparation for a soviet revolution. At best such artificial, greenhouse "soviets" become small propaganda societies for soviet power. At worst, however, these unsuccessful "soviets" can only compromise the idea of soviet power in the eyes of wide layers of the population.

11. A special situation has arisen in Austria, where the working class has succeeded in maintaining workers' councils encompassing broad masses of workers. The situation there is reminiscent of the period from February to October 1917 in Russia. The workers' councils in Austria are an important political factor and are the seed of the new power.

It is self-evident that under such circumstances Communists must participate in the workers' councils and help them permeate the country's entire social, economic, and political life. They must form Communist fractions in the workers' councils and assist their development in every way.

12. Soviets without revolution are not possible. Soviets without proletarian revolution must inevitably turn into a parody of soviets.

True mass soviets appear as the historically necessary form of the dictatorship of the proletariat. All honest and serious supporters of soviet power must treat the concept of soviets with caution. They must propagate it constantly among the masses but proceed to realize it in life only when the conditions stated above are present.

## REPORT FROM THE COMMISSION ON TRADE UNIONS

RADEK: Comrades, in keeping with the decision of the plenary session, the Commission on the Trade Union Question took the Executive Committee's theses as its starting point, merely supplementing them with several amendments. Before proceeding to them, I would like to point out that on one important point the commission failed to arrive at a common decision, and a representative of the commission minority will therefore speak as well.

The issue is that the amendment proposed by the American comrades in fact canceled out the main content of the theses. The position of the congress as expressed in the vote is, first of all, that we establish the duty of all comrades, of all Communist parties, to work in the unions. The minority on the commission, primarily the American comrades, seemed to accept this decision. But while making no motion explicitly nullifying the congress's decision, they proposed amendments that nullified it in effect.

I have already pointed out in my report that, in a certain sense, the theses we proposed are worded too narrowly. They do not take into account that in America 80 percent of workers are unorganized. Moreover, the labor federation not only does nothing to organize these unskilled workers but uses very high initiation fees to prevent them from joining the unions. Therefore we propose mentioning an additional basis for quitting the old unions and forming new ones, besides when revolutionary agitation in the unions is suppressed. New trade unions must be formed whenever the old craft organizations fail to organize unskilled workers, because the aristocratic upper layers of the working class hold sway in them. But this does not satisfy the American comrades. They propose a different wording aimed at making it possible for the American Communists to sabotage the congress's decision.

I will read out here not the entire amendment, which is to replace three points in our resolution, but only the relevant part. It says: (*Reads from "The new trade unions" down to "represent."*)[9] These three headings, establishing when it is permissible to leave the old trade unions and form new ones, encompass every possible case. Communists who have no desire to work in the unions and think it much more communist to stay outside them and fill reams of paper with articles on the worthlessness of the trade union bureaucracy can always offer the excuse either that the union's structure makes change impossible or that given the powerful revolutionary sentiments built up in the proletariat there is no room left for revolutionary work in the unions. The best proof that we are not imagining things, that this is a strict call to boycott the big American unions on principle, is provided by the resolution of the United Communist Party of America. We have just received the issue of their newspaper with their resolution on the unions. This resolution says:

"Craft unionism has become the bulwark of capitalism in this country. In every recent struggle of moment the workers have been betrayed by the reactionary officials of the American Federation of Labor and the railroad brotherhoods. The officials of the latter organization even went so far as to call upon the government to use the courts against the workers engaged in what they chose to call 'outlaw' strikes. The tactics of the trade union leaders are those of dickering with the capitalists and their governmental representatives to secure privileged positions for their trade groups, at the expense of the mass of workers.

"The concentration of industry rapidly enlarges the new class of industrial workers, the unskilled laborers and semiskilled machine tenders. It is among these workers particularly that there has developed the new form, industrial unionism—and the new method of struggle, mass strikes of all the workers in the industry. The common level of labor and wages and the common interest of workers by the millions bring class solidarity in opposition to craft disunity.

"The United Communist Party rejects the conception, as advocated by the IWW, that industrial unionism is of itself the means through which industry can be transferred from the capitalists to the workers. The proletarian revolution cannot be achieved by direct seizure of industry by the workers, without the workers first having conquered the power of the state and establishing themselves as the government. While pointing out that industrial unionism cannot transform society, the United Communist Party recognizes that industrial unionism is a revolt against the existing trade unionism and offers more efficient methods of struggle."

Now comes the decisive point:

"The Socialist Party policy of 'boring from within' the AFL is vicious in that it is only an indirect and hypocritical method of supporting an inherently reactionary labor organization. A Communist who belongs to the AFL should seize every opportunity to voice his hostility to this organization, not to reform it but to destroy it. The struggle against the AFL must not be purely negative. The IWW is the obvious medium for giving the advocacy of industrial unionism affirmative character. The IWW must be upheld as against the AFL. At the same time the work of communist education must be carried on within the IWW."[10]

Thus, this resolution flatly negates the resolution we adopted making it the duty of every Communist to fight to win the unions from within. In other words, the question here is not merely whether to go into the unions to destroy them. Boring from within, any struggle at all inside the unions, is rejected. This position stands opposed to our theses, and what the comrades of the United Communist Party are advocating here is nothing less than an obvious negation of our position.

To rescue their position, the comrades try to go from the defensive to the attack. They point out that just a few months ago the position that the United Communist Party has now adopted was held by the Executive Committee.

They refer to an Executive Committee letter to the American party that said: "Aiding by all means the more rapid process of rupture in the American Federation of Labor, and other allied trade unions and their branches, the party must strive to establish a closer connection with those economic organizations of the working class, in which one can notice tendencies toward industrial unionism (IWW, One Big Union, WIIU, and insurgent unions breaking away from the AFL)."[11]

I do not hesitate to say openly that this letter from the Executive Committee—which certainly was not adopted by its full membership—was wrong. Formally the comrades can cite this position, although it is not quite identical with their own, since this letter dealt specifically with the American Federation of Labor.

But the issue here is not whether in the past the Executive Committee took an incorrect position in a letter. Rather the question now is whether the United Communist Party representatives here are openly expressing their party's position. They had the opportunity to present it here and did not do so, claiming they oppose splitting as a matter of principle. They are trying to insert a Trojan horse in the resolution. I believe it is up to the congress not only to reject this amendment but also, in a separate resolution, to draw attention to the American comrades' position as one that contradicts that of the Communist International. The congress must proceed quite forcefully here because it is not just a question of giving the American comrades the right to destroy this counterrevolutionary organization if they can. Rather, the question is whether they will destroy themselves.

This point struck a chord with Comrade Bombacci as well, and that deserves a comment. Bombacci's position differs from that of the American comrades in that he is not taking a revolutionary stand but just playing games. Although the Americans say, "Down with the AFL," they also cry, "For the IWW! Let us build new unions!" Not so Comrade Bombacci, who nonchalantly declares, "I do not care a hoot for the unions; they are doomed to be counterrevolutionary forever." But if he bases himself on the fact that the unions in Italy are in the hands of syndicalists or of gray-bearded reformists, we must tell him openly that he is playing games with us; that is not a communist policy. If Bombacci defends a Marxist position, he should fight for it in the Italian unions and not say here that the unions are unimportant and will always be counterrevolutionary. We object to such treatment of the most serious question before the workers' movement, and we attach great importance to inducing the congress to take a completely clear position on this.

I said earlier that I would be prepared to consider other amendments. In the present situation, however, after this resolution by the United Communist Party, any compromise or retreat is impossible. Communism must be led toward beginning to do communist work and away from forming communist sects and playing sectarian games.

The next question up for debate is that of our position on factory committees. We propose an amendment that says the following: "Communists should support efforts to turn the factory committees into trade union factory groups only to the extent that the unions overcome the counterrevolutionary tendencies of their bureaucracy and become conscious instruments of the revolution." This means that in countries where the union bureaucracy holds the reins, it is the duty of Communists to support the struggle of factory committees and all similar organizations for an independent existence. Communists can take the reins of the unions only by turning these factory organizations into basic units of the new unions and of their Communist factory units.

I wish to supplement and clarify these amendments with two remarks. First, where it says: "Wherever organizations such as the Shop Stewards or factory committees emerge in the factories, inside or outside the union framework—bodies that adopt the aim of struggling against the counterrevolutionary tendencies of the trade union bureaucracy and support direct, spontaneous actions by the proletariat—Communists must of course support them with all their energy." The objection was raised, "You oppose forming small, revolutionary unions counterposed to the large ones, when there is no need to set up something separate. How can you demand support for all the factory organizations?" Let me point out that we say here, "that are formed inside the trade unions or outside of them," but not in opposition to them. The factory committees in Germany are by no means organizations meant to threaten the unions' existence. In part they have separate functions, but in part they are supposed to put pressure on the union bureaucracy. They are not directed against the unions' existence as organizations. We do not support organizations opposed to the unions. No exceptions can be made, apart from the cases described in our theses where we think it necessary to form separate trade unions.

Now to the second question. We say that we will support the unions' efforts to absorb the factory committees as subordinate bodies only to the extent that the unions become revolutionary organizations. In response, the question was raised of the situation in Germany. Most factory committees there are legally constituted,[12] we were told, and the Communists' task there was to stretch the councils' activities beyond the provisions of the law. These factory committees, we heard, were already subordinate to the unions.

Judging from the material at my disposal, I maintain that this is not the case. The union bureaucracy's struggle to dominate and absorb these factory committees has only begun. Here we say that we see it as the duty of Communists to struggle against attempts by the Legiens to gain control of the factory committees, even if it should turn out later that we are not strong enough to prevent this. I believe it is wrong to abandon the struggle at the outset, because it will decide not only a formal question but also the Communists' future course in the factory committees. Even if the great majority of factory committees were to spontaneously subordinate themselves to the unions, and it were not advantageous to maintain the revolutionary factory committees separate from the others, our present struggle to warn the masses about Legien and his goals would clearly put us in a stronger position for the future in factory committees subordinate to the unions.

It is a different question whether, should the struggle indeed turn out to be hopeless, we still ought to be dead set on keeping the small groups isolated. If the battle failed for the moment to lead to victory, would we still continue to struggle in factory committees subordinate to the unions?

But that is not the question right now. A struggle is raging in large areas of central Germany and in Berlin. The German Communists say that the great battle against the Legiens should not be turned into a struggle over external form. We reply that it is up to you to see to it that this struggle is fought out over principle, not just over who should control these factory committees. There is a principle involved: strengthening the spirit of resistance against the trade union bureaucracy.

Finally, we proposed an amendment that brought together in a separate clause the various remarks scattered throughout the resolution on the unions' future role. It reads: "By turning the trade unions and factory committees into powerful weapons of the revolution, Communists prepare these mass organizations for the great task that will devolve upon them after the proletarian dictatorship is established, that of being a principal element in reorganizing economic life on a socialist basis. The unions, consolidated into industrial unions and based on the factory committees as their factory organizations, will then acquaint the working masses with their production tasks and train the most experienced workers as managers of the factories. They will supervise the technical specialists and, together with representatives of the workers' government, design and execute the plans of socialist economic policy."

I would like to point out briefly what a difference there is between this conception of the unions' functions after the proletariat conquers political power and that of the syndicalists. In the syndicalist vision of socialist development, after the proletariat overthrows the bourgeoisie through general strikes, it organizes into a federation of industrial trade unions, linked by free agreement, which runs the economy together with the Communists without a proletarian state.

We think this conception is wrong. First, without the dictatorship, without establishing the proletarian state as an instrument to break the bourgeoisie's resistance, the proletariat cannot gather power into its hands. Second, running the economy is something that cannot be done by each union on its own or by free agreement among the unions. That is because some categories of the working class play a prominent role in the industrial process and could create an aristocratic, privileged position for their members in the economy as a whole. By exploiting this position, they manage to obtain privileges for themselves vis-à-vis less developed, less important groups in the working class.

Under the proletarian state, the working class must direct the economy in a way that not only brings workers together in an organization for each branch of industry but also gives them tasks for overall production. Alongside organizations that view their tasks from the angle of one industrial branch, the working class, through its proletarian state, must champion the interests of the proletariat as a whole. The entire economic plan and its implementation must be subordinated to the overall interests of the proletariat. We see here that alongside the unions' prominent and decisive role, the regulative function of the state has developed primarily in the form of the councils. The unions help to run the economy through the organs of the state as a whole.

Those are the main amendments to the theses. More than the first draft, we have taken into account the fact that in many countries the unions pursue an aristocratic policy. In those cases we made it the duty of Communists to begin organizing the masses into trade unions independently. Second, we make it the duty of Communists to support the new proletarian economic bodies that are appearing spontaneously: the factory committees. Communists must defend the factory committees' independence from encroachments by the union bureaucracy, yet regard them as part of the unions when those unions are revolutionary.

The third amendment defines the unions' tasks after the conquest of political power.

Fourth, there was a question about the international trade union association.

On this question the commission decided that it was adequate for now to accept the third point of our theses, which has already been printed. But that point did not address the current, concrete situation, that is, the establishment of the international council of revolutionary trade unions formed here in Moscow by representatives of the Italian, Russian, and Bulgarian unions and part of the British. Before us was the position advanced by the American and British comrades, who think this organization in its present form is inappropriate and premature, and that of the Russian comrades, who submitted a resolution.[13] Since one resolution had already been rejected by some members of the Executive Committee,[14] and since it was already four in the morning yesterday, I declined to take any position at all. Zinoviev will explain his position here.

There are profound differences of opinion over the trade union question. True, at this congress they have not assumed the character of a conflict over principle. But we should not be blind to the fact that the ferment in the working class has led to attempts in every country to launch new trade unions and many members in every Communist party support this. We should have no illusions about the dangers this entails. The congress must take these dangers into account and give the Communist parties a clear line of march.

The second point that requires the congress's attention—and it will need the International's attention in the future more than it has in the past—is the question of the factory committees, all the new organizations, the Shop Stewards' committees, and so forth. One thing must be said here: it is not that the question has been insufficiently clarified but rather that it is still evolving. The task is not one of clarification. We must weigh the possibility that as the revolution develops it will create entirely new phenomena in this regard, and Communists should not take an inflexible, negative position on them. We have tried to set down in the theses what can be said so far. But all of us sense that this cannot be the last word. These organizations are developing, and they will confront us with entirely new questions. We must be willing to consider this issue in light of new facts. The Communist International was launched in a time of revolutionary ferment, when many things seemed chaotic that later became solid, valuable creations. I intentionally stress the nascent character of these phenomena in order to prepare the Communist International for them and to avoid lapsing into the old trade union habit of disapproving of everything new.

We do not yet know what will become of the British Shop Stewards; they are just coming into existence. We do not know what will become of the German factory committees. For the moment they are still products of the receding wave of revolution. They arose when the workers seized the idea of councils but did not form political councils. We do not yet know what new life the next wave of revolution, which is no doubt approaching, will bring into these organizations. We do not know yet even whether these organizations will be a fully revolutionary force in the trade unions. But one thing can be said. As things stand today, it is the task of Communists to tell workers, "You must not forsake the unions. They are the proletariat's largest mass organizations."

The second thing we can say is that we are groping for an approach to the factory committees' tasks, trying to determine which tasks are theirs and which belong to the unions. We are trying to achieve clarity about the relationship between the two organizations. But this is far from our last word on the topic. If the tempo of the revolution in western Europe lags, if capitalist decay spreads and the proletariat fails to take power in a succession of quick blows, this area can provide a new field of work for the masses we have prepared, provided we approach these bodies not with rigid formulas but with critical minds and the willingness to act and to mold the new phenomena.

I will not say much now about the tasks of Communists in the trade unions. We are guided by the unshakable conviction that we are quite capable of carrying out communist propaganda in the proletarian mass movement and its organizations, although we cannot count on their adopting a fighting communist policy.[15] In formulating a policy for Communists, we act on the simple idea that organizations uniting millions of workers are not crystals that must be shattered. The analogy between the bourgeois state and the trade unions is lame in both legs. No matter how villainous the union bureaucracy may be, no matter how much it may be the lackey of the bourgeoisie, it can determine the unions' character only so long as the unions' development has not really gotten under way. When that happens, the workers will determine the character of their unions.

Gorter, the current theoretician of left communism, says in his pamphlet, "The union bureaucracy's power lies in the masses' lack of independence." And yet he claims that the unions cannot be taken over. This means that this comrade, who thinks the revolution is just around the corner, for whom nothing is radical enough, is convinced that he can make the revolution despite the masses' existing submissiveness and dependency. Because if he expects their dependency to vanish, he cannot defend the formulation that the unions are the basic units of the capitalist social order and are doomed to remain so.

We look forward to developments with the healthy revolutionary optimism on which a revolutionary movement must be founded. We are convinced that the masses will begin to move and cast off their servile submissiveness. In this belief, we make the call to struggle against the union bureaucracy. We do this only because we know that history does not take place independently of our will; rather we ourselves must be factors in its development. Thus we are firmly convinced that the unions are the broad arena in which the Communist parties must win the great masses of workers to communism, not through propaganda and pamphlets alone but by participating in the struggle. It is in this spirit that we ask the congress not only to adopt the theses but to make them its guide in day-to-day trade union activity.

## MINORITY REPORT FROM THE COMMISSION ON TRADE UNIONS

REED: I object to the assertion that sabotage of the commission's motion was intended.[16] The question is not at all one of sabotage but of fundamental differences and contradictions. It is not as if the English and American comrades were of the opinion that the trade unions must be abandoned. At issue is changing as far as possible the spirit and structure of the unions. Radek does not deal with the essence of the amendments. What he proposes amounts to nurturing the old reactionary spirit in the trade unions,[17] as has been done in the past. While the amendments aim at changing the old spirit in the unions, Comrade Radek proposes nothing to destroy this spirit. Radek limits himself to mechanical "capture" of the unions, while our amendments propose a fundamental alteration of their spirit, forms, and purposes. The whole discussion must be based on the differences between these two conceptions.

By numerous documents I can show that Radek is contradicting himself in various theses. This contradiction may be particularly seen in the letters addressed by the Communist International to the IWW and the American workers.[18]

I find that the theses of Comrade Radek do not contain the communist conception of unionism. There is nothing in them on the necessity of altering the spirit of the trade unions as such. Here I am referring to clause 2 of the amendments. Clauses 4, 5, 6, and 7 of the theses might be cut out altogether because some of them are not clear, others are not precise, and still others are not broad enough. Generally they contrast with the clarity of the other theses. The only comrade who really expressed the opinion of the west European labor movement on this question was Comrade Bombacci. His position was clear, but some have evaded the question by silence and others have expressed a wrong conception.

I leave it to other speakers to express the final views of the minority on the subject of the Red trade union International.

It should not be forgotten that there is a difference of principle between Radek's position and that of the minority. I shall read our amendments, particularly those which define the conditions under which Communists have the right to leave the old unions. Radek claimed these were of such a nature that might fit all and every condition and might afford to any Communist a pretext to leave the unions. I challenge this statement. It is refuted by the very conditions that are intended to enable us to implement our position in a principled way.

In conclusion, I believe that this question, which is one of principle, must be discussed here. There are so many contradictions in the theses of Comrade Radek, as well as in his conception and that of the Communist International of relations between the labor unions and the

International, that it raises the question of what their position is on parliamentary struggle and the workers' movement. No clear picture of this position can be gotten from the theses. The Third International will have to express itself definitely and clearly on this matter. For the English and American minority the key thing was not any wish to quibble but a desire to see their position carry, through amendments that could not have been new to Comrade Radek.

The English and American delegations are interested in imbuing the old trade unions with the new spirit, and this will be out of the question if the theses in their present form are adopted. The transformation of the unions must be undertaken by the Communists. If they do not, the Communists will stand alone and remain a small party. They will become an officer corps without an army, because the rank and file will stand outside their influence.

## DISCUSSION

GALLACHER: When I came to Russia and arrived in Petrograd, Lenin's booklet *"Left-Wing" Communism—an Infantile Disorder* came into my hands, and I found my name mentioned in it in connection with my activity. I have taken this rebuke as a child takes the rebuke of a father. Now comes Comrade Radek and attempts to do the same, but he will not succeed. If he insists upon his point of view, he will see that the problem he has to solve is not so easy.

It is simply ridiculous to talk of winning the old unions, with their hardened bureaucracy. Setting the masses of the working classes into motion can be achieved by agitation not only inside but also outside the unions, under the banner of a left trade union organization. The English comrades have been active for the last twenty-five years in the trade unions without, however, being able to revolutionize them from within. They found that when they succeeded in getting some of their comrades appointed as union officials, the unions, instead of changing their tactics, only corrupted their own comrades. We have very often managed to get our comrades into big posts in the unions, but we have found that the work of communism and of the revolution was not furthered in any way by this. There are actually no masses in the unions. For instance, in a union that counts five hundred members, usually not more than thirty attend the meetings, and these are under the control of the bureaucracy. But we can reach the masses by working in the workshops and factories.

I myself was for many years active in the union movement and was myself a union official. The conclusions I came to are the result of my own experience. When Lloyd George came to Glasgow, the officials prepared a festive reception. I was then one of the officials, and I fought against it. While I gained my point in the official committee, an unofficial committee was formed to arrange the reception. I and my comrades carried on an agitation in the works and factories.[19] The result is that Glasgow is now a city where Lloyd George dares not appear, because the workers in Glasgow have been revolutionized by the agitation carried on in the works and factories.

If Radek's theses are adopted and the masses are in consequence told that they must remain loyal to the old unions and their officials, we shall be laughed at. Talk of winning the trade unions from within is as ridiculous as talk of winning the capitalist state from within. The English and American comrades must be given the opportunity of working and fighting for communist ideas outside the trade unions.

ZINOVIEV: We propose to take one speaker for the theses and one speaker against alternately.

(*The motion carries.*)

ZINOVIEV: Comrades, we must have absolute clarity on this question, and I assume here that we will not make a single concession to the British comrades, because what they want amounts to the destruction of the Communist International. If we adopt their position, the result will be that we destroy not the trade unions but communism.

On the one hand, the British and American comrades are very optimistic: the social revolution will arrive overnight, the triumph of the social revolution is in the bag, and so forth. But where the unions are concerned, all at once we see a tremendous pessimism with regard to the working class. They say, "We will eliminate the Morgans and Rockefellers, we will eliminate capitalism, but the union bureaucracy—we will never be able to eliminate that. The reactionary statutes will always be with us." But these statutes will do them no good. The working class will seize the bureaucracy by the collar as surely as it will the bourgeoisie.

To the British and American comrades it seems as if the union bureaucracy were the worst thing in the world. That is not true. There are far worse creatures than Gompers. His teeth are already rotten, and we will not need surgical implements to knock out every last one of them. Of course the statutes are reactionary. That is true. The membership fees are high. But what do you expect? The working class is becoming more revolutionary not by the day but by the hour. It wants to overthrow capitalism completely, and it will do with those union statutes what it must: throw them out the window.

You cannot deny that the unions have organized millions of workers. Our slogan is "To the masses!" and it applies to our British and American parties most of all. They must go to the masses, because they are not yet with the masses.

Comrades, when you listen to the speeches of the British and American comrades you can formulate a law, namely, that an inverse proportion applies here: the fewer workers you have organized, the more radical you are. They say, "We do not need the old trade unions; we will establish new ones." Meanwhile, Britain and America have an enormous working class numbering in the millions, and workers are oppressed by a highly developed, large-scale capitalism. The working class there is becoming more revolutionary from one day to the next, but so far, the number we have organized is insignificant. The United Communist Party of America has approximately twelve thousand members. That is simply ridiculous. Our comrades have not yet taken the first steps; they should be in these unions, which have organized millions of workers. And what do we have in Britain? In Britain there are several communist parties, each having a few hundred members. There is an enormous working class there that is becoming ever more revolutionary. It is our task to be with the masses, to lead them, to show them the way when they are in motion and are evolving. Should we not take part in the unions, when millions of workers belong to them? I have read the resolution of the American Communists' unity convention. I cannot imagine confusion greater than that in the part that says the American trade unions must be destroyed.

Comrade Gallacher said we should proceed against the unions just as we would against the bourgeois state. That is absurd. The unions consist of workers, the state consists of the bourgeoisie, and here we are told they are the same. Where are we heading? Do we want to make a laughingstock of the International? We do not need to destroy unions that millions of workers belong to. We must revolutionize them and lead them onto our path. We will never make a proletarian revolution if millions of union members are against us. Comrade Gallacher says we will be a laughingstock if we continue to work in the unions. My response to this is: you should make the unions revolutionary. You did well to refuse to receive Lloyd George. You should form illegal groups in the unions in order to fight not only with words but also with weapons. In Germany they are already fighting, arms in hand. Our comrades in the Communist Party have fought against the Yellow trade unions many times, arms in hand.

If we left the unions, however, that would be the best possible gift to Legien and his gang. They would say, "The Communists are really stupid; they left the workers to us." That is exactly what Gompers and Legien need. But we will never do that. We are not a sect. We want to be a really communist International, one that will win. And in order to win, we need the millions in the working class.

There are plenty of difficulties. It is easy to say, "We will leave. We want nothing to do with these people. We will establish a pure workers' union." There might be 20,000 workers in this union—and 8 million with Legien. That is what the KAPD did; it formed a workers' union in opposition to Legien's 8 million workers. That is childish. Where are the masses with whom we will make the proletarian revolution in Germany? In this workers' union, which is not the least bit centralized, not the least bit organized? We must go into the trade unions.

We often see you pay homage to the experiences of the Russian revolution. But we ask you to study them as well. Here too there were treacherous trade unions, but within a few months of the triumph of the Bolshevik revolution, we gained the majority in them. We won over the trade unions—a goal for which we had fought for decades. But if we had run away, the Mensheviks would have had what they wanted.

The British and American comrades say, "We will not go into the unions. We are Communists, good and pure, but the working masses are with the traitors." Well, comrades, does this not mean being the instrument of the opportunists? What Comrade Reed proposes is exactly what Gompers wants. That is all he needs. If we had done that, the Huysmans and Vanderveldes would have rubbed their hands in glee and said, "These people have done our work for us."

Our slogan is "With the masses always!" But that does not mean that we always praise the masses. We tell them, "You are wrong, but we will not leave. We will stay here with you so that we can lead you at all times." The Communist International must not commit the error of running away. If it does that, we are lost. Socialism would still triumph, of course, but perhaps in ten years, and our task is precisely to hasten its triumph.

That is why we must tell our British and American comrades: if you want to belong to the Communist International, you may not walk away from the trade unions. You must go into the trade unions, fight there, revolutionize the masses, show them the right road, and establish a strong Communist party that revolutionizes the trade unions and leads the proletarian masses on to the revolution.

FRAINA:[20] I am surprised that Comrades Radek and Zinoviev are so wrought up. At issue here is clarifying the basic differences between the two currents. Both speakers insist on emphasizing the necessity of working in the unions—but that is an argument against only the representative of the United Communist Party of America, who is opposed to working in the old unions. But the position of that party is emphatically not that of the other comrades who are criticizing Comrade Radek's theses. In my opening address I emphasized our acceptance of working in the old unions, not simply because of the arguments made here, but because the whole experience of the American movement imposes that policy upon us.

The Shop Stewards—are they against working in the old unions? It would be preposterous to assert that. The Shop Stewards and similar organizations are part of the old unions; they are the most adequate expression of the Radek-Zinoviev policy of working in the labor unions. I consider it essential to form committees of factory stewards and similar organizations as independent formations inside the unions that do not, however, replace them. I must stress that Comrade Tanner and others belong to unions by the mere fact that they participate in the Shop Stewards' committees, which are a component part of the unions.

I have said, as concerns the United States, that approximately 80 percent of the workers are unorganized. Nevertheless, it is impossible to abandon the old, reactionary unions, if for no other reason than because the majority of the unorganized workers are foreigners, the majority of the organized workers, Americans. We must make our contact with these American workers, since they will necessarily assume the leadership in the revolution—not in theory but in revolutionary action.

The speakers for the minority were misunderstood. They referred to the fact that it was precisely in America where the first example was seen of a militant upsurge following the Communists' intervention in the unions. Thus we saw strikes, undertaken against the will of the leaders, that drew the masses into struggle.

But how are you going to work in the old unions? That is the crucial question—the question of methods and means. When you say, "Work in the old unions," you say much—and nothing. It is necessary to have Communist groups in the old unions, but what are they to do? Are they simply to preach abstract communism? Radek answers, "No, they must become the leaders of the workers' economic struggle." Very well; but that requires means, and the means, we insist, do not consist of peaceful penetration of the unions, of simply trying to elect new officials in place of the old, of making a fetish of maintaining the old organizations and forms of unionism. The means consist of aggressive struggle in the unions, of mobilizing the masses against the bureaucracy and liberating them, of the agitation for and construction of extraunion organizations and industrial unions. It is essential to call the masses to action, and for this appropriate organizations are needed within the unions. Comrade Radek recognizes and accepts this, but does not make it a living and pulsating part of his theses. Radek is so absorbed with the problems in Germany, where certain people have issued the slogan "Abandon the old unions," that he overemphasizes the other policy.

Again, because of his concentration on Germany, Radek is extremely cautious regarding the problem of organizing new and breakaway unions. Under certain conditions a split is necessary; it must not be forced. But equally we must not allow a split to be imposed on us. We must not be like lambs; we must possess a policy on new unions that gives the initiative in the matter to us and not to our enemies. After all, a split is to a certain extent a revolutionary act. It may accomplish more in driving the masses onward than months and years of ordinary agitation. Sometimes it may be necessary even to force a split.

Splits should not, however, hinge on whether the union supports or opposes the dictatorship of the proletariat; there must be real grounds for them. It is action that we insist upon. It is on the basis of action, and not theoretical divergences, that splits must come.

Moreover, we insist upon recognition of the new forms that are developing in unionism. Particularly in England and America, this development is of the utmost importance. We must objectively study these developments and learn from them, adapting our theory to the peculiar variations and infinite forms of life itself. That is revolutionary practice; that is what is necessary, particularly on problems of unionism.

We must liberate the masses in the unions for action. Through their economic struggles, through understanding and adapting ourselves to the variations they develop in forms of organization and action, we mobilize them for the revolution. We must not be abstract or doctrinaire; we must always realize that it is the action of the masses that potentially develops the means and the forms of the final revolutionary struggle.

I repeat again: our differences with Comrade Radek are not of principle but of emphasis. But the Russian comrades must realize the new and variegated forms of unionism that are developing. They must realize that in our countries unionism is a much more vital factor in the revolution than in their revolution.

At the next congress I believe we will be in agreement.

SERRATI:[21] I have before me a motion of closure. It is agreed.

REED: I propose that the vote also be taken on the minority resolution, taking the amendments first.

(*The vote is taken on Radek's theses. They are approved by a vote of 57 for, 8 against, and 1 abstention.*[22] *Personal statements follow.*)

BOMBACCI: I am astonished to hear it said that I am playing games on the trade union question. On the contrary, I think it is Comrade Radek who is playing games here, because he himself admitted that he neither heard nor read my speech. I have been in the union movement for fifteen years, and for ten years I was secretary of a union; I have a very clear attitude toward them. It has never occurred to me to say that Communists should take no interest in the trade union question. I remind you that since 1914 the Italian communists have made every effort to wrest leadership of the unions away from the reformists and to take it themselves. Innumerable times I have said that the unions are a mine from which the revolution must extract precious metal, whereas parliament is a petty platform by comparison. But the unions are not revolutionary and never will be.

RADEK: Comrade Bombacci's last statement confirms what I said of him earlier. He declares that the trade unions never have been, are not now, and never will be revolutionary organizations. His comparing the unions to parliament confirms what I said. In his view, our relationship to the unions must be the same as our relationship to parliament: we should take advantage of the unions for propaganda purposes, but they will never become revolutionary organizations whose purpose is to establish the dictatorship. Comrade Bombacci says the same thing in his detailed report published in *Izvestia*. I find the contradiction all the more incomprehensible given that not only did his opponents understand his speech that way, but every Italian delegate whom I asked about the speech confirmed its meaning. Comrade Bombacci has worked in the trade unions for fifteen years, but why did he do so? If he views the trade unions as counterrevolutionary institutions yet does not work with a party to destroy them, he is presenting a position that a revolutionary cannot take seriously.

(*Reed moves that a vote be taken on the amendments before the vote on the theses themselves. The vote is taken.*)[23]

ZINOVIEV: As Comrade Radek indicated in his report, the commission still has to work out its position on the Red trade union International. I have an additional proposal on this point.[24] Permit me to say a few words in motivation. As you know, an international association of trade unions that support the Communist International's platform was established here in Moscow on July 15, and several unions joined it: Comrade Rosmer for the minority of the French unions, all the Russian unions, the Italian unions, and so forth. A statement has been drafted that is inadequate as a platform but represents a first step,[25] and we should support it and organize the international congress of Red trade unions as rapidly as possible. I propose adopting that as a separate motion. We will continue this effort with the aim of quickly certifying the Red trade unions. Second, I move that we leave it to the Executive Committee to issue an appeal to the trade unions of the world explaining the significance of the Amsterdam Yellow International and calling on them to join the new trade union International.[26]

(*Tanner asks for the floor to explain relations between the Yellow and Red trade union Internationals.*)

TANNER:[27] I am against this proposal. I maintain that if we take into account the persons who participated in forming the trade union council and the council's general character, we must characterize it as a miscarriage.

ZINOVIEV: Comrades, the Red trade union International that is being organized encompasses five million members of the Russian trade unions; two million revolutionary Italians (even though D'Aragona is a reformist); the

French union minority represented here by Rosmer, who are revolutionary and have several million members; the trade unions of Bulgaria, which have several hundred thousand members;[28] and a few others—altogether, approximately eight million workers organized in unions. We now want to unite these eight million organized workers into a trade union International. Comrades, I ask you, is that bad?

D'Aragona endorses this because the Italian workers are for us, for the soviets, for the dictatorship of the proletariat. And we hope that when another congress of the Italian unions is finally convened, after an interval of seven years, it will be led by a revolutionary Marxist, not a reformist. Here we have almost ten million workers who support the Communist International, and we are told that we should not organize them. Tanner says, "We have contact with the masses." How many members does the Shop Stewards' organization have? Two hundred and fifty thousand. We invited them too because we say it is a mass organization, and we must support it. But it is really very modest of you to say you have sufficient contact with the masses in a country like Britain. Rather than be satisfied with that, we should act as an international organization. The main enemy is Amsterdam, not Brussels.[29]

We keep hearing talk about the trade union bureaucracy. D'Aragona is a bureaucrat. Does that mean we should not set up an International?

Amsterdam is a force. It represents many millions of workers, but they are led by the Messrs. Social Democrats and are therefore reactionary. We must split them and bring them over to our side. That is the main task, and our first step is a big step forward. Now we can say to every trade union: You should resign from the Amsterdam International. Now you have the Red trade union International, and you should join it. It may be only a Zimmerwald, and from there you must proceed to Kienthal and then to Moscow, yet that is quite a step forward.

We invited the Shop Stewards, but they did not want to sign the manifesto because it mentioned the dictatorship of the proletariat. Now they have listened to reason.

So do not come to us and say, "Why did you not build it on a broader basis?" We built it on this basis because we have ten million members. Sooner or later every trade union will join this International.

Tanner believes it is a contradiction to say we must remain in the unions at the national level, while internationally we want a separate body. We want to remain in the unions nationally in order to bring people over to our side. Rather than abandon the unions to the Amsterdam International, we want to unite them and place them under the leadership of the Communist International. We want to win the unions in every way possible, at the national level if necessary. You would have to be doctrinaire from head to toe to stand aside now, when on one side there is the Yellow International and on the other the Moscow association. There are those who want to stand on the sidelines. Should I not make a deal with Robert Williams against Henderson? Of course. But is he not the leader of the Triple Alliance? Why are the Shop Steward comrades not leading that multimillion-member union? That shows they are sectarians and not revolutionaries. Revolutionaries must drive out the likes of Williams and put themselves in the leadership. These people form small groups, and when mass movements of millions grow, they stand on the sidelines. But you do not fight by standing on the sidelines. You fight by placing yourself at the head of the masses and going with them.

I believe it is a big step forward that we have a center for the trade union International. That is the most important blow we can deal the bourgeoisie. What if D'Aragona is an opportunist? That does not matter—he will go, but the Italian workers will remain. We will shove the union bureaucracy aside, and millions will go with us against capitalism and against the Yellow trade union International.

ENDRE RUDNYÁNSZKY [COMMUNIST PARTY OF HUNGARY]: I move that debate be ended.

(*The motion carries. A vote is taken on the motion by Tanner and Reed to refer this question to the commission for consideration. There are 13 votes for this motion, but the majority supports Zinoviev's motion, with 1 abstention.*[30] *The session is adjourned.*)

SESSION 16

AUGUST 6, 1920

# Tasks of the Comintern; Part 4 of conditions for admission, and other business

(*Zinoviev opens the session.*)

ZINOVIEV: The Bureau proposes bringing the congress to a conclusion with today's session.

MÜNZENBERG: In the name of the youth organization representatives present here, I move that we not end the congress without taking up the question of the youth movement. The representatives of the youth movement are greatly interested in discussing the Communist youth movement and its relationship to the Communist International in plenary session. Moreover, the youth movement has such great importance for the Communist Party that this question should be discussed before the entire congress. If it can be dealt with today, we are not opposed to the Bureau's motion. Otherwise we are opposed, since the question of the youth movement should be discussed regardless.

SYLVIA PANKHURST [BRITAIN]: We have been in session so long, we could meet for a little while longer. The question before us now has not yet been sufficiently discussed. I am against ending congress deliberations.

GOLDENBERG: I support Münzenberg's position. The youth question must be discussed before the congress ends.

ZINOVIEV: I would like to defend the Presiding Committee's proposal. As comrades who unfortunately arrived very late, like Sylvia Pankhurst, are aware, we have been discussing these questions for two weeks here, and previously we discussed them for two or three months in the Executive Committee. Therefore we propose to conclude today. We cannot take up the youth question thoroughly today. For a rounded discussion of this question, it is necessary that the youth movement representatives also take part in the discussion. Perhaps it would be advisable for the youth movement and for the entire International to have a special conference to discuss their movement. But it will be well for comrades who have been away from home for more than two weeks to be able to return. Therefore, we want to resolve the question quickly and without debate so we can end today. (*The motion is adopted.*)

(*Rosmer reports on behalf of the Commission on the International Situation and the Tasks of the Communist International, outlining the amendments made to the theses on this question.*)[1]

ZINOVIEV: Comrades, we have decided to terminate the congress today, and we must therefore be economical with time. Already twelve speakers have signed up for every question. I propose that new amendments not taken up in the commission only be read out and not discussed. The commission will then make the final decision. Second, on the question of entering the Labour Party, I propose to allow only two speakers for and two against.[2]

WIJNKOOP: Comrades, I am opposed to this proposal because the question of the Labour Party and the British

Socialist Party is of paramount importance. It is very important not only for Britain, but for the whole world, and it therefore seems to me necessary to be able to discuss this question quite freely. If we allow only two speakers for the one position and two for the other, in reality only the British delegation will be able to say anything on the question. Maybe two against, one in favor, and perhaps one other party besides the British will have the opportunity to say something. That will not do. The workers of the entire world have the right to know why we take one side or another. This is particularly important, and I am for a free discussion of the question. But even if we do not decide to have a free discussion, I think that two speakers in favor and two against are too few. At least a few other parties should have a chance to express their position. As a counterproposal to that of the Presiding Committee, I move that we have a free discussion on this question.

(*A vote is taken and Zinoviev's motion is adopted.*)

## AFFILIATION TO BRITISH LABOUR PARTY

PANKHURST: It is quite impossible to make clear to workers what the differences are between the Communist Party, the BSP, and the Labour Party. It is very characteristic of Britain in general that no clear demarcation exists between the policies of the various parties inside the Labour Party that would allow anyone—especially the workers—to distinguish one party from the other. Therefore, it would be very difficult to explain to them how the adherents of the Communist Party differ from those of their own party.

I want to use the example of Comrade Williams to illustrate this lack of clarity. He was thought to hold a pro-Soviet position, and now it has come out that he favored

British workers loading ammunition for Poland. That helps show how easy it is to be mistaken. They declare that they believe in communism, but they are compelled to carry out such policies because they belong to the Labour Party. The discipline of the party binds them.

Then again, take for example the situation during any phase of the election campaign. One would like to know the difference between the candidates, that is, who the candidates are and what they represent. I deny that this is possible, first, owing to the structure of the Labour Party, which is dominated by the old traditions; second, because we are talking here about salaried officials; and third because all members of those parties affiliated to the Labour Party are subject to the strictest discipline. Anyone who takes a position in Parliament on any question is also officially subject to party discipline. Local organizations can select their candidates for elections, but the Labour Party National Executive must approve any candidate who runs. It is the same with speeches and votes. All this has already made it clear to the members of the Independent Labour Party that it is very difficult to be an adherent of the ILP and at the same time belong to the Labour Party, because one is bound hand and foot by discipline.

Comrade Newbold, a very radical member of the ILP, is an example. He was put up as a candidate and read his appeal, his program, to his electors before presenting it to the Labour Party. After it was reviewed by the Labour Party, he again read the program to his electors. There was a big stir because the Labour Party had considerably altered its member's program. Once again I emphasize the tremendous dependence and discipline. When we speak of the Labour Party we must not forget its extremely ossified structure and the character of the trade unions that belong to it, which are also bureaucratic, ossified organizations. So the structure we find is very different than you think. It is impossible to remain in the party and alter this organization in any manner.

As for parliamentarism, the situation in Britain is more difficult than anywhere else. This is a country with old parliamentary traditions and real democratic traditions, deeply rooted in the working class. If you propose to British workers to participate in the elections in order to damage the Labour Party, they do not understand such advice. They are not open to this because they have been strongly influenced by the bourgeois press.

The experience in Britain cannot be compared to that in Russia. In Britain every worker reads the bourgeois press after he has finished his daily work. I myself have seen—and I am one of those speakers who spoke most on the question of the Russian revolution—that what was most difficult to explain to workers was precisely the Russians' attitude toward parliamentarism. They ask why the Constituent Assembly was first convoked and then dispersed. Democratic prejudices are deeply rooted in the British working class, and we have to take that into consideration.

There is another reason why I am against the standpoint being advanced here by the International. If we tell the parties they should affiliate to the Labour Party and let themselves be bound by common discipline and action, we are putting the fate of the proletarian revolution in Britain into the hands of the old trade unions. All the arguments that have been discussed here go against this viewpoint, and one sees daily how difficult it is to fill the unions with a new spirit. Also in Russia the unions were against a dictatorship in the factory committees. The proposal that the British Communist Party affiliate to the Labour Party would abandon the trade unions and soviets of workers' deputies to the old ossified trade unions.

I ask you, therefore, to consider the special conditions prevailing in Britain.

Concerning what Comrade Lenin said, that we should not be too extreme, I think we should be even more extreme than we are. Especially in Britain there is a great scarcity of courageous people. Although I am a socialist, I have fought a long time in the suffrage movement and I have seen how important it is to be extreme and to have the courage to stand up for one's ideas. In politics it is necessary to stand up for the most extreme positions. This was proven on the question of supporting soviet power in Britain, and on every question where courageous conduct was necessary. I therefore hold to my point of view and ask the congress *not* to accept the resolution on entering the Labour Party.

MCLAINE: Comrades, nothing new has been said here, because we all know Comrade Pankhurst's views on parliamentarism in general. The resolution proposed to the congress by the commission is only the logical development of those resolutions that have already been adopted on other questions. I think it is no coincidence that the comrades who are most in favor of the Communist Party affiliating to the Labour Party are representatives of a country where proletarian dictatorship already exists, that is, mostly the Russian comrades.

What does the Labour Party really represent? The Labour Party is nothing other than the political expression of the workers organized in trade unions. The Labour Party represents the economic standpoint of the workers on one question or another. Nine-tenths of those who belong to the Labour Party are at the same time members of the unions.

I think Comrade Pankhurst's example is childish, because she singled out the most reactionary unions. On the whole, no one can deny that the workers organized in unions are turning to the left. We can see the union movement changing under the pressure of time and events. We cannot look upon the trade unions and their members as something set in stone. I remember the big strike of the Manchester engineers in 1917,[3] in which several comrades present here participated. Communists appeared there, expressing the strikers' standpoint in the light of the communist movement. We achieved the best possible results.

We can also refer to the results obtained lately in the Labour Party. At first it was proposed that the Labour Party should affiliate to the Third International, but this was not even put to the vote. However, the fact that this question was raised stirred up great political interest. The question has been discussed throughout Britain and in all the sections of the Labour Party, which otherwise would never have heard anything at all about the Third International. A vigorous agitation developed out of this.

Contrary to what has been stated here, although the BSP is affiliated to the Labour Party, it retains full freedom of criticism. I myself and comrades of my party have repeatedly criticized the leaders of the Labour Party in the press and on other occasions at congresses without any adverse consequences for us.

I insist on two points: first, that the Labour Party is the political expression of the workers organized in unions and must be seen as a political organization, and second, that the adherents of other parties belonging to the Labour Party keep their full freedom of action and criticism.

GALLACHER: I regret indeed that this congress has to occupy itself with the same hackneyed phrases that have been put forward for twenty years in the British working-class movement by the BSP, which argued for the same positions it has here. They say they favor affiliation to the Labour Party because they believe they can get into better contact with the masses through it. But we *are* in contact with the masses. We must distinguish between those who really are in contact with the masses and those who do not wish to be so. I could cite you many examples from the last period of the struggle in Scotland, where the adherents of the BSP and ILP proved to be very modest and, together with the reformists, got in touch with the bourgeoisie, never venturing to stand up against them.

It was we who organized the big demonstrations in Scotland. The greatest speakers in Britain came to Scotland and wanted to make social-patriotic speeches. They had brought their clique along with them, the worst part of the population, to give them support. Although the representatives of the Labour Party advised us to keep quiet, we succeeded in preventing those speakers from getting hold of the crowd. We arranged large popular counter-demonstrations, despite all difficulties. This is what I call close contact with the masses.

I would like to recall our experience during the war, when, in spite of the chauvinism dominating at that time, the Scottish workers were able to obtain humane treatment for the families of the interned Germans, while the other workers' parties, hindered by their attachment to the bourgeoisie, could not participate in this work.

I also ask you not to forget the various well-known social patriots, like Thomas and Henderson, who have betrayed the working class many times. I ask you, how can we speak in the name of the very same party that Henderson represents? I want to explain to you the relations existing in reality between the "intransigent" British Socialist Party and the Labour Party. An excellent example is provided by my article against chauvinism. The paper that at the time refused to publish it was the *Call*.

It seems very strange to me that Comrade Lenin and other comrades should share McLaine's standpoint. Surely the responsibility Comrade McLaine has taken upon himself is a very weighty one; he has converted the other Communists to his ideas, which are not in the real interests of the movement. To me the most important thing is to use agitation and action to make the masses understand the present situation. We should arouse the indignation of the proletariat and use every means possible to set the masses into motion, not choose detours or means that only divert them from their revolutionary struggle.

I close with the request that you not accept the motion made here, which would deform the Communist Party's character. I ask all the comrades who represent the various parties at this congress not to support this motion. Leave us free to create a genuine Communist party on a really communist basis, and let us find the ways and means to speak to the masses. We shall then make the masses able to decide this question themselves. You cannot expect us to work and speak against all for which we have been fighting for years and years. This is the opinion of the revolutionary and communist elements. I urge you not to make the position of the Scottish comrades difficult and unbearable by forcing upon them a resolution they cannot defend, since it contradicts all they have stood for until now, all that has made them respected and popular among the workers.

LENIN: Comrades, Comrade Gallacher began his speech by expressing regret at our having been compelled to listen here for the hundredth and the thousandth time to sentences that Comrade McLaine and other British comrades have reiterated a thousand times in speeches, newspapers, and magazines. I think there is no need for regret. The method of the old International was to refer such questions for decision to the individual parties in the countries concerned. That was a grave error. We may not be fully familiar with the conditions in one or another party, but in this case we are dealing with the principles underlying a Communist party's tactics. That is very important and, in the name of the Third International, we must clearly state here the communist point of view.

First of all, I should like to mention a slight inaccuracy on the part of Comrade McLaine, which cannot be agreed to. He called the Labour Party the political organization of the trade union movement, and later repeated the statement when he said that the Labour Party is "the political expression of the trade union movement." I have met the same view several times in the paper of the British Socialist Party. It is erroneous and is partly the cause of the opposition, fully justified in some measure, coming from the British revolutionary workers. In fact, the concepts "political organization of the trade union movement" or "political expression" of that union movement are erroneous.

Of course, most of the Labour Party's members are workers. However, whether or not a party is really a political party of the workers does not depend solely on whether its members are workers but also on who leads it and the content of its actions and its political tactics. Only the latter determines whether we really have before us a political party of the proletariat. Regarded from this point of view, the only correct one, the Labour Party is a thoroughly bourgeois party, because, although made up of workers, it is led by reactionaries, and the worst kind of reactionaries at that, who act quite in the spirit of the bourgeoisie. It is an organization of the bourgeoisie, which exists to systematically dupe the workers with the aid of the British Noskes and Scheidemanns.

We have also heard another point of view, defended by Comrade Sylvia Pankhurst and Comrade Gallacher, who have voiced their opinion on the matter. What was the substance of the speeches delivered by Gallacher and many of his friends? They told us that they are insufficiently linked with the masses. But take the case of the British Socialist Party, they went on. It is still less linked with the masses and it is a very weak party. Comrade Gallacher told us here how he and his comrades had organized, and done so really splendidly, the revolutionary movement in Glasgow, in Scotland; how in their wartime tactics they maneuvered expertly; how they gave skillful support to the petty-bourgeois pacifists Ramsay MacDonald and Snowden when they came to Glasgow, and used this support to organize a mass movement against the war.

It is our aim to integrate this new and excellent revolutionary movement—represented here by Comrade Gallacher and his friends—into a communist party with genuinely communist, that is, Marxist, tactics. That is our task today. On the one hand, the British Socialist Party is too weak and is incapable of properly carrying on agitation among the masses. On the other hand, we have the younger revolutionary elements so well represented here by Comrade Gallacher who, although in touch with the masses, are not a political party. In this sense they are even weaker than the British Socialist Party and are totally unable to organize their political work.

Under these circumstances, we must express our frank opinion on the correct tactics. When, in speaking of the British Socialist Party, Comrade Gallacher said that it is "hopelessly reformist," he was undoubtedly exaggerating. But the general tenor and content of all the resolutions we have adopted here show with absolute clarity that we demand a change in this spirit in the tactics of the British Socialist Party. The only correct tactics of Gallacher's friends will consist in their joining the Communist party without delay, so as to modify its tactics in the spirit of the resolutions adopted here. If you have so many supporters that you are able to organize mass meetings in Glasgow, it will not be difficult for you to bring more than ten thousand new members into the party. The most recent conference of the British Socialist Party, held in London three or four days ago, decided to assume the name Communist Party and introduced into its program a clause providing for participation in parliamentary elections and affiliation to the Labour Party. Ten thousand organized members were represented at the conference. It will therefore not be at all difficult for the Scottish comrades to bring into this "Communist Party of Great Britain" more than ten thousand revolutionary workers who are better versed in the art of working among the masses and thus to modify the old tactics of the British Socialist Party in the sense of better agitation and more revolutionary action.

In the commission Comrade Sylvia Pankhurst pointed out several times that Britain needed "lefts." I, of course, replied that this was absolutely true, but that one must not overdo this "leftism." She also said that "we are better pioneers, but for the moment we are rather noisy." I do not take this in a bad sense, but rather in a good one, namely, that they are more able in carrying on revolutionary agitation. We do and should value this. We expressed this in all our resolutions, for we always emphasize that we can consider a party to be a workers' party only when it is really linked up with the masses and fights against the old and quite corrupt leaders, against both the right-wing chauvinists and those who, like the right Independents in Germany, take up an intermediate position. We have asserted and reiterated this a dozen times and more in all our resolutions, which means that we demand a transformation of the old party, in the sense of bringing it closer to the masses.

Sylvia Pankhurst also asked, "Is it possible for a communist party to join another political party that still belongs to the Second International?" She replied that it was not. It should, however, be borne in mind that the British Labour Party is in a very special position: it is a highly original type of party, or rather, it is not at all a party in the ordinary sense of the word. Made up of members of all trade unions, it has at present a membership of about four million, and it allows sufficient freedom to all affiliated political parties. It thus includes a vast number of British workers who follow the lead of the worst bourgeois elements, social traitors who are even worse than Scheidemann, Noske, and similar people.

At the same time, however, the Labour Party has let the British Socialist Party into its ranks, permitting it to have its own press organs, in which members of the selfsame Labour Party can freely and openly declare that the party leaders are social traitors. Comrade McLaine has cited quotations from such statements by the British Socialist Party. I too can certify that I have seen in the *Call,* organ of the British Socialist Party, statements that the Labour Party leaders are social patriots and social traitors. This shows that a party affiliated to the Labour Party is able not only to severely criticize the old leaders but openly and specifically to call the old workers' leaders social traitors, mentioning them by name.

This is a very original situation: a party that unites enormous masses of workers, so that it might seem a political party, is nevertheless obliged to grant its members complete latitude. Comrade McLaine has told us here that at the Labour Party conference the British Scheidemanns were obliged to openly raise the question of affiliation to the Third International and that all party branches and sections were obliged to discuss the matter. In such circumstances, it would be a mistake not to join this party.

In a private talk Comrade Pankhurst said to me, "If we are real revolutionaries and join the Labour Party, these gentlemen will expel us." But that would not be bad at all. Our resolution says that we favor affiliation insofar as the Labour Party permits sufficient freedom of criticism. On that point we are absolutely consistent. Comrade McLaine emphasized that the conditions now prevailing in Britain are such that, should it so desire, a political party may remain a revolutionary workers' party even though connected with a special kind of labor organization of four million members, which is half trade union and half political and is headed by bourgeois leaders. In such circumstances it would be highly erroneous for the best revolutionary elements not to do everything possible to remain in such a party. Let the Thomases and other social traitors, whom you have called by that name, expel you. That will have an excellent effect upon the mass of the British workers.

The comrades have emphasized that the labor aristocracy is stronger in Britain than in any other country. That is indeed true. After all, the labor aristocracy has existed in Britain not for decades but for centuries. The British bourgeoisie, which has had far more experience—democratic experience—than that of any other country, has been able to buy off workers and to create among them a sizable stratum, greater than in any other country, but one that is not so great compared with the masses of the workers. This stratum is thoroughly imbued with bourgeois prejudices and pursues a definitely bourgeois reformist policy.

In Ireland, for instance, there are 200,000 British soldiers who are applying ferocious terror methods to suppress the Irish. The British Socialists are not conducting any revolutionary propaganda among these soldiers, though our resolutions clearly state that we can accept into the Communist International only those British parties that conduct genuinely revolutionary propaganda among the British workers and soldiers. I emphasize that we have heard no objections to this either here or in the commissions.

Comrades Gallacher and Sylvia Pankhurst cannot deny that. They cannot refute the fact that the British Socialist Party, while remaining in the ranks of the Labour Party, enjoys sufficient freedom to write that certain leaders of the Labour Party are traitors; that these old leaders represent the interests of the bourgeoisie; that they are agents of the bourgeoisie in the working-class movement. All this is the absolute truth. When communists enjoy such freedom, it is their duty to join the Labour Party if they take due account of the experience of revolutionaries in all countries, not only of the Russian revolution (for here we are not at a Russian congress but at one that is international). Comrade Gallacher said ironically that in the present instance we are under the influence of the British Socialist Party. That is not true; it is the experience of all revolutions in all countries that has convinced us. We think we must say that to the masses. The British Communist Party must retain the freedom necessary to expose and criticize the betrayers of the working class, who are much more powerful in Britain than in any other country. That is readily understandable.

Comrade Gallacher is wrong in asserting that by advocating affiliation to the Labour Party we shall repel the best elements among the British workers. We must test this by experience. We are convinced that all the resolutions and decisions that will be adopted by our congress will be published in all British revolutionary socialist newspapers and that all the branches and sections will be able to discuss them. The entire content of our resolutions shows with crystal clarity that we are representatives of working-class revolutionary tactics in all countries and that our aim is to fight against the old reformism and opportunism. The events are revealing that our tactics are indeed defeating the old reformism. In that case the finest revolutionary elements in the working class, who are dissatisfied with the slow progress being made—and progress in Britain will perhaps be slower than in other countries—will all come over to us.

Progress is slow because the British bourgeoisie is in a position to create better conditions for the labor aristocracy and thereby to retard the revolutionary movement in Britain. That is why the British comrades should strive not only to revolutionize the masses—they are doing that splendidly (as Comrade Gallacher has shown)—but at the same time to create a real working-class political party. Comrade Gallacher and Comrade Sylvia Pankhurst, who have both spoken here, do not as yet belong to a revolutionary communist party. Such an excellent proletarian organization as the Shop Stewards' movement has not yet joined a political party. If you organize politically you will find that our tactics are based on a correct understanding of political developments in the past decades, and that a real revolutionary party can be created only when it absorbs the best elements of the revolutionary class and uses every opportunity to fight the reactionary leaders, wherever they show themselves.

If the British Communist Party starts by acting in a revolutionary manner in the Labour Party, and if the Hendersons are obliged to expel this party, that will be a great victory for the Communist and revolutionary working-class movement in Britain.

ZINOVIEV: Now we must vote on the question of the British party entering the Labour Party. All those in favor of the commission's motion, that is, in favor of the British party joining the Labour Party, raise their hands. (*The motion is adopted* 58 *to* 24 *with* 2 *abstentions.*)

## TASKS OF THE COMMUNIST INTERNATIONAL

ZINOVIEV: Now we must vote on the resolution as a whole, but first a few comrades want the floor to make statements.

SERRATI: I am voting against the theses, first because of differences on the British and American questions, and second because of the criticism directed against the leadership of the Italian Socialist Party. I do not want to hold up the congress with overly long explanations. I will submit to the Bureau a detailed explanation to be inserted into the proceedings.[4]

GRAZIADEI: We propose that thesis 17 be formulated as follows:

"Concerning the Socialist Party of Italy, the Second Congress of the Third International considers the revision of the party program adopted by the Bologna congress last year a very positive step on the party's road to communism. The proposals submitted to the National Council of the Socialist Party of Italy in the name of the party's Turin section, as set forth in *L'Ordine Nuovo* of May 8, 1920, correspond to the fundamental principles of the Third International.[5]

"Accordingly, the Second Congress of the Third International requests the Socialist Party of Italy to convene its next congress in accordance with its statutes and with the conditions for admission to the Communist International and to discuss there, along with these proposals, all the decisions of the two congresses of the Communist International, especially regarding the questions of the parliamentary fraction, the trade unions, and the noncommunist elements in the party." Signed: Graziadei, Bombacci, Polano.

ZINOVIEV: On behalf of three members of the Russian delegation, Lenin, Bukharin, and myself, I declare that we accept this version by Graziadei and hope that the majority of the commission will also adopt it.

WIJNKOOP: I would like to say here that even though the theses do not correspond to my view on the British question I will vote for them because they take a sharp position against the opportunists and because they were sharpened even more in the commission, precisely on the Italian question.

SERRATI: Despite the statements of Graziadei and the commission members, I stick to what I said in my declaration, given that in fact there is no difference between what was stated in the theses and what was just said. Maybe a lawyer could find one or read one into it, but this is not a congress of lawyers but of Communists. The theses are a repudiation of the Italian party leadership and of *Avanti!* That should be openly stated.

ZINOVIEV: I must say that Serrati is right. In fact there is no difference, but this is a proposal from the Italian comrades, and we have obliged them. We are always ready to make accommodations of form for comrades who want to fight against lawyers. On this question I would say that the majority of the commission and of the congress sides with Comrade Serrati.

BORDIGA: Speaking on behalf of the Communist-Abstentionist faction of the Italian Socialist Party, I attach no importance to the form of the theses concerning the Italian Socialist Party.

Based on everything that was said here about this party, particularly by Comrades Lenin and Zinoviev, I see that the party as such is being criticized here because at its Bologna congress it did not do what was required on the question of its parliamentary activity. Given the presence of opportunist and Social Democratic forces in its ranks, its conduct since the Bologna congress is out of line with its affiliation to the Communist International.

On the question of antiparliamentarism, we will submit to the discipline of the congress, but we ask that all other resolutions of the congress be strictly observed by the Italian party—specifically with respect to noncommunist members of the party, the parliamentary fraction, and reformist-led trade unions. We are firmly convinced that the Executive Committee of the International will see that these decisions are implemented.

Should the Italian party have the opportunity to carry out the obligations laid on it here, it will do so. The Central Committee is capable of ensuring that the decisions made here command respect.

ZINOVIEV: We now move to the vote on the theses as a whole. (*The theses are adopted with* 2 *votes against and* 1 *abstention.*)

That concludes the matter.

## THESES ON THE BASIC TASKS OF THE COMMUNIST INTERNATIONAL

1. The present stage in the development of the international Communist movement is marked by the fact that the finest representatives of the revolutionary pro-

letariat in all capitalist countries have fully grasped the fundamental principles of the Communist International, namely, the dictatorship of the proletariat and soviet power, ranging themselves with unbounded enthusiasm on the side of the Communist International.[6] An even bigger and more important step forward is the definite sympathy with these fundamental principles that has taken shape everywhere among the broadest masses, not only of the urban proletariat but of the advanced section of the rural workers as well.

On the other hand, two errors or weaknesses are to be observed in the very rapidly growing international Communist movement. One is very grave and constitutes an immense and immediate danger to the success of the cause of proletarian emancipation. It is that some of the old leaders and old parties of the Second International—in part yielding half unconsciously to the wishes and pressure of the masses, and in part deliberately deceiving the masses in order to retain their function of agents and assistants of the bourgeoisie within the working-class movement—declare their qualified or even unqualified adherence to the Third International, while actually remaining, in all their practical party and political work, on the level of the Second International.

Such a state of affairs is absolutely intolerable. It leads to downright corruption of the masses, detracts from the Third International's prestige, and threatens a repetition of the same acts of treachery as were perpetrated by the Hungarian Social Democrats, who so hastily assumed the title of Communists.

The other error, which is far less significant and is more in the nature of growing pains of the movement, consists in a tendency toward "leftism." This results in a wrong appraisal of the role and the tasks of the party with regard to the class and the masses, and a wrong attitude toward the revolutionary Communists' obligation to work in bourgeois parliaments and reactionary trade unions.

Communists are duty-bound not to gloss over shortcomings in their movement but to criticize them openly, so as to remedy them the more speedily and radically. For this purpose it is necessary, first, to define as concretely as possible, particularly on the basis of the practical experience already acquired, the content of the concepts "dictatorship of the proletariat" and "soviet power." Second, the precise content of the immediate and systematic preparatory work to be carried on in all countries so as to give effect to these slogans must be specified. Third, the methods and means of rectifying the faults in our movement must be demonstrated.

### I. The essence of the dictatorship of the proletariat and of soviet power

2. The victory of socialism (as the first stage of communism) over capitalism requires that the proletariat, as the only really revolutionary class, accomplish the following three tasks:

First, overthrow the exploiters—and first and foremost the bourgeoisie, as their principal economic and political representative—utterly rout them, crush their resistance, and absolutely preclude any attempt on their part to restore the yoke of capital and wage slavery.

The second task is to win over and bring under the leadership of the Communist Party—the revolutionary vanguard of the proletariat—not only the entire proletariat, or its vast majority, but all who labor and are exploited by capital. It is to educate, organize, train, and discipline them in the very course of a supremely bold and ruthlessly firm struggle against the exploiters. It is to wrest this vast majority of the population in all the capitalist countries from dependence on the bourgeoisie, and imbue it, through its own practical experience, with confidence in the leading role of the proletariat and of its revolutionary vanguard.

The third task is to neutralize or render harmless the inevitable vacillation between the bourgeoisie and the proletariat, between bourgeois democracy and soviet power, to be seen in the class of petty proprietors in agriculture, industry, and commerce—a class that is still fairly numerous in nearly all advanced countries, although comprising only a minority of the population—as well as in the stratum of intellectuals, salary earners, etc., that corresponds to this class.

The first and second tasks have an independent character, each requiring its own special methods of action with regard to the exploiters and the exploited. The third task follows from the first two, and requires merely a skillful, timely, and flexible combination of measures for the first and second tasks, depending on the specific circumstances in each separate instance of vacillation.

3. In the concrete situation created throughout the world—and above all in the most advanced, powerful, enlightened, and free capitalist countries—by militarism, imperialism, the oppression of colonies and weak countries, the worldwide imperialist butchery, and the Versailles "peace," the very idea of the capitalists peacefully submitting to the will of the majority of the exploited, the very idea of a peaceful, reformist transition to socialism, is not merely sheer philistine stupidity but also downright deception of the workers, a whitewash of capitalist wage slavery, and a concealment of the truth. The truth is that the bourgeoisie, even the most enlightened and democratic, no longer hesitates at any fraud or crime, even the

massacre of millions of workers and peasants, in order to preserve private ownership of the means of production.

Only the forcible overthrow of the bourgeoisie, the confiscation of its property, the destruction of the entire bourgeois state apparatus from top to bottom—parliamentary, judicial, military, bureaucratic, administrative, municipal, etc.—right down to the wholesale deportation or internment of the most dangerous and stubborn exploiters and the institution of strict surveillance of them so as to foil their inevitable attempts to resist and to restore capitalist slavery—only such measures can ensure real submission of the whole class of exploiters.

Just as much a whitewash of capitalism and bourgeois democracy, just as much a deception of the workers, is the view—common among the old parties and the old leaders of the Second International—that the majority of the exploited toilers can achieve complete clarity of socialist consciousness and firm socialist convictions and character under capitalist slavery, under the yoke of the bourgeoisie. This yoke, moreover, assumes an infinite variety of forms that become more subtle and at the same time more brutal and ruthless the higher the cultural level in a given capitalist country.

In fact, it is only after the vanguard of the proletariat, supported by the whole or the majority of this, the only revolutionary class, overthrows the exploiters, suppresses them, emancipates the exploited from their state of slavery, and immediately improves their conditions of life at the expense of the expropriated capitalists—it is only after this, and only in the actual process of an acute class struggle, that the masses of the toilers and exploited can be educated, trained, and organized around the proletariat, under whose influence and guidance they can get rid of the selfishness, disunity, vices, and weaknesses engendered by private property. Only then will they be converted into a free union of free workers.

4. Victory over capitalism calls for proper relations between the leading (Communist) party, the revolutionary class (the proletariat) and the masses, that is, the entire body of the toilers and the exploited. Only the Communist Party, if it is really the vanguard of the revolutionary class, if it really comprises all the finest representatives of that class, if it consists of fully conscious and staunch Communists who have been educated and steeled by the experience of a persistent revolutionary struggle, and if it has succeeded in linking itself inseparably with the whole life of its class and through it with the whole mass of the exploited, and in completely winning the confidence of this class and this mass—only such a party is capable of leading the proletariat in a final, most ruthless, and decisive struggle against all the forces of capitalism.

On the other hand, it is only under the leadership of such a party that the proletariat is capable of displaying the full might of its revolutionary onslaught and of overcoming the inevitable apathy and occasional resistance of that small minority, the labor aristocracy, that has been corrupted by capitalism, the old trade union and cooperative leaders, etc. Only then will it be capable of displaying its full might, which, because of the very economic structure of capitalist society, is infinitely greater than its proportion of the population.

Finally, it is only after they have been really emancipated from the yoke of the bourgeoisie and of the bourgeois state machinery, only after they have found an opportunity of organizing in their soviets in a really free way (free from the exploiters), that the masses—that is, the toilers and exploited as a body—can display, for the first time in history, all the initiative and energy of tens of millions of people who have been crushed by capitalism. Only when the soviets have become the sole state apparatus is it really possible to ensure the participation in the work of administration of the entire mass of the exploited. Even under the most enlightened and freest bourgeois democracy, these masses have actually always been 99 percent excluded from participation in the work of administration. It is only in the soviets that the exploited masses really begin to learn—not in books but from their own practical experience—the work of socialist construction, of creating a new social discipline and a free union of free workers.

### II. What immediate and universal preparation for the dictatorship of the proletariat should consist of

5. The present stage in the development of the international Communist movement is marked by the fact that in the vast majority of capitalist countries, the proletariat's preparations to effect its dictatorship have not been completed, and, in many cases, have not even been systematically begun. From this it does not follow, however, that the proletarian revolution is impossible in the immediate future; it is perfectly possible, since the entire economic and political situation is most inflammable and abounds in causes of a sudden flare-up. The other condition for revolution, apart from the proletariat's preparedness, also exists, namely, a general state of crisis in all the ruling and in all bourgeois parties.

It follows from this, however, that the Communist parties' current task consists not in accelerating the revolution, but in intensifying the preparation of the proletariat. It must be prepared for a revolution through action.[7] On the other hand, the facts cited above from the history of many Socialist parties make it incumbent on us to see to it that "recognition" of the dictatorship of the proletariat does not remain a matter of mere words.

Hence, from the point of view of the international proletarian movement, the Communist parties' principal task at the present moment is to unite the scattered Communist forces, to form a single Communist party in every country (or to consolidate or renovate the already existing party) in order to increase tenfold the work of preparing the proletariat for the conquest of state power—political power, moreover, in the form of the dictatorship of the proletariat. The usual socialist work conducted by groups and parties that recognize the dictatorship of the proletariat has by no means undergone the fundamental reorganization, the fundamental renovation, that is essential for this work to be considered communist and adequate to the tasks to be accomplished on the eve of the proletarian dictatorship.

6. The proletariat's conquest of political power does not put a stop to its class struggle against the bourgeoisie; on the contrary, it renders that struggle most widespread, intense, and ruthless. Owing to the extreme intensification of the struggle, all groups, parties, and leaders in the working-class movement who have fully or partly adopted the stand of reformism, of the Center, etc., inevitably side with the bourgeoisie or join the waverers, or else (what is the most dangerous of all) land in the ranks of the unreliable friends of the victorious proletariat.

Hence, preparation for the dictatorship of the proletariat calls not only for an intensification of the struggle against reformist and centrist tendencies, but also for a change in the character of that struggle. The struggle cannot be restricted to explaining the erroneousness of these tendencies; it must unswervingly and ruthlessly expose any leader of the working-class movement who reveals such tendencies. Otherwise the proletariat cannot know who it will march with into the decisive struggle against the bourgeoisie.

This struggle is such that at any moment the weapon of criticism can be replaced by criticism with weapons—and, as experience has already taught, this does happen. Any inconsistency or weakness in exposing those who show themselves to be reformists or centrists means directly increasing the danger of the power of the proletariat being overthrown by the bourgeoisie, which tomorrow will utilize for the counterrevolution that which shortsighted people today see merely as "theoretical differences."

7. In particular, we must not restrict ourselves to the usual repudiation, in principle, of all cooperation between the proletariat and the bourgeoisie, of all "collaborationism." Since private property in the means of production will be preserved under the dictatorship of the proletariat, which will never be able to abolish private property completely at one blow, simple defense of "freedom" and "equality" will be transformed into a kind of "cooperation" with the bourgeoisie that actually undermines the power of the working class.

The dictatorship of the proletariat means that the state uses its whole machinery of power to uphold and perpetuate "unfreedom" of the exploiters to continue their oppression and exploitation, "inequality" between the owner of property (that is, one who has appropriated for himself certain means of production created by social labor) and the nonowner. What prior to the victory of the proletariat seems merely a theoretical difference on the question of "democracy" inevitably becomes, on the day following victory, a question that is settled by force of arms. Consequently, even preliminary work to prepare the masses to effect the dictatorship of the proletariat is impossible without a radical change in the entire character of the struggle against the centrists and the "champions of democracy."

8. The dictatorship of the proletariat is the most determined and revolutionary form of the proletariat's class struggle against the bourgeoisie. This struggle can be successful only when the most revolutionary vanguard of the proletariat has the backing of its overwhelming majority. Hence, preparation for the dictatorship of the proletariat entails more than explaining the bourgeois character of all reformism, of all defense of democracy while private ownership of the means of production is preserved. It entails more than exposing such trends, which are in fact a defense of the bourgeoisie within the labor movement. It also calls for old leaders being replaced by Communists in proletarian organizations of absolutely every type—not only political but also trade union, cooperative, educational, etc.

The more complete, long-standing, and firmly established the rule of bourgeois democracy has been in a given country, the more the bourgeoisie will have succeeded in securing the appointment to such leading posts of people whose minds it has molded and imbued with its views and prejudices, and whom it has very often directly or indirectly purchased. These representatives of the labor aristocracy—bourgeoisified workers—should be ousted from all their posts a hundred times more sweepingly than hitherto. They should be replaced by workers, even by wholly inexperienced men, provided they are connected with the exploited masses and enjoy their confidence in the struggle against the exploiters. The dictatorship of the proletariat will require the appointment of such inexperienced workers to the most responsible posts in the state; otherwise the workers' government will be impotent and will not have the support of the masses.

9. The dictatorship of the proletariat means that all toiling and exploited people—who have been disunited, deceived, intimidated, oppressed, downtrodden, and crushed by the capitalist class—come under the full leadership of the only class trained for that leadership by the whole history of capitalism. Therefore, preparation for the dictatorship of the proletariat must begin everywhere and at once and must include the following measures:

In all organizations, unions, and associations without exception, first and foremost in proletarian organizations, but also in those of the nonproletarian toiling and exploited masses (political, trade union, military, cooperative, educational, sports, etc.), groups or cells of Communists should be formed. These groups should preferably be open, but underground groups are also needed and are essential whenever there is reason to expect their suppression, or the arrest or banishment of their members on the part of the bourgeoisie. These cells, which are to be in close touch with one another and with the party center, should, by pooling their experience, carry on work of agitation, propaganda, and organization. They should adapt themselves to absolutely every sphere of public life and to every variety and category of the toiling masses, systematically educating themselves, the party, the class, and the masses by means of such diversified work.

In this connection, it is of the utmost importance that necessary distinctions between the methods of work should be evolved in practice. As for the "leaders," or "responsible representatives," who are very often hopelessly beset with petty-bourgeois and imperialist prejudices, such "leaders" must be ruthlessly exposed and expelled from the working-class movement. But as for the masses, particularly after the imperialist war they are for the most part inclined to listen to and accept the doctrine that guidance from the proletariat is essential as the only way of escaping from capitalist slavery. We must learn to approach the masses with particular patience and caution so as to be able to understand the distinctive features in the mentality of each stratum, occupation, etc., of these masses.

10. In particular, there is a group or cell of Communists that deserves exceptional attention and care from the party. That is the parliamentary fraction: the party members who are deputies to bourgeois representative institutions, primarily national, but also local and municipal. On the one hand, it is this platform that is held in particular regard by large sections of the toiling masses who are backward or imbued with petty-bourgeois prejudices. It is therefore imperative for Communists to utilize this platform to conduct propaganda, agitation, and organizational work and to explain to the masses why the dispersal of the bourgeois parliament by the national congress of soviets was legitimate in Russia (and, at the proper time, will be legitimate in any country). On the other hand, the entire history of bourgeois democracy, particularly in the advanced countries, has converted the parliamentary rostrum into one of the principal—if not the principal—venues of unparalleled fraudulence, financial and political deception of the people, careerism, hypocrisy, and oppression of the working people. The intense hatred of parliaments felt by the best representatives of the revolutionary proletariat is therefore quite justified.

The Communist parties and all parties affiliated to the Third International—especially those that have not arisen by splitting away from the old parties and by waging a long and persistent struggle against them but through the old parties accepting (often nominally) the new political positions—should therefore adopt a most strict attitude toward their parliamentary fractions. These fractions must be brought under the full control and direction of the central committees of the parties and they must consist, in the main, of revolutionary workers. Speeches by members of parliament should be carefully analyzed in the party press and at party meetings from a strictly communist standpoint. Deputies should be sent to carry on agitational work among the masses. Those who manifest Second International leanings should be expelled from the parliamentary groups. And so on.

11. One of the chief causes hampering the revolutionary working-class movement in the developed capitalist countries is the fact that because of their colonial possessions and the superprofits gained by finance capital, etc., the capitalists of these countries have been able to create a relatively larger and more stable labor aristocracy, a section that comprises a small minority of the working class. This minority enjoys better terms of employment and is most imbued with a narrow-minded craft spirit and with petty-bourgeois and imperialist prejudices. It forms the real social pillar of the Second International, of the reformists and the centrists. At present it might even be called the social mainstay of the bourgeoisie.

No preparation of the proletariat for the overthrow of the bourgeoisie is possible, even in the preliminary sense, unless an immediate, systematic, extensive, and open struggle is waged against this stratum, which, as experience has already fully shown, will no doubt provide the bourgeois White Guards with many a recruit after the victory of the proletariat. All parties affiliated to the Third International must at all costs put the following slogans into effect: "Deeper into the heart of the masses," "Closer links with the masses"—meaning by the masses all those who toil and are exploited by capital, particularly those who are least organized and educated, who are most oppressed and least amenable to organization.

The proletariat becomes revolutionary only insofar as it does not restrict itself to the narrow framework of craft interests, only when, in all matters and spheres of public life, it acts as the leader of all the toiling and exploited masses. It cannot achieve its dictatorship unless it is prepared and able to make the greatest sacrifices for the sake of victory over the bourgeoisie. In this respect, the experience of Russia is significant both in principle and in practice. The proletariat could not have achieved its dictatorship there or won the universally acknowledged respect and confidence of all the toiling masses, had it not made the most sacrifices, suffering more from hunger than any other section of those masses at the most crucial moments of the onslaught, war, and blockade effected by the world bourgeoisie.

In particular, the Communist Party and all advanced proletarians must give all-around and unstinting support to the spontaneous mass strike movement. It alone is capable, under the yoke of capital, of really rousing, educating, and organizing the masses, of imbuing them with complete confidence in the leadership of the revolutionary proletariat. Without such preparation, no dictatorship of the proletariat is possible. People capable of publicly opposing strikes, such as Kautsky in Germany and Turati in Italy, cannot possibly be tolerated in the ranks of parties affiliated to the Third International. This applies even more, of course, to those trade union and parliamentary leaders who so often betray the workers by using the experience of strikes to teach them reformism and not revolution. These include such people as Jouhaux in France, Gompers in America, and J.H. Thomas in Britain.

12. In all countries, even in those that are freest, most "legal," and most "peaceful" in the sense that the class struggle is least acute there, the time has now come when it is absolutely indispensable for every Communist Party to systematically combine legal and illegal work, legal and illegal organizations. Notwithstanding their false and hypocritical declarations, the governments of even the most enlightened and freest of countries, where the bourgeois-democratic system is most "stable," are already systematically and secretly drawing up blacklists of Communists. They constantly violate their own constitutions so as to give secret or semisecret encouragement to the White Guards and to the murder of Communists in all countries, making secret preparations for the arrest of Communists, planting agents provocateurs among the Communists, etc.

Only a most reactionary philistine, no matter what cloak of fine "democratic" and pacifist phrases he may don, will deny this fact or the conclusion that of necessity follows from it, namely, that all legal Communist parties must immediately form illegal organizations for the systematic conduct of illegal work and for complete preparations for the moment the bourgeoisie resorts to persecution. Illegal work is especially necessary in the army, the navy, and the police. For since the imperialist holocaust, governments the world over have begun to stand in dread of people's armies that are open to the workers and peasants. They are secretly resorting to all kinds of methods to set up military units specially recruited from the bourgeoisie and equipped with the most up-to-date weapons.

On the other hand, it is likewise necessary that, in all cases without exception, the parties should not restrict themselves to illegal work but should conduct legal work as well, overcoming all obstacles, starting legal publications and forming legal organizations under the most varied names, which should be frequently changed if necessary. This is being practiced by the illegal Communist parties in Finland, Hungary, partly in Germany, Poland, Latvia, etc. It should be practiced by the Industrial Workers of the World in America and by all Communist parties that are at present legal, should public prosecutors see fit to initiate proceedings against them on the grounds of resolutions adopted by congresses of the Communist International, etc.

A combination of illegal and legal work is an absolute principle dictated not only by all features of the present period—that of the eve of the proletarian dictatorship—but also by the necessity of proving to the bourgeoisie that there is not, nor can there be, any sphere of activity that cannot be won by the Communists. Above all, it is dictated by the fact that broad strata of the proletariat and even broader strata of the nonproletarian toiling and exploited masses still exist everywhere who continue to believe in bourgeois-democratic legality and whom we must undeceive without fail.

13. In particular, the condition of the working-class press in most advanced capitalist countries strikingly reveals the utter fraudulence of liberty and equality under bourgeois democracy, as well as the necessity of systematically combining legal work with illegal work. Both in vanquished Germany and in victorious America, the entire power of the bourgeoisie's state machinery and all the machinations of the financial magnates are employed to deprive the workers of their press. These methods include legal proceedings, the arrest (or murder by hired assassins) of editors, denial of mailing privileges, the cutting off of paper supplies, etc., etc. Besides, the news services essential to daily newspapers are run by bourgeois wire ser-

vices, while advertisements, without which a large newspaper cannot pay its way, depend on the "good will" of the capitalists. To sum up: through skulduggery and the pressure of capital and the bourgeois state, the bourgeoisie is depriving the revolutionary proletariat of its press.

To combat this the Communist parties must create a new type of periodical press for mass distribution among the workers: first, legal publications that, without calling themselves Communist and without publicizing their links with the party, must learn to make use of any legal opportunity, however slight, just as the Bolsheviks did under the tsar after 1905; second, illegal leaflets, even the briefest and published at irregular intervals, but reprinted at numerous printshops by workers (secretly, or, if the movement has become strong enough, by the revolutionary seizure of printshops), and providing the proletariat with outspoken revolutionary information and revolutionary slogans.

Preparation for the dictatorship of the proletariat is impossible without a revolutionary struggle, into which the masses are drawn, for the freedom of the Communist press.

### III. Correcting the political line—partly also the composition—of parties that belong to the Communist International or wish to join it

14. The degree to which the proletariat in countries most important to world economics and politics is prepared to establish its dictatorship can be seen with the greatest objectivity and precision in the fact that the most influential parties of the Second International—namely, the French Socialist Party, the Independent Social Democratic Party of Germany, the Independent Labour Party of Britain, and the Socialist Party of America—have withdrawn from this Yellow International, and have decided, on certain condi-

tions, to affiliate to the Third International. This proves that not only the vanguard of the revolutionary proletariat but its majority too have begun to come over to our side, convinced by the entire course of events. The main thing now is the ability to consummate this process and to consolidate firmly on organizational terms what has been achieved, so as to be able to advance all along the line, without the slightest wavering.

15. All the activities of the parties mentioned (to which should be added the Socialist party of Switzerland,[8] if the telegraph reports of its decision to join the Third International are true) show—as any periodical of these parties will strikingly confirm—that they are not yet communist, and quite often run directly counter to the fundamental principles of the Third International, namely, the recognition of the dictatorship of the proletariat and soviet power in place of bourgeois democracy.

Accordingly, the Second Congress of the Communist International declares that it cannot immediately accept the affiliation of these parties. It endorses the reply given by the Executive Committee of the Third International to the German "Independents." It confirms its readiness to conduct negotiations with any party that withdraws from the Second International and desires to enter into closer relations with the Third International. It will admit the delegates of such parties in a deliberative capacity to all its congresses and conferences. It sets the following conditions for the complete adhesion of these (and similar) parties to the Communist International:

a) All decisions of all congresses of the Communist International and of its Executive Committee are to be published in all the periodicals of the parties concerned.

b) These decisions are to be discussed at special meetings of all sections or local organizations of the parties.

c) After such discussion, special congresses of the parties are to be convened to sum up the results. This congress must be convened as soon as possible and not more than four months after the Second Congress of the Communist International.[9]

d) The parties are to be purged of elements that continue to act in the spirit of the Second International.

e) All periodical publications of the parties are to be placed under exclusively Communist editorship.[10]

f) Parties that now wish to join the Communist International but have not yet broken radically with their old policies must see to it that two-thirds of the members of their central committees and their central leadership bodies are composed of comrades who spoke out publicly and unambiguously in favor of joining the Communist International before its Second Congress. Exceptions can be made only with the approval of the Executive Committee of the Communist International. The Executive Committee also has the right to make exceptions for the representatives of the Center mentioned in thesis 7.[11]

g) Party members who fundamentally reject the conditions and theses formulated by the Communist International must be expelled. The same also applies to delegates of the special congress.

The Second Congress of the Third International should instruct its Executive Committee formally to accept these and similar parties into the Third International after first ascertaining that all these conditions have actually been met and that the activities of the parties have assumed a Communist character.

16. As to the question of the conduct of communists now holding a minority of the responsible posts in these and similar parties, the Second Congress of the Communist International resolves that, in view of the swiftness

with which a revolutionary spirit is now growing among the masses, it would be undesirable for communists to resign from these parties, as long as they can carry on work within them for the recognition of the dictatorship of the proletariat and soviet power, and as long as it is possible to criticize the opportunists and centrists who still remain in these parties. However, whenever the left wing of a Center party becomes strong enough—and when such action would further the development of the Communist movement—it may leave the party as a unit and form a Communist party.[12]

At the same time, the Second Congress of the Third International should declare in favor of Communist groups and organizations, or groups and organizations sympathizing with communism, joining the Labour Party in Britain, despite its membership in the Second International. As long as this party ensures its affiliated organizations their present freedom of criticism and freedom to carry on work of propaganda, agitation, and organization in favor of the dictatorship of the proletariat and soviet power, and as long as this party preserves the character of a federation of all trade union organizations of the working class, it is imperative for Communists to do everything and to make certain compromises in order to be able to exercise their influence on the broadest masses of the workers, to expose their opportunist leaders from a higher tribune—one in fuller view of the masses—and to hasten the transfer of political power from the direct representatives of the bourgeoisie to the "labor lieutenants of the capitalist class," so that the masses may be more quickly weaned away from their last illusions on this score.

17. Concerning the Socialist Party of Italy, the Second Congress of the Third International considers the revision of the party program adopted by the Bologna con-

gress last year a very positive step on the party's road to communism. The proposals submitted to the National Council of the Socialist Party of Italy in the name of the party's Turin section, as set forth in *L'Ordine Nuovo* of May 8, 1920, correspond to the fundamental principles of the Third International.[13]

Accordingly, the Second Congress of the Third International requests the Socialist Party of Italy to convene its next congress in accordance with its statutes and with the conditions for admission to the Communist International and to discuss there, along with these proposals, all the decisions of the two congresses of the Communist International, especially regarding the questions of the parliamentary fraction, the trade unions, and the noncommunist elements in the party.

18. The Second Congress of the Third International considers as erroneous a number of views on the party's relation to the class and to the masses, as well as the view that it is not obligatory for Communist parties to participate in bourgeois parliaments and in reactionary trade unions, and it has refuted these positions in detail in special decisions of the present congress. They are advocated most fully by the Communist Workers Party of Germany, and partly by the Communist Party of Switzerland, by *Kommunismus,* organ of the East European Secretariat of the Communist International in Vienna, by several Dutch comrades,[14] by several communist organizations in Britain, as for example, the Workers' Socialist Federation, etc., and also by the Industrial Workers of the World in the U.S.A. and the Shop Stewards' committees in Britain, etc.

Nevertheless, the Second Congress of the Third International considers it possible and desirable that those of the above-mentioned organizations that have not yet officially affiliated to the Communist International should do so immediately. For in the present instance, particularly as regards the Industrial Workers of the World in America and Australia, as well as the Shop Stewards' committees in Britain, we are dealing with a profoundly proletarian and mass movement, which in all essentials actually stands by the basic principles of the Communist International. The erroneous views held by these organizations regarding participation in bourgeois parliaments can be explained not so much by the influence of elements coming from the bourgeoisie, who bring their essentially petty-bourgeois views into the movement—views such as anarchists often hold—as by the political inexperience of proletarians who are quite revolutionary and connected with the masses.

For this reason the Second Congress of the Third International requests all Communist organizations and groups in the Anglo-Saxon countries—even if the Industrial Workers of the World and the Shop Stewards' committees do not immediately affiliate to the Third International—to pursue a very friendly policy toward these organizations, to establish closer contacts with them and the masses that sympathize with them, and to explain to them in a friendly spirit—on the basis of the experience of all revolutions, and particularly of the three Russian revolutions of the twentieth century—the erroneousness of their views as set forth above, and not to desist from further efforts to amalgamate with these organizations to form a single Communist party.

19. In this connection the congress draws the attention of all comrades, particularly in the Latin and AngloSaxon countries, to the fact that since the war a profound ideological division has been taking place among anarchists all over the world regarding the attitude to be adopted toward the dictatorship of the proletariat and soviet power. Moreover, a proper understanding of these principles is

particularly to be seen among proletarian elements that have often been impelled toward anarchism by a perfectly legitimate hatred of the opportunism and reformism of the parties of the Second International. That understanding is growing more widespread among them the more familiar they become with the experience of Russia, Finland, Hungary, Latvia, Poland, and Germany.

The congress therefore considers it the duty of all Communists to do everything to help all mass proletarian elements to abandon anarchism and come over to the side of the Third International. The congress points out that one of the criteria for measuring the success of the work of genuinely Communist parties is how able they are to win the genuine proletarian elements away from anarchism.

## CONDITIONS FOR ADMISSION (PART 4)

ZINOVIEV: We will move on to the report of a second commission: on the conditions for joining the Communist International. Comrade Meyer has the floor for the report.

MEYER: The conditions for joining the Communist International, as formulated in Comrade Lenin's theses, were also discussed by the commission on the tasks of the Second Congress. On page 7, five conditions for affiliation are listed.[15] In discussing them, it was noted that the congress had already adopted conditions for joining. So discussions took place in a joint commission, composed of seven members from the Commission on Conditions for Admission and seven from the commission on tasks of the Communist International. This joint commission proposes to the congress that the theses on joining the Communist International be changed somewhat. In section 7 of the conditions for joining, on page 82 of the German edition, Kautsky, Turati, Hillquit, MacDonald, and others are named as notorious reformists. This new commission decided to insert Hilferding as well.

The commission also took up suggestions made here in the plenary and referred to it for consideration. The joint commission adopted the Russian delegation's motion that two-thirds of all central leadership bodies of parties that now want to join the Communist International must be composed of comrades who had already come out in favor of this before the congress of the Communist International. Furthermore, a motion was adopted that the parties that now belong to or want to belong to the Communist International must call a special national congress as soon as possible and at least within four months of the Second Congress of the International to examine all the conditions adopted here. In addition, the commission approved a motion whereby parties that want to belong to the Communist International are obliged to expel members who reject the principles. The same goes for delegates to the special party congress who vote against joining the Communist International.

Today the subcommission of the Commission on Conditions for Admission also took up the decisions of the joint commission and made a few small changes. The Executive Committee is to retain the right to allow exceptions with respect to making up party bodies out of supporters of the Communist International and expelling notorious reformists. The relevant passages now read:

"19. All parties that belong to the Communist International or have applied to join it are required to call a special congress as soon as possible but no later than four months after the Second Congress of the Communist International to consider all these conditions. In doing so, the central leaderships must see to it that all local organizations become acquainted with the resolutions of the Second Congress of the Communist International.

"20. Parties that want to join the Communist International now but have not radically changed their previous policies must, before joining, make certain that not less than two-thirds of the members of their most important central bodies consist of comrades who even before the Second Congress of the Communist International publicly and unambiguously advocated that the party join it. Exceptions are permissible with the consent of the Executive Committee of the Communist International. The Executive Committee also has the right to make exceptions for representatives of the Center tendency mentioned in thesis 7.

"21. Party members who reject on principle the conditions and theses laid down by the Communist International must be expelled from the party. This applies in particular to delegates to the special congress."

The commission, which adopted these changes by majority vote, recommends that you approve them. The theses on the tasks of the Second Congress must make reference to these twenty-one conditions.[16]

ZINOVIEV: I have received two requests to speak, but I suggest we vote without further discussion. (*Adopted with a small minority opposed.*)

## THESES ON THE CONDITIONS FOR ADMISSION

The First Congress of the Communist International did not draw up precise conditions for admission into the Communist International.[17] When the First Congress was convened, only Communist *tendencies* and *groups* existed in most countries.

The Second Congress of the Communist International assembles under different circumstances. Today in most countries there are not merely Communist currents and movements but Communist *parties* and *organizations.*

The Communist International is now frequently approached by parties and groups that only recently belonged to the Second International and now want to join the Communist International, although they have not in fact become communist. The Second International has been definitively smashed. The intermediate parties and the groups of the Center, seeing that the Second International has no prospects at all, try to lean on the Communist International, which is becoming ever stronger. However, they hope to preserve enough "autonomy" to continue their former opportunist or "centrist" policies. The Communist International is becoming rather fashionable.

The desire of some leading Center groups to join the Communist International indirectly confirms that it has won the sympathy of the overwhelming majority of the class-conscious workers of the whole world and is becoming a more powerful force every day. It is in danger of being diluted by vacillating and irresolute groups that have not yet broken with the ideology of the Second International.

Moreover, in some large parties in countries such as Italy, Sweden, Norway, and Yugoslavia,[18] where a majority takes a communist position, there remains to this day a significant reformist and social-pacifist wing. This wing is just waiting for the moment when it can raise its head again and begin actively sabotaging the proletarian revolution, thereby helping the bourgeoisie and the Second International.

No Communist may forget the lessons of the Hungarian soviet republic. The Hungarian proletariat paid dearly for the unification of the Hungarian Communists and the so-called left Social Democrats.[19]

Accordingly, the Second Congress of the Communist International considers it necessary to define very precisely the conditions for admission for new parties and to call to the attention of parties accepted into membership the duties that are incumbent upon them.

The Second Congress of the Communist International establishes the following conditions of membership in the Communist International:

1. *All propaganda* and *agitation* must have a truly communist character and correspond to the program and resolutions of the Communist International.[20] All of the party's publications must be directed by reliable Communists who have demonstrated their dedication to the proletariat's cause. The dictatorship of the proletariat may not be spoken of simply as if it were a stock phrase to be learned by rote. Instead, it must be popularized so that every ordinary working man and woman, every soldier and peasant, can understand the need for it from the facts of everyday life, facts that our press must systematically follow and utilize every single day.

Periodical and nonperiodical publications as well as all party publishing houses must be completely subordinate to the party executive committee, regardless of whether the party as a whole is legal or illegal at any given time. It is impermissible for the publishing houses to misuse their autonomy to pursue policies that do not correspond entirely to those of the party.[21]

In the columns of the newspapers, at public meetings, in the trade unions, in consumer cooperative societies—anywhere that supporters of the Communist International can gain admission—it is necessary to denounce systematically and unmercifully not only the bourgeoisie but also its accomplices: the reformists of every shade.

2. Every organization wishing to join the Communist International must consistently and systematically remove reformists and centrists from all positions of any responsibility in the workers' movement (party organizations, editorial staffs, trade unions, parliamentary fractions, cooperative societies, local governments) and replace them with reliable Communists without being deterred by the prospect that, especially at first, ordinary workers from the masses will replace "experienced" opportunists.

3. In almost every country of Europe and America the class struggle is entering the phase of civil war. Under such conditions the Communists can place no faith in bourgeois legality. It is their duty to create everywhere a parallel organizational apparatus that in the crucial hour can help the party discharge its duty to the revolution. In all countries where a state of siege or emergency laws make it impossible for Communists to carry out all their work legally, it is absolutely necessary that legal and illegal activity be combined.

4. The duty to disseminate communist ideas carries with it a special obligation to conduct vigorous and systematic propaganda in the army.[22] Where emergency laws hinder such agitation, it is to be conducted illegally. Refusal to carry out such work would be tantamount to a betrayal of revolutionary duty and incompatible with membership in the Communist International.

5. Systematic and consistent agitation is necessary in the countryside. The working class cannot be victorious unless it has the support of the rural proletariat and at least a part of the poorest peasants and has, through its policies, neutralized part of the remaining rural population.[23] At the present time, communist work in the countryside is gaining exceptional importance. It must be carried out principally by revolutionary Communist *workers* of

town and country who have ties with the countryside.[24] To renounce this work or to leave it in unreliable, semi-reformist hands is tantamount to renouncing the proletarian revolution.

6. Every party that wishes to belong to the Communist International is duty-bound to expose not only overt social patriotism but also the duplicity and hypocrisy of social pacifism; to explain systematically to the workers that without the revolutionary overthrow of capitalism, no international courts of arbitration, no treaties of any kind curtailing arms production, no manner of "democratic" renovation of the League of Nations will be able to prevent new imperialist wars.

7. Parties wishing to belong to the Communist International are duty-bound to recognize the need for a complete break with reformism and the policies of the Center and must conduct propaganda for this among the broadest layers of the party membership. Without this, no consistent communist policy is possible.

The Communist International demands unconditionally and as an ultimatum that this break be carried out at the earliest possible date. The Communist International cannot accept that notorious opportunists as, for example, Turati, Modigliani, Kautsky, Hilferding, Hillquit, Longuet, and MacDonald should have the right to consider themselves members of the Communist International.[25] That could lead only to the Communist International coming to resemble in large measure the ruined Second International.

8. In countries whose bourgeoisies possess colonies and oppress other nations, it is necessary that the parties have an especially clear and well-defined position on the question of colonies and oppressed nations. Every party wishing to belong to the Communist International is obligated to expose the tricks of "its own" imperialists in

the colonies, to support every liberation movement in the colonies not only in words but in deeds, to demand that the imperialists of its country be driven out of these colonies, to instill in the hearts of the workers of its country a truly fraternal attitude toward the laboring people in the colonies and toward the oppressed nations, and to conduct systematic agitation among its country's troops against all oppression of colonial peoples.

9. Every party wishing to belong to the Communist International must carry out systematic and persistent activity in the trade unions, the workers' and factory committees,[26] the cooperatives, and other mass workers' organizations. In these organizations it is necessary to organize Communist cells that win the unions and other organizations to the cause of communism through persistent and unremitting work. In their daily work everywhere the cells are duty-bound to expose the betrayal by the social patriots and the fickleness of the Center. The Communist cells must be completely subordinate to the party as a whole.

10. Every party that belongs to the Communist International has the obligation to wage a tenacious struggle against the Amsterdam "International" of Yellow trade unions. It must conduct forceful propaganda among workers organized in unions on the need to break with the Yellow Amsterdam International. It must use all available means to support the emerging international association of Red trade unions affiliated to the Communist International.

11. Parties that wish to belong to the Communist International have the duty to review the individual composition of their parliamentary fractions, removing all unreliable elements from them, and to subordinate these fractions to the parties' executive committees not just in words but in deeds, demanding that each Communist member of

parliament subordinate all of his activity to the interests of truly revolutionary propaganda and agitation.

12. Parties belonging to the Communist International must be organized on the basis of the principle of democratic *centralism.* In the present epoch of intensified civil war, the Communist Party will be able to fulfill its duty only if it is organized in the most centralized way possible and governed by iron discipline,[27] and if its central leadership, sustained by the confidence of the party membership, is strong, authoritative, and endowed with the fullest powers.

13. Communist parties of countries in which Communists pursue their work legally must from time to time carry out purges (reregistrations) of the party membership in order to systematically cleanse the party of the petty-bourgeois elements that worm their way into it.

14. Every party that wishes to belong to the Communist International is obligated to render unconditional assistance to every soviet republic struggling against the forces of counterrevolution. Communist parties must conduct unambiguous propaganda aimed at preventing the shipment of war matériel to enemies of the soviet republics. In addition, they must use every possible means to carry out propaganda, etc.—legally or illegally—among troops sent to strangle workers' republics.

15. Parties that still have their old Social Democratic programs are required to change them as rapidly as possible and to formulate a new, communist program that corresponds to the specific conditions in their country and is in keeping with the resolutions of the Communist International. As a rule, the program of each party belonging to the Communist International must be approved by a regular congress of the Communist International or by the Executive Committee. If the Executive Commit-

tee of the Communist International does not approve a party's program, that party has the right to appeal to the congress of the Communist International.

16. All decisions by congresses of the Communist International as well as by its Executive Committee are binding on all parties that belong to the Communist International. The Communist International, working under conditions of most acute civil war, must be organized in a far more centralized way than was the Second International. At the same time, of course, in all their activity the Communist International and its Executive Committee must take into account the diverse conditions under which each party has to struggle and work, adopting universally binding decisions only on questions in which such decisions are possible.

17. Taking all this into consideration, all parties that wish to belong to the Communist International must change their name. Every party that wants to belong to the Communist International must bear the name: *Communist* Party of such and such country (Section of the Communist International). The question of name is not just a formality but a matter of great political importance. The Communist International has declared war on the whole bourgeois world and all Yellow, Social Democratic parties. It is necessary that the difference between the Communist parties and the old, official "Social Democratic" or "Socialist" parties, which have betrayed the banner of the working class, be clear to every ordinary toiler.

18. The leading publications of parties in all countries are required to print all important official documents of the Executive Committee of the Communist International.[28]

19. All parties that belong to the Communist International or have applied to join it are required to call a special congress as soon as possible but no later than

four months after the Second Congress of the Communist International to consider all these conditions. In doing so, the central leaderships must see to it that all local organizations become acquainted with the resolutions of the Second Congress of the Communist International.[29]

20. Parties that want to join the Communist International now but have not radically changed their previous policies must, before joining, make certain that not less than two-thirds of the members of their central committees and of all their most important central bodies consist of comrades who even before the Second Congress of the Communist International publicly and unambiguously advocated that the party join it. Exceptions are permissible with the consent of the Executive Committee of the Communist International. The Executive Committee also has the right to make exceptions for representatives of the Center tendency mentioned in thesis 7.

21. Party members who reject on principle the conditions and theses laid down by the Communist International must be expelled from the party. This applies in particular to delegates to the special congress.[30]

ZINOVIEV: Now we must vote on the twenty-one conditions as they are now formulated. (*Adopted with 2 votes cast against.*)

## OTHER BUSINESS

ZINOVIEV: Now we come to the question of the statutes. Here only one change was proposed, namely, that the Executive Committee be set up with five representatives from the country that is the seat of the committee and ten representatives from other countries. On behalf of the Russian party, I would like to propose that we say not ten representatives, but between ten and thirteen. As we put together the list, it turned out that a number of significant parties would be excluded from participating in the Executive Committee if we said ten. If we say between ten and thirteen, then we have a committee of at most eighteen members.

If no one wishes to speak, then we will vote on whether ten to thirteen representatives of other parties should be included. (*The new proposal is unanimously adopted.*)

Now we must vote on the statutes with this change. (*From the floor: "The statutes were adopted yesterday."*)

Then we do not need to vote on them again. Now we want to decide where the seat of the committee should be in the next period, until another world congress decides otherwise. Russia has been proposed. (*It is unanimously decided that the committee will remain in Russia for the next period.*)

That leaves the women and youth questions. We propose to refer these two questions to the new Executive Committee to be decided with the participation of women and youth representatives. We do this not because we do not think they are important—they are very important—but because we cannot decide them here in half an hour. That is why we want to leave these questions, together with that of representation from the women's and youth organizations, to the new committee, which will be somewhat expanded.

(*It is decided, with a minority against, to refer the woman and youth questions to the committee.*)[31]

Now we come to the report of the Commission on Parliamentarism.

WOLFSTEIN: The commission has yet to vote on the changes proposed by Comrades Levi and Bukharin. All commission members have expressed their support. We put before you the theses as discussed in the plenary with the corresponding amendments. We should vote on them now. (*Adopted*)

MEYER: Graziadei's motion on cooperatives still needs to be added to the theses [on the agrarian question]. The commission agrees on this. If the congress agrees, then the question is settled. I do not think that there will be any debate on this.[32]

ZINOVIEV: I move that the commission work out the final wording. (*Adopted*)

ZINOVIEV: Now Pestaña has a motion on the question of Esperanto.

PESTAÑA: Whereas the work of world congresses such as the present one is made much more difficult by the translation of everything said into several languages, I propose that in the future every speaker use whatever language they find easiest, and that translation take place only into the auxiliary language Esperanto. This language is readily learned and quite appropriate to our needs. We can save much time and labor by using it for translation.

ZINOVIEV: With Comrade Pestaña's agreement we propose referring the motion to the new committee. (*Adopted*)

With that we have finished the agenda.

Tomorrow we plan to hold a ceremonial session of the congress together with the Moscow soviet and the All-Russia Central Executive Committee of the Workers', Soldiers', and Peasants' Soviets, in order to evaluate the congress, deliver a few speeches, and then close the congress. The session will take place tomorrow afternoon at four o'clock in the Bolshoi Theater.

MÜNZENBERG: Unfortunately it was not possible for the congress to take up the youth question. For this reason we have decided to call a conference of the youth representatives tomorrow at twelve noon, and we invite to it all comrades interested in the youth movement. It will begin promptly at twelve o'clock in the Kremlin in the Central Executive Committee building.

RADEK: Since the delegates will probably want their passports, I ask that for their own peace of mind they pay attention to the following: tomorrow the committee will discuss the ordering of the "evacuation." One comrade will make all the arrangements, so you can relax in the hotel.

ZINOVIEV: The question of the [Executive] Committee is not yet settled. We decided how many parties, but not yet which. I have a preliminary list I would like to read to you:

Russia (five), Britain, Germany, France, America, Italy, Austria, Hungary, Bulgaria, Yugoslavia, Scandinavia, Poland, Finland, the East.[33]

These are the parties that should have the right to have one member each with decisive vote on the committee.

WIJNKOOP: I want to say that I cannot agree with this list. The Netherlands has been excluded from the Executive Committee. I have already given the arguments for including the Netherlands. I think the Netherlands is the only real, fighting revolutionary party that has been excluded from the committee. I will not go into this matter and hope that the committee will rethink it. If you persist in not giving the Netherlands a vote on the committee, then I maintain my protest.

RADEK: We have exchanged so many unpleasant words with the Dutch comrades during the congress that it is painful for me to have to speak once again in opposition to Comrade Wijnkoop's protest. The Netherlands is not on the list proposed to the congress of those to be represented on the Executive Committee, not for reasons of political orientation but for purely objective reasons of party size. The political current expressed by and large by the Dutch party is also represented by the American and a portion of the British delegations. Which countries are on the list? They are either countries with a big revolutionary movement, like Russia, Germany, and Italy; countries that already were soviet republics, like Hungary and Finland; Poland, which has a thirty-year-old mass revolutionary movement; or countries like Britain, France, and America, whose revolutionary movements, it is true, are still weak, but that are of decisive importance for the International's politics, and with whose representatives we have to consult on every matter.

The Dutch Communist Party has merits that none of us would want to belittle. It was one of the first parties that dared to split from the Social Democratic party, and the Dutch comrades stood true to the banner of communism in a difficult situation. No one can take that away from them, and we recognize it fully. But it is a small party that does not play a decisive role in the international situation. It would perhaps be considered if it could claim theoretical forces. But Comrades Pannekoek and Gorter's group is outside of the Dutch movement, as Wijnkoop said. The Dutch party's forces are too few to permit it to put some at the International's disposal. When the German comrades turned to them in great need, they could provide no help. The proposal is based on purely objective considerations, without the least animosity toward the Dutch comrades, with whom we hope to struggle together as comrades, despite differences of opinion. We hope that they will soon win more forces and will have some to spare for the International.[34]

WIJNKOOP: I thank Comrade Radek for his friendly opposition. But I must say that we do not want to be honorary members of the Executive Committee. That is not what we demand; otherwise we certainly would have it.

We are among the Communist parties with the most integrity and have always done what Communists must do. We make this demand because we are a communist force, as the committee recognized at another time. First, why did it set up an auxiliary bureau in Amsterdam? This matter was discussed in the committee. Everyone can make mistakes, and I will not go into that. We only did what we were assigned to do as Communists, and we cannot be reproached for this. We were given this bureau because of our importance, which now no one has heard of.

Radek spoke of Gorter and Pannekoek. But Pannekoek did not work in the Dutch Communist movement. Maybe in Germany, but not in the Netherlands. In any case, you cannot gauge the communist strength of a party by two people, by Gorter and Pannekoek. Those who know the *Tribune* well, know that not Gorter and Pannekoek, but Van Ravesteyn, Ceton, and I were always its editors, and that together with other comrades, we led the *Tribune*. That is the strength of the Dutch Communist movement, and it still exists.

It has been said that the movement there is not large. It seems to me that too much is being made of big numbers. Although our numbers are small, we are a disciplined, revolutionary party that holds great influence in our country. That is shown by the fact that we have a Communist daily newspaper. It is shown by the fact that many of our members sit on municipal councils, and that we exercise a great deal of influence in the union movement.

In my view the committee must reconsider this matter. It should have given us a seat on the Executive Committee—particularly in light of our conduct at this congress. We did not always agree with the committee. We do not always have to agree. In the discussions that take place in the committee, the different viewpoints must receive an attentive hearing. I think that the committee has every reason to give the Netherlands a vote. I hope that it does so. Otherwise, I must protest.

MARING: We agree that even though the Eastern peoples do not yet have an organized party they should be represented on the Executive Committee with decisive vote. This recognizes that the East is of great importance for the Communist International. Nevertheless, I would like to make the following comment. I do not think that the East is sufficiently represented in the Communist International with one delegate. The conditions in the Middle and Far East are completely different, so that it would be very difficult to find someone who can adequately represent the interests of both parts of Asia. Also, we fear that the comrades here, the Russian and perhaps other comrades, know the delegates from the Middle East better than those of the Far East. Therefore I would like to ask that our part of Asia, which is the most important for our movement and for imperialism, be given a representative on the committee. Thus we ask for not one but two representatives for the Eastern peoples, so that the Middle and Far East can each send a representative with decisive vote to the committee. I hope this will be possible, and that the congress will thereby decide to transform Lenin and Roy's theses in the next period into a reality, one that will be of great significance for the International.

ROY: For the same reasons, I ask that two delegates to the committee be approved, because it is a matter of our interests being represented.

MILOS VANEK [SOCIAL DEMOCRATIC PARTY OF CZECHOSLOVAKIA (LEFT WING)]: For the reasons given by both the previous speakers, I propose that the congress adopt the following motion: "The Executive Committee is empowered to expand its membership by cooptation in order to allow representation of parties whose strength and numbers gives them a world importance for the social revolution." I need not further substantiate this motion, because I think that this flexibility, allowing the Executive Committee to expand its ranks, corresponds with the overall mandate that it has already been accorded.

ZINOVIEV: On the question of the Netherlands, I would like to say on Radek's behalf that Wijnkoop makes it sound like a slight to the old movement and the old comrades if the Netherlands is not also given a seat on the committee. Our intention, of course, was not to treat anyone unfairly, but we cannot include every party. There is also nothing more to be said against the Middle East. Someone said that an exception was made only for Scandinavia, but there we grouped together a number of countries. We have not increased the number of representatives from the East, not because we want to curb anyone's rights but because we want a committee, not a congress. If a strong party comes that fulfills every condition, the committee should have the right to make an exception and admit such a party.

WALTHER BRINGOLF [SOCIAL DEMOCRATIC PARTY OF SWITZERLAND (LEFT WING)]: I would like to say a few more words about Switzerland. Our situation is not such that we could demand a seat on the Executive Committee, although it would be very desirable to obtain one. As Humbert-Droz already said earlier, Switzerland should be taken into account in filling out the committee because it is going through a clarification that makes it very important to be in direct contact with Russia. We went into this in our report to the committee and hope that it will be adopted.[35]

(*A motion is adopted to include the Netherlands, the Middle East, and the Far East. Vanek's motion is also adopted.*)

(*The following list is voted on and adopted: Russia (five), Britain, Germany, France, America, Italy, Austria, Hungary,*

*Bulgaria, Yugoslavia, Scandinavia, the Netherlands, Poland, Finland, the Far East, and the Middle East.*)[36]

ZINOVIEV: That ends the matter. We have on hand several drafts of manifestos. One is a draft manifesto to the KAPD. We owe them an answer, after their delegation walked away from the congress.

(*It is decided to refer the draft letter to the KAPD to the Executive Committee.*)[37]

We intend to issue a major political manifesto, which is almost finished. Comrade Trotsky, who drew up the manifesto of the First Congress, is doing most of the work. We hope to read out the manifesto tomorrow, but should that not be possible, we will give the committee a mandate on this matter as well and publish the manifesto over the signature of all the delegations, perhaps with two delegates from each country.[38] (*Adopted*)

Finally, I want to inform you that the first session of the new Executive Committee will take place tomorrow morning at eleven o'clock. I want to ask all delegations to make a preliminary choice of their representatives. The central committees of the relevant parties can substitute and send other delegates, but first the delegations must send their representatives.[39]

This session is adjourned.

(*The congress ends by singing the "Internationale" and with cheers for the Soviet republic and the world revolution.*)

SESSION 17

AUGUST 7, 1920

# Closing rally

KALININ: Comrades, I declare open the joint session of the Second Congress of the Communist International, the All-Russia Soviet Central Executive Committee, the Moscow soviet, and the plenary session of the trade unions and factory committees.[1] (*Applause; the "Internationale" is sung.*)

Comrades, the workers and peasants of the Russian Soviet Republic can be proud and happy that the Second Congress of the Communist International is taking place in our country. Comrades, the moderate Second International, which has a relationship with the bourgeoisie marked by some degree of trust—or at least by an absence of hostility—prevailed for twenty-five years. But it could not meet in Russia. It met in western Europe, in rented halls. It had no access to rooms like those where the Second Congress of the Communist International met. As you know, the Second Congress met in gilded halls, in the halls of the great Kremlin palace, where only recently the power of Russian tsarism was on display. And as this congress began, the death of the old order and the coming to life of the new proletarian order took place before our very eyes.

Comrades, we greet the Second Congress of the Communist International most especially because it frees us to a certain extent from the political responsibility that the Russian working class and the Communist Party of Russia have carried on their shoulders to this point. For some time we have thought and confidently hoped that the revolutionary energy and labor of the Russian proletariat would be transferred to the international proletariat, which would carry it forward. We thought we could count on its help soon. And today, comrades, in the course of the Second Congress, we see that already a certain portion of the revolutionary work, a part of the burden has been transferred from the shoulders of the Russian proletariat to the shoulders of the international working class. That, comrades, is the greatest service done by the western European proletariat. We need not mention here that at different times the French and British proletariat has halted the war supplies intended for White Poland. We saw the highest expression of solidarity during the days when the revolutionary committee was formed in Poland. While we participate in revolutionary work and stand unrelentingly in the fire of revolution, we pay too little heed to events of the greatest import that signify a new chapter in the history of the workers' movement. Undoubtedly the appearance of the Polish proletariat, at the moment White Poland is combating the Russian Soviet Republic, is a new stage, a new phase in the revolutionary struggle.

Besides the Russian, no other proletariat has yet managed to seize power at the moment when war raged most fiercely. But now we see how the policies of the Russian proletariat are being passed on, how the Polish proletariat takes up the struggle against the Polish bourgeoisie. It is an event of great import; not only historians but political leaders will later learn from this.

We heartily greet the delegates of the Communist International as the best representatives of the proletarian classes that want to help us. We hope they return as soon as possible to the international proletariat and that soon we will be united with the international proletariat in a common front of struggle.

Long live the Communist International!

Long live the Second Congress of the Communist International! (*Applause*)

The representative of the Scottish workers, Comrade Gallacher, has the floor.

GALLACHER: (*Speaks in English.*)

KALININ: Comrade Radek has the floor to translate.

RADEK: Comrades, allow me first of all to say a word about Comrade Gallacher, who spoke here. Moscow workers are less familiar with him than they should be. He is a worker from an area where Britain's huge munitions factories are located and was one of the main leaders of the revolutionary struggle in this region during the war. Together with Comrade McLaine, Comrade Gallacher organized an enormous struggle that was so successful that the British government ministers cannot speak of Comrade Gallacher without losing their composure.

Comrade Gallacher says:

GALLACHER: Just now, as the delegates of the Second Congress are already departing, I have received word that the British government is preparing a new attack against Soviet Russia. It intends to act in the guise of a defender of Poland's independence. This same British government that plunders and enslaves Ireland, India, and Egypt dares to say that it will act as the defender of Poland's independence. This independence is not at all threatened by the Red Army. The British government is shamelessly exploiting the banner of Poland's independence, fighting to block the uprising of the Polish working masses, to make impossible the creation of soviet power in Warsaw.

I am convinced that the British government's threats will not frighten the Russian workers. The Russian revolution has created a powerful Red Army. The entire working class of Russia must back the Red Army as one man and think only of supporting it, so that this army can break the last resistance of the enemy forces and achieve final victory. You can count not only on the Red Army but on other armies that will come forward in defense of Soviet Russia, that is, the armies of the western European proletariat, who in the last few years have come to know Soviet Russia rather well. They see Soviet Russia as their homeland, since it is the first country of the rising sun of socialism. Upon returning to Britain, I myself and my comrades will become a link calling upon the British workers to fight not only to defend Soviet Russia but also to seize power. (*Applause*)

I know the immense obstacles that block the path of the British revolutionaries. For the compromisers, still strong in Britain, the blood of the working class is cheap, blood that they spilled in the cause of the bourgeoisie. When the liberation of the proletariat is at stake, they say, "Be careful, avoid bloodletting, do not make sacrifices." But however strong these people may be, these bureaucrats in the trade union movement, however powerful they may be in Parliament, I am convinced that the British working class will send them to the devil, because it is ever more convinced that there is no way out of the situation other than the path the Russian proletariat took two and a half years ago.

On behalf of myself and my comrades I pledge that upon our return, the British comrades will have but one thought: how to help Soviet Russia in its struggles, how to make clear to the working class that here was born the great Red Army that the Russian proletariat relies upon, and that the British workers must unite with the Russians for common victory over world imperialism. (*Applause*)

KALININ: Comrades, Britain is striving to push White Finland into a war with Soviet Russia. I recognize the finest representative of the Finnish workers, Comrade Manner.

KULLERVO MANNER [COMMUNIST PARTY OF FINLAND]: (*Speaks in Finnish.*)

KALININ: Comrade Rahja has the floor to translate.

JUKKA RAHJA [COMMUNIST PARTY OF FINLAND]: Comrade Manner, the delegate of the Communist Party of Finland to the Second Congress of the Communist International, is one of the senior leaders of the workers' movement in Finland. Even when Finland was under the banner of Social Democracy, Comrade Manner was one of the best representatives of the workers' movement. When the Finnish workers had 103 out of 200 seats in the national assembly,[2] he was its chairman. In 1918 Comrade Manner was chairman of the Council of People's Commissars in socialist Finland, which fell under the blows of German imperialism. He says:

MANNER: I greet you and through you Russia's revolutionary proletariat. I do so at a time when the imperialists of the entire world, under the leadership of the British government and British capital, are again preparing a final blow to smash Soviet Russia. For this blow, they will bring to bear all the forces at their disposal, especially the small border areas, which like watchdogs await the master's command. At the very moment when the Finnish bourgeoisie is negotiating peace with the Russian Soviet

Federated Socialist Republic in Dorpat [Tartu], Britain is trying to influence the White Guard troops, trying to induce them to attack Petrograd.

Two years ago, in 1918, the Finnish proletariat was the first to answer the Russian proletariat's call and begin its revolutionary struggle alongside the Russian proletariat. At that time the Finnish proletariat had no idea how to carry out a revolution and suffered a defeat. But the Finnish proletariat, defeated two years ago, has learned now, under the frightful blows of the terror, that to win it must have a revolutionary, tightly knit organization. Such an organization, small but well organized, now exists in Finland. On behalf of the revolutionary proletariat of Finland, I declare that if the Finnish bourgeoisie dares to carry out Britain's instructions and attack Petrograd, the revolutionary proletariat of Finland will deal it a blow from the rear. (*Applause*) The two years of the terrible White Terror have taught the Finnish proletariat one thing: a small country, a country that can barely be seen on the map, has in the international revolutionary struggle at least one destiny—to die, if its death can help the working class of the entire world to victory. The Finnish proletariat will know how to do this. (*Applause*)

KALININ: Comrade Levi, member of the congress and representative of the Communist Party of Germany (Spartacus League), has the floor.

LEVI: (*Speaks in German.*)

KALININ: Comrade Radek has the floor to translate.

RADEK: Comrades, Comrade Levi has led the entire illegal work of the Communist Party of Germany after the deaths of Comrades Rosa Luxemburg and Karl Liebknecht. He says:

LEVI: World capital thinks it ended the World War at Versailles. But now, after four years of war and one and a half years after the "end" of this war, the whole world is still where it was in August 1914. Again it stands on the eve of a great war. This war may well break out between Soviet Russia and the Entente, but it cannot leave Germany on the sidelines. It will draw Germany into the struggle, causing the German proletariat and bourgeoisie to participate in solving the major questions before the world.

The German bourgeoisie returned from the war defeated. It expected a handsome sum from British capital in order to turn once again against the German proletariat. But now this proletariat is not the same as it was in 1914, when it accepted without protest the decision of the bourgeoisie that sent its sons to the battlefield in the bourgeoisie's cause. Then it still saw no way forward of its own. The German proletariat lost millions of its sons on the battlefield. Now it knows that capitalism means death and poverty. When it returned from the four and a half years of war forced on it by the bourgeoisie, it found on the streets of Germany the marks of the spilled blood of the proletariat, for whose liberation Rosa Luxemburg and Karl Liebknecht had fallen. The proletariat understood that there is no salvation other than in revolutionary war; otherwise slavery will be reestablished. This proletariat has already learned to fight. Although it has not yet been able to take power into its hands, it certainly knows how to use the means at its disposal.

Hundreds and thousands have been thrown out of work. Conditions are terrible for the proletariat, and it will now have to choose between its ruin and a fight against the entire capitalist world. The moment the Entente dares incite Germany against Soviet Russia, the moment they try to reach White Poland through Germany, the German proletariat will understand that the decisive hour has struck, that it must make its stand for the world revolution. I am deeply convinced that the German working class will do this without hesitation, because the struggle to save Soviet Russia is the struggle of the German proletariat against destitution and slavery. I am convinced that the cry that resounds through Russia, the cry "Long live Soviet Russia," will find a loud response among the millions of the German proletarian masses. And if the Red Army, in its battle against the White army of Poland, approaches Germany's borders, it will hear from the other side, over the bayonets, a cry of the German proletariat, the cry "Long live Soviet Russia!" (*Applause*)

KALININ: Comrade Radek has the floor as representative of the Polish proletariat.

RADEK: Comrades, I am convinced that our Red Army's capacity to deal blows to the Polish estate owners attacking Soviet Russia will continue. I am convinced that no efforts by Polish capital or the Polish estate owners can strangle the Polish proletariat.

In the last few days we received news that Pilsudski's government, the government of bankrupts, has been trying to halt the course of events by throwing hundreds more Communists into prison. Most of the leaders of the Polish Communist movement known to us are now under lock and key. The Polish government is threatening them and their families, saying that if the Polish White armies have to evacuate Warsaw, they will leave behind in the city the bodies of the Polish Communists, just as they previously murdered our old comrades, Wesolowski and Fabierkewicz. This desperate cry of the Polish bourgeoisie is exactly what proves that the Red Army is threatening its rule. Even more, it shows that the Polish working class is very well aware that far from threatening the independence of the Polish people, Russia will help it break the chains with which the capitalists of Poland and the Entente have shackled it.

Today Poland is an absolutely dependent country. Today even the Polish bourgeoisie admits that its army gets its weaponry from the Entente, that its army is fed by the bread supplied by the Entente so that Poland can fight. But the campaign that Soviet Russia is conducting against White Poland is supporting Poland, not conquering it. It is the assistance of Russia's working class, which for twenty years fought in alliance with Poland's working class against its opponents and now wants to reunite with the Polish proletariat. There was a time when the Polish insurgents, trying to link up with the Russian revolutionaries, raised the slogan "For our freedom and yours." We have not buried this slogan. Now we are striding to victory, so that together we may, with our own hands and our own strength, get the work under way in the devastated countries to build the temple of socialism.

Comrades, I am firmly convinced that the Polish proletariat, which all along fought side by side with the Petrograd and the Moscow proletariat in the front ranks of the Russian revolution, will prove in action that it knows how to deal with the terrible, savage pressure of the world bourgeoisie. I am certain that our Red Army, which is bearing the full weight of the struggle and whose powerful blows are coming to the aid of the Polish proletariat, will find there iron divisions of veteran Polish workers, steeled in struggle, marching, I am firmly convinced, as your allies until the final victory. (*Applause*)

TROTSKY: (*Thundering ovation; the "Internationale" is sung.*) Comrades, the Second Congress of the Communist International convened one and a half years after the First Congress. A year and a half is only a few months, but these months have more historical content than whole years did previously. For us the Second Congress of the Communist International is not just a periodic event or an international roll call. Comrades, on the path leading upward, over obstacles and chasms, we must take a look back, without letting the enemy out of our sight, to determine the path we have traveled. We must erect signposts on the road before us and advance without losing time. If we look back now on these seventeen or eighteen months between the first and second congresses of the International and most carefully examine our consciousness, our revolutionary conscience, we have the right to say that the path we charted at the First Congress of the International of the world commune was the correct one, and that when we scored successes, they were achieved along this path. When the world proletariat suffered defeats and occasionally had to retreat, it was because it did not take the path indicated by the Communist International.

The eighteen months that have passed since the First Congress have drawn a line in blood under this entire period of humanity's development. This epoch had its laws, its methods, its uniformity, its world relations, its alliances, its struggle, its lies, the democratic lie of official doctrines, the lie of the church. The World War drew a balance sheet on all this. And the bourgeois classes, who called the peoples out for this world slaughter, simultaneously promised them a new dispensation, a new order, a new regime.

But what do Europe and the entire world show us? What do they look like after the World War? In what condition have they emerged from the workshops of the Versailles treaty? The bourgeois order has no secure point of support. Everything is in motion, all the foundations are shaking, all the bourgeoisie's state programs canceled, all international associations torn apart. And the bourgeoisie, trembling at what tomorrow will bring, searches in vain for a way out of this situation, created by centuries of plunder and rape.

England, France, and the United States promised to give the peoples a world association, the "League of Nations," that would put an end to imperialist collisions, to international wars. And now we have before us the League of Nations. Barely was it out of the diplomats' chancelleries when its own creator, the American president Wilson, shrank back from it in fright.[3]

Comrades, only recently, ten or twelve months ago, all the leaders of the Second International greeted Wilson's plans and called upon the workers to support them. Our International, on the contrary, had already declared a year and a half ago in Moscow that Wilson's campaign was an attempt by the American plutocracy, the New York Stock Exchange, to subordinate Europe and the entire world to itself, that the League of Nations would be nothing but a world corporation headed by the United States. American capital is accustomed to extending itself through combinations and to pulling ever-increasing millions upon millions of people into the reach of its exploitation. And it tried to extend its conditions to Europe, Asia, and the entire world.

But when Wilson came from his big American province to Europe and ran head-on into the whole world's life-and-death questions, he saw that the helm was in British hands. Britain has the strongest fleet, the most extensive transoceanic cables, the richest experience in matters of world plunder and rape. And this small-town American, Wilson, with the dollar's favorable exchange rate not only tucked in his pocket but imprinted on his forehead, who thought that his Fourteen Points would become the gospel of the world, ran into the British fleet, and into something even more threatening: he ran into Soviet Russia and communism. So the aggrieved American apostle returned to the White House in Washington, to his Sinai. However, comrades, we should not assume that this signifies renouncing world domination. American capital has no other choice.

While American capital was in the opening stage of accumulation, expansion, and liberation, it advanced its theory, the Monroe Doctrine, which reads, "America for the Americans," that is, let no one dare mix in the affairs of America, where American capital alone reigns, exploits, and robs.

American capital found the borders of the Americas, which it had made its colony, too constricting. As American heavy industry rose up during the war like a huge pillar to the heavens, American capital discarded the slogan "America for the Americans," or better, changed it to read, "Not just America for the Americans, but the whole world for the Americans." Then it sent its apostle Wilson out with a new dispensation. We know that Wilson did not accomplish his mission. But the mission remains to be accomplished and now the American oligarchy draws its conclusion and says, "Our fleet is weaker than Great Britain's by so many tons and so many guns of this and that caliber." And the American naval war department works out a new program that is supposed to make the American fleet stronger than Britain's by the year 1925—some say sooner, in three years.

But what does that mean? Britain's strength lies in its fleet, its ships. Britain watches over all the sea-lanes, and that gives it the power to rob the world. Britain's naval program consists of its fleet being stronger at all times than the combined fleets of the two next largest naval powers. Now America with its wonderful dollar, its rate sky-high on the foreign exchanges, says, "In three years my fleet must be stronger than Britain's." So for British imperialism, the question is posed: To be or not to be.

That means further that Britain and the United States are steering at full steam toward a new, big, bloody conflict, because in the world of imperialist states there cannot be two masters. The crown of world domination must in the end belong to Britain or America, if the world proletariat does not take it from them first. And after four years of terrible world war, which laid waste the powerful states of central Europe, devastated Europe, and ruined the entire world, we see how a new, more powerful struggle is being prepared on the bones of the fallen.

France is Soviet Russia's main enemy, the most bitter, rabid enemy of the world proletariat. It now considers itself the victor. Actually, the simpletons, the petty bourgeoisie, the social patriots, and a deluded section of the workers think that France has won. That is a cruel delusion. Long before German imperialism was defeated, Austria-Hungary was a beaten land. It was maintained by German militarism, just as German imperialism, later, was maintained by the Entente. And France today is one of the most exhausted and ruined of the independent countries of the world. Of course France can plunder in the Black Sea, but only until it is Britain's turn. France can dictate laws to little Belgium, which it has made into its province, but with respect to Great Britain, France itself is nothing but a larger Belgium. Naturally France would be economically and militarily defenseless without American and British support, but in its petty-bourgeois mindlessness it nevertheless raises claims to mastery and thinks that it will play the role of chairman and arbitrator between the United States and Britain. The United States did not even join the League of Nations. And France, almost on its knees, had to beg for alms, for assurance of its state independence.

And what about the little nations, the little states? Freedom and independence were promised them, but dominant Britain has laid its claim upon them all—on Finland as on White Estonia and Latvia. What is left of the independence of Sweden and Norway? It has disappeared. What does the Baltic Sea represent? A bay in which Britain takes little outings. What does the Indian Ocean represent, ringed as it is by peoples subject to Britain? What with Egypt, Persia, Afghanistan, Baluchistan, and India, the Indian Ocean has become a British lake.

From the body of Austria-Hungary, from the old tsarist Russia, a whole number of little states have been carved. They are not at all viable, yet the Entente and the League of Nations, that is Britain, do not allow them to die—for now. We have a crucified and mangled Austria. We have Hungary, which made the heroic attempt to lead central Europe out of the chaos, to take the great road of soviet federation, that is, a fraternal alliance, economic, cultural, and in every other way, of the victorious workers. It was trampled and thrown back into chaos.

We have Poland, that wretched Poland, whose liberation fills the first pages of the history of the First International. It was created by dying imperialism for its sordid goals and tasks. This democratic republic, goal of the struggle of entire generations of Polish revolutionaries who fled tsarism in great waves and fought and died on all the barricades of the revolution, this democratic Poland is today a dirty and bloody tool in the hands of French capital. Comrades, just as the First International in its struggle against tsarism inscribed an independent Poland in the first pages of its history, so too Russia, freed from tsarism, now fulfills its great mission and gives the crucified, ravished Poland back to the Polish workers and the Polish peasants. (*Applause*)

From every parliamentary rostrum there is talk of Europe's economic reconstruction. There is no greater lie than this. In the year and a half that has passed since our first congress, Europe has been unable to right itself. It is a great deal poorer and more hopeless than it was, and with it the entire world. Can Europe be reconstructed without Russian raw materials, without Russian grain? Can Europe be reconstructed without German technology, without the German working class? That is not possible. Upon returning home, the representatives of all lands will say, "Workers of Europe and the entire world, on the basis of the little that we saw, we testify that once imperialism leaves Soviet Russia in peace, if we help Soviet Russia with our technology, even only on a small scale, then in two or three, at most five years, Soviet Russia, precisely because it is a soviet republic based on the principles of communism, will give you six times more grain and raw materials than tsarist, bourgeois Russia gave."

Hot on the tracks of victory, Anglo-French capital believed that boundless colonial territories lay before it. Formerly tsarism was Britain's competitor in Asia, and Germany was an even greater competitor of Britain's on the world market. Germany is defeated. Germany has been nailed to the cross. Austria even more so. And Anglo-French capital believes that the colonies begin immediately to the east: from the German people, subject to France, right on through Soviet Russia. Overrun Soviet Russia, seize Russian raw materials and Russian grain, force German workers to work like slaves to transform Russian raw materials into finished products that Anglo-French capital will control. That is the dazzling program of the League of Nations in its first period.

It tried to accomplish that. It tried to overthrow the Soviet republic, to bring our steppes, our seas, forests, our underground riches under its control and to use German coal and German labor to process it. One and a half years of hard fighting have passed, and with justifiable pride we can say to our western European brothers: Your bourgeoisie did not overthrow us. We live still, and we receive you in Moscow.

And that happened not only thanks to the powerful efforts of the Russian working class and the army it created. We know our efforts and our sacrifices, and now the delegates of the world working class are better acquainted with them. But we must say that we held out mainly because we felt and were aware of the growing help in Europe, America, and all parts of the world. Every strike of the Scottish proletariat on the Clyde, every movement in the cities and towns of Ireland, where flies not only the green flag of Irish nationalism but also the red flag of the proletarian struggle, every strike, every protest, every uprising in any city in Europe, America, and Asia, the powerful movement of Britain's colonial slaves in India and the growth in the development of consciousness, the growth of one central slogan, the slogan "Soviet world federation"—that is what gave us the certainty that we are on the right path, so that in the darkest hours, when we were surrounded on all sides, when it seemed that we would be strangled and executed, we could say: We are not alone. The proletariat of Europe and Asia and the entire world is with us. We will not give up, we will stand firm.

And we stood firm. (*Applause*)

Without Russia and without Germany, Europe cannot be reconstructed. In order to reconstruct Germany, it must be allowed to live, to feed itself, to work. But if Germany, crucified and oppressed, is not allowed to live, to feed itself, and to work, then it will rise up against French imperialism. French imperialism knows only *one* commandment—pay up! Germany must pay! Russia must pay! Therefore these French profiteers are prepared to put to the torch all four corners of the earth just to get their interest payments. They cannot allow Germany to work, because a working, upright Germany means an independent Germany, which will be against them.

They have but one recipe to achieve the conditions of the Versailles treaty. This recipe is the Senegalese, the African Negroes, the Arabs they send over the Rhine to occupy German cities. And when in France too little coal arrives from Germany, when the German gold does not come on time, the French bourgeoisie says with gritted teeth, "Why are they not paying on time? Does Marshal Foch have no more Blacks?"

Comrades, at this congress we greet Comrade Roy, representative of the toiling masses of India. (*Applause*) I hope, comrades, that at the third congress of our International, African Communists, Arabs, Senegalese, and other Negro peoples from the colonial possessions of France and Britain will be among us. Today some four to five hundred Senegalese brought our Russian soldiers, who were slaves in France for years, into the harbor of Odessa. Despite the precautionary measures that were taken to keep the Senegalese separate from the Russian soldiers, we know that no foreign regiment, no foreign company, has ever entered a Russian harbor and remained untouched.[4]

Comrades, the policy of Marshal Foch, who supplies seaplanes to Wrangel, who helps Poland in its hopeless fights, will not restore Europe's economy. This is the policy of a gambler who has lost hopelessly, who has already lost billions. Just recently the French parliament discovered that, of the 4 billion that was marked for the restoration of the devastated northern departments of France, Clemenceau spent only 1.5 million for this purpose. He used 3.9985 billion not to restore the devastated departments of France, but to devastate Russia's provinces and districts.

This policy, this squandering of billions, is the policy of a gambler, possessed by the hope of winning something back with his last bets—and normally he never wins anything back. Right now we can say with calm certainty that the hour is near when we, in alliance with the French proletariat, will break the bank of the French croupier. (*Applause*) The Senegalese in the Odessa harbor, the French generals in Warsaw—today perhaps they are still there, but they are not preparing to move east anymore, but west. (*Stormy applause*) All together they will not increase by a single pood the amount of coal and other raw materials, the amount of grain that France needs.[5]

The entire world is suffering from a very profound crisis. The shortage of raw materials and fuel and the fact that during the war years all labor was directed not toward creating values but toward destroying them cannot remain without consequences. For the most basic labor is that by which man uses all his thoughts and machines to draw from the bosom of the earth the essential materials, grains, and coal. This labor has continually decreased. Now the entire policy of world production must be directed toward ensuring free trade with Germany, Russia, and Austria-Hungary. All countries have been existing on leftover stocks, and the entire policy of imperialism takes as its starting point that trade relations in the next year will be marked by mutual blockade. Now we have the politics of plunder. But we have seen that the British, in the many months they were in Baku, managed to take out only a few million poods of oil, when they could have taken out tens of millions. The world economy suffered an extremely important loss when British and French mercenaries devastated the Don region, when the French blew up bridges and destroyed railroads, when British warships blocked passage to all countries and thereby undermined production—the main loser in all this was the world economy. That is the outcome of the Entente's economic policy.

Therefore comrades, when we look back on our year and a half of work in the Soviet economy, familiar with all its shortcomings, all its privations, we have no cause to cover up these shortcomings. Instead, we reveal this picture of our work to our Western brothers, the Americans and other representatives from all countries, all parts of the globe. I think that if anyone came here with any doubts at all, he will have been convinced that we have chosen the right path. The only possible way out of the world's misery is through a planned nationalization and socialization of the economy, whereby all artificial state obstacles and barriers are cleared away and the policy necessary for an integrated economy is followed. And, comrades, if despite the blockade and despite the war, we were in a position not only to supply our army but also to survive these three years, especially the last year and a half—this is in and of itself the greatest historic fact—we were able to do this because our economy was based on the principles of communism.

Finally, comrades, if we proceed from the questions of international politics and economics to those of the political struggle, we must say that the road charted by the First Congress of the Communist International was the correct one, confirmed by experience in all its principal features. If there are still honest, thinking workers who expect something from democracy, they are in a fantasyland. Where is there democracy in Europe? The newborn democracy of Germany has a democratic form, the right to vote. The Social Democrat Ebert stands at its head. This democracy murders the best workers' leaders, the best representatives of the working class, in whose name Comrade Levi spoke. Who rules there? The magnates of capital, who arrange their most important business in the stock-market pits.

During the war the French bourgeoisie and the bourgeoisies of other countries still clung to some remnants of the old democratic ideology. The bourgeoisie had to deceive the workers. They spoke of defense of the fatherland, they said that this war would be the last, they promised a league of nations. But now, after the wars and the Versailles treaty, now the hangman shows himself in all his nakedness. Now the toiling masses are robbed and reduced to beggary. Now the last shreds of this ideology are tossed aside. Now the bourgeoisie itself dispenses with virtually any allusion to the old testament of democracy, which earlier had served it to deceive the working class. Now it demands a firm, steeled will. If we take a look at any parliamentary report in any country, we see that even the most pitiful bourgeois ministers or any petty official who wants to reap a storm of applause need but shake a threatening fist in the direction of the revolutionary proletariat. The bourgeoisie demands blood and iron from its protégés, minions, and ministers, because it has understood that we—we, the entire world—have entered not the epoch of parliamentary mediation between the classes, but the epoch of fierce, brutal, and hard struggle.

And what did the working class—or at least the portion of it that made it back home—find on returning from the World War? In its cities and towns the working class found a new bourgeoisie, even more insolent and bloody than the one it left behind. War contractors, black marketeers of world repute, upstarts with shady backgrounds, who have robbed millions and yet more millions by speculating in blood, have climbed to the top. These greedy and dissolute scum have contaminated the air of the European and American cities with their poisonous breath.

Their love of ostentation has taken on the character of a crazy fever, a drunken madness, a nervous frenzy. The workers, home from the trenches, see before them this licentious, gilded bourgeoisie, which brought everything under its control, which tramples on everything, wants everything, ready at any moment to gun down the working class with its cannon just to assure its chance to live, to rule, to revel in its pleasures.

Working-class outrage in all countries flares to an ever brighter flame. Inflation provokes strikes and demonstrations of hungry men and women workers. And what a tremendous factor in the workers' movement, in the history of all humanity, is the fact that women, these downtrodden slaves, have awakened, and that proletarian youth are rising up in ever greater masses, coming to our aid and relieving us. With women and with proletarian youth, a new, more powerful stream of revolutionary lava pours into the revolutionary movement of the world proletariat, which will provide the movement of the Communist International with a new, inexhaustible supply of energy. (*Applause*)

Comrades, there is no doubt that the proletariat of all countries would already have taken power if a big, strong, intricate machine did not still stand between the masses and power, between the revolutionary masses as a whole and their advanced layers. This machine is the parties of the Second International and the trade unions of the world, which use their apparatus to serve the bourgeoisie, even in the epoch of its collapse and death. It was the Second International that tied its fate during the war to that of the bourgeoisie through mutual guarantees, that took upon itself responsibility for the old world, that intercepted the toiling masses' rush of outrage and indignation. Its authority sank, it disintegrated. Ever larger parts, millions of toiling masses, are splitting off from it. But like a buffer the Second International countered the first rush of the proletariat, the first outbreak of indignation against bourgeois society. And if the German working class is sacrificing tens of thousands and will sacrifice tens of thousands more, German Social Democracy is guilty. At this moment in world history, one that confers grave responsibility, this party has transformed itself into a counterrevolutionary machine, just as the leading parties of the Second International transformed themselves into a counterrevolutionary machine in the service of bourgeois society.

When we look back on the whole of past history for counterrevolutionary forces, we find nothing comparable. We know the history of the world Catholic church, which, like all other churches, was a powerful tool, a powerful and strong means in the hands of the possessing classes in defense of their privileges and domination. But the service rendered to the possessing classes by the church and world Catholicism is pitiful compared to the role that the parties of the Second International are playing at the critical moment of world history. For decades they have led the working class, enjoyed its confidence, organized and sustained it through their authority. But at the moment when the working class had to direct all its energy toward its liberation from the yoke of capital, they used this machine to bind the working class hand and foot, to enslave it to world capital not only materially, not only bodily, but also in spirit.

While we here in Moscow live through these days of the Second Congress, meeting in Geneva is the congress of the Second International, counterposed in program and spirit to our International of the Red proletarian commune. And from this day forward, from this congress forward, from these two congresses the split in the world working class will proceed ten times faster. Program against program, strategy against strategy, method against method. The German Independent Socialist party wobbled and wavered and to this day its upper layers are still wavering. But we, the Communist International, saw to it that this party, impelled by the pressure of the German workers, sent its representatives here. The party of French parliamentary socialism was also forced by the outrage of its proletarian masses to send delegates here to us.

But we are not going to make any concessions. The Communist International is no International of compromises and deals. We have a banner and a program. Whoever wants can place themselves under this banner. That is what we said to the representatives of the German Independent Social Democratic Party and the French parliamentary party. We asked them, "Do you hope to realize reforms through your parliament that will gradually lead to the realm of socialism?" We asked that ironically, because the facts of life have already given us the bitter response. And although the German Independent party and even the party of the French parliamentary Socialists have not yet learned to lead the proletariat onto the path of civil war and proletarian dictatorship, they certainly have learned not to believe in the path of parliamentary reformism. And the French and German workers have learned not to believe in their wavering and wobbling leaders anymore.

This congress coincides with the congress of the Second International. Moreover—and this is important and meaningful for us and for the workers of the entire world—it coincides with the threatening battles that the Entente, using White Poland, is leading against the Soviet republic. It coincides with the glorious victories of the Red Army on the western and southwestern fronts. The congress will erect great signposts for the further development of the proletarian world revolution. In its resolutions, this congress has drawn the balance sheet of the total experience of the world working class. You have read these resolutions. This congress also turns to the men and women workers of the entire world with a manifesto whose basic content I have laid out in this report, which will be published in all languages. It draws the balance of imperialism's work in international relations and the economic arena. It correctly appraises the final remnants of bourgeois democracy and bourgeois parliamentarism. It shows the proletariat of the entire world and the subjected toiling masses of the colonial countries the sure, clear, and distinct road of struggle.

What joy, what pride we Moscow workers and the workers of all Russia feel that for the second time we could assemble among us the best fighters of the world working class, that based on our experience we have helped you to forge your weapons. With your hands, comrades, we have kindled a fire in our Moscow foundry. In this fire we have made the proletarian steel glow. We have worked it with the hammer of our proletarian soviet revolution. We have tempered it in the experience of the civil war and have forged a superb, incomparable sword for the international proletariat. With this sword we will arm ourselves, with it we will arm others. We say to workers around the world: We have forged a strong sword in the Moscow fire. Take it in hand and drive it into the heart of world capital. (*Applause*)

ZINOVIEV:[6] Comrades, for three weeks representatives of the workers' organizations around the world have been meeting in Moscow, and with every day the fraternal alliance of the workers around the world has grown stronger.

Some time ago, when we first raised the question of calling the congress openly in Moscow, many doubted this could succeed. The very idea seemed too daring. Surely the world bourgeoisie, which persecutes its worst enemy, the Communist International, with the greatest hatred and venom would prevent this from happening.

But, comrades, so great was the striving of workers around the world to reach us, so widespread was the cry "To Moscow!" that, despite all the resistance of the world bourgeoisie, despite all obstacles laid in our path, we convened the congress, as you see. We can now say to the entire world that this congress has been a complete success and that it has been a genuine *world* congress of the proletariat. (*Applause*)

Comrades, just as the earth thirsts for rain after a long drought, so too the workers of the world have thirsted for international unity since the accursed war ended. This thirst, this striving by the workers for unity, is the greatest factor in world history; it is the main driving force of the Communist International. Especially important is the recognition by the workers of every land that only through close unity can they achieve what is foreordained for them by history. This consciousness is the greatest living force of the Communist International and of world history. Thanks to this consciousness, even though the blockade has not yet been broken and our sister parties in a great many countries must work illegally, the congress was a success.

I have before me a list of delegations, which fills several pages. I will only mention the *countries* that were represented: Britain, Germany, France, Sweden, Austria, Spain, Hungary, Bulgaria, Yugoslavia, Italy, Mexico, Switzerland, Turkey, Poland, East Galicia, Lithuania, Belorussia, Georgia, Latvia, Persia, Korea, America, Dutch [East] Indies,

Norway, Denmark, Finland, Estonia, Czechoslovakia, the Netherlands, Armenia, Belgium, Azerbaijan, and Russia—thirty-seven countries in all.[7]

From several of these countries we had only a few representatives, but the delegations nonetheless represent everything there is in the world that is living, fighting, revolutionary.

Of immense significance is the fact that among us are not only representatives of the European and American proletariat, but also no small number of representatives of the workers and the poorest peasants of the East: Turkey, Persia, India, the British colonies, and so on. We see this as a pledge that the movement in the East is beginning. It is a guarantee that there is no force on earth the bourgeoisie can use to take this movement of the oppressed nations of the East in tow. No! The national movement in the East will unite with the movement in Europe and America to deal a final blow to capitalism.

Various shadings of the revolutionary workers' movement were represented at our congress. The workers' movement is still in a process of fermentation and crystallization. That is understandable. After the terrible crisis experienced by the world working class, after the monstrous collapse of the Second International, and after the dreadful bloodletting endured by the workers of the world, it is quite understandable that we cannot expect to find total political clarity among workers now. But if the working class were united, if it fully understood its basic tasks, we would have defeated the bourgeoisie long ago.

The curse of our class is this: in the course of many decades some of our brothers were deceived by our enemies and others were organized into parties and federations that objectively help the bourgeoisie. In several countries the working class now stands at a crossroads. After the terrible storm that all humanity endured during the imperialist war, the working class is looking for the right path. And here we have set ourselves the task of uniting all that is living, honest, and revolutionary in the working class under the banner of the Communist International in order to fight the bourgeoisie. We intentionally called upon organizations that are not fully consolidated to join the Communist International. The best representatives of the syndicalists and anarchists participated in our congress. Representatives of the British Shop Stewards, of the Austrian factory committees, and of the Industrial Workers of the World were among us.

The mainstream of the world workers' movement flows in a communist channel. We see a powerful communist river before us, but next to that there are smaller rivers and streams that still must flow together into our Communist International. We see a large number of such proletarian movements, still in ferment, that have come to us only halfway. They are infected with many anarchist and syndicalist prejudices and do not entirely share our program. Nevertheless, they fight together with us in a common front against the bourgeoisie, and we thus see them as brothers.

We break with the hated traditions of the Second International, which snubbed with haughty disdain all the revolutionary-minded workers who dared to raise criticisms. A small handful of respectable "Socialist" grandfathers ran the Second International with a heavy hand, slamming the door against every group of workers that attempted to criticize their politics. We open our doors wide to all honest proletarian revolutionary organizations that are not yet fully communist today but will be tomorrow, since they are already prepared today, rifles in hand, to fight together with us against world capital. (*Applause*)

A group took part in our congress that some call a "left opposition," but which is actually nothing of the kind, since for communism there cannot be any opposition from the left. The "leftism" of this group in fact denoted only a certain backwardness. Alongside the "left" group, there was a rightist current at the congress, a group of repentant sinners. I mean the representatives of the French Socialist Party, the Independent Social Democratic Party of Germany, and the American Socialist Party. All these parties represent large workers' organizations that stand with one foot in the old camp, while trying with the other foot to head out on a new path. It seems to me that the presence of these groups gave our congress even more importance. These representatives of the old parties have appeared before the bar of the congress for judgment. What it all boiled down to was that some of them pleaded for amnesty. So the Communist International declared: Guilty with extenuating circumstances. (*Applause*)

However, as for the leaders who are responsible for the imperialist war, we were absolutely irreconcilable. Our answer to the representatives of the French Socialist Party is in our letter, which has already been published.[8] In it we gave a detailed description of the French Socialist Party, as personified by the leaders, their central committee, and their activists in Yellow parliamentarism. We have given them what the Germans call a *steckbrief,* that is, a letter with a description by which every honest worker can immediately recognize the malefactor who is now standing in the way of the world proletariat. Such a worker will say, "Look, workers, such a person should not be a leader of the working class."

Comrades, a significant number of workers are found in the ranks of the French party. The central organ comes out in runs of 250,000 copies. The Independent party in

Germany has about a million members. Some eleven thousand members of the party, mostly workers, languish in the prisons of the German "republic." Obviously we are filled with the greatest respect for them, and we are ready to take our hats off to them. Of course we speak to them as comrades; we try to explain their mistakes to them and we try to unite with them.

In this connection our congress worked out a series of conditions—twenty-one of them—for admission into the Communist International. I believe that every Communist worker, on becoming acquainted with these conditions, will agree with us that just as it is not easy for a camel to pass through the eye of a needle, so too, I hope, those who remain the supporters of the Center will not easily slip through these twenty-one conditions set by the Third International. (*Applause*)

We have set out these conditions so that the workers in the ranks of the French party and in the ranks of the German Independents can know what the international staff of the proletarian revolution demands, so that they can confront their leaders, shove them up against the wall, and demand a *straight answer* to all the questions raised in these conditions. And, comrades, we hope that these conditions will achieve their purpose.

A year and a half ago we were told that the danger threatening the Communist International was one of too few members. But now we face a different danger: the Communist International is becoming fashionable for some gentlemen. The Brussels International, now meeting in Geneva, has, they say, passed a resolution calling for a general strike.[9] Apparently the Second International is attempting to follow in Moscow's footsteps. We do not know yet exactly how many living shadows are meeting there, but it is clear to everyone that the Second International is now a total wreck. And among the old leaders, among these, so to speak, official Socialists, there are many who always want to be in the majority and who will lean for support on any force that is available. What international force like this is there today? The Communist International. They want to lean on us for support and make *verbal* concessions to us, reserving for themselves enough "autonomy" to continue their old ways. We hope that our Second Congress of the Communist International has bolted the door strongly enough against these gentlemen. The resolutions we passed will be sufficient to pry open the old parties. Whoever honestly wants to fight for communism should join our ranks. Everything rotten will blow away like dust and will never again obstruct the forward march of the working class.

Of the many questions before the congress, the most important was that of the role of the Communist Party. In this hall where, as I can safely say, a tremendous majority of those assembled are members of a Communist party, it is ridiculous to prove the necessity for a Communist party. But at an international congress where people from the most varied countries with different histories and different traditions were present, it was necessary to clarify thoroughly the role and significance of a Communist party.

The old parties are bankrupt, and this has clearly caused a whole number of workers to believe in the collapse not only of the Second International but also of socialist politics, of the idea of a party in general. It was essential to clarify the role and significance of the party in the proletarian revolution. I hope you realize that it was the greatest victory for us when the best representatives of revolutionary syndicalism voted for our resolutions, as did the best representatives of the other workers' organizations that are not fully communist.

Now we must say to the syndicalist workers, the anarchists, and other forces that did not believe in the significance of the party: You did not believe that there could be a party different from the Scheidemann type, that there could be a true workers' party that leads the working class into battle against capital. Look and see for yourselves: Here is the Communist Party of Russia, here is what the Russian worker has accomplished. Here is the Hungarian Communist Party. Here is the German party of the Spartacists—look what it has done to educate the working class of Germany! Here are the workers' Communist parties of a whole number of countries. Look and learn! They are a model of what we want. They are the kind of parties you must create!

In addition, the national and colonial questions were discussed. It seems to me that the unanimous adoption of this resolution is also our greatest moral victory. You know that in the Second International they did not once consider the question of so-called colonial policy. The Second International regarded bourgeois colonial policy "tolerantly." In 1907 the Stuttgart majority took the position that Socialists could support a so-called cultural colonial policy—that is, in fact, the piratical colonial policy of imperialism.[10] The Second International caused the peoples with yellow and black skins to adopt an attitude of the greatest distrust. Here too, the Third International had to return to the traditions of the First International. It had to say and it did say that it did not want to be an International only of the working people with white skin, but also an International of the working people with black and yellow skin as well, an International of the working people of the whole world. (*Applause*)

I consider that the fraternal alliance we have concluded at the congress with the representatives of India, Korea,

Turkey, and a whole number of other oppressed countries will strike straight at the heart of international capital. This is a very great conquest of the working class.

In addition, we discussed the question of the trade unions. You know that in Moscow we created the first international unit of Red trade unions. I contend that this also had a world-historic significance. Capitalism's final support is the Yellow Amsterdam international organization of trade unions. If we draw over to our side the best part of the workers, this will cause the Yellow Second International to be entirely abandoned by the masses; we will gather around us all that is living in the working class. We had to conduct a sharp polemic in the congress with a whole number of our British and American comrades, who have gone through a distinct history, fighting a monstrous betrayal by their leaders. They do not have a strong Communist party, and they want nothing whatsoever to do with parliamentarism. The Second Congress of the Third International told all these parties that our first concern is that in Britain, in America, everywhere, Communists must always be with the working masses. That is the first lesson of the Russian revolution. Sometimes you will make mistakes together with them, but never quit the mass organizations of the working class, however reactionary they may be at the given moment.

We must *destroy* the bourgeois states, but we must *win* the workers' unions, reeducate them, and take them into our own hands. Without this the victory of communism is impossible. We have had to cross swords on this question more than once with some of our comrades, but what the Communist International has decided on this shall become law for us all, including the minority who defended a different point of view.

In America, Britain, and other countries there are now two Communist parties.[11] The Communist International sets itself the task of ensuring that there shall be only *one* Communist party in every country. All the really healthy revolutionary currents of the proletarian movement must flow into a single powerful river. The tremendous authority that the Communist International enjoys in the eyes of the working class around the world is committed to accomplishing this task readily and to achieving success in the struggle for unity.

Comrades, it is especially interesting to compare our congress with what is happening in bourgeois circles. Comrade Trotsky has clearly portrayed what is happening in the upper circles of the ruling bourgeoisie.[12] Really, is it not wonderful that during these brief weeks in Moscow we came to essential agreement on a large number of the most important questions with workers who came from America and Australia and all the countries of Europe, despite the differences in culture, history, and tradition. Our fraternal alliance became stronger by the hour. Is it not truly instructive that at the very same time, in the governing bourgeois circles, one group is tripping up the other. The British bourgeoisie comes out against us and hopes to outfox its French rival. There is mutual backbiting. The bourgeoisie cannot put anything solid together.

The Second International, attempting in 1919 to come back to life, tied its fate to the League of Nations and decided that no beast was mightier than the league.[13] It had to cuddle up to the league, which it felt sure would lord it over the world for a few decades. A little more than a year has gone by, and now we see the League of Nations disintegrating before our eyes, turning into a fiction. All the "Allies" plot against each other and cheat each other.

The Second International tied its fate to the League of Nations, and together they will crash and perish.

But at the same time the real international brotherhood of the workers of the world is growing. I am deeply convinced that the Second World Congress is the precursor of another world congress—the world congress of soviet republics. (*Applause*)

Most remarkable of all, the only resolution that was adopted by the congress unanimously, by all the representatives, and without the slightest debate was the resolution on the soviets.[14] The idea of a soviet state, as a form of the proletarian dictatorship, has penetrated into the broadest masses of workers, reaching the workers' deepest layers and winning the minds of millions and tens of millions of the working class. As a result, not only was this question not disputed at the world congress of the Communist International, but it was not even discussed. This idea was considered to be our basic acquisition. It is a simple idea. It is the firm, iron foundation on which our Communist International stands.

Our work is coming to an end. We have exchanged experiences with representatives from a large number of countries. We have weighed a whole number of disputed questions. We have projected a course for long months of struggle. We do not know what turns of fate await this or that sister party, what kind of blow may fall. But one thing we know for certain: we have built an organization that at any given moment will be able to offer the workers of the world the greatest possible support.

We adopted the Statutes of the Communist International. That is no mere formality. It is confirmation of the fact that we are creating a *single, unified international party of Communists whose units in each country are no more than branches*. (*Applause*) In these statutes we recall the words from the statutes of the First International, founded by Marx, "If until now the working class has been enslaved and unfree, it is because there was no unity in the working class, there was not enough solidarity among the workers of different countries."[15] It is a simple truth, a simple thought. Still, several decades were needed for the working class around the world to absorb this idea. And in the Statutes of the Communist International we have added, "The first words that the Communist International addresses to the workers of the whole world are: 'Remember the imperialist war, the war that cost us tens of millions of victims—if you leave capitalism whole and inviolable, you will get just such wars again!'[16] Our international brotherhood was born after hard trials with fire and iron. And when you make responsible decisions, start from this: the imperialist war that destroyed the workers' organizations cost the working class tens of millions of lives. And remember, such a war can flare up again at any minute if we do not wipe capitalism off the face of the earth."

Adopting the statutes means that we have finally closed ranks, that we now have an International Workers Association,[17] with an organization welded together in blood and centralized on an international scale. We told our comrades how in the course of the civil war we in Russia had to create a centralized organization of iron, cast from a single pour, with military discipline that is sometimes extraordinarily hard on every one of us, on the individual member of the party, and demands the greatest effort and sacrifice. In the same way, we must now create on an international scale an International that is cast from a single pour with the same iron discipline and the same centralization, in which we have unconditional confidence in each other and the same selfless readiness to sacrifice ourselves for the common cause of the victory of the proletarian revolution. (*Applause*)

Comrades will depart from here for a great many countries, where awaiting them are the state of siege, prison, torture, and betrayals by western European Social Democrats and other capitalist hirelings. We wish our comrades courage in this struggle. And we ask them to remember in difficult moments that the Soviet republic is ready to share everything it has with them. The Communist Party of Russia considers its most sacred duty to be to come to the assistance of all sister parties with all means at its disposal. We wish more strength, courage, and confidence to our brothers who set out now to carry out the highest historic mission and the greatest tasks that have ever faced the fighting proletariat.

Long live the Third International!

Long live our comrades, who set out for the bourgeois countries to advance the propaganda for communism throughout the world! (*Thunderous applause, cries of "Hurray!"*)

Comrades! I declare the Second Congress of the Communist International to be closed.

# Manifesto of the Second Congress of the Communist International

## 1. International relations after Versailles

The bourgeoisie around the world looks back sorrowfully on days gone by.[1] All the foundations of foreign and domestic political relations have been overthrown or unhinged. Tomorrow looms like a dark threat over the exploiters' world. The imperialist war destroyed forever the old system of alliances and mutual assurances that underlay the international balance of power and the armed peace. The Versailles peace created no new equilibrium to replace it.

First Russia, then Austria-Hungary and Germany lost their roles as actors on the world stage. Mighty countries that held top rank in the system that divided up the world are now themselves the booty of thieves and robbers. For victorious Entente imperialism, a new, immeasurable field of colonial exploitation opened up, beginning just across the Rhine, including all of central and eastern Europe, and stretching beyond to the Pacific Ocean. Can the Congo or

Syria, Egypt or Mexico really compare with Russia's steppes, forests, and mountains or Germany's skilled labor force? The victors' new colonial program follows automatically: overthrow the workers' republic in Russia; steal Russia's raw materials; force the German workers to process them using German coal; set up armed German entrepreneurs as overseers—while the victors seize the finished products and thereby rake in the profits. The program of organizing "Europe," advanced by German imperialism at the moment of its greatest military successes, was inherited by its successors, the victorious Entente. The defeated bandits of the German Empire, put in the prisoners' dock by the rulers of the Entente, are thus truly facing a court of their peers in crime.

But even in the victors' camp there are vanquished. Intoxicated by its chauvinism and the victories it won for others, the French bourgeoisie felt that it was Europe's master. Actually, never since the beginning of its existence has France found itself in such a slavish dependence on stronger countries—Britain and North America. France dictates a specific economic and military program to Belgium, transforming its weaker ally into a subjugated province. But with respect to Britain, France itself plays the role of Belgium, only on a somewhat larger scale.

From time to time the British imperialists permit the French profiteers to command and rule within the areas of the continent assigned them, thus diverting the sharpest outrage of Europe's, and even of Britain's, toilers from themselves onto France. With France bled white and ravaged, its power has a deceptive, almost absurd character, which sooner or later will penetrate the brains of even the French social patriots.

Italy's world importance fell even more. Without coal, without bread, without raw materials, yanked completely out of its inner equilibrium by the war, Italy's bourgeoisie is incapable, though not from any lack of malice, of fully exercising its rights to robbery and rape, even in the colonial nooks and crannies assigned to it by Britain.

Japan, torn within its feudal shell by capitalist contradictions, stands on the verge of the deepest revolutionary crisis, which even now, despite advantageous international conditions, blocks its imperialist takeoff.

Thus there remain only two true world powers: Great Britain and the United States.

British imperialism freed itself from the Asiatic rivalry of tsarism and from the threatening competition of Germany. Great Britain's sea power reached its zenith. Britain encircles the continents with a chain of its subject peoples. Having seized Finland, Estonia, and Lithuania, it deprives Sweden and Norway of the last vestiges of their independence and transforms the Baltic Sea into a British lake. In the North Sea Britain faces no opposition. With the Cape Colony [South Africa], Egypt, India, Persia, and Afghanistan, it is transforming the Indian Ocean into a British sea. Because Britain rules the waves, it controls the mainland. Its commanding world role is limited only by the American dollar republic and the Russian Soviet Republic.

The World War finally dislodged the United States from its continental conservatism. The program of national capitalism as it unfolded its wings—"America for the Americans" (the Monroe Doctrine)—has been replaced with the program of imperialism: "The whole world for the Americans." After exploiting the war commercially, industrially, and through the stock market, after neutral profiteering at the expense of European blood, America went on to intervene in the war, played a decisive role in smashing Germany, and stuck its fingers into all questions of European and world politics.

Under the banner of the "League of Nations," the United States tried to extend to the other side of the ocean its experience with the federated unification of great masses of peoples of different origins. It tried to yoke to its golden chariot the peoples of Europe and other parts of the earth, bringing them under Washington's rule. The League of Nations was really meant to be a world monopoly corporation: Yankee and Company.

The president of the United States, the great prophet of platitudes, descended from Mount Sinai, his Fourteen Points in hand, to conquer Europe. The bourgeois stockbrokers, cabinet members, and businessmen were not fooled for a moment about the meaning of this new revelation. But the European "Socialists" fell quivering, Kautsky-like, into a state of religious rapture and danced like King David around Wilson's holy Ark of the Covenant.

As attention turned to practical questions, it became clear to the American apostle that despite the dollar's advantageous exchange rate, first place on all the sea-lanes that unite and divide the peoples belongs, as before, to Britain, because it has a stronger fleet, more extensive transoceanic cables, and longer experience in world plunder. Furthermore, in his travels Wilson ran up against the Soviet republic and communism. The offended American messiah renounced the League of Nations, which Britain had transformed into its diplomatic chancellery, and turned his back on Europe.

Nevertheless, it would be childish to assume that American imperialism, whose first offensive was repulsed by Britain, will retreat into the shell of the Monroe Doctrine. No. Continuing ever more violently to subordinate the American continent and transforming the countries of Central and South America into its colonies, the United States intends, through both its ruling parties, the Democrats and Republicans, to create a league of its own as a counterweight to the British League of Nations, that is, a league with North America as the center of the world system. To do the job properly, it intends to build up its war fleet more powerfully than the British over the next three to five years. Thus imperialist Britain is faced with the question: To be or not to be. Alongside these two giants' insane competition in shipbuilding goes the no less frantic struggle for the petroleum monopoly.

France, which had counted on playing the role of arbiter between Britain and the United States, sees itself drawn into Great Britain's orbit like a second-rate satellite. It discerns in the League of Nations an intolerable bridle, which it seeks to escape by inflaming the conflicts between Britain and North America.

Thus do powerful forces prepare a new world duel.

The program of liberating the small nations, posed during the war, led to the total destruction and enslavement of the Balkan peoples, victors and vanquished alike, and to the Balkanization of a large part of Europe. Imperialist interests pushed the victors to create small separate national states from the territory of the great powers that they destroyed. There is not even a semblance here of the so-called national principle. The essence of imperialism lies in surmounting the national framework, even among the great powers. The new bourgeois small states are merely by-products of imperialism. As temporary points of support for itself, imperialism created a series of smaller national states; some openly oppressed, others officially protected, but in reality vassals all: Austria, Hungary, Poland, Yugoslavia, Bohemia, Finland, Estonia, Latvia, Lithuania, Armenia, Georgia, and so on. It rules them through banks, railroads, and coal monopolies and condemns them to unbearable economic and national hardships, endless conflicts, and bloody collisions.

What a monstrous irony of history it is that the restoration of Poland, which was part of the program of revolutionary democracy and initial activity of the international proletariat, was accomplished by imperialism to oppose the revolution; that "democratic Poland," whose pioneers died on the barricades throughout Europe, now plays the role of the most foul and bloody tool in the thievish hands of the Anglo-French gangsters against the first proletarian republic in the world.

Alongside Poland, "democratic" Czechoslovakia, which has sold itself to French capital, supplies White Guard detachments for use against Soviet Russia and soviet Hungary.

The heroic attempt of the Hungarian proletariat to blaze a path out of the governmental and economic chaos of central Europe toward soviet federation—the only road to salvation—was strangled by the united capitalist reaction at a time when the proletariat of the strongest countries of Europe, deceived by its parties, proved to be still unable to fulfill its duty to socialist Hungary and to itself.

The soviet government in Budapest was overthrown with the help of the social traitors, who were pushed aside after three and a half days in power by the unbridled counterrevolutionary rabble, whose bloody crimes exceed even those of Kolchak, Denikin, Wrangel, and other agents of the Entente. But even though temporarily suppressed, soviet Hungary is like a beacon to the toilers of central Europe.

The Turkish people do not want to submit to the vile peace worked out by the despots in London. In order to enforce its terms, Britain has armed Greece and incited it against Turkey. The Balkan Peninsula and the Near East—

Greece and Turkey alike—are thereby condemned to utter devastation and mutual destruction.

In the Entente's fight with Turkey, Armenia played the same role in the script as did Belgium in the fight with Germany, as Serbia in the fight with Austria-Hungary. After Armenia was created—without borders nor any possibility of survival—Wilson spurned the Armenian mandate offered him by the "League of Nations": Armenia's soil holds neither petroleum nor platinum. "Liberated" Armenia is now less protected than ever before.

Almost every newly created national state has its unredeemed areas, that is, its internal national ulcer.

At the same time, the tension of the national struggle within the possessions of the victorious countries has risen to a peak. The British bourgeoisie, which wants to be guardian over the peoples of the four corners of the earth, is incapable of resolving the Irish question right under its very nose.

Even more threatening is the national question in the colonies. Egypt, India, and Persia are convulsed by uprisings. The toilers of the colonies are taking over the slogan of soviet federation from the leading proletarians of Europe and America.

Official, governmental, national, civilized, and bourgeois Europe, as it has emerged from the war and the Versailles peace, resembles a madhouse. Artificially splintered little states, economically suffocating within their borders, snarl at each other and wage war over harbors, provinces, and insignificant towns. They seek the protection of larger states, whose antagonisms are again increasing daily. Italy, hostile toward France, would support Germany against France if Germany were able to raise its head. France is consumed with envy of Britain and, in order to preserve its dividends, is ready to ignite Europe anew at all four corners. Britain, with help from France, holds Europe in a state of chaotic impotence and thereby achieves a free hand for world operations, which are directed against America. The United States permits Japan to get bogged down in eastern Siberia in order meanwhile to secure for itself supremacy over the British fleet by the year 1925, provided that Britain does not decide to measure forces with it sooner.

Consistent with this picture of international relations, General Foch, the military oracle of the French bourgeoisie, predicts that the next war will begin technologically where the last one left off, that is, with airplanes and tanks, with automatic arms and machine guns instead of handguns, with grenades instead of bayonets.

Workers and peasants of Europe, America, Asia, Africa, and Australia: You have sacrificed ten million dead, twenty million wounded and crippled. Now at least you know what you achieved at this price!

### 2. The economic situation

Meanwhile, the devastation of humanity proceeds apace.

The war destroyed economic ties whose development was among the most important accomplishments of capitalism. England, France, and Italy have been cut off since 1914 from central Europe and the Near East, and since 1917, from Russia.

A few years of war destroyed what it took a succession of generations to create; human labor was reduced to the minimum; and labor was employed chiefly where available raw material supplies had to be converted to arms and means of destruction.

In the basic branches of the economy, where humanity is in direct struggle with nature's stinginess and tenacity, where fuel and raw materials are torn from the earth, work has more and more approached a standstill. The Entente's victories and the Versailles peace have halted neither the economic collapse nor the economic destruction, but only altered its paths and forms. The blockade of Soviet Russia and the artificial incitement of civil war in its fertile border areas have inflicted and inflict even today incalculable harm on the well-being of all of humanity. With a minimum of technical assistance, Russia, thanks to its soviet form of economy, could give Europe two or three times more foodstuffs and raw materials than tsarist Russia supplied—and the International attests to this before the entire world. Instead, Anglo-French imperialism compels the toilers' republic to devote all its strength to defense. To rob the Russian worker of fuel, Britain holds Baku in its claws, although it can carry away only a minuscule portion of the booty for its own use. The rich coal regions of the Don were periodically laid waste by the Entente's bands of White Guards. French advisers and sappers labored not a little in the destruction of Russian bridges and railroads. Japan presently robs and ravages eastern Siberia.

German technology and the high productivity of German labor, crucial factors in restoring the world economy, are even more paralyzed after the Versailles peace than they were during the war. The Entente faces an insoluble contradiction. To force payment, it has to make it possible to work. To make work possible, it has to make it possible to live. But allowing shattered, fragmented, exhausted Germany the possibility of living provides it with the possibility of resisting. Fear of Germany's revenge dictates Foch's policy of continuously tightening the military vice to prevent Germany's rebirth.

Everyone suffers shortages, everyone has needs. There is a marked deficit in the trade balances of not only Germany but also France and Britain. The French national debt has risen to 300 billion francs. A third of this sum can be traced to embezzlement, theft, and disorganization, as was attested by the reactionary French senator Gaudin de Villaine.

The projects that have been carried out in France to reconstruct regions destroyed by the war are drops in the ocean of devastation. The lack of fuel, raw materials, and labor power constitute insurmountable obstacles.

France needs gold, France needs coal. Pointing to the countless graves in the military cemeteries, the French bourgeoisie demands its dividends. Germany must pay! After all, General Foch still has Blacks to occupy German cities. Russia must pay! To drum this idea into the heads of the Russian people, the French government squanders billions, which were collected for France's rebirth, to devastate Russia.

The international financial agreement, which was supposed to ease France's tax burden as a step toward more or less completely canceling the war debts, did not come about. The United States did not show the least interest in giving Europe ten billion pounds sterling.[2]

Paper money continues to be issued in ever greater quantities. In Soviet Russia the growth in paper money and its devaluation, taking place alongside the development of the socialized economy, the planned distribution of goods and the steadily increasing payment of wages in kind, is merely the result of the withering away of the commodity-money economy. In the capitalist states, on the other hand, the growth of the mass of printed paper money testifies to the deepening of the economic chaos and the inevitable crash.

The Entente's conferences travel from place to place, seeking inspiration in every European spa. All hands are outstretched, demanding interest proportional to the number killed in the war. This wandering stock exchange of death, which every two weeks decides anew whether France should receive 50 or 55 percent of the reparations—which Germany cannot pay—is the crowning glory of the promised reorganization of Europe.

During the war capitalism was transformed. The systematic extraction of surplus value *in the production process*—the basis of the profit economy—appears to be an insufficiently alluring pursuit for the bourgeois gentlemen, who have grown accustomed to increasing their capital two and ten times over in a couple of days through speculation and international robbery.

The bourgeois has shed certain prejudices that hampered him and acquired certain skills that he did not have. The war taught him the hunger blockade against entire countries, aerial bombardment and incineration of cities and villages, the spreading where expedient of cholera bacteria, shipment of dynamite in diplomatic pouches, counterfeiting the enemy's bank notes, bribery, espionage, and smuggling on a scale never before seen. The usages of war continued after the conclusion of peace as the usages of commerce. Big-business operations are now one with the activity of the state, which makes its appearance as a world robber gang, armed with all the instruments of destruction.

The narrower the world's productive base becomes, the more savage and wasteful its methods of appropriation. Robbery! That is capitalist policy's final word, which has replaced free trade and protective tariffs. The attack by the Romanian thieves and murderers on Hungary, where they carried off locomotives and jewels, is the symbol of Lloyd George and Millerand's economic policy.

In its domestic economic policy the bourgeoisie reels desperately back and forth between the program of further nationalizations, regulations, and controls on the one hand, and protests against the state intervention that grew up during the war on the other. The French parliament is busy trying to square the circle, creating "unified command" of the republic's railways without hurting the private capitalist interests of the railroad companies. At the same time, France's capitalist press is carrying on a vicious campaign against the all-devouring state *(étatisme),* which restricts the spirit of private enterprise.

America's railroads, run down by the state during the war, fell into an even more wretched condition after state control was lifted. Meanwhile, the Republican Party campaign platform promises to free economic life from arbitrary state intervention. Samuel Gompers, capital's old watchdog and leader of the American trade unions, is leading the fight against nationalizing the railroads, which is demanded as the cure-all by the nincompoops and quacks of reformism in America, in France, and elsewhere. In fact, the sporadic, violent interventions by the state into the economy only vie with speculation in causing even greater chaos in the capitalist economy in its epoch of collapse. Transferring the most important branches of production and transport from the hands of individual trusts into the hands of the "nation," that is, the bourgeois state, the most powerful and predatory capitalist trust, does not get rid of the evil, but only generalizes it.

The fall in prices and the improvement in the currency exchange rates are only superficial and passing phenomena against the background of continuing destruction. The price fluctuations do not eliminate the underlying facts: shortage of raw materials and decline in labor productivity. The working masses who survived the terrible strain of the war are unable to work at the previous speed and under the previous conditions. The destruction, carried out in a few hours, of so much value, which took years to create; the brazen dance of billions in the hands of the financial clique, which climbs ever higher on the bones and the ruins—this object lesson in history is poorly suited to holding the working class to the automatic discipline of wage labor.

Bourgeois economic theoreticians and journalists speak of a "wave of laziness" that is sweeping over Europe and undermining the economic future. Plant managers try to help by granting the skilled workers certain privileges. In vain! In order to reestablish and increase labor productivity, the working class will have to be certain that by every blow of its hammer it will raise its own well-being and educational level and not again expose itself to the danger of renewed mutual destruction. Only the social revolution can give it this assurance.

The rise in food prices is a powerful factor in all countries for revolutionary ferment. The bourgeoisie of France, Italy, Germany, and other countries is trying to alleviate with petty alms the hardship caused by inflation and ward off the increase in strikes. In order to subsidize a portion of the landowners' production costs for labor power, the indebted state launches into desperate speculation: it steals from itself in order to postpone the moment of disintegration. Even if certain sectors of the working class are for the moment living better than they did before the war, that has no relationship with the real economic situation in the capitalist countries. This temporary result is achieved by recklessly borrowing against the future, which is moving toward us with all its catastrophic shortages and destitution.

And the United States? "America is the hope of humanity"—thus the French bourgeois, through the mouth of Millerand, repeat Turgot's phrase in hopes of being excused from their debts, although they themselves excuse no one. But the United States is incapable of leading Europe out of the economic dead end. It too has exhausted its raw material reserves over the last six years.

The adaptation of American capitalism to the demands of the World War narrowed its industrial base. Emigration from Europe came to a standstill. The return flow pulled many hundreds of thousands of Germans, Italians, Poles, Serbs, and Czechs out of American industry. Some were drafted, some attracted by the illusion of the newly constituted fatherland. Shortages of raw materials and labor power weigh on the transatlantic republic and produce a deep economic crisis, which presses the American proletariat into a new phase of revolutionary struggle. America is quickly becoming "Europeanized."

The neutral countries were also not spared the consequences of the last war and the blockade. Like liquid in connected vessels, the economies of the interconnected capitalist states, large and small, warring and neutral, victors and vanquished, are pushed down to one and the same level of misery, hunger, and death.

Switzerland lives from hand to mouth, and now every unforeseen occurrence threatens to throw it out of balance. In Scandinavia the abundant influx of gold does not solve the food supply problem. Hat in hand, coal must be begged from Britain in dribbles. Despite the hunger in Europe, the Norwegian fishing industry is experiencing an unprecedented crisis.

Spain, whence France drew people, horses, and food, cannot emerge from severe food shortages that have brought in their wake tumultuous strikes and street unrest by the hungry masses.

The bourgeoisie is relying heavily on the countryside. Their economic theoreticians assert that the well-being of the peasantry has improved immensely. That is an illusion. Certainly, the peasants who brought their products to market during the war prospered to varying degrees in all countries. They sold their products at high prices and used cheap money to pay off their debts, which they had acquired in times when money was dear. Therein lies their profit. But their farms declined and were devastated during the war. They need industrial products, whose prices rise in the same proportion as the value of money declines. The demands of the state treasury become ever more outrageous and threaten to devour the peasant, together with his produce and his land. Thus, after a period of rising prosperity, the small peasantry has fallen into all the more unbearable difficulties. Their discontent with the results of the war will continue to grow, and as a standing army they have not a few unpleasant surprises in store for the bourgeoisie.

The economic restoration of Europe, which its ministers speak of, is a lie. Europe is going under, and with it the entire capitalist world.

There is no salvation under capitalism. Imperialism's policy does not lead to abolishing misery, but to sharpening it through plundering of available supplies.

The question of fuel and raw material supplies is international in scope and can be solved only on the basis of planned, collectivized, socialist production.

The state debts must be canceled, labor and its fruits freed from the enormous tribute to the world plutocracy, and the plutocracy overthrown. The borders between states, which fragment the world economy, must be abolished. The Supreme Economic Council of the Entente imperialists must make way for the Supreme Economic Council of the world proletariat, to achieve centralized use of all of humanity's economic resources.

Imperialism must be killed, so that humanity can live again.

### 3. The bourgeois order after the war

The propertied classes are concentrating all their energies on two questions: holding their own in the international struggle and not allowing the proletariat to become master of the house. The previous bourgeois political groupings have lost their strength in this effort. The previous programs, which divided the various layers of the bourgeoisie, have disappeared without a trace before the revolutionary assault of the proletariat. This is true not only in Russia, where in the decisive period of struggle the Cadet party banner became the banner of all propertied classes against the workers' and peasants' revolution, but also in the countries with an older and higher political culture.

Lloyd George comes forward to herald the unification of Conservatives, Unionists, and Liberals in common struggle against the emerging power of the working class. At the pinnacle, the old demagogue places the holy church, like a central power station that supplies equally all parties of the propertied classes.

In France the epoch of anticlericalism, until recently so lively, seems like an antediluvian apparition. Radicals, Royalists, and Catholics are now forming a bloc for national order against the rising proletariat. By extending its hand to all the forces of reaction, the French government supports the Black Hundred gangster Wrangel and renews diplomatic relations with the Vatican.

Giolitti, the Germanophile and supporter of neutrality, has taken over the rudder of the Italian state as the joint leader of the interventionists, the neutralists, the clericals, and the Mazzinists. He is prepared to maneuver on subordinate questions of foreign and domestic politics, in order to deliver all the more ruthless a blow in city and country against the revolutionary proletariat's offensive. The Giolitti government rightly considers itself to be the last high card of the Italian bourgeoisie.

After the fall of the Hohenzollerns, the policy of all the German governments and governmental parties, together with the ruling classes of the Entente, has been to generate an atmosphere of hatred against Bolshevism, that is, against the proletarian revolution.

While the Anglo-French shylock throttles the German people ever more brutally, the German bourgeoisie asks the parties of its enemy, without distinction, to loosen the noose enough so that they can strangle the vanguard of the German proletariat with their own hands. This is what the periodic consultations and agreements on disarmament and the export of war matériel culminate in.

In America the differences between Republicans and Democrats have been totally obliterated. These powerful political organizations of exploiters, until now appropriate for the narrow circle of American conditions, exposed their complete lack of content when the American bourgeoisie entered the arena of world robbery.

Never before have the intrigues of individual leaders and cliques, in the opposition as well as in government, stood out with such cynical openness as now. But at the same time all leaders, cliques, and bourgeois parties are building a common front against the revolutionary proletariat.

While the Social Democratic philistines continue to counterpose the path of democracy to the violent path of [soviet] dictatorship, the last vestiges of democracy are being trampled and destroyed in all countries of the world.

After the war, when the peoples' representatives played the role of an impotent but noisy patriotic facade for the ruling imperialist cliques, the parliaments fell into a state of total powerlessness. All important questions are decided outside of parliament. The superficial extension of parliamentary prerogatives, which the imperialist jugglers proclaimed so solemnly in Italy and elsewhere, changes nothing. The actual lords and masters of the destiny of nations—like Lord Rothschild and Lord Weir, Morgan and Rockefeller, Snyder and Lusher, Hugo Stinnes and Felix Deutsch, Rizello and Agnelli—the gold, coal, oil, and steel barons—are busy behind the scenes, sending low-level stand-ins into parliament to lead the parliamentary work. The French parliament, the most discredited because of its lying rhetoric and cynical venality, a body that amuses itself with the procedure of multiple readings of trivial bills, suddenly learns that four billion that had been earmarked for the devastated regions of France were spent by Clemenceau for wholly different purposes, mostly to further devastate Russia.

In the seemingly all-powerful British Parliament, the overwhelming majority of the deputies know as little about Lloyd George and Lord Curzon's real intentions toward Soviet Russia and even France as do the old Indian women in the villages of Bengal.

In the United States, Congress is the docile or disgruntled chorus for the president, who in turn is but the servant of the electoral machine, that is, of the political apparatus of the trusts—more so since the war than ever before.

Germany's belated parliamentarism, a miscarriage of the bourgeois revolution, which itself was a miscarriage of history, suffers already in its infant stage from all the ailments of a feeble old idiot. The Reichstag of Ebert's republic, the "most democratic" parliament in the world, is not only powerless before Foch's marshal's baton, but also before the stock market manipulations of its own Stinneses and the military conspiracies of its officers' clique as well. German parliamentary democracy is a void between two dictatorships.

The very composition of the bourgeoisie underwent deep-going changes during the war. The general pauperization of the entire world allowed the concentration of capital to make a colossal leap forward in a single bound. Previously obscure companies came to the fore. Solidarity, stability, tendency toward reasonable compromise, observance of a certain decorum in the exploitation as well as the enjoyment of its fruits—all that has been washed away by the torrent of the imperialist flood.

New propertied classes pushed to the fore: war contractors, base speculators, parvenus, international adventurers, racketeers, crooks decked out in diamonds, licentious, luxury-seeking rabble all ready to commit the worst brutality against the proletarian revolution, which promises them nothing but the hangman's noose.

The existing system stands before the masses in all its nakedness as the rule of the rich. Luxury rose to perverse heights of ecstasy after the war in America, France, England. In the words of *Le Temps,* Paris, packed full with international patriotic parasites, resembles Babylon on the eve of destruction.

Politics, the courts, the press, art, and the church fall in step with this bourgeoisie. All restraints have fallen. Wilson, Clemenceau, Millerand, Lloyd George, and Churchill do not shirk from the most brazen fraud or the crudest lie, and when caught red-handed, they calmly go on to new criminal acts. Old Machiavelli's classic rules of political perfidy are the innocent aphorisms of a provincial simpleton compared to the principles that guide the present bourgeois governments.

The courts, previously decked out in democratic tinsel to hide their bourgeois character, now become open organs of class outrages and counterrevolutionary provocation. The judges of the Third Republic acquitted Jaurès's murderer without batting an eye. The courts of Germany, which was proclaimed as a "socialist republic," embolden to new exploits the murderers of Liebknecht, Rosa Luxemburg, and other martyrs of the proletariat. The tribunals of bourgeois democracy transformed themselves into organs for solemnly legalizing all the crimes of the White Terror.

The bourgeois press openly bears on its mastheads, like a trademark, the stamp of bribery. The leading newspapers of the world bourgeoisie are monstrous factories for lies, slanders, and spiritual poisoning.

The bourgeoisie's moods fluctuate just as nervously as the prices on its market. In the first months after the end of the war, the international bourgeoisie, especially the French, was feverish with fear of advancing communism. They measured the level of immediate danger by the scope of their bloody crimes. But they withstood the first assault. The Socialist parties and the trade unions of the Second International, bound to the bourgeoisie by chains of common guilt, rendered it the final service of absorbing the toilers' first, angry blow. The bourgeoisie won a reprieve at the cost of the total collapse of the Second International. Clemenceau's counterrevolutionary parliamentary elections, several months of unstable equilibrium, and the fiasco of the May strike were enough to instill in the bourgeoisie the belief that its regime is as solid as a rock. Its class arrogance reached the same heights as did its fears of yesterday.

Threats have become the bourgeoisie's only argument. They do not believe in words but demand deeds: arrests, the breakup of demonstrations, deportations, confiscations, firing squads. Trying to impress the bourgeoisie, the bourgeois ministers and members of parliament pose as men of steel. Lloyd George dryly advises the German ministers to follow the example of France in 1871 and simply gun down their Communists. Any third-rate functionary can count on stormy applause in the parliamentary chamber if his inane report ends with a threat against the workers.

At a time when the official state apparatus is transformed ever more openly into an organization for bloodily suppressing the toilers, various private counterrevolutionary organizations are meanwhile being formed under its auspices and at its disposal for violently breaking up strikes, for acts of provocation, for staging frame-up trials, for destroying revolutionary organizations, for seizing Communist facilities, for pogroms and arson, for killing revolutionary leaders, and for other such measures to protect private property and democracy.

The younger sons of the big landowners and the big bourgeoisie, petty bourgeois who have lost their bearings, and all declassed elements, first among them the bourgeois and noble refugees from Soviet Russia, constitute an inexhaustible reservoir for the volunteer units of the counterrevolution. At their head stands the officer corps that came through the school of the imperialist slaughter. Some twenty thousand career officers from the Hohenzollern army make up a solid counterrevolutionary core, which, especially after the Kapp-Lüttwitz putsch, German democracy does not have the strength to disperse. It can be smashed only by the hammer of the proletarian dictatorship. This centralized organization of old-regime terrorists is supplemented by White Guard detachments on the Junker estates.

In the United States such groups as the National Security League[3] or the Knights of Liberty constitute capitalism's shock troops. On their extended flanks, true gangs of thieves operate in the form of detective agencies.

In France the Civic League represents a distinguished organization of strikebreakers, at a time when the reformist General Confederation of Labor has been proscribed.[4]

The officer-mafia of White Hungary, which exists parallel to the British-supported government of counterrevolutionary hangmen, has given the proletariat of the entire world a view of the civilization and humaneness that Wilson and Lloyd George counterpose to soviet power and revolutionary force. The "democratic" governments of Finland, Georgia, Latvia, and Estonia exhaust themselves emulating the splendid Hungarian example. In Barcelona the police have a secret death squad at their disposal.

And so it goes, and so it is everywhere. Even in destroyed and devastated Bulgaria, unemployed officers are building secret units that are preparing for the first opportunity to prove their patriotism on the skulls of the Bulgarian workers.

In light of the bourgeois order that emerged from the World War, the program of smoothing over contradictions, class collaboration, parliamentary reforms, socialism by stages, and national unity looks like a grim joke.

The bourgeoisie resolutely renounced reconciliation with the proletariat through reforms. It corrupts the minuscule upper level with sops and forces obedience from the great mass with blood and iron.

There is not a single important question that could now be decided by the ballot. Democracy still exists only as a memory in the minds of the reformists. The state organization more and more returns to its primordial form, to groups of armed men. The bourgeoisie no longer counts votes; it only counts the number of rifles, machine guns, and cannon it will have at its disposal when the question of power and property hangs in the balance.

No longer is there room for collaboration or negotiations. Only the overthrow of the bourgeoisie can bring salvation. But that can be achieved only by the uprising of the proletariat.

## 4. Soviet Russia

Amidst the unrestrained forces of chauvinism, greed, and destruction, only the principle of communism exhibits vitality and creative power. Although first consolidated in the most backward and ruined country in Europe, ringed by the massed armies of powerful enemies, soviet power has not only held out in struggle against enormous, unprecedented obstacles, but in fact has shown the great potential for development inherent in communism. The development and consolidation of soviet power in Russia is the most important historical fact since the founding of the Communist International.

Class society is accustomed to see the establishment of an army as the best test of its economic and governmental organization. It judges the strengths and weaknesses of the economy and the state by the strengths and weaknesses of its army.

Soviet power created a great armed force while under fire. The Red Army showed its unquestionable superiority fighting against old bourgeois and monarchist Russia, which imperialism tried to restore with help from the White armies of Kolchak, Denikin, Yudenich, Wrangel, and others, as well as fighting against the national armies of the "democracies" that world imperialism set up for its purposes (Finland, Estonia, Latvia, Poland).

In the economic sphere the Soviet republic has performed a great miracle simply by surviving during the first three difficult and most trying years.[5] It remains inviolate and continues to develop because it has taken the tools of exploitation from the hands of the bourgeoisie and changed them into instruments of the planned economy. Amidst the clash of battle on endless fronts, soviet power did not let slip a single opportunity for economic and cultural development. In the interval between the destruction by Denikin and the rapacious attack by Poland, the Soviet government undertook to organize comprehensively the conscription of labor,[6] to record more precisely and better utilize productive forces and resources, to draw portions of the army into economic work, and above all to reestablish the transportation system.

Only the socialist state monopoly in the principal foodstuffs together with a relentless struggle against speculation saved the Russian cities from starvation and made it possible to supply the Red Army. Only the state consolidation of individual businesses, factories, and privately owned railroads and ships made production and transportation possible.

Centralizing industry and transport in the hands of the state led to socializing technology itself by standardizing it. Only on the basis of socialism is it possible to set a minimum number of types of locomotives, freight cars, and ships to be manufactured and repaired as well as to periodically regulate machine parts for standardized mass production, which offers immeasurable advantages for productive relationships. Further economic progress, scientific organization of industry, and application of the methods of the Taylor system—without its capitalist, exploitative features—no longer face obstacles in Soviet Russia, except those imposed from without by imperialist force.[7]

At a time when national interests clash with imperialist usurpation, producing an unbroken stream of conflicts, uprisings, and wars around the world, socialist Russia proves that the workers' state is capable of smoothly combining national with economic needs by purging the former of chauvinism and freeing the latter from imperialism. Socialism wants to unite all regions, all areas, all nationalities in an integrated economic plan. Economic centralization is wholly consistent with true freedom of national development because it frees one class from exploitation by another, as well as one nation by another, and therefore is equally beneficial for all.

The peoples of central Europe, the southeast Balkans, the British possessions, all the oppressed nations and tribes—the Egyptians and Turks, Indians and Persians, Irish and Bulgarians—are becoming convinced from the experience of Soviet Russia that comradely collaboration of all the national components of humanity can be accomplished only through the federation of soviet republics.

The revolution created in Russia the first proletarian power. In the three years of its existence, its borders have continuously changed. They retreated under the external military pressure of world imperialism; they advanced when the pressure eased.

The fight for Soviet Russia merges with the fight against world imperialism. The question of Soviet Russia has become the touchstone for all working-class organizations. The German Social Democrats' most vile betrayal, second to that of August 4, 1914, took place when, as head of the German state, they sought the protection of the imperialism of the West, rather than striving for an alliance with the revolution in the East. Soviet Germany in alliance with Soviet Russia would be stronger than all the capitalist states put together!

The Communist International has made the cause of Soviet Russia its own. The international proletariat will not lay down its sword until Soviet Russia is but a link in the world federation of soviet republics.

### 5. The proletarian revolution and the Communist International

Civil war is on the agenda around the world. Its banner is soviet power.

Capitalism has proletarianized huge masses of humanity. Imperialism throws these masses out of their equilibrium and sets them into revolutionary motion. The meaning of *masses* has itself changed in recent years. Those who were counted as masses in the period of parliamentarism and trade unionism are now converted into the upper layers. Millions upon millions who previously stood outside of political life are now transformed into a revolutionary mass. The war roused everyone, awakened the political attention of even the most backward layers, fired their illusions and hopes—and deceived them.

The social foundations of the old forms of the workers' movement—labor's division into closed crafts and the relatively stable standard of living among the proletariat's upper layers; the impassive and apathetic hopelessness of the lower layers—belong irrevocably to the past. New millions have been drawn into the fight.

Women, who lost fathers and husbands whose labor must be replaced with their own, are pouring into the movement in broad torrents. The working youth, who grew up under the thunder and lightning of the World War, feel right at home in the revolution.

The struggle went through different stages in different countries. But this is the final struggle. The waves of the movement often flow into antiquated organizational forms, temporarily reviving them. Old catchwords and half-obliterated slogans bob up now and again on the surface of the torrent. Many mistakes, unclarities, prejudices, and illusions are still knocking about. But the movement as a whole has a deeply revolutionary character. It is all-embracing and unstoppable. It spreads, consolidates, and purifies itself, sweeping aside all the old rubbish. It will not stop until the world proletariat has come to power.

The basic form of this movement is the strike. Its most simple and powerful cause is the increase in prices of daily necessities. The strike often arises out of individual local conflicts. It breaks out as the masses' impatient response to the Socialists' parliamentary ruckus. It mixes economic and political demands. It is born out of a sense of solidarity with the oppressed at home and abroad. It often contains fragments of reformism together with slogans of the revolutionary social program. It recedes, dies out, is born again, disrupts production, strains the state apparatus, and rattles the bourgeoisie—all the more since it seizes every occasion to send greetings to Soviet Russia. The exploiters' premonitions are not unfounded, for this chaotic strike is in fact a revolutionary social signal and a mobilization of the international proletariat.

The great dependence of every country upon the others, which became so catastrophically evident during the war, gives special importance to those branches of industry that connect one country with another, putting the railroad workers, and transport workers in general, into front-row seats, as it were. The proletarians in transport had an opportunity to display some of their strength in the boycott of White Hungary and White Poland. The strike and the boycott, methods that have been used by the working class since the dawn of its trade union struggles, that is, before it began using parliamentarism, now assume unprecedented scope and a new, threatening significance—like the artillery barrage that precedes the final assault.

All the growing helplessness of the individual before the onslaught of historic events drives into the ranks of unions new layers not only of working men and women but also of salaried personnel, civil servants, and the petty-bourgeois intellectuals. Before the course of the proletarian revolution compels the formation of soviets, which immediately stand out above all old workers' organizations, the toilers assemble in traditional trade unions, temporarily tolerating their old forms, official program, and top officials. But they carry into these organizations the growing revolutionary momentum of a colossal mass of millions.

The lowest of the low—the agricultural proletariat, the farm workers—are raising their heads. In Italy, Germany, and elsewhere we see a tremendous growth in the revolutionary movement of the agricultural workers and their fraternal convergence with the urban proletariat.

The poorest layers of the peasantry are changing their attitude toward socialism. If the parliamentary reformists' flirtation with the peasants' property-owning superstitions failed to bear fruit, the truly revolutionary movement of the proletariat and its implacable fight against the oppressor arouses a flicker of hope in the soul of the most backward, earthbound, ruined peasant.

The ocean of human misery and spiritual gloom is bottomless. Behind every rising layer stands another, already on the verge of rising up. But the vanguard cannot await a mass following before it enters into struggle. The working class will be able to accomplish the work of awakening, elevating, and educating its most backward layers only *after* conquering power.

The toilers of the colonial and semicolonial countries have awakened. In the immense regions of India, Egypt, and Persia, across which lies sprawled the gigantic octopus of British imperialism, in this immeasurable human ocean, vast internal forces are constantly at work, tossing up high waves and causing the London bankers' stocks and hearts to tremble.

In the movement of the colonial peoples, the social element is bound up with the national in very diverse forms, but both are directed against imperialism. The distance from the first baby steps to the mature forms of struggle in the colonies and the backward countries in general will be traversed at a forced march under the pressure of modern imperialism and under the leadership of the revolutionary proletariat.

There is a promising convergence of the Muslim and non-Muslim peoples, who are everywhere welded together by the common chains of British and foreign domination. Their movement is purging itself internally, eliminating the influence of the clergy and of chauvinist reaction. Their struggles are waged not only against the foreign oppressor but simultaneously against their own landlords, feudalists, clerics, and usurers. All this is transforming the growing army of the colonial uprising into a powerful historic force, a mighty reserve of the world proletariat. The pariahs are rising up. They turn their awakened imagination warmly toward Soviet Russia, toward the fighters on the barricades in the streets of German cities, toward the raging strike battles in Great Britain, toward the Communist International.

The Socialist who directly or indirectly supports the privileged position of one nation at the cost of others, who has made his peace with colonial slavery, who makes a distinction between peoples of different races and skin colors, who helps the bourgeoisie of the metropolis to preserve its domination over the colonies instead of helping the cause of the armed rebellion of the colonies, the British Socialist who fails to support by all possible means the rebellion in Ireland, Egypt, and India against the London plutocracy—such a Socialist deserves, if not the bullet, then certainly the mark of infamy, and no mandate or confidence from the proletariat.

Furthermore, the proletariat, in its international revolutionary actions, runs up less against the half-destroyed barbed wire entanglements from the war, still standing between the countries, than against the egoism, conservatism, pigheadedness, and treachery of the old party and trade union organizations it has been saddled with since the previous period.

The leaders of the old trade unions use all means to work against the revolutionary struggles of the working masses, hamper them, or, when nothing else works, take charge of them, all the better to strangle them with dark machinations behind the scenes.

The historic betrayal by international Social Democracy has no parallel in the history of oppression and struggle. This was shown most clearly and terribly in Germany. The collapse of German imperialism took place at the same time as the collapse of the capitalist economic system. No class other than the proletariat could have laid claim to state power. The development of technology and the numerical strength and cultural level of the German working class were certain guarantees for the success of the socialist uprising. But German Social Democracy blocked the road to carrying out this task. Through refined maneuvers combining cunning and stupidity, the force of the working class was deflected from its natural and necessary goal: conquering power. Over the decades Social Democracy had won the confidence of the masses only in order, at the decisive moment when the fate of bourgeois society hung in the balance, to throw the weight of their authority to the side of the oppressors.

The treachery of liberalism and the collapse of bourgeois democracy proved to be insignificant episodes compared with the monstrous betrayal by the Socialist parties. Even the role of the church—the conservatives' power station, as Lloyd George puts it—is minor when compared to the antisocialist role of the Second International.

Social Democracy justified its betrayal during the war with the slogan of national defense. Since the conclusion of peace, they disguise their counterrevolutionary policies with the slogan of democracy. National defense and democracy are the triumphant slogans for the proletariat's capitulation before the will of the bourgeoisie.

But the plunge does not stop there. The Social Democrats' policies, which serve to defend the capitalist order, necessarily led them, as servants of the bourgeoisie, to openly trample on "national defense" and "democracy." Scheidemann and Ebert kiss the hand of French imperialism—seeking its support against a soviet revolution. Noske personifies the bourgeois counterrevolution's White Terror. Albert Thomas has become a paid agent of the League of Nations, that squalid imperialist agency. Vandervelde, that phrasemongering embodiment of superficiality of the Second International, which he headed, has become a royal minister and underling of the clerical Delacroix, defender of Belgium's Catholic priests and lawyer for capitalist atrocities against the Congo's Blacks. Henderson apes the great men of the bourgeoisie and plays now royal minister, now His Majesty's most loyal Labour opposition. Tom Shaw demands strict proof from the Soviet government that there really are robbers, thieves, and liars in the London government. What are these gentlemen but outspoken enemies of the working class?

Renner and Seitz, Nemec and Tusar, Troelstra and Branting, Daszynski and Chkheidze, every one of them translates the disgraceful shipwreck of the Second International into the roguery of their petty governments. And Kautsky, the former Marxist and theoretician for the Second International, has become a babbling shyster for the Yellow press of the world.

Under pressure from the masses, the resourceful elements of the old Socialism change their appearance and their skin without changing their essence. They break with the Second International or prepare to do so, while shrinking from any real revolutionary and mass action and even from any serious preparation for action.

In order to both characterize and stigmatize this masquerade, it suffices to point out that the Polish Socialist Party, the party of petty-bourgeois cynicism and chauvinist fanaticism, whose leader is Daszynski and whose patron is Pilsudski, has also announced its withdrawal from the Second International.

The leading parliamentary clique of the French Socialist Party, which now votes against the budget and against the Versailles treaty, remains in essence one of the mainstays of the bourgeois republic. Their oppositional gestures go only so far as is necessary occasionally to halfway restore the confidence of the most conservative layers of the proletariat.

In the basic questions of the class struggle, French parliamentary Socialism continues as before to blunt the will of the working class by teaching it that this is not the moment for seizing power because France is totally exhausted, just as yesterday it was the wrong moment because of the war, and before the war the industrial upswing stood in the way, and before that the industrial crisis. The jabbering and lying syndicalism of Jouhaux and company stands on the same level as parliamentary Socialism and not a whit higher.

The creation of a strong Communist party, forged in the spirit of unity and discipline, is a life-and-death question for the French proletariat.

A new breed of German worker is being trained and steeled in strikes and uprisings. This experience is gained at a price: a toll of victims that can only grow, as long as the Independent Socialist party of Germany remains under the influence of the stick-in-the-mud Social Democratic saviors of the government, who always look back to the Social Democracy of Bebel's time, do not understand the character of the present revolutionary epoch, flinch at civil war and revolutionary terror, and dodder along behind events, hoping for a miracle to save them from bankruptcy. In the heat of battle the party of Rosa Luxemburg and Karl Liebknecht is teaching the German workers to find the right road.

The stagnation at the top of the British workers' movement is so great that they do not even notice the need for new weapons. The leaders of the British Labour Party are stubbornly bent on remaining in the ranks of the Second International. At a time when the course of recent events has shattered the rigidity of economic life even in conservative Britain, making the masses most receptive to a revolutionary program, the official machinery of the bourgeois nation—the royalty, the House of Lords, the Commons, the church, the trade unions, the Labour Party, George V, the Archbishop of Canterbury, and Henderson—all this remains intact, a powerful automatic brake on any progress. The proletarian masses can counterpose to this officialdom only a Communist party, free of routinism and sectarianism and closely linked to the mass organizations.

In Italy, where even the bourgeoisie openly recognizes that the key to the country's future destiny is held by the Socialist Party, the policies of the right wing, led by Turati, are to entice the powerfully evolving proletarian revolution into the bed of parliamentary reformism. This internal sabotage poses the greatest present danger.

Proletarians of Italy, think of Hungary, whose example belongs to history, as a terrible warning that in the fight for power and after its seizure, the proletariat must stand firmly on its own feet by weeding out all outlived and wavering elements and relentlessly condemning all attempts at betrayal.

In the United States, as in other countries on the American continent, the convulsions of the war and the severe economic crisis resulting from it open a new chapter for the labor movement. The end of Wilsonian bombast and lies is at the same time the end of American Socialism, that mixture of pacifist illusions with the bustle of county fair barkers that amicably supplements Mr. Gompers's trade unionism from the left. The revolutionary proletarian parties and organizations of the American continent, from the Alaskan peninsula to Cape Horn, must be welded tightly together into an intimately linked American section of the Communist International opposing the powerful enemy—U.S. imperialism. This is a task that must and will be fulfilled in the struggle against all the forces that the dollar mobilizes in its defense.

Governmental and quasi-governmental Socialists of different countries use many pretexts to condemn the Communists, saying that our intransigent tactics provoke the counterrevolution and thereby help it to close ranks. This political accusation is nothing more than a belated parody of the lamentations of liberalism. According to liberalism, the independent struggle of the proletariat drives the propertied classes into the camp of reaction. That is undoubtedly true. If the working class attempted no assault on the foundations of capitalist rule, the bourgeoisie would need no reprisals. The very concept of counterrevolution would not exist if history had never known revolution. The uprisings of the proletariat inevitably entail bourgeois consolidation in self-defense and counterattack. But that only proves that the revolution is the struggle between two implacable classes that can end only in the definitive victory of one or the other.

Communism scornfully rejects this policy, which amounts to holding the masses in check by intimidating them with the whip of counterrevolution. The Communist International responds to the collapse and chaos of the capitalist world, whose death agony threatens to eradicate human culture, with the united struggle of the international proletariat, the abolition of all private property in the means of production, and the reorganization of the national and world economy on the basis of an integrated economic plan, which will be drawn up and carried out in common solidarity by the associated producers.

Uniting millions of toilers from the four corners of the earth under the banner of the dictatorship of the proletariat and the soviet system, the Communist International cleanses, broadens, and assembles its own ranks in the heat of battle. The Communist International is the party of the revolutionary uprising of the international proletariat. It excludes all groups and organizations that overtly or covertly lull, demoralize, or weaken the proletariat. It urges the proletariat on, not to bow down before the false gods of legality, democracy, national defense, and the like, which conceal the dictatorship of the bourgeoisie. Nor can the Communist International take into its ranks those organizations that, while recognizing the dictatorship of the proletariat in their program, nevertheless carry out policies that rely on a peaceful resolution of the historic crisis. The mere recognition of the soviet system solves nothing. The soviet form of organization possesses no miraculous powers. Revolutionary power lies in the proletariat itself, which has to rise up in insurrection and fight its way to power. Only then can soviet organization manifest its merits as an incomparable weapon in the hands of the proletariat.

The Communist International demands the expulsion of all those leaders of the workers' movement who are connected with the bourgeoisie through direct or indirect collaboration. We need leaders who have no other attitude toward bourgeois society than that of mortal hatred, who call and guide the proletariat to tireless struggle, who are ready to lead an army of insurgents into battle, who will not stop halfway, and who, come what may, will not refrain from pitilessly punishing those who use force in the attempt to hold them back.

The Communist International is the international party of proletarian uprising and of proletarian dictatorship. It has no goals or tasks separate from those of the working class as a whole. The pretensions of the little sects, each of which tries to save the working class according to its own model, are alien to the spirit of the Communist International and are hostile to its views. It offers no universal recipes nor incantations but is grounded in the past and present international experience of the working class. It purges this experience of all mistakes and deviations, generalizes the results, and recognizes and adopts only those slogans that are slogans for mass action.

Trade unions, economic and political strikes, boycotts, parliamentary and local elections, the parliamentary rostrum, legal and illegal agitation, secret points of support in the army, work in consumer cooperatives, barricades—the Communist International does not reject a single one of the forms of organization or struggle created in the development of the workers' movement, nor does it consider any single form to be a panacea.

The soviet system is no abstract principle that Communists counterpose to the principle of parliamentarism. The soviet system is a class instrument that must defeat and replace parliamentarism in struggle and through struggle. While leading a merciless fight against reformism in the unions and against parliamentary idiocy and careerism in parliaments, the Communist International condemns the sectarian calls to quit the many-millioned ranks of the unions, or to turn our backs on parliamentary and municipal institutions. The Communists do not separate themselves in any way from the masses, who are deceived and betrayed by the reformists and the patriots. Rather they engage the reformists in an implacable struggle within the mass organizations and institutions created by bourgeois society in order to thereby overthrow it all the more quickly and certainly.

When, under the aegis of the Second International, the methods of class organization and struggle were almost exclusively legal, they fell ultimately under the control and leadership of the bourgeoisie, which reined in the revolutionary class through its reformist agents. The Communist International tears the reins from the bourgeoisie's hands, masters all the methods of the working class and wins all its organizations, unites them under revolutionary leadership, and through them sets a single goal for the proletariat: to fight its way to power in order to destroy the bourgeois state and found the communist society.

In all work, as leader of revolutionary insurrections, as organizer of underground groups, as secretary of trade unions, as agitator at mass meetings or as parliamentary deputy, as member of a cooperative or as barricade fighter, the Communist remains himself, the disciplined member of the Communist Party, ruthless fighter and mortal enemy of capitalist society—its economic foundations, its state forms, its democratic lies, its religion, its morality. He is the most self-sacrificing soldier of the proletarian revolution and the tireless herald of the new society.

Working men and women! On this earth there is but one banner worth fighting and dying for: this is the banner of the *Communist International.*

MOSCOW, AUGUST 1920

Second Congress of the Communist International[8]
RUSSIA: *V.I. Lenin, G. Zinoviev, N. Bukharin, L. Trotsky*
GERMANY: *P. Levi, E. Meyer, J. Walcher, R. Wolfstein*
AUSTRIA: *K. Steinhardt, K. Tomann, Ströhmer*
FRANCE: *A. Rosmer, J. Sadoul, H. Guilbeaux*
ENGLAND: *T. Quelch, W. Gallacher, S. Pankhurst, W. McLaine*
AMERICA: *Flynn, L. Fraina, A. Bilan,*[9] *John Reed*
ITALY: *G.M. Serrati, N. Bombacci, Graziadei, A. Bordiga*
NORWAY: *Friis, Scheflo, A. Madsen*
SWEDEN: *K. Dahlström, Samuelson, Winberg*
DENMARK: *Å. Jørgensen, M. Nielsen*
NETHERLANDS: *Wijnkoop, Jansen, Van Leuven*
BELGIUM: *Van Overstraeten*
SPAIN: *Pestaña*
SWITZERLAND: *Herzog, J. Humbert-Droz*
HUNGARY: *Rákosi, E. Rudnyánszky, Varga*
GALICIA: *Lewicky*
POLAND: *J. Marchlewski*
LATVIA: *Stuchka, Krastins*
LITHUANIA-BELORUSSIA: *Mitskevich-Kapsukas*
CZECHOSLOVAKIA: *Vanek, Hula, Zápotocky*

ESTONIA: *R. Vakmann, H. Pöögelmann*
FINLAND: *J. Rahja, Letonmäki, K. Manner*
BULGARIA: *Kabakchiev, Maksimov, Shablin*
YUGOSLAVIA: *Milkic*
GEORGIA: *M. Tskhakaya*
ARMENIA: *Nazaretian*
TURKEY: *Nueret*
PERSIA: *Sultanzadeh*
INDIA: *Acharya, Shafiq, Roy*
DUTCH EAST INDIES: *Maring*
CHINA: *Liu Shaozhou*
KOREA: *Pak Chin-sun, Kim Tu-lin*[10]

## APPENDIX 1
ORGANIZING THE CONGRESS

# 1A
# Minutes of the Credentials Commission

### EXTRACT FROM THE MINUTES OF THE JULY 17, 1920, MEETING OF THE PROVISIONAL CREDENTIALS COMMISSION

Resolved:[1]

To leave open the question of the mandate of the following comrades:

Britain: [Marjory] Newbold (National Young Labour League). We delegated Comrade Shatskin to clarify the question of Comrade Newbold's mandate with Quelch and McLaine.

France: (1) Delinières (Third International Committee on Economic Questions). In view of Comrade Rosmer's objections, we leave the question open until the other comrades who are on their way from France arrive and can give their view. (2) Goldenberg (communist opposition in the French youth league).

Cuba: Jesús Ramírez (Communist Party of Cuba). To be left open until credentials are delivered.[2]

Italy: D'Aragona (General Confederation of Labor). To be left open pending clarification of this organization's relations with the Third International.

We leave open, pending presentation of credentials:

Switzerland: Humbert-Droz.

Latvia: Paul Blank-Berzins, Jan Berzins-Andersons, and David Beika (bureau abroad).

We refuse:

Kohn (Poale Zion): The Poale Zion organization has not yet overcome its nationalist prejudices. Its delegation cannot therefore be included among participants in the congress, nor can the organization be accepted into the Third International, for reasons of principle. The Credentials Commission of the Executive Committee cannot give the delegation either a decisive or a consultative vote. In the hope that the Poale Zion organization will eventually come over to the positions of the Communist International, the Credentials Commission considers it permissible and desirable to admit two delegates from Poale Zion to the congress as guests.

No decision was reached on:

Germany: Rühle and Merges (Communist Workers Party of Germany). These comrades declared that because they disagree with the theses submitted to the congress by the Executive Committee, they have requested instructions from the Central Committee of their party. Until they receive these, they feel they cannot take part in the congress.

## MINUTES OF THE MEETING OF THE CREDENTIALS COMMISSION, JULY 28, 1920

Present: Comrades Radek, Meyer, Bombacci, Shablin, Rudnyánszky, Sultanzadeh, Rosmer.

The Credentials Commission elected by the Communist International congress has considered the list of those participating in the congress with full and consultative voting rights that was drawn up by the Provisional Credentials Commission appointed by the Executive Committee. The commission resolves to approve this list, with the following changes and additions:

We grant Ireland, represented by Comrades Gell and Johnson, a full instead of consultative vote.

We withdraw the status of delegate with consultative vote granted to Comrades Vacirca, Colombino, Paverani, and D'Aragona from Italy.

We withdraw the status of delegate with consultative vote granted to Comrade Leutner of Hungary.

We recognize Comrades Avanesov and Katanian as delegates with consultative vote for Armenia.

We grant a consultative vote to the Socialist Party of Palestine, represented by Comrade Kohn, and we remove this comrade from the Austrian delegation.[3]

We refuse the Young Bukharans' request for voting rights at the congress.

We transfer the Netherlands from the second to the third group on the list of distribution of votes, giving it 4 votes instead of 7.

## 1B
## Preliminary list of delegates

[*Editor's note:* A list of delegates appears in the German, Russian, and English editions of the Second Congress proceedings printed in 1920 and 1921. A comparison of congress records shows that this list is a preliminary enumeration of delegates drawn up prior to the July 17 session of the Credentials Commission. It does not reflect the commission's changes and does not include some late arrivals.

[The list as printed here is based on one that appears in the German edition of the proceedings. A few corrections have been made, based on versions in the two Russian editions, the English edition, and the 1920 Vienna edition, as well as the list of Russian CP delegates published during the congress in *Pravda,* and other research. Names of organizations are given as they appear in the original text.

[The notes to this appendix record available information on congress delegates and guests whose presence is not indicated in the delegates list.

[The number of votes held by each country's delegation is taken from the Credentials Commission report in session 10 supplemented with data from a list in the 1920 Vienna edition.

[In addition to the delegations given here, the 1920 Vienna edition lists delegations from Argentina (1 delegate with 2 votes),[4] Portugal (1 delegate with 2 votes), Romania (2 delegates with 5 votes), Scotland (3 delegates with 2 votes), and, inexplicably, Greenland (2 delegates with 5 votes). *Berichte zum zweiten Kongress,* the collection of national reports submitted to the congress, includes a contribution by Hendrik Ottósson of Iceland, who was a guest at the congress, and one by a delegate from Luxembourg, E. Reiland, who was not able to arrive at the congress until after it ended.]

**Armenia**[5]

Communist Party: Avis, Nazaretian

**Australia**

Communist League: *consultative:* Freeman

IWW: *consultative:* Suzenko

**Austria** (7 votes)

Communist Party: Reisler, Steinhardt, Ströhmer, Tomann

Poale Zion: *consultative:* Kohn[6]

**Azerbaijan**

Communist Party (trade union majority): Sapunov

**Belgium** (2 votes)

Walloon Communist Federation: Van Overstraeten

**Britain** (10 votes)[7]

British Socialist Party: McLaine, Quelch

Shop Stewards: Murphy, Ramsay, Tanner

Industrial Workers of the World: Beech

National Young Labour League: *consultative:* [M.] Newbold

**Bukhara**

Communist Party: *consultative:* Muhamadiev

**Bulgaria** (4 votes)

Communist Party: Kabakchiev, Maksimov, Shablin

**China** (2 votes)

Chinese Socialist Workers Party (Central Bureau): *consultative:* Han En-hak, Liu Shaozhou

**Czechoslovakia** (3 votes)

Communist Party: Olbracht

Social Democratic Party (left wing): Hula, Zápotocky

Communist Group: *consultative:* Malírová, Sonnenstein

**Denmark** (3 votes)

Communist Teachers Club: Nielsen

Left Socialist Party: Jørgensen

**Dutch East Indies** (2 votes)

Communist Association: Maring, (unknown)

**East Galicia** (2 votes)

Communist Party of Galicia and Bukovina: Baral, Lewicky, Mitra

**Estonia** (4 votes)
Communist Party: Pöögelmann, Vakmann
Independent Socialist Workers Party: *consultative:* Joonas
**Finland** (7 votes)
Communist Party: Kohonen, Kuusinen, Letonmäki, Lumivuokko, Manner, Rahja
Socialist Workers Party: *consultative:* Gylling, Rovio, Tammenoksa
**France** (10 votes)[8]
Committee for the Third International: Vanini, Lefebvre, Rosmer
Communist Group: Sadoul
Communist Federation of Soviets: Guilbeaux
Communist Party: *consultative:* Abramovich
Socialist Party: *consultative:* Cachin, Frossard
Socialist Youth Federation: Goldenberg[9]
**Georgia** (3 votes)
Communist Party: Makharadze, Mikadze, Todria, Tskhakaya, Vashakidze
Youth League: Vardanian
**Germany** (10 votes)[10]
Communist Party (Spartacus League): Budich, Levi, Meyer, Walcher, Wolfstein
Free Socialist Youth: Leinhardt
Independent Social Democratic Party: *consultative:* Crispien, Däumig, Dittmann, Schiller,[11] Stoecker
Syndicalists: *consultative:* Souchy, Sturm
**Hungary** (7 votes)
Communist Party: Rákosi, Rudnyánszky
**India** (2 votes)[12]
Indian Revolutionary Association: *consultative:* Acharya
(unaffiliated): *consultative:* Mukherji
**Ireland** (2 votes)
Labour Party: Quinlan

Industrial Workers of the World: Connolly
Communist Party: *consultative:* Gell, Johnson, MacAlpine[13]

**Italy** (10 votes)
Socialist Party: Bombacci, Graziadei, Serrati; *consultative:* Bordiga, Colombino, D'Aragona, Paverani, Vacirca[14]
Socialist Youth Federation: Polano

**Korea**
Communist Party: Pak Chin-sun

**Latvia**
Communist Party: Blank-Berzins, Krastins, Stuchka; *consultative:* Beika, Berzins-Andersons

**Lithuania-Belorussia** (3 votes)
Communist Party: Mitskevich-Kapsukas, Rasikas

**Mexico** (2 votes)
Communist Party: Roy, Seaman; *consultative:* [H.] Allan

**Netherlands** (4 votes)[15]
Communist Party: Van Leuven, Wijnkoop

**Norway** (3 votes)
Labor Party: Åsen, Friis, Kristensen, Krogh, Langseth, Madsen, Scheflo, Syvertsen
Social Democratic Youth League: Gerhardsen, Medby

**Persia** (2 votes)
Communist Party: Sultanzadeh; *consultative:* Hassanzadeh, Orudshev

**Poland** (7 votes)
Communist Workers Party: Marchlewski

**Russia** (10 votes)[16]
Communist Party (Russia): Akhundov, Aliyev, Andreyev, Armand, Artem, Baytursunov, [I.] Berzin, Blakytnyi, Bukharin, [M.] Chernov, Dzerzhinsky, Firstov, Gopner, Ibrahimov, Ignat, Joffe, Kalinin, Kollontai, Krasnoshchekov, Krestinsky, Krupskaya,

Lenin, Lozovsky, Lunacharsky, Manuil'sky, Merezhin, Moyrova, Ol'minsky, Osinsky, Pavlovich, Pestkowski, Pokrovsky, Preobrazhensky, Radek, Rakovsky, Ramonov, Rudzutak, Ryazanov, Rykov, Sadovskaya, Serebryakov, Shlyapnikov, Skrypnyk, Smidovich, Sokolnikov, Steklov, Taratuta, Tomsky, Trotsky, Tsyperovich, Vatin, Voronova, Yanson,[17] Yaroslavsky, Yenukidze, Zinoviev, Zorin

Youth League: Dunayevsky, Ryvkin, Tsetlin

Communist Party (Crimea): Idrisov

Communist Party (South Ossetia): Kodzayev

Communist Party (Ukraine)(7 votes): Kon

Communist Party (Tatar): Safarov, Said Galiev, Sultan Galiev

Communist Bund: *consultative:* Litvakov, Vaynshteyn

Party of Revolutionary Communism: *consultative:* Sapozhnikov, Ustinov

**Spain** (2 votes)

National Federation of Labor: Pestaña

**Sweden** (3 votes)

Left Social Democratic Party: Dahlström, Linderot

**Switzerland** (3 votes)

Communist Party: Bäcker, Herzog

Social Democratic Party (left wing): Bringolf, Humbert-Droz

Socialist Youth Organization: Bamatter

**Turkey** (3 votes)

Bureau of Communist Organizations: Hakki, Slavutski

Constantinople Communist Group: Nihat Nueret

**United States** (10 votes)[18]

Communist Labor Party: Bilan, Jurgis, Reed

Communist Party of America: Fraina, Stoklitsky

Independent Young People's Socialist League: Chabrow; *consultative:* Gildei

**Yugoslavia** (5 votes)
Communist Party: Milkic
Communist Youth International: Münzenberg, Shatskin; *consultative:* Leutner[19]
Executive Committee of the Communist International: *consultative:* Balabanoff, Karakhan, Klinger, Men'shoy

# 1C
# Composition of Presiding Committee and commissions

*Presiding Committee:* Lenin and Zinoviev (Russia), Levi (Germany), Rosmer (France), Serrati (Italy).[20]

*Credentials Commission:* Rosmer (France), Meyer (Germany), Bombacci (Italy), Bukharin and Radek (Russia), Rudnyánszky (Hungary).[21]

*International Situation and the Tasks of the Communist International:* Kabakchiev (Bulgaria), Milkic (Yugoslavia), Rosmer (France), Bäcker (Switzerland), Van Leuven (Netherlands), Levi (Germany), Rudnyánszky (Hungary), Tomann (Austria), Lenin and Bukharin (Russia), Fraina (U.S.), Friis (Norway), McLaine (Britain), Murphy (Britain), Liu Shaozhou (China), Pak (Korea).

*Role of the Party:* Fraina (U.S.), Ramsay and McLaine (Britain), Meyer (Germany), Graziadei (Italy), Bukharin (Russia), Kabakchiev (Bulgaria), Steinhardt (Austria), Wijnkoop (Netherlands), Zinoviev (Executive Committee).

*National and Colonial Questions:* Kabakchiev (Bulgaria), Milkic (Yugoslavia), Guilbeaux (France), Wijnkoop (Netherlands), Levi (Germany), Rudnyánszky (Hungary), Tomann (Austria), Lenin and Kamenev (Russia), Reed (U.S.), Maring (Dutch East Indies), Roy-Allan (Mexico), [H.] Allan (British India), Quelch (Britain), Sultanzadeh (Persia), Connolly (Ireland), Ramsay (Britain), Slavutski (Turkey), Liu Shaozhou (China), Pak (Korea).

*Conditions for Admission to the Communist International:* Maksimov (Bulgaria), Sadoul (France), Humbert-Droz (Switzerland), Wijnkoop (Netherlands), Meyer (Germany), Rákosi (Hungary), Zinoviev and Sokolnikov (Russia), Fraina (U.S.), Connolly (Ireland), Steinhardt (Austria).

*Parliamentarism:* Kabakchiev (Bulgaria), Milkic (Yugoslavia), Lefebvre (France), Herzog (Switzerland), Jansen (Netherlands), Wolfstein (Germany), Rudnyánszky (Hungary), Steinhardt (Austria), Trotsky and Bukharin (Russia), Stoklitsky (U.S.), Friis (Norway), McLaine (Britain), Beech (Britain).

*Trade Union Question:* Rosmer (France), Maksimov (Bulgaria), Beika (Lithuania), Van Leuven (Netherlands), Walcher (Germany), Rákosi (Hungary), Tomann (Austria), Zinoviev and Tsyperovich (Russia), Reed (U.S.), Madsen (Norway), Quelch and Tanner (Britain), Pestaña (Spain), D'Aragona (Italy).

*Agrarian Question:* Stuchka (Latvia), Shablin (Bulgaria), Milkic (Yugoslavia), Vanini (France), Bringolf (Switzerland), Jansen (Netherlands), Meyer (Germany), Rákosi (Hungary), Steinhardt (Austria), Pöögelmann (Estonia), Lenin (Russia), Jurgis (U.S.), Langseth (Norway), MacAlpine (Ireland), Hakki (Turkey), Sultanzadeh (Persia).

*Organizational Questions:* Victor (Lithuania), Kabakchiev (Bulgaria), Goldenberg (France), Bamatter (Switzerland), Wijnkoop (Netherlands), Levi (Germany), Rudnyánszky (Hungary), Ströhmer (Austria), Zinoviev and Osinsky (Russia), Bilan (U.S.), Scheflo (Norway), MacAlpine (Ireland), [M.] Newbold (Britain).

*Translation of Resolutions:* Meyer (German), Rosmer (French), Reed (English), Sokolnikov (Russian).

APPENDIX 2

NATIONAL AND COLONIAL QUESTIONS

# 2A
# The editing of M.N. Roy's draft theses on the national and colonial questions

[*Editor's note:* M.N. Roy substantially revised his draft theses on the colonial and national questions in the course of discussions with Lenin and other delegates.[1] The changes are indicated in this appendix. Roy's original draft is printed in the left-hand column. Struck-through passages were deleted from the version he submitted to the congress. Italicized passages were substantially rewritten; the final substitutions are given in the right-hand column. Locations where Roy added new passages are marked by a gap in the left-hand column; the addition is printed in the right-hand column opposite the gap.]

| **Original draft theses by M.N. Roy** | **New and rewritten passages** |
|---|---|
| 1. To determine the relation of the Communist International to the revolutionary movements in | |

| | |
|---|---|
| the countries dominated by capitalistic imperialism | , for instance, China and India, |
| is one of the most important questions before the Second Congress of the Third International. The history of the world revolution has come to a period when a proper understanding of this relation is indispensable; the great European war and its results have shown clearly that the masses of the non-European subjected countries are inseparably connected with the proletarian movement in Europe, as a consequence of the centralized world capitalism | (for instance, the sending of colonial troops and huge armies of workers to the battlefronts during the war, and so on). |
| 2. *The fountainhead from which European capitalism draws its main strength is no longer to be found in the industrial countries of Europe but in the colonial possessions and dependencies.* Without the control of the extensive markets and vast fields of exploitation in the | 2. One of the main sources from which European capitalism draws its strength is to be found in the colonial possessions and dependencies. |

colonies, the capitalist powers of Europe cannot maintain their existence even for a short time. England, the stronghold of imperialism, has been suffering from overproduction since more than a century ago. But for the extensive colonial possessions acquired for selling her surplus products and as a source of raw materials for her ever-growing industries, the capitalist structure of England would have crushed under its own weight long ago. By enslaving the hundreds of millions of inhabitants of Asia and Africa, English imperialism succeeded so far in keeping the British proletariat under the domination of the bourgeoisie.

3. Superprofit gained in the colonies is the mainstay of modern capitalism, and, so long as it is not deprived of this source of superprofit, it will not be easy for the European working class to overthrow the capitalist order. Thanks to the possibility of intensive and extensive exploitation of human la-

bor and natural resources in the colonies, the capitalist nations of Europe are trying, not without success, to recuperate their present bankruptcy. By exploiting the masses in the colonies, European imperialism will be in a position to give concession after concession *to the proletariat at home.*

to the labor aristocracy at home. While European imperialism seeks to lower the standard of living of the home proletariat by bringing into competition the production of the lower-paid workers in subject countries,

it will not hesitate to go to the extent of sacrificing the entire surplus value in the home country so long as it continues in the position to gain its huge superprofits in the colonies.

4. *Without the breaking up of the colonial empire, the overthrow of the capitalist system in Europe does not appear possible.*

4. The breakup of the colonial empire, together with the proletarian revolution in the home country, will overthrow the capitalist system in Europe.

Consequently, the Communist International must widen the sphere of its activities. It must establish relations with those revolutionary forces that are working for the overthrow of imperialism in the countries subjected politically and economically.

These two forces must be coordinated if the final success of the world revolution is to be assured.

5. ~~Such relation of the Communist International with the revolutionary movement in the subject countries is not tantamount to the former's upholding the doctrine of nationalism.~~ The Communist International is the concentrated will of the world revolutionary proletariat. Its mission is to organize the working class of the whole world for the overthrow of the capitalist order and the establishment of communism. The Third International is a fighting body *which has outgrown the realm of pure doctrinairism.*

which must assume the task of uniting the revolutionary forces of all the countries of the world.

Dominated as it was by a group of politicians, permeated with bourgeois culture, the Second International failed to appreciate the importance of the colonial question. For them the world did not exist outside of Europe.

They could not see the necessity of coordinating the revolutionary movement in Europe with those in the non-European countries. Instead of giving moral and material help to the revolutionary movements in the colonies, the members of the Second International themselves became imperialists.

6. Foreign imperialism imposed on the Eastern peoples prevented them from developing socially and economically side by side with their fellows in Europe and America. Owing to the imperialistic policy of preventing industrial development of the colonies, a proletarian class in the strict sense of the term could not come into existence until recently. The indigenous craft industries were destroyed to make room for the prod-

ucts of the centralized industries in the imperialistic countries; consequently a big majority of the population was driven to the land to produce food grains and raw materials for export to foreign lands. On the other hand, there followed a rapid concentration of land, *the proprietary right of which was vested in the state,*

in the hands of the big landowners, financial capitalists, and the state,

thus creating a huge landless peasantry. The great bulk of the population was kept in a state of illiteracy. As a result of this policy, the spirit of revolt latent in every subject people found its expression only through the small, educated middle class.

The foreign domination has obstructed the free development of the social forces—therefore its overthrow is the first step towards the revolution in the colonies. So, to help overthrow the foreign rule in the colonies is not to endorse the nationalist aspirations of the native bourgeoisie but to open up the way to the smothered proletariat there.

7. ~~The revolutionary movements in the colonies are essentially an economic struggle. The bourgeois-democratic nationalist movements are limited to the small middle class which does not reflect the aspirations of the masses. Without the active support of the masses, the national freedom of the colonies will never be attained. But in many countries, especially in India, the masses are not with the bourgeois-nationalist leaders—they are moving towards revolution independently of the bourgeois-nationalist movement.~~ There are to be found in the dependent countries two distinct movements which every day grow further and further apart from each other. One is the bourgeois-democratic nationalist movement, *with a program of political independence and the other is the mass action of the ignorant and poor peasants and workers.*

with a program of political independence under the bourgeois order, and the other is the mass action of the ignorant and poor peasants and workers for their liberation from all sorts of exploitation.

The former endeavor to control the latter and often succeed to a certain extent. *But it would be a mistake to assume that the bourgeois-nationalist movement expresses the sentiments and aspirations of the general population.*

For the overthrow of foreign *imperialism,* the first step towards revolution in the colonies, the cooperation of the bourgeois-nationalist elements *may be useful. But the Communist International must not find in them the media through which the revolutionary movement in the colonies should be helped. The mass movements in the colonies are growing independently of the nationalist movements. The masses distrust the political leaders who always lead them astray and prevent them from revolutionary action.*

8. The real strength of the liberation movement in the colonies is no longer confined to the narrow cir-

But the Communist International and its affiliated parties must struggle against this and help to develop class consciousness in the working masses of the colonies.

capitalism

is useful. But the foremost and necessary task is the formation of Communist parties that will organize the peasants and workers and lead them to the revolution and the establishment of soviet republics. Thus the masses of the backward countries may reach communism not through capitalist development but led by the class-conscious proletariat of the advanced capitalist countries.

cle of bourgeois-democratic nationalists. In most of the colonies there already exist organized *Socialist or Communist parties, in close relation to the mass movement.*

The relation of the Communist International with the revolutionary movement in the colonies should be through the medium of these parties or groups, because they are the vanguard of the working class in their respective countries. They may not be very big today, but they reflect the desire of the masses and the masses will follow them to the revolution. The Communist parties of the different imperialistic countries must work in conjunction with these proletarian parties of the colonies and through them give all the moral and material support to the revolutionary movements in general.

9. ~~The supposition that, owing to the economic and industrial backwardness, the peoples in the colonies are~~

revolutionary parties that strive to be in close connection with the working masses.

~~bound to go through the stage of bourgeois democracy is wrong. The events and conditions in many of the colonies do not corroborate such a supposition. It is true that~~ the revolution in the colonies is not going to be a communist revolution in its first stages. But if from the beginning, the lead of the revolution is in the hands of a Communist vanguard, the revolutionary masses would not be led astray but would go straight ahead through the successive periods of development of revolutionary experience. Indeed, it would be *very difficult*

extremely erroneous to try

in many of the oriental countries to solve the agrarian problem along pure communist principles. In its first stages, the revolution in the colonies must be carried on with a program in which will be included many petty-bourgeois reform clauses—for instance, division of land, etc. But from this it does not *necessarily* follow that the leader-

at all

ship of the revolution will have to be surrendered to the bourgeois democrats.

10. ~~The bourgeois national democrats in the colonies strive for the establishment of a free national state, whereas the masses of workers and poor peasants are revolting, even though in many cases unconsciously, against the system which permits such brutal exploitation. Consequently, in the colonies, we have two contradictory forces; they cannot develop together. To support the colonial bourgeois-democratic movements would amount to helping the growth of the national spirit which will surely obstruct the awakening of class consciousness in the masses; whereas to encourage and support the revolutionary mass action through the medium of a Communist party of the proletarians will bring the real revolutionary forces to action which will not only overthrow the foreign imperialism, but lead progres-~~

~~sively to the development of soviet power, thus preventing the rise of a native capitalism in place of the vanquished foreign capitalism, to further oppress and exploit the people.~~

11. ~~To initiate at as early a stage as possible the class struggle in the colonies means to awaken the people to the danger of a transplanted European capitalism which, overthrown in Europe, may seek refuge in Asia, and to defeat such an eventuality before its beginning.~~

*M.N. Roy*
INDIA

# 2B
# Theses by Ahmed Sultanzadeh

1. Commercial capital in the colonial and semicolonial countries of the East began to flourish as far back as the 1870s.[2] Together with it, banking capital commenced its sway. Things have changed little since. The colonial policy of the great powers blocks the development of home industry in those countries and has converted them into markets for their manufactured products and into inexhaustible sources of supply of raw material for the industrial centers of Europe. The import of cheap factory products in great quantities has altogether ruined the handicraftsmen and small producers, who, having lost all their property in an unequal competitive struggle, are speedily swelling the ranks of the urban paupers.

In the European countries this painful period of original accumulation did not last very long. In those countries the vigorous growth of factories and mills constantly absorbed these elements and, in the maelstrom of new economic formations, has converted them into actual proletarians with a clearly defined class ideology. In the East, on the other hand, that period has given rise to a continual emigration. Over ten million starving paupers emigrate yearly into the industrial centers of Europe and America, and there is no power that could stop this stream of emigration even for a moment.

2. At the same time there are in these colonial and semicolonial countries masses of peasants living in extremely oppressive conditions. The clang of the feudal chains of slavery is still heard everywhere in the East. Government taxation and levies fall as a crushing burden mainly upon these unfortunate victims of the landlords' rule. The peas-

ants here are almost the sole producing class. They must feed not only themselves and their families, not only the insatiable landlords, numerous traders, and merchants, but they must also satisfy the excessive appetites of the government officials, who swoop down upon them at harvest time like hungry ravens.

3. Owing to the economic and political backwardness of the East, the oppressed and enslaved masses have not yet succeeded in creating a firmly organized revolutionary party, in spite of the great potential revolutionary energy latent in them. On the other hand an extreme antagonism of interest prevails among the ruling classes. The big landowners are interested in continuing the colonial policy of the great powers, whereas the urban bourgeoisie opposes foreign interference with all its might. The clergy protest against the import of goods from the infidel lands of the *ghayer* [foreigner], while the merchants and traders fiercely oppose this stand. There can be no unanimity among the ruling classes in countries where for some the possibility of exploiting the toilers depends on the markets of the metropolis, while others cherish the illusion of independence.

4. All this creates the greatest possibility for a revolution, which though national in character will inevitably become social, owing to the weakness of the bourgeoisie. The proximity of Russia, that great reservoir of revolutionary energy, will have an almost decisive influence in the movement of liberation of all the oppressed and exploited classes of the Near and Far East. Now when the epoch of world revolution has set in, the victorious war cry of the toilers of Asia should be to organize Communist parties. Stormed from the East and the West, the capitalist stronghold will inevitably come down under the spontaneous onslaught of the revolutionary and united proletariat of the world.

5. The working people of the East, having conquered political power and solved the agrarian question in the spirit of the communist program, must immediately begin to unite the small producers of the towns. The first step in the economic program on the morrow of the social revolution is to bring about cooperation between craftsmen and small producers. At the same time, in order to utilize all the productive forces of the country, the proletarian government will have to start immediately to organize large factories and mills, exploit the natural resources, lay out railroads, and so on, in order to speedily end the painful period of primitive accumulation caused by the colonial policy of the great powers.

Ruined by the preceding four years of war and revolution, communist Europe will at first not be able to provide Asia with any large amounts of machinery and manufactured products. But the heroic proletariat of the West, supported by the revolutionary nations of the East, will speedily overcome the economic disintegration inherited from capitalism. Only by means of mutual aid, only through firm proletarian solidarity, will the world be saved from ruin and the banner of the world social revolution be firmly planted upon the ruins of decayed capitalism.

# 2C
# Article and theses by Pak Chin-sun

## THE REVOLUTIONARY EAST AND THE NEXT TASKS OF THE COMMUNIST INTERNATIONAL

The First and Second Internationals were associations that actually included the masses only of Europe and America.[3] They paid very little attention to the "Eastern question" and, in general, to the "question of the colonial peoples." The majority of the official leaders of the Second International strove to keep the "colonial question" in the background and to fence off the western European workers' movement from the revolutionary struggle of the enslaved colonial nationalities. They were afraid to address this question openly and clearly.

Whenever they took up the "Eastern question," the official leaders of the Second International trembled just as much as did the bourgeois politicos, with their constant sham devotion to "democracy," civilization, and culture. The complex questions of the revolutionary struggles of the enslaved colonial peoples, who make up the majority of struggling humanity, were quite alien to the ideologues of parliamentarism. Even at the founding of the Communist International, Asia was weakly represented, which necessarily had an effect on the work in the East.

But consciousness of the necessity of a common revolutionary struggle by the working masses of the East and West grew ever stronger. The great, victorious October revolution in Russia was the first bridge between the proletarian West and the revolutionary East, and Soviet Russia became a connecting link between two hitherto separate worlds. The necessity of a common proletarian struggle in the East and West was never as sharply felt as at the present time, when the ruling classes have transformed flourishing fields into barren desert and laid peaceful towns and villages to ruin, when the working class has decided to raise the banner of an implacable revolutionary struggle for the power of the toiling masses, for a new, free life for all humanity.

Today the specter of social revolution haunts the whole world. The bourgeoisie is straining every nerve to briefly delay the hour of its downfall. The Second World Congress of the Communist International should thus direct serious attention to the East, where the fate of the world revolution may be decided; for whoever understands the need to go to the enslaved nations of the East and win them as allies will emerge as victor in this last war between labor and capital.

The acute economic crisis in Asia, which is inevitable at the moment of the transition from feudalism to capitalism, and the imperialist great powers' barbaric policy in the colonies have created favorable conditions for revolution there. This policy has aroused strong nationalist tendencies in the East. Granted, the first stage of the revolution in the East will be the victory of the liberal bourgeoisie and the nationalist intellectuals. Nevertheless, we must begin now to prepare our forces for the second stage by drawing from the depths of the peasant masses, enslaved by the feudal regime, organized forces to carry out an agrarian socialist revolution in Asia as soon as possible. The industrial proletariat in Asia, excluding Japan, is too weak for us to entertain any serious hopes of an early communist revolution, but the victory of the agrarian revolution is certain if we are able to master the immediate tasks of the great and bloody struggle.

Russia's proletariat, standing at the outpost of the world social revolution, was able to withstand the desperate three-year onslaught of the world bourgeoisie only because it knew how to win the poorer and middle peasantry to its side. The vanguard of the European and American proletariat, uniting around the Communist International, must fight hand in hand with the many-millioned masses of the revolutionary East if it desires a speedy and successful victory over the capitalist class. The impossibility of such a victory without the collaboration of the "colonial" peoples is so evident that further proof is superfluous. The history of the inglorious downfall of the Second International showed clearly that so long as the world bourgeoisie has a reserve of strength in the colonies in general and in Asia in particular, it will be able to repulse the most desperate attacks of the insurgent proletariat.

By directing the awakening East on the right path of revolution, the Communist International will destroy the very roots of opportunism and irresolution in the proletariat of the Western countries. Action, however, must be coordinated in such a way that the European proletariat delivers a blow to capitalism's head just at the moment when the revolutionary East is dealing it a mortal wound in the heart. The victorious rising of the colonial peoples will sign the death warrant of any "Bernsteinism" and petty-bourgeois trade unionism. The prompt execution of this task will accelerate the triumph of the Communist International on a world scale.

The question now is, what forces are propelling the revolution in the East? The majority of the former nobility, the liberal bourgeoisie, and the petty-bourgeois intelligentsia, which represent the intellectual forces of the revolution in Asia, have learned from the long years of struggle against foreign subjugation and from a process of agonizing mental struggle. They have understood that the rebirth of the East is not possible except through the rule of the broad toiling masses.

The bankruptcy of the Second International promoted the rapid development of revolutionary ideas in the East and deprived these forces of any hope that their people could enjoy a free existence without the triumph of the social revolution in Europe, Asia, and elsewhere. Two opposite roads lie open to Asia's nationalists: the one leading to personal prosperity, based on the perpetual suffering and gradual degeneration of the great masses of the people; the other leading to the social revolution, which will deprive them of material privileges to a certain degree but will bring liberation to their people.

To our great joy, the majority of the idealistic nationalists took the side of the revolution.

Certainly, even in the revolutionary milieu there are also elements that unite with us, internationalists, only to attain national political liberation, but we shall use their revolutionary zeal for the struggle against world capitalism and for the triumph of the social revolution in the whole world. But should the revolution one day require it, we will know how to turn our arms against our "allies" of yesterday. Victory will undoubtedly be ours, because the masses of the East, just liberated from foreign political and economic slavery, will hardly resign themselves to the violence of new masters.

Such a policy of supporting the nationalist movements in the colonies is impossible for those so-called Socialist governments that are afraid of "outraged patriotic feelings" in the unenlightened toiling masses of the countries whose ruling classes are carrying on a barbaric colonial policy.

But the Communist International has no reason to fear such "outrage," because the vanguard of the international revolutionary proletariat, whose ranks are growing every hour, will judge its actions at their worth, and give its farseeing tactics complete approval. Thus although we are struggling together with the nationalist elements, we cannot look upon them as our comrades, with whom we may go on to the end without fear.

Without the slightest hesitation we must make clear to the working masses of the East that national political liberation alone will not give them what they are fighting for, and that only social liberation will guarantee them complete freedom.

The victory of the first stage of the revolution in Asia will coincide with that of the socialist revolution in the West. Proletarian Europe, groaning under the yoke of bourgeois democracy, cannot remain impassive before the sufferings of the broad toiling masses of the East. The European proletariat, imbued with a sense of international solidarity, will come to their aid. Of course, we can predict with certainty that a dreadful howl will be raised in the bourgeois camp. But our Western comrades (we can be certain) will meet with a hearty and fraternal reception from the proletariat and working peasantry of Asia. The East always opposed only *that* form of foreign intervention that brought with it chains and slavery, but the intervention of the socialist proletariat of the West will be a great and even needed help to the toiling masses of Asia in their struggle against every kind of exploitation. The proletariat of the East yearns for such "intervention."

The Second Congress, which must give the revolutionary proletariat a plan of action for a successful struggle against world imperialism, will most certainly not forget the great role of the revolutionary East in the international workers' movement.

And the toiling masses of the East, with the help of their European and American comrades, after having vanquished the foreign and native oppressors, will transform Asia—the land of religious achievements—into a Communist oasis of revolutionary achievements.

## THESES ON THE TASKS OF THE COMMUNIST INTERNATIONAL IN THE EAST

1. At the very moment when the two opposed forces of labor and capital are locked in fierce combat, the libera-

tion movement of the so-called colonial peoples has taken the form of gigantic uprisings, lending great aid to the fighting proletariat of the advanced capitalist countries.[4]

2. As the gulf between labor and capital grows wider and deeper, the necessity for the closest unity and firmest solidarity between the communist West and the revolutionary East impresses itself more and more.

3. The European proletariat has long years of experience in a revolutionary struggle that will end with the liberation of all of suffering humanity. This experience, together with the bloody example of the liberation war waged for long years by the colonial peoples, imposes the need for coordinated revolutionary campaigns on the continent [of Asia] as well as in the imperialist centers in order to achieve a rapid victory over the exploiters.

4. The highest leading body of this gigantic struggle cannot be the rapacious "League of Nations" and its ally, the Second, "Yellow" International. It can be only the International of labor, of revolutionary struggles, and of the Communist proletariat—the Third, Communist International.

5. The Communist International is duty-bound to expose all the double-dealing of the agents of world capital. These agents, operating under the trademark "League of Nations," are preparing a campaign against those who fight for the happiness and free existence of the hitherto oppressed working masses of the world. Furthermore, the Communist International is duty-bound to tirelessly expose the unviability, the revolutionary destitution, and consequently the absolute uselessness of the "Yellow" Second International in the great liberation struggle of the peoples of the East.

6. Under the pretext of "civilization" and "culture," the Second International openly upholds the predatory and

barbaric policy of the bourgeois governments. In contrast to this, the Communist International directly leads the struggle of the subjugated colonial peoples against imperialist plunder.

7. The Communist International wages an implacable struggle against petty-bourgeois trade unionism, opportunism, and revisionism, which hamper the revolutionary momentum of the proletariat in the advanced countries. The Communist International is arousing the mighty East, just awakening to a new life, and will destroy the very roots of irresolution, this poisonous cancer in the healthy body of the revolutionary movement of international socialism.

8. The peculiar features of the economic and cultural conditions of the West and the East set their special stamp on each of these two armies of toiling humanity. The proletariat of the advanced capitalist countries is undoubtedly the more developed and more conscious section of the international working masses. But the task of the Communist International does not, of course, lie in separating into a special caste the industrial workers of the more industrially developed countries, who make up only a minority of toiling humanity. On the contrary, it lies in organizing, with the help of the most staunch and conscious Western industrial workers, the whole working mass of the awakening East and leading its great forces into the broad current of the revolutionary struggle between labor and capital.

9. Tireless struggle is needed against bourgeois pacifism, which dams up the fighting energies of the revolutionary East, and against Pan-Mongolism and Pan-Islamism, enemies of the international solidarity of the toiling masses and of their collaboration in the struggle for freedom and the fraternity of peoples.

10. The agrarian revolution must be tirelessly advocated among the peoples of the colonies, especially in Asia, in order to give their liberation movement not only political but also economic content. The class consciousness of the masses must be raised to draw them into the social movement and to transform it from an intellectual into a mass movement. The historic mission of the proletariat, which is ready for power, must be explained to them.

11. In expectation of this socialist agrarian revolution in the East, the Communist International must immediately work out a revolutionary method to organize the new society—the communist society. It must create an economic plan for the most painless transition possible from the agrarian to the socialist order, avoiding the cruel period of the development of private capitalism in the East.

## 2D
## Excerpt from the discussion at the July 25, 1920, meeting of the Commission on the National and Colonial Questions

SNEEVLIET: Socialist propaganda has been carried on [in the Dutch East Indies] for five years. "Imported" capitalism prevents the development of a native bourgeoisie.[5] But imported capitalism's development has gone a long way, and the native population is being deprived of both its land and its small industry. Out of 30 million Muslims in Java, 24 million are peasants and 3 million, proletarians. Of the 40,000 railwaymen—the most revolutionary element—10,000 are organized. The revolutionary socialist party [Communist Association in the Indies] numbers 1,500, of whom 100 are Europeans.

SULTANZADEH: The destruction of peasant ownership and of domestic industries [in Persia] is being hastened by the import of cheap manufactured goods from abroad. The peasants are ruled by the shah's clique and the feudal aristocracy, who control estates equal in size to Belgium and the Netherlands together. There is, however, no unity among the ruling classes, of whom the landed section favors a foreign "protectorate," while a section of the mercantile class desires independence. These quarrels, which began with the Russian invasion of 1912, and the acute agrarian question, must inevitably lead to a gigantic social upheaval.

ROY: The nationalist movement in India began to take on more or less definite forms from the 1880s, finding expression in the [Indian] National Congress.

As it developed, this movement attracted broad layers of students and of the middle classes, especially in south India, but the nationalists' call to fight for India's independence found no response in the masses.

The masses of India are not infected by a nationalist spirit. Only questions of a socioeconomic character are of interest to them. India's population lives in the most difficult conditions.

From the moment British capitalism was firmly established in India, 80 percent of the country's agricultural population lost their land and became farm laborers, dependent upon the six or seven hundred princes who rule nearly the whole country. These millions of people are destitute. Even as they work the land, they go hungry, since everything their labor produces is exported. These tens of millions of people are absolutely not interested in bourgeois-nationalist slogans. Only one slogan can interest them: "Land to the tillers."

Compared to the rural proletariat, the industrial proletariat is not numerous. In India as a whole there are five million workers. The union movement is expanding rapidly among these workers. Recently a powerful strike movement has been spreading among India's working class. The first significant strike, which took place in 1906, involved railroad workers and took on the character of a genuine uprising.

Forces are present in India that can establish a strong Communist party. But insofar as we are considering the broad masses of the people, the revolutionary movement in India has nothing in common with a national liberation movement.

On the basis of this analysis, in point 11 of the theses on the national question, the paragraph taking up the necessity for all Communist parties to aid the bourgeois-democratic liberation movement in the Eastern countries must be deleted. The assistance of the Communist International should be directed solely toward establishing and developing the Communist movement in India, while the Communist Party of India must concern itself exclusively with the organizations of the broad masses in the fight for their own class interests.

The fate of the revolutionary movement in Europe depends entirely on the course of the revolution in the East. Without the triumph of revolution in the Eastern countries the Communist movement in the West could be reduced to nothing. World capitalism draws most of its raw materials and profits from the colonies, especially those in Asia. As a last resort European capitalism can give back to workers all the surplus value and thus win them over, killing their revolutionary aspirations. But these very capitalists will continue their exploitation of Asia with the help of the proletariat. Such a result would be very advantageous for the capitalists. It is therefore necessary to channel energy toward developing the revolutionary movement in the East, toward its ascent, and to adopt as our basic thesis that the fate of world communism depends on the triumph of communism in the East.

QUELCH: We are obligated to help any kind of movement against imperialism. It may be that the national liberation movement in India has not yet won the sympathy of the broad masses of the people, but this does not mean it will not do so in the very near future. The British government today will have no trouble at all in dealing with purely communist propaganda in the colonies and in crushing the Communist movement there. It will find it much harder to defeat the national liberation movement there.

For a thorough study of all these questions I propose that a bureau be organized within the Comintern to deal with Eastern questions, with departments to take up each point.

LENIN: In Russia we supported the liberal liberation movement at the time of the actions against tsarism. Hindu communists are obligated to support a bourgeois-nationalist movement, without, however, merging with it. Comrade Roy goes too far when he claims that the fate of the West depends solely on the degree to which the revolutionary movement in the Eastern countries has developed and gained strength. In spite of the fact that there are five million proletarians and thirty-seven million landless peasants in India, Hindu communists have so far not succeeded in launching a Communist party in that country. This fact alone shows that Comrade Roy's views are to a considerable extent without foundation.

LIU SHAOZHOU: Revolutionary nationalism, led by the students, who help the workers and even shopkeepers organize strikes, is making rapid strides in China. The industrial district of Shanghai is the center of the revolutionary movement, and carries on a struggle against both the northern and southern governments. Sun Yat-sen, at first a member of the southern regime, left it on finding himself surrounded by mere military adventurers. A Socialist party, standing for union with Soviet Russia and publishing a daily organ, exists in Shanghai.

The main problem in China, apart from the existence of the ruling class of governors and generals who are selling the country piecemeal to foreign powers, is land hunger, owing to the immense population. There are no large estates, however, and Sun Yat-sen advocates as a remedy the colonization of the border territories.

PAK CHIN-SUN: Until 1914 the nationalist movement [in Korea] existed only among the nobility and propertied classes, but it has assumed mass proportions during the last eighteen months. Japanese rule means the development of only commercial capitalism. The north is a country of small holdings, but in the south the majority of the population is of a semilaborer, semirenter type, the latter giving up 70 percent of his produce.

REED: The Negroes are only one of three groups of oppressed nationalities in the marvelous "democracy" of the United States, the others being the immigrants and the subject nations, like the Filipinos. In spite of the constitution, the ten million Negroes are practically devoid of political rights. In South Carolina, for example, $35 per student per year is spent in the schools on white children and only $1 per student on Black. Many trade unions, until quite recently, refused to accept Negroes.

The first impulse—to return to Africa—has not had much success, as the Negroes feel themselves bound up with America. Their competition on the labor market, particularly after the return of four million soldiers from Europe, has provoked many conflicts. But the Negroes are now no longer what they were. About half a million served in the army, and they acquire revolutionary ideas with facility. The IWW has begun work among them.

RUDNYÁNSZKY: The experience of the proletarian dictatorship in Hungary has produced striking results among the working classes, who previously labored under purely nationalist illusions. In the trans-Danube area, in the mining district at Pecs, 40,000 to 50,000 purely Hungarian workers have, in a series of gigantic meetings, refused to accept the Versailles treaty, which hands them back to White Hungary. They call for admission into Yugoslavia, which stands, from a social point of view, much higher than the Hungary of Admiral Horthy. Similarly, in the agricultural districts of the northwestern Carpathians, a mixed population of Romanian, Slovak, Hungarian, Ruthenian, and Jewish peasants are demanding admission into Czechoslovakia rather than remain under the White Terror. This is entirely the result of the [Hungarian] soviet dictatorship.

KABAKCHIEV: Bulgarian Communists cannot fight for national self-determination, despite the grip of foreign powers on their country and separation of over one million Bulgarians in Macedonia, Dobruja, and Thrace. It was just this nationalism that led the Bulgarian people, through two terrible disasters in 1912 and 1918, into its present condition.[6] The same applies to Serbia and Greece, and the only way out is a Balkan socialist revolution.

In Turkey the situation is different. There a bourgeoisie does not exist, and the country is practically nothing but a colony of the great ruling powers. The dominant classes can therefore genuinely enlist the support of the widest masses of the people against European capitalism, and the international proletariat can and should support the Turkish nationalist movement.

## 2E
## Comments by Lenin on Sultanzadeh's report

1. Disintegration of the propertied exploiting classes;[7]

2. A large part of the population are *peasants* under *medieval exploitation;*

3. *Small* artisans—in industry;

4. Deduction: *adjust* both Soviet institutions and the Communist Party (its membership, special tasks) to the level of the *peasant* countries of the colonial East.

This is the crux of the matter. It is necessary to think about this and to *seek* concrete answers.

## 2F
## Note by Lenin on a proposal by Levi

1. This is formulated in too general terms, as if it applied to *all* peoples. What about Persia today?[8]

I'm sorry, but it is *you* who are falling into "National Bolshevism" by regarding Germany as the *only* nation in the world.[9]

2. And what if *the bourgeoisie* (in Bulgaria, in Germany, in other countries) *initiates* war against Britain, France, or other countries?

What should the workers do?

Boycott?[10] That would be completely wrong. Participate, but defend their independence and utilize the *joint* struggle *in such a way* as to overthrow the bourgeoisie.

ΣΣ = Either write *only* against *German* National Bolshevism, or write nothing at all.

# 2G
# Revolutionary Ireland and communism

*by Thomas Darragh [Roderic Connolly]*

Ireland is of importance to international communism primarily for the following two reasons: (1) its strategic position with regard to England, the seat of British imperialism; (2) the influence of Ireland's political development on the broad masses of its nationals scattered throughout the British Empire and the United States of America.[11]

For the purpose of this report it is necessary to give a brief survey of the Irish labor and socialist movements and the personalities who played and are playing a part in their development. The recent history of the Irish labor movement may be said to start from the coming of Jim Larkin to Ireland in 1907. Up to this time very few of the Irish workers were organized in trade unions, and of these about 75 percent were in Irish branches of English unions. They were mere dues-paying members who exercised little or no effect upon the policy of these unions, whose executive offices were in England.

Larkin, who was identified with the Independent Labour Party of England from its inception, came over as organizer of the English dockers' union, and within a short time of his arrival the first big strike in Ireland took place in Belfast. This strike is noteworthy inasmuch as, along with the dock and transport workers of the city, the police came out on strike. It was marked by much rioting and military activity. Within a few months of the settlement of the Belfast dispute the dockers in Cork went on strike. As a result of the treatment meted out to the Belfast strikers by the executive of the union in England and a continuation of the same policy with regard to the Cork workers, Larkin broke away from the English dockers' union and organized the Irish Transport and General Workers' Union [ITGWU] on the lines of industrial unionism. After a series of fiercely fought strikes the transport workers' union got a permanent foothold in the bigger ports and industrial centers.

[James] Connolly returned from America in 1910 and immediately went to see Larkin, who was in Mountjoy Prison in Dublin. As a result of this meeting Connolly took over the management of the union during Larkin's imprisonment, and on his release they joined forces. From this time onward they worked together until Larkin went to America to raise funds for the union treasury, which had been completely exhausted by the great Dublin strike of 1913–14.

Connolly had spent his early life in the Social Democratic movement in Britain, particularly in Scotland. He was one of the few intrepid young Marxists who in the early days of the Social Democratic Federation split from the first manifestations of Hyndman's social patriotism and reformism to form the Socialist Labour Party, of which he was the first chairman and organizer. Up to the last he was in constant touch with it and his influence is still felt in this organization, which is one of the few fighting socialist bodies in Britain. In 1896 he returned to Ireland, where he founded the Irish Socialist Republican Party, the first socialist party in Ireland. He was editor of its official organ, the *Workers' Republic,* by means of which the revolutionary doctrines of the party began to make themselves felt on the Irish working masses. It is noteworthy to record that alone of all other parties, no matter how extreme in nationalism, the Irish Socialist Republican Party was the first to openly advocate the establishment of an Irish republic. The party was small, though active, and contested some few municipal elections, without success.

In 1902 Connolly went to America to raise funds for the party by a lecture tour. The tour completed, he stayed on and was identified with the foundation of the IWW and was for a time an organizer of the American Socialist Labor Party.[12] In 1908 he founded the Irish Socialist Federation in America and was editor of its official organ the *Harp,* which was later transferred to Ireland. In 1910, on his return to Ireland, he published *Labour in Irish History,* the only Marxian interpretation of the history of the development of the Irish proletariat and peasantry.

From 1910 Larkin and Connolly dominated the Irish labor and socialist situation. Their work consisted in organizing the Irish Transport and General Workers' Union, educating the masses in the use of the mass strike and the sympathy strike, and transforming the Irish Trades Union Congress into an Irish labor party. So powerful did the transport union become, with its revolutionary cry for the abolition of the wage system, that in 1913 the Irish bourgeoisie and English capitalist interests in Ireland combined to crush it. This resulted in the Dublin strike and lockout, which lasted for over ten months and was the first great proletarian upheaval in Ireland. The radical section of the British workers rallied to the aid of their Irish comrades, sending money and food into Dublin. But the British labor leaders, true to their position as henchmen of the capitalist class and saboteurs of every revolutionary act of the workers, killed the demand for sympathy actions in Britain, and the Irish workers were forced back to the shops. This proved a Pyrrhic victory for the bourgeoisie, the transport union emerging from the struggle depleted in membership and in funds, but still with its organization intact, and with a bitterness in the minds of the workers that flared into action in 1916.

The outbreak of the World War found the transport union sufficiently recovered to make vigorous protest against the social traitors of British laborism, who, rallying to the defense of the British imperial state, assisted in the doubly brutal coercion of Ireland as a small nationality and the Irish workers as a class. Larkin and Connolly held meetings throughout the country, baring the capitalist-imperialist nature of the conflict, urging the workers to utilize the crisis by every means in their power, and ruthlessly criticizing British laborism. They revealed the essentially bourgeois-imperialist content of the Irish Parliamentary Party, which had hitherto masqueraded as the party of democratic opposition to British imperialism and now supported the war, and the equally bourgeois reactionary tendencies of Sinn Féin, which declared Ireland to be neutral.

Realizing that the difficulties of British imperialism must necessarily be the opportunity of the Irish proletariat, they set about the development of the Irish Citizen Army, extending its scope, arming its members, and intensifying the military nature of its organization. In order to raise funds, Larkin went to America. He was exiled as soon as the British government found he was out of the country. Connolly took full charge of both the union and the Citizen Army and carried on the work alone. From now until Easter 1916, the Irish Citizen Army dominated Irish labor politics.

### The Irish Citizen Army

The Irish Citizen Army was founded in Cork in 1908. Its purpose was to protect the strikers from the brutality of the police. Beyond this it was little heard of and of no particular importance until the latter end of 1913, when it figured in several riots arising out of the Dublin strike. With the outbreak of the World War, serious attention was paid to its organization, military instructors were obtained, and the systematic arming of its members was begun. The first military instructor was Captain White, son of British Field Marshal Sir George White. Captain White was identified with the Dublin strike and subsequently, in 1916, was arrested in South Wales for attempting to bring the miners out on strike to prevent Connolly's execution.

As commandant, Connolly surrounded himself with a socialist staff, the chief of whom was Michael Mallin, a silk weaver executed by the British in 1916. National-revolutionary ferment developing rapidly all over the country was met by British military suppression, which resulted in the establishment of military staff cooperation between the Irish Volunteers (the nationalist republican armed forces) and the Irish Citizen Army. This was on the initiative of the Citizen Army, which dominated the alliance until the 1916 rebellion. British activity in suppressing all revolutionary papers resulted in Connolly's paper, the *Workers' Republic,* being published under an armed guard of the Citizen Army, which also provided a guard for Liberty Hall, the headquarters of the transport union. This condition of affairs lasted for about three months, the last number of the *Workers' Republic* being issued two days before the rebellion.

The army was designed along proletarian lines. The commandant, staff officers, and ordinary officers were elected by the soldiers. There was also a governing committee consisting of equal representatives of the officers and the men. Its activities were confined to the neighborhood of Dublin city. It was of first-rate efficiency, outmatching in many competitions the rival Irish Volunteers, holding on several occasions demonstrations of actual street fighting. Its well-trained officers, especially the commandant, lectured and instructed the Irish Volunteers, particularly in street fighting. The Irish Citizen Army, being drawn from the proletariat, had within its ranks many men who through economic necessity had served in the British army.

It was the Citizen Army that set the pace in the months preceding the rebellion. Despite the usual wavering of the middle-class leaders of the Irish Volunteers, when faced with the actual crisis, the iron determination of the Citizen Army and its leader forced the participation of the Volunteers in the uprising. The immediate cause of the failure of the revolutionary forces was that at the eleventh hour the timid, right-wing bourgeois leaders countermanded the order to mobilize Irish republican troops throughout the country. These leaders had always opposed Connolly and the cooperation of the Irish Volunteers with the Citizen Army. Nevertheless, 1,000 raw republican troops defended the captured capital against 47,000 disciplined and modernly equipped British soldiers. A victorious onslaught on Dublin from the north took place, and there were several attempts at uprisings in the west of Ireland.

In the rising, the Citizen Army, as a unit of the republican forces, attacked and seized Dublin Castle, the executive headquarters of the British government in Ireland, as well as holding several strategic positions throughout the city. Connolly was commander in chief of all the fighting forces of the republic during the rising. After the surrender, Connolly, who had been severely wounded during the fighting, and Michael Mallin, chief of staff of the Citizen Army, were executed along with several of the left-wing nationalist leaders, while the majority of the remainder of the prominent proletarian leaders were killed during or after the fighting. An overwhelmingly greater percentage of the Citizen Army than of the Irish Volunteers participated in the fighting. As a result, during the arrests that followed, the Irish Citizen Army was practically destroyed as an organization, while the Irish Volunteers was able to preserve its organization intact throughout the greater portion of the country, where no fighting had occurred.[13]

On its reorganization after the release of all prisoners in December 1917, the Irish Citizen Army retained its proletarian basis. But the situation was now dominated by the Irish Volunteers. All the leaders of the Citizen Army had been killed. The Citizen Army therefore weakened steadily and is not now an effective influence on Irish political life. It must be remembered that the Citizen Army is not a communist organization, though it is hostile to the present Social Democratic tendencies of the Socialist Party of Ireland. The Citizen Army cooperated with it only once, when, despite the military, it forced the holding of a meeting in favor of the Russian Bolshevik revolution.

The Irish Citizen Army's program is the establishment by force of arms of a workers' republic in Ireland, though the form and structure of such a republic are not consciously understood by the majority of its members.

**Sinn Féin and the Irish Volunteers**

In order properly to understand Sinn Féin it is necessary to deal with its political predecessor, the Irish Parliamentary Party. This party dominated Irish national politics for well over forty years. Its aim was to secure home rule for Ireland within the British Empire by constitutional means. Out of a total of 104 Irish members in the British Parliament, the Irish Parliamentary Party numbered about 80, the remainder being mostly Unionists returned from the Protestant constituencies of northeast Ulster, who stand on the anti–home rule platform and are a wing of the English Tory Party.

Under the leadership of Parnell, the Irish Parliamentary Party pursued a policy of obstruction in the British Parliament. It maintained its independence by refusing to ally itself with any British party, throwing its weight now to this side and now to that. This policy led to its gradually compromising, until finally it became the tail of the English Liberal Party. Though still protesting its independence in Ireland, this attachment to the Liberal Party caused it to become identified with English imperial politics, thus relinquishing its so-called democratic opposition to English imperialism. The final expression of this position was its opposition to the Boer War of 1899–1902.

While this party was losing its hold on the national-revolutionary mind of the people a new national policy, in the form of Sinn Féin, made its first appearance. A pamphlet called *The Resurrection of Hungary: A Parallel for Ireland* began to attract attention. In this work Arthur Griffith, an independent bourgeois journalist, traced Hungary's fight for political independence against Austria, and advocated the adoption in Ireland of the tactics employed by the Hungarian nationalists. He sketched a program, subsequently amplified as his party's power increased after 1916. Its most salient points were (a) the election of members through the English electoral system pledged to abstention from the British Parliament; (b) the actual setting up of an Irish parliament or general council; (c) refusal to pay taxes to the English imperial exchequer; (d) establishment of a policy of protection, especially against England; (e) the encouragement of Irish industries; (f) the building up of an Irish consular service; and (g) the general encouragement of all Irish national movements, such as the Gaelic League, the organization of the Irish-language revival movement, the Gaelic Athletic Association for the revival of old Irish sports and games, the Irish literary and dramatic renaissance, and the Irish Boy Scouts (Fianna), organized in opposition to the English military Baden-Powell Boy Scouts.

Sinn Féin was a party designed to use political and extraparliamentary action, but it did not advocate the use of arms for the accomplishment of its object, nor did it aim at the establishment of an Irish republic. It remained true to the Hungarian parallel and urged the establishment of an Irish parliament that should be united to the British Parliament only in the person of the British monarch, who would also be king of Ireland, thus ratifying the decrees of both parliaments. In fact in the first decade of the twentieth century no party except the Irish Socialist Republican Party openly advocated an Irish republic.

For many years, even up to the rebellion, despite the waning popularity and political bankruptcy of the Irish Parliamentary Party, Sinn Féin made little headway, existing rather as a critic of the Irish Parliamentary Party than as a definite political party. In its economic doctrine it followed the obsolete bourgeois economist Friedrich List, and its pronouncements on economic questions were reactionary in the extreme. In 1913 it assumed an attitude of hostility to the Dublin strike.

From the outbreak of the war to the rebellion, Sinn Féin assumed a more revolutionary role, being largely influenced by the Irish Volunteers movement, which, rather than Sinn Féin itself, was the dominant national force in Irish politics. Though Sinn Féin played no actual active part in the struggle, after the rebellion it shed the more reactionary portions of its doctrines and harmonized its program with the now-popular demand for an Irish republic, assuming the position of the political leader of the Irish people. It leaped from success to success until, in the 1918 parliamentary elections, it swept the country. Following this it set up its own parliament, Dáil Éireann, and attempted to form ministries and assume the government of the country. It was immediately declared illegal. Since then it functions whenever possible, though most of its members and prominent officials are being continually imprisoned in English jails from which they escape by hunger-striking, jail deliveries [escapes], and other means.

With the increasing oppression of English militarism, Sinn Féin is coming more and more under the dominance of the Irish Volunteers, so that now it is actually the Volunteers that implement Sinn Féin's political and economic principles using armed force. They raid and destroy British revenue offices and police stations, set up justice committees to try criminals and settle land ownership disputes, and so forth. In the recent elections Sinn Féin captured the majority of the municipalities and rural councils, its nearest competitor being the Irish Labour Party, which cooperates with it in the local government of the country. The whole policy of Sinn Féin is to make

British governance impossible in Ireland, and at the same time to establish as many of its own institutions as possible, so that it may step in and function as the government of the country.

In its outward form, the Irish Volunteers is a purely military organization with a general staff and officers elected by the rank and file. Many of its officials are members of the Sinn Féin parliament and form the link between the two organizations. Through these officials the Irish Volunteers guides Sinn Féin's activities as well. Its program originally consisted in the establishment of an Irish republic by force of arms. Now the idea of a republic has crystallized and is well maintained by the united efforts of the Volunteers and Sinn Féin. Its membership consists mostly of proletarians and the peasantry, though on the average mostly officered by the younger members of the petty bourgeoisie and farmers. The majority of the rank and file look upon the establishment of the Irish republic as of the first importance and are inclined to subordinate the solution of social problems to the successful accomplishment of this aim. The allegiance of the rural members to this ideology is being somewhat undermined by their being now mostly organized in the ITGWU. The consequent spark of class consciousness derived from this and the increasing economic difficulties force them into opposition to the farmer-class members of the Irish Volunteers. On the whole there are but few socialists within their ranks, but many sympathizers and admirers of Connolly and the idea of a workers' republic.

Owing to the constant national-revolutionary ferment that dominates the activity of all classes of the population and the almost universal opposition to England, which throws otherwise antagonistic classes into spasmodic cooperation, it is difficult to actually determine of what classes the various organizations are the political expression. Roughly speaking, Sinn Féin is controlled in the rural districts by the small farmers and petty peasantry or tenant farmers, in the towns by the small shopkeepers and middlemen, and in the cities by the smaller manufacturers, merchants, and bourgeois intellectuals. There are practically no big landowners or even moderately big capitalists in this movement, this class in Ireland being economically dependent upon English capitalism and having as its political expression the English Tory and Liberal parties.

The conglomeration of classes comprising Sinn Féin necessarily causes antagonism to develop within the party. As long as the cooperation of these classes and the working masses continues—and such cooperation is unavoidable if political independence is really to be achieved—the Sinn Féin movement will be unable to formulate any definite socioeconomic program. Its aim being political independence, it finds it necessary to draw all classes of the population to it to accomplish this object. To preserve the cooperation of the classes, it dare not issue any *definite* political and economic program. Instead it has issued a so-called democratic program, breathing all the false glittering generalities of bourgeois democracy—the will of the sovereign people, the ownership of the land and resources of the country by and in the interests of the whole people, the equality of all citizens, and so forth. But it reveals its essential class content by promising international regulation of the conditions under which the *working class* will live. The ideology of the two allied movements, Sinn Féin and the Irish Volunteers, is similar to that of any small nationality. Finally the hope of Sinn Féin is the development of the already existing antagonism between America and England, and the tendency is to rely more and more on American capitalism and to become subservient to its interests.

### The Irish labor movement

The Irish labor movement is composed of the Irish Transport and General Workers' Union, local or national craft unions, and branches of the big English trade unions, such as the National Union of Railwaymen and the Amalgamated Society of Engineers. It functions nationally through the Irish Trades Union Congress and Labour Party, and locally through trades councils composed of representatives of the various unions in the district. By far the most powerful body is the Irish Transport and General Workers' Union, which now numbers 120,000 members. It was originally organized on the lines of industrial unionism, and though small in numbers and restricted to the larger towns, it wielded with tremendous efficiency and success the weapons of the mass and the sympathy strikes, at the same time carrying on an almost incessant revolutionary propaganda campaign.

Since the rebellion, with the loss to the union of its two leading figures and the indiscriminate increase of its membership, its revolutionary outlook has deteriorated, until now it has become a federation of unskilled workers with a large sprinkling of craft unions and with bureaucratic and strong centralization tendencies. It is not a craft union, but neither has it kept abreast of the later developments of industrial unionism, consequently tending to become an unwieldy and ineffective weapon for the proletariat either against alien imperialism or native capitalism.

The larger portion of its membership at the present time consists of the poorer peasantry and agricultural laborers, who are not in close sympathy and whose activities are not in coordination with those of the industrial proletariat. It should not be forgotten, however, that the organization of the rural proletariat has been a tremendous accomplishment, and has imbued them with a certain amount of class consciousness. On account of the form of the organization and the failure of the ITGWU to sufficiently educate these rural workers as to their class position, it has been demonstrated that this is not the organization to bridge the gulf between the agricultural and industrial proletariat.

The general condition of Irish life being nationalistically revolutionary, the ITGWU, in common with the craft unions, has a much stronger fighting spirit than its English prototypes. In alliance with the nationalists, the Irish labor movement defeated conscription in 1918; on May 1, 1919, it stopped industry throughout the greater portion of the country; and only recently, again in alliance with the nationalists, by a two-day general strike it forced the British government to release more than one hundred political prisoners who were on hunger strike. In the majority of these cases, however, the general sentiment of the people practically forces the labor movement to take action, and the strike is carried out by unionists and nonunionists alike.

It is only comparatively recently that the ITGWU has entered the political arena as a dominant force, and its successes in the late municipal elections have only strengthened its tendency toward reaction. The Irish Labour Party and Trades Union Congress, acting through its local trades councils, emerged from the municipal elections as the second party in numerical strength, and of the labor members elected, the ITGWU secured an overwhelming majority. This solidifies the domination of the Irish Labour Party and Trades Union Congress by the ITGWU, which gave them their present form and program. Despite the insistence of the Labour Party that this program was constructed by Connolly and must therefore be revolutionary, it refuses to understand that such a program was designed for use by the proletariat in a pre–world revolutionary period.

The attempt of the ITGWU, under the slogan of One Big Union, to absorb the craft unions has led to the development of antagonisms within the Labour Party. The craft unions object to such absorption primarily because of their craft ideology. They also claim that the transport union does not represent industrial unionism, but the growth of a federation that is tending to bring the whole labor movement under a bureaucracy. The craft unions in Ireland are small and constantly dwindling. They are of little political importance with the exception of one or two big branches of English unions, the tendency of which is to break away from the parent bodies and form national unions. A large section of the Amalgamated Society of Engineers has already done so recently.

The transport union publishes the only labor paper in Ireland, the *Watchword of Labour,* a weekly with a circulation of about ten thousand. It shares the common fate of all nationalist and rebel papers in Ireland—continual suppression by the government. This paper, while claiming to be the successor of Connolly's revolutionary *Workers' Republic,* in fact constantly emasculates his application of revolutionary Marxism to Ireland in much the same manner as Kautsky emasculates the general principles of Marxism. It voices or represents the views of the dominant section of the ITGWU, the Irish Labour Party, and the Socialist Party of Ireland.

Internationally the Irish labor movement is affiliated to the Yellow International, the delegates from Ireland being Cathal O'Shannon, the editor of the *Watchword of Labour,* executive member of the Irish Labour Party, and at present president of the Socialist Party of Ireland; Thomas Johnson, treasurer of the Irish Labour Party; William O'Brien, secretary of the Irish Labour Party, treasurer of the ITGWU, and one of the biggest forces in the Irish labor movement; and another Irish Labour Party executive member; together with [James J.] Hughes, assistant secretary of the ITGWU, who represented the Socialist Party of Ireland. O'Shannon and Johnson, who were equipped with supplementary mandates from the Irish Socialist Party, were the only two to reach Bern. They signed the Adler-Longuet resolution and generally adopted the policy of that wing of the conference.[14]

The Socialist Party of Ireland, which was founded in 1896, underwent many changes of program and name, until now it is a very small and ineffective party with no bearing upon national politics. The same personalities who dominate the Irish Labour Party and the ITGWU influence and direct its policy and tactics. For one brief spell it was captured by the left wing, which during its brief term of power, against the violent opposition of the rest of the party, succeeded in introducing a few revolutionary conceptions into its long-established program, ordered the revocation of the affiliation to Bern and secured a majority vote in favor of the Third International, and held a meeting in Dublin on the last anniversary of the Bolshevik revolution. Before it had time to consolidate its forces it lost power; consequently its orders regarding the Internationals were never put into force. It is now a party numbering scarcely 150 members in Dublin, about 30 of whom may be considered effective members, and a few hundred members throughout the country, badly organized and having no direct connection with each other or the Dublin headquarters. It is very inactive, has no paper and but a few pamphlets by its own members, none of which deal with the problems facing the Irish proletariat.

A force that will undoubtedly play an important part in the revolutionary development of Ireland is the cooperative movement, led by George Russell. There are several well-organized branches of this movement, which now form a considerable part of the economy of the country and may readily be utilized by the proletarian state for the solution of such immediate problems as that of food distribution during the first period of the proletarian dictatorship. Communists will be chiefly interested in cooperative production on the land by the poor peasantry. This movement, which tends even now to destroy the ideology of small private property ownership among the land-hungering poorer peasantry, is of paramount importance to Communists. For it actively tends to the solution of one of the most important and difficult problems of the proletarian state by initiating the organization of the poorer peasantry on the basis of large-scale cooperative production, thus mentally harmonizing the two sections of the working class and making certain the unity of the industrial proletariat and peasantry under the dictatorship of the proletariat.

Ulster, or more properly the northeast corner of Ireland, is the big manufacturing and industrial center. Industrially it bears a greater resemblance than any other part of the country to the highly industrialized portions of England and Scotland. It is dominated by the only big capitalists in the country, who are closely allied with the British bourgeoisie. Economically the workers are organized in branches of English trade unions, and politically the vast majority adhere to the Unionist Party, the party of extreme opposition to Sinn Féin and any form of Irish nationalism. One of the main factors, though steadily declining of late years, is its religious antagonism to the rest of the country.

In many respects the problems of the Communists are much easier here, it being possible to rally the proletariat to their banner on the straight issue of the capitalist state versus the proletarian state. The lack of any nationalist republican feeling on the part of the majority of the proletariat renders them hostile to the establishment of an Irish bourgeois republic. With the exception of the anti-nationalist feeling, which is partly the outcome of religious bigotry, Ulster presents a problem similar to that presented by any large industrial center, and for this reason may become one of the chief centers of the proletarian struggle against an Irish bourgeois state.

We have attempted here to show the major factors and tendencies in modern Ireland that must be grasped to form an opinion on Ireland's general situation. We make no claim to have delivered a complete report. The present events in Ireland have the character of an uninterrupted guerrilla war between the imperialists and nationalists, the latter enjoying the support of the Irish labor movement.

# 3A
# Minutes and notes of commission meetings

## MINUTES OF THE SESSION OF JULY 25, 1920

*Sunday, July* 25
Convened: 5:00 p.m.
Chairman: Meyer (Germany)
Members of the commission: Maksimov (Bulgaria), Steinhardt (Austria), Sadoul (France), Humbert-Droz (Switzerland), Wijnkoop (Netherlands), Rákosi (Hungary), Zinoviev, Sokolnikov (Russia), Fraina (U.S.), Connolly (Ireland).[1]

Invited with consultative vote: Cachin and Frossard (France), Crispien, Däumig, Stoecker, and Dittmann (Germany, USPD).

General discussion is opened on the theses put forward by the Executive Committee.

CRISPIEN: I am in basic agreement with the proposed theses on admission. Only a few specific points, like the question of the party name, need to be taken up in the discussion of the different theses.

DITTMANN: I am likewise in overall agreement with the proposed theses. At its last congress in Leipzig the Independent party took a clear stand in favor of the theses and general principles of the Third International. We would like to direct the discussion to one point, however. If these theses are adopted in their present form, our party will lose its legal character, and we believe we must avail ourselves in our activity of all legal means in order to draw in and educate the masses. We know that in practice legal means are not enough. We have seen that the general strike will not suffice to take power, that an armed uprising is necessary. But if we openly affirm this in the theses, our party will cease to be a legal party.

ZINOVIEV: Dittmann is wrong to think that the theses will alter the character of the USPD. In Finland too an Independent Social Democratic party was founded, which had a legal existence up to the moment it declared its adherence to the Third International.[2] At that moment the police moved in and broke up the congress. The mere fact of joining the Third International is enough to call forth repressive measures from the capitalist governments. In the eyes of capitalist governments it is enough for the Independents to call for the dictatorship of the proletariat and the soviet form of government.

RADEK: I do not believe that the Central Committee of the USPD can deal directly with illegal work and propaganda in the army. This work must be assigned to illegal organizations responsible to the party. In Germany the political situation is such that the leaders of the Independents can be executed at any moment without trial. The discussion must go deeper. We have to examine the party's policies.

DITTMANN: Radek is in error to hold that the leaders of the Independents can be executed at any time without trial. The parties of the right, Helfferich especially, have labored in vain to have us declared outside the law,[3] so as to legalize all manner of persecution. We maintain that we must exercise our legality to the utmost. We have more than fifty daily papers. This press is a means of propaganda and revolutionary action that we must hold on to and that will be lost to us in illegality. Our press has already been repressed once, and we know how hard that makes our work.[4] The Communists know from experience how difficult propaganda is for a party when it is illegal. Thus it seems to us necessary to use all possible legal means.

Another question is centralization. I personally have favored strong centralization for a long time, even in the old Social Democracy. But the experience of bureaucratic Social Democracy is precisely what has repelled a large body of revolutionary workers from centralization. This is an understandable reaction against the centralist bureaucratization of the old Social Democracy. So we come up against a tendency that is hostile to the centralization of the party. The [1917] Gotha congress, for example, opposed the central leadership having control over the press. It will take a certain period of time before this attitude can be overcome.

The leaders of the Independents are happy to find support in the Third International for their efforts to carry through centralization.

CRISPIEN: My remarks at the beginning of the debate require some elaboration. Four points in the theses seem to me to be important:

1. The organization of the International. We agree with the statement that the International cannot be a federation of autonomous national sections, as the Second International was. We too want a strongly centralized organization that supervises the sections and guides

the general line of the International. An international assessment for every member should be initiated alongside the national dues.

2. Centralization. Our party is basing itself more and more on centralization and will definitely fulfill this condition.

3. The party program as well is already an accomplished fact for us. The decisions at Leipzig have aligned us with the basic principles, and now we have only to bring our program into line with the theses proposed to the congress.

4. Means. We live in the period of the struggle for power. Our movement must hold on to its legal character; the masses would not understand an illegal party. We cannot take a public stand for the arming of the proletariat. This must happen, but alongside the legal organization. Russia also has a legal movement, the soviets, that deal with governments in an official capacity, and an illegal movement, the Communist Party. A purely illegal organization is out of the question for us.[5] We want to make use of all means of struggle, but we cannot declare it openly and publicly.

MEYER: It is important to go deeper beneath the surface. The theses call for the expulsion of centrist elements. I am very skeptical about the USPD leaders' assurances that their party's conduct is already in accord with the theses. The attitude the USPD has adopted in the past toward Soviet Russia and the Third International is not a satisfactory assurance for the future. How the USPD intends to work closely with the Third International must also be determined. Until now the only thing mentioned has been an international [financial] assessment. For the USPD leaders, party unity appears to be the most important question, and they fear that the theses will threaten their unity. The break with the spirit of the Second International is not complete. You see this in the fear expressed of government persecution. The USPD has little experience in illegal work.

Ströbel, Kautsky, Hilferding—all anticommunists—are still in the USPD. It is quite true that many workers in the USPD took part in revolutionary battles. But the leaders have not gotten there yet. The relations between the USPD and the KPD must also be discussed.

ZINOVIEV: It is certainly important for a revolutionary party to have fifty newspapers. But the number of papers is not the most important thing. The experience of the Bolsheviks proves this. They were not afraid of their paper being suppressed. This happened frequently but it always rose anew and emerged victorious and stronger from the battle. What is important in the revolutionary period is not maintaining the press but spreading the ideas. Often the banning of a newspaper can do more to spread ideas than the newspaper itself, especially if it is a paper like *Freiheit*. The right wing of the USPD has not acted in the spirit of the proposed theses.

It is true that we are entering a new era in which we can set aside the past. We are revolutionaries and not bureaucrats. With this Second Congress a new period is opening. We have to break with Hilferding as long as he is what he is. Under his direction *Freiheit* is not a revolutionary publication. If the questions posed do not allow us to open up a new period now we will wait a month. We would rather wait than leave these questions undecided. We do not want to draw up a list of all those who should be expelled; we want a new orientation, a new policy, new tactics. If that is not possible we will wait. In Italy we demand the expulsion of Turati and company. We say the same to the Swedish and Yugoslav parties. We have to cut ourselves loose from the deadweight of the right wing in these parties. We want a centralized International ready for revolutionary action. If the congress proves to us that this is impossible now, the alternative will be an International of propaganda.

HUMBERT-DROZ: Up to now we have debated only the special case of the USPD. This case can be handled most easily of all, because the USPD adopted a program in Leipzig that accepts the general principles of the Third International. But there are other parties that have left the Second International and want to join the Third International: the French party, the English Independent Labour Party, the Swiss party, the American party, and others. To meet the danger of being overrun by centrist elements, the true continuators of the spirit of the Second International, the conditions for admission have to be made sharper and the theses more decisive.

The main point for me is to demand of the parties that want to join that they completely abandon any idea of restoring the [old] International to encompass the Third International or exist side by side with it. The USPD and the French party, on the other hand, who are talking here about joining, have still not given up their negotiations with the thoroughly centrist parties, for example with the leadership of the Swiss party. While Cachin and Frossard were here, Paul Faure, Böhm from the USPD, and the Swiss party leadership were in Bern discussing the restoration of the International, with or without the Third International.[6] At the National Council meeting of the French party that discussed the participation of Cachin and Frossard at the Moscow conference, Mayéras stated quite openly that the party ought not to orient itself to Moscow, but that the Third International should be allowed to restore the International. His resolution was adopted by a large majority.[7] A rejection of this quest for restoration seems to me to be the first condition for negotiations on affiliation.

Many centrist elements, such as the American Socialist Party and the right wing of the Swiss Socialist party, want to join the Communist International in order to transform it from within and corrupt it. We have to be more vigilant than ever before, testing the sincerity of this affiliation and preventing these opportunist elements from getting in.

CRISPIEN: The USPD has conducted itself in such a fashion that it can stand shoulder to shoulder with the other revolutionary parties. Our party has developed more and more to the left. It has unloaded its right-wingers: Bernstein has left; Kautsky has no influence and no longer plays a role in the party. It cannot be said that Kautsky and Ströbel constitute a right wing. They stand alone and isolated. The party must apply revolutionary principles, and those who cannot agree may leave.

Our party has always guided and led revolutionary struggles. During the Kapp putsch we conducted ourselves no differently than the KPD. At the start of the struggle the KPD hesitated more than we did, and we had the truly revolutionary policy. The KPD Central Bureau conducted negotiations with the government together with us. We worked together and we agreed on numerous points. We could not replace the unions in this struggle; we could not do without them—but we fought everywhere. We always supported the Russian Soviet Republic.

Hilferding cannot be placed in the same category as Kautsky. Already before the war his writings acknowledged the necessity of the dictatorship of the proletariat.

We are ready to put out illegal leaflets when our press is banned. *Freiheit* is not the central organ of the party but the paper of the Berlin district.

We wanted to discuss the conditions for admission before joining. We never wanted to form a fourth International. When we wanted to speak with the other parties it was only about going to Moscow, and we pushed them forward along this road. But we have been ill-used by the Third International, and before our entry we wanted to negotiate so that we would be respected. We did not want to do as the Italians have done. They entered the Third International but today they have to purge their party. We want to negotiate before joining.

SCHEFLO: There is also a Norwegian question. Our party numbers 110,000 members in a population of 2.5 million, but these 110,000 are not communists. Our party is composed of unions, youth organizations, and various clubs. It has fifteen dailies, all completely under the control of communists. The party's great majority is communist, but about 10 percent is antisocialist and Social Christian. We cannot expel them, however, because they are organized in the unions. The youth and the political clubs are the real political strength of the party. Sweden has to get rid of Lindhagen so we can clean house in Norway.

RADEK: Listening to Crispien gave me an odd feeling. Behind him you can make out Hilferding, Ströbel, and others. Is Däumig in agreement with the policies of the congress? At the Leipzig congress Ledebour made statements on Soviet Russia and the civil war that are unacceptable.

No party can overcome its past without recognizing its errors. And the Independent party has made many errors. A political line that favors the Americans and the British, the coquetry with Wilson that was in vogue for a while, the entire international political line right up to the Spa conference[8]—these are not communist. In the unions Dissmann pursues a purely reformist line, yet he belongs to your left wing. True, the political line of a party is determined by the masses, but the party apparatus can, for a time, corrupt the best politics of the best masses. Such is the apparatus of the USPD. Sixty percent of your parliamentary fraction is actually hostile to revolutionary struggle. Quite often Hilferding writes in *Freiheit* in Kautsky's spirit. Granted, the worker base of the party is revolutionary, but the party tops are a layer of members that carry out a counterrevolutionary line. What measures will be taken against the minority when it rejects the conditions of the Third International at the next congress? You cannot retain a minority that rejects the Third International. The question is very important. Every party has its right wing, but yours is especially strong and influential. What are you going to do about it?

MEYER: The right in the USPD is not so uninfluential as Crispien says. We have to know how the USPD is going to handle this right wing. In practice the left wing has less influence. Its attitude is characterized by silence, a silence observed by its representatives here in the commission, Däumig and Stoecker, who certainly do not agree with the remarks of Crispien and Dittmann.

CACHIN: I want first to address the questions raised by Humbert-Droz on the restoration of the International. Paul Faure, with his trip to Switzerland, was only carrying out the decision of the Strasbourg party congress. We are delegated to come here to ascertain the conditions for admission. In the event that the Third International should decline the proposal that will subsequently be made by the French party, we have to know what attitude we should take. We have to take a look at the other parties that have left the Second International. Paul Faure did no more than this when he traveled to Switzerland. We do not contemplate a reconstruction. The very concept and word are absurd. We do not want to reconstruct anything outside of the Third International. So much for the principled aspect of the question.

We have received and examined the theses and conditions. We understand that we are being subjected to a critique that is fully justified. We were guided above all by the idea of party unity. You will agree that in a party such as ours, with a left, a center, and a right, its policies cannot be as rigid as those of other parties. We were bound to party unity by the [1904] Amsterdam resolution and the memory of Comrade Jaurès, who embodied party unity in France. During our stay here we have read and seen a great deal. Driven forward by ever more serious circumstances, we sense and understand that we must of necessity make a radical break with our present policies. We have to start fresh and elucidate the principles of socialism in an understandable form for all to see. On our return to France we will propose such a radical break and the beginning of a new policy. That much is clear.

We have had our errors and weaknesses. We feel that we have to defend the dictatorship of the proletariat and that we have to prepare for ever more serious battles leading up to the social revolution. We were delegated to make an informational trip; on our return we will step down as editor of the paper and party secretary, in order to work toward this new plan. We will distribute the documents of the Communist International widely. We will demand the speedy convocation of an extraordinary party congress. At the congress we will defend the theses of the Third International openly, for all to see.

As to the theses themselves we can say that we have no reservations about the four theses of Comrade Lenin. An article of Trotsky's posed four questions to which we will now respond:[9]

1. Defense of the fatherland. French militarism is so imperialistic and hateful that it must be the party's duty

to reject war credits in peace as in war. We cannot possibly vote for any kind of war credits under any circumstances whatsoever. We will always place class interests above national interests.

2. Can we keep members in our ranks who work for the League of Nations?[10] We think these comrades have to choose. The new statutes must contain a ban on editing a nonsocialist paper, and the parliamentary fraction must be brought under control.

3. Are we ready to support the efforts of the colonies to liberate themselves? We did not wait for this call. A special envoy of the party is right now on the scene in North Africa, working together with the natives for their liberation.[11]

4. The opposition within the French unions will be very hard for us to overcome.[12] An enormous gulf divides the unions from the party. Prejudices have to be overcome. The General Confederation of Labor (CGT) was founded by anarchists, and the anti-Marxist currents within it are still strong. If political party activists want to join the fight against opportunism they will encounter big difficulties.

FROSSARD *(INTERRUPTING)*: The minority in the unions is not united. It includes in its ranks oppositionists of my tendency, communists like Monatte and Rosmer, and anarchists as well. Collaboration with the anarchists will be impossible. We can collaborate with the communist syndicalists if they sincerely accept the Moscow theses on the necessity of the Communist Party and make an effort to understand them. We are ready to lead the fight against reformism together with the syndicalist minority in the political as well as the union arena.

CACHIN: As for Zinoviev's theses,[13] we accept them as a whole. One point that appears difficult to us is propaganda in the army. This entails major practical difficulties. The army is not in France but on the Rhine and in the hands of the officers.[14] Propaganda can be carried out through the youth, in the press, and from parliament. Immediately on our return to France we will set up illegal organizations to conduct propaganda in the army. We admit that propaganda for an armed uprising has not been carried out so far, and we consider it urgent to do so. You will see what we do. We ask you not to take our word but to wait and judge us by our deeds. We will work with all our strength for the party's affiliation to the Third International. We personally have already taken our decision and made our choice.

ZINOVIEV: I do not have much to say on the statements of the French comrades. They say they want to break with the old line. Now we will wait to see the success and fruit of their propaganda. As for the USPD, its errors are greater than those of the Communist Party because it holds influence over the mass of workers and wields more power. Despite the USPD's wide influence, especially in Berlin, Legien was nevertheless able to negotiate in the name of the workers.[15] The USPD dawdled, it did not act, although Berlin, where they are dominant, was the center of the struggle. We demand a break with this old system. Dissmann likewise carries out a counterrevolutionary policy among the metalworkers.

In Norway we cannot accept a situation where 10 percent of the party is antisocialist. In Sweden, also, something has to be done about the situation. In Yugoslavia and Switzerland the left wing is likewise made up not just of communists. We have to part company with all these people. Today the Communist International is in vogue. The Bulgarians (*unintelligible*), but it is necessary to separate ourselves from the right wing in every party.

DITTMANN: The French delegates have told us what they intend to do. They are in a better situation than we are because they were able to speak with the Executive Committee before the congress. We can speak on the questions posed to us only insofar as they relate to our minority. If a German makes a promise he keeps his word, and we do not want to make any promise we cannot keep. The theses pose the question of the illegality of our party, and they will be discussed. The experience of the KPD is no encouragement to us along this road, but we do not want to get into all the small matters separating us from the KPD in daily struggle.

It is a comfort to me to hear that all parties have their faults even though they joined the International. Until now, however, those of the Communist Party of Russia have not been mentioned. The Bolsheviks also made compromises forced on them by the struggle. We understand that. But they must understand our compromises. Trotsky is wasting his time in literary assaults against Kautsky, whose influence is nil and whose book is unread.[16] Our party did its revolutionary duty in the Kapp putsch. In the Rhineland, in Westphalia, in Saxony, it came to the point of an armed uprising. If you want to expel Dissmann, the working class will not follow you. The difficulties of our affiliation would grow larger and you would have to bear the responsibility. We truly wish for the German proletariat to be in closer contact with the Russian proletariat.

(*Crispien makes some personal remarks to prove his revolutionary past.*)

DÄUMIG: The next USPD party congress has to determine precisely what it understands by the dictatorship of the proletariat. We must also prepare the proletariat for revolutionary action. (*He gives a historical retrospective of the Social Democracy and the USPD, which since January 1918, he affirms, has been the instrument of the German revolution.*)[17] The centralized bureaucracy still holds sway in the unions. When we affirm that the unions must be revolutionized, we understand it is more than just a change of personnel. Legien still has the whole union army behind him. In Berlin the Independents who are union functionaries can neither leave the union bureaucracy nor destroy it. There are definitely several tendencies in our party, but nothing is so harmful to the German and to the world revolution, in my opinion, as the splintering and division of the German working class.

We will place the theses adopted by the congress before our party for discussion as quickly as possible, with the goal that the party in its entirety join the Third International. We want revolutionary centralization. We believe it is impossible to get good results by posting an expulsion list. We do not want to say that so-and-so is excluded or expelled. We want to make life in our party impossible for them through our principled decisions and our action.

TROTSKY: I am not satisfied with the response Cachin gave to my first question, on defense of the fatherland. This question is key and it must be answered so there is no misunderstanding. Putting class above nation is not enough. *Le Temps,* the paper of the French financial bourgeoisie, endlessly repeats that patriotism is the only rampart that can be erected against Bolshevism—patriotism of the Ukrainians, the Poles, the Finns, and above all the French. In France no progress can be made on the road to revolution unless an open and unambiguous fight is waged against patriotism and defense of the fatherland. Patriotism and defense of the fatherland must be denounced before the working class as lies. We have to fearlessly proclaim in all our propaganda that we combat patriotism, we sabotage the defense of the fatherland. Longuet is a hard-bitten patriot despite the affected phraseology he substitutes for nation and fatherland. This conception of nation must also be combated. In recent strikes the French union federation raised the slogan of nationalization, a thoroughly obscure slogan. They speak of nationalization in order to keep quiet about the social revolution. The socialists have to have the courage to counterpose the social revolution to nationalization and therefore must fight against defense of the fatherland and patriotism.

CACHIN: I agree.

TROTSKY: Dittmann's speech is very pretty rhetoric, but in reality a gulf stands between us. Dittmann charges us with getting literary and writing against Kautsky. I remind him, by the way, that, aside from our literary activity, we had something more urgent to do. The proof that the polemic against Kautsky was not useless is that Dittmann himself, while claiming not to have read Kautsky (Kautsky is losing influence), puts forward all the arguments of this same Kautsky who also accuses us of opportunism. It would be interesting to have a thorough discussion of this. If you are serious about the theses proposed to you here, then we do not need to propose an expulsion list. You would find for yourselves those you have to drive away. The KPD is no doubt a small party, but it is an advance that there is a center around which revolutionary forces in Germany can be assembled. The same was true of the Bolsheviks in Russia. In Germany the bureaucracy is the greatest counterrevolutionary force.

When Dittmann says a German keeps his word, I do not follow him. You are comrades here, not Germans. You are forgetting, by the way, that Bethmann-Hollweg was also a German.[18] How many pledges did the German Social Democracy make in Basel in 1912? How can you say, after the bankruptcy of the Social Democracy, after its betrayal, that Germans keep their word? The Independents, at the beginning of the revolution, turned down peace with Soviet Russia. Haase, Kautsky, and Dittmann, who took part in the previous government, rejected an alliance with Russia.

DITTMANN: That is a lie!

RADEK: We will present the evidence for examination.[19]

TROTSKY: Now Scheidemann is in the opposition and is orienting to the left. The convergence between him and the right wing of the USPD is public.[20] To this must correspond another convergence: between the left wing of the USPD and the KPD. Given this, if the USPD wants to join the Third International, it must make energetic decisions and part company with its right wing.

## NOTES BY MEYER ON THE SESSION OF JULY 26, 1920

*Since it was impossible to take stenographic minutes in German, the following notes were taken by Comrade Meyer.* [Footnote in *Rote Fahne*][21]

### Thesis 1: Party propaganda and agitation

CRISPIEN: It has been raised here that the press has to be directed by Communists. I would simply like to inquire whether this is to be interpreted strictly to the letter or just in a general sense. There are parties that want to enter the Third International and still have a different name, so it takes them a while before they meet the preconditions. So I would like to know if the demand is that Communists be placed on the newspapers.

ZINOVIEV: It would be better if tomorrow *Freiheit* could already be full of Communists. But the thesis is to be taken in the general rather than the formal sense.

**Thesis 3: Legal and illegal work**

DITTMANN: This is what we were discussing yesterday. The question for us is merely whether we want to broadcast this all over the world.

ZINOVIEV: We have to look at this from an international point of view. A widespread prejudice prevails in west European countries against illegal work. People think you do not need it. I do not believe there is any principled difference here; we can come to an understanding. But while we take into account the German comrades' considerations, we have to stick to an international point of view. When we conclude this, we will set up an editing commission. We can confidently leave this question to the editing commission, instructing it to meet the concerns of the German comrades, and to some extent the French comrades as well.

CRISPIEN: Before the editing commission completes its final draft, we would like to have the opportunity to look it over.

MEYER: As regards the USPD's misgivings, let me say that we stress that illegal work exists to be used in times of a state of siege, when the conditions of legality are broken by the bourgeoisie and the government.

**Thesis 4: Agitation in the army**

DITTMANN: Here the same misgivings arise to the same degree. When a large legal party officially declares it is going to undertake agitation for communist ideas in the army in order to sweep away those presently in power, such a party runs the risk that the state's authority will be brought to bear against it, and it will be suppressed. As for the basic notion, we have stressed our agreement with it.

MEYER: I would like to say that no juridical considerations stand in the way of our setting the task of agitational activity in the army. There are no clauses of the constitution that forbid carrying out propaganda in the army. Given the nature of our activity, it is certainly possible for them to take measures against us in any area. When a strike call is considered treason, no statutory provision is going to help; you are going to go to prison. And when civil war proceeds to a still sharper stage, no formulation is going to be of any help. Then they will move against us still more sharply.

Working in the army for the ideas of communism is not forbidden. And to leave this passage out completely is excluded, unless we are going to establish secret conditions for admission. That is simply not going to work. We can perhaps formulate this passage a little differently, but we cannot and should not leave out the fact that we are required to carry out propaganda in the army.

### Thesis 5: Agitation in the countryside

MEYER: In the subcommission I will propose some changes here, specifically concerning conditions in our country. The sentence saying that a part of the rural workers must support us can go because the entire rural working class, organized in unions, supports the revolutionary parties, the Communists and the USPD.

DITTMANN: That is inaccurate.

MEYER: We can take that up in the subcommission.

### Thesis 2 (in the French edition): Removal of reformists and centrists from leading posts

MEYER: "Every organization wishing to join the Communist International must consistently and systematically remove reformists and centrists from all positions of any responsibility in the workers' movement (party organizations, editorial staffs, trade unions, parliamentary fractions, cooperative societies, local governments) and replace them with reliable Communists without being deterred by the prospect that, especially at first, ordinary workers from the masses will replace 'experienced' opportunists."[22]

ZINOVIEV: What is at stake here is that we must accept the duty to disseminate our ideas through all posts of responsibility, through all wings of the party organization, through editorial boards, parliament, trade unions, cooperatives, and so forth. We must quite systematically replace wavering leaders on the right with Communists, without being afraid of the fact that often we are replacing an experienced politician with a new face or a simple worker.[23]

DITTMANN: I consider that totally superfluous.

MEYER: It relates to thesis 1. Not only must agitation be carried out along Communist lines, but posts must also be held by reliable comrades.

ZINOVIEV: Comrades sometimes come to us, inspired by our example—the Czech comrades, for example—and say, "We are Communists, we want a firm grip on everything, but we don't have the strength." All we can say to them is: Don't do it all at once; be circumspect but very systematic. That has practical significance.

CRISPIEN: Comrade Zinoviev's reasoning defies response. When the movement reaches a certain age, a veritable inquisition is to be set up. The question is, aren't we acting too much like a church? And doesn't that lead to the danger of persecution and inquisition?

DITTMANN: People are appealing to texts and using sophistry.

ZINOVIEV: In my opinion this is very important for the simple worker. You should not be afraid of replacing a lawyer with a simple worker.

MEYER: It applies to the first stage, that of joining the Third International.

DITTMANN: There is one thing we must not forget. Even in revolutionary parties there are elements strongly motivated by ambition. There are circumstances where this provision can be an excuse for ambitious elements to drive people out of their positions and take these posts for themselves. There is the danger that adopting such detailed provisions will favor troublemakers.

As the largest party, we suffer from a lack of organizers and editors. We have to make do with forces who, we are convinced, are not yet up to snuff. We hope that later the situation will be different. The Communists will be in the same position. Theses formulated in such detail will carry weight and give the whole movement a servile character.

CRISPIEN: Maybe you could say "replace" instead of "remove."

**Thesis 7: The break with the reformists**

DITTMANN: In Germany we have carried out the break with the reformists.

Zinoviev: We have to recognize that the movement in Germany has recovered more easily than that in other countries. We do not condemn you for having carried out a split; the problem is that part of the Scheidemanns are still in your ranks.

DITTMANN: A new paragraph 2 has been introduced—we do not have it yet but the sense has been expressed—specifying just which people should hold the leading posts. Given that, it is quite sufficient to refer here to the reformists without naming any names. It is really not tactically smart to complicate the question by naming names. You kindle arguments against specific people. We believe naming names holds up the process of transforming parties. A lot of workers see it as an inquisition, and it prevents merging the parties into a single current.

CRISPIEN: I agree, and I will show why this will not work. In each country you want to pick out a name and expel that person, excommunicate them. First you have to give them the opportunity to defend themselves. (*Interjection: "Kautsky has done enough of that."*) I would consider that a dubious procedure, and I do not see why it is necessary. The general foundation already provides sufficient grounds to do what is required.

I can speak only for my party. Based on our statutes, we cannot expel someone without giving them the opportunity to vindicate themselves. It cannot be done this way. Some of them are known, others are not. But maybe these people will quit on their own.

ZINOVIEV: There has been talk of inquisitions. To say, "We ought to listen to them first"—that is childish. Should we listen to Kautsky after he has written twenty pamphlets and stabbed us in the back? He belongs with the bourgeoisie and we are revolutionaries. Kautsky does not want in any way to belong to the Third International. According to Huysmans, Kautsky told him at the Belgian party congress that if the USPD decides to enter the Third International, Kautsky's choice is clear: he will stay with the Second International, not the USPD. We have to lay it out as the workers understand it to the marrow of their bones. We do not want to insult Turati. We know he is an honorable man. But he is a bourgeois democrat. If they become something different tomorrow, so much the better.

STOECKER: I am astonished by the proposal to say "opportunists" instead of "reformists."[24] Kautsky is worse than that, he is a reformist. We want to combat those who base themselves on bourgeois democracy but are in a party that bases itself on the dictatorship [of the proletariat].

### Thesis 9: The trade unions and producers' and consumers' cooperatives

DITTMANN: In the trade unions in Germany, especially in the metalworkers' union, fractions have been built, instigated by the right-wing Socialists. There have been extended discussions over this in the unions. This dispute has been ironed out inasmuch as the right-wing Socialists have given up their fractions. If our own people come now and build fractions, they are giving the right-wing Socialists cause to do likewise at a time when our people are increasingly gaining control of the organization. In addition, the question arises whether establishing as a condition that certain bodies must carry out agitation may not just make the work of the unions all the more difficult. In Germany it is not necessary to speak of setting up special bodies. We have influence over the members we have inside.

ZINOVIEV: I followed this dispute in the press, and it seems to me that you have a point. We cannot hold it against the social pacifists and social reformists when they organize their members in the unions. How can you argue that these are organizations where politics have no place? Ten years ago Kautsky said it very well: there is no neutrality—in such fights you are either on the bourgeoisie's side or on our side.

You are allowing yourself to be guided by the fact that in Berlin you have the majority. In this dispute such a course would be opportunistic and unprincipled, given that in Germany Legien is still managing the affairs of millions of members and in America nine-tenths of the entire union movement is in the hands of our enemies *(Garbled)*. If we want to win there, we must organize inside the movement and systematically and persistently fight for our ideas.

CRISPIEN: If we build bodies inside unions where we are the minority, we run the danger of being kicked out of them. Then all we have is a splintered organization and we accomplish nothing. In Germany it has happened that by-laws were brought to bear and the comrades were driven out. Therefore we should say, work *in* the unions.

DÄUMIG: I do not share Dittmann and Crispien's reservations. I think that a fight will ensue in the unions between reactionary and revolutionary forces. Since the factory councils have remained nothing but an eloquent scrap of paper, we must give more unity to our forces in the unions. Two days after our departure from Berlin, the SPD metalworkers' fraction called its people together. They see no problem in that, and we have no reason not to unite our forces as well.

DITTMANN: We all are striving for the same thing. It is only a question of achieving our goals as easily as possible and accomplishing the most with the least possible exertion. We do not want to expose ourselves to unnecessary resistance. In general, with regard to what we want to accomplish, we are advancing along the same course.

But we must take into account not only what happened in the metalworkers' union, but also what happened in the miners' union, and not only in the Ruhr Valley. This time it was possible for the miners, who had gone over to the syndicalist union, to make their way back. In Germany the danger exists that whenever there is a split, the syndicalists come out on top. Even you do not want people to be unnecessarily driven into the arms of the syndicalists.

I prefer the word *cell* to *fraction,* a word that in this context has a political flavor.

I only wish that these reservations were not correct.

**Thesis 11: Parliamentarism**

DITTMANN: I draw to your attention that our party first arose out of the SPD as the Working Group, formed because as Reichstag deputies we put party discipline above fraction discipline. Eventually the party was built from this. We have no doubts about this clause, since for us too party discipline still stands above fraction discipline.

**Thesis 12: The party press and publishing houses**

DITTMANN: I do not think it necessary to repeat what we said on the press in the general debate.[25] I want only to remind you of it, so that it cannot be said that we let this point pass without comment. Because our Social Democracy was robbed of its newspapers,[26] we did not want to continue granting the party Executive Committee significant proprietary rights. This gives us a better guarantee that the newspapers will be run more in the spirit of the party. To the extent that we can have an influence on this spirit, it will become more uniform. But more we cannot do.

ZINOVIEV: Soon you will do more.

**Thesis 17: Name of the party**

DITTMANN: For us in Germany the situation is different. There already is a Communist Party there, and if we were to join the International, there would be a second Communist Party, so long as the two parties did not merge. In general it is better for the parties to have different names. Besides, when the party was founded in Gotha, the name Communist Workers Party was proposed. That was rejected because communism has a somewhat archaic sound to it—

RADEK: Primitive communism!

DITTMANN: —and the name Independent Socialist party was chosen because of the particular situation the party was in. With that name, we wanted to make the statement that the party pursues a political line that is independent of the government, independent of the right-wing Socialist party, and independent of the bourgeois parties. That is how the name came to be. It has existed for some time now and has come to mean something. Many members are of the opinion that this thesis need not be an obstacle to our joining, that at some point the name will disappear, giving way to "Communist Party." If affiliation is decided upon, the logical consequence is to merge with the Communist Party, and the name Communist Party can then be adopted.

ZINOVIEV: For twenty-five to thirty years we called ourselves Social Democrats and for fifteen years Bolsheviks. We got used to that name, we became well known with it.

We can find no other expression [except Communist]. It comes from the good old days and was put on a scientific foundation by Marx. Obviously, if the USPD really belongs to the International, then the name will become United Communist Party of Germany.

RADEK: Independent of the United Communist Party of Germany!

ZINOVIEV: Now we are discussing the conditions. The question of the name comes later.

### Lenin's amendment

*Regarding Lenin's proposal that before a party can be accepted into the Communist International two-thirds of the members of its leadership body must be made up of those who supported communism before the Third International met in congress:*[27]

DITTMANN: Our party leadership is reelected at every congress. If the congress decides to join the Third International, that can happen only at a special party congress that we call. If the congress decides to join, it will elect to the leadership people in whom it has confidence. Of course it will elect people in whom it has confidence to carry out the decisions.

CRISPIEN: This passage reduces us to the level of parties that are just now starting to carry out revolutionary policies. The workers will not be able to understand this. They will take this as a blow. I would like to ask that this be stricken.

MEYER: If Dittmann thinks that the masses will not understand this, after the policies the USPD has been pursuing, then I disagree. Nevertheless, I do not support Lenin's proposal. You could not come up with very many people in the USPD who have carried out entirely communist policies. If we charge the Executive Committee, or better yet the Communist International, with checking on this, we will find that all the conditions have been fulfilled.

The USPD commission itself declared that it will give a report when it returns to Germany. Cachin and Frossard said the same. There they will say that such and such are the conditions for our party to be accepted. Only the party as a whole can make a decision.

By the time the application of the party as a whole gets to the Third International, a certain time will have passed, and it will also take a certain time for joining the International to be carried out in practice. That time will be sufficient for the Communist International to make a decision on whether the practice corresponds to what the Communist International demands. In this commission, where we are establishing the general conditions, we do not need to get too technical.

DITTMANN: I have the impression that we are weaving a web of technicalities. We are here to negotiate affiliation. Our task is to make known the basis for joining and to see to it that the masses understand what this means. Once this takes place, a party congress will be called that will deal almost exclusively with this question. If the majority decides in favor of joining, then of course a leadership will be elected that adheres to the conditions. Obviously the statutes will be published, and from the outset the International will be able to judge these things. I want to very strongly request that these formalistic conditions be dropped.

*Lenin's proposal is adopted by a vote of 5 to 3.*

## 3B
## Letter to the French Socialist Party from the Presiding Committee

*July 29, 1920*

To all members of the French Socialist Party;

To all class-conscious proletarians of France:

The last congress of the French Socialist Party decided by an overwhelming majority to withdraw from the Second International, which all class-conscious workers of the world now consider a traitorous organization.[28] But the same congress rejected immediately joining the Communist International by a two-thirds majority, confining itself to an equivocal resolution that it would enter into only certain relations with the Third International and would undertake to organize the intermediate parties situated between the Second and Third Internationals.

Two delegates of the congress majority, Marcel Cachin and Frossard, arrived in Russia to conduct negotiations with us regarding the congress resolution. An expanded Executive Committee of the Communist International (with the participation of delegates from Italy, Britain, America, Austria, Hungary, Germany, Bulgaria, and other countries) devoted two full sessions to studying the matters related to the arrival of Cachin and Frossard. In addition, the Executive Committee had a number of smaller meetings with the two delegates of the French Socialist Party. We received from them three written reports, which have been printed in the official press of the Communist International in all languages.[29] We invited Cachin and Frossard to the Second World Congress of the Communist International with consultative voice. We heard Cachin and Frossard at length in the congress commission. It goes without saying that the Executive Committee of the Communist International takes as its duty giving the closest attention to every delegation of a party or group that wishes to break with the Second International and join the ranks of the Communist International.

We are grateful that the French Socialist Party, by sending its delegates, gave us the opportunity to discuss with you frankly and openly, as is proper for revolutionaries. From what follows you will learn how we regard the state of affairs in France. Our answer, we are confident, will be printed promptly in France and read and discussed attentively by all class-conscious French workers.

Our assessment of the French Socialist Party's situation is based on two primary factors: (1) the role the French bourgeoisie is now playing in the world; and (2) the internal situation of the French Socialist Party itself.

For a number of reasons the French bourgeoisie today plays without a doubt the most reactionary role possible around the world. It has become the bulwark of world reaction. Before the eyes of the whole world, French imperialist capitalism has assumed the role of international gendarme. The French bourgeoisie did more than any other to strangle the proletarian soviet republic in Hungary. The French bourgeoisie has always played and is still playing the star role in organizing the criminal campaign against Soviet Russia. The French bourgeoisie has assumed the part of the most foul hangman in the Balkans.[30] And finally, the same French bourgeoisie took on the main duties for stifling the developing proletarian revolution in Germany. To it went the key role in working out the predatory Versailles peace. It sent Black troops to occupy German cities. Indeed it entered into an alliance with the German bourgeoisie against the German working class. There is no monstrous crime that the government of the French bourgeoisie would not commit. There is no worse enemy of the developing world revolution than the government of the French capitalists.

This places an especially important internationalist duty on the French workers and their party. You, French proletarians, are assigned by history a highly responsible, difficult, but rewarding mission to deliver a counterblow to the most violent, the most unrestrainedly reactionary detachment of the international bourgeoisie.

But regretfully, the Executive Committee of the Communist International is compelled to note—and here we pass to the second factor mentioned above—that the internal situation of the French Socialist Party is not at all conducive to your being able to fulfill the historic mission assigned to you by the course of events.

The advanced workers of France will agree with us in saying that apart from Germany, nowhere during the four-year imperialist war was there such a base betrayal of socialism as that committed in your very country by the former majority of your party. The actions of the former majority's leaders (Renaudel, Thomas, Sembat, and others) after August 4, 1914, was not a bit better than the vicious, traitorous conduct of Scheidemann and Noske in Germany. Your party's leaders not only voted for war credits but also placed the whole party press, the entire party apparatus at the service of the murderous imperialist bourgeoisie. These leaders poisoned the spirit of the rank-and-file soldier and worker. They helped the imperialist bourgeoisie summon up across the whole country a murky wave of unheard-of and monstrous chauvinism. They helped the bourgeoisie institute a despotic regime in the factories and abolish even the most moderate labor legislation.

They assumed complete responsibility for the imperialist carnage. They sat in the French bourgeoisie's government. They carried out the most repulsive tasks for the ringleaders of the Entente. When the February revolution of 1917 began in Russia, Albert Thomas arrived in Russia on the instruction of the French imperialists to persuade the Russian workers and soldiers, in the name of his party, to continue the imperialist bloodletting. The French social patriots helped the French capitalists organize the campaign of the Russian White Guards, who had declared war on the working class and peasantry of Russia.

As for the former minority of your party, it never carried out a principled, strong, and clearly defined struggle against its loathsome majority, a struggle it was duty-bound to conduct. Once it became the majority, it went on as before and even today carries out an equivocal policy, showing neither the proper determination nor the appropriate energy, and continuing the former sorry opportunist line.

Even now, Albert Thomas, Renaudel, Jouhaux, and others continue to play a most reactionary role as servants of the bourgeoisie. In the ranks of your party are not only notorious social patriots but many prominent representatives of the Center as well (Longuet and others). They still insist that for France the predatory imperialist war of 1914–18 was defense of the fatherland *(défense nationale)*. Your party, in the person of its centrist majority, has yet to say clearly to the workers of France that for the French as well as the German bourgeoisie the last World War was a predatory war, a war of oppressors, a war of robbers. Speeches by Longuet, Faure, Pressemanne, and others of your leaders about "defense of the fatherland," given as recently as the Strasbourg congress, are close to social patriotism.

We must tell you frankly, comrades, that the internal situation of the French Socialist Party is worse even than that of the German Independents. You have lagged behind even the German pace of development. You still have not split with your open social patriots. You still have not done even what the German Independents did as far back as 1916.[31] Turncoats like Albert Thomas, who did not shrink from occupying a responsible post in the piratical League of Nations, have remained in your party as before. It still includes such personages as Pierre Renaudel, a most zealous lackey of the bourgeoisie. You still tolerate betrayers of the workers' cause like Jouhaux and his cothinkers, who are now reviving the Yellow International of trade unions. In your ranks you tolerate people who, at the bidding of the Entente capitalists, staged the farce of founding the International Labour Office. Deputies of your party who shamelessly abstained from voting when the disgraceful, blood-soaked, criminal Versailles treaty was ratified by the French Chamber of Deputies remain members with full rights.

You will agree, comrades, that such a situation in the party in no way equips you to fulfill the mission history has entrusted you with.

Given such a state of affairs, comrades, it is not surprising that the present official majority of the French Socialist Party, which considers itself internationalist and revolutionary, is in practice carrying out a policy of vacillation, equivocation, and half-baked compromise.

Let us look at your most important daily tasks in this order: (1) your parliamentary work, (2) your press, (3) your propaganda in the countryside and the army, (4) your relations with the trade unions, (5) your position on the French government's most recent acts of violence, (6) your relations with the communist left wing of your own party, (7) your relations with the International.

1. The *parliamentary work* of your Socialist fraction in the Chamber of Deputies continues as before: neither revolutionary, proletarian, nor socialist. Each Socialist deputy does what he wishes. The parliamentary fraction as a whole does not subordinate itself to the work of the party. It carries out only those majority party decisions that suit its fancy. It does not speak for the French proletarian masses, who are burning with indignation at the base acts of the French bourgeoisie. It does not report back to the working masses. It does not expose the crimes of the French government. It does not conduct revolutionary agitation among the millions of war veterans. It does not take on the task of fully depicting the criminal character of the recent imperialist war to the toiling masses. It does not call on the workers to arm themselves.

In a word, your parliamentary fraction not only fails to prepare for the proletarian revolution but, on the contrary, does all in its power to sabotage the revolution. Many of your parliamentary deputies remain, as before, not fighters for the working class but petty intriguers. The overall conduct of your deputies evokes feelings of disgust among the French working masses and this adds grist to the anarchists' mill. The opportunism of your parliamentary fraction only feeds into and enhances the mistakes and prejudices of syndicalism. Your deputies' conduct only increases the masses' contempt for parliamentary schemers and for those who call themselves Socialists but in practice hobnob with the worst enemies of the working class.

2. Your *daily press,* mainly *L'Humanité* and *Le Populaire,* are not revolutionary publications. We do not see these newspapers propagandizing and agitating in a daily, systematic way for the idea of proletarian revolution. At best the newspapers use dry and uninspired words to speak of the dictatorship of the proletariat—but these words do not take on flesh and blood in all your daily written agitation. Often your newspapers are as indistinguishable from those of the bourgeoisie as two drops of water. You too allocate most of the space to parliamentary trifles and petty "events" in bourgeois "circles." Your newspapers neither attempt nor succeed in being the true voice of the rising revolutionary anger of the proletarian masses. Your newspapers do not describe the disasters French working people are experiencing as a result of the war. Your newspapers are limited to dry, formal, pedantic, and passionless protests. You handed over editorship of your party paper among the peasants to Compère-Morel, a notorious social patriot.

You must repudiate the intolerable policy of proportional representation, which opens up the pages of the party press to the poisonous writings of Renaudel and company.

3. The same can be said about *your agitational work in the countryside and among soldiers*. Either it does not exist at all, or it has a clearly reformist character. Where and when has your party explained to the French soldiers their revolutionary proletarian duty? As far as we know—*nowhere and never*. If the relationship of forces today in France is such that Socialists cannot do this legally, *the duty of every honest proletarian consists in supplementing legal with illegal work*. This is essential to fulfilling your responsibility to the working class of your own country as well as to the proletarians around the world.

4. Your *attitude to the trade unions* is completely ambiguous. Not only do you fail to conduct a systematic ideological struggle against the social-patriotic leaders of the General Confederation of Labor, but you are covering up for them. When Jouhaux and company helped the bourgeoisie restore the Amsterdam trade union International, when the same group together with Albert Thomas went to the imperialist-organized international labor conference, when leaders of the General Confederation of Labor most treacherously sabotaged the July 21, 1919, strike, you did not campaign against them. You did not pillory them before the entire French working class. You did not expose them as the basest traitors to the workers' cause. No, you continued to "collaborate" with them. At best you give them a good-natured warning; you do not fight them. You failed to set as your task winning the French unions away from the pernicious influences of the agents of capital.

At the time of the last big strikes in May, when the government threw you in jail and the companies fired you, one of your comrades, Paul-Boncour, accused the government in parliament of only one thing. He said they had forgotten the patriotism exhibited by Jouhaux on August 2, 1914, and his great service during and after the war.

5. The French bourgeoisie has recently committed *unspeakable acts of violence* directed specifically against the left wing of the French workers' movement. They have thrown into prison Loriot, Monatte, Souvarine, and a number of other comrades. What have you done to repulse this campaign by the French capitalists? Why have you not sounded the alarm? Why have you not organized a nationwide campaign? Why do you limit yourselves to merely philanthropic agitational work?

6. Your relation to the *communist left wing* of your own party leaves much to be desired. You do not seek closer contact among French communists. On the contrary, you are organizing a struggle against them. You place on your agenda joining the Communist International, but at the same time you do nothing, or almost nothing, to establish sincere and comradely rapprochement with the communists of your own country.

7. Finally, on your attitude toward the *International.* You stayed in the ranks of the treacherous, Yellow Second International until the German Independents left it and the French workers forced the current leaders of the French Socialist Center to break with it. You sent delegates to the infamous Bern conference. True, some of them defended the Russian revolution there, but there were also attempts to save the dying Second International. You tried to create a new intermediate current, the so-called reconstructors. Even now you have not made a direct statement of your intention to join the Communist International. You announced your departure from the Second International, but at the time you also stated your solidarity with the Belgian "Socialists," that is, with the social traitor Vandervelde, leader of the Second International. You

declared your desire to join the Third International, but meanwhile, during the Kapp insurrection, your official representative, Mistral, signed a joint statement with the bureau of the Second International calling on the German proletariat to defend the republic along with Noske and Scheidemann. Either you are silent concerning the existence of the Third International or you conduct a semi-open campaign against it.

In his report to us in Moscow, your representative, Frossard, continues even now to explain that the reason you have not yet entered the Communist International is that the largest parties in western Europe have not yet joined. But you must not forget: if by the largest parties in western Europe you mean those infected with social patriotism, we do not need those parties and we will never accept them into membership in the Communist International. All the truly revolutionary parties of Europe and America are in our ranks.

The Communist International has become such a powerful force that for some Socialists it has become *fashionable*. Some supporters of the Center have begun to call themselves Communists and think that they can join the Third International while continuing with their former semireformist politics. The Communist International cannot tolerate this. We will not allow our organizations to be diluted. The Communist International must remain the international *combat* association of Communist workers.

Now we turn to the questions that your representative Frossard put to us directly in his first written report. Among other things, this report asked about our relations with the *French trade unions*. This question is of the utmost importance and must be taken up.

From our theses and other official documents of the Communist International you know that we are firmly opposed to the suggestion of a handful of "left" Communists that we leave the ranks of the reactionary trade unions. They suggest we wash our hands of these unions and counterpose some new amorphous "General Workers Union." Our view applies not only to the free Yellow Social Democratic unions of Legien and company but to the French trade unions under the leadership of Jouhaux and company. *We are against* revolutionaries and Communists leaving the mass trade unions, even in cases where the unions have the misfortune of being led by Legien and Jouhaux. Revolutionaries and Communists must be where the masses are. Russian communists, as well, were a minority in the unions for a long time. Russian communists learned how to fight for their ideas within the most backward and openly reactionary workers' organizations.

We demand that our supporters in France under no circumstances *abandon* the trade unions. On the contrary, if they wish to fulfill their duty to the Communist International, they must strengthen their work in the unions.

The unions today are the last refuge for the social patriots. As a political organization, the Second International has collapsed like a house of cards. The new Amsterdam International of Yellow trade unions, however, is still a significant base for the social traitors. The Yellow Amsterdam International is now more harmful and dangerous to the world revolution than the League of Nations. Through Legien, Gompers, and Jouhaux the bourgeoisie is trying to make the Amsterdam trade union International into a tool in their drive for plunder, just as they did with the Social Democratic parties around the world during the imperialist war.

This means that we Communists must pay ten times more attention to the union movement. We must at all costs wrench these unions from the hands of the capitalists and social traitors. To do this we must be *inside* these unions. We must therefore send our best forces there.

Our supporters will stay in the trade unions, but they will not act in an uncoordinated way, like human dust. *In every union, in every branch of the union, we must organize a Communist group, a Communist cell.* Within the unions we must expose the tricks of the big and small Jouhauxes through daily struggle. We must open the eyes of the rank-and-file union members. We must drive the social traitors out of the unions. Through systematic and persistent struggle we must wrench one union after another from the influence of the social traitors and Yellow unionists such as Jouhaux. Only after long years of work did the Russian Bolsheviks succeed in accomplishing this task. Even on the eve of the October revolution, the Russian communists were a minority in the unions. After taking power into their hands and giving new means of propaganda to the class-conscious workers, the Russian Bolsheviks managed in a short time *after the revolution* to win over the great majority of the trade union movement. Communists and revolutionaries around the world must follow this path.

In his written report in Moscow, Frossard said, "The General Confederation of Labor will not make a revolution without us (the party); we will not make a revolution without them (the unions)."[32] This formulation, to say the least, is not sufficiently clear. The revolution cannot be made with those who do not want to make it. The proletarian revolution will not be made with gentlemen like Jouhaux, who exert all their intellect, all their strength to block the proletarian revolution. You will make the proletarian revolution only *in spite of* Jouhaux and *against him,* and in spite of Albert Thomas and Pierre Renaudel. If you cleanse the party of opportunism, if your deputies in parliament begin to carry out communist propaganda, if you drive out the Yellow traitors from the ranks of your own party, in a word if you become Communists, then rank-and-file workers, trade union members, will follow you in opposing Jouhaux. The sooner you overcome your syndicalist prejudices, the sooner you will shed your opportunism.

Red trade unions have begun to organize on an international level. On the initiative of the Executive Committee of the Communist International, the left-wing trade unions of Italy, Russia, and Britain have formed a tripartite alliance, which will call an international congress of Red trade unions in August or September.[33] This congress will be an alternative to the Amsterdam International of Yellow trade unions. Support this initiative in France. Persuade your unions to join with the Red International of trade unions and break once and for all with the Yellow International. That is the task of real revolutionaries in France.

In his report Frossard handed us a semireprimand when he asked whether we still insisted on the expulsion of certain figures from your party.

This question, of course, is quite important, but it alone does not determine our relationship with you. We say to you quite frankly that you are lagging behind in comparison even to the German Independents. Although the German Independents have finally faced up to the question of expelling Kautsky (which means the Kautskyites),[34] Albert Thomas and Renaudel—that is, the French Noske and Scheidemann—are still in your party, enjoying full rights. We must declare quite emphatically that despite the struggle that Longuet leads on behalf of the Russian revolution and despite his verbal acceptance of the dictatorship of the proletariat, Longuet's ideological positions and general activity in the press and parliament are as identical to Kautsky's propaganda in Germany as two peas in a pod. You will have to abandon a whole number of right-wing leaders who are infected with reformism to the marrow of their bones.

But the main question we put to you is not that of expelling individuals but that of breaking with a definite reformist tradition. The Communist International does not demand that you "make" a soviet revolution forthwith. Anyone who presents the Communist International's demand to you in this light is distorting our position. We require only this: in your day-to-day work, in the press, in the unions, in parliament, and at meetings, you must systematically and unswervingly conduct honest, unequivocal propaganda for the ideas of [proletarian] dictatorship and communism. You must do this to clear the road for the proletarian revolution and fight conscientiously against bourgeois-reformist ideas.

That is the main thing that we wanted to say to you, comrades.

On the eve of their departure, your delegates Cachin and Frossard declared to us officially that they agree to the conditions proposed by the Second World Congress of the Communist International. They declare that upon returning to France they will propose that the French Socialist Party break radically with the old reformist policies and switch over to communist rails.

Needless to say we will be very glad if the French workers' movement at last actually turns out to have found the right path. We will follow the further course of events in the French Socialist Party very closely. And the congress is giving the Executive Committee the authority to admit your party to the ranks of the Communist International if you accept and truly implement the conditions the congress has established.

In conclusion we shall state several particular points that seem to us to be central. We will expect you to reply to them quite clearly and definitely.

We reaffirm entirely our reply to the German Independents, which was also printed in the Paris communist press. Almost in its entirety, this answer was also addressed to you, the majority of the French Socialist Party.

We make the following ten points with reference to the situation in France:

1. The press of the French Socialist Party must radically change the character of its day-to-day propaganda and agitation along the lines we have indicated.

2. In countries where the bourgeoisie holds dominion over the colonial peoples, it is especially necessary for parties to have a precise and clear line on the question of colonies. The French party must mercilessly expose the tricks of the French imperialists in the colonies, support every liberation movement in the colonies not just in word but in deed, popularize the slogan "Imperialists out of the colonies," cultivate among the workers of France a truly fraternal attitude to the laboring population of the colonies, and conduct systematic agitation among the French troops against colonial oppression.

3. The French party must expose the falsity and hypocrisy of social pacifism, systematically demonstrating to the workers that without the revolutionary overthrow of capitalism, no international arbitration courts, no arms reduction negotiations can save humanity from new imperialist wars.

4. The French Socialist Party must begin to organize the revolutionary communist forces inside the General Confederation of Labor for a struggle against the social traitors leading the federation.

5. The French Socialist Party must obtain, not only in words but also in deeds, the strictest subordination of the

parliamentary fraction to the party as a whole. It must accept into the party fraction only those delegates who conscientiously fulfill party decisions and who change all their day-to-day parliamentary activity in the spirit described above.

6. The present majority of the French Socialist Party must radically change its relationship with the communist left wing of the French workers' movement. The party must grant representatives of the communists access to the pages of all its publications. The present majority must search out a sincere rapprochement with the communist forces in France.[35]

7. The French party must radically break with reformism and systematically cleanse its ranks of elements that do not want to enter on a new, revolutionary road.

8. The French party must also change its name and appear before the world as the Communist Party of France.

9. The French comrades must recognize the necessity of combining legal and illegal work in an epoch when the bourgeoisie is creating a state of siege for the workers and their leaders.

10. The French party, like all parties that want to take part in the Third International, must recognize that all decisions of the Communist International are unconditionally binding. The Communist International is fully aware of all the diverse conditions in which the workers in different countries have to struggle. Congresses of the Communist International will always consider these conditions and will make decisions binding on everyone only on questions where such decisions are possible.

We ask you to acquaint all the French workers with this reply.

Comrades, we have quite frankly told you our opinion on a whole number of major questions. We know that at present only a small number of your leaders will subscribe to what we have said. But we are confident that the vast majority of conscious worker-socialists and the honest revolutionary syndicalists of France are one with us. However our mutual relations may develop in the immediate future, we are unshakably confident that the French proletariat will forge a mighty Communist party, occupying a foremost place in the international family of the militant proletariat. We cannot accept that the revolutionary working class of France with its wonderful revolutionary traditions, with its culture, with its readiness for self-sacrifice, and with its excellent militant temperament, would be unable to create a powerful Communist party in this epoch when the bourgeois system has clearly begun to breathe its last.

Comrades, in the coming year the international proletariat will celebrate the fiftieth anniversary of the Paris Commune—the great workers' uprising, which found its continuation in the proletarian revolution in Russia. From the bottom of our hearts we wish that this fiftieth anniversary of the great Paris Commune finds you organized into a powerful proletarian Communist party, continuing the best traditions of the Paris Communards and ready to storm the strongholds of capitalism.

Long live the working class of France!

Long live a united and mighty French Communist party!

With communist greetings,

*The Presiding Committee of*
*the Second Congress of the*
*Communist International*[36]

# 4A
# Appeal to the IWW

Comrades and fellow workers:

The Executive Committee of the Communist International, in session at Moscow, the heart of the Russian revolution, greets the revolutionary American proletariat in the person of the Industrial Workers of the World.[1]

Capitalism, ruined by the World War, unable any longer to contain within itself the tremendous forces it has created, is breaking down.

The hour of the working class has struck. The social revolution has begun, and here, on the Russian plain, the first vanguard battle is being fought.

History does not ask whether we want revolution or not, whether the workers are ready or not. Here is the opportunity. Take it and the world will belong to the workers; leave it—there may not be another for generations.

Now is no time to talk of "building the new society within the shell of the old." *The old society is cracking its shell. The workers must establish the dictatorship of the proletariat, which alone can build the new society.*

An article in *One Big Union Monthly,* your official organ, asks, "Why should we follow the Bolsheviks?" According to the writer, all that the Bolshevik revolution in Russia has done is "to give the Russian people the vote."

This is, of course, untrue. The Bolshevik revolution has taken the factories, mills, mines, land, and financial institutions out of the hands of the capitalists, and transferred them to the *whole working class.*

We understand, and share with you, your disgust for the principles and tactics of the Yellow Socialist politicians, who all over the world have discredited the very name of socialism. Our aim is the same as yours—a commonwealth without state, without government, without classes, in which the workers shall administer the means of production and distribution for the common benefit of all.

We address this letter to you, fellow workers of the IWW, in recognition of your long and heroic services in the class war, of which you have always borne the brunt in your own country, so that you may clearly understand our communist principles and program.

We appeal to you, as revolutionists, to rally to the Communist International, born in the dawn of the world social revolution.

We call you to take the place to which your courage and revolutionary experience entitles you, in the front ranks of the proletarian Red army fighting under the banner of communism.

### Communism and the IWW

The American capitalist class is revealing its true colors.

The constantly rising cost of living, the growing unemployment, the savage repression of all efforts of the workers to better their condition, the deportation and imprisonment of "Bolsheviks," the series of antistrike laws, "criminal syndicalist" laws, laws "against red flags," and laws against propaganda advocating the "forcible overthrow of government and the unlawful destruction of property"—all these measures can have but one meaning for every intelligent worker.

Industrial slavery is as old as capitalism, and other forms of slavery existed before it. *But now the capitalists of the world—the American capitalists as well as those of France, Italy, England, Germany, and so on—are planning to reduce the workers once and for all to absolute and hopeless serfdom.*

Either this, or the dictatorship of the working class—there is no other alternative. And the workers must choose *now*.

Capitalism is making desperate efforts to reconstruct its shattered world. The workers must forcibly take state power and reconstruct society in their own interests.

**The coming slave state . . .**

Before the American Civil War, the Negro slaves of the South were bound to the land. The industrial capitalists of the North, who needed a floating population to operate their factories, declared slavery to be an outrage and abolished it by force. Now the industrial capitalists are attempting to bind the workers to the factories.

In every country during the World War, it was practically forbidden for the workers to strike, or, in general, to quit their jobs. You will remember the "work or fight" laws in your own country.

And now that the war is over, what has happened? The cost of living has gone up and up, while the capitalists have actually tried to reduce wages. And when the workers, faced by starvation, are forced to strike, the whole power of the state is mobilized to drive them back to the machines. When the railway shopmen walked out, the U.S. marshal of California threatened to bring in federal troops to force them to work. When the railroad brotherhoods demanded higher wages or the nationalization of the railways, the president of the United States menaced them with the full armed power of the government. When the United Mine Workers laid down their tools, thousands of soldiers occupied the mines, and the federal court issued the most sweeping injunction in history, forbidding the union leaders from sending out the strike order or in any way assisting in conducting the strike and forcibly preventing the payment of strike benefits. And finally, the attorney general of the United States declared officially that the government would not permit strikes in "industries necessary to the community."

Judge Gary, head of the steel trust, can refuse the demand of the president of the United States to meet a committee of his workers. But when the steelworkers dare to go on strike for a living wage and the elementary right to join a union, they are called Bolsheviks and shot down in the streets by the Pennsylvania cossacks.[2]

And you, fellow workers of the IWW, with your bitter memories of Everett, of Tulsa, of Wheatland, of Centralia, in which your comrades were butchered;[3] with your thousands in prison—you who nevertheless must do the "dirty work" in the harvest fields, on the docks, in the forests—you must see plainly the process by which the capitalists, by means of their weapon, the state, are trying to inaugurate the slave society.

Everywhere the capitalists cry, "More production! More production!" In other words, the workers must do more work for less wages, so that their blood and sweat may be turned into gold, to pay the war debts of the ruined capitalist world.

In order to accomplish this the workers must no longer have the right to leave their jobs; they must be forbidden to organize to wring concessions from the bosses or take advantage of capitalist competition. At all costs the labor movement must be halted and broken.

To save the old system of exploitation, the capitalists must unite and chain the workers to the machines of industry.

**. . . or the social revolution**

Will the capitalists be able to do this?

They will unless the workers declare war on the whole capitalist system, overthrow the capitalist governments, and set up a government of the working class, which shall destroy the institution of capitalist private property and make all wealth the property of all the workers in common.

This is what the Russian workers have done, and this is the *only way* for the workers of other countries to free themselves from industrial slavery and to make over the world so that the worker shall get *all he produces,* and nobody shall be able to make money out of the labor of other men.

But unless the workers of other countries rise against their own capitalists, the Russian revolution cannot last. The capitalists of the entire world, realizing the danger of the example of Soviet Russia, have united to crush it. The Allies have quickly forgotten their hatred for Germany, and have invited the German capitalists to join them in the common cause.

And the workers of other countries are beginning to understand that in Italy, Germany, France, and England, the tide of revolution is rising. In America, too, even the conservative members of the American Federation of Labor (AFL) are realizing that strikes for higher wages and better conditions don't mean anything, because the cost of living is always climbing higher and higher. They have proposed all sorts of remedies, reforms, such as the Plumb Plan,[4] nationalization of mines, and so on. They have founded a so-called "Labor Party,"[5] which works for municipal and government ownership of industry, more democratic electoral machinery, and so forth.

But these reforms wouldn't solve the problem, even if they could be achieved. *So long as the capitalist system exists, the same men will be making money out of the labor of others. All reforms of the present system of society simply fool the worker into believing that he isn't being robbed as much as he was before.*

The social revolution has begun, and the first battle is on in Russia. It will not wait for the workers to experiment with reforms. The capitalists have already destroyed the Hungarian soviet republic. If they can dominate and break the labor movement in the other countries, then will follow an industrial slave state.

*Before it is too late,* the class-conscious workers of the world must prepare to meet the shock of the capitalist assault, to attack and destroy capitalism, and root it out of the world.

## The capitalist state

The war and its aftermath have revealed with startling clearness the real function of the capitalist state, with its legislatures, courts of justice, police, armies, and bureaucrats.

The state is *used* to defend and strengthen the power of the capitalists and to oppress the workers. This is particularly true in the United States, whose Constitution was framed by the great merchants, speculators, and landowners with the deliberate purpose of protecting their class interests against the majority of the people.

*At the present time the government of the United States is openly acting as the weapon of the capitalists against the workers.*

The IWW should realize this more clearly than any other body of workers, for it has been savagely persecuted by the government—its leaders imprisoned, its papers suppressed, its members deported, jailed on false charges, refused bail, tortured, its headquarters closed, and its propaganda declared illegal in many states.

Any worker can see this fact with his own eyes. All the people vote for governors, mayors, judges, and sheriffs; but in time of strike the governor calls in the militia to protect the scabs, the mayor orders the police to beat up and arrest the pickets, the judge imprisons the workers for "rioting," "disturbing the peace," and the sheriff hires thugs as deputies to break the strike.

Capitalist society all together presents a solid front against the worker. The priest tells the worker to be contented, the press curses him as a "Bolshevik," the policeman arrests him, the court sentences him to jail, the sheriff seizes his furniture for debt, and the poorhouse takes his wife and children.

In order to destroy capitalism, the workers must first wrest the state power out of the hands of the capitalist class. They must not only *seize* this power, but *abolish the old capitalist apparatus entirely.*

For the experience of revolutions has shown that the workers cannot take hold of the state machine and use it for their own purposes—as the Yellow Socialist politicians propose to do. The capitalist state is built to serve capitalism, and that is all it can do, no matter who is running it.

And in place of the capitalist state the workers must build their own *workers' state,* the dictatorship of the proletariat.

### The dictatorship of the proletariat

Many members of the IWW do not agree with this. They are against the "state in general." They propose to overthrow the capitalist state and to establish in its place immediately the industrial commonwealth.

The Communists are also opposed to the "state." They also wish to abolish it—to substitute for the government of men, the administration of things.

But unfortunately this cannot be done immediately. The destruction of the capitalist state does not mean that capitalism automatically and immediately disappears. The capitalists still have arms, which must be taken away from them. They are still supported by hordes of loyal bureaucrats, managers, superintendents, foremen, and trained men of all sorts, who will sabotage industry—and these must be persuaded or compelled to serve the working class. They still have army officers who can betray the revolution, preachers who can raise superstitious fears against it, teachers and orators who can misrepresent it to the ignorant, thugs who can be hired to discredit it by evil behavior, newspaper editors who can deceive the people with floods of lies, and Yellow Socialists and labor fakers who prefer capitalist "democracy" to the revolution. All these people must be sternly suppressed.

To break down the capitalist state, to crush capitalist resistance and disarm the capitalist class, to confiscate capitalist property and turn it over to the *whole working class in common*—for all these tasks a government is necessary; a state, the dictatorship of the proletariat, in which the workers, through their soviets, can uproot the capitalist system with an iron hand.

This is exactly what exists in Soviet Russia today.

*But this dictatorship of the proletariat is only temporary.*

We, Communists, also want to abolish the state. The state can only exist as long as there is class struggle. The function of the proletarian dictatorship is to abolish the capitalist class as a class; in fact, do away with all class divisions of every kind. And when this condition is reached, then the *proletarian dictatorship, the state, automatically disappears*—to make way for an industrial administrative body which will be something like the General Executive Board of the IWW.

In a recent leaflet, Mary Marcy argues that although the IWW does not theoretically recognize the necessity for the dictatorship of the proletariat, it will be forced to do so *in fact* at the time of the revolution, in order to suppress the capitalist counterrevolution.

This is true. But unless the IWW acknowledges beforehand the necessity of the workers' state and prepares for it, there will be confusion and weakness at a time when firmness and swift action are imperative.

### The workers' state

What will be the form of the workers' state?

We have before us the example of the Russian Soviet Republic, whose structure, in view of the conflicting reports printed in other countries, it may be useful to describe briefly here.

The unit of government is the local soviet, or council, of workers', Red Army, and peasants' deputies.

The city workers' soviet is made up as follows: each factory elects one delegate for a certain number of workers, and each local union also elects delegates. These delegates are elected from lists submitted by political parties—or, if the workers wish it, from among candidates standing as individuals.

The Red Army delegates are chosen by military units.

For the peasants, each village has its local soviet, which sends delegates to the township soviet, which in turn elects to the county soviet, and from this to the provincial soviet.

Nobody who employs labor for profit can vote.

Every six months the city and provincial soviets elect delegates to the All-Russia Congress of Soviets, which is the supreme government body of the country. This congress decides upon the policies which are to govern the country for six months and then elects a Central Executive Committee of two hundred, which is to carry out these policies. The congress also elects the cabinet—the Council of People's Commissars, who are heads of government departments—or people's commissariats.

The people's commissars can be recalled at any time by the Central Executive Committee. The members of all soviets can be recalled very easily, and at any time, by their constituents.

These soviets are not only *legislative* bodies, but also *executive* organs. Unlike your Congress, they do not make laws and leave them to the president to carry out. Rather the members carry out the laws themselves, and there is no Supreme Court to say whether or not these laws are "constitutional."

Between the all-Russia soviet congresses the Central Executive Committee is the *supreme power* in Russia. It meets at least every two months, and in the meanwhile, the Council of People's Commissars directs the country, while the members of the Central Executive Committee go to work in the various government departments.

### The organization of production and distribution

In Russia the workers are organized in industrial unions, all the workers in each industry belonging to one union. For example, in a factory making metal products, even the carpenters and painters are members of the metalworkers' union. Each factory is a local union, and the shop committee elected by the workers is its executive committee.

The All-Russia Central Executive Committee of the federated unions is elected by the annual trade union convention. A wage-scale committee elected by the convention fixes the wages of all categories of workers.

With very few exceptions, all important factories in Russia have been nationalized and are now the property of all the workers in common. The business of the unions is therefore no longer to fight the capitalists but to *run industry.*

Hand in hand with the unions works the department of labor of the Soviet government, whose chief is the people's commissar of labor, elected by the soviet congress with the approval of the unions.

In charge of the economic life of the country is the elected Supreme Council of National Economy, divided into departments, such as the metal department, chemical department, and so on, each one headed by experts and workers, appointed, with the approval of unions, by the Supreme Council of National Economy.

In each factory, production is supervised by a committee of three, made up of the head of the factory committee and of representatives of the trade union central executive committee and the Supreme Council of National Economy.

**Democratic centralization**

The unions are thus a *branch of the government*—and this government is the *most highly centralized government that exists.*

It is also the most democratic government in history. For all the organs of government are in constant touch with the working masses and are constantly sensitive to their will. Moreover, the local soviets all over Russia have complete autonomy to manage their own local affairs, provided they carry out the national policies laid down by the soviet congress. Also, the Soviet government represents *only the workers* and cannot help but act in the workers' interest.

Many members of the IWW are opposed to centralization, because they do not think it can be democratic. But where there are great masses of people, it is impossible to register the will of individuals; only the will of majorities can be registered, and in Soviet Russia the government is administered only for the common good of the working class.

The private property of the capitalist class, in order to become the *social* property of the worker, cannot be turned over to individuals or groups of individuals. It must become the property of *all in common,* and a centralized authority is necessary to accomplish this change.

The industries, too, which supply the needs of all the people, are not the concern only of the workers in each industry, but of *all in common,* and must be administered for the benefit of all. Moreover, modern industry is so complicated and interdependent that in order to operate most economically and with the greatest production, it must be subject to one general scheme and one central management.

The revolution must be defended against the formidable assaults of the combined forces of capitalism. Vast armies must be raised, drilled, equipped, and directed. This means centralization. Soviet Russia has for two years almost alone fought off the massed attacks of the capitalist world. How could the Red Army, more than two million strong, have been formed without central directing authority?

The capitalist class has a strongly centralized organization, which permits its full strength to be hurled against the scattered and divided sections of the working class. The class war is war. To overthrow capitalism, the workers must have a military force, with its general staff—elected and controlled, of course, by the workers.

In time of strike every worker knows that there must be a strike committee—a centralized organ to conduct the strike, whose orders must be obeyed—although this committee is elected and controlled by the rank and file. *Soviet Russia is on strike against the whole capitalist world. The social revolution is a general strike against the whole capitalist system. The dictatorship of the proletariat is the strike committee of the social revolution.*

Probably the coming proletarian revolutions in America and other countries will develop new forms of organization. The Bolsheviks do not pretend that they have said the final word in the social revolution. But the experience of two years of workers' government in Russia is naturally of the greatest importance and should be closely studied by the workers of other countries.

## Politics

The word *politics* is to many members of the IWW like a red flag to a bull—or a capitalist. Politics, to them, means simply politicians—usually Yellow Socialist candidates trying to catch votes to elect themselves to some comfortable office, where they can comfortably forget all about the workers.

These "antipolitical" fellow workers oppose the Communists for calling themselves a "political party" and sometimes taking part in election campaigns.

This is using the word *politics* in too narrow a sense. One of the principles upon which the IWW was founded is expressed in the saying of Karl Marx, *"Every class struggle is a political struggle."*[6] That is to say, every struggle of the workers against the capitalists is a struggle of the workers for the *political* power—the state power.

This is the sense in which we Communists also use the word *politics*.

The Yellow Socialists believe that they can gradually gain this political power by using the political machinery of the capitalist state to win reforms, and when they have elected a majority of the members of Congress and the legislatures and the president, governors, mayors, and sheriffs, they can proceed to use the state power to legislate capitalism peacefully out, and the industrial commonwealth in.

This leads the Yellow Socialists to preach all sorts of reforms of the capitalist system, draws to their ranks small capitalists and political adventurers of all kinds, and finally causes them to make deals and compromises with the capitalist class.

The IWW does not believe in this and *neither do the Communists*.

We Communists do not think that it is possible to capture the state power by using political machinery of the capitalist state. The state being the particular weapon of the capitalist class, its machinery is naturally constructed so as to defend and strengthen the power of capitalism. Capitalist control of all agencies molding public opinion—press, schools, churches, and labor fakers—capitalist control of the workers' political conduct through control of their means of living, make it extremely improbable that the workers under the present capitalist "democracy" could ever legally elect a government devoted to their interests.

And at this time when the capitalist class the world over is launching a desperate campaign of repression against all conscious working-class organizations, it is unthinkable.

But even if it were possible for the workers to win the state power by means of the political machinery, the capitalist state could never be used to introduce the industrial commonwealth. The real source of capitalist power lies in *capitalist ownership and control of the means of production.* The capitalist state exists for the purpose of protecting and extending this ownership and control—it cannot therefore be used to destroy it.

So far the Communists and the IWW are in accord. The capitalist state must be taken by storm, by an uprising—it must be attacked by *direct action.* This, in the correct meaning of the word, is also *political* action, for it has a *political* aim—the seizure of state power.

The IWW proposes to attain this end by the general strike. The Communists go further. History indicates clearly that the general strike is not enough. The capitalists have arms—and the experience with White Guards in Russia, Finland, and Germany proves that they have sufficient organization and training to use these arms against the workers. Moreover, the capitalists possess stores of food, which enable them to hold out longer than the workers, always on the verge of actual want.

The Communists also advocate the general strike, but they add that it must turn into *armed insurrection.* Both the general strike and the insurrection are forms of *political action.*

### Revolutionary parliamentarism

If this is so, if the Communists do not believe in capturing the state power by means of the ballot box, why do the Communist parties participate in elections and nominate candidates for office?

The question of whether or not Communists should participate in elections is of secondary importance. Some Communist organizations do, others do not. But those who *do* act on the political field, do so only for *propaganda.* Political campaigns give an opportunity for revolutionists to speak to the working class, pointing out the class character of the state and *their* class interests as workers. They enable them to show the futility of reforms, to demonstrate the real interests that dominate the capitalist—and Yellow Socialist—political parties, and to point out why the entire capitalist system must be overthrown.

Communists elected to Congress or the legislatures have as their function to make propaganda, to ceaselessly expose the real nature of the capitalist state, to obstruct the operation of capitalist government and show its class character, to explain the futility of all capitalist reform measures, and so forth. In the halls of the legislative assembly, against the sounding board of the nation, the Communist can show up capitalist brutality and call the workers to revolt.

Karl Liebknecht showed what a Communist in parliament can do. His words, spoken to the German Reichstag, were heard around the world.

Others in Russia, in Sweden (Höglund), and in other countries have done the same thing.

The most common objection to electing candidates to capitalist legislatures is that no matter how good revolutionists they are, they will invariably be corrupted by their environment and will betray the workers.

This belief is born of long experience, chiefly with Socialist politicians and labor fakers. But we Communists say that a *really revolutionary party will elect real revolutionists and will know how to keep them under its control.*

Many members of the IWW are bitterly opposed to making *any* use of legislatures and other government institutions for purposes of propaganda. But the IWW as an organization has often used them. In the Lawrence strike of 1912 the IWW made good use *even of Victor Berger, the Socialist congressman,* who advertised the strikes and the IWW on the floor of the House of Representatives. William D. Haywood, Vincent St. John, and many other IWW leaders voluntarily testified before the Industrial Relations Commission of the United States government, using this method to make propaganda for their organization. But the most striking example of using the political machinery of the state for purposes of propaganda occurred in 1918, when the federal court in Chicago was turned into a three-month-long IWW agitational meeting—extremely valuable for us—by one hundred IWW leaders on trial there.

These are all cases of using the political machinery of the capitalist state to make revolutionary propaganda among the masses. This method of propaganda should be used as circumstances dictate—as should parliamentary action. *No* weapon should be totally condemned.

The special and particular business of the IWW is to train workers for the seizure and management of industry. The special function of the Communist political party is to train the workers for the capture of political power and the administration of the proletarian dictatorship. All workers should at the same time be members of the revolutionary industrial union of their industry and of the political party that advocates communism.

**The social revolution and the future society**

The aim of the IWW is "to build the new society within the shell of the old." This means to organize the workers so thoroughly that at a given time the capitalist system will burst asunder and the industrial commonwealth, fully developed, will take its place.

Such an act requires the organization and discipline of the great majority of the workers. Before the war there was reason to believe that this might have been feasible—

although in the fourteen years of its history the IWW has been able to organize comparatively only a small fraction of the American workers.

But at the present time such a plan is utopian. Capitalism is breaking down, the social revolution is upon us and *history will not wait until the majority of the workers are organized 100 percent according to the plan of the IWW or any other organization.* There is no longer before us the prospect of normal industrial development which would alone allow the carrying out of such a plan. The war has hurled the peoples of the world into the great cataclysm, and they must plan for *immediate action*—not for the working out of schemes that would take years to accomplish.

The new society is not to be built, as we thought, within the shell of the capitalist system. We cannot wait for that. *The social revolution is here.* And when the workers have overthrown capitalism and have crushed all attempts to reestablish it, then, at their leisure, through their soviet state, they can build the new society in freedom.

In the face of the social revolution, what is the immediate important work of the Industrial Workers of the World?

They, as the most important organization based on revolutionary unionism in America, should take the initiative in trying to establish a basis for the uniting in one organization of all unions that have a class-conscious revolutionary character, of all workers who accept the class struggle—such as the Workers International Industrial Union, the One Big Union, and certain insurgent unions in the AFL. This is no time to quibble about a name or minor questions of organization. The essential task is to draw together all workers capable of revolutionary mass action in time of crisis.

They, as revolutionists, should not repel the attempts of the American Communists to come to an agreement with them for common revolutionary action. The political party and the economic organization must go forward shoulder to shoulder toward the common goal—the abolition of capitalism by means of the dictatorship of the proletariat and the formation of soviets, and the disappearance of classes and the state.

The Communist International holds out to the IWW the hand of brotherhood.

*Gregory Zinoviev*
*Chairman of the Executive Committee of the Communist International*
JANUARY 1920

# 4B
# Formation of the International Council of Trade and Industrial Unions

*July 15, 1920*

Whereas the conditions of proletarians in all countries resulting from the imperialist war demand with every day a clearer and more energetic class struggle to put a definitive end to capitalist exploitation and to establish a communist system;[7]

Whereas such a struggle must be conducted on an international scale through the very closest unity of all workers, united not by individual craft but by industry;

Whereas so-called social reforms—for example, reduction of the working day, an increase in wages, regulating the conditions of labor and so on—may under certain circumstances alleviate the class struggle but are in themselves unable to resolve the social question;

Whereas during the dark years of the war, in most countries that took part in it, most of the unions that had supported neutralism (nonpolitical unions) became servants of imperialist capitalism,[8] playing a fateful role in delaying the final liberation of the working people;

Whereas the primary responsibility of the working class is to gather all organized union forces into a powerful revolutionary class association, which, working side by side with the political organization of the international Communist proletariat and in close connection with it, would be able to develop all its forces for the final victory of the socialist revolution, for the establishment of the world republic of soviets;

Whereas the ruling classes use all their forces and take every measure to suffocate the liberation movement of the exploited;

Whereas to the dictatorship of the bourgeoisie it is necessary to counterpose the dictatorship of the proletariat, as a decisive transitional instrument that alone is capable of suppressing the resistance of the exploiters and ensuring and consolidating the achievements of proletarian power;

Whereas the Amsterdam International Federation of Trade Unions is incapable in its program and its tactics of achieving the triumph of these principles and ensuring the victory of the proletarian masses in all countries;

The undersigned representatives of trade unions of Russia, Italy, Spain, France, Bulgaria, Serbia, and Georgia, convened by the Executive Committee of the Third International, resolve:

1. To condemn the policy of withdrawing the advanced revolutionary forces from the existing unions. These forces

must, on the contrary, take every measure to expel the opportunists from the unions. The opportunists have collaborated and are collaborating even now with the bourgeoisie by accepting the imperialist war. They continue to serve the interests of capitalist imperialism by participating in the deceitful activity of the League of Nations;

2. To conduct methodical communist propaganda inside these unions around the world, creating in every organization Communist and revolutionary cells for propaganda work and to affirm our program;

3. To organize a militant international committee for the rebuilding of the trade union movement along these lines.

This committee functions as an *International Council of Trade and Industrial Unions,* working in accord with the Executive Committee of the Third International under conditions to be determined by congresses. All trade and industrial workers' organizations that join the council must be represented in it. One representative of the International Council of Trade Unions must be included on the Executive Committee of the Third International, and vice versa.

*S. Lozovsky,* All-Russia Central Trade Union Council

*L. D'Aragona,* Italian General Confederation of Labor

*A. Pestaña,* National Federation of Labor of Spain

*Shablin,* General Workers Union of Bulgaria

*A. Rosmer,* Revolutionary-Syndicalist Minority of the General Confederation of Labor of France

*Mikadze,* Communist Minority of the Trade Unions of Georgia

*Milkic,* General Federation of Labor of Yugoslavia (Serbia and others)

# 4C
# Provisional statutes of the International Council of Trade and Industrial Unions

### I. Name

The body, formed by representatives of trade unions of each country, shall be known as the International Council of Trade and Industrial Unions.[9]

### II. Aims and objectives

1. To carry on incessant and continuous propaganda and agitation in broad layers of the proletariat for the ideas of revolutionary class struggle, social revolution, dictatorship of the proletariat, and mass revolutionary action aimed at destroying the capitalist system and the bourgeois state.

2. To fight against the disease of class collaboration, which weakens the labor movement, and against the widespread hope for a peaceful transition from capitalism to socialism.

3. To unite all revolutionary forces in the world trade union movement and conduct a determined struggle against the International Labour Office of the League of Nations and against the program and tactics of the Amsterdam International Federation of Trade Unions.

4. To take the initiative in organizing international campaigns at especially critical moments in powerful class struggles, as well as organizing the collection of funds to support strikers in great social conflicts.

5. To collect background, statistics, and documents on the international labor movement and keep all orga-

nizations affiliated to the International Council of Trade and Industrial Unions informed about the movement in other countries.

6. To publish books, leaflets, and pamphlets on all questions concerning the international trade union movement.

### III. Composition

The council is composed of one representative each from the union councils of Russia, Italy, Spain, Yugoslavia, Bulgaria, France, and Georgia, and one delegate from each national trade union federation or individual union belonging to the International Council of Trade and Industrial Unions. The council also includes a representative of the Executive Committee of the Communist International. The council elects an executive bureau of three persons, including a general secretary and a delegate to the Executive Committee of the Communist International.

### IV. Bulletin

The council shall publish its own organ in four languages, entitled *Bulletin of the International Council of Trade and Industrial Unions*.

### V. Conferences

Only those trade unions or trade union minorities that conduct a revolutionary struggle in their country and accept the dictatorship of the proletariat are entitled to representation at international conferences.

National trade union federations, individual unions, and international federations may be represented on the following basis: Those national trade union federations, individual unions, and union minorities with a membership of less than 500,000 have the right to send two delegates; organizations having a membership greater than 500,000 may send an additional delegate for every 500,000 members. International federations such as textile workers or metalworkers may send a delegate with a consultative vote. Individual national unions are allowed representation on the condition that their national federation is not taking part in the conference.[10]

With regard to those trade unions such as the IWW that have not yet clearly expressed themselves on the question of the dictatorship of the proletariat, the council instructs the Executive Committee to issue an appeal asking them to submit this question to their local organizations and inviting them to take part in the international conference.

### VI. Headquarters

Until the meeting of the international conference, scheduled to take place on January 1, 1921, the headquarters of the International Council of Trade and Industrial Unions will be Moscow.

## 4D
## To the trade unions of all countries

*by the Executive Committee*

Workers, trade union members of all countries:[11]

The most backward worker and the most backward workers' organization must now recognize that the bourgeois world is crumbling. The old social relations have been upset; the stability of the bourgeois order has turned out to be illusory. The bourgeoisie cannot restore the war-ravaged economy. A bloody civil war is giving birth to a new, free world of labor and true brotherhood.

All humanity has now been divided into two parts. One part—excellently organized, possessing all the technical means of the modern state, permeated by a high degree of class consciousness—is the *bourgeoisie*. The other—less conscious than the bourgeoisie, more poorly organized than its class enemy, and, most important, insufficiently welded together on an international scale—is the *proletariat*.

The last several years have brilliantly demonstrated the bourgeoisie's high degree of class consciousness. Despite the sharp rivalry of national imperialisms, despite acute economic competition, despite even the war, from the first days of the October revolution in Russia the ruling classes of all countries created a united, international antiworker, antirevolutionary front. The rout of the bourgeoisie in one country is perceived by the ruling classes of another country—and of course correctly so—as their own defeat.

Soviet Russia and soviet Hungary have felt the lash of this class solidarity of the exploiters of all countries. There is no corner of the globe, from Japan to Canada, from Brazil to Norway, including the great powers, where the bourgeoisie and its dependent press does not rant and rave against the "barbarism" of the Russian revolution, against the "monstrous pretensions" of the proletariat and its "criminal attempts" on the "sacred" foundations of private property. Moreover, the countries that yesterday were waging war among themselves quickly find a common language whenever the question of proletarian revolution comes up. This was shown at the last conference at Spa, where Lloyd George, the British minister, and Simons, the representative of the German bourgeois republic, both approached the question of disarmament from the angle of the "Bolshevik peril."

The international bourgeoisie presents a united bloc as soon as matters touch on "sacred profit." Both the British and the French bourgeoisie willingly help the German bourgeoisie to crush the revolutionary workers' movement, and the German bourgeoisie and its military butchers are prepared to drown in blood the socialist movement in France or England.

This high degree of consciousness, an acute class sense of common interests, and excellent organization are the basic strengths of the bourgeoisie in its struggle against the working class. But this alone cannot explain the victory of the bourgeoisie along the whole international front except for Russia. The international bourgeoisie is strong not only in its high degree of organization and its excellently functioning apparatus, but above all because of the workers' backwardness and insufficient consciousness and because *in its struggle against the revolution the bourgeoisie relies on some of the workers' organizations*. This is monstrous, but it is an unquestionable historic fact. It is enough to examine the main countries of Europe and America to be convinced that the strength of the bourgeoisie and its victory are based on the trade unions of these countries.

Indeed, during the long years of war, the unions of almost every country were the support and foundation of the military policy of their own governments. Who raised and promoted the idea of class truce? The "neutral" trade unions. Who preached to the workers during the war for abstention from any revolutionary actions whatsoever and even from economic strikes? The free Social Democratic trade unions. Who was the advocate of extending the working day, intensifying exploitation of female and child labor, abolishing rights that had been won? Who sharpened the nationalist and chauvinist feelings that gripped wide masses of the population? Who led a brutal and merciless struggle against those still loyal to the precepts of international solidarity who were conducting agitation against the imperialist war? The "Socialist" and "syndicalist" unions.

The war dragged on endlessly. On the fields of Europe tens of millions of people perished. Humanity was brought to an extreme degree of exhaustion. The bourgeoisie managed during this war to subordinate to itself hundreds of millions of people, while drawing unheard-of profits from the mutual slaughter of the peoples. And for all this, an immense part of the guilt falls on the leaders of the union movement, who had forgotten the elementary principles of international class solidarity and who had placed the stamp of approval of the workers' organizations on the bloody predatory war.

And when the war ended, these very same union leaders who had promised the workers miracles when their governments won, these very same leaders who had said that the "sacred union" and class collaboration were temporary phenomena called forth by the nation's peril, and that after the war the class struggle would be restored—when the war ended these very same leaders failed to call for the workers to struggle. Even worse, they moved from agreement with the bourgeoisie on a national scale to class collaboration internationally.

As soon as the war ended, the leaders of national trade union movements—the Legiens, Oudegeests, Jouhauxes, Appletons, Gomperses, and others—moved to establish international unity in order to consolidate internationally what earlier they had practiced in each country, during the truce between proletariat and bourgeoisie. To this end, these proven traitors to the working class set up two institutions: one is called the "League of Nations Labour Office" and the other the "International Federation of Trade Unions."

Consisting of six representatives from unions, six from employers' organizations, and twelve from "neutral" governments, the "League of Nations Labour Office" serves as a safety valve to counter the revolutionary movement of each country. Headed by such a specialist in betrayal of the workers as Albert Thomas, the Labour Office is to enable the international bourgeoisie to fend off the social demands of the broad working masses, bribing them with little handouts. Here, before "neutral" representatives of bourgeois governments, the representatives of labor and capital *are to come to an understanding and find a common language. It goes without saying that the basis of negotiations and agreements is the inviolability of private property, the stability of the rule of capital.*

The representatives of the employers' organizations are all the more willing to *talk* about social reforms, since all this talk does not obligate them to anything. They only obligate these workers' "representatives" to preach a peaceful solution to the social question in their own countries and to sow the illusion that the predatory "League of Nations" and its organs can help the working class get out of the dead end into which the long years of imperialist war have driven it. And that is precisely what the international bourgeoisie needs.

Simultaneously with the creation in Bern of the Labour Office, the "International Federation of Trade Unions" was founded in Amsterdam, at the head of which stand those very same lackeys who are the errand boys for the imperialist League of Nations. What is the program of the Amsterdam International Federation of Trade Unions? What is this federation's view on the events that we have lived through? How does it hope to solve the problems before the working class? How does it regard all the forces aggravating the civil war? What does it think about social revolution? What has it done in order to help the proletarians in struggle in different countries? Even the Amsterdam federation of trade unions would be hard put to answer these questions. But from all its actions, as well as its composition, it is clear that it holds entirely to the standpoint of the League of Nations Labour Office, that is, to the standpoint of the utterly bourgeois League of Nations.

This is obvious, first, because the chief leaders of the Amsterdam federation of trade unions are at one and the same time representatives in the League of Nations Labour Office, and, second, because the May declaration of the Amsterdam international federation concluded with the slogan "Implement the resolutions of the Washington Conference."[12]

In this way, the social-patriotic and renegade elements' hold on the trade unions of the largest countries has led to the creation of two *Yellow* organizations, whose very existence lends the bourgeoisie the best possible support in its struggle against the revolutionary proletariat. It could not have been otherwise, since the Second International, composed of traitors to the working class of every country, cannot represent anything other than a union of traitors. Thus the betrayal of the workers' interests has now been consolidated on an international scale. The working class has in its own ranks *an organized agency of the bourgeoisie.* The Amsterdam association is an agency of the bourgeoisie in the camp of the working class. And the working class must therefore know that the class struggle consists now not only of a fight against the ruling classes, but first and foremost of a fierce, merciless struggle against the "lieutenants of capital" in its own midst.[13]

The struggle against the legacy of the imperialist war and the bourgeoisie's organized agency in the workers' organizations is easier because today the working masses are streaming into the trade unions. Where unions' members were previously counted in hundreds or thousands, now they are counted in tens and hundreds of thousands. The worker looks to the unions for an answer to all the obstinate questions posed by the imperialist war. Old ties were destroyed, old relations were broken. The most backward workers, bound to bourgeois culture, absorbing the petty-bourgeois and bourgeois prejudices of a whole epoch—even these workers, torn from their habitual conditions, enter the unions in search of a better life, looking for solid support for their extremely shaky economic position. The workers join the unions in order to solve collectively the problems before each proletarian, since the individual worker is even more powerless than he was on the eve of the war.

The working masses are filling the trade unions. Around the world unions encompass more than thirty million members. This is a colossal army, and the fate of humanity depends on how it directs its activity. Such an army, if permeated with a spirit of revolutionary class struggle, could overturn the world. Nevertheless, this colossal army, including tens of millions of undoubtedly revolutionary-minded proletarians, is still under the ideological influence and organizational leadership of the old leaders who have gone over to the bourgeoisie.

What forms the basis of all Lloyd George's bourgeois demagogy? What sustains with its strength Britain's entire colonial system? The old British trade unions.

During the whole revolutionary period in Germany, who sent battalions against the social revolution? At the time of most acute crisis, during the reactionary Kapp uprising, who came out as a savior of the unnatural alliance of the bourgeoisie and the proletariat? Who is the bearer of the ideology of social peace and of solving the social question in Germany gradually? The so-called free trade unions of Germany that follow the Legiens.

In France today, who hampers the road of revolutionary struggle? Who wrecks the revolutionary movement in this country? The famous General Confederation of Labor, an organization that for many long years preached social revolution. And when social revolution was placed on the agenda, the leaders of this federation with all their baggage went over to the camp of the bourgeoisie.

This is what we observe in America, Austria, Belgium, Hungary, and other countries. It results in the following monstrous phenomenon: the revolutionizing working masses flow in a broad stream into the unions, which meanwhile continue their old policy of "class collaboration and social peace"—a tool in the hands of the bourgeoisie.

What explains the backwardness of the unions? Why do the unions in most countries still act as a barrier against social revolution? It is because the unions, despite their enormous influx of new members, despite their manyfold expansion, have preserved their old apparatus, their old organizational forms, their old habits, and the old bourgeoisified leaders. The workers join unions in order to tackle collectively the question of liberating labor from the yoke of capital. But once in the unions, the workers encounter the bureaucrats—the very people who compromised during the war, the very leaders who sold the workers of their countries down the river. And at just the moment when social hatred is growing in the working masses, when class energy is accumulating, when all the growing destitution and capitalist barbarism are impelling the working masses to rebellion—at just this moment the unions, which should reflect the revolutionary energy of the masses and convert it to action, act instead as a conservative force, holding back the workers. *The working masses are for revolution, while the old trade union organizations are against it.*

What must each revolutionary worker do in face of such treachery by the trade union movement? What must revolutionaries do when they run up against the social sabotage of the leadership? Get out of the unions, abandon these mass organizations, and create their own little unions? Walk away from millions of workers inspired by class hatred, leaving them under the ideological leadership of the old leaders, tearing out of the union the most revolutionary and active elements? This would be a suicidal policy! This is hara-kiri!

The Second Congress of the Communist International knows perfectly well the value of the Yellow leaders and the measure of their treachery. It nonetheless speaks sharply and categorically *against* withdrawing from the mass workers' organizations. Communists must be where the working masses are. Every worker must know and understand that in western Europe and America social revolution without the million-membered army of trade unions is impossible. That is why it is necessary to win the unions that put a brake on the revolutionary movement. That is why it is necessary to throw out of the ranks of the working class and its organizations the elements who, when the battle between labor and capital reaches its peak, act as strikebreakers against their own class. *Not by passively leaving the unions, but by struggling actively within them and by expelling from them the traitors, the Yellow leaders.* That is the slogan to be implemented with all revolutionary determination and with all necessary energy.

This struggle against the treacherous policy of the heads of the union movement must be conducted through *factory committees*. To win the factory committees, to subordinate them to the influence of the Communist and revolutionary parties, to make them a tool for converting the craft unions into industrial organizations, into a powerful battering ram to smash the economic order of capitalism—that is the task of the day. The Communist Party, carrying with it all those who are aware of the great social catastrophe happening before our eyes, can and must carry out this task in every country.

This is all the easier since the new layers of workers filling the old unions are not reconciled to the union leadership's tradition of treachery. This last year was rich with facts testifying to a shift in this respect. In Britain, Germany, and even America two extremely important phenomena can be seen. Union after union is emerging from the influence of the old sellout leadership, and is shifting, be it slowly, to the left. In addition, tremendous strikes are taking place despite the decisions of the union bureaucracy—bypassing it and opposing it. These facts prove best of all that the union bureaucracy, even the most reactionary, may find itself in an iron grip—*it is necessary only to know how to win the working masses.*

Drive the traitors out of the union movement and make the unions a powerful instrument of social revolution on an international scale—that is the only way to resolve the problem. But the socialist revolution is international. The tug of war between labor and capital, beginning separately in each country, will be resolved and this solution consolidated only when our international organization is permeated with the revolutionary energy and communist consciousness indispensable to overthrow international capital. That is why, simultaneous with the task of winning the union movement in each country, the union members of all countries face the task of *creating an international center for the union movement.* This center, together with the Communist International, would represent a single whole, a single steel block.

This task will be realized when the unions turn away from the Labour Office created by the traitors of the union movement of different countries under the imperialist League of Nations and break away from the international federation of Yellow trade unions in Amsterdam, which is spiritually and materially connected to the capitalist world.

On July 15, in Moscow, an *International Council of Trade and Industrial Unions* was created by the unions of Russia, Britain, Italy, Spain, Yugoslavia, Bulgaria, France, and Georgia. The Communist International calls on all workers who stand for social revolution and the dictatorship of the proletariat to conduct a decisive struggle for their unions to join this council, and for the trade unions of all countries to withdraw from the brothel bearing the name of the League of Nations Labour Office and from the Amsterdam federation of Yellow trade unions connected with it.

The program of the International Council of Trade and Industrial Unions is the program of the Communist International, that is, the revolutionary overthrow of the bourgeoisie and the installation of a dictatorship of the proletariat. It strives for a worldwide republic of soviets and a close, indestructible alliance between the Communist parties and the unions. From this it is clear that the Amsterdam trade union center, a refuge for political invalids from the bankrupt Second International and the final bulwark of international capital, must be destroyed. All revolutionary class-struggle unions must, through their own International Council of Trade and Industrial Unions, become an indissoluble part of the Third, Communist International.

Rank-and-file members of the trade unions, Communists, revolutionaries:

The Second World Congress of the Communist International summons you to an active struggle for the unions. Win the factory committees, reshape the narrow shop and craft unions into industrial unions! Take these powerful organizations into your own hands. Do not shrink from the most decisive struggle against those who convert the workers' organizations into tools of bourgeois policy. You are often threatened with split and expulsion. But this will frighten only weak-willed and passive people. The Communist International does not want a split of the unions and does not strive for one, but neither does it fear one. The same will be said by every revolutionary worker, by every fair-minded socialist.

Like any workers' organization, a trade union is not an end in itself but a means to an end. That is why neither split nor unity is an absolute. The union movement does not need a split, but it does need to expel from the unions those treacherous groups of leaders who make the workers' organizations into playthings of imperialism. Such is the task that stands before the Communists of all countries, before all conscious, honest, and revolutionary-minded proletarians.

Drive the Yellow traitors in leadership out of the trade unions!

Long live the revolutionary proletarian trade unions, fighting for the dictatorship of the proletariat!

Long live an indestructible alliance between the Communist parties and the trade unions of all countries!

Long live the Communist International!

# 5A
# The agrarian question and the world revolution

*by Julian Marchlewski*

It is no accident that the Second International never placed the agrarian question on its agenda, while the Communist International feels itself called upon to take up this question right away.[1] So long as the Socialist parties talked a lot about revolution but were never confronted with its reality, their connection to the countryside amounted at best to agitation among farm workers and small peasants. Now and then, in their parliamentary work, they dealt with limited agrarian reforms. Since conditions of agriculture in individual countries appeared infinitely varied, however, it did indeed make little sense to take up this topic in an international framework.

Now that revolutionary action is at hand, things are different. Here we run up against the banal but quite fundamental fact that the social division of labor in capitalist society, which has led to a deep gulf between the city and the countryside, must be of decisive importance for the revolutionary movement. The makers of the revolution, the proletarians of the cities and industrial districts, must be fed. Their power is paralyzed if the countryside is counterrevolutionary and denies them food. This is especially so in the present situation, where the mass slaughter has led to an unheard-of shortage of food throughout Europe. Every revolutionary action poses the question of the attitude of the rural population, which is tightly bound up with that of the nourishment of the cities. This is an exceptionally important matter.

The Russian revolution has provided uncommonly rich material in this regard. But while these experiences must not be disregarded, we must also note that the situation that arose in Russia cannot be repeated in any other country. First of all, the Russian peasantry found itself in an objectively revolutionary situation, although the masses lacked the corresponding subjective consciousness. This revolutionary situation is explained by historical facts. Serfdom in Russia was eliminated only a half century ago, and capitalist relations in agriculture had not yet been consolidated. Russia remained until 1917 a land of enormous latifundia, but in Great Russia there were scarcely any large-scale capitalist operations on these latifundia.[2] The landlords did not cultivate their property, but rented the land to peasants, almost always on a short-term basis, because the wretched peasants, in contrast to the American or English farmers, could offer no guarantee of organized, intensive cultivation.

Thus arose a most backward form of agriculture with a dispersal of operations the likes of which is hardly to be found in the capitalist world. Hence also the unbelievably low yields. Even in good soil the peasants harvested crops only half the size of those from less fertile soil in central and western Europe. Russia nevertheless exported great quantities of grain. But it was not the surplus after its own needs had been met that the tsarist empire offered on the world market. The government's economic policies forced the peasants to sell even though they were starving and literally dying from hunger.

Thus everything pressed toward a revolutionary solution. The peasant became an ally of the proletariat, which guaranteed him possession of the land and use of the products of his labor. But this peasant, quite radical in dealing with the ownership rights of the large landlords, was not at all revolutionary in the subjective sense and was far removed from consciously collaborating in the construction of a proletarian state. Were the will of the peasantry to prevail, an economic order would take shape in the countryside with unlimited private ownership by the peasants of their individual plots of land. Because of this, we see a large part of the peasantry in the counterrevolutionary camp. Only the hard fact that the leading elements of the counterrevolution—the large landlords, the bourgeoisie, and the tsarist officials—are not willing to condone the "theft of landed property" by the peasants brings the peasantry to its senses. Furthermore, the animalistic egoism of the peasantry led inevitably to holding back food from the cities, even when the peasants had a surplus. The proletarian government, if it was not to abandon the large cities to famine, had to use force against this animalistic egoism. All the more since the ruin caused by war and the chaos of the civil war meant that industry was not in a position to provide products for a rational exchange of goods between city and countryside.

The thinly populated character of the countryside, the relatively small urban population, and finally the fact that in Russia a very large part of the working class has not yet fully broken its ties to the village, but remains in close touch through family connections—all this made it possible to gain time in order to solve the conflict between city and countryside in an organic manner. Despite the terrible destruction of means of transportation, the cities were supplied with a modest amount of provisions, and a large part of the working class fled the starving cities for the villages.

In western Europe and America the situation is different. The revolutionary proletariat, in a time of struggle, will meet with even greater difficulties with regard to feeding the cities, and the relationship between city and countryside demands solutions different from those possible in Russia. That alone makes it necessary to clarify the agrarian question in its totality, above all from the standpoint of the revolutionary transformation.

These lines cannot assume the task of presenting a program of the Communist International on the agrarian question, especially since, given the variation of conditions in different countries, a single program is not at all possible. It is rather a matter of noting the questions as they arise and posing them for discussion.

### The structure of rural property and production relations in the countries of Europe

In order to make possible an overview, we would like to propose examining the agrarian conditions in the countries of Europe in two groups: (a) countries in which large-scale agriculture plays a predominant role, and (b) countries in which peasant land ownership and cultivation is decisive.

This ought to make it possible to come to agreement on the general lines of a revolutionary agrarian policy. Of course a certain schematism must be allowed for, but it is of no consequence, insofar as we are concerned only with the most general features of a program that will need adjustment in every individual country.

The first group, then, comprises "central Europe," not in its usual meaning, but a region with a peculiar agrarian formation in which large-scale agriculture plays a predominant role. This zone stretches roughly from the Dnieper on the east past the Elbe on the west and from the Baltic to the mountains of the Balkans. Outside of this region, in the west, south, and north of Europe, we face a different type of agrarian system.

This central European zone, of course, is by no means homogeneous in its agrarian system, but in all the countries within it—Latvia, Lithuania, Poland, the Ukraine, Romania, Hungary, Bohemia, eastern Germany, and a part of Austria—we observe the preponderant role of large-scale agriculture. The historical reason is everywhere the same: the relatively late abolition of serfdom. Thus we can recognize everywhere more or less clear vestiges of the agrarian system based on the peasants' lack of freedom. In this connection, of course, the conditions in individual countries are quite varied. Yet the point is that in this zone the large estates are what matter, since they comprise 30 to 50 percent or more of the land area in the individual countries, and on these estates the economy is organized on capitalist principles—large-scale agriculture dominates.

It follows that in these countries we are dealing with a relatively sizable layer of propertyless farm workers, that is, true proletarians. Moreover, in almost all these countries a second layer is strongly represented: owners of small plots, who are not "peasants" proper, since they possess too little land to eke out an existence from the yields of their own farms. They support themselves mainly through wage labor on the large-scale agricultural estates and are thus "semiproletarians."

The peasantry in these countries comprises a very substantial part of the population, but not in every case the absolute majority, if the semiproletarians are separated out. However much Schäffle's reference to the "anticollectivist peasant skull" may apply to the peasants of our "central Europe," they still do constitute a revolutionary element to some degree, insofar as the contradiction between peasants and the estate owners ("barons" in Latvia; "*szlachta*" in Poland, Lithuania, and the Ukraine; "magnates" in Hungary; "Junkers" in eastern Germany) is a substantial force in the political and social life of these countries. As capitalist entrepreneurs, the estate owners still have extensive prerogatives over the peasants, which result in numerous conflicts that lead the peasantry to be, in a certain sense, revolutionary.

In the countries of this "central European" zone, therefore, we are dealing in the countryside with proletarian and semiproletarian elements, landless farm workers and owners of small plots, who can certainly be won to the revolution, as well as with a peasantry that is revolutionary to the extent that it has a compelling interest, come what may, in overthrowing the political supremacy of the owners of large estates. Only the large peasants, who are but few in number in almost all these countries, can be regarded as a counterrevolutionary force, ready to make common cause with the Junkers.

It is easy to arrive at the idea of winning the proletarian, semiproletarian, and peasant elements through a program that simply decrees the partition of the large estates among the rural population. Such a measure would, however, signify a step backward with regard to the relations of production. Despite all the talk of "democratic" and "revisionist" theoreticians,[3] it is precisely in this zone—for climatic reasons a zone of grain cultivation—that the superiority of large-scale over small-scale agriculture is beyond any doubt. Destruction of the large enterprises, which are administered more or less rationally throughout the area, would mean an absolute reduction in yields.

Finally, the way things stand today, dividing up the large estates can offer no real benefits to the peasantry, since there is not enough land to give out. The first to be considered would have to be the farm workers and the owners of small plots, who would lose their livelihood with the liquidation of the large estates. Yet this land would hardly suffice to provide these two categories even minimally with land, and so nothing would remain for the working peasants. Moreover it is false to say that the farm workers are obsessed with becoming property owners no matter what. They know quite well that the lot of a more or less well-paid farm worker is superior to that of an indebted small peasant, who works his fingers to the bone on his few hectares and is still never free of worry and want.

As noted, the working peasant population in the countries of this zone is favorable to the revolution insofar as it finds itself in sharp political conflict with the large estate owners, but it is certainly not going to be won to a communist economic system. There is, however, no necessity for a revolutionary assault on peasant property relations. Without renouncing its communist goal, the proletariat can leave the development of social relations in this field to the passage of time. Only experience can persuade the peasantry of the advantages of large-scale communist agricultural enterprises. But the proletarian revolution can immediately offer the working peasants quite substantial advantages. *These peasants undergo crushing debt slavery to finance capital.* When the proletariat, after establishing its dictatorship, in one stroke declares the debts of these peasants null and void, it makes them a gift that is tantamount to a significant increase in wealth. Besides, the peasantry can only gain by this transformation since, based on the council system, it will achieve true self-administration, which can advance its interests, its commercial relations, and its cooperative affairs. This means not winning the peasantry to the communist program but neutralizing it for now in the decisive battle between the proletariat and capital, a compromise that secures advantages to both sides.

This, then, is the agrarian program for Communist parties in this zone:

- For political as well as economic reasons the large estate owners are the main enemy and must be brought down at all costs.
- Their landholdings, together with attached equipment and livestock, will be expropriated without compensation.
- The agricultural enterprises will be declared nationalized property and will be administered, under state supervision, by estate councils made up of the farm workers, both those without land and the semi-proletarian owners of small plots.
- The surplus product of these operations, after meeting the needs of the farm workers, will serve the needs of the urban population.
- The farm workers will be state employees at steady, decent wages who will supply the cities with food and will in turn be provided by the cities with all necessary industrial products.
- The property and operations of the working peasant will not be touched. The debt burden of the peasants will be canceled, and they will enjoy all the advantages of effective self-administration based on the council system.

It is well known that there are numerous "issues" regarding peasant property, all of which amount to reforming relations within the capitalist economic system. These include the use of entailment to limit the partition of peasant holdings through inheritance, getting rid of "common lands" through their becoming municipal property, the question of credit, and others. It is unnecessary for a revolutionary program to go into these detailed questions. That will be up to the peasantry to work out, with the proletarian state having its say, of course. Moreover, these are things that can be left to the near future; given a fundamentally new political order they will take on quite a different form than they have had up to now. Thus we can put these questions off for now.

One question, however, which was resolved in Russia in a revolutionary fashion, may be of particular interest. There all wage labor for the benefit of a private landowner was absolutely forbidden, in order to head off the formation of new, large-scale private land ownership. This specific measure appears to be aimed against the large peasants, who cannot operate without wage labor. Nevertheless it seems questionable whether such a radical intervention will be necessary in the countries of our zone. Such a law would antagonize the peasantry no end, since, given the very complex conditions of production, even the working peasant cannot get by without any wage labor at all.

On the other hand, given the general "labor shortage" in agriculture in most of the countries under consideration, such a ban could impose itself naturally. For when the large enterprises go over to intensive cultivation and offer the workers favorable conditions, the large peasants will be hard put to find workers. They would probably soon be forced to reduce their property to a size on which they could till the soil, while the remaining land would become the property of working peasants who have no land. Such peasant holdings are poorly suited to nationalization, since once a portion has been set aside for the previous owner, the remaining land will as a rule be too small for any rational exploitation.

At any rate this question would have to be weighed carefully in each of the countries concerned.

### Countries with small peasant property

To the west of our "central European" zone begins the region where the large landed estate plays a minimal role and agrarian conditions are characterized by a thoroughly petty-bourgeois breadth and scope. This includes western Germany, part of Austria, France, Switzerland, Belgium, the Netherlands, the south of Italy, Spain, and Portugal.

The situation in Italy is exceptional inasmuch as a particular form of latifundium has survived here, and the peasantry has long been in revolutionary ferment. Small in size, these latifundia are hardly worthy of the name by eastern European standards. Only seldom are they worked as large-scale operations. Mostly the land is rented out to peasants, who cultivate it in uncommonly intensive small-scale operations bordering on garden farming. The conditions of rent are extremely harsh for the peasantry, who, driven nearly to desperation, are constantly rising up in revolt. A quick transition to rational, large-scale operations appears hardly possible under present conditions. We are dealing here not with grain farming, but with the cultivation of rice, vegetables, wine, garden produce, and, in several areas, very intensive cattle raising. So here we have scarcely any choice but to divide up the latifundia, bowing to the will of the oppressed small peasant and leaving the land in the hands of the peasantry.

Here, therefore, the revolutionary proletariat has in the peasantry a firm ally. The only way to open the road to communism is through the systematic development of cooperatives.

To a certain degree things are similar in Spain and Portugal.

The prospects for revolution are less favorable in western Germany, France, Belgium, and the Netherlands, where petty-bourgeois property is firmly rooted and the peasantry is extremely conservative if not outright reactionary in every respect. Any hope of winning the broad masses of the peasantry to revolutionary action might seem futile. Nevertheless, the way things stand in Belgium, in various regions of western Germany such as Baden, the Rhineland, and Westphalia, and in the industrial regions of France, the working class makes up the solid majority of the population. At any rate, the revolutionary proletariat has potential comrades-in-arms in the countryside: the agricultural workers, not so numerous in these "peasant countries" as in countries with many large landed estates, but a significant layer nevertheless.

Therefore it would be illusory to attempt to win this peasantry through agitation for the ideas of the proletarian revolution. The task must consist in neutralizing them by means of compromise.

The peasantry of these countries is much deeper in debt than in central Europe and emancipation from the debt slavery of finance capital has enormous significance for them. Dividing up the large estates is another concern here. In general there is no strong reason to maintain the large-scale operations. Here and there, of course, there are large operations of general economic importance such as stud farms and farms producing seed grain. With these exceptions, however, large enterprises play no decisive role. Thus it is in no way an economic step backward to divide up the large estates in these countries in order to provide the suffering, land-hungry small peasants with the means to sustain themselves. The difficulty lies in what attitude to take toward the property of the large peasantry. This question seems eminently political. In countries where the reactionary large peasantry is numerous and, because of its numbers, plays a prominent role, a revolutionary struggle must necessarily be waged against it. This might be the case in parts of Bavaria and Württemberg as well as parts of Scandinavia. And here the movement will be such that the small peasants and farm workers, relatively numerous in such regions, will unite with the urban proletariat in carrying out a thoroughgoing agrarian reform.

In any event, for all these regions with overwhelmingly peasant property it should be firmly grasped and emphasized that expropriation of working peasants who do not exploit outside labor power is absolutely foreign to the program of the revolutionary Communist proletariat. With respect to industry we are dealing with a social revolution, with expropriating the expropriators. But the countryside, in these countries with overwhelmingly peasant property, will be directly affected only by the political reverberations of this social revolution. The council system, as already mentioned, leads by its very nature to the authentic realization of *self-management.* It can offer the working peasantry nothing but advantages, and no disadvantages. We can safely assume that with moderately skillful agitation these advantages can become clear to even the most backward peasants. Here the main opponent may well be the counterrevolutionary clergy—which is counterrevolutionary as a matter of principle. Since what is involved here are overwhelmingly Catholic regions, the opponent is not to be underestimated, and must be fought relentlessly with all means.

Britain is a special case due to its quite special agrarian conditions: on the one hand, large estates laden with feudal privileges; on the other, purely capitalist operations based on the rental system. Without a doubt the parasitic layer of landlords must be overthrown; the dictatorship of the proletariat is unthinkable so long as the landlords hold sway over the ground the British proletariat lives on.

To what extent is the tenant farmer a partisan of the landlord and to what extent his social opponent? One part of these tenants consists of working peasants. For them the expropriation of the landlords is an immediate gain. With the nationalization of land in Britain, the British proletariat, as master of this land, can guarantee the working peasants formidable advantages. It will cede them this land for cultivation under favorable conditions, which may include the total suppression of the rents formerly gouged from them by the landlords.

Another section of tenants is quite thoroughly different in character. These are capitalist entrepreneurs, who conduct extremely intensive operations on rented land with hired wage labor. Clearly, these capitalists would gladly rid themselves of the burden of paying rent to the landlord. But just as clearly they see that in the social revolution their capitalist property cannot retain a "do not disturb" status. Therefore they will prefer to defend the status quo.

Thus both the capitalist renters and the landlords must be combated, while the working peasants, farmers, and landless workers appear as allies of the revolutionary proletariat.

We would like to forgo judgment here on the extent to which large operations in Britain, organized until now on a capitalist basis, should be retained, and on the desirability of dividing up the land among the farm workers and working peasants. It is the task of the British communists to carefully decide on and answer these questions, which will urgently demand categorical solutions with the outbreak of the revolution.

As noted, we consider it the main task of these lines to point to the urgent necessity of a clear program regarding agricultural conditions. Unfortunately, in this respect there are still huge gaps, for in most countries the Communist parties have of necessity sorely neglected precisely these questions. This should in no way be taken as a reproach. Certainly there have been urgent tasks that absorbed all available energy. But time is pressing. In no country of Europe can we be sure that "tomorrow" the Communist Party will not face a situation where it must take power, whether it wants to or not. It will not do for these parties to confront the problems of agrarian conditions in helpless confusion. The example of Russia should teach us how difficult these problems are and how important a thought-out position on them is for the success of the social revolution, for the triumph of our communist idea.

Let us hope that the international congress will advance the urgent resolution of these problems.

## 5B
## Preliminary draft theses on the agrarian question

*by V.I. Lenin*

In his article Comrade Marchlewski gave an excellent explanation of the reasons why the Second International, which has now become the Yellow International, failed not only to define the revolutionary proletariat's tactics on the agrarian question but even to pose that question properly.[4] Comrade Marchlewski then went on to set forth the theoretical fundamentals of the Third International's communist agrarian program.

These fundamentals can (and, I think, should) serve as the basis of the general resolution on the agrarian question for the Communist International congress, which will meet on July 15, 1920.

The following is a preliminary draft of that resolution:

1. Only the urban and industrial proletariat, led by the Communist Party, can liberate the working masses of the countryside from the yoke of capital and landed proprietorship, from ruin and the imperialist wars that will inevitably break out again and again if the capitalist system remains. There is no salvation for the working masses of the countryside except in alliance with the Communist proletariat, and unless they give the latter devoted support in its revolutionary struggle to throw off the yoke of the landowners (the large landed proprietors) and the bourgeoisie.

On the other hand, the industrial workers cannot accomplish their epoch-making mission of emancipating mankind from the yoke of capital and from wars if they confine themselves to their narrow craft or trade interests and smugly restrict themselves to attaining an improvement in their own conditions, which may sometimes be tolerable in the petty-bourgeois sense. This is exactly what happens to the "labor aristocracy" of many advanced countries, who constitute the core of the so-called Socialist parties of the Second International. They are actually the bitter enemies and betrayers of socialism—petty-bourgeois chauvinists and agents of the bourgeoisie within the working-class movement.

The proletariat is a really revolutionary class and acts in a really socialist manner only when it comes out and acts as the vanguard of all the working and exploited people, as their leader in the struggle for the overthrow of the exploiters; this, however, cannot be achieved unless the class struggle is carried into the countryside, unless the rural working masses are united about the Communist Party of the urban proletariat, and unless they are trained by the proletariat.

2. The working and exploited people of the countryside, whom the urban proletariat must lead into the struggle or, at all events, win over, are represented in all capitalist countries by the following classes:

First, the agricultural proletariat, wage laborers (by the year, season, or day) who obtain their livelihood by working for hire at capitalist agricultural enterprises. The organization of this class (political, military, trade union, cooperative, cultural, educational, and so on) independently and separately from other groups of the rural population, the conduct of intensive propaganda and agitation among this class, and the winning of its support for the soviets and the dictatorship of the proletariat constitute the *fundamental* tasks of the Communist parties in all countries.

Second, the semiproletarians or peasants who till tiny plots of land, that is, those who obtain their livelihood partly as wage laborers at agricultural and industrial capitalist enterprises and partly by working their own or rented plots of land, which provide their families only with part of their means of subsistence. This group of the rural working population is very numerous in all capitalist countries. Its existence and special position are played down by the representatives of the bourgeoisie and by the Yellow "Socialists" belonging to the Second International, partly by deliberately deceiving the workers and partly by blindly submitting to the routine of petty-bourgeois views and lumping together this group with the mass of the "peasantry."

This bourgeois method of duping the workers is to be seen mostly in Germany and in France, but also in America and other countries. If the work of the Communist Party is properly organized, this group will become its assured supporter, for the lot of these semiproletarians is a very hard one and they stand to gain enormously and immediately from soviet government and the dictatorship of the proletariat.

Third, the small peasantry, that is, the small-scale tillers who, either as owners or as tenants, hold small plots of land that enable them to satisfy the needs of their families and their farms and who do not hire outside labor. This stratum, as such, undoubtedly stands to gain by the victory of the proletariat, which will fully and immediately bring it (a) deliverance from the necessity of paying the large landowners rent or a share of the crop (for example the *métayers* in France, also in Italy and other countries); (b) deliverance from mortgages; (c) deliverance from the numerous forms of oppression by and dependence on the large landowners (forest lands and their use, etc.); (d) immediate aid for their farms from the proletarian state (the use of the agricultural implements and part of the buildings on the large capitalist farms confiscated by the proletariat and the immediate conversion, by the proletarian state, of the rural cooperative societies and agricultural associations from organizations that under capitalism served above all the rich and middle peasants into organizations that will primarily assist the poor, that is, proletarians, semiproletarians, small peasants, etc.), and many other things.

At the same time the Communist Party must clearly realize that during the transitional period from capitalism to communism, that is, during the dictatorship of the proletariat, this stratum, or at all events part of it, will inevitably vacillate toward unrestricted freedom of trade and the free enjoyment of the rights of private property. That is because this stratum, which, if only in a small way, is a seller of articles of consumption, has been corrupted by profiteering and by proprietary habits. However, if a firm proletarian policy is pursued, and if the victorious proletariat deals very resolutely with the large landowners and the large peasants, this stratum's vacillation cannot be considerable and cannot alter the fact that, on the whole, it will side with the proletarian revolution.

3. Taken together, the three groups enumerated above constitute the majority of the rural population in all capitalist countries. That is why the success of the proletarian revolution is fully assured, not only in the cities but in the countryside as well. The reverse view is widespread. However, it persists only, first, because of the deception systematically practiced by bourgeois science and statistics, which do everything to gloss over both the gulf that separates the above-mentioned classes in the countryside from the exploiters—the landowners and capitalists—and that which separates the semiproletarians and small peasants from the large peasants.

Second, it persists because of the inability and unwillingness of the heroes of the Yellow Second International and of the "labor aristocracy" in the advanced countries, which has been corrupted by imperialist privileges, to conduct genuinely proletarian revolutionary work of propaganda, agitation, and organization among the rural poor. The attention of the opportunists has always been and still is wholly concentrated on inventing theoretical and practical compromises with the bourgeoisie, including the large and middle peasants (who are dealt with below), and not on the revolutionary overthrow of the bourgeois government and the bourgeoisie by the proletariat.

It persists, third, because of the obstinate refusal to understand—so obstinate as to be equivalent to a prejudice (connected with all the other bourgeois-democratic and parliamentary prejudices)—a truth that has been fully proved by Marxist theory and fully corroborated by the experience of the proletarian revolution in Russia, namely, that although the three enumerated categories of the rural population—who are incredibly downtrodden, disunited, crushed, and doomed to semibarbarous conditions of existence in all countries, even the most advanced—are economically, socially, and culturally interested in the victory of socialism, they are capable of giving resolute support to the revolutionary proletariat only *after* the latter has won political power, only *after* it has resolutely dealt with the large landowners and capitalists, and only *after* these downtrodden people see in *practice* that they have an organized leader and champion, strong and firm enough to assist and lead them and to show them the right path.

4. In the economic sense, one should understand by "middle peasants" those small farmers who (a) either as owners or tenants, hold plots of land that are also small but, under capitalism, are sufficient not only to provide, as a general rule, a meager subsistence for the family and the bare minimum needed to maintain the farm, but also produce a certain surplus that may, in good years at least, be converted into capital; (b) quite frequently (for example, one farm out of two or three) resort to the employment of hired labor.

A concrete example of the middle peasants in an advanced capitalist country is provided by the group of farms of five to ten hectares [twelve to twenty-five acres] in Germany, in which, according to the census of 1907, the number of farms employing hired laborers is about one-third of the total number of farms in this group.* In France, where the cultivation of special crops is more developed—for example, grape growing, which requires a very large amount of labor—this group probably employs outside hired labor to a somewhat greater extent.

The revolutionary proletariat cannot set itself the task—at least not in the immediate future or in the initial period of the dictatorship of the proletariat—of winning over this stratum, but must confine itself to the task of neutralizing it, that is, rendering it neutral in the struggle between the proletariat and the bourgeoisie. This stratum inevitably vacillates between these two forces. In the beginning of the new epoch and in the developed capitalist countries, it will, in the main, incline toward the bourgeoisie. That is because the world outlook and the sentiments of the property owners are prevalent among this stratum, which has a direct interest in profiteering, in "freedom" of trade and in property, and stands in direct antagonism to the wageworkers.

By abolishing rent and mortgages, the victorious proletariat will immediately improve the position of this stratum. In most capitalist countries, however, the proletarian state should not at once completely abolish private property. At all events, it guarantees both the small and the middle peasantry not only the preservation of their

* Here are the exact figures: the number of farms of five to ten hectares—652,798 (out of a total of 5,736,082); these employed 487,704 hired laborers of various kinds while members of the farmers' families *(Familienangehörige)* working on the farms numbered 2,003,633. In Austria, according to the census of 1902, this group comprised 383,331 farms, of which 126,136 employed hired labor; the hired laborers working on these farms numbered 146,044 and the working members of the farmers' families 1,265,969. The total number of farms in Austria was 2,856,349. [*Note by Lenin.*]

plots of land but also their enlargement to cover the total area they usually rented (the abolition of rent).

A combination of such measures with a ruthless struggle against the bourgeoisie fully guarantees the success of the policy of neutralization. The proletarian state must effect the transition to collective farming with extreme caution and only very gradually, by the force of example, without any coercion of the middle peasant.

5. The large peasants *(Grossbauern)* are capitalist entrepreneurs in agriculture, who as a rule employ several hired laborers and are connected with the "peasantry" only in their low cultural level, habits of life, and the manual labor they themselves perform on their farms. These constitute the biggest of the bourgeois strata, who are open and determined enemies of the revolutionary proletariat. In all their work in the countryside, the Communist parties must concentrate their attention mainly on the struggle against this stratum, on liberating the toiling and exploited majority of the rural population from the ideological and political influence of these exploiters, etc.

Following the victory of the proletariat in the cities, all sorts of manifestations of resistance and sabotage, as well as direct armed action of a counterrevolutionary character on the part of this stratum, are absolutely inevitable. The revolutionary proletariat must therefore immediately begin the ideological and organizational preparation of the forces necessary to completely disarm this stratum and, simultaneously with the overthrow of the capitalists in industry, to deal this stratum a most determined, ruthless, and smashing blow at the very first signs of resistance. For this purpose, the rural proletariat must be armed and village soviets organized, in which the exploiters must have no place, and in which proletarians and semiproletarians must be ensured predominance.

However, the expropriation even of the large peasants can in no way be made an immediate task of the victorious proletariat, because the material and especially the technical conditions, as well as the social conditions, for the socialization of such farms are still lacking. In individual and probably exceptional cases, those parts of their land that they rent out in small plots or that are particularly needed by the surrounding small-peasant population will be confiscated. The small peasants should also be guaranteed, on certain terms, the free use of part of the agricultural machinery belonging to the large peasants, etc. As a general rule, however, the proletarian state must allow the large peasants to retain their land, confiscating it only if they resist the power of the working and exploited people.

The experience of the Russian proletarian revolution, in which the struggle against the large peasantry was complicated and protracted by a number of special conditions, showed nevertheless that, when taught a severe lesson for the slightest attempt at resistance, this stratum is capable of loyally fulfilling the tasks set by the proletarian state, and even begins to be imbued, although very slowly, with respect for the government that protects all who work and is ruthless toward the idle rich.

The special conditions that, in Russia, complicated and retarded the struggle of the proletariat against the large peasants after it had defeated the bourgeoisie were, in the main, the following: after November 7, 1917 [October 25, old style], the Russian revolution passed through the stage of the "general democratic"—that is, basically the bourgeois-democratic—struggle of the peasantry as a whole against the landowners; the cultural and numerical weakness of the urban proletariat; and, lastly, the enormous distances and extremely poor means of communication.

Inasmuch as these retarding conditions do not exist in the advanced countries, the revolutionary proletariat of Europe and America should prepare far more energetically and achieve far more rapidly, resolutely, and successfully complete victory over the resistance of the large peasantry, completely depriving it of the slightest possibility of offering resistance. This is imperative because, until such a complete and absolute victory is achieved, the masses of the rural proletarians, semiproletarians, and small peasants cannot be brought to accept the proletarian state as a fully stable one.

6. The revolutionary proletariat must immediately and unreservedly confiscate all landed estates, those of the large landowners, who, in capitalist countries—directly or through their tenant farmers—systematically exploit wage labor and the neighboring small (and, not infrequently, part of the middle) peasantry, do not themselves engage in manual labor, and are in the main descended from the feudal lords (the nobles in Russia, Germany, and Hungary, the restored seigneurs in France, the lords in Britain, and the former slave owners in America), or are rich financial magnates, or else a mixture of both these categories of exploiters and parasites.

Under no circumstances is it permissible for Communist parties to advocate or practice compensating the large landowners for the confiscated lands, for under present-day conditions in Europe and America this would be tantamount to a betrayal of socialism and the imposition of new tribute upon the masses of working and exploited people, to whom the war has meant the greatest hardships, while it has increased the number of millionaires and enriched them.

As to the mode of cultivation of the land that the victorious proletariat confiscates from the large landowners, the distribution of that land among the peasantry for their use has been predominant in Russia, owing to her economic backwardness; it is only in relatively rare and exceptional cases that state farms have been organized on the former estates that the proletarian state runs at its own expense, converting the former wage laborers into workers for the state and members of the soviets, which administer the state. The Communist International is of the opinion that in the case of the advanced capitalist countries it would be correct to keep *most* of the large agricultural enterprises intact and to conduct them on the lines of the "state farms" in Russia.

It would, however, be grossly erroneous to exaggerate or to stereotype this rule and never to permit the free grant of *part* of the land that belonged to the expropriated expropriators to the neighboring small and sometimes middle peasants.

First, the objection usually raised to this, namely, that large-scale farming is technically superior, often amounts to an indisputable theoretical truth being replaced by the worst kind of opportunism and betrayal of the revolution. To achieve the success of this revolution, the proletariat should not shrink from a temporary decline in production, any more than the bourgeois opponents of slavery in North America shrank from a temporary decline in cotton production as a consequence of the Civil War of 1863–65.

What is most important to the bourgeois is production for the sake of production; what is most important to the working and exploited population is the overthrow of the exploiters and the creation of conditions that will permit the working people to work for themselves and not for the capitalists. It is the primary and fundamental task of the proletariat to ensure the proletarian victory and its stability. There can, however, be no stable proletarian government unless the middle peasantry is neutralized and the support is secured of a very considerable section of the small peasantry, if not all of them.

Second, not merely an increase but even the preservation of large-scale production in agriculture presupposes the existence of a fully developed and consciously revolutionary rural proletariat with considerable experience of trade union and political organization behind it. Where this condition does not yet exist, or where this work cannot expediently be entrusted to class-conscious and competent industrial workers, hasty attempts to set up large state-conducted farms can only discredit the proletarian government. Under such conditions, the utmost caution must be exercised and the most thorough preparations made when state farms are set up.

Third, in all capitalist countries, even the most advanced, there still exist survivals of medieval, semifeudal exploitation of the neighboring small peasants by the large landowners, as in the case of the *Instleute* [tenant farmers] in Germany, the *métayers* in France, and the sharecroppers in the United States (not only Negroes, who, in the southern states, are mostly exploited in this way, but sometimes whites too). In such cases it is incumbent on the proletarian state to grant the small peasants free use of the lands they formerly rented, since no other economic or technical basis exists and it cannot be created at one stroke.

The implements and stock of the large farms must be confiscated without fail and converted into state property, with the absolute condition that *after* the requirements of the large state farms have been met, the neighboring small peasants may have the use of these implements gratis, in compliance with conditions drawn up by the proletarian state.

In the period immediately following the proletarian revolution, it is absolutely necessary not only to confiscate the estates of the large landowners at once but also to deport or to intern them all as leaders of counterrevolution and ruthless oppressors of the entire rural population. However, with the consolidation of the proletarian power in the countryside as well as in the cities, systematic efforts should be made to employ (under the special control of highly reliable Communist workers) those forces within this class that possess valuable experience, know-how, and organizing skill, to build large-scale socialist agriculture.

7. The victory of socialism over capitalism and the consolidation of socialism may be regarded as ensured only when the proletarian state power, having completely suppressed all resistance by the exploiters and assured itself complete subordination and stability, has reorganized the whole of industry on the lines of large-scale collective production and on a modern technical basis (founded on the electrification of the entire economy). This alone will enable the cities to render such radical assistance, technical and social, to the backward and scattered rural population as will create the material basis necessary to boost the productivity of agricultural and of farm labor in general, thereby encouraging the small farmers by the force of example and in their own interests to adopt large-scale, collective, and mechanized agriculture.

Although nominally recognized by all socialists, this indisputable theoretical truth is in fact distorted by the opportunism prevalent in the Yellow Second International and among the leaders of the German and the British "Independents," the French Longuetists, etc. This distortion consists in attention being directed toward the relatively remote, beautiful, and rosy future; attention is deflected from the immediate tasks of the difficult practical transition and approach to that future. In practice, it consists in preaching a compromise with the bourgeoisie and a "class truce," that is, complete betrayal of the proletariat, which is now waging a struggle amid the unprecedented ruin and impoverishment created everywhere by the war, and amid the unprecedented enrichment and arrogance of a handful of millionaires resulting from that war.

It is in the countryside that a genuine possibility of a successful struggle for socialism demands, first, that all Communist parties should inculcate in the industrial proletariat a realization of the need to make sacrifices, and be prepared to make sacrifices so as to overthrow the bourgeoisie and consolidate proletarian power—since the dictatorship of the proletariat implies both the ability of the proletariat to organize and lead all the working and exploited people, and the vanguard's ability to make the utmost sacrifices and to display the utmost heroism to that end.

Second, success demands that, as a result of the workers' victory, the laboring and most exploited masses in the countryside achieve an immediate and considerable improvement in their conditions at the expense of the exploiters—for without that the industrial proletariat cannot get the support of the rural areas and, in particular, will be unable to ensure the supply of food for the cities.

8. The enormous difficulty of organizing and training for the revolutionary struggle the masses of rural working people, whom capitalism has reduced to a state of great wretchedness, disunity, and frequently semimedieval dependence, makes it necessary for the Communist parties to devote special attention to the strike struggle in the rural districts, give greater support to mass strikes by the agricultural proletarians and semiproletarians, and help develop the strike movement in every way.

The experience of the Russian revolutions of 1905 and of 1917, now confirmed and extended by the experience of Germany and other advanced countries, shows that the growing mass strike struggle (into which, under certain conditions, the small peasants can and should also be drawn) alone is capable of rousing the countryside from its lethargy, awakening the class consciousness of the exploited masses in the countryside, making them realize the need for class organization, and revealing to them in a vivid and practical manner the importance of their alliance with the urban workers.

This congress of the Communist International brands as traitors and renegades those Socialists—to be found, unfortunately, not only in the Yellow Second International but also in the three very important European parties that have withdrawn from that International—who are capable not only of remaining indifferent to the strike struggle in the countryside, but even (like Karl Kautsky) of opposing it on the grounds that it threatens to reduce the output of articles of consumption.

Neither programs nor the most solemn declarations are of any value whatever unless it is proved in practice, in deed, that the Communists and workers' leaders are able to place above everything else in the world the development and the victory of the proletarian revolution, and to make the greatest sacrifices for it, for otherwise there is no way out, no salvation from starvation, ruin, and new imperialist wars.

In particular, it should be pointed out that the leaders of the old Socialist movement and representatives of the "labor aristocracy"—who now often make verbal concessions to communism and even nominally side with it in order to preserve their prestige among the worker masses, who are rapidly becoming revolutionary—should be tested for their loyalty to the cause of the proletariat and their suitability for responsible positions in those spheres of work where the development of revolutionary consciousness and the revolutionary struggle is most marked, the resistance of the landowners and the bourgeoisie (the large peasants, the kulaks) most fierce, and the difference between the Socialist compromiser and the Communist revolutionary most striking.

9. The Communist parties must exert every effort to begin, as speedily as possible, to set up soviets of deputies in the countryside, and in the first place soviets of hired laborers and semiproletarians. Only if they are linked up with the mass strike struggle and with the most oppressed class can the soviets perform their functions and become consolidated enough to influence (and later to incorporate) the small peasants.

If, however, the strike struggle has not yet developed, and the agricultural proletariat is as yet incapable of strong organization owing both to the severe oppression by the landowners and the large peasants and to lack of support from the industrial workers and their unions, then the formation of soviets of deputies in the rural areas will require lengthy preparation by means of the organization of Communist cells, even if only small ones, intensified agitation—in which the demands of communism are enunciated in the simplest manner and illustrated by the most glaring examples of exploitation and oppression—and the arrangement of systematic visits of industrial workers to the rural districts, and so on.

# 6A
# To the working women of the world

Women in your millions![1] You, the millions of women working in the factories, in the mills, in offices, on the railways; you, domestic servants and you who are enslaved by capital in all countries of the world; you whose husbands, brothers, and children are maimed and murdered on the battlefields by that same, insatiable capital for the sake of its own gain; you whose children, not yet grown to strength, are persecuted in the street and driven to prostitution and crime—it is to you, the half of toiling humanity subjected to grave oppression, that this appeal goes out from the first International Conference of Communist Women, called by the Third International.

Women who are workers, farm laborers, peasants! The Communist International, this great fellowship, this brotherhood of the workers of the whole world, has set as its goal the total liberation of workers from the triple slavery in which the majority of humanity is still bound. The Communist International, which already numbers in its ranks millions of the most advanced working men and women around the world, calls on all of you to swell its ranks in the struggle for that liberation. Only you yourselves, through your participation in organization and in struggle, can ensure the victory of labor over capital.

You have just lived through all the horrors of imperialist slaughter. Millions of your brothers, husbands, fathers, and sons were thrown by the capitalists into the jaws of death on the battlefield. For four years death reaped a rich harvest, and millions of people will never return; millions have been left crippled, and hundreds of thousands fill the lunatic asylums; and you, their mothers, wives, sisters, and daughters, stand, wretched, faced with the inevitability of ever more sacrifices, ever more world wars, which will be yet more terrible and bloody.

Woe to the workers of countries defeated in this war! The women of Russia, Germany, Austria, and other countries have experienced not only the suffering brought by the loss of their loved ones, but also the unparalleled torment of hunger, cold, and other forms of deprivation. But are not the women of the "victorious" countries suffering in the same way? The women workers of Britain, France, Italy, America, Japan, and the other "victorious" countries—are not they too seeing their need become fiercer, harsher each day, each day feeling the yoke of capital becoming more intolerable?

There is only one path that can lead us out of this oppression, these sufferings, these inevitable new world wars, and that is the path of social revolution, of armed struggle and the dictatorship of the proletariat. The Communist International is the commander, the general staff that organizes and leads the forces of social revolution. We, the working women of the whole world, are a great force that can hasten and smooth the way for the downfall of the capitalist world if we realize, if we come to understand that our place is there in the struggle for the liberation of the toilers, in the ranks of the Communist International.

The Communist International is a great army liberating the oppressed around the world.

It is the duty of each one of us to join the ranks of that army. In each separate country, in each town, each village, in the darkest, most remote corner, workers must come to realize that their liberation can come about only through the victory of this international brotherhood. And when the workers of any country rise in struggle, the knowledge that they are supported by the workers of all countries will make them invincible. That is what our union, the Communist International, must represent; that is what we must make it.

Fearing revolution, fearing insurrection, dreading their downfall, the capitalists, the bourgeois democrats, and all their multifarious lackeys sometimes resign themselves to concessions—they throw us a miserable sop, a meager bone, such as voting rights for women.[2] But even now more than half the women in the world do not enjoy equal political rights. Women will never have equal rights under capitalism. Only the victory of the Communist International will make them equal—comrades instead of slaves. Do not yield to these traps set so hastily by the bourgeoisie; do not satisfy yourselves with the sop of voting rights. Use your right to vote to organize, to unite, to gather your strength—the strength of working women—in pursuit of the common goal.

Our common and immediate goal, a goal clear to all, is the creation of a soviet republic. In this commune of labor the relics of political, economic, and spiritual slavery are being swept away. Do not rest until you have created a soviet republic in your country. Do not rest even when your soviet republic has been formed, for it will be a living, liberating force only when women take an equal part in the work of its soviets.

We are suffering from poor living conditions, from poverty; the victory of the Communist International, the victory of the social revolution will enable us to distribute all the riches of the world so that all poverty is abolished. It will enable us to increase the productivity of labor many times over, since we will know that we are working not for parasites and exploiters but for ourselves.

We are suffering because we are burdened by the cares of housework, cooking, and child rearing. The victory of communism will enable us to organize public child care, liberating us in reality, not in empty words. It will give women equality and free them from ignorance and backwardness.

Working women of Russia, peasant women of Russia! You have achieved the greatest revolution; step by step, you are truly laying the foundations for new ways of living. Over the short period of the revolution, you have done more for the liberation of humanity than was achieved over centuries of existence in slavery. During this short time you have created in our soviet republic thousands of crèches, nurseries, children's homes, children's canteens, and kindergartens. You are active in the party, in the soviets, in trade unions, in agricultural communes and cooperatives. You have gained access to the organization of all areas of society; all the despicable laws that still restrict the rights of women in other countries are a thing of the past for you. And if you are suffering, it is because in other countries the yoke of the bourgeoisie, of the bankers and large landowners has not yet been thrown off, and this holds back you too from concluding your struggle for the complete rebuilding of society on communist principles.

The Communist International and toilers the world over will never forget how on that international day of working women, the Russian woman took to the streets under the Red banner and began the greatest of revolutions, sealing it with her blood.[3]

You, the women of Europe, America, and Australia, women of the capitalist states, you whom capital is increasingly turning into a simple tool for its own enrichment, you hundreds of thousands thrown hungry onto the streets of the cities, into the arms of prostitution—you are doomed to untold suffering if you stand aside from the great movement of social revolution.

War with all its disasters condemns you to an ever more painful existence. As the growth of capital in the hands of a few billionaires becomes more and more irrepressible, so your deprivation and poverty will grow ever faster.

The capitalist system does not and cannot bring peace to all. The predatory "League of Nations" did not stop the criminal war that bourgeois Poland waged against the proletarian Russian Soviet Republic. It is the guilty party behind the White Terror in Hungary and Bavaria, the oppression of Ireland, the plunder of the East, and the endless wars in so many countries.

You fear the unavoidable sacrifices for revolution. Of course revolutionary struggle demands sacrifices and heroism, it entails suffering; but it also gives the supreme joy of the struggle, the supreme joy of liberation. When they call on you to be content, when they frighten you with the horrors of revolution and civil war, remember how many perished in the imperialist war and how many more will die in wars like it, remember the horrors you lived through in this war. Cry out, "If we had listened in 1914 to the appeals of the Communists, of Lenin, Liebknecht, and the others, if our brothers and we ourselves had turned our arms against the true instigators of the war—the world's bourgeoisie—there would be none of these sacrifices and horrors now, and we would now be living as free human beings in the bright realm of communism, no longer in dread of new wars."

The Communist International strives for the overthrow of capitalist oppression the world over. It knows that more than any others the peoples of the East have suffered the harshest forms of colonial exploitation at the hands of the imperialists of the West, robbers of the whole world, as well as Japan, the imperial power of the East. The overthrow of capitalist rule is the only way to liberate the toiling masses of the East.

If the nations of the East are more backward, that is precisely because of this merciless exploitation that has held back their natural free development, and their economic, social, political, and intellectual emancipation.

The Communist International calls on the peoples of the East to struggle both against the landlords and capitalists of their own countries and against the imperialist yoke. If you, working women, want to see yourselves and your children free, if you want to end the enslavement of the colonies and the enslavement of the East, your place is in the ranks of our union, the Communist International. For it is only side by side with your more liberated brothers and sisters in the other countries of Europe and America that you will liberate yourselves.

Working women the world over! Come out of your basements, your hovels, and your garrets, come out of your workshops, factories, and mills, your offices and shops, to join the struggle for total liberation. Become Communists! Join the Communist Party in your country. Follow the examples from the great revolutionary past and the even greater present of the proletarian movement and learn to build up your mighty strength, hand in hand with working men.

And know this: there is no force in the world that can hold out against the Communist International if we join its ranks—we, the workers of the world, working men and working women, peasant men and peasant women.

Long live the Third, Communist International!

*First International Working Women's Conference*

## 6B
## Theses for the communist women's movement[4]

*edited by Clara Zetkin*

1. The Second Congress of the Third International reaffirms the decision of the First Congress on the need to rouse the broadest masses of proletarian women to class consciousness.[5] They must be armed with communist ideas and rallied as fighters and fellow workers, clear in their aims, determined in their actions, and prepared for any sacrifice. It is imperative that proletarian women play a powerful role in the revolutionary struggle for the overthrow of capitalism and realization of communism. The goal is to secure for all women complete and unrestricted social rights, so that in their education and employment and as mothers they can develop every aspect of their full human personality, linked by bonds of solidarity with society as a whole. The proletariat must attain greater unity

and strength so that, in the revolutionary struggle against the bourgeois order as in the revolutionary construction of the new order, it may create the social preconditions for achieving this goal for women.[6]

2. Past and present history teach that private property is the ultimate and fundamental cause of the superior and privileged position of men over women. Only with the arrival and establishment of private property could the wife and child, like the slave, become the property of the man. Only then was it possible, on the basis of the domination of one human being over others, for class divisions to arise between rich and poor, exploiters and exploited. So too arose the dependency of the woman as wife and mother on the man, her subordination to him, her pariah status in the family and in public life. Even today these conditions still prevail in the practices and prejudices of the so-called civilized nations; in the denial of rights or at least in the second-class status of the female sex before the law; in its disadvantaged position in family, state, and society; in its patronized and backward intellectual condition; in the inadequate appreciation of the social importance of maternal activity. Among the peoples of Europe this state of affairs was consolidated and deepened by the development of the guilds, which drove women out of social production and strictly limited their field of activity to housework and the family proper.

For women to achieve full social equality with men in truth and fact and not just on the passive pages of dead law books, for women as well as men to win the possibility of unrestricted achievement and free development of their full human personality, two primary conditions must be met. First, private property must be uprooted and replaced by social property. Second, the activity of women must be integrated into the social production of a new order free of exploitation and subjugation. Only the realization of these two conditions will prevent women from becoming economically dependent on men as wives and mothers in the family, or, as a result of the class conflict between exploiter and exploited, falling under the economic subjugation and exploitation of the capitalist as proletarian women working a job. Only this will prevent one-sided, excessive demands—whether of household duties and motherhood or of work on the job—from squandering valuable talents and gifts and making impossible a harmonious integration of both spheres of duty. Only the realization of both these conditions guarantees that women will participate as workers and producers, with fully developed abilities and powers, with equal duties and equal rights, in a community of similarly charged workers and producers, and that work and motherhood will form an unbroken circle for a full life.

3. The demands of the bourgeois women's movement have proved incapable of securing full rights and humanity for the whole of womenkind. Carrying through these demands, of course, entails a fundamental change—and one not to be underestimated—namely, that bourgeois society and its state officially abandon the old prejudice about inferiority of the female sex and recognize women's social equality with equal rights. In practice, however, realizing feminist demands results primarily in reforming the capitalist order for the benefit of wives and daughters of the possessing classes. Meanwhile the huge majority of proletarian women, the women of the toiling people, still unfree and exploited, are abandoned, their humanity stunted, and their rights and interests neglected.

As long as capitalism survives, a woman's right to dispose freely of her property and her person signifies the final stage of the emancipation of property and a broadening of the scope for capitalists to exploit proletarian women. Women's right to education and employment equal to that of men leads to opening up the so-called higher professions to the women of the possessing class, bringing to bear in this realm too the fundamental law of unlimited capitalist competition, and sharpening economic as well as social conflict between the sexes.[7] Even the most important and far-reaching of feminist demands—that of full political equality of the sexes, especially recognition of women's right to vote and to be elected—is thoroughly insufficient to guarantee women of little or no property their full rights and freedom.

Under capitalism the right to vote serves only to realize purely formal, political, bourgeois democracy; in no way does it signify real, economic, proletarian democracy. The general, equal, secret, and direct right of all adults to vote and to be elected signifies nothing more than the highest stage of development of bourgeois democracy and becomes a foundation and cover for the most perfected form of the class rule of owners and exploiters. In this period of imperialism, of revolutionary social development, class rule intensifies into the most violent, brutal dictatorship against the propertyless and exploited, despite the democratic right to vote. The right to vote does not get rid of private ownership of the means of production or class conflict between bourgeoisie and proletariat. In addition, therefore, it does not remove the cause of economic dependence and exploitation of the vast majority of women and men by the minority—propertied women and men. It simply covers up this dependence and exploitation with the treacherous smoke screen of political equality.

Thus for proletarian women, even full political equality can in no wise be the goal of their movement and struggle. For them the right to vote and run for office is only one means among many to organize and train themselves to work and struggle for the construction of a social order cleansed of the domination of private property over human beings and thus, after the elimination of class conflict between exploiters and exploited, a social order of free producers with equal rights and responsibilities.

4. Communism is the only social order that meets these conditions and, in so doing, guarantees full freedom and rights for the whole of the female sex. The foundation of communism is the social ownership of the large, economically dominant means of production, distribution, and commerce. In doing away with private ownership in this realm, communism eliminates the cause of the subjugation and exploitation of man by man, the social conflict between rich and poor, exploiter and exploited, oppressor and oppressed. In so doing it also eliminates the economic and social conflict between men and women. In a social sense, women are fellow owners, fellow administrators, fellow users of the means of production and distribution, and fellow recipients of the material and cultural results of their application and use. In this capacity, women are dependent, in their development and activity, solely and exclusively on their bond of solidarity with society as a whole. No longer are they, because of their sex, dependent on an individual man, or even on the small moral unit of the family, and even less so on a profit-hungry capitalist and an exploitative ruling class.

The highest law of a communist economy is meeting the material and cultural needs of all members of society, gauged according to the highest, most advanced productive and cultural possibilities available at the time. This goal can be reached only by instituting general obligatory labor for all normal, healthy adults, without regard to sex. It can be reached only in a social organization that recognizes the equal worth of all socially necessary and useful labor, that also values the toil and trouble of motherhood as a social task, that bases the conditions of development of its members from birth on free social labor and the greatest conscious effort.

5. Communism, however, the great emancipator of the female sex, cannot, now or ever, be the result of the united struggle of women of all classes for reform of the bourgeois order along the lines of the demands of the feminist movement, that is, demands against the privileged social position of the male sex. It can be realized only through the common class struggle of women and men of the exploited proletariat against the privileges and power of men and women of the possessing and exploiting classes. The goal of this class struggle is to overturn bourgeois society, to overturn capitalism. The proletariat can be victorious in this struggle only by breaking the power of the exploiting bourgeoisie and its class domination in the economy and the state through revolutionary mass action. It must conquer political power and construct its own class dictatorship based on the soviet system. Not bourgeois democracy but proletarian class rule and the proletarian state, which follows on the defeat of this democracy—that is the unavoidable first step toward the communist society of free workers, equal in rights and responsibilities.

In the struggle for state power the exploiting and dominating classes throw the most brutal means of violence of their class dictatorship against the advancing proletariat. The revolutionary mass actions of the exploited and oppressed culminate finally in civil war. The victory of the proletariat through revolutionary mass actions and in civil war is impossible without the participation of the women of the toiling people—confident of their goal and of the road forward, prepared to sacrifice, determined to struggle. For they constitute half (among the most advanced peoples even more than half) of the working people, and their role in social economy as well as in the family is very often decisive for the outcome of class struggles between exploiters and exploited, as well as for the conduct of individual proletarians in these struggles. The proletarian conquest of power must also be the work of convinced, communist, proletarian women.

The same holds true, after the establishment of the proletarian class dictatorship, for the construction of the soviet system, for the realization of communism. Without the active and conscious participation of the broadest masses of communist-minded women, this deep-going, massive transformation of society, of its economic base, of all its institutions, is an impossibility. The participation of the masses of women signifies not merely a greater quantity of work for the realization of communism but also qualitatively different accomplishments, richer and of greater dimension. This participation is a precondition for the necessary increase in the material wealth of society and for advancing, refining, and deepening its culture.

Just as the revolutionary class struggle of the proletariat in each country combines internationally and reaches its high point in the world revolution, so the revolutionary struggle of women against capitalism—*against its highest stage, imperialism*—and for the dictatorship of the proletariat, for the construction of the proletarian class dictatorship and the soviet system, must be unified on an international scale.

6. The imperialist World War—a diabolical crime by the great capitalist states—and the conditions this war created, have enormously aggravated the social ills and contradictions faced by the overwhelming majority of women.

These ills are the inevitable consequences of capitalism and will disappear only with its overthrow. This holds true not only in the belligerent countries but in the so-called neutral ones as well, since all of them were, to a greater or lesser extent, sucked into the bloody maelstrom of the World War; they all suffered its consequences.

The monstrous, growing tension between extortionate prices for the necessities of life and the income, the means of support, of untold millions of women inflicts intolerably greater worries, privations, suffering, and burdens on them as employees, housewives, and mothers. The housing shortage has become a fearful scourge. The health of women in particular is worsening at a rapidly increasing rate due to chronic undernourishment and the suffocating burden of work on the job and in the home.

Fewer and fewer mothers are able to give birth normally and bring healthy, strong babies into the world. Infant mortality rates are skyrocketing. Sickness and infirmity, the unavoidable consequences of inadequate nourishment and wretched living conditions in general, strike down hundreds of thousands, even millions of proletarian children, to the despair of their mothers.

A special phenomenon intensifies the torment of women in all the countries where capitalism still holds sway. During the war an extraordinary number of women gained employment. At that time the slogan in the belligerent countries was, "Women into the trenches of the economy, of administration, of all social activity." Prejudice against the "weak, inferior, backward sex" was silenced by the bugle call of imperialist greed for world power and exploitation, the most powerful expression of world capitalism. Pressure to earn money and the lie about defense of the fatherland combined with the search for capitalist profit to drive women to take employment in industry and agriculture, in business and commerce. Women's labor pressed forward impetuously and irresistibly into all branches of municipal and state administration, into so-called public service and learned professions.

Today, as a result of the World War, the capitalist economy is breaking down and collapsing. Today capitalism, where it still reigns, is proving itself incapable of the economic development required to provide the physical and cultural needs of the broad layers of the toiling masses. Today the decay of the economy and its conscious sabotage by the capitalists have conjured up an unprecedented crisis of stagnating production and unemployment. In all this women are the first and most numerous victims of this crisis.

Individual capitalists, like the local and state capitalist administrations, have less fear of unemployed women, who are mostly unorganized and less politically conscious, than they do of unemployed men. And they calculate that these women, faced with destitution, can as a last resort put their body on the market and sell it. In every country where the proletariat has not taken power through revolutionary struggle, the slogan rings out loudly again today, "Women out of the jobs, women back to the home!" It finds its echo even in the trade unions, impeding and arresting the struggle to get equal pay for equal work by both sexes. It gives new life to the old petty-bourgeois, reactionary ideology of the "only true, natural calling" and the inferior worth of the female. Parallel to the increasing joblessness and growing want of untold numbers of women appears the increase in prostitution in the most varied forms, from marriage as a means of economic survival all the way to the naked sale of female bodies in sexual "commerce."

The increasing tendency toward forcing women out of the realm of social labor stands in glaring contrast to the growing need of the broadest masses of women for independent income and satisfactory occupations. The World War killed millions of men and made further millions into cripples needing total or partial care and support. The disintegration of the capitalist economy makes it impossible for millions of men to provide for their families through their labor as they used to do.

This tendency also stands in the sharpest opposition to the interests of the overwhelming majority of the members of society. Only when the strengths and talents of women, too, are made available to society in the most varied areas of activity will it be possible to make up for the war's colossal destruction of social and material goods and to bring about the necessary increase in wealth and culture.

The mounting tendency to displace women as coworkers in social production and culture is ultimately rooted in the greed of capitalist profiteers seeking to perpetuate their power to exploit. It shows the incompatibility of the capitalist economy, the bourgeois order, with the most important interests of the overwhelming majority of women and of members of society in general.

All the immediate and pressing hardships of women hinge on one key point: these hardships are unavoidable, essential expressions of capitalism, which exploits and enslaves. The war has intensified these hardships to the utmost and imposed them as the tragic fate of the great mass of women. They are not, however, passing phenomena that will disappear in time of peace—to say nothing of the fact that capitalism's continued existence threatens humanity with new imperialist predatory wars, which can be quite clearly seen taking shape in today's events.

It is the many millions of proletarian women, women of the toiling masses, who feel the oppression of today's social evils most sharply. For the combined effect of the exploited character of their class and the disadvantaged condition of their sex makes them victims to the highest degree of the capitalist order. All their want and suffering, however, is only a partial expression of the fate of the exploited and oppressed proletarian class as a whole in every country still under capitalist rule. These evils can thus never be reversed through reforming the bourgeois order for a "struggle against the poverty left over from the war." They will disappear once and for all only together with that order itself, through the revolutionary struggle of the exploited and disinherited women and men of all countries, through the revolutionary action of the world proletariat. Only world revolution and it alone, as history's Last Judgment, can put an end in each country to the World War's legacy of poverty, spiritual and moral decay, bloody mass suffering, and the complete bankruptcy of capitalism.

7. Given the social phenomena and interrelationships just described, the Second Congress of the Communist International, held in Moscow, calls all *women of the working people,* who thirst for freedom and full humanity, to the ranks of the Communist Party of their country and to the ranks of the Communist International itself, in which these parties have united to act with greater effectiveness and determination. Clear in its goals, sure of its path, and ready for action, the Communist International fights to defeat capitalism and establish communism through world revolution. It has also shown itself to be the most discerning and loyal champion of the rights of women.

The Communist International carries forward, on a higher historical plane and in the interests of women the work that the Second International began but was unable to carry out consistently. Given the growing influence on the workers' movement of opportunist reformism, the Second International failed to change from a community of belief to a community of the deed. Ultimately, in August 1914, it shamefully betrayed its historic task. It failed to rally proletarians of all countries to a common, international, revolutionary struggle against imperialism, against the capitalist order. On the contrary, it gave its blessing to the fraternization of exploiter and exploited in the national armies. Imperialism hurled these armies against each other in the interests of capitalist profits and the capitalist craving for world-power status. It drove the working class to mutual fratricide and to suicide. And by this act the Second International also abandoned the rights and interests of women.

When it was founded the Second International inscribed on its banners the struggle for full social liberation and full equal rights for the female sex. There is no question that by taking these demands propagandistically into the broadest circles it achieved much of value and lasting influence. Moreover, it explained that achieving these goals required the destruction of capitalism and the realization of socialism. It demonstrated the irreconcilable class contradiction between women of the exploiting minority and those of the exploited majority. It called for national and international solidarity of all capitalist wage slaves without distinction of sex. It obliged all trade unions and Socialist parties to rally women to their ranks as members with equal rights and responsibilities in the economic and political class struggles of the proletariat.

The Second International demanded laws to limit the scope of capitalist exploitation, to establish social services that could ease the burden of housewives and mothers, and to grant women full and equal political rights—measures aimed at increasing the capacity of proletarian women to resist and to fight in the struggles of their class. The Second International demanded that the Socialist women's movement demarcate itself sharply from the bourgeois women's movement. Whether or not these obligations were realized, whether these demands became the focus of action, of struggle—all that was left by the Second International to be decided by the trade unions and the Social Democratic parties of each country. On the whole, where the interests and rights of women were concerned the International's decisions were carried out only to the degree that organized Socialist women were able to wrest this from the proletarian organizations in each country.

The gulf between theory and practice, between decision and deed was particularly flagrant with regard to the demand for women's right to vote. The Second International permitted its member organization in Britain to call for many years for women to receive a limited right to vote, whose introduction would have reinforced the political power of the propertied and thus the resistance against universal suffrage for all adults.[8] The Second International permitted the Social Democratic party in Belgium and later the party in Austria to abstain during its major voting rights struggle from also demanding universal women's suffrage.

It is true that the Stuttgart congress of the Second International obliged Social Democratic parties of all countries to make the fight for universal women's suffrage an essential part of the overall struggle for proletarians' right to vote and for proletarian power.[9] A sharp demarcation was to be maintained, it stated, against bourgeois-democratic strivings for women's rights, and no regard was to be taken of reformist opportunist politics. But in most countries this decision too remained no more than mere words. Specifically, it did not prevent the unified party of French Socialists from contenting itself with platonic parliamentary resolutions for the introduction of women's suffrage, while even today the proposals of the social-democratic Belgian Workers Party lag behind those of even the clericals.

Within the entire world workers' movement, it was the Socialist women of the warring and neutral countries that took the first tentative step to place the need for international solidarity of the exploited above the bellicose commands of the traitorous social patriots. These women called for international revolutionary mass action to compel the imperialist regimes to make peace and to free up the historic terrain for the workers' international struggle to achieve political power and vanquish imperialism and capitalism. The Second International's response to this was feeble, shameful, and dishonorable. What is more, far from lending its support, the Second International gave tacit encouragement to its member parties in each country to fulminate against this initiative, to denounce it, and to obstruct it in every way. Setting the pace in all this was the "model party"—a model first in organizational strength and in its policies, and then in decay and bankruptcy—the German Social Democracy.[10]

Even today, the Second International strives to reinforce capitalism's power of exploitation and thus to obstruct the full liberation of the female sex. It does this by misleading the masses through democratic and parliamentary hocus-pocus, social patriotism, and social pacifism.

Moreover, the Second International never established a publication with the mission of working internationally to achieve the principles and demands adopted by the International in the interests of women. It was outside the framework of the International's structure that the first steps were taken, quite autonomously, to bring together women Socialists and women workers internationally for united action.[11] It is true that representatives of the Socialist Women's International were permitted to attend congresses of the Second International. But they had no formal right to take part in its proceedings. And in the International Socialist Bureau, the Socialist Women's International enjoyed no representation and no voice.

Women who are communists, revolutionary socialists, or revolutionary proletarians must therefore break their ties with the Second International and join the Communist International, which will fight for women's rights and women's liberation as it fights elsewhere—not as a resolution-writing machine but as an association for action. To repeat, the most complete and consistent way to become part of the Communist International is to join the national party affiliated to it. Women who belong to parties and organizations in which the struggle for affiliation to the Third International has not yet been decided must of course apply all their energy toward winning these organizations to recognize the Communist International's basic principles, policies, and organizational guidelines. They must strive for these organizations to affiliate fully with the Communist International and to act with loyalty toward its character and its demands.

Communist women, consistent revolutionary socialist women, proletarian women must turn their backs on those organizations that persist in their basic opposition to the Communist International, that struggle against it and cripple the proletarian class struggle by infesting it with opportunist and reformist slogans. Forward into the Third International of the revolutionary deed! That must be the overriding and unambiguous rallying call of all women of the toiling people who wish to be rid of class and sexual slavery.

8. The Second Congress of the Communist International requires all its member parties to implement the preceding theses by reaching out to the broadest masses of women and awakening, assembling, and schooling them. These parties must raise to the utmost women's capacity to work and struggle for communism and prove to them through word and deed that only the revolutionary class struggle of the proletariat and the achievement of its goals can ensure full rights, full freedom, and a fully harmonious humanity for the entire female sex. In accordance with these theses, the Communist parties should:

a) *In countries such as Russia where the proletariat has already conquered power, establishing its rule in the form of the soviet system*

(1) Mobilize women fully in all struggles and measures needed for the fight at the front and at home against domestic and foreign counterrevolutionaries and for the defense and consolidation of the soviet system. Involve them in service in the women's militia and as Red nurses, in educational work in the Red Army, and so forth. The widespread, conscious collaboration of women is equally indispensable to completely overcome all the economic and social remnants of capitalism and, what is more, its egoistic morality.

(2) Vigorously and thoroughly educate women of the proletariat and small peasantry and all employed, working women. Explain to them that shortening the difficult transition period from capitalism, which is decaying but must still be torn down, to the higher, communist form of society, lies in their hands too, in their growing understanding, in their unshakable will, and in their dedicated

action. This difficult transition period, during which suffering, misery, and sacrifice are unavoidable, hits women and their children hardest.

(3) Explain to these women that the new, liberating social order of full communism, which will mature by struggling against the forces of the old, foundering bourgeois world and by wrestling with new problems, must also be in large part their own work, the fruit of each one of them being clear as to the goal, unbreakable in will, and always ready to sacrifice.

(4) Draw all employed women into full collaboration in the work of economic development through the soviet bodies, the trade unions, and the cooperatives and their various institutions.

(5) Achieve women's full collaboration in the soviets and their various supervisory, administrative, and development bodies as well as in every other area, including science.

(6) Establish working conditions for employed women that take into account the characteristics of the female organism and the physical as well as intellectual and moral needs of motherhood. These conditions must facilitate a harmonious combination of motherhood with employment. This combination must enable women, by fully applying their strengths and capacities, to develop fully their female humanity.

(7) Incorporate traditional family housekeeping—the most backward, deformed, and stultifying of the old guild handicrafts—into the general social economy. Transform the housewife from the slave of the small individual economy into the free toiler of the larger social economy.

(8) Create model social institutions that take over women's present economic tasks in the family as it has existed up to now and ease, round out, and improve the work mothers do.

(9) Create model social welfare institutions to protect maternity, children, and youth.

(10) Create similar institutions to assist the ill, the infirm, the old, and those unable to work. Take economic and pedagogic measures that will lead prostitutes—an inheritance from the bourgeois order—out of the lumpenproletariat and back into the community of working people.

(11) Establish a system for upbringing and instruction, based on coeducation and education rooted in labor, that guarantees the right to develop individuality, fulfills the duty of teaching solidarity, and thereby ensures the female sex the conditions for rounded human development.

(12) Achieve women's full collaboration in determining and implementing measures to establish, plan, and administer institutions designed to ease the workload of housewives and mothers and to promote social services, particularly those serving women, children, and youth.

b) *In all countries where the proletariat is still fighting for political power*

(1) Enlist women as members with equal rights and duties in the Communist Party and in the economic organizations of the proletariat for the class struggle. Ensure their collaboration with equal rights and duties in all bodies and at all levels of the party, trade unions, and cooperatives.

(2) Educate the broadest masses of women of the proletariat and the small peasantry about communism, about the nature, goal, methods, and means of revolutionary campaigns and struggles of the proletariat. Secure the participation of the broadest masses of women in all these campaigns and struggles, which provide an extremely effective, practical, and educational lesson. Use all means, measures, and institutions that serve to strengthen and

clarify the class consciousness of proletarian women and increase their revolutionary energy and capacity to struggle.

(3) Achieve total equality of rights of both sexes before the law and in practice in all areas of private and public life.

(4) Utilize in a revolutionary and class-conscious way women's right to vote and to stand as candidates for local and national parliaments and for all public bodies. Strongly emphasize the limitations on the usefulness of the right to vote, parliamentarism, and bourgeois democracy for the proletariat, and the historically determined necessity for it to overcome parliamentarism and bourgeois democracy through the soviet system and the dictatorship of the working class.

(5) Achieve the active participation of women workers, salaried employees, civil servants, and all working women in the city and the countryside as voters, clear on their goals, in electing revolutionary economic and political workers' councils. Secure the zealous participation of women workers and salaried employees as delegates in these workers' councils and their subordinate bodies. Reach out to housewives of the proletariat and of layers of the population with limited means as voters for the revolutionary workers' councils and secure their participation in them as delegates. Extend and implement the idea of councils among women of the small peasantry and socially related layers of the population of the countryside.

(6) Fight for the right of women to equal, unrestricted, and free general and occupational education; for women's inclusion as employees with equal rights and duties in the social division of labor and in all areas; and for the recognition and appreciation of maternal tasks as a social contribution.

(7) Fight for equal pay for equal work by men and women.

(8) Fight for the drastic reduction of capitalist exploitative power through effective legal protection of women workers, office employees, and civil servants—including so-called domestics—in all areas of the economy and with due consideration for measures required by young and pregnant women, women with newborns, and nursing mothers.

(9) Demand comprehensive labor inspection by a sufficiently large staff of independent officials, consisting of doctors, technicians, and workers with full powers, in which women must be represented in accordance with the extent of female labor.

(10) Demand social measures and institutions that ease the burdens working women bear as housewives and mothers, that transfer traditional domestic work out of the family economy and into the social economy, and that complement and fill out the raising of children in the home with a social upbringing, giving their education the necessary characteristic of an upbringing that instills solidarity.

(11) Establish the required institutions not only in the cities and industrial centers but also in the countryside for the benefit of women farm workers, peasant women, and so forth.

(12) Educate women on the backward character of old-style housekeeping; on the waste of time, energy, and materials that it entails; and on the use of the household by capitalism to keep men's wages low (since housewives' labor is unpaid) and to keep women intellectually and politically backward by blocking them from participating in society.

(13) Demand a thorough reform of the housing system, a reform that does not respect the rights of bourgeois property—the right to luxury and superfluous dwellings. Women must participate in implementing this.

(14) Demand an extended and organic regulation of the public health system so as to provide, among other

things, free medical clinics in the cities and countryside, in which woman doctors also serve, as well as trained pediatric, general, and home-care nurses.

(15) Demand economic and social measures to fight prostitution; hygienic measures against the spread of venereal diseases; an end to the housing of prostitutes in barracks, to their supervision by vice squads, and to social contempt for them. Do away with the sexual double standard for men and women.

(16) Demand the collaboration of women in all measures and institutions that significantly affect the right of women to education, work, protection against capitalist exploitation, and so forth.

c) *In countries still at a precapitalist level of development*

(1) Fight to overcome the prejudices, morals, practices, and religious and legal rules that reduce women to men's slaves at home, at work, and sexually. This effort will require educating not only women but also men.

(2) Strive for the full legal equality of women with men in education, in the family, and in public life.

(3) Struggle for thorough protection of poor and exploited women against exploitation and subjugation by the dominant, property-owning classes. This sometimes takes the form of cottage industry, whose worst effects can be moderated by cooperatives, among other ways.

(4) Demand measures and institutions that lead from precapitalist forms of economy and social life to communism, especially through efforts to prove by example, by object lessons, that individual housework enslaves women, whereas social labor frees them.

In agitational and organizational work among women in countries with a precapitalist level of development, special use should be made of the experiences acquired by the Russian comrades since the Russian revolution in their work among women of the Eastern peoples.

9. To permit the Communist International's member parties to work for these goals as successfully as possible, the Second Congress adopts the following *organizational* measures:

a) *National organization*

(1) Within the Communist Party of each country, women are not to be organized in separate units but rather integrated into the local party branches as members with equal rights and obligations. They must be drawn into the work of all party bodies and all levels of the party structure.

Nonetheless, the Communist Party takes special measures and establishes special institutions in order to reach women with its agitation, keep them organizationally in its ranks, and educate them. In all this, it recognizes women's distinctive intellectual and moral characteristics, the backwardness imposed upon them by history, and the special position they still often assume as a result of their household activity.

(2) Every local party branch will have a women's agitation committee, to which male comrades may also belong. Its tasks are

(a) to agitate in a planned and consistent way among women still unsympathetic to the party through public meetings, factory-based discussions and meetings, meetings of housewives, delegated conferences of those outside the party, door-to-door agitation, and production and distribution of appropriate leaflets, newspapers, pamphlets, and literature of every kind;

(b) to lead the women reached by this agitation to join the party, the trade unions, the cooperatives, and other proletarian organizations of struggle and of economic development;

(c) to strive to prevent the female members of the party, the unions, the cooperatives, the workers' councils, and other bodies of the militant revolutionary proletariat from being carried along as dead and passive ballast; to inspire them with communist ideals so that they take part in the life and activity of these bodies with vigor and with full understanding;

(d) to ensure that female party members receive the necessary theoretical and practical education, whether it be through the party's general educational institutions, special evenings where women read or discuss together, or other such events;

(e) to see to it that women with agitational and organizational ability receive a thorough education and can participate fully;

(f) to establish a women's page in every party newspaper, name a woman as editor of this section, and ensure that women from the proletarian ranks collaborate with her.

The local women's agitation committee consists of five to seven members, who are proposed by the women members and approved by the local party leadership. This committee works in close collaboration with the local leadership, whose approval is required for its measures and decisions. A woman comrade serves as the standing representative of this committee in the local leadership, taking part in all its meetings and activities with consultative vote in questions affecting the party as a whole and decisive vote in questions affecting the women's movement.

(3) Linked to the leadership of every party district organization is a district women's agitation committee. Its task is to stimulate local women's agitation committees

throughout the district to carry out their tasks and to lend these committees effective support. To this end, its tasks are

(a) to maintain continual and regular contact with all local women's committees in the district and with the national women's agitation committee or the national women's secretariat;

(b) to assemble important factual material on the work of each local women's agitation committee and make this information available to all the committees;

(c) to supply agitational and educational literature to the district as a whole;

(d) to stimulate, prepare, and carry out broader agitational events of every kind for the entire district, assembling the agitational and organizational forces this requires;

(e) to undertake and carry though every measure that helps mobilize women of the working people in the district for all the party's major projects and campaigns, transforming women from passive observers into active participants;

(f) to organize district women's conferences, to which each local women's agitation committee must send one or two representatives. In addition, the women party members in each locality will elect delegates—one delegate is to be chosen for each fifty women party members. The committee will call the district women's conferences as needed, but at least once every six months. The district women's committee also initiates and conducts other delegated conferences for women in the district who do not belong to any party.

The district women's committee consists of five to seven members, proposed by the women members of the district at their conference and approved by the district party leadership. The committee works in closest collaboration with the district party leadership, whose approval is required for its measures and decisions. Within the district party leadership, the committee is represented by one or several women comrades, who take part in all its sessions with consultative vote for questions affecting the party as a whole and decisive vote for questions affecting the women's movement.

(4) Linked to the national party leadership is a national women's agitation committee or national women's secretariat. Its tasks are

(a) to maintain continual and regular contact with the district and local women's agitation committees and to place them in close touch with the national party leadership;

(b) to assemble all factual material on the work of each district women's agitation committee and to provide for an exchange of this information, including of the lessons and proposals that flow from it, among these committees;

(c) to distribute agitational and educational literature to the district women's committees across the country as a whole;

(d) to give close attention to the employment, education, and legal status of women, to laws protecting women workers, and to developments and disputes affecting women's economic, political, and social interests; to encourage the district and local women's agitation committees to take up controversial questions;

(e) to publish regularly a magazine that serves to educate women comrades theoretically, deepen their understanding of communism, and give them an intimate feel for the intellectual essence of the party and its current revolutionary tasks. The national women's committee selects the woman who edits this publication and strives to provide her with contributions and collaborators from among women workers;

(f) to promote and organize agitational events of every kind for the entire country and to provide the necessary agitational and organizational forces;

(g) to take up and drive through every appropriate measure to summon the broadest masses of working women across the country to join in the party's overall tasks and struggles and lead women to participate actively and with a readiness for sacrifice;

(h) to convene national women's conferences composed of one or two representatives of each district women's committee and elected delegates of the women party members in every locality. One delegate is to be chosen for every one hundred women party members. Where there are fewer than one hundred women members, one delegate is sent nonetheless. National women's conferences will be called when necessary, but at least once a year. The national women's agitation committee also convenes delegated conferences of women across the country who do not belong to any party.

(i) to select an international correspondent who maintains continual contact with the International Women's Secretariat.

The national women's agitation committee consists of seven to ten members proposed by the national women's conference and approved by the national Communist Party convention. The committee works in closest contact with the national party leadership, and the committee's decisions are subject to its approval. The committee's representatives take part in all meetings and activities of the party leadership, with decisive vote in all matters affecting women and consultative vote in all matters affecting the party as a whole.

b) *International organization*

An International Women's Secretariat will be established associated with the Executive Committee of the

Communist International. It will consist of three to five comrades nominated by the conference of Communist women and confirmed by the congress of the Communist International, or by the Executive Committee as its representative. The women's secretariat works in close collaboration with the International's Executive Committee, whose approval is required for its decisions and measures. A woman comrade serves as representative of the secretariat in all meetings and activities of the Executive Committee with consultative vote on overall questions and with decisive vote on questions particular to the women's movement.[12]

Its tasks are

(a) to establish and maintain active ties with national women's committees of each Communist Party, as well as active ties among these committees;

(b) to assemble and make available informational and agitational material produced by the work of each national women's committee;

(c) to assemble Communist women's and party literature produced in each country, such as "women's pages," periodicals, leaflets, and so forth, and to organize their exchange among different countries;

(d) to study and to assemble material on the development of women's employment, their political and civil rights and their public position, their occupational training and overall education, and on questions of the protection of female workers, public welfare services for mothers and children, housing conditions, and so forth. In short, all problems relating to women's life and activity must be studied, the relevant material collected, and the national women's committees made aware of questions and tasks of international significance and referred to the available study material;

(e) to urge the international correspondents of each national organization to submit reports, doing so rapidly on especially important events and phenomena but at least every three months;

(f) to produce a publication for international information that contains general, all-embracing reports as well as particularly important individual reports and that draws attention to current general problems, tasks, and campaigns;

(g) when the proletariat, led by the Communist International, conducts international campaigns, to immediately take all necessary steps to enroll the broadest toiling masses of women into the revolutionary ranks as intelligent, self-sacrificing, and courageous partners in struggle;

(h) to call together and lead international conferences of Communist women that will facilitate the exchange of knowledge won through experience, provide a new stimulus for action, strengthen the ties between comrades, and unite the great masses of toiling women internationally in revolutionary work and struggle.

International women's conferences must appeal to the exploited and enslaved women of the entire world.

Proletarian women of all countries! Unite with the proletarian men of all countries under the banner of the Communist International, against capitalism and its deceitful democracy, in the struggle to conquer political power and establish the dictatorship of the proletariat and the soviet system! Even more than of proletarian men, it can be said of you, proletarian women, that in this struggle you have only your chains to lose and a world to win.

APPENDIX 7

COMMUNIST YOUTH MOVEMENT

# Theses on the youth movement

1. The founding of proletarian youth organizations around the world results from several factors: the increased capitalist exploitation of young workers in all factories and workshops and in home industry, which can only lead to their spiritual and physical degeneration; militarism, whose burdens are born above all by working-class youth; the danger that their ranks will be permeated by bourgeois-nationalist ideology through the schools, the press, bourgeois youth organizations, and so on; and the special psychological characteristics of the younger generation.[1]

2. Communist youth groups arose in every country as part of the development of the workers' movement as a whole during and after the imperialist war. This occurred in part through old Socialist youth organizations going over to the camp of the Communist International and in part through splits in these organizations.

3. The Communist youth organizations have the following tasks: the communist education of working-class

youth, active participation in bringing down capitalism (the defense of the proletarian dictatorship and soviet construction after taking power), and the struggle to reorganize work and education on a new socialist basis. As much as possible, the Communist youth organizations promote the cultural development of young workers along the lines of the Marxist worldview as well as physical education, which currently must aim primarily at military preparation.

4. The most important element in the communist education of youth, aside from theoretical education, is their taking an active part in the daily political struggles of the working class. It is in this respect that the Communist youth organizations are different from the social-patriotic and centrist youth groups. Their political struggles, in addition to their educational significance, have great and real importance for the international Communist movement.

5. The entire history of the proletarian youth movement in every country shows that only independent, that is, self-governing, youth organizations develop bold and determined revolutionary fighters and astute organizers of the proletarian revolution and soviet power. The independent action of working-class youth is the first prerequisite for their revolutionary communist development. By contrast, the social patriots' exercise of tutelage over the youth results in an opportunist, petty-bourgeois development. The communist development of young people requires special methods of work that reflect the special characteristics of their age group.

6. The relationship between the Communist parties and the Communist youth organizations will take different forms as a result of differences in objective conditions and in the state of the party in each country. In some countries, where the formation of Communist parties is

still in flux and the youth organizations are just breaking away from the social-patriotic and centrist parties, our main slogan is that of the absolute political and organizational independence of the youth movement. Under such conditions this slogan is objectively revolutionary! The slogan of absolute independence is wrong, however, in countries where there are already strong Communist parties, and where this slogan is used by the social patriots and the centrists against the Communist youth and to mislead the youth. There the Communist youth organizations have based themselves on the program of the Communist Party.

7. In all countries where old and active Communist parties existed, a strong relationship between the Communist Party and the Communist youth organization was established. The form this took was that the Communist youth organization adopted the program of the Communist Party and functioned in the framework of its political positions. At the same time, in these cases, the youth (1) had their own centralized organization; (2) decided for themselves how to carry out their organizational, agitational, and propaganda activities; (3) decided the place and the forms of their participation in political struggle; and (4) discussed the main political questions. All youth organizations must arrive at this relationship with the Communist Party, not through compulsion by the party, but by being convinced and making their own free decision.

8. The Communist parties support the Communist youth organizations intellectually and materially, without tying this support to petty interference in the activity of the youth organization or the exercise of tutelage over it. For their part the Communist youth organizations support the Communist parties in the full range of their organizational activity, legal and illegal, and their political work.

9. The Communist International hails the formation of the Communist Youth International, whose basic tasks are the centralized leadership of the Communist youth movement, support of the national Communist youth groups, the formation of Communist youth groups where none yet exist, and international agitation around the ideas of communism and the youth movement.

10. The Communist Youth International is part of the Communist International. As such it subordinates itself to the decisions of the congresses of the Communist International and the political directives of its Executive Committee. It carries out independently its work of leading, organizing, strengthening, and broadening the youth International.

11. The Communist Youth International and its groups take part in the congresses of the Communist International. The executive committees of the Communist International and the youth International exchange representatives with decisive vote.

12. The Communist International assigns to its Executive Committee and its member parties the task of spreading the idea of the Communist youth movement among party members and the broad working masses.

# Notes to volume two

### Session 11: Trade unions and factory committees, part 1

1. At the German Communist Party's founding congress, Luxemburg expressed the view that workers' councils were taking over the functions of trade unions. "The workers' councils," she said, "are the organizations at the factory level that lead and watch over the economic struggles. . . . As you can see, the [party] platform leads straight to completely assuming all the functions of the unions. We expropriate from the trade unions the functions entrusted to them by the workers, whom they betrayed." She cautioned, however, against the proposal that Communists quit the unions. "What will become of the enormous power those gentlemen control?" she asked. "I would not be in favor of a split that left even a part of the power in their hands." Riddell, John, ed., *The German Revolution and the Debate on Soviet Power* (Pathfinder, 1986), pp. 270–71 [2021 printing].
2. Schröder and Wendel, *Betriebsorganisationen,* p. 5.
3. J.H. Whitley (1866–1935) chaired the British government's Committee on Relations between Employers and Employed. Its main report, presented in 1917, proposed a permanent arbitration court, joint labor-management councils in factories and on a district and national basis, and other similar measures. Many such joint bodies, called "Whitley councils," were established in the next few years.
4. John Spargo (1876–1966), a former Socialist, a collaborator of Samuel Gompers, and an opponent of Soviet Russia, wrote *Russia as an American Problem.*
5. The value of the German mark was falling steadily during this period. In 1914 it was worth U.S. $.24; by mid-1921 it was worth just over U.S. $.01.

6. The translation of this sentence follows the French and English texts. The German text reads, "We must induce the Communists in America and Britain to consider the possibility and necessity of forming new trade unions in all large organizations in America." The Russian texts read, "We must agree with the general tendency of American Communists to form new trade unions."
7. The syndicalist unions are discussed in thesis 5 of the resolution on the role of the party (session 3, pp. 264–66) and in thesis 6 of the resolution on the trade unions (session 12, pp. 844–45). These passages, however, do not take up their admission to the International. All syndicalist groups were invited to the congress in the Executive Committee's congress call, found after the Prologue to this book.
8. The translation here follows the Russian and English texts. The German and French texts read, "What the USPD accomplished by entering the trade unions . . ."
9. Radek is referring to trade union theses submitted by John Reed. The text of these theses is not available.
10. The union statement, issued July 15, 1920, is found in appendix 4b. In fact, no British unionists signed this statement. Purcell and Williams, the British unionists, had agreed to the calling of a congress to found a new trade union International but left Moscow before subsequent meetings that led to the July 15 statement.
11. Under the tsars the Central Asian province of Khorezm, then known as Khiva, was a khanate subject to a Russian protectorate. Early in 1920 the revolutionary nationalist Young Khivan Party, backed by units of the Red Army, drove out the khan. In June 1920 a democratic republic was established, organized along soviet lines. In 1925 Khorezm was incorporated into the Soviet Union as part of the Uzbek and Turkmen soviet socialist republics.

    The placement here of the greetings from Khorezm follows that in the Russian edition of 1934. The German edition, however, puts these greetings at the beginning of session 12.

12. Fraina's report conveys the main points of the theses that he and Murphy submitted to the trade union commission. Their theses are found in the Communist Party of America's April 1921 issue of the *Communist.*
13. See point 1 of the July 15 declaration in appendix 4b.
14. This topic is taken up in the last sentence of article 5 of the trade union council's provisional statutes in appendix 4c.
15. See article 3 of the trade union council's statutes in appendix 4c.
16. Tanner is referring to the declaration in appendix 4b.

### Session 12: Trade unions and factory committees, part 2

1. For Luxemburg's remarks on this question, see note 1 to session 11, p. 1321.
2. In a coup on October 4–5, 1910, the constitutional monarchy in Portugal was overthrown and a republic proclaimed.
3. Wolffheim and Rühle were prominent figures in the KAPD, which had organized a small, separate trade union federation under its leadership. See remarks by Zinoviev in session 15 (p. 968).
4. The term "civil peace" *(Burgfrieden)* was used by revolutionaries after 1914 to refer to the right-wing Social Democratic Party and trade union leadership's policy of support to the government in prosecuting the war effort and opposing workers' struggles to defend their interests.
5. In most European countries, including in factories where trade unions were strong and negotiated collective agreements on behalf of all the workers, joining the union remained a matter of individual choice, and many workers did not belong.
6. The translation of this sentence follows the Russian and French texts.
7. Following the congress, Fraina wrote in his party's newspaper that he and Stoklitsky did not join Reed and other U.S. delegates in abstaining. See *Communist* (Communist Party of America), vol. 3, no. 1, April 1921.

8. According to the 1920 Vienna edition, this vote was 57 to 8, with one abstention.
9. The trade union theses were drafted by Radek. In the German edition of the congress proceedings, these theses appear as an appendix.
10. In place of "sharpening class antagonisms," the draft resolution reads, "They [the masses] . . ."
11. The words "in the interests of the bourgeoisie" are not found in the draft resolution.
12. This sentence is not found in the draft.
13. This sentence is not found in the draft.
14. The rest of this sentence is not found in the draft.
15. This sentence is not found in the draft.
16. The rest of this sentence is not found in the draft.
17. The rest of this sentence is not found in the draft.
18. This sentence is not found in the draft.
19. The words "and factory committees" are not found in the draft.
20. In place of the rest of this sentence and the sentence that follows, the draft resolution reads, "must be most energetically supported by the Communist parties."
21. At this point the draft contains the following passage, absent from the final version: "After the proletariat gains power, the factory committees will be the first organs of management of industry until the establishment of overall state economic organs, through which the working class can administer the factories and lead, in the interests of society as a whole, the country's entire economic life, utilizing to that end the scientific resources bequeathed by capitalism."
22. In place of this sentence, the draft reads, "Only after the taking of power can the factory committees become factory units of the trade unions, which together with the local and central organs of workers' power will create special economic organs."
23. Point 14 is not found in the draft.

### Session 13: The agrarian question

1. Julian Marchlewski had left the congress to head the provisional Polish revolutionary government just established in the Polish city of Bialystok.
2. For a discussion of the German Social Democracy's agrarian policy, which was typical of that of most parties affiliated to the Second International, see Riddell, *German Revolution,* pp. 297–307.
3. See Kautsky, *Agrarian Question,* and Lenin's review of the book in *CW,* vol. 4, pp. 94–99.
4. The Settlement Laws of 1919 aimed to strengthen the German government's claim to eastern regions inhabited by many Poles through providing marginal or defaulted-upon land there to army veterans and peasants who needed land.
5. In July 1919 the German Communist Party began publication of *Der Pflug* (The plow), a weekly newspaper for small peasants.
6. In fact, the draft theses refer here not to the total population on these farms but to the number of farms of this size. See Lenin's footnote in appendix 5b on p. 1272.
7. See "Agrarprogramm der Kommunistischen Partei Deutschlands (Spartakusbund)," *Kommunistische Internationale,* no. 9 [April 1920], pp. 129–35.
8. This formulation is not found in the final text of the resolution.
9. Beginning in the spring of 1919 and continuing through 1921, agrarian revolts were widespread among Italian small peasants and farm workers, especially in the south. Many land occupations and local insurrections took place. Farm workers' organizations grew rapidly and won improved wages and working conditions, and in some areas landowners were forced to recognize the closed shop. Growing support from rural toilers enabled the Socialist Party to win sweeping electoral victories in important agricultural regions.

10. Graziadei misread this passage in the draft theses, which states that small peasants and rural workers made up the majority not of the population as a whole but of that in the countryside.
11. A decare, which is one-tenth of a hectare, equals about one quarter of an acre.
12. By "socialization" of the land, Shablin means convincing farm laborers and peasants to join together in cooperative or state farms for large-scale cultivation. This is not the same as nationalization of the land, which was carried out by the Soviet government in Russia in 1917. Nationalization abolished private property in land, thus putting an end to the renting, selling, or mortgaging of land. This freed the peasant from the capitalist rents and mortgages system under which many were driven off the land by their incapacity to maintain rent and interest payments. Following nationalization of the land, the Soviet government guaranteed peasants full freedom to decide themselves whether to cultivate individually or collectively. The Bolsheviks saw this as the best road toward the voluntary expansion of cooperative and collective farming on a socialist basis. Lenin discusses these concepts in "The Proletarian Revolution and the Renegade Kautsky," in *CW,* vol. 28, pp. 305–15.
13. In 1920 the Communist Party of Bulgaria began publishing *Selski Vestnik* (Country herald), a newspaper aimed at peasants and farm workers.
14. Explaining why French peasants had supported the 1851 coup d'état of Louis-Napoléon Bonaparte (Napoléon III) against the bourgeois parliament, Karl Marx described their conditions as follows: "Their mode of production isolates them from one another instead of bringing them into mutual intercourse. The isolation is increased by France's bad means of communication and by the poverty of the peasants. . . . Each individual peasant family is almost self-sufficient; it itself directly produces the major part of its consumption and thus acquires its means of life more through exchange with nature than in intercourse with

society." Marx, "The Eighteenth Brumaire of Louis Bonaparte," in *MECW,* vol. 11, p. 187.

15. In France during and just after the war, trade in grain was put in the hands of a government monopoly, which purchased peasants' grain surpluses at fixed prices that were held below free-market levels. Although this policy met strong opposition from the better-off peasants, who sold grain on the market, it actually benefited most poorer peasants, who purchased some of the grain they needed on the market. The French government announced in the early summer of 1920 that, while maintaining the grain monopoly, it was increasing the price of grain. Price controls were abolished in 1921.
16. The Italian delegation was so divided that it could not agree on delegates to the programmatic commissions and participated in only two of them.
17. The initial draft of these theses was written by Lenin and is included as appendix 5b to this volume. Substantive differences between this draft and the final version are noted.

    In the German edition of the congress proceedings, these theses appear as an appendix.
18. This paragraph is not found in Lenin's draft.
19. Lenin's draft includes a footnote giving precise data on this point. See appendix 5b, p. 1272.
20. In Lenin's draft this paragraph ends as follows: "That is because the world outlook and the sentiments of the property owners are prevalent among this stratum, which has a direct interest in profiteering, in 'freedom' of trade and in property, and stands in direct antagonism to the wage-workers. By abolishing rent and mortgages, the victorious proletariat will immediately improve the position of this stratum."
21. This sentence is not found in Lenin's draft.
22. In Lenin's draft this sentence is expressed as follows: "The proletarian state must effect the transition to collective farming with extreme caution and only very gradually, by the force of example, without any coercion of the middle peasant."

23. All of the remainder of thesis 6 in Lenin's draft, except for the last two paragraphs, is substantially reworked in this final version.
24. At this point three sentences in Lenin's draft are omitted from this final version.
25. Lenin's draft specifies only Germany here.
26. The final three sentences of this paragraph are not found in Lenin's draft.
27. Lenin's draft refers specifically to "three very important European parties" that left the Second International and names only Kautsky, not Scheidemann and the trade union bureaucracy.
28. At this point a sentence in Lenin's draft has been omitted from this final version.
29. This sentence is not found in Lenin's draft.
30. In Lenin's draft this sentence reads: "Only if they are linked up with the mass strike struggle and with the most oppressed class can the soviets perform their functions and become consolidated enough to influence (and later to incorporate) the small peasants."

## Session 14: Statutes

1. The names of those nominated here as editors are not found in any of the 1921 editions of the proceedings. They appear, however, in the notes of the congress secretaries.
2. Marx and Engels, "Manifesto of the Communist Party," in *MECW,* vol. 6, p. 519. See also *The Communist Manifesto* (Pathfinder, 1970, 2008), p. 73 [2021 printing].
3. Levi is apparently referring here to the Executive Committee's decision to establish a regional bureau in Amsterdam. The bureau members appointed by the Executive Committee were Wijnkoop, Willem Van Ravesteyn, Henriette Roland-Holst, Anton Pannekoek, and Herman Gorter. Inclusion of the last two would have seemed an error even to the Dutch party leaders, with whom they were at odds. The Amsterdam bureau's activities and the decision to dis-

solve it are discussed in the Executive Committee's report found before session 1.

4. Gallacher's speech and the subsequent remarks of Reed have been translated from the German edition and edited after a comparison with the English and Russian editions.
5. In December 1919 the British Trades Union Congress authorized a delegation to visit Soviet Russia on a fact-finding tour. Representatives of the Labour Party and Independent Labour Party joined the group, which visited Russia in May and June 1920.

   On May 26 the delegation met briefly with Lenin, who gave them his "Letter to the British Workers." See Lenin, *CW,* vol. 31, pp. 139–43.
6. Zinoviev is apparently referring to the proposed changes he has just discussed.
7. The statutes were drafted by Zinoviev.
8. Marx and Engels, "General Rules," in *MECW,* vol. 23, pp. 3–4.
9. This sentence encompasses an amendment adopted in session 16, which raised the maximum number of parties represented in the Executive Committee to thirteen from ten.
10. The 1921 and 1934 Russian texts of this sentence read, "united internationally under the leadership of the Executive Committee of the Communist International . . ."
11. The third Comintern congress, held in 1921, decided that structuring the association of revolutionary trade unions as a section of the Comintern, as proposed in this clause, would be premature. This was the "ideal solution," the congress trade union resolution stated. "Undoubtedly this is the organization of the future. However, in the present transitional period, given the diverse types of trade unions that actually exist, the essential need is for an independent international association of Red trade unions which supports the general outline of the platform of the Communist International, but sets less strict conditions for membership than the Communist International can allow." Adler, *Theses, Resolutions,* pp. 268–69.

## Session 15: Forming workers' councils; Part 3 of trade unions and factory committees

1. The remarks of Edward Lindgren (Flynn) have been translated from the German text and edited after comparison with the English version.
2. Total membership in the U.S. Communist movement as a whole was then probably closer to eight thousand, divided more or less evenly between the United Communist Party and the Communist Party.
3. The German text of this paragraph reads, "It is quite wrong to say, as Flynn did here, that if the congress continues to support the two comrades from the Communist Party it is sanctioning the split. On the contrary, if the congress excludes these two comrades, it will be exacerbating the differences. I maintain that I have the right to attend the congress as a delegate because my party can and must and will contribute much to the cause of the communist revolution in general."
4. See Kautsky, *Dictatorship of the Proletariat,* pp. 70–74. Lenin's reply, together with another article by Kautsky on this theme, can be found in Riddell, *German Revolution,* pp. 145–60 and 464–72.
5. Kerensky was a minister in the bourgeois Provisional Government from its inception after the February 1917 revolution until its overthrow in October. He did not become prime minister in that regime, however, until early July.
6. Zinoviev is probably referring to the Communist Federation of Soviets.
7. The result of the vote is taken from the 1920 Vienna edition.
8. The theses on forming workers' councils were drafted by Zinoviev. A comparison of that draft with the final version found here shows that no significant changes were made in the course of the congress. In the German edition of the congress proceedings, these theses appear as an appendix.
9. The proceedings contain no record of the amendment by U.S. delegates.

10. The 1921 editions of the congress proceedings give only the opening and closing phrases of these passages from the United Communist Party program. The text of these quotations is taken from *Communist* (United Communist Party), vol. 1, no. 1, June 12, 1920.
11. This quotation is not found in any previous version of the congress proceedings. Radek was evidently referring to the Executive Committee letter, "The Communist International to the American Comrades," published in *Communist International,* no. 11/12, June–July 1920, cols. 2498–99. The passage from this letter that deals with the American Federation of Labor has been inserted in this edition of the proceedings.
12. A law passed in January 1920 established a system of worker-elected factory committees, authorized to negotiate with and advise the employers on many questions of plant management. The law's thrust was to convert the committees from an instrument of struggle built by the workers into a government-regulated institution of collaboration between workers and employers.
13. The Russian delegation's resolution submitted to the Second Congress trade union commission proposed that the July 15 union council declaration serve as a platform for the trade union International and that this International should form part of the Comintern. This latter point was not included in the trade union theses, although it is reflected in thesis 14 of the Comintern statutes in session 14, p. 935.
14. The resolution that had been rejected was probably an August 1 statement adopted by a meeting of trade union delegates to the congress, which established a provisional structure for the revolutionary trade union council. This statement, included in the 1934 Russian edition of the proceedings, was not widely publicized at the time. Much of its content was incorporated into the Executive Committee appeal to trade unions found in appendix 4d.
15. The translation of this sentence is based on the Russian text of 1921.

16. This heading, not found in any previous edition of the proceedings, is given in the notes of the congress secretaries.
17. The German text reads, "changing the old revolutionary spirit in the trade unions . . ."
18. The letter to the IWW is found in appendix 4a.
19. British Prime Minister David Lloyd George visited Glasgow in December 1915 to urge on union leaders the need for "dilution." This meant the introduction of unskilled labor, especially that of women, into skilled job classifications in a manner that drove down wage rates and undercut union rights. The Clyde Workers' Committee, a precursor of the Shop Stewards' movement, demanded to meet with him, but was refused. When Lloyd George toured the factories December 24, however, workers refused to talk to him and referred him to the Clyde Workers' Committee. Progovernment union officials had arranged an areawide meeting on Christmas Day at which specially invited workers would meet with Lloyd George. Gallacher persuaded the official local labor council to repudiate the meeting, while he simultaneously cornered the invitations, giving them to the Workers' Committee for distribution. The Christmas meeting thus turned into a tumultuous confrontation between the prime minister and several thousand militant metalworkers.
20. The text of Fraina's speech, taken from the English edition, has been expanded by adding a number of passages found only in the Russian edition of 1921. The final sentence is taken from the German edition.
21. These remarks by the chair and by Reed are taken from the English edition.
22. The result of the vote is taken from the 1920 Vienna edition.
23. The meaning of Reed's motion is unclear, given that the proceedings record earlier the taking of a vote on the theses.
24. The text here follows the Russian edition of 1921. No reference to Zinoviev's "additional proposal" is found in the

French or English texts. According to the German edition, Zinoviev read out a motion at this point. The text of such a motion, however, is found neither in the German edition nor in any other available congress records.

25. This is a reference to the July 15 call to form an International Council of Trade and Industrial Unions, in appendix 4b.
26. See "To the Trade Unions of All Countries," in appendix 4d.
27. Tanner's remarks, not found in any previous version of the proceedings, are taken from the notes of the congress secretaries.
28. The size of the revolutionary trade unions of Bulgaria was given by the Bulgarian Communist Party, in its written report to the congress, as just over 30,000 members.
29. Zinoviev's meaning is that the main enemy is not the Second International but the reformist-led trade union International. Brussels was the seat of the pre-war Second International and of the "Bern International" sponsored by procapitalist forces trying to reconstitute the Second International under their leadership. Meeting in Geneva simultaneously with the second Comintern congress, these forces shifted their center to London.
30. This is a reference to Zinoviev's motion that the Executive Committee issue an appeal on behalf of the newly formed trade union council.

### Session 16: Tasks of the Comintern; Part 4 of conditions for admission, and other business

1. No text is available of Rosmer's report. There is no record of it in any edition of the proceedings. It is mentioned, however, in the notes of congress secretaries, in Rosmer's *Moscow under Lenin,* and in the congress supplement to *Pravda, Vestnik 2-go kongressa,* no. 7.
2. Thesis 16 of the draft resolution on tasks advocated that communists in Britain join the Labour Party. In the commission on this resolution, this proposal was strongly opposed by the British delegates present, as well as by Fraina, Rosmer, and Wijnkoop. Although a clear majority favored

the thesis, Lenin requested a special plenary discussion on the topic, asking Rosmer to present the commission's report on this resolution.

3. In May 1917 a walkout of metalworkers near Manchester opened the biggest wartime strike in Britain, which embraced 200,000 workers. The strikers were protesting moves to extend "dilution" of skilled labor from government munitions factories to private firms, as well as to cut back the skilled machinists' exemption from conscription. Though the strikes were broken, the government dropped plans to expand dilution. The strikes strengthened the Shop Stewards' movement and established it as a national force.
4. No record is available of such a statement by Serrati.
5. The resolution adopted at the Bologna congress is printed in *Communist International,* no. 6, October 1919, cols. 901–2. The Turin section's report can be found in no. 13 [September 1920], pp. 71–74.
6. The theses were drafted by Lenin. This translation, from Lenin, *CW,* vol. 31, pp. 184–201, has been edited on the basis of comparison with the German and 1934 Russian editions of the proceedings. In the German edition of the congress proceedings, these theses appear as an appendix.
7. This sentence is not found in the draft resolution.
8. The Central Committee of the Swiss party had decided April 17 to propose to the party's 1920 congress that it join the Communist International. Prior to the congress, which was not held until December, the Central Committee reversed itself and advocated rejecting the Twenty-one Conditions. The congress majority adopted this latter position.
9. This sentence is not found in the draft.
10. Points (f) and (g) are not found in the draft.
11. This reference is to thesis 7 of the Twenty-one Conditions. This sentence is not found in the German text.
12. This sentence is not found in the draft.

13. Mention of the Bologna congress decision in this sentence is not found in the draft.

14. Rosmer later recounted that a proposal was placed before the commission that the resolution explicitly condemn the *Bulletin* published by the Amsterdam bureau. Rosmer spoke against this measure, arguing that the *Bulletin* was published on the authority of the Comintern leadership, which must accept responsibility for its actions. Insertion of the criticism was defended by Zinoviev and Levi. The commission vote was tied, and Lenin, who was chairing, then cast the deciding vote against this proposal. See Rosmer, *Moscow under Lenin,* p. 75.

15. Meyer is referring to point 15 of the "Theses on the Basic Tasks of the Communist International," which appear earlier in this session.

16. The published version of the theses on tasks does not refer to the Twenty-one Conditions.

17. An early, seventeen-point version of these theses was published in 1920 in German in Zinoviev's pamphlet *Brennende Tagesfragen,* pp. 99–107. A subsequent draft, with an eighteenth point (thesis 2 in the final version that appears here), appeared prior to the congress in the French- and English-language editions of the Comintern magazine; for the English version, see *Communist International,* no. 11/12, June–July 1920, cols. 2221–26. During the congress, Bordiga and Humbert-Droz drew up what became thesis 19; Bordiga proposed it in session 6. A draft including nineteen points was published in Russian listing Zinoviev as the author. See *Tezisy ko Vtoromu kongressy,* p. 83. This version can also be found in Lenin, *CW,* vol. 31, pp. 206–11. After further discussion Lenin proposed what became thesis 20, and thesis 21 was suggested by Bordiga. In a 1924 address, Zinoviev said that the Twenty-one Conditions "were drafted by me, but, to the last detail, inspired by Lenin." See "W.I. Lenin: Genie, Lehrer, Führer, und Mensch," *Kommunistische Internationale,* no. 31/32 [1924], p. 13.

In the 1921 German edition of the proceedings, these theses are placed in session 8 (July 30).

In the notes that follow, the comparison is between the final text and the nineteen-point draft published in Lenin's *Collected Works*.

18. Norway and Yugoslavia are not mentioned in the draft resolution.
19. In place of "the so-called left Social Democrats," the draft reads "the reformists."
20. The words "and correspond . . . the Communist International" are not found in the draft.
21. In the draft this paragraph is thesis 12.
22. At this point the draft adds, "Communist cells must be formed in every military unit."
23. In the Russian editions of 1921 and 1934, as in the draft, this sentence begins, "The working class cannot consolidate its victory unless it has the support of at least a part of the rural proletariat and poorest peasants."
24. The words "of town and country" are not found in the draft.
25. In the draft only Turati and Modigliani are mentioned in this sentence.
26. The workers' and factory committees are not mentioned at this point in the draft.
27. The Russian texts of 1921 and 1934, as well as the draft, read at this point, "governed by an iron, almost military discipline."
28. This thesis is not found in the draft.
29. This thesis was introduced by Bordiga in session 6. In the nineteen-point draft, this thesis reads, "After the Second Congress of the Communist International has finished its work, all parties wishing to join it are required to call a special congress as soon as possible, in order, on behalf of the party as a whole, to approve the measures laid down above."
30. Theses 20 and 21 are not found in the draft resolution.

31. The draft theses on work among women and on the youth movement were adopted and published by the Executive Committee (see appendixes 6b and 7).

32. Graziadei's proposal, presented in session 13, is reflected in the addition made to the end of the first paragraph of thesis 8 of the agrarian theses on p. 897.

33. The list given here is reconstructed from the notes of the congress secretaries. The English, French, and Russian texts do not contain any indication here of the proposed composition of the Executive Committee. The German text contains a list, giving names as well as countries, that differs markedly from the secretaries' notes and from the list published in *Pravda* on August 10, 1920.

    In the German edition's list, Radek represents Poland not Russia; Java is represented by Maring; Latvia by Stuchka; Georgia by Tskhakaya; and Turkey by Shatskin. Lazar Shatskin was, in fact, a representative of the youth International, not of Turkey. No representatives are named for the Communist Party of Russia.

34. The secretaries' notes refer at this point to a speech by Sverre Krogh of Norway but give no indication of its contents. There is no mention of his speech in any edition of the congress proceedings.

35. Reports on Switzerland were printed in *Berichte zum zweiten Kongress,* pp. 77–111.

36. This list is not found in any previous edition of the proceedings; it is taken from the notes of congress secretaries.

37. The Executive Committee's August 26, 1920, letter to the KAPD appears in *Communist International,* no. 13 [September 1920], pp. 154–56.

38. The manifesto appears immediately following session 17.

39. The membership of the new Executive Committee, according to *Pravda* of August 10, 1920, was as follows: "Germany, Levi (candidate member, Meyer); France, Rosmer; Britain, Quelch (for all British parties and groups including the Shop Stewards, but not including the Pankhurst group); America, John Reed; Italy, Serrati; Austria, Steinhardt; Scandina-

via, Friis (Norway, Sweden, Denmark; it was subsequently decided to give Sweden separate representation); Bulgaria, Shablin; Yugoslavia, Milkic; Hungary, Rudnyánszky (candidate member, Varga); Middle East, Sultanzadeh; Far East, Pak; Finland, Manner; the Netherlands, Wijnkoop. As decided by the congress, the Russian Communist Party chose five delegates, Zinoviev, Bukharin, Radek, Tomsky, and Kobetsky, as well as the candidate members Lenin, Stalin, Trotsky, Berzin, Pavlovich, and Chicherin." The Communist Youth International elected Shatskin as its representative.

A bureau was elected to coordinate the Executive Committee's day-to-day business. Usually called the Narrow Bureau, it was initially composed of Zinoviev, Bukharin, Kobetsky, Meyer, and Rudnyánszky. By June 1921 its membership had been altered through the addition of Radek, Rosmer, Béla Kun, and Wilhelm Koenen.

### Session 17: Closing rally

1. The closing rally was conducted in Russian. The Russian and French editions of 1921, however, omit any record of this rally, and the Russian edition of 1934 includes only Zinoviev's closing speech. Apart from this last speech, therefore, the translation of this session is taken from the German text.
2. The Finnish Social Democratic Party won a majority in the 1916 elections for a parliament that, under the tsar, had no real authority. Bourgeois parties regained the majority in the October 1917 elections.
3. Wilson was frustrated in several of his attempts to win gains for U.S. capitalist interests in trade and other issues at the Paris conference of Allied powers. He quit the conference in June 1919, leaving the impression that he considered the "humane" peace he had promised in his Fourteen Points to have been sabotaged by the European powers' greed.
4. The Russian soldiers brought to Odessa had been sent to France during World War I to fight on the western front.

Following the outbreak of the Russian revolution, many of the forty thousand Russian troops in France refused to fight. They were imprisoned and put to forced labor by the French authorities.

Soldiers from Senegal and other French colonies made up more than half the armed forces sent by France to the Black Sea to intervene against Soviet Russia. In April 1919 troops on the French ships in the Black Sea port of Sebastopol mutinied, demanding an end to the French intervention.

5. The pood is a Russian unit of weight equal to about 36.1 pounds (16.4 kilograms).
6. The translation of Zinoviev's remarks, taken from the Russian edition of 1934, has been edited on the basis of a comparison with the German text.
7. For a fuller list of countries represented see appendix 1b.
8. See appendix 3b.
9. The published resolutions of the 1920 Geneva congress contain no call for a general strike.
10. In fact, the position Zinoviev refers to here was taken not by the Stuttgart congress as a whole but by its commission on colonialism. The plenary session defeated the commission report by a narrow margin. See Riddell, John, ed., *Lenin's Struggle for a Revolutionary International* (Pathfinder, 1984, 1986), pp. 35–50 [2022 printing].
11. The larger of the two Communist parties in Britain was formed through the fusion of the British Socialist Party and a wing of the Socialist Labour Party at a convention held July 1–August 1, 1920. One month earlier, the Workers' Socialist Federation led by Sylvia Pankhurst had launched a rival Communist party. Other revolutionary currents stood aside from both groups. A united Communist Party was finally established at a January 1921 conference in Leeds.
12. This sentence, excised from the 1934 edition, is taken from the 1921 German edition.
13. This is a reference to the Russian proverb "For the mouse, no beast is mightier than the cat."

14. See "Theses on the Conditions under Which Workers' Councils May Be Formed," in session 15.
15. This is a paraphrase from the General Rules of the First International. See Marx and Engels, *MECW,* vol. 23, p. 3.
16. This is a paraphrase of a passage in the Communist International statutes found in session 14 on pp. 930–31.
17. The First International, founded with the participation of Marx and Engels in 1864, took the name International Working Men's Association.

### Manifesto

1. The manifesto was drafted by Trotsky.
2. The debt of the European Allied powers to the United States was ten billion dollars, not pounds sterling.
3. The National Security League was established in December 1914 by prominent representatives of U.S. capital to push for U.S. entry into World War I. After the war it participated in whipping up antilabor sentiment.
4. Civic League refers to the Civic Unions, gangs organized by the extreme right in France in the first half of 1920.

   In May 1920 the rail workers' strike won the formal support of the French labor federation and spread to other industries. In its zeal to crush the strike, the French government obtained a court order dissolving the labor federation. This order was never enforced, however.
5. This sentence, taken from the Russian edition, is not found in the German text.
6. In January 1920, as a military measure to deal with the extreme economic hardship resulting from the civil war and imperialist intervention, the Soviet government decreed that all working people could be conscripted to carry out various forms of essential labor services. In the first half of 1920 nearly six million people were rallied to chop wood and do other work in the timber industry. Many army units were put to work during this period to carry out urgently needed tasks. See Trotsky, "Problems of the Organization

of Labor," in *Terrorism and Communism,* pp. 128–76. These measures were phased out in 1921 after the end of the civil war.

7. In early 1918 Lenin wrote: "The Taylor system . . . like all capitalist progress, is a combination of the refined brutality of bourgeois exploitation and a number of the greatest scientific achievements in the field of analysing mechanical motions during work, the elimination of superfluous and awkward motions, the elaboration of correct methods of work, the introduction of the best system of accounting and control, etc. The Soviet Republic must at all costs adopt all that is valuable in the achievements of science and technology in this field." Lenin, "The Immediate Tasks of the Soviet Government," in *CW,* vol. 27, p. 259.
8. The list of signatures that follows, not found in the proceedings, is taken from *Communist International,* no. 13 [September 1920], p. 22.
9. In the 1920 Vienna edition of the proceedings, "Williams" appears here instead of Bilan.
10. The 1920 Vienna edition of the proceedings includes "Mexico: R. Allan, F. Seaman."

### Appendix 1: Organizing the congress

1. The Provisional Credentials Commission was established by the Executive Committee before the congress convened. Full minutes of its sessions are not available. The following extract is translated from the 1934 Russian edition of the proceedings.
2. Jesús Ramírez was another pseudonym of Charles Phillips, who attended the congress as a delegate of the Mexican Communist Party under the name Frank Seaman. Phillips had passed through Cuba on the way to the congress, and it may have been proposed that he represent revolutionaries there at the congress. The Communist Party of Cuba was not formed until 1925.
3. See note 6 to this appendix.

4. This is probably a reference to Tom Barker of Britain, who had been active in the IWW in Argentina and Australia and attended the congress.
5. In addition, the Credentials Commission session of July 28 granted consultative votes to Avanesov and Ruben Katanian.
6. The Credentials Commission session of July 17 refused to grant the Austrian Poale Zion voting rights, but admitted two observers as guests. The session of July 28 granted Kohn a consultative vote representing the Socialist Workers Party of Palestine, but in the Credentials Commission report to the congress during session 10 on August 2, Radek noted that a protest had been received that needed to be resolved.
7. In addition to the delegates listed, William Gallacher and Sylvia Pankhurst arrived at the congress after the opening session and actively participated in the debates. John Clarke of the Glasgow Shop Stewards' movement and Tom Barker of the IWW also attended. Helen Crawfurd, sent by the Independent Labour Party left wing, did not arrive until after the congress ended.
8. In addition, Marcel Vergeat and Lepetit (Bertho), syndicalists from the French General Confederation of Labor (CGT), attended the congress as observers. Returning from the congress, they were lost at sea on a fishing boat along with Raymond Lefebvre. The anarchist Mauricius, from Péricat's Communist Party, also attended.
9. Also listed as a Socialist Youth Federation delegate is "Thal," apparently a pseudonym of Goldenberg.
10. Eduard Fuchs of the German Communist Party was also present at the congress.
11. This may be a pseudonym for Wilhelm Herzog, a left-wing member of the USPD, who also attended the congress.
12. Mohammad Shafiq also attended the congress as an observer.
13. The Credentials Commission session of July 28 granted Gell and Johnson full voting status.

14. When D'Aragona, representing the Italian General Confederation of Labor (CGL), refused to certify that this organization would break with the Amsterdam International, he, together with Vacirca, Colombino, and Paverani were refused credentials. D'Aragona, Vacirca, and Colombino then left Moscow on July 29.

15. Jan Proost (Jansen) from the Dutch Communist Party also attended the congress and served on two of its commissions.

16. The July 22, 1920, issue of *Pravda* contains a list of the members of the Russian delegation that includes, in addition to the names that follow, Moshe Rafes, who had led the left wing of the Bund into the Communist Party; Oleksandr Shums'ky, who had led the Ukrainian Borotbists into the CP; and Alekseyev. Names listed below that are not found on the *Pravda* list are Berzin, Blakytnyi, Skrypnyk, and Steklov. The 1921 English edition of the proceedings also lists Mariya Frumkina, who participated in the debates, as a consultative delegate from the Bund. Lev Kamenev, a member of the party's Political Bureau, served on one of the congress commissions.

    In the list of Russian delegates, the indications of the national parties represented is clearly not complete.

17. Other sources identify this delegate as Karl Ernestovich Yanson, a representative of the United Communist Party of the United States.

18. During the congress Edward Lindgren (Flynn) arrived representing the newly formed United Communist Party and was seated as a delegate. Chabrow's credentials were not accepted. Owen Penney, an anarchist, and Jarokoshiharo of the U.S. IWW also attended the congress.

19. The Credentials Commission session of July 28 withdrew Leutner's credentials.

20. Commission membership is taken from the 1934 Russian edition of the congress proceedings, except for the commissions on organizational questions and on translating resolutions, whose memberships are given in the notes of

congress secretaries (as recorded in *Komunisticka internacionala,* vol. 2, p. 478).

21. This is how the Credentials Commission's membership is recorded in the German and the 1921 and 1934 Russian editions of the congress proceedings. In the notes of the congress secretaries, however, Meyer's name is omitted from this list. The French and English editions of the congress proceedings give Serrati's name in place of Meyer. As reported in *Pravda,* the Credentials Commission had a somewhat different makeup, consisting of Rosmer, Bombacci, Bukharin, Radek, Rudnyánszky, Shablin, Marchlewski, and Ahmed Sultanzadeh. The first seven names were given in *Pravda,* July 25, 1920; the addition of Sultanzadeh to the body was reported in the congress supplement to *Pravda, Vestnik 2-go kongressa,* no. 1, July 27, 1920.

### Appendix 2: National and colonial questions

1. The draft version is taken from Adhikari, *Documents of the CPI,* vol. 1, pp. 173–89. The revisions have been identified by comparing this text to the final version found in session 4.
2. The following theses, submitted by Sultanzadeh, formed part of the discussion in the Commission on the National and Colonial Questions. The text is taken from the *Communist* (Communist Party of Great Britain), September 2, 1920.
3. This article by Pak appeared in *Pravda* on July 27, 1920, as part of the Second Congress discussion of the national and colonial questions. It has been translated from *Pravda* and edited after comparison with the German- and English-language versions printed in *Kommunistische Internationale,* no. 12 [August 1920], cols. 2219–22, and in *Communist International,* no. 11/12, June–July 1920, cols. 2315–19.
4. Pak's theses have been translated from the German version printed in *Kommunistische Internationale,* no. 12 [August 1920], cols. 2222–24, and edited after comparison with the text in *Communist International,* no. 11/12, June–July 1920, cols. 2319–20.

5. The following notes of a session of the Commission on the National and Colonial Questions were taken by Safarov and Mikhail Pavlovich. A portion of the notes appear in the congress supplement to *Pravda, Vestnik 2-go kongressa,* no. 1, July 27, 1920. Another, more extensive version is found in the *Communist* (Communist Party of Great Britain), August 26, 1920. The text in this volume is based on both these sources.
6. Kabakchiev is referring to the Balkan wars of 1912–13 and World War I. In both cases Bulgaria was ultimately defeated.
7. Lenin wrote these comments on the typewritten copy of a report by Sultanzadeh apparently prepared for the Commission on the National and Colonial Questions. The text has been taken from Lenin, *CW,* vol. 42, p. 202.
8. The following note by Lenin, which does not appear in the English-language edition of his works, is translated from the original German text found in Lenin, *Polnoye sobraniye sochineniy,* vol. 41, p. 458. No record is available of the proposal by Levi to which Lenin is replying.
9. It appears that Levi had raised objections to the national and colonial draft theses' unconditional defense of oppressed nations against imperialist domination (regardless of the class character of the government or of the leadership of a national movement), comparing this stand to that of a German political current, the "National Bolsheviks." This current, led by Heinrich Laufenberg and Fritz Wolffheim, left the German CP in 1919 as part of the ultraleft split and was expelled from the KAPD in August 1920. The National Bolsheviks opposed "counterrevolutionary civil war" against Germany's capitalists and called instead for unity with the German capitalist class for a "revolutionary people's war" against the Allied powers and the harsh terms of the Versailles treaty.
10. By a "boycott," Lenin means an attempt by workers to refuse or evade compulsory military service.

11. A version of this report was read into the congress record by Connolly during session 5. The present text is taken from *Communist International,* no. 11/12, June–July 1920, cols. 2281–94, and has been edited on the basis of a comparison with the text in the German edition of the magazine.
12. Although Connolly visited the United States briefly in 1902, he did not move there until the following year.
13. For contrasting assessments of the Easter Uprising by Lenin, Radek, and Trotsky, see Riddell, *Lenin's Struggle,* pp. 561–73.
14. At the February 1919 Bern conference, Friedrich Adler and Jean Longuet headed a centrist minority that opposed open condemnation of the Bolsheviks as likely to obstruct the reconstruction of the Second International.

### Appendix 3: Conditions for admission

1. The following condensed records of the July 25 and July 26, 1920, meetings of the Commission on Conditions for Admission to the Communist International are translated from the October 10, 1920, issue of *Rote Fahne.*
2. Zinoviev is referring to the Finnish Socialist Workers Party. See note 3 to the report of the Comintern Executive Committee on page 647.
3. Karl Helfferich gained notoriety in November 1919 through his charge that the USPD had financed the November 1918 German revolution with money obtained from the Soviet embassy.
4. Following the government attack on a January 13, 1920, demonstration in front of the National Assembly, a state of siege was declared in northern Germany, and at least thirty-five USPD newspapers were banned for varying periods of time.
5. An apparent misprint in the original text gives this sentence the opposite meaning.
6. At the Bern meeting, held June 8, Faure proposed the calling of an international conference of Socialist parties. The USPD

representative, who was in fact Wilhelm Koenen, objected that this would seem an attempt to organize a rival to the Comintern. It was ultimately agreed by those present that the French and USPD delegates in Moscow would suggest to the Comintern Executive Committee that it call a conference of all parties to the left of the Second International.

7. At the July 4 National Council meeting, Barthélémy Mayéras and Paul Louis of the Socialist Party majority leadership presented a motion that Cachin and Frossard be authorized to participate in the second Comintern congress; the motion received 2,735 votes. The party's left wing, stressing that Cachin and Frossard did not speak for them, called for abstaining on this motion and was supported by 1,362 votes. Another 454 votes supported a motion by Renaudel that Cachin and Frossard attend the Second International gathering in Geneva.

8. At the July 5–16, 1920, international conference in Spa, Belgium, the Allied powers pressed their claims for German disarmament and war reparations, against vigorous protests by representatives of German capitalism.

9. The theses of Lenin referred to here are probably the five conditions for admission found in his draft of the theses on Comintern tasks. The final version, with two additional conditions, is found in thesis 15 of the resolution on tasks. See session 16, pp. 1014–15. Trotsky's four questions were posed in his article, "To the Forthcoming Congress of the Communist International," *Communist International,* no. 11/12, June–July 1920, cols. 2207–8.

10. Trotsky's question cited Albert Thomas, head of the International Labour Office.

11. According to Frossard, Cachin informed the commission that "the Strasbourg congress has set up a standing propaganda committee in North Africa" to carry out "propaganda on behalf of the natives." Frossard, *Le Parti socialiste,* p. 24. Nonetheless the French Socialist Party in North Africa, which counted very few Arabs among the approximately one thousand members of the party there, failed to speak out against French colonial rule during this period.

12. Trotsky's question asked whether the French Socialists intended to work hand in hand with Rosmer and other revolutionary syndicalists to combat the right-wing majority in the syndicalist union federation.
13. The reference is to the "Theses on the Conditions for Admission," in session 16, pp. 1021–29.
14. Cachin is referring to the French army then occupying the German Rhineland.
15. The reference is to events during the Kapp putsch in the spring of 1920.
16. Dittmann is referring to Trotsky's book *Terrorism and Communism,* written in reply to a book by Kautsky of the same name.
17. The reference here is to the prominent role of USPD members in the antiwar strikes by one million workers that swept across Germany in late January 1918.
18. Theobald von Bethmann-Hollweg (1856–1921), German chancellor from 1909 to 1917, played a leading role in the secret diplomatic maneuvers that unleashed World War I and in the public explanations that the German government had carried out nothing more than unavoidable acts of self-defense.
19. See Radek's speech in session 6 on July 29 and Dittmann's reply in session 7.
20. Philipp Scheidemann was cochairman of the SPD, whose governmental coalition lost its majority in the June 6, 1920, elections. Alarmed at the USPD's major inroads among its former supporters, the SPD proposed that the two Social Democratic parties form a joint government. When the USPD rejected this offer, the SPD decided against forming another coalition with the openly bourgeois parties, and went into opposition.
21. Subheads have been adapted from those found in *Rote Fahne*. The numbering of the theses has been changed to conform to that of the final text of the Twenty-one Conditions.
22. Thesis 2 was omitted from the German text published in *Brennende Tagesfragen,* which served as the basis for the

commission's discussion. Meyer introduced this point by translating the missing thesis from the French text.

23. In *Rote Fahne,* this paragraph was placed in the discussion on thesis 3, following Dittmann's remarks.

24. In both the draft and final texts of thesis 7, Kautsky and other centrists are referred to as "notorious opportunists."

25. Thesis 12 in the draft resolution is incorporated into thesis 1 in the final text.

26. In October 1916 the SPD right-wing majority leadership arranged for the German government to seize *Vorwärts,* then controlled by centrists. The government turned the paper over to the party's Executive Committee, which soon reopened it under right-wing control. In subsequent months the majority leadership took over most of the remaining opposition SPD newspapers.

27. See thesis 20, in session 16, p. 1021.

28. The circumstances in which this letter was written are discussed in the section of the Introduction on the Twenty-one Conditions. The text has been translated from the Russian edition of 1934, which reprints the Russian text originally published July 29, 1920. Three days before its publication, a French-language version of the letter, which differed in some respects, had been given to Cachin and Frossard; it can be found in Frossard, *Le Parti socialiste,* pp. 30–38. The present translation has been edited after comparison with the French text.

29. Cachin and Frossard's reports are printed in *Kommunistische Internationale,* no. 12 [August 1920], cols. 2131–42, and in Frossard, *Le Parti socialiste,* pp. 9–15, 18–20.

30. French troops participated in the Entente military thrust from Greece into Bulgarian-occupied Serbia in September 1918. After Bulgaria's surrender these Entente forces were used to crush incipient workers' and peasants' councils in Serbia. In 1920–21 the French government organized the "Little Entente," a military alliance between Czechoslovakia, Yugoslavia, and Romania, to promote the interests of French capitalism in the area.

31. When eighteen deputies of the German SPD broke party discipline in March 1916 by voting against continued war credits, they set in motion a chain of events that led to a split in the SPD the following year and the formation of a separate party, the USPD.
32. See Frossard, *Le Parti socialiste,* p. 14.
33. In fact, no such trade union conference was held until July 1921, when the congress convened that founded the Red International of Labor Unions.
34. No disciplinary action was taken against Kautsky or others of the USPD right wing, although after the Leipzig congress some of them resigned. Kautsky himself withdrew from the party in all but name until after its split later in 1920.
35. This paragraph is not found in the text of the letter in Frossard, *Le Parti socialiste.*
36. After receiving the text of this letter, Frossard and Cachin wrote the Executive Committee as follows:

   "Moscow

   "July 29, 1920

   "We have read your appeal to the French Socialist Party. We will give your document all the publicity you ask—it will be submitted to all branches of the party. As for us, we must express our reservations on its form and on the ramifications of several of the judgments it contains. But we came to you here mandated to carry out only a mission of investigation. We will submit all the details to our party, which has the final say.

   "We extend our cordial thanks to our comrades of the Third International for the fraternal welcome they gave us during the six weeks of our stay in Russia.

   "L.-O. Frossard and M. Cachin"

   Frossard, *Le Parti socialiste,* p. 29.

### Appendix 4: Trade unions and factory committees

1. This statement was drafted by Zinoviev, probably in collaboration with John Reed, the one central leader of the U.S.

Communists who was in the Soviet republic at the time. The text has been taken from the August 14, 1920, issue of the U.S. IWW paper *Solidarity* and has been checked against the Russian version in *Kommunisticheskiy internatsional,* no. 9 [April 1920], cols. 1369–82.

2. A massive campaign to organize steelworkers was undertaken in 1919 by a committee working within the AFL. At one stage in the drive, the committee prevailed upon President Wilson to ask Elbert H. Gary, head of U.S. Steel Corporation, to meet with the workers' representatives. Gary refused. The ensuing strike involved at its peak about 365,000 workers in several states. The workers were eventually defeated, in part by ferocious repression on the part of the Pennsylvania State Constabulary, dubbed "cossacks" by the largely immigrant workers.

3. In November 1916 a vigilante gang organized by sawmill owners in Everett, Washington, fired on several hundred workers on their way to an IWW-organized free speech rally. The vigilantes killed at least five and wounded thirty-one, and seventy-four of the survivors were arrested.

   On November 5, 1917, eleven IWW organizers working in an oil field near Tulsa, Oklahoma, were arrested and turned over to vigilantes, who whipped them, tarred and feathered them, and drove them out of town at gunpoint.

   On August 3, 1913, police attacked a peaceful gathering of more than two thousand farm workers organized by the IWW in Wheatland, California. In the ensuing melee, four were killed, including two of the attackers. Two IWW organizers, Richard Ford and Herman Suhr, were framed up for murder and sentenced to life in prison.

   On November 11, 1919 (Armistice Day), the Centralia, Washington, American Legion chapter attacked the local IWW headquarters. One IWW militant, Wesley Everest, was captured by the legionnaires, castrated, and lynched. Seven others were framed up for trying to defend the hall, convicted, and sentenced to long prison terms.

4. In 1919 railroad union officials had an attorney, Glenn E. Plumb, draw up a plan for the federal government to buy

the railroads from their private owners and to sponsor a corporation to run them. The 1920 AFL convention backed the plan, over Gompers's opposition. When the proposal was introduced into the U.S. Congress, it died in committee.

5. Numerous local and statewide political parties based on the trade unions were established during 1918–20. The most important were the Cook County Labor Party in Chicago and the American Labor Party in the New York City area. Formation of a national labor party was blocked, however, by the opposition of Gompers and other top leaders of the AFL. See Dobbs, Farrell, *Revolutionary Continuity: Birth of the Communist Movement* (Pathfinder, 1983), pp. 167–75 [2019 printing].
6. This idea was expressed numerous times by Marx. See for example, "Manifesto of the Communist Party," in *MECW,* vol. 6, p. 493. See also *The Communist Manifesto,* Pathfinder, p. 42.
7. This statement was drafted by Serrati. The circumstances in which it was adopted are discussed in the section of the Introduction on the trade union debate.
8. The "nonpolitical" unions mentioned here are syndicalist associations, which traditionally rejected any alignment with political parties. The majority leadership of some of these unions, such as those in France, supported their national ruling class during World War I.
9. These statutes were adopted in conjunction with the launching on July 15, 1920, of the International Council of Trade and Industrial Unions. The text has been taken from Lozovsky, *International Council,* pp. 53–55. It has been edited after comparison with the German version in Lozovsky, *Der Internationale Rat,* pp. 75–77, and compared with another version printed in an article by J.T. Murphy, in *Kommunistische Internationale,* no. 14 [1921], pp. 210–11.
10. This sentence is missing from the version reported by Murphy in *Kommunistische Internationale,* no. 14 [1921]. Fraina had raised objections on this topic in his minority report on the trade unions during session 11.

11. This statement was written after the congress by Lozovsky and adopted by the Comintern Executive Committee. It incorporates the ideas contained in an August 1 statement by the International Council of Trade and Industrial Unions, which is found in the 1934 Russian edition of the proceedings.
12. A conference, sponsored by the League of Nations International Labour Office, brought representatives of employers and governments together with right-wing union officials in Washington, D.C., from October 29 to November 29, 1919. Recommendations included the forty-eight-hour workweek (but not for China, India, Iran, Japan, Thailand, or Greece), unpaid pregnancy leave for women, and an end to child labor.
13. Up to this point the Presiding Committee statement closely follows the August 1 statement of the International Council of Trade and Industrial Unions. Material from this point on, especially concerning growth of the unions and the importance of Communists' participation in them, is not found in the August 1 statement.

### Appendix 5: The agrarian question

1. This article was published as part of the discussion preparatory to the Second Congress. The differences between the policy toward the small-scale and middle peasantry reflected in this document and that proposed by Lenin's draft theses on the agrarian question were the main focus of discussion in the congress commission on the agrarian question. The text of Marchlewski's article is translated from *Kommunistische Internationale,* no. 12 [August 1920], cols. 2085–94.
2. The term *Great Russia* referred to the territory inhabited chiefly by Russian speakers, who made up less than half the population of the pre-1917 Russian Empire.
3. In the 1890s and subsequently, the revisionist wing of the German Social Democracy oriented toward winning the support of the richer peasants and tended to glorify the virtues of small-scale farming.

4. The following is the draft resolution submitted by the Executive Committee to the Commission on the Agrarian Question of the Second Congress. The text is taken from Lenin, *CW,* vol. 31, pp. 152–64. The final, revised text of this resolution appears in session 13 on pp. 885–98.

## Appendix 6: Communist women's movement

1. This appeal was adopted by the International Conference of Communist Women, which was held July 30–August 2, during the Second Congress. About two dozen delegates attended from close to twenty countries. The conference appeal was first published in *Pravda,* on August 6, 1920. The text here is translated from the 1934 Russian edition of the congress proceedings.
2. A number of capitalist countries granted women the right to vote in the years just preceding the congress, including the Netherlands (1917); Austria, Czechoslovakia, Poland, and Sweden (1918); Germany and Luxembourg (1919); and the United States (1920).
3. Demonstrations in Petrograd marking International Working Women's Day on March 8, 1917 (February 23, old style), initiated the revolutionary uprising that toppled the tsar.
4. An initial draft for this resolution was sent to Moscow by Clara Zetkin, who was then living in Germany. An expanded version was submitted by the Russian delegation to the July 30–August 2 International Conference of Communist Women. The draft was then referred to an editing commission headed by Zetkin, which made few substantive changes. The reworked resolution found here was adopted by the Executive Committee and published later in 1920. This translation is taken from *Kommunistische Internationale,* no. 15 [1921], pp. 530–55, and has been edited after comparison with the draft found in the 1934 Russian edition of the congress proceedings.
5. For the First Congress resolution, see Riddell, John, ed., *Founding the Communist International* (Pathfinder, 1987), pp. 347–48 [2021 printing].

6. The previous two sentences are taken from the Russian draft. The German text reads: "The goal is to ensure all women can develop, in their education and employment and as mothers, every aspect of their full human personality linked by bonds of solidarity with society as a whole, so that they may achieve complete and unrestricted social rights. The goal is to create the social preconditions for achieving the new order, so that the proletariat may attain the unity and strength required for the revolutionary struggle against the bourgeois system and the revolutionary construction of the new order."
7. The resolution is referring to the entry of women in large numbers into any highly paid profession, a process that tends to break down its character as a male job trust and reduce its privileges.
8. In 1911 a bill was introduced into the British Parliament, backed by Labour deputies among others, which proposed limited women's suffrage based on a property qualification that would have excluded working-class women from the vote.
9. See *Stuttgart* 1907, pp. 40–48 and 120–23, and Lenin, "The International Socialist Congress in Stuttgart," in *CW,* vol. 13, pp. 89–91.
10. The only international Social Democratic body that took action against the betrayal by the Second International's leadership in August 1914 was the International Bureau of Socialist Women, headed by Clara Zetkin. It called an international conference, held March 26–28, 1915, where delegates from seven countries adopted the resolution summarized in this paragraph. The resolution is printed in Riddell, *Lenin's Struggle,* pp. 423–26. In May 1917 the SPD Executive Committee removed Clara Zetkin from editorship of the women's magazine, *Gleichheit* (Equality), which served to coordinate the international Socialist women's movement, because of the campaign against the World War she had carried out in its pages.
11. International Socialist women's conferences were held simultaneously with the 1907 and 1910 congresses of the Second International. In 1907 a coordinating center for

the International Bureau of Socialist Women was set up within the *Gleichheit* editorial board. These structures were often called the Socialist Women's International.

12. An International Communist Women's Secretariat had been established by the Executive Committee in April 1920 as a section of the Comintern, with Clara Zetkin as its secretary. On August 8, 1920, Aleksandra Kollontai was appointed the secretariat's representative on the Executive Committee. Following the initial conference in 1920, further international conferences of Communist women were held in 1921 and 1924. In April 1921 the secretariat began publication of *Kommunistische Fraueninternationale* (Communist women's International), a monthly magazine edited by Zetkin and published in Germany. After 1923 the magazine appeared irregularly; in 1925 it ceased publication.

### Appendix 7: Theses on the youth movement

1. These theses were drafted by Communist Youth International Executive Committee members Shatskin of Russia and Luigi Polano of Italy shortly before the second Comintern congress. The congress was not able to discuss the theses, but they were taken up by a conference held August 7–10, 1920, of youth delegates who had attended the congress. The theses were adopted August 13, 1920, by the new Comintern Executive Committee at a joint meeting with youth representatives; they were published in 1921. The text is translated from *Kommunistische Internationale,* no. 14 [1921], pp. 311–13.

# Chronology

### 1917

**November 7** – Bolshevik-led insurrection establishes workers' and peasants' government in Russia.

### 1918

**Summer** – Imperialist armies invade Russia on several fronts; Russian landlords and capitalists launch civil war against workers' and peasants' government.

**November 9** – German workers' and soldiers' uprising overthrows kaiser, opening revolution in Germany and central Europe.

**December 30** – Communist Party of Germany founded in Berlin.

### 1919

**January 5** – Uprising of Berlin workers begins against repressive actions of SPD government.

**January 15** – Luxemburg and Liebknecht murdered by SPD-instigated Freikorps.

**February 3–10** – International conference of right-wing and centrist Social Democratic parties in Bern, Switzerland.

**March 2–6** – Founding congress of Communist International in Moscow.

**March–April** – Broad strike movement in Egypt against British colonial domination.

**Early 1919** – Extended wave of strikes, land occupations, and other mass protests opens in Italy.

**March 1–April** – Massive uprising in Korea against Japanese occupation.

**March 19** – Italian Socialist Party breaks with Second International and resolves to join the Comintern.

**March 21** – Hungarian Communist and Social Democratic parties fuse; workers' and soldiers' councils take power in Budapest.

**March–April** – Rising wave of mass opposition to British domination in India met by massacre at Amritsar; hundreds killed by British troops.

**April–May** – French and British intervention troops forced to withdraw from southern Russia.

**April 13–27** – German Communists lead workers' and soldiers' government in Bavaria.

**May** – First issue of *Communist International* magazine published in Moscow.

**May 3** – Beginning of Afghanistan war of independence from British domination.

**May 4** – Student demonstration in Beijing protesting Allied powers' violations of Chinese sovereignty launches broad revolutionary upsurge for national liberation.

**June 7–10** – Norwegian Labor Party congress votes to quit Second International and join Comintern.

**June 16–July 7** – Soviet republic established in Slovakia with support of Hungarian Red Army.

**June 28** – Treaty of Versailles signed.

**July 20–21** – Solidarity strikes in several European countries opposing imperialist intervention against soviet Hungary and Russia.

**July 28–August 2** – Amsterdam trade union International founded.

**August 1** – Hungarian soviet republic overthrown.

**August 1–9** – Right-wing and centrist Social Democrats meet in Lucerne, Switzerland.

**September 1–2** – Communist Party of America and Communist Labor Party founded in Chicago.

**September 22–January 8** – Strike of up to 365,000 steelworkers in U.S.

**October 5–8** – Italian SP holds congress in Bologna.

**October 20–23** – Split with ultralefts at German CP Heidelberg congress.

**November 1–December 9** – Up to 400,000 miners strike in U.S.

**November 16** – Italian SP wins 32 percent of vote in national parliamentary elections.

**November 20–26** – Communist Youth International founded in Berlin.

**November 30–December 6** – USPD holds congress in Leipzig.

## 1920

**Early 1920** – British government introduces "Black and Tans," a special police force that terrorizes rising Irish independence struggle.

**January 2** – Thousands of supposed Communists arrested in U.S. in largest of raids organized by Attorney General Palmer; hundreds of immigrant workers subsequently deported.

**January 13** – German security police fire on demonstration in Berlin, killing 42.

**February** – 71,000 Black miners strike in South Africa for higher wages and against color bar.

**February 25–29** – French SP holds congress in Strasbourg.

**March 13** – Kapp putsch in Berlin met by general strike of German workers.

**March 17** – General strike topples Kapp regime in Berlin.

**April–May** – Alvaro Obregón launches uprising that topples Carranza regime in Mexico.

**April 5** – Two-day general strike in Ireland wins release of 100 political prisoners.

**April 13–24** – 500,000 workers participate in general strike in Turin, Italy.

**April 22** – Comintern Executive Committee decides to call Second Congress.

**April 23** – Rebel Turkish government established in Ankara to fight for national independence.

**April 24** – Polish government launches attack against the Ukraine.

**May 1–28** – General strike by rail workers in France, supported by other unions, ends in defeat.

**May 5** – Anarchists Sacco and Vanzetti arrested, framed up in U.S.

**May 7** – Polish army occupies Kiev.

**May 11** – British trade union delegation arrives in Moscow.

**May 14** – Red Army launches counteroffensive against Polish invasion.

**June 5** – Soviet government established in Gilan, northern Iran.

**June 6** – USPD scores major gains in elections to German Reichstag.

Italian SP and trade union delegation arrives in Petrograd; reaches Moscow June 15.

White General Wrangel launches offensive against Soviet republic from Crimea.

**June 12** – Polish army forced to evacuate Kiev.

**June 14** – Comintern Executive Committee announces that Second Congress will convene July 15.

**June 16** – French SP delegation arrives in Moscow.

Russian, British, and Italian trade unionists hold first of several discussions in Moscow on forming revolutionary trade union International.

**June 22** – Communist Party of Iran founded in Enzeli, Iran.

**June 29** – Comintern Executive Committee issues call for Congress of Peoples of the East in Baku.

**June 30** – Mass uprising begins in Iraq against British domination.

**July** – Faisal I, leader of Arab revolt, driven from Damascus by French army.

**July 15** – Provisional International Council of Trade and Industrial Unions formed in Moscow.

**July 19** – Second Comintern congress opens in Petrograd; moves to Moscow July 23.

**July 21** – Comintern Executive Committee meets with delegates from USPD two days after their arrival in Russia.

**July 29** – French SP delegation and Italian trade union leader D'Aragona leave Moscow.

**July 30** – Polish provisional revolutionary government established in Bialystok.

**July 30–August 2** – International Conference of Communist Women held in Moscow.

**July 31–August 5** – Right-wing Social Democrats meet in Geneva.

**August 1** – Beginning of noncooperation campaign in India against British rule.

**August 7** – Closing session of second Comintern congress in Moscow.

**August 16** – Red Army forced to retreat by counterattack of Polish government forces.

**Late August–September** – Mass strikes, factory and land occupations in Italy.

**September 1–7** – Comintern congress of Eastern peoples held in Baku.

**October 12–17** – USPD splits at Halle congress, majority votes to accept Twenty-one Conditions and join Comintern.

**December 25–30** – French SP splits at Tours congress, majority changes name to CP.

## 1921

**January 15–21** – Italian SP splits at Livorno congress, minority forms CP.

# Glossary to both volumes

**Abramovich, Aleksandr Yemelyanovich (b. 1888)** – joined RSDLP 1908; Bolshevik; Comintern emissary to central and western Europe from 1919; French CP delegate to second Comintern congress; deported from France 1921; worked in Comintern staff until 1931, then in Russian CP staff; retired 1961.

**Acharya, M. Pratiwadi Bhayankar (b. 1888)** – joined Indian revolutionary group in Britain before World War I; leader of Indian Revolutionary Association in soviet Tashkent 1919, which he represented as consultative delegate at second Comintern congress; a founder and Central Committee member of Indian CP in Tashkent 1920; member of Indian CP bureau abroad in Berlin 1922; developed anarcho-syndicalist views and left Comintern 1920s.

**Adler, Friedrich (1879–1960)** – led opposition in Austrian SDP to collaboration with government war policy during World War I; assassinated Austro-Hungarian Prime Minister Stürgkh as protest against war 1916; played key role in limiting left-wing split in SDP; opposed foundation of Comintern; principal organizer and president of Two-and-a-Half International 1921–23; secretary of Socialist International 1923–39.

**Adler, Victor (1852–1918)** – a leader of Austrian SDP and of European Social Democracy from 1880s until his death; chauvinist during World War I; foreign minister of provisional government after collapse of monarchy October 1918.

**AFL** – *see* American Federation of Labor.

**Akhundov, Rukhulla (1897–1938)** – newspaper editor from Azerbaijan; joined Russian CP 1919; Russian CP delegate to second Comintern congress; secretary of Azerbaijani CP 1924–30; shot during Stalin's frame-up purges.

**Aliyev, B.** – Bolshevik delegate to second Comintern congress; leader of Azerbaijani CP; expelled during Stalin purges.

**Allan, Helen** – *see* Roy, Evelyn.

**Allan-Roy, Robert** – *see* Roy, Manabendra Nath.

**All-Russia Soviet Central Executive Committee** – supreme executive body of Russian soviets; first elected June 1917 with Menshevik and Socialist Revolutionary majority until Bolsheviks won majority at second soviet congress November 7–9 (October 25–27), 1917; highest body of Soviet government after October revolution.

**American Federation of Labor (AFL)** – U.S. craft union federation formed 1881; largely restricted to organizations of skilled workers; membership grew from under 2 million to over 4 million 1915–20; split with rise of Congress of Industrial Organizations 1935–37; merged with latter 1955.

**Amsterdam International** – *see* International Federation of Trade Unions.

**Andreyev, Andrey Andreyevich (1895–1971)** – joined Bolsheviks 1914; member of CP Central Committee 1920–21 and from 1922; supporter of Stalin; CP Political Bureau from 1932; removed 1952.

**Andrews, William H. (1870–1950)** – a founder of International Socialist League of South Africa 1915 and of CP 1921; a leader of Rand strike 1922; expelled as "right opportunist" in early 1930s; later readmitted; remained leader of CP until death.

**Anfu** – militarist faction that controlled Peking government 1918–20 with support of Japan.

**Appleton, William A. (1859–1940)** – secretary of British General Federation of Trade Unions 1907–38; chair of Amsterdam international trade union federation 1919–20.

***Arbejdet* (Labor)** – newspaper of Left SP of Denmark November 1919–May 1921.

**Armand, Inessa (Elizabeth d'Herbenville) (1874–1920)** – born in France; joined RSDLP in Moscow 1904; Bolshevik; in exile from 1909; returned to Russia 1917; headed women's section of party; Bolshevik delegate to second Comintern congress; organized International Conference of Communist Women 1920; died of cholera.

**Artem** – *see* Sergeyev, Fedor Andreyevich.

**Åsen, Augusta (1878–1920)** – secretary of Norwegian Social Democratic Youth League 1912–14; member of Norwegian Labor Party Oslo leadership 1914–20; Central Committee alternate; delegate to second Comintern congress; died in accident in Moscow.

**Aubry, Albert Jules Marie (1892–1951)** – French SP deputy 1919–24; active in SP until death; high officer in French Legion of Honor.

**Avanesov, Varlaam Aleksandrovich (Suren Karpovich Martirosian) (1884–1930)** – joined RSDLP 1903 and Bolsheviks 1914; member of Petrograd Military Revolutionary Committee 1917; member of All-Russia Soviet Central Executive Committee 1917–27; Armenian CP consultative delegate to second Comintern congress; deputy commissar of Workers' and Peasants' Inspection 1920–24.

***Avanti!* (Forward!)** – central organ of Italian SP, founded 1896; banned 1926 and published abroad until 1944.

**Avis** – *see* Nurijanian, Avis.

**Baars, Adolf (1892–1943)** – member of Dutch SDP; moved to Indonesia 1915; leader of Indies Social Democratic Association and Communist Association in the Indies; worked as engineer in Soviet Russia 1921–26 and in Soviet trade mission in Berlin from 1927.

**Balabanoff, Angelica (1878–1965)** – born in Russia; joined Italian SP 1900; secretary of Zimmerwald committee and editor of its *Bulletin* 1917; joined Bolshevik Party 1917; secretary of Comintern 1919–20; ECCI consultative delegate to second Comintern congress; left Russia 1922; broke with communism and rejoined Italian SP.

**Balkan Communist Federation** – Balkan Revolutionary Social Democratic Federation founded July 1915 by Bulgarian (Tesnyaki), Greek, Romanian, and Serbian SDPs opposed to chauvinism and "civil peace"; favored founding new, revolutionary International; renamed Balkan Communist Federation 1920; Comintern coordinating body for Balkan parties until 1930s.

**Bamatter, Siegfried (Sigi) (1892–1966)** – Swiss SDP member; leader of international revolutionary socialist youth organization during World War I and of Communist Youth International from its founding 1919; Swiss SDP youth organization delegate to second Comintern congress; represented Communist Youth International in Europe and U.S. until 1924; subsequently in Comintern apparatus; appointed by Moscow to head Swiss CP during purge of "rightists" 1929; himself purged 1931; died in Moscow.

**Baral, Arnold (Wladyslaw Sawko) (1890–1957)** – anarchist from 1907; East Galician CP member 1919; represented it at second Comintern congress; Central Committee member of CP (Bolsheviks) of the Ukraine 1920 and of Austrian CP from 1921; returned to Russia and worked with Red International of Labor Unions from 1925.

**Barth, Emil (1879–1941)** – German anarchist before 1910; later active in SPD and USPD; chair of Berlin-area Revolutionary Shop Stewards February–November 1918; member of SPD-USPD government November–December 1918; rejoined SPD 1921.

**Barthélémy, Georges (1882–1933)** – French SP parliamentary deputy 1919–24; signed statement opposing Comintern July 1920; went with SP after CP founded 1920.

***Basler Vorwärts*** **(Basel forward)** – Swiss SDP daily newspaper established 1897; daily of SDP left wing, then of CP 1921.

**Bauer, Otto (Heinrich Weber) (1881–1938)** – a leader of Austrian SDP and theoretician of "Austro-Marxism"; foreign minister of German Austria 1918–19; opposed

Comintern and helped found centrist Two-and-a-Half International; remained in SDP until death.

**Bebel, August (1840–1913)** – collaborator of Marx and Engels; founder and central leader of German SPD; prominent in Second International; opposed revisionist current in SPD but eventually adopted centrist positions.

**Beech, Dick (1892–1955)** – delegate from British IWW to second Comintern congress; affiliated with Pankhurst's CP 1920–21; elected to provisional executive committee at CP Leeds unity conference January 1921; active in CP-led trade union Minority Movement mid-1920s; left CP, collaborated with but did not join Left Opposition in Britain; later Chemical Workers' Union president.

**Beika, David Samuelevich (Bernard) (1885–1946)** – joined RSDLP 1903; member of U.S. SP Latvian federation 1908–17; returned to Latvia 1917; official of Comintern Executive Committee 1920–22; Latvian CP consultative delegate to second Comintern congress; member of USSR Council of People's Commissars 1932–37; in Spain during civil war 1937–38; returned to Moscow and was arrested; died in prison camp.

**Belgian Workers Party** – founded 1879 as Socialist Party of Belgium; merged with trade unions and cooperative societies to form Workers Party 1885; took chauvinist position during World War I; 450,000 individual members and 650,000 affiliated through unions and cooperatives May 1920; left-wing currents within party broke away 1919 and 1921 to form two Communist groups that fused to form CP of Belgium September 1921.

**Benisch, Josef (1881–1937)** – Austrian rail worker; a leader of Social Democratic Working Group of Revolutionary Workers Councils, a left tendency in SDP; secretary of Austrian workers' councils' executive body; joined CP 1921.

**Berger, Victor (1860–1929)** – right-wing leader of U.S. SP; held chauvinist, anti-immigrant, and racist positions; opposed SP joining Comintern and argued for rejoining Second International.

***Berliner Tageblatt und Handelszeitung* (Berlin daily news and commerce gazette)** – liberal bourgeois paper founded 1871.

***Berner Tagwacht* (Bern daily herald)** – official organ of Swiss SDP; founded 1893.

**Bern International** – *see* Second International.

**Bernstein, Eduard (1850–1932)** – German Social Democrat; Engels's literary executor; leading exponent of revisionism from 1890s; adopted pacifist stand during World War I; joined USPD 1917; rejoined SPD December 1918; reelected to Reichstag for SPD 1920–28.

**Berzin, Ian Antonovich (1881–1938)** – joined Latvian SDP 1902; Bolshevik; emigrated 1908; represented Latvian party at Zimmerwald where he supported Zimmerwald Left; Bolshevik Central Committee member 1917–18; Comintern Executive Committee secretary 1919–20; Russian CP delegate to second Comintern congress; subsequently active in Comintern and Soviet diplomatic service; arrested during Stalin purges 1937; died in prison.

**Berzins-Andersons, Jan (1875–1934)** – Latvian SDP Central Committee alternate member from 1914; Latvian CP consultative delegate to second Comintern congress.

**Bettelheim, Ernö (1889–1959)** – member of first Hungarian CP Central Committee; claimed to be Comintern emissary and ordered Austrian CP to launch abortive uprising in support of Hungarian soviet republic June 1919; expelled from CP March 1922; lived in Russia until return to Hungary 1945; managed Hungarian CP publishing house until death.

**Bilan, Alexander** – leader of U.S. SP left wing in Ohio; founding member of Communist Labor Party and its delegate to second Comintern congress.

**Bjarnason, Brynjólfur** – *see* Brynjólfur Bjarnason.

**Black Hundreds** – monarchist gangs formed by tsarist police; murdered revolutionaries and organized pogroms against Jews.

**Blakytnyi** – *see* Ellansky, Vasyl.

**Blum, Léon (1872–1950)** – joined Jaurès's French SP 1902; backed chauvinist right wing of party 1914; parliamentary deputy 1919; opposed SP affiliation to Comintern 1920; prime minister of Popular Front government 1936–37; imprisoned during Nazi occupation; leader of SP after World War II.

**Bolsheviks** – *see* Communist Party of Russia (Bolsheviks).

**Bombacci, Nicola (1879–1945)** – Italian SP member before World War I; in SP Maximalist wing led by Serrati during war; represented SP at second Comintern congress; founding member of Italian CP and Central Committee member from 1921; expelled from CP for supporting fascism 1927; supported Mussolini and executed with him.

**Bordiga, Amadeo (1889–1970)** – joined Italian SP 1910; led left faction in SP during World War I; represented "Communist-Abstentionist" SP faction at second Comintern congress; became party head at Italian CP founding congress at Livorno 1921; member Comintern Executive Committee 1922–28; defended Trotsky 1928; expelled from CP 1930; led small ultraleft current until death.

**Borghi, Armando (1882–1968)** – secretary of Italian anarcho-syndicalist union federation (USI), which claimed 800,000 members summer 1920; arrived in Moscow just after second Comintern congress and pledged USI affiliation to Comintern, but remained hostile to Comintern after returning to Italy; emigrated to United States 1926; resumed work in Italian anarcho-syndicalist movement 1945.

**Borotbist party** – *see* Ukrainian Communist Party (Borotbist).

**Brandsteder, Jacobus Andries (b. 1887)** – leader of Dutch sailors' union; moved to Dutch East Indies 1913; a founder of Indies Social Democratic Association and associated with left wing from 1914; functionary in Dutch CP 1919–24; expelled from CP 1929; leader of transport workers' union 1929–45.

**Branting, Hjalmar (1860–1925)** – longtime leader of Swedish Social Democrats; leader of Second International; chauvinist during World War I; prominent in efforts to revive Second International after World War I; Swedish prime minister 1921–23.

**Braun, M.I.** – *see* Brónski, Mieczyslaw.

**Breitscheid, Rudolf (1874–1944)** – German Social Democrat; joined USPD 1917; Prussian interior minister 1918–19; rejoined SPD 1922; died in Nazi concentration camp.

**Bringolf, Walther (1895–1981)** – joined Swiss SDP 1919; represented Swiss SDP left wing at second Comintern congress; Swiss CP founding member 1921; broke with Swiss CP and Comintern 1930; worked with Left Opposition; rejoined SDP late 1930s; elected to high government posts early 1960s.

**British Independents** – *see* Independent Labour Party.

**British Labour Party** – founded as federation of trade unions and Socialist organizations and societies 1906; affiliated to Second International; more than 1.6 million members in 1914, predominantly through union affiliation; supported British imperialism in World War I; 3.5 million members late 1919; 4.25 million late 1920.

**British Socialist Party** – founded through fusion of Social Democratic Federation and other groups 1911; antichauvinist during World War I; right-wing pro-war minority split 1916; 10,000 members early 1919; joined Comintern 1919; majority fused with other groups in August 1920 to found CP of Great Britain.

**Broido, G.I. (1885–1956)** – Menshevik through 1917; chair of Turkestan soviet 1917–18; joined Russian CP 1918; deputy people's commissar of nationalities 1921–23;

a founder of Communist University of the Toilers of the East and its rector until 1926; first secretary of Tadzhikistan CP until 1933; deputy people's commissar of education 1934–41.

**Brónski, Mieczyslaw (M.I. Braun) (1882–1941)** – joined Social Democracy of Poland 1902; emigrated to Switzerland 1907; active in Swiss SDP; represented Polish party at Kienthal conference and supported Zimmerwald Left; participated in Russian October revolution 1917; part of Comintern West European Secretariat in Berlin 1919–21; held government posts in USSR after 1924; arrested 1937, died in prison.

**Brynjólfur Bjarnason (1898–1989)** – attracted to communism as Icelandic student in Europe 1918; observer at second Comintern congress; founding member of Icelandic CP 1930; leader of CP and its successor SP through 1960s; minister in Icelandic government 1944–47.

**BSP** – *see* British Socialist Party.

**Budich, Willi (1890–1941)** – joined German SPD before World War I and Spartacus group during war; founder and leader of Red Soldiers League; German CP delegate to second Comintern congress; officer in Red Army 1920; numerous posts in USSR and in German CP until 1933; arrested and tortured by Hitler's Gestapo 1933; fled to Russia; arrested there 1937; died in prison.

**Bukharin, Nikolai (1888–1938)** – joined Bolsheviks 1906; in exile in western Europe and United States 1911–17; member of Bolshevik Central Committee from 1917; led Left Communist faction of Bolshevik Party 1918; editor of *Pravda* 1919–29; one of main Bolshevik leaders of Comintern 1919–29; headed Right Opposition to Stalin and was expelled from Soviet CP 1929; later recanted and was readmitted; executed on Stalin's orders after third Moscow frame-up trial.

**Bund (General Union of Jewish Workers in Lithuania, Poland, and Russia)** – founded in Vilna 1897; affiliated to RSDLP

1898–1903 and from 1906; advocated "national-cultural autonomy" within capitalist states for Jews from 1905; aligned with liquidators 1907–8 and Mensheviks from 1912; included chauvinist and centrist wings during World War I; Russian group supported Provisional Government after February 1917; opposed October revolution; split by March 1919 and left-wing majority took name Communist Bund; majority joined Bolsheviks 1920; minority soon ceased activity; Polish group split 1921; Communist wing eventually joined Polish CP; right wing continued functioning into World War II.

**Bureau of Communist Organizations** – *see* Central Bureau of Communist Organizations of the Peoples of the East.

**Cachin, Marcel (1869–1958)** – joined Guesde's French Workers Party 1891; French SP member from 1905; chauvinist during World War I; French SP delegate to second Comintern congress; managing editor of *L'Humanité* 1918–58; supported SP joining Comintern 1920; CP Political Bureau member 1923–58.

**Cadets (Constitutional Democrats)** – liberal bourgeois party in Russia founded 1905; supported constitutional monarchy; participated in Russian Provisional Government 1917; worked for overthrow of Soviet government after October revolution.

***The Call*** – published in London 1916–20; founded by left wing of British SP; later organ of party leadership; merged with the *Communist* August 1920.

**Carranza, Venustiano (1859–1920)** – president of Mexico during Mexican revolution 1914–20; opposed implementing land reform championed by Pancho Villa and Emiliano Zapata; ousted by uprising led by Alvaro Obregón.

**Center Party (Zentrum)** – German bourgeois party founded 1870, supported privileges for Catholic hierarchy.

**Central Bureau of Communist Organizations of the Peoples of the East** – coordinating body for groups of Communists working among Asian minority peoples in Soviet republics; affiliated to Russian CP; sent delegates to first and second Comintern congresses.

**Ceton, Jan Cornelis (1875–1943)** – secretary of Dutch Social Democratic Workers Party; editor of opposition *Tribune* newspaper from 1908; part of left-wing split that formed Social Democratic Party 1909; later joined CP.

**Chen Duxiu (Ch'en Tu-hsiu) (1879–1942)** – took part in Chinese bourgeois revolution of 1911; a central leader of May 4 Movement against terms of Versailles treaty 1919; CP founder 1920 and general secretary 1920–27; removed from leadership positions 1927; expelled from CP and a founding leader of Chinese Left Opposition group 1929; imprisoned by Kuomintang 1932–37; broke with communism 1941.

**Chernov, Mikhail Aleksandrovich (1891–1938)** – Menshevik from 1909, later associated with Martov; left Mensheviks; joined Russian CP early 1920; Russian CP delegate to second Comintern congress; CP Central Committee member 1934 until purged.

**Chernov, Viktor Mikhailovich (1873–1952)** – a founder and central leader of Russian Socialist Revolutionary (SR) Party; opposed October revolution; chair of Constituent Assembly 1918; active in SR-led antisoviet regime in Samara (Kuibyshev) 1918; emigrated 1920.

**Chicherin, Georgiy Vasilevich (1872–1936)** – tsarist diplomat until 1904; supported 1905 revolution and joined RSDLP in exile; Menshevik before 1914; antichauvinist during World War I; returned to Russia January 1918 and joined Bolsheviks; people's commissar of foreign affairs 1918–30; key organizer of first Comintern congress.

**Chinese Socialist Workers Party** – formed January 1919 by Chinese workers living in Russia who led the Union of Chinese Workers. *See also* Socialist Party (Shanghai).

**Chkheidze, Nikolai Semyonovich (1864–1926)** – Menshevik leader in Russia and Georgia; chairman of Petrograd soviet after February revolution 1917; chairman of Georgian Constituent Assembly 1918–21; emigrated 1921.

**Christian Socialist Party** – Hungarian party representing higher clergy, monarchy, and landowners; organized alternative labor unions to counter CP influence after fall of soviet republic.

**Churchill, Winston (1874–1965)** – British Conservative Party politician; key in prolonging British intervention against Soviet Russia 1919–20.

**Clemenceau, Georges (1841–1929)** – French prime minister, 1906–9, 1917–20; chief organizer of 1919 Paris conference and architect of Treaty of Versailles.

**Cohn, Oskar (1869–1937)** – German Social Democrat; joined USPD 1917; adviser to Soviet embassy in Berlin 1918; rejoined SPD 1922; lawyer for Trotsky's son Leon Sedov early 1930s; fled Nazis to Soviet Union 1933; arrested and disappeared during Moscow trials.

**Colombino, Emilio (1884–1933)** – joined Italian SP before 1905; part of Italian General Confederation of Labor (CGL) delegation to Soviet Russia May–July 1920; SP consultative delegate to second Comintern congress but walked out during congress; critical of Soviet regime on his return; collaborated with fascist government from 1923.

**Committee for the Third International (France)** – established May 1919 from fusion of syndicalist and anarchist forces with Committee for the Resumption of International Relations, which had been formed January 1916 to support ideas of Zimmerwald in France; its members promoted Comintern from within existing parties and unions; dissolved mid-1921.

**Committee to Reconstruct the International (France)** – centrist current in French SP calling for unification of parties that had left Second International but had not joined Comintern, those of Comintern, and forces in Second International; organized by Longuet, Frossard, Faure, and others December 1919; opposed Twenty-one Conditions; split in two September 1920; when SP split December 1920, Frossard wing joined CP, Longuet wing joined SP.

***Communismo*** – Italian SP newspaper published twice monthly in Milan; edited by Serrati.

**Communist Association in the Indies** – Indies Social Democratic Association took this name May 1920; 1,300 members with dominant influence in trade unions 1922; changed name to Communist Party of Indonesia 1924.

**Communist Bund** – *see* Bund.

**Communist Federation of Soviets (France)** – *see* Communist Party (France).

***The Communist International*** – official magazine of Comintern, published in German, Russian, French, and English 1919–39.

**Communist Labor Party (U.S.)** – founded September 1919 by former members of SP left wing led by Reed and Benjamin Gitlow with 10,000 members; joined Comintern; 3,000 members early 1920; fused with Ruthenberg group of CP of America to form United Communist Party with 4,000 members May 1920; fused with remainder of CP 1921.

**Communist League (Australia)** – formed late 1918 by fusion of members of Queensland Industrial Trade Union Council, Queensland Socialist League, One Big Union Propaganda League, and League of Russian Workers in Australia; took name CP in unsuccessful merger with SP late 1920; CP and SP participated in third Comintern congress; SP disintegrated and many members joined CP 1922.

**Communist Party (Bolsheviks) of the Ukraine** – originated out of first Ukraine Bolshevik structure established December 1917; held first congress as autonomous component of Russian CP with 4,000 members July 1918; 23,000 members March 1919; 75,000 1920.

**Communist Party (France)** – originated out of small group influenced by anarchism formed by Raymond Péricat June 1919; split into Communist Federation of Soviets and CP December 1919; both groups hostile to CP of France by 1921. *See also* Socialist Party of France.

**Communist Party in the Netherlands** – originated from Dutch SDP, formed by expelled left-wing *Tribune* group of Social Democratic Workers Party 1909; leaders aligned with Zimmerwald Left during World War I; became CP November 17, 1918; 1,000 members late 1918; joined Comintern April 1919; claimed 3,000–4,000 members 1920.

**Communist Party of America** – founded by former members of SP left wing representing language federations, Ruthenberg-Fraina group, and Michigan organization with more than 20,000 members September 1, 1919; Michigan group split away January 1920 and degenerated into sect; 5,000 members early 1920, Ruthenberg minority split and fused with Communist Labor Party to form United Communist Party with 4,000 members May 1920; remainder of CP fused with United CP 1921; 12,000 members 1921.

**Communist Party of Armenia** – originated out of Caucasus regional committee of Russian CP 1918; Communists in Armenia worked in Armenian component of Russian CP with 400 members 1919; CP of Armenia founded 1920; 3,000 members summer 1920; headed Armenian soviet republic from December 1920.

**Communist Party of Austria** – initial nucleus founded November 3, 1918; strengthened in following months by fusions; 3,000 members at first congress February 1919; 40,000 members June 1919; 14,000 1921.

**Communist Party of Azerbaijan** – founded with 4,000 members at underground congress February 1920; first Marxist circles in Baku 1898; Bolsheviks active in Azerbaijan from 1903; led Baku soviet regime November 1917–

July 1918; functioned underground until soviet power reestablished April 1920.

**Communist Party of Bukhara** – organized November 1918; Bukhara People's Soviet Republic proclaimed in city of Bukhara October 1920; civil war continued in eastern Bukhara until late 1922; led formation of Tadzhik Autonomous Soviet Socialist Republic October 1924.

**Communist Party of Bulgaria** – originated in Social Democratic Party of Bulgaria, which was founded 1891; it split into revolutionary Tesnyaki (Narrow) and opportunist Shiroki (Broad) wings 1903; Tesnyaki won mass support during World War I; joined Comintern and changed name to CP May 1919; 35,000 members 1920.

**Communist Party of Czechoslovakia** – founded in Russia among soldiers in Red Army from Czechoslovakia as section of Russian CP May 1918; headed by Alois Muna; most members returned to Czechoslovak SDP 1918 and became part of its Marxist Left faction, which founded CP 1921. *See also* Social Democratic Party of Czechoslovakia; Czechoslovak Communist Group.

**Communist Party of Denmark** – revolutionary wing of Social Democratic Party of Denmark formed Socialist Workers Party of Denmark April 1918; Independent Social Democratic Party of Denmark also formed April 1918; these two groups fused with revolutionary SDP youth to form Left SP of Denmark November 1919; joined Comintern, took name CP of Denmark November 1920; 1,200 members 1921.

**Communist Party of Estonia** – originated from RSDLP Revel (Tallinn) committee formed 1904; Estonian component of Bolshevik Party had 10,000 members late 1917; led Estonian soviet governments November 1917–February 1918 and November 1918–January 1919; 700 members represented at first congress November 1920; underground until Estonia's incorporation into USSR under Stalin-Hitler Pact 1940.

**Communist Party of Finland** – originated in left wing of Finnish SDP, which won majority early 1918 and led unsuccessful revolution; forced into exile by White Terror; CP founded in Moscow August 29, 1918; banned in Finland until after World War II; underground Communists in Finland participated in left-wing split from SDP that founded Socialist Workers Party of Finland May 1920.

**Communist Party of France** – *see* Communist Party (France).

**Communist Party of Galicia and Bukovina** – originated as Communist Party of East Galicia through fusion of several local Communist groups February 1919; admitted to Comintern August 1919; participated with CP of Ukraine–sponsored group in forming CP of Galicia, which headed Galician soviet republic July–August 1920; affiliated to CP of the Ukraine, then to Polish CP late 1920; split on Ukrainian national question 1921, reunited 1923; 1,500 members 1923; became CP of West Ukraine 1923; leadership expelled from Comintern 1928.

**Communist Party of Georgia** – originated from first Marxist Social Democratic organization, Mesame-dasi, established in Tiflis 1892; Tiflis committee of RSDLP established 1898; Bolsheviks driven underground by Menshevik regime February 1918; CP founded as component of Russian CP May 1920; 9,000 members early 1921; led formation of soviet regime February 1921; 16,000 members 1925.

**Communist Party of Germany (Spartacus League)** – founded December 30, 1918, by Spartacus League with participation of International Communists of Germany; joined Comintern 1919; lost half its membership in 1919 split of ultraleft forces; 66,000 members July 1920; 350,000 members after fusion with USPD left wing December 1920.

**Communist Party of Great Britain** – founded July 31, 1920, by Socialist Labour Party and British Socialist Party; joined by several communist and radical groups around William Gallacher, Sylvia Pankhurst, and others January 1921; about 4,000 members 1921.

**Communist Party of Hungary** – founded November 1918; claimed 10,000 members January 1919; fused with SDP to form Socialist Party March 1919, which led Hungarian revolutionary government March–July 1919; SP disintegrated; CP severely repressed, functioned in exile and isolated cells in Hungarian SDP 1919–25; 250 members in Hungary late 1921; reorganized September 1925.

**Communist Party of India** – founded in exile in Tashkent by M.N. Roy and six other émigré revolutionaries October 1920; Communist groups functioning in India by 1922; party reorganized within India December 1925.

**Communist Party of Iran** – founded in Baku as Adalet (Justice) Party 1916; changed name to CP at first congress in Enzeli with several thousand members and supporters June 1920; joined Comintern soon after; destroyed under intense repression by monarchy from 1925 and Stalin in 1930s.

**Communist Party of Ireland** – *see* Socialist Party of Ireland.

**Communist Party of Korea** – originated from first Korean Communist groups formed in Soviet Siberia 1918–19; rival factions in Irkutsk and Shanghai wracked by dispute for several years from 1919; first Communist groups established inside Korea 1921; first Korean CP organized in Seoul April 1925.

**Communist Party of Latvia** – originated in Social Democracy of the Latvian Territory, which affiliated to RSDLP 1904 and allied with Bolsheviks; 1,000 members February 1917; led Latvian soviet republic November 1917–February 1918 and again 1919; took name CP March 1919; soviet republic overthrown by German and Entente intervention May 1919; 7,500 members 1919.

**Communist Party of Lithuania-Belorussia** – originated in Lithuanian SDP founded 1896; fused with Polish SDP 1899;

Lithuanian CP founded as component of Russian CP August 1918; first congress, representing 800 members, held underground October 1918; led Lithuanian soviet republic December 1918–April 1919; underground 1919–40; Belorussian CP founded as component of Russian CP December 1918; led Belorussian soviet republic from January 1919; 1,700 members November 1920; Lithuanian and Belorussian CPs functioned as united organization 1918–20.

**Communist Party of Mexico** – *see* Mexican Communist Party.

**Communist Party of Poland** – *see* Communist Workers Party of Poland.

**Communist Party of Russia (Bolsheviks)** – originated from Russian Social Democratic Labor Party founded 1898; majority (Bolshevik) faction originated at second congress 1903; led 1917 October revolution and establishment of soviet government; changed name to CP March 1918; 611,000 members April 1920.

**Communist Party of Spain** – first Spanish CP founded April 1920 by Federation of Socialist Youth; 2,000 members 1921; Spanish Socialist Workers Party split up over Comintern's Twenty-one Conditions April 1921, minority left wing founded Communist Workers Party of Spain; the two CPs formed united CP of Spain November 1921; forced underground 1923–31.

**Communist Party of Switzerland** – originated from ultraleft wing in Swiss SDP and youth alliance, which founded *Forderung* newspaper late 1917; expelled and launched first CP in Zurich ("Old Communists") October 1918 and nationwide May 1919; 800 members 1921; joined with SDP left wing to form united CP with 6,000 members March 1921.

**Communist Party of the Netherlands** – *see* Communist Party in the Netherlands.

**Communist Party of Yugoslavia** – originated in Social Democratic Party of Serbia founded 1903; opposed war credits 1914; participated in Balkan Revolutionary Social Democratic Federation from 1915; called conference that united several Yugoslav Socialist parties to form Socialist Workers Party (Communist) April 1919, which joined Comintern; 40,000 members May 1920; changed name to CP of Yugoslavia June 1920.

**Communist Teachers Club (Denmark)** – small organization affiliated to United Trade Union Opposition (FS), left trade union opposition movement with syndicalist leanings.

**Communist Workers Party of Germany (KAPD)** – originated from ultraleft wing of German CP, including majority of Berlin and Ruhr regions; expelled from CP October 1919; decided after Kapp putsch to organize separate party, which had 38,000 members April 1920; admitted as sympathizing section of Comintern November 1920; declined rapidly and split 1921; many members joined German CP.

**Communist Workers Party of Poland** – founded December 16, 1918, through fusion of Social Democracy of the Kingdom of Poland and Lithuania with Polish Socialist Party–Left; 6,000 members July 1919; dissolved 1938 and most leaders murdered during Stalin purges.

**Communist Youth International** – originated from Socialist Youth International, which was reconstituted with antichauvinist policy 1915; organized clandestine congress in Berlin where representatives of fourteen revolutionary youth organizations with 140,000 members formed Communist Youth International November 1919; transferred seat from Berlin to Moscow 1921; 800,000 members 1921; dissolved by Stalin together with Comintern as gesture to imperialist allies 1943.

**Communist Youth League of Georgia** – originated from small revolutionary youth groups formed in the Caucasus 1917 and 1918; united youth organization of the Caucasus founded September 1919; Georgian Communist youth organized underground under Menshevik government; 2,000 members with Red Guard of 800 by April 1920; joined Communist Youth International June 1920; 12,000 members 1921.

**Communist Youth League of Russia** – founded October 1918 with 22,100 members from existing youth leagues in cities throughout old Russian empire; 75,000 of its members participated in Red Army 1918–20; affiliated to Communist Youth International; 482,000 members October 1920.

**Compère-Morel, Adéodat (1872–1941)** – French SP parliamentary deputy 1909–36; member of SP highest leadership body 1914–15, 1921–32; supported Committee to Reconstruct the International 1920; went with SP after Tours split congress 1920; part of right-wing split from SP with Renaudel 1933; left politics 1936.

**Connolly, James (1868–1916)** – Irish revolutionary; a founder of Marxist movement in Ireland; a founder of U.S. IWW while in U.S. 1903–10; a leader of Irish Transport and General Workers' Union; founder of Irish Labour Party 1912; internationalist during World War I; central leader of Easter Uprising against British rule April 1916; executed by British.

**Connolly, Roderic (Thomas Darragh) (1901–1980)** – son of James Connolly; fought in Irish Easter Uprising 1916; listed as Irish IWW delegate to second Comintern congress; active in SP; first president of Irish CP 1921; Irish Labour Party chair 1971–77.

**Constantinople Communist Group** – group of Turkish intellectuals around the journal *Kurtulus* (Liberation); founded by exiles in Berlin; functioned in Constantinople (Istanbul) from May 1919; founded what became Turkish CP.

**Council of People's Commissars** – government of Russian Soviet Republic established after October 1917 revolution.

**CP** – Communist Party.

**Crispien, Artur (1875–1946)** – German SPD newspaper editor 1894–1917; supported Spartacus current briefly 1915;

leader of USPD from 1917 and its cochair from January 1919; USPD consultative delegate to second Comintern congress; opposed USPD joining Comintern at Halle split congress; participated in formation of Two-and-a-Half International 1921; rejoined SPD 1922; member of SPD leadership; fled Nazis 1933, died in Switzerland.

***Critica Sociale* (Social critique)** – published 1891–1926 in Milan; edited by Turati.

**Cunow, Heinrich (1862–1936)** – leader of German SPD; close to Bebel and Kautsky before World War I; chauvinist during World War I; replaced Kautsky as editor of *Neue Zeit* 1917–23; opposed Russian October revolution.

**Curzon, George Nathaniel (1859–1925)** – British politician and lord; secretary of state for foreign affairs 1919–24.

**Czechoslovak Communist Group** – Czechoslovak Communists resident in Russia; affiliated to Federation of Foreign Groups of the Russian CP.

**Dahlström, Katarina (Kata) (1858–1923)** – joined Swedish SDP 1893; first woman elected to national committee 1900; leader of left wing from 1910; supported Zimmerwald during World War I; founding leader of Left SDP 1917 and of CP 1921; delegate to second Comintern congress; supported Twenty-one Conditions; supporter of Russian revolution until death.

**Dan, Fyodor Ilyich (1871–1947)** – a central leader of Russian Mensheviks; leading opponent of October revolution; deported 1922; edited émigré Menshevik journal.

**Danish Left** – *see* Communist Party of Denmark.

**D'Aragona, Ludovico (1876–1961)** – joined Italian SP 1892; Italian General Confederation of Labor (CGL) secretary general 1918–25; SP deputy 1919–24; SP consultative delegate to second Comintern congress, where he participated in founding International Council of Trade and Industrial Unions 1920; walked out during congress; opposed founding CP 1921; joined United SP 1922.

**Darragh, Thomas** – *see* Connolly, Roderic.

**Daszynski, Ignacy (1866–1939)** – headed Galician SDP 1892–1919; leader of unified Polish SP (PPS) from 1919; selected by Polish military to head government during war with Soviet Russia August 1920; headed SP parliamentary fraction 1920s; supported Pilsudski's coup d'état 1926.

**Däumig, Ernst (1866–1922)** – an editor of *Vorwärts* 1911–16; dismissed for opposing German SPD war policy; leader of USPD and Revolutionary Shop Stewards 1918; became USPD cochair December 1919; USPD consultative delegate to second Comintern congress; joined CP with USPD majority 1920; German CP cochair 1920; left CP 1921; rejoined USPD.

**David, Eduard (1863–1930)** – leader of German SPD right wing and outspoken supporter of German imperialism; first president of National Assembly 1919; minister without portfolio 1919–20.

**De Ambris, Alceste (1874–1934)** – Italian SP founding member 1892; active in workers' movement in Brazil 1898–1903, 1908–11; revolutionary syndicalist at turn of century; advocated Italy's entry into World War I; sympathetic to fascism 1919; later opposed fascists; stripped of Italian citizenship 1926.

**Delacroix, Léon (1865–1929)** – Belgian prime minister 1919–21.

**Delinières, Lucien (1857–1937)** – part of chauvinist majority in French SP during World War I; attended second Comintern congress; on Moscow Comintern staff 1920–25; later returned to France and left Communist movement.

**Delory, Gustave Emile (1857–1925)** – a founder of Socialist movement in northern France; follower of Guesde; mayor of Lille 1896–1904 and 1909–25; SP parliamentary deputy 1902–25; prisoner in Germany during World War I; went with SP after CP founded at Tours congress 1920.

**Denikin, Anton Ivanovich (1872–1947)** – tsarist general; White army commander in chief in southern Russia in civil war 1918–20; emigrated 1920 after defeat by Red Army.

**Dimitrov, Stanke (1889–1944)** – joined Bulgarian workers' movement 1904; early member of revolutionary wing of Bulgarian SDP; Bulgarian CP founding member 1919; elected to Central Committee 1920; CP organizational secretary 1923–25; emigrated to USSR 1925; again active in Bulgarian CP 1935–37 and in underground resistance to Bulgarian regime during World War II; killed in plane crash.

**Directory** – antisoviet government of Ukraine established after collapse of German-backed Skoropadsky government late 1918; led by Petlyura and Vinnichenko; supported by Entente powers; ousted by prosoviet forces early 1919.

**Dissmann, Robert (1878–1926)** – German Social Democrat; union official 1900–1908; joined USPD 1917; president of metalworkers' union from late 1919; opposed joining Comintern at Halle congress and remained in USPD after split 1920; member of Reichstag 1920–26; rejoined SPD 1922.

**Dittmann, Wilhelm (1874–1954)** – joined German SPD 1894; edited party newspapers from 1899; SPD Reichstag deputy from 1912; joined centrist opposition 1915; USPD party secretary 1917–22; member of Ebert cabinet November–December 1918; USPD delegate to second Comintern congress 1920; opposed Twenty-one Conditions and unification with German CP; returned to SPD 1922.

**Domes, Franz (1863–1930)** – founder of Austrian metalworkers' union, became its secretary 1898 and president 1918; SDP member of parliament from 1911; prominent figure in SDP government from 1918; founder and president of Austrian Chamber of Workers and Employers 1920.

**Dugoni, Enrico (1874–1945)** – Italian SP member from turn of century; member General Confederation of Labor

National Council from 1908; SP delegate to Kienthal conference 1916; in SP right wing after World War I; participated in labor and SP delegation to Soviet Russia spring 1920; stayed with SP after CP's formation 1920; arrested for antifascist activities 1930 and 1932.

**Dunayevsky, Vladimir Abramovich (1902–1983)** – leader of Bolshevik youth organization from 1917, which he represented at second Comintern congress.

**Dutch Communist Party** – *see* Communist Party in the Netherlands.

**Dyer, Reginald Edward Harry (1864–1927)** – British general; commanded troops at Amritsar massacre, where 379 unarmed Indian protesters murdered 1919.

**Dzerzhinsky, Feliks (Józef) (1877–1926)** – Polish revolutionary, a founder of Social Democracy of the Kingdom of Poland and Lithuania; Bolshevik Party Central Committee member 1917–26; headed Cheka (Soviet security police) after revolution; Russian CP delegate to second Comintern congress.

**Ebert, Friedrich (1871–1925)** – German SPD leader; close collaborator of Bebel from 1906; cochair of SPD 1913–19; chauvinist during World War I; led Council of People's Representatives government 1918–19; worked with army high command to crush January uprising 1919; German president 1919–25.

**ECCI** – Executive Committee of the Communist International.

**Ellansky, Vasyl (Blakytnyi) (1894–1925)** – Ukrainian writer; spokesperson for Ukrainian Left SRs (Borotbist) and editor of their newspaper *Borotba;* joined CP (Bolsheviks) of the Ukraine and elected to its Central Committee 1920; delegate to second Comintern congress; joined Red Army, fought against Polish invasion 1920; theoretician of "proletarian literature."

**Engels, Frederick (1820–1895)** – lifelong collaborator of Karl Marx and cofounder with him of modern communist workers' movement; coauthor of Communist Manifesto; a leader of revolutionary democratic forces in 1848 German revolution; lived in England 1841–44 and again from 1849 to his death; in last years the outstanding figure in Second International.

**Estonian Independent Socialist Workers Party** – formed by forces from SRs and SDP March 1920; left wing majority supported Comintern and split 1922; left wing, allied with underground CP, took name Estonian Working People's Party, which was banned 1924; right wing fused with Estonian SDP 1925.

**Fabierkewicz, Zbigniew (1882–1919)** – Polish revolutionary; contributor to and editor of many socialist and communist newspapers; returned from Russia to Poland to help lead CP work 1918; shot by Polish police.

**Fabri, Ernst (1891–1966)** – Austrian Social Democrat; led antiwar work among soldiers during World War I; an organizer of January 1918 mass strike; a leader of Social Democratic Working Group of Revolutionary Workers Councils, a left tendency in SDP, 1920; joined CP 1921; emigrated to Soviet Union 1932; Soviet secret police agent; died in Soviet Union.

**Faisal I (1885–1933)** – son of ruler of the Hejaz in Arabia; a leader of Arab revolt, aided by Britain, against Ottoman Empire 1916; led Arab forces that occupied Damascus 1918; declared king of Syria 1920; forced out by French 1920; installed as king of Iraq with British support 1921.

**Faure, Paul (1878–1960)** – leading figure in centrist opposition in French SP during World War I; opposition delegate to 1919 Bern conference; secretary of Committee to Reconstruct the International; opposed SP affiliation to Comintern 1920; general secretary of French SP 1920–39; sympathized with pro-Nazi Vichy government during World War II; expelled from SP 1944.

**Federation of Foreign Groups of the Russian Communist Party** – formed May 1918 by Russian CP to organize among prisoners of war and immigrant workers in Russia; dissolved 1920.

**Ferri, Enrico (1856–1929)** – Italian criminologist; joined SP 1893; theorist of antiopportunist wing of Italian SP at turn of century; editor in chief of *Avanti!* 1898, 1904–8; moved to U.S.; returned to Italy and supported Mussolini 1922.

**First International (International Working Men's Association)** – founded 1864; united revolutionary working-class organizations in a number of European countries and North America; Marx became its central leader; campaigned to defend 1871 Paris Commune; faced stiff repression after defeat of Commune and went into decline; seat moved to New York 1872; dissolved 1876.

**Flynn** – *see* Lindgren, Edward.

**Fraina, Louis (Lewis Corey) (1894–1953)** – born in Italy, emigrated to U.S. 1897; member of Socialist Labor Party 1909–14; campaigned for revolutionary International during World War I; active in SP left wing 1917–19; a founding leader of CP of America 1919; participated in International Communist Conference in Amsterdam and second Comintern congress 1920; Comintern emissary to Mexico 1920–21; left Comintern 1922; wrote under name Lewis Corey from late 1920s; supported Lovestone's pro-Bukharin opposition group in U.S. in 1930s; repudiated Marxism 1940.

**Freeman, Paul (1884?–1921)** – probably born in Germany; emigrated to Australia from U.S. 1911; joined Australian SP and IWW; active in antidraft campaigns during war; deported repeatedly for antiwar activities 1919; consultative delegate for Australian IWW at second Comintern congress; returned illegally to Australia 1920; participated in third Comintern congress 1921; died in Russia in rail accident.

**Freemasonry** – teachings and practices of the secret fraternal order of Free and Accepted Masons; evolved from stonemasons' guilds of Middle Ages into a worldwide secret society; largely petty bourgeois in composition; democratic in professed goals; in solidarity with the bourgeois order.

**Free Socialist Youth of Germany** – revolutionary national opposition group founded in SPD youth early 1916; fused with USPD youth early 1918; 4,000 members October 1918; won over to CP 1919; 35,000 members October 1919; centrist minority expelled October 1919; joined Communist Youth International November 1919; won over majority of USPD youth November 1920; renamed Communist Youth League of Germany late 1920.

**Free Workers Union of Germany (Syndicalists)** – grew out of pre-war anarcho-syndicalist unions; founding congress December 1919 with 110,000 members; rejected dictatorship of proletariat; degenerated into sect by 1923 as many members joined CP; banned 1933.

***Die Freiheit* (Freedom)** – daily newspaper of German USPD published in Berlin 1918–22; edited by Hilferding.

**French Communist Group** – organized by French Communists resident in Russia 1918; affiliated to Federation of Foreign Groups of the Russian CP; carried out educational work that helped prepare ground for mutinies among French intervention troops in 1919.

**Friis, Jacob (1883–1956)** – correspondent for Norwegian Labor Party newspaper *Social-Demokraten* from 1909; joined Comintern with Norwegian Labor Party; delegate to second Comintern congress; representative to Comintern Executive Committee 1920–21; supported Labor Party withdrawal from Comintern 1923; broke with Labor Party and joined CP 1928; left CP 1933 and rejoined Labor Party; opposed asylum for Trotsky in Norway.

**Frossard, Louis-Oscar (1889–1946)** – joined French SP 1905; a leader of its centrist opposition during World War I; SP general secretary from October 1918; SP consultative delegate to second Comintern congress 1920; French

CP general secretary 1920–23; split from CP 1923; member SP 1927–35; subsequently minister in several governments including pro-Nazi Vichy government 1940.

**Frumkina, Mariya (Ester) (1880–1938)** – joined General Union of Jewish Workers (Bund) 1901; editor in chief of Bund newspaper *Der Veker* from February 1917; close to Mensheviks until October revolution; joined Russian CP 1919; delegate to second Comintern congress; edited Russian CP Jewish press from 1920; head of Comintern Jewish section; arrested during Stalin purges and executed.

**Fuchs, Eduard (1870–1940)** – longtime German SPD member; leader of Spartacus group during World War I; met with Bolshevik leaders late 1918 on founding of Comintern; attended second Comintern congress; left German CP 1929.

**Gallacher, William (1881–1965)** – joined British Social Democratic Federation 1903; opposed World War I; leader of British Shop Stewards' movement and president of Clyde Workers' Committee during World War I; Shop Stewards' representative at second Comintern congress; member of British CP from 1920 and of Central Committee 1921–65; held numerous Comintern posts from 1924; member of Parliament 1935–50.

**Gandhi, Mohandas (Mahatma) (1869–1948)** – central leader of India's independence movement; president of Indian National Congress 1925–34; advocated pacifist civil disobedience as political strategy.

**General Confederation of Labor (CGL) (Italy)** – founded 1906; grew from 250,000 members 1918 to 2 million late 1920; led by reformists Turati and D'Aragona; remained affiliated with Amsterdam International; dissolved 1927.

**General Confederation of Labor (CGT) (France)** – founded 1895; anarcho-syndicalist in orientation; 600,000 members 1914; majority leadership backed war effort; internationalist minority rallied to Comintern; 2.5 million members early 1920; hurt by failed general strike May

1920; 600,000 members spring 1921; revolutionary wing expelled with 350,000 members December 1921 and organized United CGT June–July 1922.

**General German Trade Union Federation (ADGB)** – organized 1919, replacing former federation founded 1890; politically aligned with SPD; 7.4 million members late 1919; affiliated to Amsterdam International.

**General Workers Union of Germany (AAUD)** – union federation founded February 1920 by ultralefts expelled from German CP; saw factory organizations as basic unit to replace trade unions and political parties; became union arm of KAPD; 80,000 members 1920; membership declined from mid-1921; split 1922; existed as sect until banned 1933.

**Gerhardsen, Einar Henry (1897–1987)** – joined Norwegian Social Democratic Youth League 1914; youth league delegate to second Comintern congress; Norwegian Labor Party Central Committee member 1921–69; Labor Party secretary 1923–26 and 1936–39; jailed by Nazis 1941–45; Labor Party chair 1945–65; prime minister after World War II.

**Giolitti, Giovanni (1842–1928)** – Italian politician; opposed Italy's entry into World War I; prime minister numerous times, including 1920–21; aided fascists during their rise to power.

**Goldenberg, Boris (Robert Thal) (1897–1973)** – leader of French Socialist Youth Federation during World War I and its delegate to second Comintern congress; arrested in Germany returning to France; worked in Marx-Engels Institute in Moscow 1923–28; left Russia and Communist movement 1928.

**Golovin, Nikolai Nikolayevich (1875–1944)** – tsarist general; emigrated to France after October revolution 1917 and worked with counterrevolution; collaborated with Nazis during World War II.

**Gompers, Samuel (1850–1924)** – founder and president of American Federation of Labor 1886–1924 (except 1895);

advocated policy of collaboration with employers; opposed industrial unionism; supported U.S. entry into World War I; chair of Labor Commission at Versailles conference 1919.

**Gopner, Serafima Il'inichna (1880–1966)** – Bolshevik from 1903; held important party and government posts in the Ukraine after 1917; member of Comintern Executive Committee secretariat 1929–38.

**Gorter, Herman (1864–1927)** – Social Democrat from 1897; expelled from Dutch Social Democratic Workers Party with left-wing *Tribune* group and cofounder of Dutch SDP 1909; supported Zimmerwald Left during World War I; cofounder of Dutch CP 1918; worked with German ultraleft from November 1918; supported formation of Comintern; negotiated KAPD affiliation to Comintern as sympathizing organization November 1920; part of KAPD break with Comintern July 1921; active in ultraleft groups in Germany and Netherlands until death.

**Graber, Ernst Paul (1875–1956)** – leading Swiss Social Democrat; supported right wing in Swiss SDP after 1917.

**Gramsci, Antonio (1891–1937)** – joined Italian SP 1914; founder of *L'Ordine Nuovo* 1919; leader of revolutionary current in SP; CP founding member 1921; Comintern Executive Committee member from 1922; replaced Bordiga as party's central leader 1926; imprisoned 1926 until death.

**Graziadei, Antonio (1873–1953)** – joined Italian SP 1893; active in right wing; supported party's antiwar stand in World War I; delegate to second Comintern congress; supported joining Comintern at Italian SP Livorno split congress 1921; expelled from CP 1928; recanted and rejoined Italian CP late 1940s.

**Grimlund, Otto (1893–1969)** – cofounder of Swedish Left SDP 1917; delegate to first Comintern congress; Comintern Executive Committee member 1920; Swedish CP Central Committee member until 1925; rejoined Social Democrats 1929.

**Grimm, Robert (1881–1958)** – leader of Swiss SDP and longtime *Berner Tagwacht* editor; centrist during World War I; chair of Zimmerwald International Socialist Committee in Bern 1915–17; helped organize Two-and-a-Half International 1920; later returned to Second International.

**Guesde, Jules (1845–1922)** – veteran of Paris Commune; one of first Marxists in France; a founder of first French socialist party 1880; led French Workers Party from 1882, which became Socialist Party of France 1901; a leader of Second International and opponent of revisionism until 1914; chauvinist and government minister during World War I.

**Guilbeaux, Henri (1885–1938)** – French anarcho-syndicalist before World War I; later joined SP; supported Zimmerwald Left at Kienthal conference 1916; delegate of French Communist Federation of Soviets to second Comintern congress; broke with communism in 1930s and became extreme reactionary.

**Gylling, Edvard (1881–1944)** – joined Finnish SDP 1905; parliamentary deputy 1908–18; finance minister of Finnish soviet government and Red Guard chief of staff 1918; Finnish CP Central Committee member 1919; Finnish Socialist Workers Party delegate to second Comintern congress; joined Russian CP 1920; headed government of Autonomous Soviet Socialist Republic of Karelia 1923–35; purged for "nationalism" 1935; arrested 1937; executed.

**Haase, Hugo (1863–1919)** – German SPD Reichstag member from 1897; with Kautsky in SPD Center current before World War I; SPD cochair 1911–16; voted in Reichstag against war credits from 1916; USPD cochair from 1917; government minister November–December 1918; assassinated by monarchist.

**Hakki** – *see* Ismael Hakki of Kayseri.

**Han En-hak** – consultative delegate of Central Bureau of Chinese Socialist Workers Party to second Comintern congress.

**Hapsburg** – ruling dynasty of Austro-Hungarian Empire until 1918.

**Hassanzadeh** – *see* Nikbin, Hassan.

**Haywood, William D. (Big Bill) (1869–1928)** – a founder of U.S. IWW 1905 and for years a prominent spokesperson; sentenced to 20 years in prison for opposing World War I 1918; jumped bail while on appeal and escaped to Soviet Russia 1921.

**Helfferich, Karl (1872–1924)** – German banker and politician; government minister 1915–18; National People's Party chair from 1919; leader in restabilizing capitalist economy after World War I; opposed abiding by Versailles treaty.

**Henderson, Arthur (1863–1935)** – general secretary of British Labour Party 1911–34; chauvinist during World War I; government minister 1915–17; central organizer of 1919 Bern conference; chair of Second International 1925–29; British foreign secretary 1929–31.

**Henke, Alfred (1868–1946)** – German Social Democrat; edited *Bremer Bürger-Zeitung* 1910–17; Reichstag member 1912–18, 1919–32; USPD founding member 1917; head of Bremen workers' and soldiers' council 1918; leader of insurgent Bremen council republic 1919; rejoined SPD 1922; member of parliament.

**Herzog, Jakob (1892–1931)** – Swiss Social Democrat, influenced by anarchism; leader of Swiss SDP youth during World War I; headed radical *Forderung* group; expelled from SDP October 1918; founded first Swiss CP ("Old Communists") 1918, which he represented at second Comintern congress; part of fusion that formed united Swiss CP 1921; leader of CP through 1920s.

**Hilferding, Rudolf (1877–1941)** – Austrian Social Democrat and author of *Finance Capital;* supported German SPD centrist opposition during World War I; USPD member from 1917; *Freiheit* editor in chief 1918–22; anti-Bolshevik; opposed USPD joining Comintern and fusion with German CP; returned to SPD 1922; German finance minister 1923, 1928–29; killed by Hitler's Gestapo.

**Hillquit, Morris (1869–1933)** – leader of U.S. SP; centrist during World War I; nominal head of legal department of Russian Soviet Government Information Bureau in New York 1919; opposed Comintern.

**Hindenburg, Paul von (1847–1934)** – German general; army chief of staff 1916–18; president 1925–34; appointed Hitler chancellor.

**Höglund, Karl Zeth (1884–1956)** – joined Swedish SDP 1904; leader of SDP youth movement and party left wing; internationalist in World War I; supported Zimmerwald Left; founding leader of Left SDP 1917; elected to Comintern Executive Committee 1922, 1924; broke with CP and Comintern 1924; rejoined SDP 1926; elected to SDP Central Committee 1928.

**Hohenzollern** – ruling dynasty of Prussia and German Empire until November 1918.

**Hornik-Ströhmer, Anna (1891–1966)** – active in Austrian SDP youth and women's movements from 1910; cofounder of Left Radicals 1915–16; supported Zimmerwald Left; an organizer of January 1918 strike wave; with Left Radicals joined newly founded Austrian CP late November 1918; CP delegate to second Comintern congress; Central Committee member from 1923; in exile during Nazi regime; resumed activity in Austrian CP after 1945.

**Horthy de Nagybánya, Miklós (1868–1957)** – Hungarian aristocrat; organized reactionary forces that massacred thousands 1919; dictator of Hungary 1919–44; allied with Hitler during World War II.

**Hueber, Anton (1861–1935)** – Austrian Social Democrat; central leader of Social Democratic trade unions 1895–1931; a founder of Chamber of Workers and Employers after World War I.

**Huggler, August (1877–1944)** – secretary of Swiss SDP; opposed SDP joining Comintern 1919.

**Hula, Bretislav (1894–1937)** – joined Bolsheviks while in Russia late 1917; secretary of Czechoslovak Communist section of Russian CP 1918; returned to Czechoslovakia and advocated Czechoslovak SDP joining Comintern; delegate of SDP left wing to second Comintern congress; CP founding member; expelled from CP as "rightist" 1925.

***L'Humanité* (Humanity)** – founded 1904 by Jean Jaurès; newspaper of French SP until 1920; controlled by chauvinist majority 1914–18, then by centrists; managing editor was Cachin 1918–58; newspaper of CP from 1921.

**Humbert-Droz, Jules (1891–1971)** – delegate of Swiss SDP left wing at second Comintern congress; founding member of Swiss CP 1921; headed Comintern secretariat responsible for Latin America and Latin countries of Europe through 1920s; relieved of all Comintern functions 1928; capitulated to Stalin; resumed activity in Swiss CP 1931; removed from CP leadership 1941 and expelled 1943; joined Swiss SDP and was its secretary 1947–58.

**Huysmans, Camille (1871–1968)** – leader of Belgian Workers Party; secretary of International Socialist Bureau from 1904; took chauvinist stand 1914; helped organize 1919 Bern conference; subsequently served in Belgian government.

**Hyndman, Henry Mayers (1842–1921)** – founded British Social Democratic Federation 1881, which participated in founding British SP 1911; chauvinist during World War I and opposed women's suffrage; left British SP 1916; hostile to Russian revolution.

**Ibrahimov, Veli (d. 1928)** – Crimean Tatar; leader of left wing of Crimean National Party after February 1917; joined Russian CP 1919; head of Crimean CP and president of Crimean Autonomous Soviet Socialist Republic 1920;

delegate to second Comintern congress; accused of "nationalist deviation" and arrested 1927; executed.

**Ignat, Samuil Iosifovich (1898–1939)** – Menshevik from 1915; Bolshevik from mid-1919; youth movement leader in Odessa and Kharkov August 1917–22; Ukrainian Bolshevik youth delegate to second Comintern congress; later held leading government posts.

**Independent Labour Party (ILP) (Britain)** – founded January 1893; component of Labour Party 1900–1932; pacifist during World War I; 50,000 members April 1919; 45,000 members April 1920; withdrew from Second International 1920; minority split to join CP, majority joined Two-and-a-Half International 1921; broke with Labour Party to form centrist group 1932.

**Independents** – *see* Independent Social Democratic Party of Germany.

**Independent Social Democratic Party (Denmark)** – *see* Communist Party of Denmark.

**Independent Social Democratic Party of Germany (USPD)** – began to coalesce when centrist SPD deputies were expelled from parliamentary fraction March 1916; formed Social Democratic Working Group, then separate USPD with 120,000 members April 1917; participated in provisional government under Friedrich Ebert November–December 1918; included Spartacus current until December 1918; 100,000 members November 1918; 900,000 summer 1920; majority fused with CP December 1920; minority retained name until rejoined SPD 1922.

**Independent Socialist Workers Party of Estonia** – *see* Estonian Independent Socialist Workers Party.

**Independent Young People's Socialist League of America** – originally YPSL, founded by SP as national organization 1913; 150 chapters by 1916; broke ties with SP fall 1919; majority voted to join Communist Youth International forming Independent YPSL with 3,000 members December 1919; soon succumbed to effects of Palmer raids and division in Communist ranks; Young Communist League organized 1922.

**Indian National Congress (Congress Party)** – founded as all-India opposition to British rule 1885; Muslim membership split away 1906; came under leadership of wing led by Gandhi 1918; led mass resistance to British rule 1920s through 1940s; ruled India after independence 1947.

**Indian Revolutionary Association** – founded in soviet Tashkent by exiled Indian revolutionary nationalists 1919; participated in founding Indian CP in Tashkent October 1920.

**Industrial Workers of the World (IWW) (Australia)** – formed 1907 with particular influence among mine and transport workers; 2,000 members 1916; active in struggle against war and conscription during World War I; severely repressed, main leaders convicted of "high treason" 1916; remnants participated in forming Communist League 1918.

**Industrial Workers of the World (IWW) (Britain)** – originated 1905 when members of Socialist Labour Party formed British Advocates of Industrial Unionism; after split with anarchists, reorganized as Industrial Workers of Great Britain 1909; height of influence 1910–11; especially strong among Irish, Scottish, and Welsh workers; had many activists in Clyde Workers' Committee during World War I and Shop Stewards' movement.

**Industrial Workers of the World (IWW) (Ireland)** – inspired by British and U.S. IWWs, especially after tour by Haywood 1913.

**Industrial Workers of the World (IWW) (U.S.)** – founded as revolutionary industrial union movement 1905; rejected electoral participation and work in American Federation of Labor; opposed U.S. participation in World War I and suffered severe repression; 35,000 members May 1919; went into decline after formation of CP 1919; majority rejected affiliation to Comintern-led Red

International of Labor Unions 1921; some 20 percent of members joined CP.

**International Council of Trade and Industrial Unions** – established in Moscow July 15, 1920, by representatives of unions from Russia, Italy, Spain, France, Yugoslavia, Bulgaria, and Georgia representing nearly 9 million workers; represented 17 million members when it organized first congress of Red International of Labor Unions July 1921.

***Die Internationale*** **(The International)** – published one issue 1915 edited by Rosa Luxemburg and Franz Mehring; banned; resumed publication as journal of German CP 1919; banned 1933; published in exile until 1939.

**International Federation of Trade Unions (Amsterdam International)** – founded by Social Democratic trade union officials 1913; collapsed during World War I; refounded in Amsterdam July 1919; claimed 24 million members 1920; disappeared with advent of World War II.

**International Socialist Bureau** – Second International executive body; formed 1900.

**International Socialist League (South Africa)** – founded by split from reformist South African Labour Party 1915; merged with other smaller groups to form CP of South Africa July 1921.

**International Working Men's Association** – *see* First International.

**Irish Parliamentary (Home Rule) Party** – founded 1873; worked for Irish home rule in British Parliament by maneuvering between Conservatives and Liberals; agreed to suspend Home Rule Bill during World War I; denounced Easter Uprising as treasonous; discredited, virtually disappeared by 1919.

**Irish Socialist Republican Party** – *see* Socialist Party of Ireland.

**Irish Transport and General Workers' Union (ITGWU)** – founded by James Larkin in Dublin 1909; led workers in general lockout of more than 25,000 workers in Dublin

1913–14; 100,000 members late 1919; Larkin's syndicalist wing split 1924.

**Ismael Hakki of Kayseri (1901–1945?)** – delegate for Turkey of Bureau of Communist Organizations to second Comintern congress; Central Committee member of Turkish CP founded in Baku spring 1920; remained in Soviet Russia; president of Turkish CP bureau abroad from 1920; worked with Communist University of Toilers of the East; member of CP Transcaucasian provincial committee.

**Italian Socialist Party** – founded 1892; extreme reformist and chauvinist wing expelled 1912; took centrist stand on Italy's entry into World War I 1915; initiated Zimmerwald conference 1915; 81,000 members 1919, 216,000 in 1920; affiliated to Comintern 1919, but leadership refused to expel party's reformist wing; minority split to form Italian CP January 1921; Turati right wing expelled from SP summer 1922; SP reorganized in Italy, led by Pietro Nenni, 1943.

**Italian Socialist Youth Federation** – formed 1901; supported SP opposition to World War I and SP affiliation to Comintern; 6,500 members 1918; joined Communist Youth International November 1919; 55,000 members mid-1920; broke with SP, affiliated to newly formed CP, and changed name to Italian Communist Youth Federation January 1921; declined to 2,000 members by December 1922.

**ITGWU** – *see* Irish Transport and General Workers' Union.

**IWW** – Industrial Workers of the World.

**Jacobins** – political association of revolutionary bourgeoisie that provided much of the leadership and organization for French revolution 1789–94.

**Jansen** – *see* Proost, Jan.

**Jaurès, Jean (1859–1914)** – leader of French and international Socialist movements; held reformist positions; founded

*L'Humanité* 1904; central leader of French SP from its foundation 1905; spoke out against militarism; assassinated by right-wing fanatic at outbreak of World War I.

**Joffe, Adolf Abramovich (1883–1927)** – joined Russian Social Democracy before 1900; with Mezhrayontsi during World War I; joined Bolsheviks June 1917 and elected to Central Committee August 1917; member of Soviet delegation to Brest-Litovsk 1918; Soviet ambassador to Berlin April–November 1918; supported Leninist opposition to Stalin led by Trotsky in Russian CP from 1923; committed suicide to protest bureaucratic measures of Stalin faction.

**Jogiches, Leo (1867–1919)** – a founding leader and central organizer of Polish Social Democracy; imprisoned but escaped to Germany 1907; central organizer of Spartacus current during war; member Spartacus and German CP central bureaus; arrested and murdered during March 1919 struggles in Berlin.

**Joonas, Erich (b. 1893)** – active in SR party in Estonia from 1909; Estonian Independent Socialist Workers Party member from 1920; consultative delegate for this party to second Comintern congress; later Social Democrat.

**Jørgensen, Åge (1890–1960)** – member SDP of Denmark and of left wing of Social Democratic youth federation; founder of Danish Socialist Workers Party April 1918; edited party newspaper *Klassekampen;* Left SP delegate to second Comintern congress; Danish CP Central Committee member and its Comintern representative; quit CP 1935; returned to Social Democracy; edited journal sympathetic to Nazis during World War II.

**Jouhaux, Léon (1879–1954)** – French union leader; began as syndicalist; head of General Confederation of Labor (CGT) 1909–40; chauvinist during World War I; opposed Bolshevik revolution; leader of Amsterdam international trade union federation after World War

I; founded French anticommunist union federation Force Ouvrière 1948.

**Kabakchiev, Khristo Stevanov (1878–1940)** – joined Bulgarian SDP 1897; supported revolutionary Tesnyaki wing in split 1903; Central Committee member of SDP 1905–19 and of CP 1919–28; editor in chief of party newspaper 1908–23; delegate to second Comintern congress; imprisoned after failure of Bulgarian uprising 1923; released and lived in Moscow from 1926; arrested during Stalin purges 1937; released 1938.

**Kalinin, Mikhail Ivanovich (1875–1946)** – founding member of RSDLP 1898; Bolshevik; Central Committee alternate member from 1912; Central Committee full member 1919; elected Soviet head of state 1919 and remained so until death; Russian CP delegate to second Comintern congress.

**Kamenev, Lev Borisovich (1883–1936)** – joined RSDLP 1901; Bolshevik from 1903; arrested with Bolshevik Duma deputies 1914; elected to Central Committee 1917; Political Bureau member 1917–26; member of Commission on National and Colonial Questions at second Comintern congress; aligned with Stalin and Zinoviev 1923–25; joined Trotsky and Zinoviev in United Opposition to bureaucratic current led by Stalin 1926–27; expelled from CP 1927; capitulated 1928; twice readmitted and reexpelled; executed during Moscow frame-up trials.

**KAPD** – *see* Communist Workers Party of Germany.

**Kapp, Wolfgang (1858–1922)** – German politician; led failed monarchist military putsch against Weimar republic 1920.

**Karakhan, Lev Mikhailovich (1889–1937)** – joined RSDLP 1904; joined Bolshevik Party with Mezhrayontsi 1917; secretary of Soviet Brest-Litovsk delegation 1918; held other diplomatic posts; ECCI consultative delegate to second Comintern congress; executed during Moscow frame-up trials.

**Katanian, Ruben Pavlovich (1881–1966)** – active in Armenian workers' movement from 1901; joined Bolsheviks 1903; edited socialist and Bolshevik press; consultative delegate from Armenian CP to second Comintern congress; worked in public prosecutor's office from 1936; arrested 1938; rehabilitated 1955.

**Kautsky, Karl (1854–1938)** – born in Prague; a leader of German Social Democracy and of Socialist International; collaborator of Engels; author of many works on history and Marxist theory; a leader of Center current in SPD before 1914; adopted pacifist stand 1914; apologist for chauvinist SPD majority; founding member of USPD 1917 and supporter of its right wing; under secretary in German foreign ministry after November revolution 1918; opponent of Russian October revolution; opposed USPD affiliating to Comintern; leader of Two-and-a-Half International; rejoined SPD 1922.

**Kemal, Mustapha (Atatürk) (1881–1938)** – led Turkish independence struggle and establishment of Turkish republic 1919–23; elected president of provisional government 1920; remained Turkish head of state until death.

**Kerensky, Aleksandr Fyodorovich (1881–1970)** – Russian SR; leader of peasant-based Trudovik group; prime minister of Russian Provisional Government July–November 1917; emigrated 1918.

**Keynes, John Maynard (1883–1946)** – British economist and successful stock speculator; chief British treasury representative at Paris conference 1919; resigned in opposition to economic terms of Versailles treaty; later advocated use of government spending to try to counteract capitalist boom-and-bust cycles.

**Kilbom, Karl (1885–1961)** – joined Swedish SDP 1908; secretary of youth league and editor of SDP newspaper *Stormklockan* during World War I; supported Zimmerwald Left; cofounder of Left SDP 1917 and of CP 1921; worked in Comintern Executive Committee 1919–20;

elected to it 1921, 1924, and 1928; chief editor of party newspaper from 1924; expelled with majority of party as "rightist" 1929; launched dissident CP in Sweden, which was affiliated with international pro-Bukharin opposition until 1933; resigned from party 1937 and rejoined SDP.

**Kipling, Rudyard (1865–1936)** – British jingoist writer and poet.

**Klinger, Gustav K. (1876–1937)** – joined Bolsheviks 1917; leader of Volga German soviet government 1918; Comintern administrator 1919; ECCI consultative delegate to second Comintern congress; Comintern Executive Committee member 1920; killed during Stalin purges.

**Kodzayev, Rozhden Shamelovich** – delegate to second Comintern congress from South Ossetia; formerly a worker in Baku.

**Koenen, Wilhelm (1886–1963)** – joined German SPD 1904; USPD founding member 1917 and Central Committee member from August 1919; supported Twenty-one Conditions and USPD affiliation to Comintern; elected to United KPD Central Bureau 1920 and to Central Committee 1929–31; in exile 1933–45; East German CP member after World War II until death.

**Kohn, Michael (Kohn-Eber) (b. 1884)** – born in Galicia; member of Poale Zion; Austrian Left Radical, supported Zimmerwald during World War I; consultative delegate from Palestine SP to second Comintern congress; joined Austrian CP 1921; lived in exile in France 1939–46; returned to Austria; worked with Communist Jewish group.

**Kolchak, Aleksandr Vasilevich (1873–1920)** – tsarist admiral; head of White armies in Siberia and "supreme ruler" of Russian White forces 1918–19; defeated by Red Army; tried and executed for his role in armed counterrevolution.

**Kollontai, Aleksandra Mikhaylovna (1872–1952)** – Russian Social Democrat in 1890s; Menshevik from 1906; joined Bolsheviks 1915; elected to Central Committee 1917; people's commissar of social welfare 1917; Russian CP delegate to second Comintern congress; head of women's department of CP Central Committee 1920; supported Workers Opposition in CP 1920–21; secretary of Comintern International Women's Secretariat 1921–22; held diplomatic posts after 1923.

**Kon, Feliks (1864–1941)** – active in Polish socialist movement from 1882; joined Polish SP 1904; became leader of left wing when party split 1906; moved to Switzerland 1914 and supported Zimmerwald movement; moved to Russia 1917; joined Russian CP 1918; CP (Bolsheviks) of the Ukraine Central Committee secretary 1919–22; CP (Bolsheviks) of the Ukraine delegate to second Comintern congress; member of Polish provisional government during Red Army offensive 1920; criticized during purges and relieved of political positions late 1930s.

**Kornilov, Lavr Georgiyevich (1870–1918)** – tsarist general; commander in chief under Provisional Government 1917; led attempted putsch August 1917 (old style); later led White armies until killed in battle.

**KPD** – *see* Communist Party of Germany (Spartacus League).

**Krasin, Leonid Borisovich (1870–1926)** – Russian Social Democrat from 1890s; Bolshevik; Central Committee member from 1903; emigrated and withdrew from political activity 1908; rejoined Bolsheviks 1917; took central economic responsibilities in Soviet regime; people's commissar of foreign trade 1920–24; elected to Central Committee 1924.

**Krasnoshchekov, Aleksandr Mikhailovich (1880–1937)** – joined Russian Social Democratic movement 1896; lived in U.S. 1902–17, where he joined SP; returned to Russia and joined Bolsheviks 1917; central political leader of CP's Far Eastern bureau and of Far Eastern Republic 1918–21; CP delegate to Second Congress; held key posts in state economic administration from 1921; killed in Stalin purges.

**Krasnov, Pyotr Nikolayevich (1869–1947)** – tsarist general; commanded units sent against Petrograd by Kerensky late

October 1917; captured and released by Bolsheviks; officer in White Cossack army on the Don 1918–19; went abroad 1919; collaborated with Hitler 1941–45; captured, tried, and executed 1947.

**Krastins, Karl (1892–1932)** – elected to Latvian SDP Central Committee July 1917; delegate of Latvian CP to second Comintern congress.

**Krestinsky, Nikolai Nikolayevich (1883–1938)** – Bolshevik from 1903; State Duma deputy from 1907; directed Bolshevik committee in the Urals 1917; member of Central Committee 1917–21 and its secretary 1919–21; people's commissar of finance 1918–22; Russian CP delegate to second Comintern congress; worked in Soviet embassy in Berlin 1921–30; sympathized with opposition to Stalin 1923–24; deputy people's commissar of foreign affairs from 1930; arrested in purges and executed.

**Kristensen, Kristian (1889–1934)** – member of Norwegian Social Democratic Youth League Central Committee 1911–12; member Norwegian Labor Party 1912–23; delegate to second Comintern congress; Norwegian CP Central Committee member 1923–27; broke with CP and returned to Labor Party 1928.

**Krogh, Sverre (1883–1957)** – leader of Norwegian Social Democratic Youth League 1903–12; joined Norwegian Labor Party 1907; delegate to second Comintern congress; parliamentary deputy 1921–27; joined Norwegian CP 1923; rejoined Labor Party 1928; left labor movement 1937; collaborated with Nazis from 1940; imprisoned for treason 1948.

**Krupp von Bohlen und Halbach** – family of leading German capitalists; owned steel and munitions factories; during World War I, firm run by Gustav (1870–1950) and Bertha (1886–1957).

**Krupskaya, Nadezhda Konstantinovna (1869–1939)** – joined Marxist movement 1890; RSDLP founding member 1898; Bolshevik; collaborator and wife of Lenin; leader in commissariat of education after October revolution; Russian CP delegate to Second Congress; briefly supported United Opposition led by Trotsky and Zinoviev 1926; Central Committee member 1927–39; suffered harassment during Stalin purges 1930s.

**Kuczynski, Robert René (1876–1947)** – German statistician; sympathetic to left; edited *Finanzpolitische Korrespondenz* and other statistical journals from 1919; emigrated to Britain 1933; taught at London School of Economics.

**Kun, Béla (1886–1939)** – joined Bolsheviks while war prisoner in Russia; chair of Federation of Foreign Groups of the Russian CP 1918; organized and headed CP on return to Hungary November 1918; head of Hungarian soviet government March–June 1919; after its collapse, interned in Austria 1919–20; was released and arrived in Moscow just after second Comintern congress; later worked in Comintern apparatus; arrested and killed during Moscow purge trials.

**Kuusinen, Otto (1881–1964)** – participated in 1905 revolution; led center faction of Finnish SDP; member of Finnish revolutionary government 1918; Finnish CP founding member 1918; led underground CP in Socialist Workers Party split from SDP 1920–21; attended all seven Comintern congresses; member Comintern Executive Committee from 1921; Soviet CP Central Committee from 1941; signed dissolution of Comintern 1943; secretary of presidium of Soviet CP Central Committee from 1957.

**Labour Party (Britain)** – *see* British Labour Party.

**Labour Party (Ireland)** – founded 1912 by James Connolly; political arm of transport workers' union; at first supported nationalist cause and workers' republic, but later moved away from these stands; supported Adler-Longuet resolution at Bern conference 1919; opted not to affiliate to Second or Third International 1919; participated in several coalition governments after 1948.

**Labriola, Arturo (1873–1959)** – revolutionary syndicalist leader of Italian SP; expelled 1906; evolved into pro-war chauvinist by World War I; retained radical rhetoric as Giolitti's minister of labor 1920–21; joined Turati's SP.

**Landsberg, Otto (1869–1957)** – German Social Democrat; openly proimperialist during World War I; government minister November 1918–19.

**Langseth, Haavard (1888–1968)** – Norwegian Labor Party member 1917–23; delegate to second Comintern congress; Norwegian CP member from 1923; CP Political Bureau 1928; held leading party positions into 1930s; expelled from CP 1949.

**Lapinski, Pawel (Y. Lewinson) (1879–1937)** – active Socialist from 1897; Polish SP member from 1904; participated in Zimmerwald and Kienthal conferences; founding member Polish CP 1918; active in Russian CP from 1918; in Soviet diplomatic service from 1920; arrested 1937 and committed suicide in prison.

**Larkin, James (1876–1947)** – Irish labor leader; founded Irish Transport and General Workers' Union 1909; active in U.S. SP and IWW from 1914, founding member of Communist Labor Party in U.S. 1919; imprisoned for revolutionary activities 1920–23; deported to Ireland 1923; represented Ireland at Fifth Congress of Comintern in 1924 where he was elected alternate member of ECCI; drifted away from Communist Party of Ireland in 1928; remained active in unions and Irish Labour Party.

**Lazzari, Costantino (1857–1927)** – Italian SP general secretary 1912–19; attended Zimmerwald and Kienthal conferences; joined Comintern along with Italian SP 1919, but left with SP majority 1921; SP delegate at third Comintern congress 1921.

**League of Nations** – imperialist alliance created by Allied powers at Paris conference 1919; aimed to defend division of world imposed by that conference; disappeared at start of World War II.

**Ledebour, Georg (1850–1947)** – longtime German SPD leader; opposed SPD majority position during World War I; backed centrist wing of Zimmerwald movement; co-chair of USPD 1917–19; a leader of January 1919 Berlin uprising; opposed USPD majority's fusion with Communists 1920; refused to rejoin SPD and led a small left-wing group throughout 1920s; emigrated to Switzerland 1933.

**Lefebvre, Raymond (1891–1920)** – French internationalist during World War I; wounded at battle of Verdun; joined French SP 1916; a founder of left-wing veterans' organization; joined Committee for the Third International 1919, which he represented at second Comintern congress; perished on return voyage to France.

**Left Social Democratic Party of Sweden** – founded by expelled left-wing minority of Social Democratic Workers Party spring 1917; affiliated to Comintern June 1919; 23,000 members early 1920; majority adopted Twenty-one Conditions and became CP 1921; majority led by Kilbom split from party and Comintern 1929 and later dissolved.

**Left Socialist Party of Denmark** – *see* Communist Party of Denmark.

**Legien, Carl (1861–1920)** – Social Democratic head of German trade unions from 1890; avowed reformist; supported SPD right wing during World War I; backed crushing of revolutionary workers' movement 1918–19; backed and then moved to liquidate general strike against Kapp putsch 1920.

**Lékai, János (Johan Leutner) (1895–1925)** – Hungarian; former anarchist; among first members of Hungarian CP; president of Union of Young Communist Workers during Hungarian soviet republic; alternate executive committee member of Communist Youth International 1919–22; attended second Comintern congress; sent to U.S.; active in U.S. CP Hungarian Federation and editor of its newspaper *Uj Elöre* 1922–25.

**Lenin, Vladimir Ilyich (1870–1924)** – founded St. Petersburg League for the Emancipation of the Working Class 1895; exiled to Siberia 1896; went abroad and helped publish *Iskra* 1900–1903; central leader of Bolsheviks from 1903; defended revolutionary organization against liquidationism after 1907; RSDLP representative on International Socialist Bureau 1908–12; issued call for new, revolutionary International 1914; organized Zimmerwald Left to fight for this goal 1915–17; returned to Russia and led Bolsheviks' struggle for soviet power 1917; chair of Council of People's Commissars government 1917–24; Presiding Committee member at second Comintern congress; central leader of Comintern.

**Letonmäki, Lauri** – founding member of Finnish CP and elected to first Central Committee 1918; Finnish CP delegate to second Comintern congress.

**Leutner, Johan** – *see* Lékai, János.

**Levi, Paul (1883–1930)** – member of German SPD from 1906; Luxemburg's lawyer in political cases; worked with Zimmerwald Left in Switzerland 1915–16; leader of Spartacus League and central leader of German CP after deaths of Luxemburg, Liebknecht, and Jogiches early 1919; member of Comintern West European Secretariat in Berlin; headed CP delegation to second Comintern congress and served on Presiding Committee; elected CP cochair after merger with USPD 1920 but resigned February 1921; expelled for publicly criticizing party policies following March uprisings 1921; joined rump USPD and later SPD; committed suicide.

**Leviné, Eugen (1883–1919)** – born in Russia and participated in 1905 revolution; member of German Spartacus current and founding leader of German CP; arrested en route to first Comintern congress; central leader of Bavarian council republic 1919; arrested, tried, and shot after its overthrow.

**Lewicky, Mychajlo (1891–1933)** – Galician taken prisoner by Russians during World War I; joined Bolshevik Party in

Turkestan 1918; East Galician CP Central Committee member 1919–20; member of Galician soviet republic government 1920; CP delegate to second Comintern congress; ambassador of soviet Ukraine to Vienna 1921; worked in USSR from 1924; arrested 1933.

**Lieber, Mikhail Isaakovich (1880–1937)** – Bund leader and leading Menshevik during 1917; opponent of Russian October revolution; withdrew from politics after October revolution; executed during Moscow trials.

**Liebknecht, Karl (1871–1919)** – German revolutionary; son of Wilhelm Liebknecht; helped found Socialist Youth International 1907; jailed same year for book *Militarism and Anti-Militarism;* only member of Reichstag to vote against war credits December 1914; helped found Spartacus current; used parliamentary seat to lead antiwar agitation; jailed for antiwar activities 1916; released October 1918; a founding leader of German CP December 1918; a leader of Berlin uprising January 1919; arrested and murdered by SPD-instigated Freikorps.

**Liebknecht, Wilhelm (1826–1900)** – participated in German revolution of 1848; friend and collaborator of Marx and Engels; a leader of First International in Germany; cofounder of German Social Democratic Workers Party 1869; central party leader until death.

**Linderot, Sven (1889–1956)** – joined Swedish SDP 1908; founding member of Left SDP 1917 and of CP 1921; Left SDP delegate to second Comintern congress; central leader of International Red Aid in Berlin 1922–23; became party chair after Comintern purge of those linked to Bukharin 1929; held this post until 1951.

**Lindgren, Edward I. (Flynn) (b. 1879)** – leader of U.S. SP left wing; founding member of Communist Labor Party and elected to its first executive committee; United CP delegate to second Comintern congress; elected to Central Executive Committee and Executive Council of Workers Party 1922.

**Lindhagen, Carl (1860–1946)** – Swedish liberal, then Social Democrat from 1909; mayor of Stockholm 1903–30; internationalist during World War I; cofounder of Left SDP 1917; joined Comintern 1919; expelled from CP 1921 for opposing decisions of second Comintern congress; rejoined Social Democrats 1923.

**Litvakov, Moisey Il'ich (1880–1939)** – joined RSDLP 1901; Communist Bund consultative delegate to second Comintern congress; arrested 1938; died in prison.

**Litvinov, Maksim Maksimovich (1876–1951)** – joined RSDLP 1898; Bolshevik from 1903; Soviet envoy to Britain after October revolution 1917; deputy people's commissar, then people's commissar of foreign affairs 1921–39.

**Liu Shaozhou (b. 1892)** – born in China, lived in Russia from 1897; Bolshevik from 1917; chair of Union of Chinese Workers in Russia; Chinese Socialist Workers Party delegate to first and second Comintern congresses; returned to China after 1949 and held diplomatic post.

**Lloyd George, David (1863–1945)** – British Liberal politician; prime minister 1916–22; coauthored Versailles treaty and organized British intervention against Soviet republic.

**Longuet, Jean (1876–1938)** – grandson of Karl Marx; leader of French SP centrist minority after 1916; leader of centrist opposition at 1919 Bern conference; opposed SP joining Comintern; split with right-wing minority that retained SP name 1920.

**Loriot, Fernand (1870–1932)** – leader of revolutionary left in French SP during World War I; secretary of French Committee for the Third International; French CP international secretary 1921; quit party 1926; collaborated with Left Opposition currents.

**Louis, Paul (1872–1955)** – joined French SP before World War I; centrist, elected to party central leadership body October 1918; member of centrist Committee to Reconstruct the International December 1919–September

1920; CP central committee member from 1920; quit CP and founded Communist Socialist Party 1924.

**Lozovsky, Solomon Abramovich (Dridzo) (1878–1952)** – joined RSDLP 1901; in exile 1909–17; active in French trade union movement and SP; member dissident Bolshevik current that advocated conciliation with Mensheviks from 1912; contributed to Paris *Nashe Slovo* 1915; returned to Russia June 1917; elected secretary of trade union central council July 1917; expelled from Bolshevik Party December 1917; readmitted December 1919; Bolshevik delegate to second Comintern congress; general secretary of Red International of Labor Unions 1921–37; elected alternate CP Central Committee member 1927 and full member 1939; deputy minister of foreign affairs 1939–45; arrested 1949; shot in prison.

**Lukanov, Todor (1874–1946)** – lawyer and member of Tesnyaki wing of Bulgarian SDP; parliamentary deputy from 1913; jailed during World War I; Bulgarian CP Central Committee member from 1919; CP secretary from 1922; expelled from CP after 1923 uprising; readmitted after 1925; later emigrated to USSR.

**Lumivuokko, H.** – Finnish trade union leader; Finnish CP delegate to second Comintern congress; allied with Kuusinen 1920.

**Lunacharsky, Anatoly Vasilevich (1875–1933)** – joined revolutionary movement 1890s; Bolshevik from 1903; expelled as part of ultraleft current associated with *Vperyod* current 1909; took internationalist position during World War I; joined Mezhrayontsi and with them rejoined Bolsheviks 1917; people's commissar of education 1917–29; CP delegate to second Comintern congress; named ambassador to Spain 1933.

**Lüttwitz, Walther von (1859–1942)** – German baron and general; commander in chief 1919–20; leading participant in 1920 right-wing coup attempt.

**Luxemburg, Rosa (1871–1919)** – founding leader of Social Democracy of the Kingdom of Poland 1893; later lived in Germany and joined SPD 1898; Polish representative on International Socialist Bureau from 1903; supported left wing against revisionist right and, after 1910, against Center current led by Kautsky; leader of Spartacus group during war; imprisoned 1915; founding leader of German CP December 1918; arrested and murdered by SPD-instigated Freikorps after Berlin January uprising.

**Lysis** – pseudonym of Eugene Letailleur, conservative editor of French *Democratie Nouvelle.*

**MacAlpine, Eamonn** – born in Ireland; member of U.S. SP left wing; associate editor of Boston SP's *Revolutionary Age* 1918 and of *New York Communist* 1919; member Communist Labor Party in U.S.; returned to Ireland 1919; Irish CP consultative delegate to second Comintern congress.

**MacDonald, James Ramsay (1866–1937)** – joined Independent Labour Party 1894; leader of British Labour Party from 1911; forced to resign this post 1914 because of pacifist position on World War I; opposed Bolshevik revolution; head of Labour Party from 1922; prime minister 1924, 1929–31; split from party to found coalition government with Conservatives and Liberals 1931.

**McLaine, William (1891–1960)** – a leader of British engineers' (metalworkers) union; internationalist, Shop Stewards' leader, and British SP member during World War I; SP Central Committee member 1918; SP delegate to second Comintern congress; CP Central Committee member 1920; broke with CP 1929; became outspoken anticommunist.

**MacLean, Neil** – Independent Labour Party delegate to Geneva congress of Second International July–August 1920.

**Madsen, Alfred (1888–1962)** – head of Norwegian Social Democratic Youth League in Bergen 1909; editor of Norwegian Labor Party newspapers from 1914; Labor Party Central Committee member from 1919; delegate to second Comintern congress; left Comintern with Labor Party majority 1923; member of parliament 1921–45; head of trade union federation 1931–34; government minister 1928 and 1935–39.

**Makharadze, Pilipe (1868–1941)** – Georgian revolutionary from 1891; joined Bolsheviks 1903; Georgian CP delegate to second Comintern congress; chair of soviet government in Georgia from 1921; opposed Stalin in dispute on national question in Georgia 1922–23; removed from responsible political positions during Stalin purges late 1930s.

**Malírová, Helena (1877–1940)** – well-known writer; joined SDP in Czechoslovakia 1913; consultative delegate of Czechoslovak Communist Group to second Comintern congress; participated in founding Czechoslovak CP 1921; left CP in opposition to Comintern ultraleft policies 1929; continued activity in workers' movement.

**Mallin, Michael (1880–1916)** – Irish union leader; cofounder of Irish Citizen Army 1913; participated in Easter Uprising and executed by British.

**Manner, Kullervo (1880–1936)** – joined Finnish SDP 1905; party chair 1917–18; headed Finnish revolutionary government 1918; leading figure in Finnish CP and Comintern 1920s; CP delegate to second Comintern congress; expelled from Finnish CP as "Trotskyist sympathizer" 1935; condemned in Soviet Union to hard labor 1935; died in camps.

**Manuil'sky, Dmitri Zakharovich (1883–1959)** – joined RSDLP 1903; Bolshevik; went into exile 1907; associated with Otzovist dissident Bolshevik group and *Vperyod* current; internationalist during World War I; returned to Russia and joined Bolsheviks with Mezhrayontsi 1917; participated in all Comintern congresses except first; key ideologist of Stalinism; held leading Ukrainian diplomatic posts through 1953.

**Marchlewski, Julian (Karski) (1866–1925)** – joined Polish Marxist group 1885; a founding member of RSDLP and of Social Democracy of Poland; helped found German Spartacus group during World War I; jailed by German government 1916; released and moved to Soviet Russia 1918; helped reorganize German CP after January 1919 defeat; Polish CP delegate to second Comintern Congress; chair of Polish provisional revolutionary government during war with Poland 1920; chair of International Red Aid 1923.

**Maring** – *see* Sneevliet, Henk.

**Marx, Karl (1818–1883)** – cofounder with Engels of modern communist workers' movement; leader of Communist League 1847–52; coauthor of Communist Manifesto; editor of *Neue Rheinische Zeitung* in 1848–49 German revolution; central leader of International Working Men's Association (First International) 1864–76; published first volume of *Capital* 1867; partisan and defender of Paris Commune.

**Maurin, Jean (Maurice) (1879–1943)** – French Socialist; member of Committee for the Resumption of International Relations during World War I; member of SP central leadership body 1918–27; member of Committee to Reconstruct the International; went with SP after CP formed at Tours congress; expelled from SP 1933.

**Max von Baden (1867–1929)** – German prince, politician, and heir to throne of Baden; appointed imperial chancellor October 3, 1918; named Ebert as successor on November 9.

**Mayéras, Barthélémy (1879–1942)** – joined Guesde's French Workers Party; SP executive body member 1910–14 and 1920–25; centrist during World War I; part of Committee for the Reconstruction of the International; went with SP after split with Communists at Tours congress December 1920.

**Mazzinists** – Left bourgeois chauvinist current favoring Italy's entry into World War I; named after Giuseppe

Mazzini (1805–1872), Italian patriot and revolutionary republican.

**Medby, Johan (1896–1971)** – secretary of Norwegian Social Democratic Youth League; arrested for antimilitarist agitation 1917; youth league delegate to second Comintern congress 1920; edited various Labor Party newspapers; joined CP when Labor Party left Comintern 1923; edited CP newspapers, including illegal paper during Nazi occupation.

**Mensheviks** – originated as minority faction of RSDLP at its second congress 1903; moved increasingly to right after 1907; contained centrist and openly chauvinist wings during World War I; participated in Provisional Government 1917; opposed October 1917 revolution; during civil war one wing openly supported White armies; the other, led by Martov, opposed White Guards and participated in soviets but took no clear stand in defense of Soviet rule; this wing placed itself outside Soviet legality during Kronstadt crisis in 1921; thereafter functioned primarily in exile.

**Merezhin, A.N. (b. 1880)** – Menshevik 1905–16, then member of Bund; joined Bolsheviks 1919; member Bolshevik Party Central Bureau of Jewish Sections; Russian CP delegate to second Comintern congress; worked in People's Commissariat of Nationalities, then as lecturer.

**Merges, August (1870–1933)** – German Spartacus group leader of Brunswick Workers' and Soldiers' Council and president of Brunswick Council of People's Representatives 1918–19; delegated to represent ultraleft KAPD at second Comintern congress but left as congress opened; joined German CP 1921; murdered by Nazis.

**Méric, Victor (1876–1933)** – French anarchist; left Socialist; member of Committee for the Third International; member of SP central leadership body from February 1920 and of CP central committee 1920–21; increasingly opposed Comintern from rightist standpoint; expelled 1923.

***The Messenger*** – U.S. monthly founded 1917 by A. Philip Randolph, while member of SP left wing, that promoted Black rights and opposed World War I.

**Mexican Communist Party** – founded with 22 members when Mexican SP adopted this name November 1919; 1,500 members late 1922.

**Meyer, Ernst (1887–1930)** – left-wing German SPD member from 1908; delegate to Zimmerwald and Kienthal conferences; leader of Spartacus current; German CP Central Bureau member 1918–20, 1921–23 and Central Committee member 1926–29; delegate to second Comintern congress; elected to Comintern Executive Committee 1920; removed from leadership positions 1929 for opposing Stalin's policies.

**Mezhrayontsi** – Russian Social Democratic group formed 1913 with position intermediate between Bolsheviks and Mensheviks; took internationalist stand during World War I; among its leaders were Trotsky, M.S. Uritsky, and Lunacharsky; fused with Bolsheviks 1917.

**Michaelis, Georg (1857–1936)** – German chancellor and head of Prussian government July–October 1917.

**Milkic, Iliya (1882–1968)** – a founder and organizer of Serbian Social Democratic and union movements; lived in France and Switzerland during World War I, in Russia 1919–22; Yugoslav CP delegate to second Comintern congress; elected to Comintern Executive Committee 1920; lived in Vienna, active in Yugoslav CP 1922–26; returned to Belgrade and left politics 1926.

**Millerand, Alexandre (1859–1943)** – French SP politician; sparked controversy when took ministerial post in bourgeois government 1899; later moved to right of bourgeois political spectrum; premier and foreign minister January–September 1920; president 1920–24.

**Mineff, Stoyan (Vanini) (1891–1959)** – joined Tesnyaki wing of Bulgarian SDP; internationalist in Switzerland during World War I; supported Lenin in Zimmerwald movement in Switzerland 1916–17; moved to France 1920; French Committee for Third International delegate to second Comintern congress; Comintern envoy to Spain during civil war; remained on Comintern staff until retired for health reasons 1941.

**Mistral, Paul (1872–1932)** – joined French Workers Party 1893; SP member of parliament 1910–32; backed centrist opposition during World War I; mayor of Grenoble 1919–32; opposed Comintern; after split with CP, member of SP central leadership body 1920–24.

**Mitskevich-Kapsukas, Vikenti S. (1880–1935)** – joined Lithuanian SDP 1903; joined Bolsheviks 1915; edited Bolshevik newspaper in Lithuania 1917; founder of Lithuanian CP and Central Committee member from 1918; headed soviet Lithuanian government 1919; delegate from CP of Lithuania-Belorussia to second Comintern congress; held leading positions in Comintern from 1924.

**Modigliani, Giuseppe Emanuele (1872–1947)** – joined Italian SP 1894; parliamentary deputy 1913–24; opposed Italy's entry into World War I; backed centrists at Zimmerwald and Kienthal conferences 1915 and 1916; with Turati, leader of SP's openly reformist right wing; expelled; helped found United SP 1922; participated in SP reunification 1930; split again with right Social Democrats 1947.

**Monatte, Pierre (1881–1960)** – French anarcho-syndicalist from 1904; leader of antichauvinist opposition in unions during war; secretary of Committee for Third International; advocated revolutionary syndicalists joining Comintern; did not join French CP until 1923; expelled 1924 for opposing anti-Trotsky campaign; returned to syndicalism.

**Moraczewski, Jedrzej (1870–1944)** – a leader of Polish Social Democratic Party of Galicia and Silesia (PPSD) from 1893; deputy in Austrian imperial parliament; formed first procapitalist Warsaw government November 1918;

PPSD deputy in Polish parliament 1919–27; expelled from party for supporting Pilsudski; head of progovernment trade union organization 1931–39.

**Morgan** – U.S. capitalist family based on railroad, steel, and banking empire.

**Moyrova, Varvara Akimovna (1890–1951)** – joined Russian CP 1917; active in various international and Soviet bodies; CP delegate to second Comintern congress.

**Mukherji, Abaninath (1891–1937)** – born in India; studied abroad 1910–12; joined German SPD 1912; active in independence movement in India during World War I; consultative delegate to second Comintern congress; attended Baku congress 1920; a founder of CP of India in Tashkent exile 1920; active in underground in India 1922–26; returned to Soviet Union 1926; worked in Comintern apparatus and in scientific work in Moscow and Leningrad from 1926; arrested and killed in Stalin's purges.

**Münzenberg, Willi (1889–1940)** – German Socialist; moved to Switzerland 1910; secretary of reconstituted Socialist Youth International 1915–19; supported Zimmerwald Left; German CP founding member; key founder and secretary of Communist Youth International (CYI) 1919–21; CYI delegate to second Comintern congress; leader of International Red Aid from 1921; elected to German CP Central Committee 1927; broke with Stalin and expelled from CP 1937; continued political activity in France; probably killed by Stalin's secret police.

**Murphy, John T. (1888–1966)** – leader of British Shop Stewards' movement during World War I; joined Scottish Socialist Labour Party 1917; represented Shop Stewards at second Comintern congress; founding member of British CP 1920 and elected to its first Central Committee; prominent in CP-led trade union Minority Movement; jailed six months for subversion 1925; broke with CP and Comintern 1932; joined Labour Party.

**Nadolny, Rudolf (1873–1953)** – member of German foreign office from 1902; head of its Russian department 1918–19.

**Naine, Charles (1874–1926)** – a leader of Swiss SDP; member of Zimmerwald International Socialist Committee in Bern; joined right wing of Swiss party 1917; helped form centrist Two-and-a-Half International 1919–21.

**Napoléon III (Louis-Napoléon Bonaparte) (1808–1873)** – nephew of Napoléon Bonaparte; became emperor after 1851 coup; deposed 1870.

**National Democratic People's Party (Germany)** – split-off from Bavarian People's Party; participated in German National Assembly elections 1919 and Reichstag elections 1920 with little success.

**National Federation of Labor (CNT) (Spain)** – Spanish anarcho-syndicalist trade union federation founded in Madrid 1911; 109,000 members 1914; voted to join Comintern at Second Congress December 1919; grew to 700,000 members by late 1919; disaffiliated under pressure of anarchist leaders 1922; banned 1923–30.

**National Young Labour League (Britain)** – one of three small British organizations affiliated to Communist Youth International in mid-1920; probably grew out of London-based Proletarian College, which was an off-shoot of Scottish youth organization of same name; functioned publicly from May 1920.

**Nazaretian, Hamaiak (1889–1937)** – Bolshevik from 1905; member of Council of People's Commissars of Terek Soviet Republic from April 1918; organized partisan detachments in Georgia 1919; Russian CP Caucasus bureau secretary 1920–22; Armenian CP delegate to second Comintern congress; occupied key party posts until disappeared in Stalin purges.

**Nedelkov, Ivan (Nikolai Shablin) (1881–1925)** – active in Bulgarian SDP (Tesnyaki) before World War I; Bulgarian CP founder and Central Committee member 1919; delegate to second Comintern congress; elected to Comintern

Executive Committee 1920; represented Comintern at Baku congress 1920; returned to Bulgaria and carried out underground party work after right-wing coup 1923; murdered by police.

**Nemec, Antonín (1858–1926)** – centrist leader of Czechoslovak SDP; supported Tusar's participation in coalition government.

**Nenkov, Temelko (1877–1925)** – joined Bulgarian revolutionary workers' movement 1906; mine workers' union secretary 1912–24; Bulgarian CP founding member 1919; killed by government forces.

**Newbold, J.T. Walton (1888–1943)** – joined British Fabian Society and Independent Labour Party 1910; joined British CP 1921; elected to Parliament 1922; left CP 1924.

**Newbold, Marjory Neilson (1883–1926)** – joined British Independent Labour Party 1908 and became a leader of its left wing; chair of British National Young Labour League, for which she was a consultative delegate to second Comintern congress; joined CP with ILP left wing 1921.

***New Statesman*** – British Labour Party publication founded by Beatrice and Sidney Webb in 1913.

**Nielsen, Marie-Sophie (1875–1951)** – member of Danish SDP; executive committee member 1916–18; second Comintern congress delegate from Communist Teachers Club; founding member of Danish CP 1920; expelled for not supporting campaign against Trotsky 1928.

**Nikbin, Hassan (Hassanzadeh, Hassanov, Kerim-Aga Farsi) (b. 1879)** – Iranian trade union leader, Iranian CP consultative delegate to second Comintern congress; succeeded Heydar Khan as Iranian CP head September 1921.

**Nobs, Ernst (1886–1957)** – leading Swiss Social Democrat; supported Zimmerwald Left at Kienthal conference; adopted centrist position 1917 and became right-wing Social Democrat after 1920; president of Switzerland 1949.

**Norwegian Labor Party** – founded 1887; left wing won majority 1918; affiliated to Comintern June 1919; 125,000 members 1920; right-wing minority of 3,000 split to form Social Democratic Labor Party 1921; majority disaffiliated from Comintern 1923; minority founded Norwegian CP with 15,000 members.

**Noske, Gustav (1868–1946)** – German SPD leader; chauvinist during World War I; German war minister 1919–20; organized suppression of workers' uprisings in Berlin and central Germany January–March 1919.

**Nurijanian, Avis (1896–1937)** – Armenian; Dashnaktsutiun Party representative to Baku soviet Executive Committee 1918; joined Bolshevik Party 1918; secretary of Russian CP Baku committee 1918; helped found CP of Armenia 1920; represented it at second Comintern congress and Baku congress 1920; Armenian soviet republic commissar of war 1920–21; held other party and government posts 1921–37; arrested and killed during Stalin purges.

**Obolensky, Valeryan Valeryanovich (N. Osinsky) (1887–1938)** – joined RSDLP 1907; Bolshevik; first chair of Supreme Council of National Economy 1917; a leader of Left Communist opposition 1918; Russian CP delegate at second Comintern congress; Central Committee alternate member 1921 and from 1925; supported Leninist opposition to Stalin led by Trotsky in Russian CP from 1923; later aligned with Bukharin; arrested 1937 and shot.

**Olbracht, Ivan (Kamil Zeman) (1882–1952)** – delegate from Czechoslovak CP to second Comintern congress; edited Czechoslovak CP newspaper *Rudé Pravo;* denounced as "rightist" 1928–29; quit party in opposition to Comintern's ultraleft course 1929; subsequently rejoined; participated in resistance during World War II; left political activity after 1945.

**Ol'minsky, Mikhail Stepanovich (Aleksandrov) (1863–1933)** – joined revolutionary movement 1883 and RSDLP 1898; Bolshevik from 1903; leading member of People's Commissariat of Finance 1917; *Pravda* editorial staff member 1918–20; Russian CP delegate to second Comintern congress; engaged in party history and literary studies from 1920.

***L'Ordine Nuovo* (New order)** – Italian revolutionary newspaper launched by Gramsci, Tasca, Terracini, and Togliatti 1919; merged with *Avanti!* 1921; forced to cease publication October 1922; also name of left-wing current in SP that dissolved into CP 1921.

**Orlando, Vittorio Emanuele (1860–1952)** – Italian bourgeois politician; prime minister 1917–19; headed Italian delegation to Paris peace talks 1919–20.

**Osinsky** – *see* Obolensky, Valeryan.

**Oudegeest, Jan (1870–1951)** – Dutch trade union federation chair 1908–18; secretary of International Federation of Trade Unions and leader of League of Nations International Labour Office from 1919; Social Democratic Workers Party chair 1927–34.

**Pak Chin-sun** – born in Korea, settled in Russia as youth before World War I; rallied to communism 1917; delegate to second Comintern congress; elected to Comintern Executive Committee; worked in China among immigrant Korean Communists 1921; not recognized as delegate at fourth Comintern congress and relieved of Comintern duties 1922; lived in Soviet Union.

**Pankhurst, Sylvia (1882–1960)** – joined British Independent Labour Party 1898; repeatedly arrested for activity in labor and women's suffrage movements; held antichauvinist position on war; leader of Workers' Socialist Federation, which took name CP June 1920; represented this group at second Comintern congress; Pankhurst group joined unified British CP January 1921, which expelled her for indiscipline 1921.

**Pannekoek, Anton (1873–1960)** – joined Dutch Social Democrats 1902; leader of left-wing *Tribune* current from

1907; member Zimmerwald Left during World War I; cofounder Dutch CP 1918; worked closely with KAPD; broke with Comintern over Twenty-one Conditions as part of ultraleft split from Dutch CP 1921; subsequently left political activity while continuing to consider himself a Marxist and write on theoretical questions.

**Parnell, Charles Stewart (1846–1891)** – Irish nationalist; joined Parliamentary (Home Rule) Party 1875; led struggles against British landlord system 1879–82; elected chairman of Parliamentary Party 1880; central leader of Irish nationalist movement until death.

**Party of Revolutionary Communism** – founded September 1918 as split from Russian Left SRs following July uprising against soviet power; supported Soviet government but at first denied need for proletarian dictatorship; joined Russian CP fall 1920.

**Pastukhov, Krustiu Ivanov (1874–1949)** – leader of reformist Shiroki wing of Bulgarian SDP after 1903 split; harshly repressed popular mobilizations as minister of interior 1919; arrested for anticommunist activities 1946.

**Paul-Boncour, Joseph (1873–1972)** – French politician; parliamentary deputy 1909–14 and 1919–31; labor minister 1911; joined SP 1916; opposed SP joining Comintern and went with SP after split at Tours congress 1920; quit SP 1931; several times government minister; rejoined SP 1945; French signatory to United Nations Charter 1946.

**Pavlovich, Mikhail (M.L. Wel'tman) (1871–1927)** – joined Russian Socialist movement before finishing secondary school; exiled in Paris from late 1890s; collaborated with *Iskra;* Menshevik from 1903; internationalist, contributed to *Nashe Slovo* during World War I; joined commissariat of foreign affairs after Bolshevik victory; Bolshevik delegate to second Comintern congress; participated in Baku congress 1920.

**Pestaña, Angel (1888–1937)** – anarchist; leader of Spanish National Federation of Labor (CNT); CNT delegate to second Comintern congress; after congress, opposed joining Comintern and Red International of Labor Unions; founded syndicalist party 1934; deputy commissar of republican army during Spanish civil war.

**Pestkowski, Stanislaw (1882–1937)** – joined left wing of Polish Social Democracy 1902; escaped Siberian exile; active in London Bolshevik section and British SP 1914–17; participated in October revolution in Russia 1917; deputy people's commissar of nationalities under Stalin 1917–19; chair of Kirghiz Revolutionary Committee 1919–20; headed political administration of western front 1920–21; Bolshevik delegate at second Comintern congress; held various posts in Soviet diplomatic service and Comintern; disappeared during Stalin purges.

**Phillips, Charles (Frank Seaman, Jesús Ramírez, Manuel Gomez, Charles Shipman) (1895–1989)** – U.S. journalist; founder of Mexican CP 1919; traveled to Russia via Cuba; Mexican CP delegate to second Comintern congress; deported from Mexico, joined U.S. CP 1921; headed CP's All-American Anti-Imperialist League from 1925; Comintern Executive Committee member 1928; expelled from U.S. CP 1929; worked with pro-Bukharin opposition groups until mid-1930s, then quit politics.

**Pilsudski, Józef (1867–1935)** – cofounder of Polish SP 1892; led right-wing nationalist Revolutionary Faction from party's 1906 split until 1918; backed Central Powers in World War I; headed newly created Polish republic 1918; led invasion of Soviet republic 1920; resigned 1923; right-wing dictator of Poland 1926–35.

**Platten, Fritz (1883–1942)** – Swiss SDP secretary from 1912; led Swiss Zimmerwald Left; organized Lenin's return to Russia from exile April 1917; led pro-Comintern left wing of Swiss SDP 1919–21; delegate at Comintern founding congress; returned to Switzerland spring 1920; led founding of united Swiss CP 1921; party secretary 1921–23; in Soviet Union after 1923 except 1930–31; arrested in Stalin's purges 1938 and died in prison camp.

**Poale Zion (Workers of Zion)** – coalition of Jewish nationalist organizations that attempted to combine ideas of socialism with Zionism; formed in several eastern European countries from 1897; gave rise to several parties, including in Russia, Jewish Social Democratic Labor Party – Poale Zion 1904–6; 15,000 members 1917; opposed October revolution; supported right-wing Ukrainian Directory government 1918; left wing split, forming Jewish CP – Poale Zion August 1919; some members of this party joined Russian CP December 1922; Poale Zion banned in Soviet Union 1928.

**Poale Zion of Austria** – small group that developed in Vienna during World War I; supported Zimmerwald Left; active in January strikes 1918; after Russian revolution, initially sought to reconcile Zionism and communism; many members later joined CP.

**Pokrovsky, Mikhail Nikolayevich (1868–1932)** – joined RSDLP 1905; Bolshevik; in exile 1909–17; supported ultraleft current associated with *Vperyod;* contributed to *Nashe Slovo;* chair of Moscow soviet November 1917–March 1918; associated with Left Communists 1918; deputy commissar of education 1918–32; CP delegate to second Comintern congress; worked as historian; writings fiercely attacked and banned in 1930s.

**Polano, Luigi (1897–1984)** – leader of Italian Socialist youth during World War I; elected to Communist Youth International Executive Committee 1919; Italian Socialist youth delegate to second Comintern congress; elected to Italian CP Central Committee at founding congress 1921; lived in Soviet Union during fascist regime; arrested during Stalin purges and deported to Siberia; returned to Italy 1945; Italian CP elected official after 1945.

**Polish Socialist Party** – founded 1892; strongly marked by nationalist and reformist tendencies; left-wing majority founded Polish Socialist Party–Left 1906, which adopted internationalist position during World War I and merged with Social Democracy of the Kingdom of Poland and Lithuania to form Polish CP 1918; right-wing Revolutionary Faction supported Central Powers during World War I and participated in formation of Polish capitalist state 1918; joined coalition government during war with Russia 1920.

**Pöögelmann, Hans (1875–1938)** – active in Estonian socialist movement from 1905; active in U.S. exile in SP Estonian federation 1911–17; member of Estonian soviet governments 1919–20; after overthrow, lived in Soviet Union; Estonian CP founding member 1920 and Central Committee member 1925–27; Estonian CP delegate to second Comintern congress; Estonian representative to Comintern Executive Committee 1921–22; Comintern Control Commission member 1924–28; arrested during Moscow trials and shot.

***Le Populaire* (The people)** – French SP newspaper representing centrist Longuet current.

**Prampolini, Camillo (1857–1930)** – editor of Italian Socialist newspapers from 1887; Italian SP founding member 1892; Socialist deputy 1890–1926; took centrist position during World War I; part of reformist wing of Italian SP; stayed with SP when CP formed 1921; expelled from SP with right-wing faction 1922.

**Preobrazhensky, Yevgeny Alekseyevich (1886–1937)** – joined Bolsheviks 1903; alternate Central Committee member 1917–18, full member 1920–21; Left Communist 1918; *Pravda* editor 1919; CP delegate to second Comintern congress; member of Leninist opposition in Soviet CP led by Trotsky; expelled from CP 1927; readmitted 1929; arrested during Stalin purges; refused to profess guilt and was shot without trial.

**Pressemanne, Adrien (1879–1929)** – French Socialist; adopted centrist position during World War I; member of parliament 1914–29; member of Committee to Reconstruct the International 1919–20; opposed Twenty-one Conditions; went with SP when CP founded 1920; member of its central leadership body 1920–26.

**Proost, Jan (Jansen) (1890–1943)** – worked with Dutch *Tribune* current during World War I; a founding member of Dutch CP 1918; attended second Comintern congress, where he served on parliamentarism and agrarian commissions; elected to Comintern Executive Committee; remained in Moscow as Dutch CP representative through 1923; left Dutch CP when Wijnkoop and Van Ravesteyn expelled 1926; shot by Nazi troops.

**Quelch, Thomas (1886–1954)** – member Social Democratic Federation, then British SP; internationalist during World War I; advocated SP affiliating to Comintern; delegate to second Comintern congress and elected to Comintern Executive Committee; participated in Baku congress 1920; British CP Central Committee 1923–25; *Communist International* editorial staff 1920–31; withdrew from CP late in life.

**Radek, Karl (1885–1939)** – joined Social Democracy of the Kingdom of Poland and Lithuania 1904; moved to Germany 1908 and was active in SPD left; leader of Zimmerwald Left during World War I; joined Bolsheviks 1917; Bolshevik and Soviet emissary to Germany December 1918; arrested there February 1919; released and returned to Russia January 1920; elected to Bolshevik Central Committee 1919; Comintern secretary April–August 1920; a central Comintern leader; with Trotsky, part of Leninist opposition to Stalin 1923–29; expelled from CP 1927; capitulated 1929; arrested 1937 during Moscow frame-up trials and died in prison.

**Rafes, Moshe (1883–1942)** – joined Bund 1903; Central Committee member 1912–19; opposed Bolshevik revolution; fought against Bolsheviks in the Ukraine 1917–19; joined Bolshevik Party 1919; played key role in winning left wing of Bund to communism in Poland and Russia 1919–21; Russian CP delegate to second Comintern congress; Comintern representative to China 1927; arrested during purges and died in prison.

**Rahja, Jukka (1887–1920)** – Finnish Bolshevik from 1905; Finnish SP 1907–13; member Petrograd Military Revolutionary Committee 1917; participated in Finnish revolution 1918; returned to Moscow and helped form Finnish CP 1918; Finnish delegate to first and second Comintern congresses; assassinated in Petrograd by opponent current previously expelled from CP.

**Rákosi, Mátyás (1892–1971)** – joined Hungarian SDP 1910; joined Bolsheviks while prisoner of war in Russia 1918; returned to Hungary and participated in founding Hungarian CP November 1918; held key posts in Hungarian soviet republic 1919; joined Comintern staff 1920; Hungarian CP delegate to second Comintern congress; Comintern Executive Committee secretariat member 1921–24; returned to Hungary to reorganize CP, captured and imprisoned 1925–40; signed manifesto dissolving Comintern 1943; general secretary of Hungarian CP 1945–56; emigrated to Soviet Union after Hungarian uprising 1956; expelled from Hungarian CP 1962.

**Rakovsky, Christian (1873–1941)** – prominent Romanian Social Democrat from 1890s; elected secretary of Balkan Revolutionary Social Democratic Federation 1915; attended Zimmerwald conference; joined Bolsheviks 1918; elected to Central Committee 1919; head of Ukrainian soviet government January 1919–23; Russian CP delegate to second Comintern congress; supported Leninist opposition to Stalin led by Trotsky in Russian CP from 1923; expelled from party and arrested 1927; capitulated 1934; died in prison following Moscow frame-up trials.

**Ramírez, Jesús** – *see* Phillips, Charles.

**Ramonov, Yevgeny Davidovich (1883–1950)** – joined Bolsheviks 1905; active in Central Asia and southern Caucasus from July 1917; delegate to second Comintern congress from Bolshevik organization among Caucasus mountain peoples; held key Transcaucasian party posts and was USSR Soviet Central Executive Committee member; later left political activity.

**Ramsay, David (1883–1948)** – member of British Social Democratic Federation, then of Socialist Labour Party before World War I; antichauvinist and leader of Shop Stewards during World War I; Shop Stewards' delegate to second Comintern congress; joined British CP 1920; CP executive committee 1926–29.

**Randolph, A. Philip (1889–1979)** – launched radical socialist Black magazine the *Messenger* 1917; initially sympathetic to Russian revolution but stayed with SP after CP founded 1919; organized Brotherhood of Sleeping Car Porters 1925; organized March on Washington movement for Black civil rights during World War II; vice president AFL-CIO 1955.

**Rasikas, Rafail Stepanovich (1887–1938)** – Lithuanian; member of the Latvian SDP 1904–6 and of Lithuanian SDP 1906–17; joined Bolsheviks November 1917 and was leader of Lithuanian soviet of soldiers' deputies in Petrograd; Lithuanian soviet government military commissar 1919; member of Lithuanian CP Bureau Abroad 1920–22; Lithuanian-Belorussian CP delegate to second Comintern congress; held Comintern posts until 1925.

**Reconstructors** – *see* Committee to Reconstruct the International.

**Red International of Labor Unions (Profintern)** – founded July 1921 by Communist and revolutionary anarcho-syndicalist union leaders to provide alternative to reformist policies of Amsterdam International; dissolved December 1937.

**Reed, John (1887–1920)** – radical U.S. journalist; supported IWW from 1913; opposed government during World War I; supported Wilson 1916; won to Communist movement while U.S. correspondent in Russia during October revolution 1917; author of *Ten Days That Shook the World;* joined U.S. SP 1918; a founding member of Communist Labor Party 1919; Communist Labor Party delegate at second Comintern congress and elected to Comintern Executive Committee 1920; addressed Baku congress 1920; died of typhus in Soviet Russia.

**Reichpietsch, Max (1894–1917)** – mechanic; drafted into German navy 1914; worked with USPD in organizing sailors against World War I; leader of mutiny summer 1917; executed.

**Renaudel, Pierre (1871–1935)** – associate of Jean Jaurès before 1914; central leader of French SP right-wing majority during World War I; political director of *L'Humanité* 1914–18; member of parliament 1914–19, 1924–35; opposed Comintern; part of right-wing split that retained SP name 1920; led right-wing split from SP 1933.

**Renner, Karl (1870–1950)** – prominent revisionist in Austrian SDP; promoted "national-cultural autonomy" within capitalist state for minorities from 1897; chauvinist during World War I; Austrian chancellor 1919–20 and president 1931–33.

**Rockefeller** – U.S. capitalist family; founded Standard Oil and acquired vast industrial and banking empire.

**Roland-Holst, Henriette (1869–1952)** – joined Dutch Social Democratic Workers Party 1897; supported its left wing; with Zimmerwald Left; joined SDP *Tribune* group 1916; founding member Dutch CP 1918; left CP 1927; later Christian Socialist.

**Rosmer, Alfred (Griot) (1877–1964)** – French revolutionary syndicalist; joined Zimmerwald movement during World War I; Comintern Executive Committee member in Moscow 1920–21; delegate of Committee for

Third International to second Comintern congress and served on Presiding Committee; CP founding member 1920; a leader of Red International of Labor Unions; expelled from CP as supporter of Left Opposition to Stalin 1924; broke with Left Opposition 1930 but collaborated with Trotsky and movement for Fourth International after 1936.

**Rothe, Franz (1862–1941)** – writer for Austrian SDP newspaper *Arbeiter-Zeitung;* a leader of a left tendency in SDP, Social Democratic Working Group of Revolutionary Workers Councils; joined CP 1921.

**Rovio, Gustaa (1887–1938)** – born in Finland; joined Bolsheviks while living in Russia 1905; joined Finnish SDP 1910; hid Lenin August–September 1917; chief of Helsinki militia during Finnish revolution 1918; after its defeat, emigrated to Russia; founder of Finnish CP 1918; Finnish Socialist Workers Party delegate to second Comintern congress; head of CP in Autonomous Soviet Socialist Republic of Karelia from 1929 until dismissed for "nationalist deviation" 1935; arrested during Stalin purges 1937 and shot.

**Roy, Evelyn Trent (Helen Allan, Santi Devi)** – traveled to Mexico from U.S. with M.N. Roy; cofounder of Mexican CP 1919; Mexican CP consultative delegate to second Comintern congress; member of Indian CP in exile in Tashkent 1920; active in Comintern through 1925; left political activity late 1920s.

**Roy, Manabendra Nath (Bhattacharya, Robert Allan-Roy) (1887–1954)** – Indian revolutionary; active in nationalist protests against British rule 1910–15; forced into exile 1915; attracted to Marxism in U.S. 1916–17; under U.S. federal indictment, escaped to Mexico 1917; participated in founding Mexican CP 1919, which he represented at second Comintern congress; founded Indian CP in exile in Tashkent 1920; headed Comintern Far Eastern bureau 1920; elected Comintern Executive Committee alternate member 1922–24 and full member 1924–27; Comintern representative to China February–August 1927; expelled from Comintern with Bukharin supporters 1929; returned to India 1930; led current critical of Comintern's sectarianism on national struggle; imprisoned 1931–36; joined Congress Party with supporters 1936; founded Radical Democratic Party 1940 and edited its newspaper, *Radical Humanist.*

**RSDLP (Russian Social Democratic Labor Party)** – *see* Communist Party of Russia (Bolsheviks); Mensheviks.

**Rudas, László (1885–1950)** – Hungarian CP Central Committee member 1918; carried out academic work in Moscow from 1922; imprisoned 1937; returned to Hungary after World War II and directed CP school.

**Rudnyánszky, Endre (1885–1943)** – Hungarian prisoner of war in Russia; joined Bolsheviks 1917; helped found Hungarian Communist Group; chair of Federation of Foreign Groups of the Russian CP late 1918; Moscow representative of Hungarian soviet republic 1919; Hungarian CP delegate to second Comintern congress; Comintern Executive Committee member 1920; disappeared from Russia with Comintern funds and was expelled from Hungarian CP 1921.

**Rudzutak, Yan Ernestovich (1887–1938)** – Latvian; joined Bolsheviks 1905; after October revolution, member of Supreme Council of National Economy Presiding Committee; Russian CP Central Committee member from 1920; Russian CP delegate to second Comintern congress; general secretary of All-Russia Central Trade Union Council; head of Russian CP Central Asia bureau 1921–24; CP Political Bureau member 1927–32; arrested during Stalin purge trials and shot.

**Rühle, Otto (1874–1943)** – joined German SPD 1900; voted with Liebknecht against war credits in Reichstag 1915; chair of Dresden Workers' and Soldiers' Council in November 1918 revolution; delegate to German CP founding congress December 1918; part of 1919 ultraleft split that later formed KAPD; delegated to represent KAPD at second Comintern congress, but left as congress began; expelled from KAPD November 1920; returned to German SPD 1923; served on Dewey commission to investigate Moscow frame-up trial against Trotsky 1937.

**Russian Social Democratic Labor Party** – *see* Communist Party of Russia (Bolsheviks); Mensheviks.

**Rutgers, Sebald Justius (1879–1961)** – joined Dutch Social Democracy 1899; part of left-wing Tribune group from 1909; organized U.S. supporters of *Tribune* current and Zimmerwald Left in Socialist Propaganda League during World War I; delegate at first Comintern congress 1919; headed Comintern's Amsterdam bureau 1919–20; headed settlement of U.S. volunteer workers in Kuzbas, Soviet Union, 1922–25; continued to live in Soviet Union until 1938, then returned to the Netherlands.

**Ruthenberg, Charles E. (1882–1927)** – joined U.S. SP 1909 and a leader of its left wing during World War I; CP national secretary 1919–27; Comintern Executive Committee alternate member from 1922 and full member from 1924.

**Ryazanov, David Borisovich (Gol'dendakh) (1870–1938)** – active in Russian Social Democratic and trade union movements from 1890s; collaborated with *Nashe Slovo* in Paris during World War I; returned to Russia, joined Mezhrayontsi, then Bolsheviks 1917; Russian CP delegate to second Comintern congress; director of Marx-Engels Institute from 1921; included in frame-up of "Mensheviks" and expelled from CP 1931; arrested and died in Stalin purges.

**Rykov, Aleksey Ivanovich (1881–1938)** – joined RSDLP 1899 and Bolsheviks 1903; elected to Central Committee 1905; member of first Council of People's Commissars 1917; party Central Committee 1917, 1920–34; Russian CP delegate to second Comintern congress; CP Political Bureau member 1922–30; deputy chair of Council of

People's Commissars from 1921; succeeded Lenin as its chair 1924; allied with Bukharin; leader of Right Opposition 1928–29; recanted 1929; expelled from CP 1937; executed during frame-up purges.

**Ryvkin, Oskar L'vovich (1899–1937)** – joined Red Guards and Bolsheviks early 1917; central leader of Russian CP youth organization from its founding 1918; represented it at second Comintern congress; held various party posts from 1924; arrested 1937 and died in prison.

**Sadoul, Jacques (1881–1956)** – French SP member; part of French military mission to Russia 1917; won to communism and volunteered for Red Army; sentenced to death in absentia in France for desertion 1919; delegate of French Communist Group in Russia to second Comintern congress; returned to France 1924 and pardoned; remained with French CP until death.

**Sadovskaya, Bronislava Lyudvigovna** – Polish; Bolshevik Party member 1917–35; Russian CP delegate to second Comintern congress.

**Safarov, Georgy Ivanovich (1891–1942)** – joined RSDLP 1908, soon became Bolshevik; worked in exile during World War I; returned to Russia with Lenin 1917; led Comintern work for Middle and Far East from 1920; Russian CP delegate to second Comintern congress; elected to Comintern Executive Committee 1922; associated with Zinoviev in Leningrad opposition and dropped from CP Central Committee 1925; member of United Opposition 1926–27; expelled from CP 1927; capitulated 1928; reexpelled 1934 and arrested; perished in prison camps.

**Said Galiev, Sahibgiray (1894–1939)** – Tatar; began revolutionary work in army 1916; joined Bolsheviks March 1917; held numerous posts leading political work among Muslim peoples 1918–20; chair of Central Bureau of the Communist Organization of the Peoples of the East November 1919; elected chair of Council of People's Commissars of Tatar autonomous republic 1920 and of Crimean republic 1921; Tatar CP delegate to second Comintern congress; held other government posts until killed in Stalin purges.

**St. John, Vincent (1873–1929)** – one of the principal leaders of U.S. IWW and its general secretary 1908–14; became an opponent of CP.

**Samuelson, Oskar (1885–1947)** – chair of Social Democratic Youth League of Sweden, which played important role in founding Left SDP 1917; elected to Communist Youth International Executive Committee 1919; journalist for Left SDP from 1920; joined CP 1921; CP secretary from 1924; broke from Comintern with Kilbom 1929; rejoined SDP 1937.

**Sapunov, Mikhail Yefimovich (1884–1952)** – oil worker in Baku 1901–20; joined Bolshevik Party March 1917; elected to first Baku soviet of workers' deputies; Soviet oil workers' union Central Committee deputy chairman 1920–22; delegate for Azerbaijan trade union majority to second Comintern Congress; subsequently held administrative posts.

**Sarekat Islam (Islamic Association)** – formed in Indonesia out of Association of Islamic Merchants 1912; initially reflected interests of Indonesian bourgeoisie against foreign competition; became mass nationalist movement, with strong rural support, claiming 360,000 members by 1916; adopted radical democratic program under influence of mass pressure and revolutionary Social Democrats 1917; 1.5 million members 1920; played no significant role after political break with CP 1923.

**Sazonov, Sergey Dmitrovich (1860–1927)** – tsarist diplomat; minister of foreign affairs 1910–16; represented Denikin and Kolchak at Versailles conference 1919; died in exile.

**Schäffle, Albert Eberhard Friedrich (1831–1903)** – German and Austrian economist, social reformer, and politician.

**Scheflo, Olav (1883–1943)** – Norwegian Labor Party journalist from 1905; editor of central organ *Social-Demokraten* 1918–21; led struggle for Norwegian Labor Party to join Comintern; represented party at second Comintern congress; Comintern Executive Committee member 1921–27; joined CP when Labor Party split from Comintern 1923; CP Central Committee member and chief editor of *Norges Kommunistblad* 1923–26; criticized as "right opportunist" from 1925; left CP 1928; rejoined Labor Party 1929; when Trotsky was in Norway, defended him against government and Stalinist attacks 1935–36.

**Scheidemann, Philipp (1865–1939)** – German SPD member; elected to Reichstag 1898; with Ebert, a central leader of party after Bebel's death in 1913; chauvinist during World War I; SPD cochair from 1917; as member of Ebert's cabinet, participated in suppression of 1918–19 revolution; chancellor 1919; forced into exile by Nazis 1933.

**Schlicke, Alexander (1863–1940)** – chair of German metalworkers' union 1895–1919; specialist on union questions in war ministry 1917–18; minister of labor 1919–20.

**SDP** – Social Democratic Party.

**Seaman, Frank** – *see* Phillips, Charles.

**Second International** – founded 1889 as international association of workers' parties; based in Brussels; collapsed at outbreak of World War I when leaders of most constituent parties supported interests of own bourgeoisies; revolutionary left wing founded Communist International 1919; right wing formed Bern International on procapitalist basis 1919 and Labor and Socialist International based in London 1923.

**Seitz, Karl (1869–1950)** – Austrian Social Democrat; chauvinist during World War I; National Assembly president 1919–20; SDP president 1920–34.

**Sembat, Marcel (1862–1922)** – prominent right-wing French SP leader; government minister 1914–16.

**Serebryakov, Leonid Petrovich (1888–1937)** – joined Bolsheviks 1905; All-Russia Soviet Central Executive Committee secretary 1919–20; CP Central Committee secretary 1919–20; Russian CP delegate to second Comintern congress; active in Left Opposition to Stalin's anti-Leninist course from 1923; expelled from CP 1927; readmitted 1930; reexpelled for "antiparty activities" 1936; condemned in Moscow frame-up trial of "anti-Soviet Trotskyite Center" and shot.

**Sergeyev, Fedor Andreyevich (Artem) (1883–1921)** – joined RSDLP 1901; headed Bolshevik organization in Kharkov and led armed uprising there 1905; emigrated to Australia 1911 and led revolutionary Russian workers there; returned to Russia May 1917; elected to Bolshevik Central Committee 1917, 1919–21; chair of Donetsk-Krivoi Rog Soviet Republic 1918; Russian CP delegate to second Comintern congress; died in rail accident.

**Serrati, Giacinto Menotti (1874–1926)** – central leader of Italian SP during war; editor of *Avanti!* 1915–20; attended Zimmerwald and Kienthal conferences; led SP into Comintern; Italian SP delegate to second Comintern congress and served on Presiding Committee; elected to Comintern Executive Committee 1920; opposed break with reformists and remained head of SP after CP split 1921; led SP left wing into fusion with CP 1924; elected to CP Central Committee.

**Shablin, Nikolai** – *see* Nedelkov, Ivan.

**Shafiq, Mohammad** – left India in protest against British policy in Turkey May 1919; joined Indian exile revolutionary group in Tashkent summer 1920; observer for Indian Section of Council for International Propaganda, an Indian exile group, at second Comintern congress; first general secretary of Indian CP formed in Tashkent exile November 1920; played leading role in Indian CP through 1920s; left politics 1932.

**Shatskin, Lazar Abramovich (1902–1938)** – joined Bolshevik Party 1917; Communist Youth League Central Committee member from 1918 and first secretary 1919–22; elected to Communist Youth International Executive Committee 1919, which he represented at second Comintern congress; Comintern Executive Committee member from 1920; closely associated with Stalin late 1920s; accused of opposition activities and excluded from political activity 1931; expelled from party and arrested 1935; died in Stalin purges.

**Shaw, Thomas (1872–1938)** – British labor official; chauvinist during World War I; Labour member of Parliament 1918–31; cosecretary of Second International 1923–25.

**Shiroki** – right wing of Social Democratic Party of Bulgaria; Shiroki (Broad) faction split from revolutionary Tesnyaki (Narrow) faction in 1903; voted to quit Second International 1919; voted against joining Comintern 1920; left wing split and joined CP; Shiroki then had 8,000 members.

**Shlyapnikov, Aleksandr Gavrilovich (1885–1937)** – joined RSDLP 1901; Bolshevik; in exile in western Europe from 1908; organized Bolshevik Party leadership within Russia 1914–17; first commissar of labor after October revolution; Central Committee alternate member 1918–19 and full member 1921–22; CP delegate to second Comintern congress 1920; leader of Workers Opposition in CP 1920–22; Soviet diplomatic service from 1924; expelled from CP 1933; arrested and shot.

**Shop Stewards' and Workers' Committees** – originated among engineers (metalworkers) in Clyde valley strike in Scotland 1915; grew with strike wave and by early 1917 was national organization opposed to official trade union leadership no-strike policy; advanced revolutionary demands; movement declined after 1918 but many militant stewards joined British CP.

**Shums'ky, Oleksandr (1890–1946)** – leader of Ukrainian SR party and of its left wing (Borotbists); member of Ukrainian soviet government 1919; led Ukrainian CP (Borotbist) into CP (Bolsheviks) of the Ukraine March 1920; CP Central Committee member; Russian CP delegate to second Comintern congress; Ukrainian commissar of education, where he promoted Ukrainian language and culture, 1924–27; accused of "nationalist deviation"; expelled from CP and arrested 1933; died in prison camp.

**Simons, Walter (1861–1937)** – member of German delegation at Brest-Litovsk negotiations 1918; Imperial Association of German Industry president 1919–20; German foreign minister 1920–21.

**Sirola, Yrjö (1876–1936)** – joined Finnish SDP 1903; foreign affairs commissar in revolutionary government 1918; founding leader of Finnish CP 1918; elected to Comintern Control Commission 1921, 1928, and 1935; Comintern emissary to U.S. CP 1925–27.

**Skrypnyk, Mykola (1872–1933)** – joined RSDLP 1897; Bolshevik from 1903; member Petrograd Military Revolutionary Committee in October revolution; Russian CP delegate to second Comintern congress; elected alternate Russian CP Central Committee member 1924, full member from 1927; central leader of CP of the Ukraine from 1927; elected to Comintern Executive Committee 1928; supported Stalin faction in 1920s; accused of "nationalist deviation" during Stalin's assault on Ukrainian national rights; committed suicide.

**Skulski, Leopold (b. 1878)** – Polish politician; premier of Pilsudski's cabinet December 1919–June 1920; interior minister 1920–21.

**Smeral, Bohumír (1880–1941)** – joined Czech SDP 1897 and elected to Central Committee 1904; took chauvinist stand during World War I but spoke against collaboration with bourgeois parties from 1918; a leader of SDP left wing 1919–21; headed CP from its founding 1921; Comintern Executive Committee member 1922–35.

**Smidovich, Petr Germogenovich (1874–1935)** – joined RSDLP 1898; Bolshevik from 1903; member of Moscow Military Revolutionary Committee 1917; Russian CP delegate to second Comintern congress; member of All-Russia Soviet Central Executive Committee; held various government posts.

**Sneevliet, Henk (Maring) (1883–1942)** – joined Dutch Social Democratic Workers Party 1902; emigrated to Dutch East Indies 1913; became leader of rail union in Semarang and founding leader of Indies Social Democratic Association 1914; supported Russian October revolution 1917; deported December 1918; joined Dutch CP 1919; represented Communist Association in the Indies at second Comintern congress; Comintern representative in China 1921–23; returned to Netherlands 1924; left CP 1927; supported views of Left Opposition led by Trotsky; founded Revolutionary Socialist Party 1929; with Trotsky, cosigned call for new International 1933; did not participate in launching Fourth International 1938; took part in resistance to Nazi occupation forces until captured and executed.

**Social Democratic Federation (Britain)** – founded 1884; changed name to Social Democratic Party 1906; participated in founding British SP 1911; chauvinist wing of SP split from antiwar majority 1916 and retook name Social Democratic Federation 1920.

**Social Democratic Party of Austria** – *see* Social Democratic Workers Party of Austria.

**Social Democratic Party of Czechoslovakia** – originated before 1914 as national breakaway from SDP of Austria; Marxist Left faction organized December 1919, which won leadership of party 1920; 650,000 members mid-1920; split fall 1920; left-wing majority took name CP with 350,000 members and adopted Twenty-one Conditions March 1921; united with Communist groups based among other nationalities November 1921; 170,000 members 1922. *See also* Communist Party of Czechoslovakia.

**Social Democratic Party of Finland** – founded 1899; adopted this name 1903; held internationalist positions during World War I; won majority of parliamentary seats 1916; after defeat of working class in Finnish civil war, SDP left wing founded CP in Russian exile August 1918 but also continued to work in SDP; underground Communists in Finland participated in left-wing split from SDP that led to founding of Socialist Workers Party May 1920.

**Social Democratic Party of Germany (SPD)** – founded 1875 as Social Democratic Workers Party from fusion of Marxist and Lassallean parties; changed name to SPD 1891; largest and most influential party in Second International; more than 1 million members 1914; majority leadership supported German imperialist war effort; expelled oppositionists 1917; 250,000 members March 1918; headed bourgeois government 1918–19; 1 million members 1919; opposed formation of Comintern, remained in Second International.

**Social Democratic Party of Hungary** – founded 1890; initially chauvinist during World War I; shifted to pacifist position 1915; fused with CP and participated in short-lived Hungarian soviet republic 1919; refounded 1921; functioned as legal reformist opposition party.

**Social Democratic Party of Romania** – *see* Balkan Communist Federation.

**Social Democratic Party of Switzerland** – founded 1888; leadership took centrist position during World War I, helping initiate and lead Zimmerwald movement; withdrew from Second International 1919; voted for Comintern affiliation at 1920 congress, but membership referendum later that year reversed decision; left wing split and fused with other Communist groups to form Swiss CP March 1921; SDP had 54,000 members 1921.

**Social Democratic Party of Yugoslavia** – founded 1903 as Social Democratic Party of Serbia; opposed war credits 1914; participated in Balkan Revolutionary Social Democratic Federation from 1915; called April 1919 conference that united left wings of all Yugoslav Socialist parties (except Slovenian) to form Socialist Workers Party (Communist) April 1919 that joined Comintern; 50,000 members late 1919; changed name to CP of Yugoslavia June 1920.

**Social Democratic Workers Party of Austria** – founded 1888–89; loose federation of six autonomous national parties from 1896, which broke up by 1912; then functioned solely within German Austria; led governmental coalition with bourgeois parties November 1918–June 1920, left government October 1920; suffered no significant left-wing split after World War I; 335,000 members November 1920; main party in Two-and-a-Half International 1921–23; 491,000 members 1921.

**Social Democratic Working Group of Revolutionary Workers Councils** – formed October 1919 as left faction in Austrian SDP; expressed support for soviet power and Communist International; considerable influence over workers' councils late 1919; split over election tactics September 1920; reunited December 1920 and joined CP January 1921.

**Social Democratic Youth League (Denmark)** – founded 1906; youth organization affiliated to SDP of Denmark; opposed party's reformist line, supported Zimmerwald movement during World War I; split from SDP October 1919; most members fused with Socialist Workers Party to form Left SP of Denmark November 1919; minority returned to SDP; 10,000 members 1920.

**Social Democratic Youth League (Norway)** – youth organization of Norwegian Labor Party founded 1907; strong radical influence on party during war; 12,000 members 1920.

**Socialist Labour Party (Britain)** – founded with 80 members 1903 by split of Scottish sections of Social Democratic

Federation; influenced by Daniel De Leon of U.S. SLP; opposed labor movement's fighting for partial goals short of socialism; actively opposed World War I; supported Bolshevik revolution and Comintern; at first participated, then withdrew from unity talks on forming CP December 1919; 1,250 members 1920; minority split and participated in founding first CPGB August 1920; 100 members 1924.

**Socialist Party of America** – founded 1901; 1917 membership referendum denouncing U.S. entry into World War I ignored by most of leadership; 109,000 members January 1919; leadership representing right-wing minority expelled 70,000 members January–July 1919; membership referendum voted for conditional affiliation with Comintern early 1920, which was rejected by Comintern; membership dropped to 13,000 by 1921.

**Socialist Party of France (Section française de l'Internationale ouvrière; SFIO)** – founded by merger of Guesde's SP of France and Jaurès's French SP 1905; deputies voted unanimously to support war credits August 1914; 93,000 members 1914; dropped to 34,000 1918; centrists won majority July 1918; split at Tours congress December 1920; majority of 120,000 changed name to CP; right-wing minority of 50,000 split, retained name SFIO, affiliated to centrist Two-and-a-Half International February 1921.

**Socialist Party of Ireland** – founded as Irish Socialist Republican Party by James Connolly 1898; became SP in Connolly's absence 1903–10; reconstituted 1917 after Connolly's death; called for reestablishing Second International 1918; supported Adler-Longuet resolution at Bern conference 1919; included small left faction that called itself Workers' Communist Party, which sent delegates to second Comintern congress; left wing won majority September 1921 and renamed party CP, which was dissolved when Comintern transferred recognition to Irish Workers' League 1923.

**Socialist Party of Italy** – *see* Italian Socialist Party.

**Socialist Party (Shanghai)** – formed September 1919 by laborers who were exposed to revolutionary movement while working in Europe 1917–18. *See also* Chinese Socialist Workers Party.

**Socialist Revolutionary Party (SR)** – formed in Russia by rightward-moving currents from populist Narodnik tradition 1901–2; affiliated to Second International; had wings that supported and opposed war effort during World War I; supported by majority of peasant delegates to soviets 1917; Right SRs opposed October revolution and took up arms against Soviet government; Left SRs opposed World War I, supported immediate confiscation of landed estates, backed October revolution and soviet power; joined Bolsheviks in coalition government November 28, 1917 (November 15, old style); broke from Soviet government and organized attempted insurrection July 1918; minority currents split away and eventually joined Russian CP.

**Socialist Workers Party (Denmark)** – *see* Communist Party of Denmark.

**Socialist Workers Party of Finland** – *see* Communist Party of Finland.

**Socialist Workers Party of Palestine** – founded October 1919; defended Zionism; called for alliance with Arab workers; banned by British authorities in Palestine mid-1921; disintegrated shortly thereafter.

**Socialist Workers Party of Spain (PSOE)** – founded by former members of Spanish section of First International 1879; policies reflected majority views of Second International; voted for conditional affiliation to Comintern June 1920, but reversed this decision April 1921; left wing split to form Communist Workers Party of Spain 1921.

**Socialist Youth Federation (France)** – founded as national organization, affiliated to SP, 1912; adopted chauvinist position during World War I; 1,300 members 1918; opposition won leadership June 1918; 15,000 members mid-1920, with significant communist, syndicalist, and pacifist currents; application to join Communist Youth International initially rejected; adopted positions of autonomy with respect to party; pro-Communist wing won majority, changed name to National Federation of Socialist-Communist Youth of France and affiliated with Communist Youth International October 1920.

**Socialist Youth Federation of Italy** – *see* Italian Socialist Youth Federation.

**Socialist Youth Organization (Switzerland)** – developed early 1900s from existing youth groups with anarcho-syndicalist influence; renamed Social Democratic Youth Organization and adopted increasingly revolutionary stance from 1911; took name Socialist Youth Organization 1915; French- and German-speaking sections unified 1919; joined Communist Youth International and Comintern 1919; broke with SDP January 1920; participated in second Comintern congress; 2,500 members August 1920; changed name to Communist Youth League November 1920.

**Sokolnikov, Grigory Yakovlevich (1888–1939)** – joined Bolsheviks 1905; collaborated with *Nashe Slovo* in Paris during World War I; rejoined Bolsheviks April 1917; elected to Bolshevik Central Committee 1917–19, 1922–30; Russian CP delegate to second Comintern congress; headed Comintern Central Asia bureau from 1920; people's commissar of finance 1922–26; briefly supported United Opposition 1926; Soviet diplomatic service 1929–34; sentenced to ten years in prison at Moscow frame-up trial 1937 and shot.

**Solf, Wilhelm Heinrich (1862–1936)** – German colonial minister 1911–18; negotiated armistice as foreign minister 1918; ambassador to Tokyo 1920.

**Souchy, Augustin (1892–1984)** – anarchist from 1911; in Sweden and Denmark as opponent of draft during World

War I; leader of German anarcho-syndicalist Free Workers Union 1919–33; represented it at second Comintern congress; refused to join Comintern or Red International of Labor Unions; leader of anarcho-syndicalist International from 1922; fled to France 1933; active in anarchist federation in Spain during civil war 1936–39; emigrated to Mexico 1942; returned to Europe, worked with UN International Labor Organization 1950s.

**SP** – Socialist Party.

***Spartacus*** – illegal organ of German Spartacus group; appeared irregularly September 1916 to October 1918; predecessor newsletters dated from fall 1914.

**SPD** – *see* Social Democratic Party of Germany.

**SR** – *see* Socialist Revolutionary Party.

**Stalin, Joseph (1879–1953)** – joined RSDLP 1898; Bolshevik from 1903; member Central Committee 1912; people's commissar of nationalities after October revolution; general secretary of Russian CP Central Committee 1922; presided over bureaucratic degeneration of Russian CP and Comintern and their rejection of revolutionary internationalist course; organized Moscow frame-up trials in 1930s and liquidation of majority of Bolshevik leaders of Lenin's time; dissolved Comintern as political gesture to imperialist allies 1943.

**Steinhardt, Karl (J. Gruber) (1875–1963)** – member of Austrian SDP from 1891; militant antichauvinist, expelled from party 1916; Austrian CP chair from 1918; elected general secretary 1919; on return journey from first Comintern congress imprisoned in Romania April 1919–January 1920; Austrian CP delegate to second Comintern congress; still active in CP after World War II.

**Steklov, Yury Mikaylovich (1873–1941)** – active in Russian revolutionary movement from 1888; joined Social Democratic movement 1893; in exile in Siberia and abroad 1894–1914; edited *Izvestia* 1917–25; Russian CP delegate to second Comintern congress; popularizer of Marxism and historian of Russian revolutionary movement; arrested 1938; works placed under ban; died in prison.

**Stinnes, Hugo (1870–1924)** – leading German capitalist; headed industrial production during World War I.

**Stoecker, Walter (1891–1939)** – member German SPD 1908; joined USPD 1918; favored its affiliation to Comintern; USPD delegate to second Comintern congress; led USPD majority into united CP 1920; elected to CP Central Bureau 1920–21, 1923–24, and to Central Committee 1927–33; chair of CP parliamentary fraction 1924–31; arrested by Nazis night of Reichstag fire 1933; died in Nazi concentration camp.

**Stoklitsky, Alexander I.** – Russian emigrant to U.S.; head of U.S. SP Russian federation; a founder of U.S. CP 1919; CP delegate to second Comintern congress; remained in Russia.

**Ströbel, Heinrich (1869–1944)** – active in German workers' movement from 1889; editor of various Social Democratic newspapers; opposed SPD leadership during war; joined USPD; later returned to SPD; parliamentary deputy from 1924; founded journal *Klassenkampf*.

**Ströhmer** – *see* Hornik-Ströhmer, Anna.

**Ström, Fredrik (1880–1948)** – Swedish SDP party secretary 1911–16; close to Zimmerwald Left during World War I; member of parliament 1916–21, 1928–48; a founder of Left SDP 1917; head of Stockholm Comintern liaison with western Europe 1919–20; a CP founder 1921 and its general secretary 1921–24; opposed Comintern policies with Höglund from 1924; resigned from CP and returned to SDP 1926.

**Stuchka, Pyotr Ivanovich (1865–1932)** – Latvian; joined Bolsheviks 1903; Bolshevik Central Committee member 1917; people's commissar of justice 1917–18; Latvian soviet government head 1918–19; chair of Supreme Court, Russian Soviet Republic 1923–32.

**Sturm, Fritz** – *see* Zaks, Samuel.

**Sultan Galiev, Mir-Said (1880–1939)** – Tatar; central organizer of movement uniting revolutionaries from predominantly Muslim peoples from 1917; joined Bolshevik Party November 1917; member of Central Muslim Commissariat and of commissariat of nationalities central leadership; represented Tatar CP at second Comintern congress; opposed policies of Stalin and Russian CP leadership on national question from 1923; briefly arrested for "national deviation" 1923 and expelled from Russian CP; rearrested 1928 and disappeared in prison.

**Sultanzadeh, Ahmed (Avetis Mikaelian) (1889–1938)** – born in Iran, settled in tsarist Russia; joined Caucasus SDP 1907; joined Bolsheviks 1912; Iranian CP founder 1920; Central Committee member 1920–23 and 1927–32; represented Iranian CP at second Comintern congress; elected to Comintern Executive Committee and attended Baku congress 1920; left Comintern and Iranian CP posts 1923–27 to work in Soviet government; expelled from Iranian CP Central Committee 1932; arrested and died in Stalin purges.

**Sun Yat-sen (Sun Ixian) (1866–1925)** – Chinese revolutionary democrat; president of republic after first revolution 1911–12; founder of Kuomintang 1912; removed by Yuan Shikai 1912; after two failed attempts, established government in Canton 1923; accepted help of Soviet Russia from 1923.

**Suzenko, Alexander** – exiled from Russia to Australia after defeat of 1905 revolution; active in association of Russian-born workers there during World War I; deported from Australia mid-1919, returned and was again deported 1920; Australian IWW consultative delegate to second Comintern congress.

**Syvertsen, Sigrid (1885–1974)** – joined Norwegian Labor Party 1907; secretary of Labor Party Women's League 1917–23; Labor Party delegate to second Comintern congress; quit

Comintern with Labor Party 1923; Central Committee member and head of women's secretariat from 1923.

**Szamuely, Tibor (1890–1919)** – joined Bolsheviks as Hungarian prisoner of war in Russia 1917; political commissar of First Internationalist Battalion of Red Army 1918; returned to Hungary January 1919 and became Hungarian CP Central Committee chair; as leader of soviet republic, visited Moscow May 1919; captured and died after fall of Hungarian soviet republic.

**Tanner, Jack (1889–1965)** – leader of British Shop Stewards during World War I, which he represented at second Comintern congress; joined CP 1921; leader of CP-led trade union Minority Movement 1920s; became right-wing opponent of CP in 1940s; continued to hold prominent posts in British trade unions until 1954.

**Taratuta, Viktor Konstantinovich (1881–1926)** – joined RSDLP 1898; Bolshevik from 1903; elected alternate Central Committee member 1907; abroad 1909–19; joined French SP 1917; represented Russian CP at second Comintern congress; later worked in Soviet foreign commerce bank.

***Le Temps* (The times)** – daily newspaper published in Paris 1861–1942; unofficial voice of French government.

**Tesnyaki** – *see* Communist Party of Bulgaria.

**Thomas, Albert (1878–1932)** – leader of French SP right wing; chauvinist during World War I; held key government posts 1914–17; visited Russia April 1917 to promote war effort; led attempts to reorganize Second International 1919; first director of League of Nations International Labour Office.

***The Times*** – leading Conservative British newspaper founded 1785, took present title 1788.

**Todria, Sil'vestr Yaseyevich (1880–1936)** – joined RSDLP 1901; Bolshevik; participated in revolutionary movement in Azerbaijan and Georgia; held various posts after 1917;

Georgian CP delegate to second Comintern congress; held high posts in Georgian and Transcaucasian soviet governments; disappeared during frame-up purges.

**Tomann, Karl (1887–1945)** – born in Austria of Czech descent; won to Bolsheviks while prisoner of war in Russia; head of German section, Federation of Foreign Groups of the Russian CP; returned to Austria, joined Austrian CP December 1918; became general secretary February 1919; represented CP at second Comintern congress; editor in chief of CP newspaper until 1924; dropped from Central Committee 1924; expelled from CP 1931; led independent socialist grouping; became town mayor under Nazis; shot by Soviet troops after World War II.

**Tomschik, Josef (1867–1945)** – longtime national secretary of Austrian rail union; elected to Austrian SDP Central Committee 1896; parliamentary deputy 1907–34.

**Tomsky, Mikhail Pavlovich (1880–1936)** – joined RSDLP 1904; Bolshevik; chair of Revel (Tallinn) soviet in 1905 revolution; All-Russia Central Trade Union Council chair 1919–29; CP Central Committee member 1919–36 and Political Bureau member 1922–29; Russian CP delegate to second Comintern congress and elected to Comintern Executive Committee 1920; helped found Red International of Labor Unions 1921; with Bukharin, leader of Right Opposition 1928–29; stripped of all leading posts and forced to make self-criticism by Stalin 1930; committed suicide after publicly assailed during Moscow frame-up trials.

**Treves, Claudio (1869–1933)** – joined Italian SP 1893; parliamentary deputy 1906–26; editor of *Avanti!* 1909–12; called for Italian neutrality during World War I; leader of reformist, anti-Comintern wing of SP after World War I; stayed with SP when CP founded 1921; expelled from SP with rightist current that founded United SP 1922; emigrated to Paris when fascists took power.

***De Tribune* (The tribune)** – founded 1907 as publication of left wing of Dutch Social Democratic Workers Party; became newspaper of SDP of the Netherlands 1909 and of CP 1919.

**Triple Alliance** – formal agreement of mutual support among British mine, rail, and transport unions; established 1914; operation suspended by union officials during World War I; broke up over failure to support miners' strike April 1921.

**Troelstra, Pieter (1860–1930)** – right-wing leader of Dutch Social Democratic Workers Party from its foundation 1894; member of International Socialist Bureau; chauvinist during World War I.

**Trotsky, Leon (1879–1940)** – Russian revolutionary leader; aligned with Mensheviks 1903–4; president of St. Petersburg soviet 1905; took intermediate position between Bolsheviks and Mensheviks 1904–17; led Mezhrayontsi into fusion with Bolsheviks 1917; elected to Bolshevik Central Committee 1917; people's commissar of foreign affairs 1917–18; organized and led Red Army 1918–25; prominent leader of Comintern; from 1923 led opposition in Russian CP and Comintern against retreat from Leninist policies; expelled from party 1927; exiled abroad 1929; launched fight for new, revolutionary International 1933; led in founding Fourth International 1938; main defendant, in absentia, at 1936–38 Moscow frame-up trials; assassinated by agent of Stalin.

**Tsetlin, Yefim Viktorovich (1898–1937)** – Bolshevik youth movement leader 1917–22 and its delegate to second Comintern congress; Communist Youth International Executive Committee member 1922–24; active in party work until 1929, then held administrative posts.

**Tskhakaya, Mikhail Grigor'evich (Leonov Barsov) (1865–1950)** – active in revolutionary movement in Georgia and Caucasus from 1880s; joined RSDLP 1898; exiled abroad 1907–17; member of Tiflis RSDLP committee 1917–20;

Georgian CP delegate to second Comintern congress; Comintern Executive Committee member 1920; held high government and state posts in Georgia; demoted but not arrested during frame-up purges of 1930s.

**Tsyperovich, Grigory (1871–1932)** – joined Russian revolutionary movement 1888; worked in trade unions after October revolution; joined Russian CP 1919; represented CP at second Comintern congress; worked in Petrograd economic council, later chancellor of Leningrad industrial academy.

**Turati, Filippo (1857–1932)** – a founder of Italian SP; avowed reformist; voted against war credits during World War I but supported Woodrow Wilson's Fourteen Points; opposed Comintern; led right-wing split from SP 1922.

**Turgot, Anne-Robert-Jacques (1727–1781)** – high official of French monarchs Louis XV and Louis XVI; tried unsuccessfully to introduce limited reforms.

**Tusar, Vlastimil (1880–1924)** – leader of Czechoslovak SDP; prime minister of coalition government July 1919–September 1920.

**Two-and-a-Half International** – derogatory name applied to the International Association of Socialist Parties; formed 1921 by centrist parties that opposed soviet power but had left Second International, with which it reunited 1923.

**Ukrainian Communist Party (Borotbist)** – originated in Borotbist majority faction in Ukrainian Party of Socialist Revolutionaries May 1918; fought against Skoropadsky and Directory governments under banner of soviet power and Ukrainian federation with Soviet Russia; joined Ukrainian soviet government April 1919; criticized Bolshevik policy toward demands of peasantry and Ukrainian national rights; formed Ukrainian CP (Borotbist) August 1919; applied to Comintern for recognition as its Ukrainian section August 1919 but was refused; fused with CP (Bolsheviks) of the Ukraine March 1920.

**Ukrainian Communist Party (Ukapist)** – originated in left-wing split from nationalist and antisoviet Ukrainian Social Democratic Labor Party; these forces formed Ukrainian SDP (Independents) 1919, which fought both Whites and Bolshevik-led soviets; supported soviet regime from late 1919; took name Ukrainian CP (Ukapist) 1920; defended soviet power while advocating an independent soviet Ukraine and accusing the Bolsheviks of failing to respect Ukrainian national rights; its forces joined Bolsheviks in stages 1923–25.

**Ukrainian National Directory** – *see* Directory.

**United Communist Party (U.S.)** – *see* Communist Party of America; Communist Labor Party (U.S.).

**USPD** – *see* Independent Social Democratic Party of Germany.

**Ustinov, A.M. (1879–1937)** – active in Russian revolutionary movement from 1901; SR 1906–17; Left SR 1917–18; member All-Russia Soviet Central Executive Committee 1917–20; split from Left SRs with forces who formed Party of Revolutionary Communism; represented this party as consultative delegate at second Comintern congress; joined Russian CP 1920; diplomat from 1921.

**Vacirca, Vincenzo** – member of Italian General Confederation of Labor (CGL) delegation to Soviet Russia 1920; consultative delegate of Italian SP to second Comintern congress; left congress early with D'Aragona; expelled with Turati current from SP after Rome party congress 1922; joined United SP founded by Turati 1922.

**Vakmann, Rudolf (1894–1937)** – RSDLP member in Estonia from 1913; Revel (Tallinn) party committee secretary 1917; Estonian CP delegate to second Comintern congress; Central Committee member 1920–30; executed during Stalin purges.

**Vandervelde, Emile (1866–1938)** – Belgian Social Democrat; International Socialist Bureau chair from 1900; defended chauvinist positions during World War I; cabinet minister throughout World War I; an organizer of 1919 Bern conference; president of Second International 1929–36.

**Vanek, Milos (1897–1967)** – joined left wing of Czechoslovak SDP during World War I, which he represented at second Comintern congress; helped form CP 1921; worked for Comintern in Moscow 1922–26; rejoined SDP 1926; emigrated to West Germany 1948; commentator for Radio Free Europe from 1951.

**Vanini, Lorenzo** – *see* Mineff, Stoyan.

**Van Leuven, Vilem** – member of Dutch SDP from 1909; stockbroker; a founding member of Dutch CP; Dutch CP delegate to second Comintern congress; quit CP 1924.

**Van Overstraeten, Eduard (War) (1891–1981)** – active in Socialist Young Guards in Belgium at end of World War I; founded Walloon Communist Federation 1920; represented it at second Comintern congress; elected to Comintern Executive Committee 1921; elected Belgian CP national secretary at founding congress 1921; imprisoned for opposing Ruhr occupation 1923; led majority of party Central Committee in opposing expulsion of Trotsky and Zinoviev 1927; expelled 1928; founder of Belgian Left Opposition but soon withdrew from politics.

**Van Ravesteyn, Willem (1876–1970)** – Dutch Social Democrat from 1900; leader of *Tribune* current from its inception 1907; Zimmerwald Left supporter during World War I; Dutch CP founding member 1918; expelled with Wijnkoop 1926 and retired from political activity.

**Vardanian, Stepan Khristoforovich (1900–1936)** – joined Bolsheviks 1916; Transcaucasian Bolshevik youth organization chairman 1919–20, which he represented at second Comintern congress; held leading government and party posts in Armenia and Georgia 1920s; Armenian CP Central Committee secretary 1930–32.

**Varenne, Alexandre (1870–1947)** – member of French parliament 1906–10, 1914–36; part of SP chauvinist majority during World War I; opposed SP joining Comintern 1920; went with SP after CP formed 1920; member of SP central leadership body 1923–25; quit SP 1925–31 and again 1933; active in bourgeois parties; government minister 1946.

**Varga, Jenö (Eugen) (1879–1964)** – joined Hungarian SDP 1906; university economics professor; joined CP February 1919; people's commissar of finance in Hungarian soviet republic 1919; interned with Kun in Austria 1919–20 after collapse of republic; released with Kun and arrived in Moscow just after second Comintern congress; played leading role in Comintern from 1920; leading Soviet economist until criticized by Stalin 1947; restored to favor after Stalin's death.

**Vashakidze, Valerian Afanas'evich (1882–1937?)** – rail union leader 1917; Georgian trade union delegate to second Comintern congress; Georgian government commissar 1928–36.

**Vatin, Vadim Aleksandrovich (Bistriyansky) (1886–1940)** – joined Bolsheviks 1907; newspaper editor 1920–30; Russian CP delegate to second Comintern congress.

**Vaynshteyn, Aron Isakovich (1877–1938?)** – joined Bund 1897; held chauvinist positions during World War I; chairman of Bund from 1917; initially critical of October revolution; supported soviet power from 1919; joined Russian CP with Bund majority 1920; Communist Bund consultative delegate to second Comintern congress; member of Belorussian soviet government 1921–22; member of Soviet Union commissariat of finance executive board from 1923.

**Vennerström, Ivar (1881–1945)** – Swedish SDP National Committee member 1911–16 and leader of left wing; member of parliament 1914–36; Left SDP cofounder 1917; opposed Twenty-one Conditions and broke with Comintern 1921; rejoined SDP 1924; defense minister 1932–36.

**Voronova, Pelageya Yakovlevna (b. 1892)** – leader of textile workers' union and Russian CP women's department; Russian CP delegate to second Comintern congress; textile workers' union Central Committee secretary 1927–30; held government posts 1931–37.

**Vorovsky, Vatslav Vatslavovich (1871–1923)** – Social Democrat from 1894; Bolshevik from 1903; edited *Vperyod* and *Proletary* with Lenin 1905; headed Bolshevik Odessa organization 1907–12; member of Central Committee abroad 1917; ambassador in Scandinavia 1917–19; Comintern secretary and Executive Committee member 1919–20; ambassador to Italy 1921–23; assassinated by White émigré.

***Vorwärts* (Forward)** – main daily newspaper of German SPD; founded in Leipzig 1876; published abroad from 1933.

**Walcher, Jakob (1887–1970)** – German Social Democrat from 1906; active in Spartacus current during World War I; German CP founding member December 1918; Central Bureau alternate, then full member responsible for trade union work 1919–23; CP delegate to second Comintern congress; worked in Red International of Labor Unions headquarters 1924–26; returned to Germany 1926; expelled from party as "rightist" 1928; in exile in France and U.S. during Nazi regime; returned to East Germany and joined CP 1946; expelled 1951; readmitted 1956.

**Walloon Communist Federation** – originated January 1920 when first group founded in Brussels by Socialist Young Guards, youth group of Belgian Workers Party; ten groups with 200 members consolidated into federation at congress May 1920; fused September 1921 to form CP with other groups that had split from Workers Party December 1920.

**Washington, Booker T. (1856–1915)** – born a slave in U.S.; Black educator; exponent of vocational self-improvement and accommodation rather than struggle for Black rights;

founded Tuskegee Normal and Industrial Institute 1881 and National Negro Business League 1900.

**Webb, Sidney (1859–1947)** – British reformist; leading figure in Fabian Society; supported British war policy; colonial minister in Labour government 1929–31; hostile to Lenin's Bolshevik government of early 1920s but later an admirer of Stalin's regime.

***The Weekly Critic* (Hsing-ch'i p'ing-lun)** – socialist newspaper published in Shanghai from mid-1919.

**Wesolowski, Bronislaw (1870–1919)** – a founder of Social Democracy of the Kingdom of Poland and Lithuania and collaborator of Luxemburg; participated in Russian October revolution; murdered by Polish police.

**West European Secretariat** – established in Berlin by Comintern Executive Committee October 1919 as Comintern political and information center for central and western Europe.

**White, James (1879–1946)** – British captain; supported Irish home rule from 1913; organized and trained Irish Citizen Army 1913 and Irish Volunteers 1914; imprisoned for organizing Welsh miners' strike to try to block execution of James Connolly 1916.

**WIIU** – *see* Workers International Industrial Union.

**Wijnkoop, David (1877–1941)** – Dutch Social Democrat; chair of left-wing Dutch SDP 1909; supported Zimmerwald Left during World War I; leader of Dutch CP from 1918; CP delegate to second Comintern congress and elected to Comintern Executive Committee 1920, 1924; expelled from Dutch CP 1926; reinstated 1930.

**Williams, Robert (1881–1936)** – secretary of National Transport Workers' Federation 1912–25; leader of Triple Alliance of mine, rail, and transport unions; helped form action council to oppose imperialist intervention against Soviet Russia and part of labor delegation to Soviet Russia spring 1920; British SP member and founding member of British CP; expelled from CP for failure to support miners' strike 1921; Labour Party chair 1926.

**Wilson, Woodrow (1856–1924)** – U.S. president 1913–21; led U.S. into World War I; announced Fourteen Points as alternative to Soviet program for democratic peace without annexations 1918; joined in organizing invasion of Soviet republic 1919.

**Winberg, Carl (1867–1954)** – organizer of Swedish rail workers' union; member of parliament 1911–17, 1919–30; cofounder Left SDP 1917 and CP 1921; expelled along with CP majority 1929; active in opposition CP led by Kilbom 1930s.

**Wolffheim, Fritz (1888–1942)** – part of Hamburg revolutionary left during World War I; German CP founding member December 1918; split with ultraleft wing October 1919; KAPD founding member 1919; expelled from KAPD for advocating Communist bloc with right-wing German nationalists for liberation struggle against Entente August 1920; later active in Nazi groups; arrested by Nazi regime and died in concentration camp.

**Wolfstein, Rosi (Rosi Frölich) (1888–1987)** – joined German SPD 1908; internationalist during World War I; member of Spartacus group; delegate at German CP founding congress 1918; CP delegate to second Comintern congress; elected alternate member of German CP Central Bureau 1920, full member 1921–23; expelled from German CP as "rightist" early 1929; in exile 1933–50; active in groups aligned with pro-Bukharin opposition 1930s; returned to West Germany 1951 and joined SPD.

***Workers' Dreadnought*** – published by Sylvia Pankhurst 1914–24 (during first three years under name *Woman's Dreadnought*); became newspaper of Shop Stewards' movement from 1918.

**Workers International Industrial Union** – De Leonist split from U.S. IWW 1908; based primarily in Detroit; opposed IWW's militant tactics; took this name 1915; dissolved 1925.

**Working Group** – *see* Independent Social Democratic Party of Germany.

**Wrangel, Pyotr Nikolayevich (1878–1929)** – tsarist general; succeeded Denikin as head of White forces in Russian civil war April 1920; fled to Turkey after defeat by Red Army October 1920.

**Yanson, Karl Ernestovich (1882–1937?)** – joined Bolsheviks 1904; lived in U.S. and active in SP left wing 1909–April 1920; delegate to U.S. CP founding congress September 1919; political prisoner in Boston October 1919–April 1920; elected to United CP Central Committee and was its delegate to second Comintern congress; active in Communist movement and trade unions in U.S. and Canada until mid-1920s; held Comintern posts in late 1920s.

**Yaroslavsky, Yemel'yan Mikhailovich (1878–1943)** – joined RSDLP 1898; edited Bolshevik newspapers 1917; member of Moscow Military Revolutionary Committee during October revolution; Russian CP delegate to second Comintern congress; CP Central Committee secretary 1921; CP Central Control Commission secretary 1923–34; organized expulsion of United Opposition leaders 1929; authored Stalinist textbooks on party history.

**Yenukidze, Avel' Sofronovich (1877–1937)** – joined RSDLP 1898; Bolshevik; active in revolutionary movement in Tiflis and Baku; All-Russia Soviet Central Executive Committee secretary 1918–35; Russian CP delegate to second Comintern congress; CP Central Control Commission 1924–34; CP Central Committee from 1934; expelled from CP June 1936; executed.

**Young Bukharans** – revolutionary nationalist bourgeois party founded in Bukhara 1909; strengthened and radicalized under impact of Russian revolution; overthrew feudal regime August–September 1920; merged with Bukharan CP August 1920; leaders prominent in Uzbek CP until purged 1937–38.

**Yudenich, Nikolai Nikolayevich (1862–1933)** – tsarist general; White army commander 1919; emigrated to Britain 1920.

**Zaks, Samuel Markovich (Fritz Sturm, Gladnev) (1884–1937)** – joined German SPD 1904; moved to Russia; joined RSDLP as Menshevik; joined Bolsheviks 1906; sent to Germany November 1918; active with Hamburg Left Radicals; expelled with ultraleft October 1919; arrested and deported from Germany 1920; consultative delegate for German syndicalist unions at second Comintern congress; remained in Russia; backed oppositions led by Zinoviev and Trotsky 1925–27; framed up for terrorism 1937 and executed.

**Zápotocky, Antonín (1884–1957)** – joined Czech SDP 1902; part of left wing 1919; delegate to second Comintern congress for left wing of SDP; Czechoslovak CP Central Committee secretary 1922–25; general secretary of CP-led trade unions 1929–39; imprisoned by Nazis 1939–45; trade union central council chair 1945–50; president of Czechoslovakia 1952–57.

**Zetkin, Clara (1857–1933)** – joined German Social Democracy 1878; a leader of Marxist wing of Second International; editor of SPD women's newspaper; secretary of International Bureau of Socialist Women; helped organize International Conference of Socialist Women in Bern 1915; Spartacus leader during World War I; joined German CP 1919; named head of Comintern's International Secretariat for Communist Women 1920; elected to Comintern executive committee 1921; remained a prominent figure in German CP and Comintern until death.

**Zimmerwald** – the Zimmerwald conference, the first gathering of antiwar parties and currents during World War I, was held in Switzerland September 1915; groups supporting the conference manifesto were linked in the Zimmerwald movement, active through 1917; the revolutionary forces at the 1915 conference formed the Zimmerwald Left, a precursor of the Communist International.

**Zimmerwald** – theoretical journal of Swedish Left SDP, then of CP 1917–21.

**Zinoviev, Gregory (1883–1936)** – joined RSDLP 1901; Bolshevik; elected to RSDLP Central Committee 1907; in exile in western Europe 1908–17; member of Zimmerwald Left bureau; chair of Petrograd soviet 1917–26; Russian CP delegate to ECCI until 1926; chairman of Communist International 1919–26; served on Presiding Committee at second Comintern congress; aligned with Stalin and Kamenev 1923–25; joined Trotsky and Kamenev in United Opposition to bureaucratic current led by Stalin 1926–27; capitulated 1928; convicted at first Moscow frame-up trial and executed.

**Zorin, S.S. (1890–1937)** – joined RSDLP 1905; in exile, member U.S. SP 1911–17; held various Soviet government and Russian CP posts after October revolution; delegate to second Comintern congress; member of opposition in CP led by Zinoviev and Kamenev 1925; later in United Opposition 1926–27; expelled from CP after party congress 1927; readmitted 1930; arrested during frame-up purges and died in prison.

**Zubatov, Sergey Vasilevich (1864–1917)** – tsarist police official; organized police-sponsored trade unions to maintain control over workers; committed suicide at the beginning of Russian February revolution.

# Books cited

## EDITIONS OF THE SECOND CONGRESS PROCEEDINGS (BY DATE OF PUBLICATION)

*Der zweite Kongress der Kommunistischen Internationale.* Vienna: Arbeiter Buchhandlung, 1920.

*2-oy kongress Kommunisticheskogo Internatsionala: Stenograficheskiy otchet.* Petrograd: Izdat. Kommunisticheskogo Internatsionala, 1921.

*Der zweite Kongress der Kommunistischen Internationale.* Hamburg: Verlag der Kommunistischen Internationale, 1921. Reprint. Milan: Feltrinelli, 1967.

*II-e congrès de la III-e Internationale communiste : Compte rendu sténographique.* Petrograd: Editions de l'Internationale communiste [1921].

*The Second Congress of the Communist International.* N.p. Publishing Office of the Communist International, 1921.

*Vtoroy kongress Kominterna, Iyul'–Avgust* 1920 *g.* Moscow: Partiynoye izdat., 1934. Reprint. Milan: Feltrinelli, 1967.

*Second Congress of the Communist International: Minutes of the Proceedings.* 2 vols. London: New Park, 1977.

*Drugi kongres Komunisticke Internacionale.* Vol. 2 of *Komunisticka Internacionala: Stenogrami i documenti kongresa.* Gornji Milanovac, Yugoslavia: Kulturni centar, 1981.

## OTHER BOOKS AND PAMPHLETS

Adhikari, G., ed. *Documents of the History of the Communist Party of India, volume 1:* 1917–1922. New Delhi: People's Publishing House, 1971.

Adler, Alan, ed. *Theses, Resolutions and Manifestos of the First Four Congresses of the Third International.* London: Ink Links, 1980.

Balabanoff, Angelica. *My Life as a Rebel.* New York: Harper & Brothers, 1938.

Barth, Emil. *Aus der Werkstatt der deutschen Revolution.* Berlin: A. Hoffmann, 1919.

Bauer, Otto. "Bolschewismus oder Sozialdemokratie?" In *Otto Bauer Werkausgabe,* vol. 2, pp. 223–358. Vienna: Europaverlag, 1976.

*Bericht über den 4. Parteitag der Kommunistischen Partei Deutschlands (Spartakusbund) am 14. und 15. April 1920.* N.p., n.d.

*Berichte zum zweiten Kongress der Kommunistischen Internationale.* Hamburg: Verlag der Kommunistischen Internationale, 1921. Reprint. Milan: Feltrinelli, 1967.

Berthold, Lothar, and Ernst Diehl. *Revolutionäre deutsche Parteiprogramme.* Berlin: Dietz Verlag, 1967.

Braun, M.J. *Wer soll die Kriegsrechnung bezahlen? Zur Wirtschaftspolitik des kapitalistischen Bankrotts.* Leipzig: Frankes Verlag, 1920.

Bringolf, Walther. *Mein Leben: Weg und Umweg eines Schweizer Sozialdemokraten.* Bern: Scherz, 1965.

Broué, Pierre, ed. *Du premier au deuxième congrès de l'Internationale Communiste.* Paris: Études et documentation internationales, 1979.

Bukharin, Nikolai. *Imperialism and World Economy.* New York: International Publishers, 1929.

Bukharin, Nikolai, and Yevgeny Preobrazhensky. *The ABC of Communism.* Ann Arbor: University of Michigan, 1966.

*Bulletin of the Sub-Bureau in Amsterdam of the Communist International.* Reprint. Milan: Feltrinelli, 1967.

Bunzl, John. *Klassenkampf in der Diaspora – Zur Geschichte der jüdischen Arbeiterbewegung.* Vienna: Europaverlag, 1975.

Cannon, James P. *The First Ten Years of American Communism.* New York: Pathfinder, 1973.

——— *The History of American Trotskyism.* New York: Pathfinder, 1972.

Charles, Jean, et al., eds. *Le Congrès de Tours.* Paris: Editions sociales, 1980.

*The Communist International.* Reprint. New York: Greenwood, 1968.

Connolly, James. *Labour in Irish History.* London: Bookmarks, 1987.

Cortesi, Luigi. *Il Socialismo italiano tra riforme e rivoluzione.* Bari: Editori Laterza, 1969.

Crispien, Artur. *Die Internationale: Vom Bund der Kommunisten bis zur Internationale der Weltrevolution.* Berlin, 1920.

Dobbs, Farrell. *Revolutionary Continuity: Marxist Leadership in the U.S.,* vol. 2, *Birth of the Communist Movement, 1918–1922.* New York: Pathfinder, 1983.

*Dokumente und Materialien zur Geschichte der deutschen Arbeiterbewegung.* Series 2, vol. 2. Berlin: Dietz Verlag, 1957.

Ely, Richard. *Socialism: An Examination of Its Nature, Its Strength and Its Weakness, with Suggestions for Social Reform.* New York: Thomas Y. Crowell, 1894.

*The First Congress of the Toilers of the Far East.* Reprint. London: Hammersmith Books, 1970.

Frossard, L.-O. *De Jaurès à Lénine.* Paris: Nouvelle revue socialiste, 1930.

——— *Le Parti socialiste et l'Internationale : Rapport sur les négociations conduites à Moscou suivi des thèses présentées au 2e Congrès de l'Internationale communiste.* Paris: Librairie de L'Humanité et du Parti Socialiste, 1920.

Gallacher, William. *Revolt on the Clyde: An Autobiography.* London: Lawrence and Wishart, 1936.

Gorter, Herman. *Die Klassenkampforganisation des Proletariats.* Berlin: KAPD, 1920.

——— "Der Opportunismus in der niederländischen Kommunistischen Partei." In *Die Linke gegen die Parteiherrschaft,* ed. Frits Kool, pp. 260–98. Olten, Switzerland: Walter-Verlag, 1970.

Hájek, Milos, and Hana Mejdrová. *Vznik Tretí internacionály.* Typescript. Prague, 1979.

Hendrik Ottósson. *Frá hlítharhúsum til Bjarmalands.* Reykjavík, Iceland: Skuggsjá, 1979.

Hicks, Granville. *John Reed: The Making of a Revolutionary.* New York: The Macmillan Company, 1936.

Humbert-Droz, Jules. *Mon évolution du tolstoïsme au communisme : 1891–1921.* Vol. 1 of *Mémoires de Jules Humbert-Droz.* Neuchâtel: Editions de la Baconnière, 1969.

*The I.L.P. and the Third International.* London: National Labour Press, 1920.

*Die Internationale,* Zeitschrift für Praxis und Theorie des Marxismus. Reprint. Frankfurt/Main: Neue Kritik, 1971.

*Istorijski arhiv Komunisticke partije Jugoslaviye.* Vol. 2 of *Kongresi i zemaljske konferencije KPJ 1919–1937.* Belgrade, 1950.

Kautsky, Karl. *The Agrarian Question.* 2 vols. London: Zwan, 1988.

——— *The Dictatorship of the Proletariat.* Ann Arbor: University of Michigan Press, 1964.

——— *Vergangenheit und Zukunft der Internationale.* Vienna: Wiener Volksbuchhandlung, 1920.

Keynes, John Maynard. *The Economic Consequences of the Peace.* New York: Harcourt, Brace & Howe, 1920.

*Die Kommunistische Internationale*. Reprint. New York: Greenwood, 1968.

König, Helmut. *Lenin und der italienische Sozialismus* 1915–1921. Tübingen, Germany: Böhlau Verlag, 1967.

Korolev, N.Ye. "Razrabotka Leninym politiki Kominterna po natsional'nomy i kolonial'nomy voprosam." In *Vtoroy kongress Kominterna,* pp. 152–93. Moscow: Izdat. Politicheskoy literatury, 1972.

Landauer, Carl. *European Socialism.* 2 vols. Berkeley: University of California Press, 1959.

Lazitch, Branko, and Milorad M. Drachkovitch. *Lenin and the Comintern.* Vol. 1. Stanford: Hoover Institution Press, 1972.

Lenin, V.I. *Collected Works.* 45 vols. Moscow: Progress Publishers, 1960–71.

——— *"Left-Wing" Communism–an Infantile Disorder.* In *Collected Works,* vol. 31, pp. 17–118.

——— *Lenin's Final Fight: Speeches and Writings 1922–23,* New York: Pathfinder, 1995, 2010.

——— *Polnoye sobraniye sochineniy.* 5th edition. 55 vols. Moscow: Izdat. Politicheskoy literatury, 1967–70.

Leonhard, Wolfgang. *Völker hört die Signale: Die Gründerjahre des Weltkommunismus* 1919–1924. Munich: Wilhelm Goldmann, 1981.

Lozovsky, S.A. *The International Council of Trade and Industrial Unions.* New York: The Union Publishing Association [1920].

——— *Der Internationale Rat der Fach- und Industrieverbände (Moskau gegen Amsterdam).* Berlin: A. Seehof & Co. [1920].

Luxemburg, Rosa. *The Accumulation of Capital–An Anti-Critique.* Bukharin, Nikolai, *Imperialism and the Accumulation of Capital.* New York: Monthly Review, 1972.

MacDonald, J. Ramsay. *Parliament and Revolution.* New York: Scott & Seltzer, 1920.

*Manifest, Richtlinien, Beschlüsse des Ersten Kongresses. Aufrufe und offene Schreiben des Exekutivkomitees bis zum Zweiten Kongress.* Hamburg: Verlag der Kommunistischen Internationale, 1920. Reprint. Milan: Feltrinelli, 1967.

Marx, Karl, and Frederick Engels. *Collected Works.* New York: International Publishers, 1975–.

——— *Selected Works.* 3 vols. Moscow: Progress Publishers, 1969.

Morgan, David W. *The Socialist Left and the German Revolution.* Ithaca: Cornell University Press, 1975.

Münzenberg, Willi. *Die dritte Front*. Berlin: Neuer deutscher Verlag, 1930.

Murphy, J.T. *New Horizons*. London: John Lane The Bodley Head, 1941.

Nettl, J.P. *Rosa Luxemburg*. 2 vols. London: Oxford University Press, 1966.

Pannekoek, Anton. "World Revolution and Communist Tactics." In *Pannekoek and Gorter's Marxism,* ed. D.A. Smart, pp. 93–148. London: Pluto Press, 1978.

*Le Parti socialiste italien et l'Internationale communiste (recueil de documents)*. Petrograd: Editions de l'Internationale communiste, 1921.

*Parti socialiste (SFIO) : 17-e congrès national tenu à Strasbourg les 25, 26, 27, 28, 29 février 1920. Compte rendu sténographique*. Paris, 1920.

*1-ya mezhdunarodnaya konferentsiya kommunistok*. Moscow: Gosizdat., 1921.

*Protokoll der Reichskonferenz vom 1. bis 3. September 1920 zu Berlin*. Berlin, n.d. Reprint. *Protokolle der Parteitage der Unabhängigen Sozialdemokratischen Partei Deutschlands*. Vol. 2. Glashütten im Taunus, Germany: Detlev Auvermann, 1976.

*Protokoll über die Verhandlungen des ausserordentlichen Parteitages vom 30. November bis 6. Dezember 1919 in Leipzig*. Berlin, n.d. Reprint. *Protokolle der Parteitage der Unabhängigen Sozialdemokratischen Partei Deutschlands*. Vol. 2. Glashütten im Taunus, Germany: Detlev Auvermann, 1976.

Radek, Karl [pseud. Arnold Struthahn]. *Die Entwicklung der deutschen Revolution und die Aufgaben der Kommunistischen Partei*. Stuttgart: Verlag Spartakus, 1919.

——— *Die Entwicklung der Weltrevolution und die Taktik der kommunistischen Parteien im Kampfe um die Dictatur des Proletariats*. Berlin: West European Secretariat of the Communist International [1919].

——— *Pyat' let Kominterna*. Moscow: Krasnaya Nov', 1924.

Reed, John. "The World Congress of the Communist International." *The Communist* [United Communist Party of America], no. 10 [1920].

Resis, Albert. "The Profintern: Origins to 1923." Ph.D. diss., Columbia University, 1964.

Riddell, John, ed. *Founding the Communist International: Proceedings and Documents of the First Congress, March 1919*. New York: Pathfinder, 1987.

——— *The German Revolution and the Debate on Soviet Power: Documents 1918–19, Preparing the Founding Congress*. New York: Pathfinder, 1986.

——— *Lenin's Struggle for a Revolutionary International: Documents, 1907–16, The Preparatory Years*. New York: Pathfinder, 1984.

——— *To See the Dawn: Baku, 1920–First Congress of the Peoples of the East*. New York: Pathfinder, 1993.

Ritter, Gerhard A., ed., *Die II. Internationale 1918/1919*. Berlin: Verlag J.H.W. Dietz Nachf., 1980.

Rodinson, Maxime. *Israel and the Arabs*. New York: Pantheon, 1968.

Roland-Holst, Henriette. *Kapitaal en arbeid in Nederland; bijdrage tot de economische geschiedenis der 19de eevw*. Amsterdam: A.B. Soep, 1902.

Rosmer, Alfred. *Moscow under Lenin*. New York: Monthly Review Press, 1972.

Roy, M.N. *M.N. Roy's Memoirs*. Bombay: Allied Publishers Private Ltd., 1964.

Schröder, Karl, and Friedrich Wendel. *Wesen und Ziele der revolutionären Betriebsorganisationen*. Berlin: W. Vogel, 1920.

Serge, Victor. *Memoirs of a Revolutionary* 1901–1941. London: Oxford University Press, 1963.

Shirinya, K.K. "Voprosy soyuza rabochego klasa c krest'yanstvom." In *Vtoroy kongress Kominterna,* pp. 111–51. Moscow: Izdat. Politicheskoy literatury, 1972.

Sokolov, Ye.N. "Politika kommunistov po otnosheniyu k profsoyuzam." In *Vtoroy kongress Kominterna,* pp. 194–228. Moscow: Izdat. Politicheskoy literatury, 1972.

Spargo, John. *Russia as an American Problem*. New York: Harper, 1920.

*Stuttgart 1907–Basel 1912*. Vol. 2 of *Kongress-Protokolle der Zweiten Internationale*. Reprint. Glashütten im Taunus, Germany: Detlev Auvermann, 1976.

Tezisy ko Vtoromu kongressy Kommunisticheskogo Internatsionala. Petrograd: Izdat. Kommunisticheskogo Internatsionala, 1920.

Trotsky, Leon. *The First Five Years of the Communist International*. 2 vols. New York: Pathfinder, 1972.

——— *Pyat' let Kominterna*. Moscow: Gosizdat. [1924].

——— *Terrorism and Communism: A Reply to Karl Kautsky*. Ann Arbor: University of Michigan Press, 1961.

——— *The Third International after Lenin*. New York: Pathfinder, 1970.

Urquidi, Donald. "The Origins of the Italian Communist Party, 1918–1921." Ph.D. diss., Columbia University, 1962.

Varga, Eugen. *Die wirtschaftspolitischen Probleme der proletarischen Diktatur*. Vienna: Neue Erde, 1920.

Weber, Hermann, ed. *Der deutsche Kommunismus, Dokumente*. Cologne: Kiepenhewer & Witsch, 1963.

——— *Der Gründungsparteitag der KPD*. Frankfurt/Main: Europäische Verlagsanstalt, 1969.

Wheeler, Robert F. "The Independent Social Democratic Party and the Internationals: An Examination of Socialist Internationalism in Germany 1915 to 1923." Ph.D. diss., University of Pittsburgh, 1970.

Zinoviev, Gregory. Brennende *Tagesfragen der internationalen Arbeiterbewegung*. Petrograd: Verlag der Kommunistischen Internationale, 1920. Also found in *Kommunistische Internationale*, no. 9 [April 1920].

——— *Report of the Executive Committee of the Communist International to the Second World Congress of the Communist International*. Petrograd: Editions of the Communist International, 1920.

# Index

Entries are filed letter by letter. **Boldface** locators identify significant contributions by speakers in the congress sessions.

# THE COMMUNIST INTERNATIONAL IN LENIN'S TIME

## To See the Dawn

Baku, 1920—First Congress of the Peoples of the East

How can peasants and workers in the colonial world achieve freedom from imperialist exploitation? By what means can working people overcome divisions incited by their national ruling classes and act together for their common class interests? These questions were addressed by 2,000 delegates to the 1920 Congress of the Peoples of the East. $17

## The First Five Years of the Communist International

LEON TROTSKY

During its first five years, the Communist International, guided by V.I. Lenin, Leon Trotsky, and other central Bolshevik leaders, sought to build a world movement of Communist Parties capable of leading the toilers to overthrow capitalist exploitation and colonial oppression. This two-volume collection contains Trotsky's speeches and writings from the first four Comintern congresses. Volume 1, $22; volume 2, $22.

## Founding the Communist International

Proceedings and Documents of the First Congress, March 1919

Delegates from 20 countries discuss the revolutionary upsurge that swept Central Europe and Asia following World War I. Includes manifesto announcing founding of new revolutionary International. $25

## Three Study Guides on Lenin's Writings

A guide to articles, speeches, and resolutions on the contending class forces in the Russian Revolution.

- Bolshevik leader V.I. Lenin's political strategy for the democratic and socialist revolutions.
- Building a revolutionary working-class movement worldwide.
- Plus, the Marxist approach to wars, from Italian unification in 1859 to the first imperialist world war in 1914. With Gregory Zinoviev's 1916 article, "Wars: Defensive and Aggressive." $10

## The German Revolution and the Debate on Soviet Power

Documents, 1918–1919;
Preparing the Founding Congress

A day-to-day account of the 1918–19 German revolution in the words of its main leaders, including Rosa Luxemburg and Karl Liebknecht. $27

## Lenin's Struggle for a Revolutionary International

Documents, 1907–1916; The Preparatory Years

The debate among revolutionary working-class leaders, including V.I. Lenin and Leon Trotsky, on a socialist response to World War I. $30

## Questions of National Policy and Proletarian Internationalism

V.I. LENIN

Why the fight of oppressed nations for self-determination is decisive in the worldwide proletarian struggle to take and hold power. Why workers and farmers in imperialist countries have a deep class interest in championing this right. $16

PATHFINDERPRESS.COM

## THE RUSSIAN REVOLUTION'S WORLD EXAMPLE

### Lenin's Final Fight

Speeches and Writings, 1922–23

V.I. LENIN

In 1922 and 1923, V.I. Lenin, central leader of the world's first socialist revolution, waged what was to be his last political battle—one that was lost after his death. At stake was whether that revolutionary government and the world communist movement it led would remain on the revolutionary proletarian course that brought workers and peasants to power in October 1917. $17. Also in Spanish, Farsi, Greek.

### The Revolution Betrayed

What Is the Soviet Union and Where Is It Going?

LEON TROTSKY

In 1917 workers and peasants of Russia were the motor force of one of the deepest revolutions in history. Yet within ten years a political counterrevolution by a privileged social layer, whose chief spokesperson was Joseph Stalin, was being consolidated. The classic study of the Soviet workers state and its degeneration. $17. Also in Spanish, Farsi, Greek.

### The History of the Russian Revolution

LEON TROTSKY

How, under Lenin's leadership, the Bolshevik Party led millions of workers and farmers to overthrow the state power of the landlords and capitalists in 1917 and bring to power a government that advanced their class interests at home and worldwide. Unabridged, 3 vols. in one. Written by one of the central leaders of that socialist revolution. $30. Also in French and Russian.

# DEFENDING CONSTITUTIONAL FREEDOMS

*Under the constitution "the power of censorship rests with the people over the government, not the government over the people."*
—James Madison, *1794*

## 50 Years of Covert Operations in the US

Washington's Political Police and the American Working Class

LARRY SEIGLE, FARRELL DOBBS
STEVE CLARK

How class-conscious workers have defended constitutional freedoms and fought the capitalists' drive to build the "national security" state essential to maintaining their rule. $10. Also in Spanish and Farsi.

## Socialism on Trial

Testimony at Minneapolis Sedition Trial

JAMES P. CANNON

The revolutionary program of the working class presented in federal court in 1941 on the eve of US entry into World War II. The frame-up charges of "seditious conspiracy" targeted leaders of the Minneapolis labor movement and the Socialist Workers Party. $15. Also in Spanish, French, Farsi.

## FBI on Trial

The Victory in the Socialist Workers Party Suit Against Government Spying

MARGARET JAYKO

The record of a historic victory in the fight for political rights, including the 1986 federal court ruling against government spying and excerpts from trial testimony by SWP leaders Farrell Dobbs and Jack Barnes. $17

# The US rulers' political crisis and working people's response

## The Low Point of Labor Resistance Is Behind Us

The Socialist Workers Party Looks Forward

**Jack Barnes, Mary-Alice Waters Steve Clark**

The global order imposed by Washington after its victory in World War II is shattering. A long retreat by the working class and unions has come to an end. The bosses and their government are stepping up attacks on our wages, conditions, and constitutional rights. This book highlights opportunities for building a mass proletarian party able to lead the struggle to end capitalist rule, opening a socialist future for humanity. $10. Also in Spanish, French, Greek.

## Capitalism's World Disorder

Working-Class Politics at the Millennium

**Jack Barnes**

The social devastation and financial panic, coarsening of politics, cop brutality, and imperialist aggression—all are products not of something gone wrong with capitalism but of its lawful workings. Yet the future can be changed by the united struggle of workers and farmers increasingly conscious of their capacity to wage revolutionary struggles for state power and to transform the world. $20. Also in Spanish and French.

## Is Socialist Revolution in the US Possible?

A Necessary Debate Among Working People

**Mary-Alice Waters**

An unhesitating "Yes"—that's the answer given here. Possible—but not inevitable. That depends on what working people *do*. $7. Also in Spanish, French, Farsi.

## Are They Rich Because They're Smart?

### Class, Privilege, and Learning Under Capitalism

**Jack Barnes**

Exposes growing class inequalities in the US and the self-serving rationalizations of well-paid professionals who think their "brilliance" equips them to "regulate" working people, who don't know what's in our own best interest. $10. Also in Spanish, French, Farsi, Arabic, Greek.

## The Clintons' Anti-Working-Class Record

### Why Washington Fears Working People

**Jack Barnes**

What working people need to know about the profit-driven course of Democrats and Republicans alike over the last three decades. And the political awakening of workers seeking to understand and resist the capitalist rulers' assaults. $10. Also in Spanish, French, Farsi, Greek.

## Capitalism's Long Hot Winter Has Begun

**Jack Barnes**

Today's global capitalist crisis is but the opening stage of decades of economic, financial, and social convulsions and class battles. Class-conscious workers confront this historic turning point for imperialism with confidence, Jack Barnes writes, drawing satisfaction from being "in their face" as we chart a revolutionary course to take power. In *New International* no. 12. $14. Also in Spanish, French, Farsi, Arabic, Greek.

# BUILDING A REVOLUTIONARY WORKERS PARTY

## The Turn to Industry

Forging a Proletarian Party

JACK BARNES

A book about the working-class program, composition, and course of conduct of the only kind of party in the imperialist epoch worthy of the name "revolutionary." A party that can recognize the most revolutionary fact of this epoch—the worth of working people, and our power to change society when we organize and act against the capitalist class. It's about building such a party in the US and in other capitalist countries. $15. Also in Spanish, French, Farsi, Greek.

## Malcolm X, Black Liberation, and the Road to Workers Power

JACK BARNES

"The conquest of state power by a class-conscious vanguard of the working class is the mightiest weapon possible in the fight against Black oppression, the subjugation of women, Jew-hatred, and every form of human degradation inherited from class society." $20. Also in Spanish, French, Farsi, Arabic, Greek.

## Tribunes of the People and the Trade Unions

KARL MARX, V.I. LENIN, LEON TROTSKY
FARRELL DOBBS, JACK BARNES

A tribune of the people uses every manifestation of capitalist oppression to explain why working people, in class battles, will break from the bosses' parties, organize a revolutionary fight for state power, and lay the foundations of a socialist world of human solidarity. $12. Also in Spanish, French, Farsi, Greek.

# CUBA'S SOCIALIST REVOLUTION

## Women in Cuba: The Making of a Revolution Within the Revolution

VILMA ESPÍN
ASELA DE LOS SANTOS
YOLANDA FERRER

The integration of women in the ranks and leadership of the Cuban Revolution was intertwined with the proletarian course led by Fidel Castro from the start. This is the story of that revolution and how it transformed the women and men who made it. $17. Also in Spanish, Farsi, Greek.

*New!*

## Revolution and the Road to Peace in Colombia

The Example of the Cuban Revolution

FIDEL CASTRO

"No crime can be committed in the name of revolution," Fidel Castro declares, drawing from the example set by working people of Cuba as they took state power out of the hands of its capitalist rulers. In 2008, as part of efforts to end six decades of armed conflict in Colombia, he shared the exemplary record of Cuba's revolutionary struggle with the Revolutionary Armed Forces of Colombia (FARC) and the world. $10. Also in Spanish.

## The First and Second Declarations of Havana

Nowhere are the questions of revolutionary strategy that today confront men and women on the front lines of struggles in the Americas addressed with greater truthfulness and clarity than in these uncompromising indictments of imperialist plunder and "the exploitation of man by man." Adopted by million-strong assemblies of the Cuban people in 1960 and 1962. $10. Also in Spanish, French, Farsi, Arabic, Greek.

*New Edition!*

## Che Guevara on Economics and Politics in the Transition to Socialism

CARLOS TABLADA

It's essential for working people to win state power, said Ernesto Che Guevara. "Then there's the second stage, maybe more difficult than the first"—the transition from dog-eat-dog capitalism to socialism. That includes moving from work as a condition for survival, to voluntary social labor through which we express our common humanity. Includes Fidel Castro's 1987 speech "Che's Ideas Are Absolutely Relevant Today." New edition with substantially expanded selections from Guevara's writings. $17. Also in Spanish.

## Cuba and the Coming American Revolution

JACK BARNES

This is a book about the example set by the Cuban people that socialist revolution is not only necessary—it can be made. A book about the struggles of workers and other exploited producers in the imperialist heartland, and the youth attracted to them. About the class struggle in the US, where the revolutionary capacities of working people are as utterly discounted by the ruling powers as were those of the Cuban toilers. And just as wrongly. $10. Also in Spanish, French, Farsi.

## Dynamics of the Cuban Revolution

A Marxist Appreciation

JOSEPH HANSEN

How did the Cuban Revolution unfold? Why is it an "unbearable challenge" to US imperialism? Why are its lessons important to working people everywhere?

In "Cuba—The acid test: A reply to ultraleft sectarians," one of more than 20 articles here, Hansen starts with facts—not doctrine pretending to be theory—to examine the class struggle unfolding in Cuba in the 1960s. He refutes the political blindness of leftists who denied the dialectical richness of the socialist revolution and communist leadership developing before their eyes. $23

# EXPAND YOUR REVOLUTIONARY LIBRARY

## Labor, Nature, and the Evolution of Humanity

The Long View of History

FREDERICK ENGELS, KARL MARX
GEORGE NOVACK
MARY-ALICE WATERS

Without understanding that social labor, transforming nature, has driven humanity's evolution for millions of years, working people are unable to see beyond the capitalist epoch of class exploitation that warps all human relations, ideas, and values. Only the revolutionary conquest of state power by the working class can open the door to a world free of capitalist exploitation, degradation of nature, subjugation of women, racism, and war. A world built on human solidarity. A socialist world. $12. Also in Spanish and French.

## Thomas Sankara Speaks

The Burkina Faso Revolution, 1983–87

Under Sankara's guidance, Burkina Faso's revolutionary government led peasants, workers, women, and youth to expand literacy; to sink wells, plant trees, erect housing; to combat women's oppression; to carry out land reform; to join others worldwide to free themselves from the imperialist yoke. $20. Also in French.

## Opening Guns of World War III: Washington's Assault on Iraq

JACK BARNES

The murderous assault on Iraq in 1990–91 heralded increasingly sharp conflicts among imperialist powers, growing instability of capitalism, and more wars. Also includes:
**1945: When US Troops Said 'No!'** by Mary-Alice Waters
**Lessons from the Iran-Iraq War** by Samad Sharif
In *New International* no. 7. $14. Also in Spanish, French, Farsi.

*New Expanded Edition!*

## Cosmetics, Fashion, and the Exploitation of Women

MARY-ALICE WATERS
JOSEPH HANSEN, EVELYN REED

"Norms of beauty and fashion are inseparable from the class struggle" is the new opening chapter of this timely expanded edition of a lively 1950s debate in the *Militant*, a socialist newsweekly. How cosmetics and fashion monopolies rake in profits from social insecurities of women and adolescents. Why women's integration in the workforce and unions marks a major advance in the fight for their emancipation. A Marxist classic on the origins of women's oppression and the working-class road forward. $15. Also in Spanish, French, Farsi, Greek.

## U.S. Imperialism Has Lost the Cold War

JACK BARNES

The collapse of regimes across Eastern Europe and the USSR claiming to be communist did not mean workers and farmers there had been crushed. In today's sharpening class conflicts and wars, these toilers are joining working people the world over in the class struggle against capitalist exploitation. In *New International* no. 11. $14. Also in Spanish, French, Farsi, Greek.

Pathfinder Press **accessible e-books** for the blind, those with low vision, or other challenges reading print books

For a list of current accessible titles, go to: pathfinderpress.com/collections/books-for-the-blind.

Visit bookshare.org for information on how to sign up.

## PATHFINDER AROUND THE WORLD

**UNITED STATES**
*(and Caribbean, Latin America, and East Asia)*

*Pathfinder Books, 306 W. 37th St., 13th Floor*
*New York, NY 10018*

**CANADA**

*Pathfinder Books, 7107 St. Denis, Suite 204*
*Montreal, QC H2S 2S5*

**UNITED KINGDOM**
*(and Europe, Africa, Middle East, and South Asia)*

*Pathfinder Books, 5 Norman Rd.*
*Seven Sisters, London N15 4ND*

**AUSTRALIA**
*(and New Zealand, Southeast Asia, and the Pacific)*

*Pathfinder Books, Suite 2, First floor, 275 George St.*
*Liverpool, Sydney, NSW 2170*
*Postal address: P.O. Box 73, Campsie, NSW 2194*

**BUILD YOUR LIBRARY!**
**JOIN THE PATHFINDER READERS CLUB**

**$10 / YEAR**
**25% DISCOUNT ON ALL PATHFINDER TITLES**
**30% OFF BOOKS OF THE MONTH**
Valid at pathfinderpress.com and local Pathfinder book centers

**Go to: pathfinderpress.com/products/pathfinder-readers-club**

**Pathfinder**
pathfinderpress.com